RG
6.50

1408 E. Grand River
337-0115

AMERICAN WELFARE

AMERICAN

CENTER FOR APPLIED SOCIAL RESEARCH *and*

WELFARE

Alfred de Grazia & Ted Gurr

DEPARTMENT OF GOVERNMENT, NEW YORK UNIVERSITY

NEW YORK UNIVERSITY PRESS · 1961

PREFACE

IN ONE WAY OR ANOTHER, every American is concerned with welfare. He gives and receives benefits constantly, at home or on the stage of world politics. Mostly adults pay taxes to support one of the largest and most complex sets of governmental agencies ever devised. Hundreds of thousands, perhaps millions, of Americans are employed in the welfare offices of the national, State, and local governments. Many millions of other Americans depend upon the same offices for welfare assistance—a retired person for his monthly pension, a veteran for his disability pay, a mother for the vaccination of her children, or a family for its outdoor recreation.

Each year, many million Americans give time and money to churches, welfare agencies, unions, and schools, which, in part, use these resources to assist others and to improve their condition of life. Many thousands are paid salaries to perform professional welfare services— social workers, guidance counselors, teachers of blind, deaf, and handicapped children, and many doctors. Other thousands give of themselves generously without regular wage—volunteers, businessmen, and many ministers and priests.

This survey is addressed to all of the active or potentially active men and women engaged in welfare work in America, as well as to the young people, now students, who will become involved in the welfare process in the future.

These citizens have many and diverse interests. Some of them are highly specialized. The professional social worker who deals with juvenile delinquency may know little about hospital care. A union leader may know a great deal about community chests and councils, yet very little about church welfare. The volunteer may have only a vague notion of the number and complexity of groups and organizations that provide welfare services in his community, his State, and his nation. Few of these people have the opportunity to stand aside from their own special tasks and contemplate the whole panorama of welfare activity in America.

Yet some kind of panoramic view is desirable. Familiarity with the main features of the sprawling welfare picture gives one the same self-confidence and orientation that the study of a global map provides. The individual learns to recognize the main features of the world of welfare. He learns what institutions and what people provide welfare, and the nature of their welfare services. He comes to recognize how vast quantities of human energy are used to produce welfare results. He finds the key to many controversies and public issues whose echoes reach his own area of work.

Most important of all for the public good, he can acquire some knowledge of the vast account sheet of American welfare, which, together with his knowledge of the sources of welfare, will enable him as a citizen to judge whether welfare efforts are appropriately distributed in the interests of society.

To the best of our knowledge, no single book contains this broad view of welfare. Even in limited fields there are few studies that consider the relations between welfare for particular groups and what the philosophers call "the general welfare." To the senior author this survey is a diversion. He set out four years ago to write a book on the philosophy of welfare. But he discovered no collection of materials upon which he might base his theoretical work. The works that perhaps come closest to serving this purpose are the *Social Work Year Book*; the useful booklet *Giving, U.S.A.*; John Turnbull and associates, *Economic and Social Security*; and the social work texts of Walter Freidlander, Wayne Vasey, Arthur Dunham, and others. But unfortunately none of these gives a truly general description of welfare activity in America. So, with the junior author, he began to collect the fundamental information about welfare. Then, with the realization that all others concerned with welfare faced the same problem, it was decided that a general survey of the facts of the whole field might serve others as well.

This book is the result. If it increases understanding of the welfare functions of modern society and its institutions, if it helps those who work in the field of welfare, and if it brings in needed recruits, it will have well justified itself: "Knowledge puffeth up, but charity edifieth."

Many persons deserve acknowledgment for the assistance they have provided the authors. Many officers of fraternal and service organizations and welfare agencies provided materials that otherwise would have been unavailable. Religious bodies, unions, and businesses also furnished welcome materials. Mrs. Judith Pinch collected and arranged a library of materials on welfare. Miss Eileen Lanfeld also assisted in the collection of data, and prepared part of the chapter "American Welfare Abroad." Mr. Vaughn Davis Bornet offered criticism during the early stages. The authors are particularly indebted to Mr. T. H. Stevenson for his critical eye and editorial skills. Finally, the authors wish to thank the William Volker Fund of California and its officers, without whose financial assistance and personal interest this book would not have been possible.

ALFRED DE GRAZIA
TED GURR

CONTENTS

Contents

AMERICAN WELFARE

Chapter One

THE AMERICAN WELFARE SYSTEM

Welfare is the material and spiritual well-being of people. In this sense, almost every human act is for welfare—for the welfare of self, of family, of fellow citizens, or even of all mankind. Yet if welfare is so broadly conceived it goes out of focus, so men speak of certain kinds of welfare: "selfishness," that is, welfare of the self; social welfare, for the good of those who need society's special attention; general welfare, for the equal benefit of all men.

This survey centers attention on social welfare, but it does so with the knowledge that social welfare is closely akin to other kinds of welfare and that most of the institutions of society provide many types of welfare. A man can provide for his own financial security in later life and for the financial security of his family through life insurance; this is welfare. A family service agency can help keep a family together by giving it counsel and financial assistance; this is social welfare in its usual sense. The national government can protect all Americans from external aggression by maintaining the military establishment; this also is welfare, of the sort known to the philosopher and legislator as "general welfare." Hence, this survey describes the American welfare *system*: the institutions that provide welfare and the nature of the welfare that they provide.

All welfare begins with an individual and ends with an individual, so that the whole welfare process can be contained in a single question:

Who gives *what* to *whom*, by what *means* and with what *effects*? In ancient villages, this question asked of a citizen would probably have elicited a fairly specific answer. Yet ask the same question of his descendant in a modern metropolis and the answer would most likely be confined to a few personal acquaintances; it would indicate the existence of many means (or media, or institutions) of giving, and it would not be very clear as to who precisely was getting what from where. Concerning the effects of all giving and receiving, the modern man is likely to know much less than his ancestor, despite all the vaunted advances in the study of social behavior.

So intricate have the answers to the key question of welfare become that a survey such as this can only begin to reply. Moreover, it is almost inevitable that the reply, to be orderly, should take up the institutions of welfare one by one. First, the family is considered as a means for organizing welfare; from there the survey moves to more and more general institutions, and ultimately to machinery for collecting and distributing social benefits throughout the world. This chapter makes certain distinctions and definitions that are followed in subsequent chapters, then traces the historical development of welfare systems, particularly in America, outlines the general nature of giving and receiving in the present American welfare system, and concludes with some suggestions as to the capacity of the system.

SOME WELFARE DISTINCTIONS

THE WELFARE activities of all institutions can be differentiated according to whether they are performed for members or for non-members. Most of the welfare activities of the family are for family members, for example, but a family also sometimes helps others, as when it cares for a sick neighbor. Similarly, churches undertake welfare activities for their members *and* for those who are not members. The same is true of unions, businesses, fraternal and service organizations, governments, and other institutions of American society. The division of activities between those performed for members and for non-members varies from one institution to another. Most family activities are for its own members. The same is true of most churches. On the other hand, the activities of many institutions such as governmental agencies and non-governmental community welfare organizations are for non-members, that is, for persons other than those working within the institution.

The groups that perform welfare activities may be temporary and almost devoid of formal organization. By contrast they may be more or less permanent and possess a complex formal structure and body of governing rules. A group of neighbors may unite simply to petition the city council to construct a children's playground. As an intermediate stage a group that first met informally to deal with a single welfare problem may enjoy such a degree of success in dealing with this problem that it creates a formal organization for itself and acquires a professional staff so that it can deal with other problems. As an extreme case the government of the United States has one of the most involved organizational structures in the world. Although this survey deals primarily with groups having a high degree of organization, the reader should not allow himself to forget that a great many welfare activities in America are carried out by groups with little if any formal structure. *as highly organized*

In keeping with the definition of welfare given at the outset of this chapter, a welfare activity may benefit either those who are economically well-to-do or those who are economically impoverished, or both. The establishment and operation of an expensive secondary school for the children of weathy parents is just as much a welfare activity (of the type called "privilege") as the distribution of old-age assistance funds among elderly indigent persons (an activity of the "social welfare" type). The protection of natural resources presumably benefits all persons about equally, and thus is "general welfare." This survey is concerned primarily with welfare activities intended to benefit people who are economically hard-pressed, and to a lesser extent with activities for the general welfare. *as aiding the "hard pressed"*

Finally, in so far as welfare activities are concerned, any institution may simultaneously be giver and receiver. Families perform many welfare activities for themselves, yet at the same time many governmental and non-governmental agencies provide welfare services for families. As another illustration, labor unions undertake welfare activities both for their members and for the public at large, while businesses and government furnish welfare services to unions. As a concluding example, the national government provides a multitude of welfare services both for its employees and for the public. On the other hand, it can conscript men into the armed forces to protect the government; *i.e.*, it demands services as well as providing them. This survey is organized so as to deal with welfare activities in terms of the institutions that perform them. In other words, the chapters deal with the institutions chiefly as *performers* of welfare services. Discussions of institutions as *receivers* of welfare services are to be found mainly in the chapters dealing with the institutions that perform those services. *as performer*

THE HISTORICAL DEVELOPMENT OF WELFARE SYSTEMS

WELFARE systems are as old as society itself; in every society there has apparently been some system of social welfare. In each case systems of social welfare have depended upon the economic, political, and religious structure of the society. In the ancient Mesopotamian city-states, for example, a theocratic and partly collectivist economy emphasized work as a universal obligation and provided social security as a right of citizens. A 4,000-year-old hymn of Sumer describes the good goddess Nanshe,

> Who knows the orphan, who knows the widow,
> knows the oppression of man over man, is the orphan's mother,
> Nanshe, who cares for the widow,
> who seeks out justice for the poorest.
> The queen brings the refugee to her lap,
> finds shelter for the weak.[1]

Doing one's social duties well and doing well for others were common themes in East and West over the centuries. The medieval Church became the chief instrument for spreading St. Paul's Christian doctrine of charity. From St. Thomas to the humblest peasant, Western man could clearly state his obligations to give alms. An English lyric of the twelfth or thirteenth century carried the message forcefully:

> Every freeman should be kind
>   and give what Christ has let him find.
> For life must end in death alone,
>   whence he has no land but his length of bone.

Still later the English Poor Laws were unique in establishing assistance as a specialized secular function where formerly it had been a church function. In contemporary society the institutions of welfare have tended to evolve into government-controlled systems. The United States is no exception: many once-prominent non-governmental institutions now perform secondary welfare roles, whereas government activity has greatly increased. The change has come about slowly and has roots in early American tradition. But the change is by no means complete, for non-governmental welfare is rooted in the same tradition and has access to a degree of private organizational ingenuity unknown to earlier ages.

During the colonial period there were strong ties between the Anglican Church and colonial governments in the South. Hence, many welfare activities were performed under the auspices of the Church. In the northern colonies the governments were influenced by Puritan religious doctrine. Welfare problems were discussed in town meetings; solutions normally followed a combination of community action and religious pressure enforced and financed by the colonial governments. In this manner public health and education first became government func-

---

[1] S. N. Kramer. *History Begins at Sumer*. New York: Doubleday, 1959, p. 106.

tions. Still, many welfare problems were solved by families and small "neighborhood" groups.

When revolt freed the colonies of English domination, State governments carried forward the welfare role of the colonial governments. The law remained fashioned after the principles of the English Poor Laws, and provided for the use of tax funds for the relief of the poor. The federal government established in 1787 was designed to be incapable of tyranny. At the same time, it was made responsible for protecting private enterprise and promoting the welfare of its citizens. Far from being weak, the federal government possessed ample power to become a dynamic social institution. Under its aegis, business flourished. About it there developed a political system in which groups contended fiercely over issues of general welfare and, eventually, social welfare.

At the close of the colonial period seven of the chief welfare media existed in the United States, most of them flourishing, some of them nascent: the family, the church, the community, the school, business, fraternal orders (Freemasonry was established in the United States by the middle of the eighteenth century), and government. The remaining welfare institutions did not appear on the welfare scene in force for almost another hundred years, and might be considered born of the industrial revolution.

As the United States underwent the industrial revolution, the country changed radically; factories replaced family shops and cities developed to service the workers of growing business firms. Whereas in 1800 little over 6 per cent of the population lived in cities, by 1870 approximately 25 per cent of the population resided in cities. In the field of welfare, industrialization made two major contributions: on the one hand, it made available greater resources to relieve welfare problems and raised substantially the standard of living of most Americans; but, at the same time, it changed the nature of welfare problems. Potential welfare recipients lived together in large cities. The new poor seemed to be more helpless than the old to subsist without outside attention. Health conditions became of general concern. Leisure encouraged social action toward better recreation facilities. The gap between rich and poor widened.

As a result of these and related conditions, some new welfare institutions were developed. National labor unions evolved from local and regional worker affiliations that, up to this time, had been little more than professional guilds. (From their beginnings they were concerned with the welfare of their members, however.) Welfare agencies also began to develop. The Salvation Army was founded in 1880, the Red Cross in 1881. The first settlement house was established in New York City in 1886, Hull House in Chicago was founded in 1889. The

5

American Public Health Association and the National Conference of Social Work both began in the 1890's. Before the 1920's, however, relatively little energy was expended through such agencies on a national level; most of their activities were centered in communities and cities. A third American welfare institution was the foundation, through which fortunes accumulated from industrial activities were diverted to welfare purposes beginning about 1900. Finally, businessmen's service clubs, beginning with Rotary International, developed in the second decade of the twentieth century.

Summary

By World War I, then, welfare activity in the United States was spread thoroughly among the various institutions. State and local governments dominated government welfare; national activity was limited primarily to veterans' pensions, farm programs, and a few others. Non-governmental welfare activity was mainly local in character; relatively little was done on the national level.

The recent history of welfare structure in the United States has been characterized by both conflict and growth. Almost every institution has improved its position substantially during the twentieth century. Churches have grown considerably; in 1906, 38 per cent of the population claimed church membership, while by 1960 more than 60 per cent of the population was on church rolls. Most current national agency affiliations have been made since 1900. The same growth can be seen in all the other formal welfare institutions.

The greatest growth, however, has been the expansion of government into the welfare field, an expansion that actually began during the last three decades of the nineteenth century when secular non-governmental agencies began leaving to government cases involving direct relief, hopeless cases, and those requiring permanent institutional care. Functional expansion of the government during both world wars and the depression accounted for much of the growth, made permanent both by legislative acts and by court action. In 1913 the federal income tax became a permanent part of the federal revenue program and later provided the national government with the wherewithal to undertake many new welfare activities. Social security became a permanent program in 1935 and received ultimate judicial approval before the Supreme Court in 1937; the majority of justices agreed that social security activities were constitutional contributions to the "general welfare" of the country. Court action in 1939 justified federal control over activities financed by federal grants.

Governmental expansion in welfare can likewise be traced to public opinion voiced through the political parties of the country, as well as through formal and informal lobbying activity undertaken by special interest groups. In this expansion a number of welfare functions have

6

devolved on the national government through the complicated process of political action. This process, where welfare matters are involved, has six not-clearly-distinct phases:

(1) A need is discovered. This is usually done by a non-governmental agency established for some other purpose.

(2) Public concern is aroused, as the need is advertised as urgent. A "crisis psychology" is generated as the need becomes generally recognized.

(3) Experimental programs are undertaken to demonstrate or test appropriate means of remedy. Such projects may be undertaken by the non-governmental agency originally involved, by a separate agency formed for that function, or by some local governmental unit.

(4) National concern is aroused to climax the "crisis." A White House Conference may be called to study the need, or, more often, a special national commission, a Congressional hearing, or an independent national conference does such a study.

(5) The national government becomes intimately involved, either as a center of information or as a source of funds administered through grants-in-aid and State-sharing programs. A special federal agency is created and "pilot projects" are undertaken.

(6) The function is accepted as a permanent federal activity and State and local programs are expanded. Non-governmental agencies may be gradually displaced, may be converted to largely tax-supported operation, or may continue to operate both to experiment with new methods and to supplement governmental activities.

As the functional role of government has expanded the welfare structure of the country has become far more complicated. There has been some conflict over the distribution of welfare functions as the older welfare media, the family, the community, and the church, have surrendered some of their functions to the more vigorous and aggressive welfare agencies and other formal organizations. It is virtually impossible to discern any expression of a distinct philosophy of social welfare; however, there appear to be certain accepted beliefs in the realm of welfare in contemporary America:

(1) There is no practical limit to the number of welfare functions that can be undertaken by groups.

(2) Need is a relative thing; there is no absolute minimum assistance level.

(3) Any need affecting a portion of the population may be viewed as a legitimate responsibility of government.

(4) Institutions may qualify to function in an area of welfare

7

merely by demonstrating ability to satisfy a portion of a particular need.

(5) The administration of welfare requires more trained personnel.

These tenets leave a certain amount of room for non-professional, informal institutions, but they also require a highly organized structure or series of structures staffed by uniformly trained personnel, bureaucratic in approach, broad in scope. Whether those principles are the only or the major principles of contemporary American welfare, whether they should be, and whether they are changing must be left to the judgment of the individual citizen.

THE FLOW OF WELFARE: GIVERS AND RECEIVERS

ON ALMOST any day one can read news commentaries on the operation of the welfare system. These newspaper headlines one recent Spring reflected some aspects of the system:

School Volunteers—Successful Effort to Relieve Overburdened Teachers

Hugh R. Cullen, Oil Man, Dies; Gave $160,000,000 "Selfishly"— Benefactor of Schools, Other Institutions in Texas—Found Pleasure in Big Donations

New Aid Program Set Up for Areas—Boston Expert is Director of Nation-Wide Plan to Advise in Regional Self-Help

Wider Aid Pushed for Handicapped—Congress Increases Funds for Research on Four Major Forms of Disability

Aid Program Urged for Family Farmer

U.S. Curb is Urged in Pension Funds

Drive Will "Sell" Needs of Schools—NEA Ready to Double Dues and Campaign Against Cuts in Classroom Funds

M'Gill to Return Grant—Decides to Give Up $1,200,000 from Federal Government

City Set to Widen Social Security—Would Give 110,000 Employees Retroactive Coverage if State Approves Plan

State Care Lags for Chronic Ills—Hospital Survey Finds Need for 32,280 Beds but Only 6,972 Are Now Available

Charges Relief Law Fosters Pauperism

Each of these seems to be concerned with one of the following questions: Who is active in the welfare system? Who receives benefits from it? What are the programs the system undertakes? Why are they undertaken? How are they implemented? Any examination of the present

8

status of welfare in the United States must consider these same questions. The remaining chapters of this survey deal with these questions on an institution-by-institution basis. Here some of the general characteristics of all givers and receivers are outlined.

Givers

THE INPUTS of the welfare system can ultimately be traced to individuals. Four channels of giving are currently used. The first of these is used by the individual who freely gives of his time and money to welfare institutions, which in turn pass them on to the needy. The amount of individual contribution reported in itemized income tax returns for 1956 was nearly $5 billion (cf. Table 1). These voluntary contributions,

TABLE 1

INCOME TAX RETURNS SHOWING CHARITABLE CONTRIBUTIONS, 1956 [1]

Income Class	Returns With Deductions for Contributions (thousands)	Adjusted Gross Income (millions)	Deductions for Contributions (millions)	Contributions as Percentage of Income
Under $5,000	6,773	$ 25,306	$1,127	4.45
$5,000 to $10,000	7,702	53,104	1,871	3.52
$10,000 to $25,000	1,484	21,512	750	3.48
$25,000 to $50,000	288	9,917	327	3.29
$50,000 to $100,000	82	5,539	226	4.07
$100,000 to $500,000	21	3,417	237	6.98
$500,000 to $1,000,000	0.6	393	43	10.90
$1,000,000 and over	0.3	543	69	12.67
Totals	16,350 [1]	$119,731	$4,650	3.88 [2]
Non-taxable returns	1,252		$ 228	
Total contributions reported			$4,878	

Note: Totals do not necessarily add because of rounding.
Source: *Giving USA 1959*. New York: American Association of Fund-Raising Counsel, 1959, p. 35, from Internal Revenue Service Publication No. 198 (August, 1958).

[1] In addition some 43 million individuals took standard deductions, which presumably included several billions more in philanthropic contributions.
[2] Total contributions ($4,650 million) as percentage of total reported gross income.

as well as union dues, contributions to fraternal organizations, and donated time and energy, are introduced into the welfare stream in a variety of ways. They may be given in response to a federated fund-raising campaign undertaken on behalf of social welfare agencies, they may be given to a church project, to a particular community project, or even directly to a neighbor.

TABLE 2

ESTIMATED EFFECTIVE RATES OF TAX FOR 1954
(Tax as Percentage of Income)

	Spending Unit Income Brackets (thousands of dollars)							
	0–$2,000	$2,000–$3,000	$3,000–$4,000	$4,000–$5,000	$5,000–$7,500	$7,500–$10,000	Over $10,000	Total
FEDERAL TAXES								
Personal income tax	3.1	5.3	7.1	8.4	11.5	14.2	14.6	10.7
Estate and gift taxes							1.4	.3
Corporate profits tax	3.7	3.8	3.3	3.2	3.6	4.1	14.1	6.2
Excises	5.0	4.5	4.1	3.9	3.6	3.3	1.9	3.4
Customs	2.3	.3	.2	.2	.2	.2	.1	.2
Social insurance contribution	3.6	4.1	4.4	4.2	3.2	2.4	1.1	3.0
Totals	15.7	17.9	19.1	20.0	22.2	24.2	33.2	23.8
Without social insurance contribution	12.1	13.8	14.7	15.8	19.0	21.8	32.1	20.9
STATE AND LOCAL TAXES								
Personal income tax	.01	.1	.2	.2	.4	.5	.8	.4
Inheritance and gift taxes							.4	.1
Corporate profits tax	.2	.2	.1	.1	.2	.2	.6	.3
Excise and sales taxes	5.7	5.1	4.6	4.4	4.2	3.8	2.2	3.9
Property	4.8	4.3	4.1	4.1	3.8	3.6	3.4	3.8
Social insurance contribution	.5	.7	.7	.9	.7	.6	.3	5.9
Totals	11.2	10.4	9.8	9.8	9.1	8.8	7.7	9.1
Without social insurance contribution	10.7	9.7	9.1	8.9	8.4	8.1	7.4	8.5
ALL LEVELS OF GOVERNMENT								
Totals	26.9	28.3	28.9	29.8	31.3	33.0	40.9	32.9
Without social insurance contribution	22.8	23.5	23.8	24.7	27.4	29.9	39.5	29.4

Source: Computations by the Michigan School of Graduate Studies; explained in *Federal Tax Policy for Growth and Stability*, testimony by Dr. R. A. Musgrave, pp. 96–113.

The American Welfare System

A second method by which funds are introduced into the welfare system includes donations by business organizations. In 1958 corporations directly contributed about $420 million to charitable and philanthropic purposes, about 0.9 per cent of their taxable earnings. These funds, substantially reduced by the corporate income tax, would otherwise have been retained as earnings or distributed as dividends to owners.

donations by Business (margin note)

TABLE 3

GENERAL GOVERNMENTAL TAX REVENUES FOR A TYPICAL YEAR
IN THE LATE 1950's [1]

(In Millions of Dollars)

| Type of Tax | Level of Government and Amount | | | |
	Local (1958 data)	State (1959 data)	National (1960 data)	Total [2]
Individual Income	$ 215	$ 1,778	$40,306	$ 42,300
Corporation Income		979	22,200	23,200
Sales, Gross Receipts, and Customs	1,079	9,289	10,276	20,600
Property	13,514	565		14,100
Other Taxes and Licenses	652	3,220	5,818	9,700
Totals	$15,460	$15,831	$78,600	$110,000 [2]

Note: Totals do not necessarily add because of rounding.

Sources: *Statistical Abstract of the United States 1960*, U.S. Bureau of the Census, Washington, D.C.: USGPO, 1960, pp. 403, 416; "President's Budget Message," *New York Times*, Jan. 19, 1960.

[1] Excludes employment taxes (except share for administrative expenses) and other insurance taxes but includes some miscellaneous revenues.
[2] Since data are for different years, totals are artificial, but for any given year in the period 1958–1960 they are accurate within 5 per cent.

Trust funds set aside by various contributors provide a third source of money for contemporary welfare. Foundations are the most publicized of such trust funds, yet others also are important: college and university endowments; endowments and trust funds for the support of hospitals, homes, and other welfare institutions; and community trusts. In 1959 foundations alone had assets of over $10 billion, from which they made grants in excess of $700 million. In another recent year college and university endowments provided more than $125 million for operating expenses. Total funds for philanthropic and charitable purposes from foundations, endowments, and other trust funds may have been as much as $1 billion a year in the late 1950's.

trust funds (margin note)

Finally, tax funds are poured into the welfare system by governments, which essentially are acting as welfare agents for individuals and

Sou't (margin note)

businesses. Table 2 presents the sources of national, State, and local taxes in 1954 as percentages of the incomes of persons in various income brackets. The average tax burden of a man earning $3,500 was about $1,015, including all forms of taxation, indirect as well as direct. More recent data on total governmental tax revenues are given in Table 3. From 1957 to 1960 governments in the United States collected between $105 billion and $115 billion annually in general taxes. Of this total between 25 and 30 per cent was spent for social welfare, including education (c. $14 billion per year), veterans' programs (c. $5 billon per year), public health (c. $3.5 billion per year), and public assistance and social service programs (c. $4.5 billion per year). In addition, an estimated $17 billion annually was collected and distributed under governmental social insurance plans.

Thus a rough summary balance sheet of giving to social welfare (including education) can be drawn up for a typical year in the late 1950's. It includes these items: [2]

Direct individual contributions:	$8 billion	22%
Corporate and other business contributions:	$0.7 billion	2%
Contributions through foundations and other trust funds:	$1.0 billion	3%
Contributions through government taxation:	$27 billion	73%
	$36.7 billion	100%

Receivers

As SUGGESTED above, money introduced into the welfare stream through institutions can be traced from the giver to the ultimate receiver. For example, an individual gives ten dollars to a community chest. The community chest divides it among welfare agencies, which in turn pass along their share in the form of financial assistance or, more commonly, services to the welfare recipient. Federal tax funds for aid to dependent children are passed from the federal to a State government, which adds its own funds and then may allocate the total to one of its own agencies or pass it on to various local government agencies. Ultimately the funds may be paid to a family to provide care for the child or might be given directly to the child in the form of resident care by a secular or religious agency. Any welfare activity can be followed in this manner, by tracing funds out of the pocket of the individual, through the media chosen for distribution, and ultimately to the receiver.

[2] Includes certain additional estimates drawn from material in subsequent chapters, excludes social insurance.

It is no longer true that practically all beneficiaries of the welfare activities of institutions other than the family are impoverished. Nevertheless, the whole organized system of welfare rests fundamentally upon the existence of many people who are unable to care for themselves in the ways society believes that they should be cared for. Consequently it may be helpful in understanding the core problems of welfare to outline the traits of persons in the lower income groups. These people are generally the consumers of social welfare benefits (other than education and social insurance, available to most persons). Table 3 in chapter 2 shows the characteristics of low-income families and unattached individuals in 1954.

A glimpse of those who are receiving what used to be called "charity" is also in order. A study of chronic general assistance cases disclosed these eight significant case characteristics: [3]

Age of family head:	Usually 40 years or more.
Occupational classification:	Unskilled or not in labor force.
Highest school grade completed:	Eighth or less.
Previously registered by an assistance agency:	Usually yes.
Indebtedness when applying for assistance:	$50 or less.
Length of residence in county:	Less than three years.
Marital status:	Spouse often dead or divorced, institutionalized, or in armed forces.
Housing:	Housing difficulties noted in chronic cases.

Many welfare receivers must qualify in respect to a particular need, of course. A major one is chronic illness. Another area of need that has been receiving increased attention is mental illness. According to a recent survey 10 per cent of the city population, or approximately nine million people, suffer from varying degrees of mental disturbance. The National Foundation (formerly the National Foundation for Infantile Paralysis) has linked need with illness in this manner:

We are not dispensing charity in any sense of the word. While we expect a family to do what it reasonably can financially, we do

[3] Ethel G. Harrison and John C. Kidneigh, "Can We Identify the Long-Term General Assistance Case at Intake?" *Public Welfare*, XIII (October, 1955), p. 203.

not insist that it prove itself totally indigent to obtain care. If it is evident that the high cost of polio care would result in undue hardship, force the family to sell a car that it needs, mortgage its home or otherwise drastically lower its standard of living, the [National Foundation for Infantile Paralysis] Chapter should offer to pay all or that portion of the cost that cannot reasonably be met by the family.[4]

Thus, for more and more welfare receivers, it is difficult to make an income-group classification, a fact consistent with the popular slogan of community fund-raising campaigns: "Everybody gives, everybody benefits."

THE CAPACITY OF THE WELFARE SYSTEM

ON LOOKING at the welfare system and considering the resources it involves, one may ask, "How much can the system carry?" Social welfare and education already take between 9 and 10 per cent of the gross national product annually, and governmental social insurance and nongovernmental life, health, and retirement insurance plans take another 10 per cent. Many views are expressed concerning the use of the social welfare system, ranging from observations that there is an absolute limit to the needs demanding attention to the other extreme that there is no limit to the needs that can be serviced by the system. A specific view of the capacity of the welfare system has been presented by Eveline Burns of the Columbia University School of Social Work. In discussing the question, "How much social welfare can America afford?" she says, "To an overwhelming extent . . . the costs of social welfare must be considered from two major angles: how great a drain do they represent on our total basic economic resources; and how great a measure of income redistribution will the country stand for?" Mrs. Burns concludes that resources are limited by the level of national output, and continues:

Does this, then, mean that we are forced to accept the existing level of social welfare expenditures as a fixed maximum? Obviously not. Precisely because the way in which any community decides to utilize its available productive capacity is a matter of choice, our problem becomes . . . one of persuading the majority of the electorate that the forms in which we would like to see that productive capacity embodied are more worthwhile than alternative end products.

[4] *Chapter Patient Care Program.* New York: National Foundation for Infantile Paralysis, 1954, p. 4.

In this sense, and within the limits of national output, it is true that the amount of social welfare that America can afford is largely a matter of how much social welfare the people of America want, but want, mark you, as compared with other things. It is for us to persuade the taxpayers and voluntary givers that social welfare expenditures are worth the money or, if you like, the reduction in freely disposable income that they cost.[5]

It should be added that Americans need not only decide on the amount of money and energy they wish to pour into the welfare system; they must also select with care the most effective channels and, with equal care, determine which persons have the greatest need of welfare services.

[5] Eveline M. Burns, "How Much Social Welfare Can America Afford?" in *The Social Welfare Forum*, 1949, New York: Columbia University Press, 1950, pp. 63, 71–72.

Chapter Two

THE FAMILY

THE FAMILY IS THE CENTER of personal life and the principal source of well-being for most people; it is the original and fundamental institution of society, and the first resource of welfare. Most modern families are capable of caring for their sick, their aged, and their children in ways that no other institution can duplicate. The family may not have the technical skills to provide all the necessary physical care for members who are ill, crippled, or in need of special education, but it is the most important and effective source of love and emotional support for them. This chapter is concerned with the nature and the welfare functions of the contemporary family.

THE NATURE OF THE CONTEMPORARY FAMILY

Size and Composition

THE AMERICAN FAMILY has changed somewhat in both size and composition in the past 160 years. In 1800 the average family had nearly six members, in 1950 it had less than four. These statistics conceal more of the story than they tell, for the greatest decline has been in the proportion of large family units. Although statistics for the earlier periods are not available, even in the two decades from 1930 to 1950 the percentage of households having seven or more members dropped from 11 per cent to less than 6 per cent of all households. The data in Table

1 indicate that the family is still an important part of the experience of the average American, however.

Of the more than 176,350,000 people in the United States in 1959, all but about 7 per cent were members of forty-four and a quarter million families. (Some seven million persons lived alone, about three and a half millions lived with families to which they were not related, and an estimated two million persons were institutionalized.) Over the long run there have been increasing proportions of two- and three-person families, but there are still many persons who are members of large

TABLE 1

FAMILIES AND UNATTACHED INDIVIDUALS IN THE
FORTY-EIGHT STATES, 1959

	Number	*Per Cent*
All families [1]	44,202,000	100.0
Size of family:		
2 persons	14,247,000	32.3
3 persons	9,584,000	21.7
4 persons	9,062,000	20.5
5 persons	5,702,000	12.9
6 persons	2,894,000	6.5
7 or more persons	2,713,000	6.1
Primary individuals [2]	7,361,000	100.0
Male	2,386,000	32.4
Female	4,975,000	67.6

Source: *Statistical Abstract of the United States 1960.* U.S. Bureau of the Census. Washington, D.C.: USGPO, 1960, pp. 41–43.

[1] "Family" includes groups of two or more persons related by marriage, blood, or adoption, residing together. These figures on number and size of families include 261,000 so-called "secondary" families, that is, family units such as young married couples and servant families living in the same household with another family.
[2] These are individuals living by themselves, in separate households. A "household" comprises all persons living in a house, apartment, or other group of rooms, or a single room that constitutes "separate living quarters." There were 51,302,000 such households in the United States in 1959.

families. For example, in 1959 more than sixty-seven million Americans belonged to families of five or more persons. There is also evidence that in the past few years the large family has become somewhat more common. In 1953, 22 per cent of American families had five or more members; by 1959 the percentage had increased to 25.5.

The large numbers of small families do not necessarily suggest a decrease in the importance of the family either. Economic independence often encourages families to establish themselves in two or more households for the sake of convenience and privacy, while they still maintain strong affectional ties with other parts of the family. In 1953 a study was made of informal group participation of men of different socio-economic status in San Francisco. Over-all, nearly two-thirds of them got together with relatives other than those living with them at least once a month. About four men out of ten got together with relatives once a week or more.[1]

Since 1890 marriages have been occurring at an increasingly younger age; in 1890 the average newlywed husband was just over twenty-six and his wife was twenty-two. In 1950 he was not yet twenty-three years old and his wife had just passed her twentieth birthday.[2] This trend has been attributed in part to economic conditions—couples believe that they can support themselves at a younger age.

Kinship ties are still strong. Even though what was once an extended family may now be split into autonomous segments and geographically widely separated, family members maintain contact through many forms of communication and make many trips to visit relatives. The "nuclear" family that falls prey to economic disaster or to illness may not to able to rely with certainty on assistance from relatives, yet it receives this assistance in many instances.

Employment and Family Mobility

EMPLOYMENT FOR the nuclear family in an industrialized society is a different matter from employment for the extended family in a communal, agricultural society. Almost all the members of a rural family have certain occupations that contribute directly to the material betterment of the family.

Tendencies in the United States today suggest that a related phenomenon is developing, in which the contribution to the family is indirect rather than direct. More and more family members are employed, not to provide directly the food and shelter the family needs but to provide financial means of satisfying these needs by working outside the family. The number of employed women is increasing; many of them are married and use the income for family purposes. Whereas youths from low-income families have for many years joined the labor force at an early age, more and more young men from middle-income families have apparently been taking part-time and summer jobs, both to supplement family income and to provide funds for a college education. There is also an increase in "moonlighting," accompanying the shorter work week: many laborers and white-collar workers,

[1] Wendell Bell and Marion D. Boat, "Urban Neighborhoods and Informal Social Relations," *American Journal of Sociology*, LXII (January, 1957), pp. 391–98.
[2] J. Frederic Dewhurst and Associates. *America's Needs and Resources: A New Survey.* New York: The Twentieth Century Fund, 1955, p. 57.

working thirty-five and forty hours a week, take night and weekend jobs to supplement family income.

The modern family is semi-migratory in nature. In *each year* between 1950 and 1955 nearly one-fifth of the labor force moved from one house to another at least once. At this rate the average worker would change his residence about eight times in his working life, and several of these changes would involve moving from one community to another. There are indications that many of these shifts involve changes in occupation and industry, as well as employer.[3]

Economic conditions and employment mobility produce two counter-acting tendencies relating to the welfare functions of the family. On the one hand the family has much greater financial resources with which to contribute to the well-being of its members. On the other hand families that move from one area to another, particularly those that move from a rural to an urban setting, are often subject to strains that cause a breakdown in family structure and create new welfare problems. Also it is more difficult for relatives who might otherwise assist a distressed family to help if the family is in a distant part of the country.

Family Authority and Personal Relations

ONE ASPECT of the changing pattern of the American family is the decentralization of authority that characterizes the typical family. In times past the self-sufficient, economically integrated family required at its head an authoritative figure, usually the husband and father. The non-authoritative family structure with which modern American society is familiar was made largely impossible by the exigencies of survival. Nevertheless, the individual needs love and affection for well-being, and for many Americans today the family is the primary and sometimes the only source of these qualities.

One of the factors underlying the non-authoritative structure of the American family is the increasing economic contributions of the wife to the family. As the percentage of total family income contributed by the husband has decreased, the wife has come to share more and more responsibility for family activities. This tendency has been accompanied and abetted by a changing concept of the ideal marriage. The romantic ideal of young Americans is a marriage built on companionship, with great emphasis on the affective side of family life.

Families are increasingly centered on satisfying affective needs largely because of the lack of personal quality in the dealings of the individual

[3] Harold Wilensky and Charles N. Lebaux. *Industrial Society and Social Welfare.* New York: Russell Sage Foundation, 1958, p. 72.

19

with the outside world. Most of the person's contacts outside the family are with people with whom he or she has no particular emotional involvement—this is one of the dominant characteristics of an associational society. As a result, the typical individual in American society turns to the family as a source of companionship, mutual comfort, and mutual concern.

The Family and the Law

LAWS ENACTED by State governments regulate family formation, family functioning, and family dissolution. These laws partially determine the nature of the family and to some degree prescribe the obligations of the family to perform welfare functions for its members.

FAMILY FORMATION: Family life and the formation of marriages have traditionally been beyond the powers of the federal government, and the regulation of marriage has fallen within the purview of the States. All the States license those qualified to perform a marriage and require documented evidence of the ceremony.[4] Fifteen of the fifty States recognized common-law marriage in 1960 but they differed greatly in its legal definition. The effect of State regulation of marriage is the establishment of the family as a legal entity and allows the States to control, in part, the functioning of the family unit.

FAMILY FUNCTIONING: The laws of most States require that family community property and the husband's personal property be used to support the family. In other States the laws provide that the wife's property also must be available for family support. In a majority of States the wife and children can file claims of non-support against the husband and father. If it is proved to the court that he can provide support, and that the family is in need, he is guilty of the felony, or misdemeanor, of non-support and is ordered by the court to provide the support. Non-compliance ordinarily can be penalized by imprisonment.

States also require that families send their children to school. Most States have required attendance until the child is sixteen, a few States until he or she is seventeen. More recently a number of States have raised the minimum age to eighteen. In all States that require attendance beyond the age of sixteen, however, employed youths are exempted from the requirements.

FAMILY DISSOLUTION: As the States control marriage they also control divorce. The various grounds for divorce fall into six main groups:

[4] *The Book of the States 1960–1961* (Vol. XIII). Chicago: The Council of State Governments, 1960, p. 389.

(1) Conduct violating the sanctity of the marriage.
(2) Violent or gross conduct menacing life, health, or happiness.
(3) Willful or negligent disregard of marital obligations.
(4) Incapacity to fulfill marital obligations.
(5) Civil death, either through criminal status or prolonged absence without word of whereabouts.
(6) Defective marriage.

Grounds vary considerably from State to State.

Once a divorce is granted, there are problems of the division of property between the parties involved, alimony to the former wife, the custody of children, and allowances for the support of the children. In most States decisions on these matters are left largely to the discretion of the court hearing the case.

Divorce frequently results in welfare problems, child welfare problems in particular. Yet the causes and extent of divorce in American society are very much a part of an associational society. Because of the strong interpersonal and emotional relations of the modern family, friction is quite likely to develop among its members. Emotional problems and incompatability are held to be the most frequent causes of divorce, and about one marriage in four can be expected to end in divorce. In 1958, for every 10,000 persons in the United States there were eighty-three marriages and twenty-two divorces. On the average divorced couples had been married about six and a half years, but about half of the couples had no children.[5]

The fact that families with children are more likely to stay together suggests that a high divorce rate does not necessarily mean a decline in the importance of the family. Also, more than 90 per cent of Americans eventually marry, and 87 per cent of those who divorce marry again within five years, testifying to the popularity if not the stability of marriage and family life.[6]

Family Economics

THE FAMILY as an institution cannot fulfill its welfare functions, and indeed cannot exist, without economic means. Thus, although from the point of view of society the reproductive function of the family is probably paramount, for the members of any given family the fulfillment of almost all functions is contingent on the fulfillment of the economic function.

There are two indices of the financial resources of the American

[5] *Statistical Abstract* 1959, pp. 52, 73.
[6] Reuben Hill, "The Changing American Family," in *The Social Welfare Forum*, 1957, New York: Columbia University Press, 1957, pp. 68–80.

family: income and net worth. In 1958 there were 54.3 million "families and unattached individuals" in the United States, as defined by the national Office of Business Economics. The average income of these families and individuals before taxes was $6,220. Income after taxes averaged $5,610.[7]

In 1953 a study of the net worth of a sample of American families was made. "Net worth" was defined as the differences between selected assets (including liquid assets, real estate, machinery, automobiles, and investments, but excluding most consumer durable goods and corporate bonds), and total debt. The median net worth of the families surveyed was $4,100. There were significant differences between various occupational groups, of course. Self-employed individuals had a median net worth of $17,000, farm operators $13,500, skilled and semi-skilled workers $2,700, and unskilled and service workers had $400 net worth. One significant finding was that retired persons had a median net worth of $6,000.[8]

Fulfilling the economic function for the American family is not solely a matter of providing a minimum of food, shelter, and clothing for family members. On the contrary, each family unit in contemporary society is expected to supply itself with goods that constitute a comfortable standard of living. The family financially obligates itself in an almost limitless number of ways to accomplish this end, depending on its conception of what constitutes a "comfortable standard of living" and on its expected income.

A sociologist has this to say about the concept of a standard of living:

In general, a standard of living is a normative or scale of consumption that represents the goal of living which a family or group of people are striving to reach or maintain. . . . When a goal is achieved, the standard of living coincides with the actual consumption performance. But, owing to the fact that the standard set up by the group is fundamentally psychological in nature, in that it represents a desirable goal, it is usually beyond the achievement of most groups. The goal varies by individuals and groups, it changes from time to time, and it depends upon items included in a minimum standard.[9]

For most families in American society the standard of living includes a number of items that do not have a great deal of physical utility but that instead constitute a demonstration of the owner's social and eco-

[7] *Statistical Abstract* 1959, p. 317.
[8] Survey of Consumer Finances, conducted for the Board of Governors of the Federal Reserve System by Survey Research Center of the University of Michigan.
[9] Martin H. Neumeyer. *Social Problems and the Changing Society*. New York: Van Nostrand, 1953, p. 255.

nomic status. Such items have come to require a large part of the family income. In Table 2 the average expenditures for current consumption of a sample of American families are given (1950), for several income levels. There is a general similarity of percentages across the income levels.

TABLE 2

DISTRIBUTION OF CURRENT CONSUMPTION EXPENDITURES
OF URBAN FAMILIES, 1950 [1]

Type of Expenditure	All Income Levels	$1,000 to $2,000	$5,000 to $6,000	$10,000 and over
Food and Beverages	31.4%	36.4%	30.2%	24.5%
Tobacco	1.8	3.0	1.7	1.0
Housing	11.5	15.7	10.3	10.7
Fuel, Light, Refrigeration	4.1	6.1	3.7	2.8
Household Operation	4.7	4.6	4.5	9.0
Furnishings and Equipment	6.9	4.9	7.2	8.4
Clothing and Clothing Services	11.5	9.3	12.3	14.1
Transportation	13.4	7.9	15.4	12.8
Medical Care	5.2	5.4	4.8	4.1
Personal Care	2.2	2.4	2.2	1.9
Recreation and Education	5.9	3.7	6.3	7.8
Miscellaneous	1.4	1.6	1.4	2.9
	100%	100%	100%	100%

Source: *Statistical Abstract* 1959, p. 316, from data in *Survey of Consumer Expenditures in 1950*, Bureau of Labor Statistics.

[1] The sample included one-person units, and covered 12,500 families in all.

The greatest difference in absolute percentages is in food, the lower income families spending a greater percentage for food than higher income families. The monetary difference is still great however: the family unit that had a disposable income of $2,000 a year spent about $730 on food, whereas the family with $10,000 spent $2,450.

Lower income families are of particular interest to a survey of welfare since they consume a relatively large portion of welfare services. Some of their characteristics are summarized in Table 3 (see also Chapter 1, Table 4).

THE WELFARE FUNCTIONS OF THE FAMILY

THE WELFARE FUNCTIONS of the family are to provide for the physical and emotional well-being of its members. It reproduces and raises new members of society, it acquires for its members the economic goods necessary for their survival, and it offers them love and affection. Ideally the family is a setting in which all its members can achieve maximum personal satisfaction and personal development. When the family cannot or does not provide for the welfare of its members because of lack of money, lack of specialized skills, family breakdown, or emotional tensions within the family, other institutions of society are called upon to provide assistance. The extent of family care for its members—children, the aged, the sick—is discussed below. Welfare services provided the family by other institutions are dealt with in subsequent chapters.

Children

THE FUNDAMENTAL FUNCTION of the family is to reproduce and raise new members for society. This is a welfare function in the sense that child-raising is both a contribution to the welfare of society and a contribution to the welfare of the child. Through socialization the family begins the development of the ideas, habits, and attitudes that constitute the child's personality. The family is the institution that conveys many of the fundamentals of culture, its skills and moral values. Only in the first few years of life, however, does the contemporary family have sole influence in this process. Within a very few years after birth the child comes in informal contact with children and adults outside

TABLE 3

CHARACTERISTICS OF LOW-INCOME FAMILIES AND INDIVIDUALS
WITH INCOME LESS THAN $2,000, 1954

	PERCENTAGE DISTRIBUTIONS		
CHARACTERISTIC	Urban Families (6,568,000)	Urban Single Persons (6,556,000)	Rural Families (2,844,000)
Family Composition			
1 Adult and Children	16%		4%
2 Adults	46		40
2 Adults and Children	24		41
3 Adults with or without Children	14		15
Age of Head of Family			
Under 25	6	8%	4
25 to 54	45	19	47
55 to 64	17	11	25
65 and over	31	62	23
Not Ascertained	1		1
Education of Head of Family			
None	10	6	6
Grammar School	62	48	69
High School	24	36	23

CHARACTERISTIC	PERCENTAGE DISTRIBUTIONS		
	Urban Families (6,568,000)	Urban Single Persons (6,556,000)	Rural Families (2,844,000)
College	4	10	1
Not Ascertained			1
Occupation of Head of Family			
Professional, Managerial, Self-employed	6	3	4
Clerical and Sales	5	5	1
Skilled and Semi-skilled	12	5	6
Unskilled and Service	20	16	12
Protective Service, Students, Housewives	15	40	4
Farm Operator			44
Unemployed	15	5	10
Retired	26	26	18
Not Ascertained	1		1
Region			
Northeast	21	31	4
North Central	26	31	30
South	46	25	61
West	7	13	5
Place			
Metropolitan Area	27	32	
City, 50,000 or More	31	36	
Town, 2,500 to 50,000	42	32	
Town under 2,500			49
Open Country			51
Liquid Assets			
None	69	51	62
Under $500	12	24	22
$500 to $1,999	10	11	8
$2,000 or over	9	14	8
Housing Status			
Own with Mortage	12	4	15
Own without Mortgage	32	24	45
Rent	53	60	25
Other	3	12	15

Source: *Characteristics of the Low-Income Population and Related Federal Programs.* U.S. Congress, Joint Committee on the Economic Report. Washington, D.C.: USGPO, 1955, pp. 25–26.

his family. Formal contact begins with the child's schooling at the age of four or five; from this point on his knowledge and skills, his behavior patterns, and his morality are increasingly the result of forces outside the family, forces over which the family often has little influence.

Beyond the act of reproduction and early socialization the role of the family with regard to its children varies widely from one family to another. Individual parents differ on the extent and quality of the outside contacts of their children. The age at which formal education should begin—and end—is likewise a matter of dispute, though almost all families recognize such education as necessary. Parents of some social groups typically send their child to boarding school when he is nine or ten; during his adolescence he has only infrequent contacts with his parents. In some instances families have wished to educate their children entirely within the family, but in most such cases the desires of the family have been thwarted by local school boards and courts, on grounds that families do not have the technical skills to provide a complete education for their children.

Various religions make requirements on the child's schooling. With Roman Catholicism, and to a lesser extent with other religious groups, this may involve a separate educational system with a separate curriculum. A few small religious groups minimize any formal education, preferring to retain the function within the family.

How well do American families provide for the material and emotional welfare of their children? An indirect answer is provided by data on children and young people whose families have failed them in one way or another. In 1958 over two million children were receiving part of their economic support from the federal-State Aid to Dependent Children program. A third of a million children received child welfare casework services from public welfare agencies. Somewhat less than 200,000 young people were in institutions for orphans or juvenile delinquents. About 250,000 persons under eighteen years of age were arrested for criminal offenses in American towns and cities.[10] Other children received special assistance from non-governmental agencies, churches, and schools. There are many juvenile delinquents other than those arrested for specific offenses. There were perhaps as many as five million children and young people, taking all these into account, who were victims of an at least partial failure by their families to provide adequately for their welfare.

Five million inadequately cared-for children may appear to be a shockingly high figure. But the total number of children under eighteen in the United States in that year, 1958, was 60.9 million. The families of more than 90 per cent of America's children were apparently caring for them well enough that they did not have to ask for special outside help.

Also, the families of many of the five million children did not fail because of inherent weakness but because of external circumstances,

[10] *Statistical Abstract* 1959, pp. 289, 293; *Uniform Crime Reports for the United States* (Vol. XXVIII, No. 2), Federal Bureau of Investigation, Washington, D.C.: USGPO, 1958, p. 115. There is some double counting in these figures; for example, many children receiving casework services were also receiving Aid to Dependent Children funds and were thus included in both statistics.

such as unemployment or the death of one or both parents. Many juvenile delinquents, though far from all of them, are what they are because of the breakdown of the social structure in urban slums, which produces forces that even the strongest of families sometimes cannot withstand.

The evidence suggests that most American families are capable of caring for their children. Few persons believe that children should be raised outside the family. The major efforts of governmental and non-governmental agencies are directed at maintaining the child in a family. Financial assistance programs enable children to stay with their families. If there is no immediate family capable of raising them, as is sometimes true of orphans, illegitimate children, and children from broken homes, every effort is made to place them with foster families.

The Aged

CARE FOR THE AGED is still a significant function for many families. Only a very small proportion of the aged in American society become institutionalized, an estimated 4 per cent. "The rest, in sickness or health, in want or in comfort, live out their days at home." [11] Many of them live in their own homes; others live in the homes of their children or of other younger relatives.

Medical technology has prolonged the life span of the average individual, greatly increasing the proportion of persons over sixty-five in the population. The machine society also has a tendency to deprive the average worker of his productive role at an earlier stage in his life span than might be the case in an agrarian society. When the industrial laborer and the white-collar worker are retired at the age of sixty-five their productive existence is usually ended, and with it their earned income, although they have a remaining life expectancy of more than ten years.

In 1957 there were nearly fifteen million persons aged sixty-five or older in the United States. It is not known how dependent these people were on their families but it is known that most of them were not a financial burden. Nine out of ten were receiving income from employment or governmental or non-governmental income-maintenance programs. By 1980 virtually all of the aged population will be eligible for benefits.[12] A 1952 survey of the aged in California indicated that aged *couples* who did not receive social security benefits most often relied on wages as their most important source of income. Only about

[11] *The Aging in Three Catholic Parishes.* Washington, D.C.: National Conference of Catholic Charities, 1958, p. 1 (pamphlet).
[12] *Mobilizing Resources for Older People: Proceedings of the Federal-State Conference on Aging.* Washington, D.C.: USGPO, 1956, pp. 31-32.

8 per cent of them relied on help from their children. Of *single* aged persons who were not receiving governmental social security payments, about one in four said that their children and other relatives were their most important source of income. However, the survey did not take into account other forms of assistance that the aged received from families, such as food, care, housing, and so forth.[13]

A 1960 study in a lower-middle-class parish in Milwaukee gives a close and detailed portrait of 236 elderly Catholics. About 40 per cent of them lived in their own homes, though they often shared them with their children, and half of them lived in rented apartments; more than two-thirds of them said that they wanted to stay in their own places for as long as they could, even if alone. Most of them were financially able to do so; 34 per cent said that earnings were their chief source of income, while 48 per cent relied on pensions or social security. Only 5 per cent had to turn to children or Old Age Assistance for most of their support. Nine out of ten said that they "had enough to get along on" or were in "comfortable" circumstances; a few (8 per cent) said that they could not make ends meet. Complementing this picture of relative independence, more than half said that their relatives helped them, by performing services during emergencies, providing transportation, and so forth, and others said that help would be given if necessary. Of those who had children, 87 per cent said that they saw some of them at least once a week. Perhaps surprisingly, nearly two-thirds of the Milwaukee elderly said that they regularly or occasionally helped their children or close relatives, by baby sitting, doing yard work, giving them loans, and so forth. In general, this small group of elderly persons was financially independent yet at the same time kept close family ties.[14]

The Handicapped and the Sick

MANY AMERICANS are afflicted with some form of physical or mental ailment. There is increased awareness, though not necessarily an increased number, of a multitude of disorders: loss of hearing, blindness, heart disease, cancer, arthritis and rheumatism, diabetes, tuberculosis, cerebral palsy, infantile paralysis, muscular dystrophy, neurosis, schizophrenia, and mental retardation. Most of the victims of these and other ailments are leading or are capable of leading useful and satisfying lives.

[13] Vaughn Davis Bornet. *California Social Welfare.* Englewood Cliffs, N.J.: Prentice-Hall, 1956, p. 376.
[14] *The Elderly of St. Rose of Lima Parish.* Washington, D.C.: National Conference of Catholic Charities, 1960. Two more general studies of the status of the aged in American society are John J. Corson and John W. McConnell's *Economic Needs of Older People* (New York: The Twentieth Century Fund, 1956), and Henry D. Sheldon's *The Older Population of the United States* (New York: Wiley and Sons, 1958).

How useful and satisfying their lives are depends largely on their families.

The most important service the family can provide for the sick and handicapped is personal warmth and concern, qualities that few medical institutions can provide to any great extent. For the sick these personal qualities may aid recovery; for the handicapped they are often necessary for rehabilitation. Personal concern for most sick and handicapped persons is best provided in the home, though the technical skills and continuous observation and treatment required by many ailments often make it impossible for care to be given within the family.

Families must also bear much of the financial burden of medical care. Though the average American family has relatively limited resources, families do spend a considerable amount for medical services. In 1957 American families incurred medical charges totaling $15.1 billion (23 per cent of which was covered by insurance benefits), an average of about $300 per family. In 1958 medical care expenditures were $16.7 billion, 28 per cent of which was met by insurance benefits.

The Physically Handicapped: The physically handicapped are those with orthopedic and neuromuscular disabilities, and the blind and the deaf. Table 4 lists estimates of the numbers of persons suffering from certain ailments. For instance, there are 68,000 children who are partially sighted. There are some 760,000 deaf persons in the United States. There are about 200,000 amputees requiring prosthetic devices— artificial arms and legs.

Care for the handicapped or disabled person is provided by the family in many cases. Blind or deaf children are raised in the family, and may even be sent to ordinary schools. Victims of paralysis are returned to the family as soon as their physical condition allows.

The Physically Ill: There are two general categories of the physical ill, those who have chronic disorders and those whose illnesses are temporary.

Although chronic illness is ordinarily attributed to older persons, more of the chronically ill are under sixty-five years of age than are older. The aged have only a higher *incidence* of chronic illness. An estimated 3 per cent of the total population has chronic disabilities severe enough to make usual activities impossible. A third of this group comprises chronic invalids, about half of whom are in institutions and about half of whom live with their families.

The Mentally Ill: There are three groups of mentally ill persons. The smallest, numbering about one and one-half million, includes the extremely disturbed, or psychotic, personalities. These persons are incapable of carrying on most or all of the functions of ordinary life. The second group consists of individuals with personality disturbances, the emotional cripples. The anxieties, compulsions, and obsessions of these people, who number between seven and one-half and ten million

TABLE 4

Estimated Prevalence of Chronic and Disabling Illnesses

General Illness	Estimated Prevalence (Number of Cases)
Arthritis and Rheumatism	10,104,000
Blindness (Both Eyes)	200,000 to 334,000
Cerebral Palsy	570,000
	(280,000 under 21)
Deafness	
Total Deafness	760,000
Partial Deafness	3,500,000
Deaf Mutes	92,000
Diabetes	
Known Cases	1,000,000
Undiscovered	1,000,000
Disabling Chronic Diseases or Impairment	
(Long Term—over 3 months)	5,300,000
Drug Addiction	60,000
Epilepsy	500,000 to 1,500,000
Hay Fever and Asthma	3,900,000
Heart Disease	9,000,000 to 10,000,000
Homebound Persons (at Least 1 Year)	1,000,000
Mentally Retarded	4,500,000
Number of Patients Resident in Mental	
Hospitals (December, 1957)	560,000
Multiple Sclerosis	250,000 to 300,000
Muscular Dystrophy	100,000 to 200,000
Paraplegia	100,000
Amputees Needing Prosthetic Devices	200,000
Total	43,908,387 [1]

Source: *Corporate Contributions to National Health Agencies.* New York: National Better Business Bureau, 1957, p. 4.

[1] Where high and low estimates are given in the table, averages were struck to arrive at a total. The total can be considered only a very rough estimate, despite its apparent preciseness.

in the United States, are not severe enough to prevent apparently "normal" functioning. The third group comprises people who are not actually mentally "ill," but mentally deficient; about 3 per cent of the population is sufficiently retarded to have noticeable difficulty in living a normal existence.[15]

[15] *Facts and Figures about Mental Illness and Personality Disturbances.* New York: National Association for Mental Health, 1952, pp. 1–3.

The role of the family toward the mentally ill and retarded depends on the seriousness of the incapacity. The most seriously disturbed and retarded persons are often but not always beyond the family's capacity for care; they may not be capable of surviving without institutional treatment. However, many of them apparently *are* cared for by families. In 1958 there were about 560,000 patients in hospitals for mental disease in the United States. If the estimate that there were one and a half million seriously disturbed individuals in American society in the early 1950's is accurate, comparison of the figures suggests that over half of them were the direct responsibility of their families.

The less seriously ill seldom receive institutional care, though many of them have access to clinical consultation. Their care is usually provided by their families. Psychiatrists generally believe that the family has considerable potential in the care and rehabilitation of the mildly disturbed. It is usually capable of providing for the emotional needs that lie at the roots of the disturbance, if it is not their cause. Finally, only about 5 per cent of the retarded are institutionalized; the rest live in their own homes.

CONCLUDING REMARKS

THIS CHAPTER has described the nature of the American family and noted its changing roles. Though smaller, it places more emphasis on providing for the affective needs of its members than it did two generations ago. State laws concerning its formation and dissolution set the conditions under which the family operates as a welfare system. The spending behavior of the family gives a fair idea of what the typical family regards as necessary and preferable welfare expenditures, given the choices available it it. Low-income families have certain distinct characteristics; they are the recipients of much of the social welfare benefits provided by other institutions. Many of the persons who are the object of social welfare concern—dependent children, the aged, the sick and handicapped—receive some or most of their care from their families; when outside assistance is provided it is often for the purpose of helping families to care for such persons. It should be stressed that in all these problem areas much of the burden of care is carried by the contemporary American family.

Sometimes the family is held to be the perfect mechanism of human welfare. Different individuals and groups at different times have contended that nothing need be done outside the jurisdiction of the family, whether it be education, care of the sick, or provision of employment. Certainly the family is a versatile institution. It does many things well. The affectional ties that bind its members allow many mistakes, accidents, inadequacies, and diseconomies to occur without disrupting the fabric of family welfare activities.

However, the family suffers the defects of versatility as well. If all things can be done with fair success, some things in some cases are done poorly. The family is an excellent educational institution except when children seek skills not traditional in their families. The family can provide mutual economic support, but in a complex society the family must depend upon wages or other outside income to do so. The family can provide only a limited amount of physical protection. Almost no single welfare function is completely provided by the family, even when the family is intact and operating under good conditions.

On the other hand, it has been said too often that the family is declining; its demise is sometimes pictured as a matter of a few generations. A distinguished and conservative sociologist, the late William Ogburn, once listed a host of functions that had been lost to the family. The impression given was of an institution on its last legs. The materials of this chapter do not support such a view. If it did not exist, the family would have to be invented: it is the most lasting and best-known means for fulfilling economically and appropriately a number of welfare functions of primary importance. Among these are socialization of the young, providing for the emotional needs of the aged and the sick, moral instruction and experience, the teaching of manners and of physical techniques of self-care, imparting and teaching love and affection, and coaching in all manner of skills and customs. Only when internal or external circumstances prevent the family from carrying out these tasks are the other institutions of society called upon to step in and supplement or, more rarely, supplant the family.

Chapter Three

THE NEIGHBORHOOD

T HE NEIGHBORHOOD IS A GROUP OF INDIVIDUALS and families living in *defin.*
close association. It is a small area, and most of its residents can and
do have frequent face-to-face meetings with other residents. The boundaries of a neighborhood cannot always be stated precisely. For some
families their neighborhood is generally those persons living within
walking distance. In other cases a neighborhood may be defined along
lines of social grouping or national origin. For example, many cities
have well-recognized Italian, Polish, Jewish, or German neighborhoods.
Housing developments, whose residents generally have similar economic
standings and similar social backgrounds, may often be considered
neighborhoods. Small towns in which most of the inhabitants know
each other have many of the characteristics of neighborhoods. Also,
rural areas whose inhabitants share common interests, perhaps centered
in a grange, may also be neighborhoods.

The neighborhood is one of the primary groups to which the needs
of an individual or family very early become apparent, and the neighborhood possesses certain resources for dealing with these needs. The
senses of belonging to the neighborhood and of sharing responsibility
for the well-being of neighbors that typify a member of a neighborhood
underlie his or her willingness to perform welfare activities for the neighborhood and its residents. This chapter deals chiefly with the informal
groups and the formal, non-governmental neighborhood organizations
that have come into existence in response to neighborhood welfare
conditions.

33

THE PEOPLE OF THE NEIGHBORHOOD

MOST AMERICANS live in what they would consider to be neighborhoods, even though they may not be actively involved in them. Some sociologists have argued that the neighborhood is declining in importance in American society. One sociologist has written: "Distinctive features of the urban mode of life have often been described sociologically as consisting of the substitution of secondary for primary contacts, the weakening of bonds of kinship, and the declining social significance of the family, the disappearance of the neighborhood, and the undermining of the traditional basis of social solidarity." [1] Nevertheless there is evidence that the neighborhood and neighbors are still important to most people.

A recent study compared the male residents of four neighborhoods to determine the extent and nature of their informal contacts with neighbors and others, and the sources of their friendships. [2] Seven hundred men, divided about evenly among four San Francisco neighborhoods, were interviewed. Families in two of the neighborhoods had high economic status and those in the other two had low economic status. Two-thirds of the men from low-income families participated in informal groups of all kinds once or more a week. All but about 10 per cent participated in such groups at least once a month. Only some of these contacts were with neighbors, of course. Slightly less than half the men associated with groups of neighbors once or more a month. But most of those that did participated at least once a week. By comparison, about two-thirds associated with relatives at least once a month and two-thirds associated with groups of friends at least once a month.

Two-thirds of the men in the higher income neighborhoods also participated in informal groups of all kinds once a week or more. About 40 per cent of them participated with groups of neighbors at least once a month. Two-thirds of them visited relatives once or more a month, and three-quarters of them gathered with their friends that often. The authors remark that "whether a man lives in a cheap rooming-house area, an expensive apartment-house area, an area characterized by small detached houses and modest means, or one in which the dwellings are detached, large, and relatively expensive, he is very unlikely to be completely isolated." [3]

[1] Louis Wirth, "Urbanism as a Way of Life," *American Journal of Sociology*, XL (July, 1938), pp. 20–21.
[2] Wendell Bell and Marion D. Boat, "Urban Neighborhoods and Informal Social Relations," *American Journal of Sociology*, LXII (January, 1957), pp. 391–98.
[3] *Ibid.*, p. 393.

The men were also asked whom they would call on to take care of them if they were sick, even for as long as a month. Many of them gave more than one answer. Eight out of ten said "relatives," about six out of ten said "friends." Four out of ten specified "neighbors," four out of ten said "co-workers." Furthermore, neighborhoods are a source of friendships. About one-third of the men said that they had met one or more of their friends in their neighborhood.

This study, limited in scope though it may be, suggests that neighborhoods are still relatively important in the lives of families and individuals; even men in more or less randomly chosen neighborhoods have many informal group relations with their neighbors. Married women probably have even more frequent and intense contacts with neighbors than do their husbands or single men. The rest of this chapter comprises a consideration of some types of neighborhood welfare activity and a discussion of the informal and formal welfare groups of certain specific neighborhoods.

CHARACTERISTICS OF NEIGHBORHOOD WELFARE

THERE ARE two principal means by which neighborhoods can solve their problems. These are cooperative action, in which a group of individuals combine in an informal body; and assistance, the creation by some members of the neighborhood or the larger community of a formal agency, either non-professional or professional, to carry out services for those in need.

Most neighborhood services, regardless of the means by which they are carried out, fall into one or more of nine areas of interest:

(1) aid to relatively underprivileged groups or individuals;
(2) medical and nursing care;
(3) educational opportunities and programs;
(4) recreation;
(5) cultural enjoyment;
(6) improvement of existing facilities, such as homes, parks, and schools;
(7) development of new facilities;
(8) community planning;
(9) governmental reform.

The effectiveness of neighborhood welfare activities depends at least in part on three human factors. How many members of a neighborhood are likely to be involved? What are their socioeconomic positions in the neighborhood? and, What are their motives? The answers to these questions in turn depend on the type of action taken and the social composition of the neighborhood.

In any neighborhood cooperative action is likely to involve a considerable number of individuals. Car pools, baby-sitting cooperatives, and informal groups providing food and care for sick neighbors are simple and frequently seen examples. Almost every individual in a neighborhood becomes involved at some time in this type of activity. So far as motive is concerned, self-interest, satisfaction of humanitarian and religious impulses, social expectations, and group acceptance are all probably significant. Any or all of these motives may be satisfied by a single action; the presence of self-interest does not necessarily mean that the individual has no charitable or humanitarian feelings.

When a group organizes for neighborhood assistance, however, the picture changes. The percentage of individuals in a neighborhood involved drops off and a hierarchy develops. Not every person sees either neighborhood or personal benefit in providing a children's playground or a center for the aged. The men and women who do become involved establish a hierarchy, or have one established for them; the hierarchy ranges down from the leaders and initiators through the activists to the rank and file. The success of neighborhood assistance activity in fact often depends on the establishment of such a hierarchy. The idea and the desire do not become reality without effective leadership, individuals with organizational skill, and a group of individuals who are willing to give and to work.

The case of the Back of the Yards Council in Chicago, one of the most elaborate and effective neighborhood groups in the nation, provides some illustrations. A critical study made in the early 1940's indicated that popular participation in activities of the organization was between 5 and 7 per cent of the hundreds of thousands of people in the neighborhood. These figures were substantiated in later studies. Awareness of the organization or membership in a union or church that was part of the Back of the Yards movement was no criterion for participation, however. To qualify as a participant, the individual must have taken part in organizational discussions of Back of the Yards policies, served on a committee, or carried out some type of assignment for Back of the Yards organizations.

By way of comparison, similar criteria were applied to residents of precincts that were highly organized politically and to 6,000 members of a CIO union. In a sample of precincts, the degree of actual participation in political activities was about one-fourth of one per cent, excluding election day activities but including communicating with voters between elections, helping to organize annual picnics, traffic-ticket-fixing activities, and so forth. In the CIO union, counting participation as any union activity except attendance at the annual contract meetings and at strike meetings, the figure was about one per cent of union membership. As a further example, when membership in highly integrated church bodies was examined, participation in church or parish activities outside of Sunday church attendance was found to be less than one-half of one per cent of church members.

This phenomenon of a low rate of active participation in neighborhood organization may be explained in various ways. For instance, neighborhood assistance activities often benefit many persons other than the participants. A recreational area made available by the volunteer work of fifty men and women may be used by the children of a thousand families. It is a characteristic of most neighborhood assistance programs that a number of persons benefit from the intense efforts of a smaller number. Then, too, a host of people have neither the time, the money, nor the inclination to share in these doings.

The motivations for participating in these neighborhood assistance activities vary. The initial reaction on the part of families and local businessmen is likely to be "What's in it for me?" As Joseph Meegan, a Chicago recreation leader, pointed out, the success of a Back of the Yards project was frequently due to the fact that the organizers were able bluntly to demonstrate the self-interest aspects of an activity to an individual or a group whose cooperation was necessary. In a large number of cases, once an individual was attracted on the ground of self-interest he would subsequently find satisfaction in the activity itself and in certain concomitants of the activity.

Some of the concomitants of activity in neighborhood organizations are the pleasures of manipulating people and things, the enjoyment of cooperating with others, the respect and approval of other people, and the simple satisfaction of "a job well done." Often, increased knowledge of a problem itself brings greater interest. The ultimate result is that a participating individual often finds sharing in a neighborhood activity a desirable end in itself; over a long period of time he will exert maximum energy and talents to the activity, even to the detriment of his other interests.

This process is in part illustrated by the recruitment of two grocers into a Back of the Yards child welfare group. An organizer visited one of these men, a "Mr. David," who was completely unimpressed when the plight of the neighborhood children was explained to him. However, he agreed to attend a meeting of the group when it was pointed out that his attendance might benefit his business and customer relations. The organizer then pointed out the same thing to Mr. David's competitor, a "Mr. Roger," remarking that Mr. David was taking advantage of the opportunity.

At the meeting both men made financial contributions and were appointed to a children's committee; they accepted rather reluctantly but in keeping with their desires for good public relations. The organizer described their activities:

> As part of their first assignment the members of the committee were sent into some of the West Side tenements of the neighborhood. There Roger and David personally met the children who had been the subjects of their orations. They met them face to face and by their first names. They saw them as living persons framed in the squalor and misery of what they called "home." They saw the tenderness, the shyness, and the inner dignity which are in all people. They saw the children of the neighborhood for the first time in their lives. . . . Both of them came out of this experience with the anger of one who suddenly discovers that there are a lot of things in life that are wrong. One of them was violent in his denunciations of the circumstances that would permit conditions of this kind to go on unabated. Today these two rugged individualists are the foremost apostles of co-operative organization.[4]

As stated above, the ratio of participation in a particular cooperative or assistance effort rarely exceeds 5 per cent. Which individuals in a neighborhood are most likely to be among the 5 per cent? Studies have indicated that under ordinary circumstances neighborhood activity participants are not drawn from the various groups in the neighborhood in proportion to their numbers.

The same small group of individuals usually provides the leadership for a wide variety of non-professional neighborhood welfare organizations, councils, and movements. The functions of leadership are performed by the men and women who have had training and experience in leadership in their daily lives. They are businessmen, churchmen, schoolteachers, union leaders, government and political party officials, professional men, and officeholders in women's clubs and fraternal orders. Their motivations are generally strong and based not so much on self-interest in terms of other activities as on leadership as a goal in itself, along with the desire to "do something" in the face of events and conditions that do not correspond to their ideals.

A wider group supplies the individuals who do most of the work of a neighborhood movement. They are typically more representative of the neighborhood population than the leaders are, though they sometimes include members of the groups that also provide the leaders and organizers. As a rule, however, there are two groups that are absent

[4] Saul Alinsky. *Reveille for Radicals*. Chicago: University of Chicago Press, 1946, pp. 118–20.

38

from the rank and file of neighborhood welfare undertakings. One group comprises individuals of the highest income brackets and social standing, who, if they participate at all, do so as leaders; the other group consists of people at the lower end of the economic and social scale.

The absence of the first group can probably be explained in terms of interest, abilities, and social prestige. Such people feel that their abilities are put to better use at the leadership level, and seek prestige positions. The absence of the lower economic and social groups must be explained by their special attitudes toward neighborhood welfare undertakings. These people have been frequently subjected to outside attempts at assistance—they are ordinarily the consumers of most welfare activity. They often develop antagonisms toward "outsiders" and "do-gooders," and they consider most people of higher economic and social levels as "outsiders." With this frame of mind they are seldom willing to participate in work under the direction of such leaders, even if they might otherwise have the inclination to help their neighbors and neighborhood.

Some organizations have not experienced this opposition from people of the lower economic and social levels. The Back of the Yards Council in particular was highly successful in overcoming these resistances. The single most important factor in this was probably that these people were encouraged to participate at the planning and leadership levels from the beginning, and to initiate programs themselves. Also, those few leaders who came from outside the area went to great lengths to be considered as members of the neighborhood rather than "outsiders." This has been one of the most important factors in the Back of the Yards movement and in similar neighborhood movements in urban areas; their strength, when they have been successful, has rested on the interest and efforts of the lower income groups.

INFORMAL NEIGHBORHOOD WELFARE

THE TRADITIONAL AMERICAN means of dealing with community problems has been the informal group. The practice of self-help and help for neighbors has been a fundamental and sometimes essential community activity. There is a wealth of evidence that this tradition still plays an important role in American communities.

The earliest New England settlers developed their communities and their social patterns for cooperative action, out of necessity. New England towns were, and often still are, in part cooperative welfare systems. The frontier communities beyond the Appalachians, and later beyond the Mississippi, resorted to similar informal, voluntary organization.

39

They built their own schools and churches, and they formed vigilante committees. The same talents operate in contemporary society, although the stimuli are usually different. In the neighborhood people may help rebuild a burned-down house, care for aged neighbors, or spontaneously give money to pay the hospital expenses of a child with a weak heart. Such activities are initiated and performed without formal structure. Nor have the people involved considered it necessary to turn to outside sources of welfare for help. The will to act and the means of assistance are those of the people of the neighborhood.

The extent of such activities in the United States can only be estimated. They are a widespread and common part of American life. They probably occur to a greater extent in small towns and suburban areas than they do in large cities, yet even this conclusion is only hypothetical. Their contributions to the over-all picture of the welfare of a particular neighborhood may be inconsequential, or they may be so significant as to overshadow all organized welfare activity. Ultimately, their importance depends on the extent and seriousness of the welfare problems facing the neighborhood and on the willingness of families and individuals to work for the welfare of their neighbors.

FORMAL NEIGHBORHOOD WELFARE

A CHARACTERISTIC of neighborhood welfare activity is a trend from informal to formal organization. Isolated problems in an immediate neighborhood may be dealt with by informal means, but some semblance of formal organization is almost certain to develop if any one or more of the following conditions exist: First, the problem is a continuing one rather than an isolated one. Second, the problem is sufficiently complex that it cannot be adequately dealt with by informal means. Third, the number of people engaged in the activity becomes so large that certain among them decide that a formal organization would add to their efficiency in performing their tasks. Finally, the persons sharing in the activity desire a formal organization, which, with its hierarchic structure, can add to their prestige.

This section describes specific neighborhood welfare groups in four large cities: an association to develop a children's playground in Philadelphia; a tenant organization in a large New York City housing development; the Central West End Association in St. Louis; and the Back of the Yards Council in Chicago. It also describes the precinct organization of a political party as a welfare organization and discusses settlement houses.

40

The Neighborhood

Philadelphia: The Haines Street Tot Lot Association

THE HAINES STREET TOT LOT ASSOCIATION of Philadelphia was a neighborhood organization established for the specific purpose of developing a playground for children. The project stemmed from a broader movement to bring about the general betterment of the neighborhood that involved a number of other organizations. The neighborhood was old and run-down and contained many vacant lots so filled with trash that they were dangerous for children to play in. The project originated in a discussion between a neighborhood housewife and a social worker, slowly attracted the attention and interest of more neighborhood residents, and eventually acquired a formal organization.

The Tot Lot Association obtained a rent-free lease on three adjacent lots from their owner, a sympathetic businessman, as land for the playground. To secure funds for transforming these lots into a playground the Association conducted door-to-door solicitations; received contributions from business and other sources; held raffles, dances, parties, and dinners; and sold Christmas trees. Neighbors and friends contributed many hours of work for such tasks as leveling the ground, building a retaining wall, and installing equipment. Thanks mainly to such freewill donations of money, time, and energy, the playground opened a year after the project was inaugurated and has been used by dozens of children each day.[5]

New York: The Kingsborough Houses Tenant Organization

THE KINGSBOROUGH HOUSES tenant organization is an association of some residents of a New York City public housing project, containing 1,165 families, who seek to maintain order in the project and to keep the project in good physical condition. In New York City experience in particular, these have been found to be very serious problems in public housing projects and have been attributed to the breakdown of neighborhood feeling and responsibility among tenants drawn from different areas and backgrounds.[6] The Kingsborough organization indicates that such problems are not insurmountable. Among the problems confronting the organization, which was founded shortly after the project was first tenanted, are that many of the tenants have been slum dwellers; that about two-thirds of the tenants are Negroes, with con-

[5] Mrs. Aaron Okin, "Haines Street Tot Lot," in T. H. Stevenson, ed., *Building Better Volunteer Programs*, Princeton, N.J.: The Foundation for Voluntary Welfare (n.d. [1958]), pp. 81–91.
[6] For example, cf. Harrison Salisbury's *The Shook-Up Generation*. New York: Harper & Brothers, 1958.

41

sequent racial tensions; and that there are many juvenile delinquents and criminals in the surrounding area.

The tenant organization works in various ways to carry out its goals, ways that have changed considerably since the group came into being. At the outset, a tenant committee of thirty men patrolled the walks in the project to discourage criminal activity. The committee was later disbanded, after the crime problem in the six-block project decreased. Currently the organization encourages youths from outside the project to use the recreational areas of the project, so as to lessen the amount of juvenile gang warfare in the vicinity. The organization also attends to matters of physical condition such as cracked windows and bad plumbing, in cooperation with the manager—an employee of the City Housing Authority, which owns and operates the project. Furthermore, the organization supervises the community center of the project, which houses among other groups a Golden Age Club for elderly residents, and it has expanded the playground facilities for youngsters.[7]

St. Louis: The Central West End Association

THE CENTRAL WEST END ASSOCIATION of St. Louis is a group of about four hundred people devoted to preventing and eliminating blight in a section of St. Louis. The neighborhood concerned, an area of once-excellent homes, had so decayed that property owners, businessmen, and ordinary residents united to inaugurate a program of rehabilitation. Eventually they established the Central West End Association as a formal organization, with an annual budget of $20,000 and an executive director. With the help of other welfare groups and certain departments of the city government it has carried out a substantial part of its aims.

Perhaps the chief undertaking of the Association was to convince owners of both business and residential property in the neighborhood that they should improve their property, by painting, redecorating, and landscaping it. The Association has also enlisted the aid of city officials for such tasks as installing new street lights, removing wrecked and abandoned automobiles from the streets, and revising and enforcing zoning laws. Among the results of these undertakings are that large new commercial buildings are being erected in the area, property values have generally increased, and the city government has been enabled to collect a larger tax revenue from the neighborhood. In so far as decayed urban areas are associated with high crime rates and other welfare problems, the Association has indirectly had a restraining effect on their growth as well. The work of the Association in its neighborhood has encouraged the leaders of comparable bodies in other parts of St. Louis.[8]

[7] New York Times, Oct. 14, 1958.
[8] St. Louis Post-Dispatch, June 22, 1958, and July 27, 1958.

Chicago: The Back of the Yards Council

THE BACK OF THE YARDS COUNCIL in Chicago is an organization designed for the over-all improvement of a large neighborhood near the stockyards. In 1939, the "Back of the Yards," then known as "Packingtown," was a slum that was torn by every variety of crime, poverty, and disease. Hoodlumism and religious intolerance were widespread. Political offices went to the men who bought the most votes. Churchmen, union leaders, and businessmen contributed almost nothing to neighborhood feeling or interest. Yet in two decades Back of the Yards became one of the cleanest, healthiest, most united sections of the city.

The Back of the Yards Council began in 1939 in a movement led by two men: Saul Alinsky, a social worker and criminologist, and Joseph Meegan, a recreation leader. It adopted as its slogan, "We the people will work out our own destiny." Regarding those who worked with the Council, Joe Meegan, speaking as executive secretary, said:

At first most of the folks came in for an angle. The neighborhood is ninety per cent Catholic and strongly union—a criss-cross of steeples and smokestacks. We got the priests because they wanted people to be more law-abiding. We got the C.I.O. unions by saying, 'You guys have trouble keeping your members interested between strikes. We'll give them a program for every day in the year.' Then the A.F.L. came in to check the C.I.O. The merchants joined to make us cool down the boy gangs. When we pooled all the selfish objectives, we had a movement with a lot of strength. Pretty soon everyone forgot he'd joined for his own group and began working for the whole shebang.

Many people were antagonized by Council programs. For instance, some landlords were angered by efforts of the Council to have them comply with the requirements of the city housing code. To force action by the landlords, Back of the Yards children filled out questionnaires on violations of fire and health department rules in their own homes. A list of 3,600 violations was forwarded to City Hall. When no action was forthcoming the City Fathers were reminded of the voting strength of the neighborhood. City officials immediately began to enforce the laws.

In 1953 the Council started a home conservation and modernization program. In the 172 blocks of the area 150 new homes were built in the first five years of the program and another 4,000 homes were remodeled. Much of the program was financed not by the Council itself but by the twenty-two savings and loan associations in the area.

As an outgrowth of Back of the Yards, Saul Alinsky, Bishop Bernard Sheil, and G. Howland Shaw, a federal government official who was interested in social problems, organized the Industrial Areas Foundation, a national group applying similar methods to other cities. Kansas City, Kansas, Omaha, and South St. Paul, Minnesota, were among the first cities in which people developed neighborhood organizations along the lines of the Back of the Yards Council.[9]

The Political Party

THE POLITICAL PARTY provides considerable welfare services in many urban neighborhoods. The unit of party organization most closely related to neighborhood welfare is the precinct, whose boundaries may or may not correspond to those of a neighborhood as sociologically defined. The strength of precinct party organization varies widely from one precinct to another. In some precincts, especially in the West and in rural areas, there may be either no organization at all or only the skeleton of an organization. In other precincts, notably in areas of large cities populated by low-income groups, the party organization may be very strong. Precinct party organization comprises both government office-holders and influential people of the neighborhood who are not office-holders. The real strength of the organization can be measured by the number of other people in the precinct willing to work for the party.

A precinct party organization carries on welfare activities for both party members and non-members. For party members its most important professed function is to help them get elected to any government office they may seek. It also has the latent functions of supplying them with a ladder on which they can rise in society and of furnishing them with entertainment and a means for self-expression. In these latter respects it somewhat resembles fraternal and service organizations.

Most important for neighborhood welfare, it may supply food, clothing, and shelter to the needy; may attend to the legal difficulties of any residents; may draw the attention of any governmental or non-governmental agency to a welfare problem of the precinct; or may try to have the city council enact ordinances that will help the precinct. It also may secure profitable contracts or other economic advantages for the businessmen of the precinct. The main payment that the precinct party leader expects for such services is the support of the voters at election time, along with contributions of money from the more prosperous party members. In precincts where party organization is strong the precinct party leaders will be so active in seeking votes for their candidates that they may be more aware than any other group of the welfare

[9] Alinsky, *op. cit.*; Gretta Palmer, "Love Thy Neighbor," *The Kiwanis Magazine,* XXXI (February, 1946), pp. 10–11 (Meegan quotation from "Love Thy Neighbor"); *Chicago Sun-Times,* Feb. 15, 1958.

44

needs of their precinct, and more effective in satisfying those needs than some other agencies.

The Settlement House

THE SETTLEMENT HOUSE, sometimes known as the neighborhood center or the neighborhood association, is a welfare agency designed to carry out a variety of welfare activities for the people of a specific neighborhood. The first settlement house in the United States was established in 1886; today there are more than 800 of them. The settlement house is ordinarily administered by a board of directors, whose members are likely to be philanthropically minded community leaders residing outside the neighborhood. However, the boards of more and more houses include residents of the neighborhood as well. Generally the houses have a professional staff, but rely to a considerable extent on untrained, unsalaried volunteers as well. Community houses obtain their funds from numerous sources, particularly community chests and church groups.

The settlement house is often situated in a lower income neighborhood; traditionally, one of its chief aims has been to raise living standards in its area. The center also seeks to keep family ties strong, to develop friendly relations among all residents of the neighborhood, and to develop links between the neighborhood and the city, the State, and the nation. It works with both individuals and groups in the neighborhood. To benefit individuals, for instance, it may provide health services for the ill, home visiting for the aged, and schools or classes for the mentally retarded. Also, it may sponsor teams and clubs within its own confines, and may counsel groups of various kinds in the neighborhood outside the house.

The West Side Community House of Cleveland

THE WEST SIDE COMMUNITY HOUSE, one of Cleveland's fourteen settlements, "attempts to cultivate a sense of pride in, and loyalty to the neighborhood, a feeling of belonging together, a sense of responsibility for conditions in the local area, and an awareness that the neighborhood is an integral part of the wider community." It was founded in 1904 by Methodist Church parish workers in an effort to help the women and children of new immigrant families in Cleveland's "Near West Side." The neighborhood in which it is located still has a large group of newcomers, now Negroes and Puerto Ricans, who live alongside families of previous European immigrants.

The Community House has a number of programs for helping people in its area and for developing healthy neighborhood relations. It regularly provides day care for forty-five children of mothers who must work away from home. In 1958 about sixty children between six and eight years old were served in after-school clubs and classes; four hundred older children, between nine and twelve, participated in similar clubs and classes, and many of them took part in a summer day-camp program that the Community House has operated for some years. Food was provided for many children of the neighborhood. About 280 teenagers were members of interracial clubs sponsored and housed by the Community House. For adults there were evening classes in English, a mothers' club, and a Golden Age Club. The staff has a neighborhood worker to organize neighborhood groups and counsel them on economic, family, and community problems.

The West Side Community House still operates under the auspices of the Methodist Church. Its board of directors includes *ex officio* officers of local and regional organizations of the Women's Society of Christian Service of the Methodist Church. The Community House is directed and in part operated by trained personnel, with the assistance of volunteers, including people of the neighborhood, and college students. In 1958 it expended about $83,000 in providing its services. About two-thirds of this came from the community fund-raising organization of Cleveland.[10]

CONCLUDING REMARKS

THE ESSENTIAL CHARACTERISTIC of most neighborhood welfare is that the helpers and the helped live in close association with one another. In some neighborhood welfare projects, such as the Haines Street Tot Lot Association and the Back of the Yards Council, those who participate may benefit just as much as other neighborhood residents. A great deal of neighborhood welfare is informal, assistance given by one family to another; in any one case the extent of assistance is likely to be small, yet the effect of many such acts is to reduce the welfare burden of the nongovernmental and governmental welfare agencies of the larger community. The total extent of informal neighborhood welfare is unknown and perhaps never will be known, but it has a definite place in the scheme of American welfare.

Informal neighborhood welfare activities sometimes evolve into formal welfare organizations, operated primarily by people of the neighborhood for the benefit of the neighborhood. Such organizations may be quite small and have a relatively brief existence, lapsing once a particular problem is solved. Others, such as the Back of the Yards Council,

[10] From descriptive materials provided by Bernard S. Houghton, Executive Director of the West Side Community House.

46

may become formidable and enduring operations, concerned with a multitude of neighborhood welfare conditions.

There are also some neighborhood welfare activities that are initiated by persons outside the neighborhood but that become closely identified with the neighborhood and draw much of their strength from the cooperation and participation of neighborhood residents. Political party organizations on the ward level, though their primary purpose is delivering the vote on election day, may provide the setting for extensive welfare activities of this sort. The settlement house, found particularly in low-income urban neighborhoods, is usually established by persons outside the neighborhood but depends for its success on the participation of the people of the neighborhood, who usually carry out most settlement-house welfare projects and are often strongly represented on the settlement's governing board.

The neighborhood, particularly the urban neighborhood with a high concentration of population, has welfare resources that are seldom exploited to their fullest. Even people of lowest incomes and education are often ready to spend time and energy to help themselves and their neighbors, if the circumstances are right. Only a small proportion of all the people in the neighborhood may actually become involved in a particular neighborhood welfare project, but the end results may be as sweeping as they were in Chicago's "Packingtown."

Chapter Four

THE COMMUNITY

THE COMMUNITY CONSISTS either of a large enough to include several neighborhoods or of a rural area that in some way—usually geographic or economic—is a "natural" unit and that contains several small towns with characteristics similar to those of neighborhoods. Although these broader usages have the value of emphasizing that there are some feelings, problems, and conditions common to large and widely distributed groups of people, "community" as it is used in this discussion refers to a relatively small geographical area whose residents have a comparatively large number of common interests and problems.

In a community, unlike the situation in a neighborhood, most of the people do not have frequent face-to-face meetings with other people of the community (save, of course, those in their own neighborhoods); hence their relations tend to be impersonal. By contrast the leaders of the community, even though they may only rarely meet the people of their own neighborhoods, usually have fairly close relations with one another. This is so because leaders are apt to belong to the same community-wide associations and are likely to have similar community-wide business or professional interests.

Owing to its far greater resources, the community is able to undertake much more extensive welfare activities than the neighborhood. However, these community-wide activities almost always have a formal organization. The welfare problems of an entire community are usually continuing ones; they are likely to be complex; and they generally require the participation of a number of people. Finally, since the relations among the people of a community tend to be impersonal, the people are not likely to cooperate effectively save in a formal structure. Therefore this chapter deals almost exclusively with formal welfare undertakings.

One important distinction among welfare organizations is that some are *professional* and others are *non-professional*. A professional organization is one that is staffed chiefly by paid workers many of whom have had special training in welfare work. A non-professional organization, by contrast, consists almost entirely of unsalaried volunteer workers most of whom have had no special training for welfare work. Both types exist at the community level, and are discussed here.

One other important distinction among welfare organizations is that some carry out primarily line functions and others carry out primarily staff functions. For the purposes of this book, line functions are those services provided *directly* to persons or groups of persons who are believed to be in need. A family service agency that provides material assistance to a family that has been deserted by its husband and father is performing a line function. The provision of facilities such as playgrounds and clinics for people in need also is a line function. Staff functions include planning, coordination, research, and fund-raising performed by one welfare organization for another welfare organization or group of organizations. For example, community councils attempt to coordinate the activities of the non-governmental welfare agencies and sometimes the government welfare agencies in a community. Accordingly welfare bodies may be termed line organizations or staff organizations, depending on their principal functions. Figure 1 depicts the formal decision-making and staff relations among types of non-government welfare organizations at the community level and related regional and national bodies; Figure 2 suggests the flow of funds, time, and energy provided by individuals for community welfare.

This chapter deals almost exclusively with *non-governmental* community welfare activities. The welfare activities of city and county governments may also be considered community welfare activities, at least in part, but because of their distinctive characteristics they are discussed separately, in the chapter on local governments. In contrast to non-governmental welfare organizations, local government programs are initiated by law, their purposes and operations are usually explicitly defined by law, and their activities are financed from tax funds. It should be kept in mind, however, that there are many interrelations between non-governmental and governmental community welfare activities. Non-governmental welfare organizations may work for the establishment of a government welfare program, and, though less frequently, local government officials may actively encourage the development of non-

FIGURE 1

NON-GOVERNMENTAL COMMUNITY WELFARE:
Decision-Making About Who Gets What and How

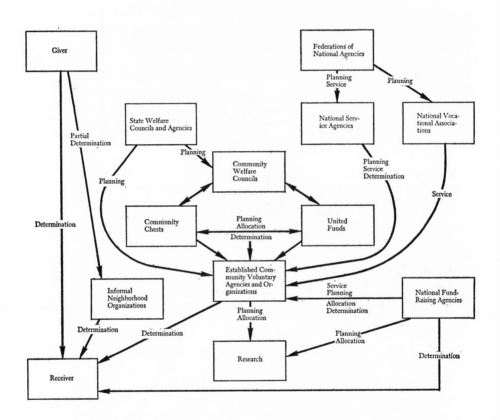

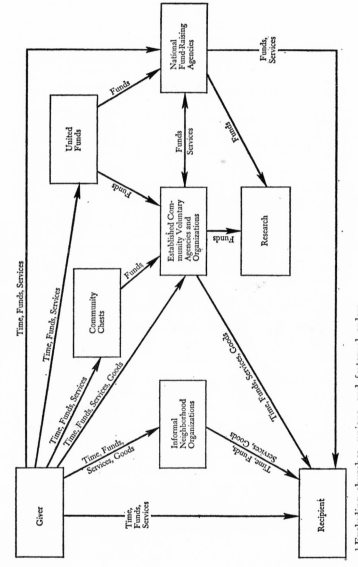

FIGURE 2

VOLUNTARY COMMUNITY WELFARE ACTIVITY [1]

[1] Excluding churches, unions, and fraternal orders.

governmental welfare programs. Local government welfare funds may be channeled into the hands of non-governmental welfare organizations. Many community-wide welfare projects are the result of close cooperation between governmental and non-governmental welfare groups. In most communities the governmental and non-governmental welfare activities complement each other, and both are deemed necessary for the community good.

COMMUNITIES AND THEIR WELFARE PROBLEMS

COMMUNITIES EXPERIENCE A HOST of welfare problems, which vary according to the nature and population of the community. Of all American communities 174 are metropolitan areas, which may be defined as central cities with populations of 50,000 persons or more and their surrounding dependent areas. In 1959 these metropolitan areas had a population of about a hundred million, about 55 per cent of the total population of the United States. Other communities are cities with smaller yet considerable populations. Still other communities are rural, consisting of parts of counties, entire counties, or groups of two or more counties. It is clear from this definition of a community that almost every American lives in a community, may experience welfare problems in a community, and may contribute to solving welfare problems in a community.

Among welfare problems, many are common to both urban and rural communities; some, chiefly to urban communities; and a few, chiefly to rural communities. In all communities welfare efforts are directed, for example, to problem families, the aged, the mentally ill, health, and medical facilities. Especially in urban communities, such efforts are directed to juvenile delinquents, organized crime, vocational rehabilitation, unemployment in depressed areas, natural disaster, housing, planning, streets, and sanitation. Especially in rural areas, welfare efforts are made to decrease cultural isolation and to assist migrant workers.

LINE WELFARE ORGANIZATIONS

Non-professional

THIS SECTION DESCRIBES four non-professional community welfare organizations, two urban and two rural. Because of the great variety of such organizations they cannot be called either "typical" or "unique."

However, they do serve to give some idea of the range of non-professional community welfare interests and activities.

THE BERKELEY BIG BROTHER PROJECT: The Big Brother Project of Berkeley, California, is designed to keep young boys from becoming delinquents by providing them with the company of an adult. There are many such Big Brother projects in American communities; the Berkeley project is unusual in that it is staffed by carefully chosen male students from the University of California, who are paid nominal sums for their services.

Between 1946 and 1956, 117 boys were referred to the Berkeley YMCA, which supervises the project, by the Juvenile Bureau of the Berkeley Police Department. The fathers of most of the boys were dead or had deserted their families. Sixty-eight Big Brothers were recruited to act as the boys' friends and counselors. Only nine of the boys that entered the project were subsequently sent to Juvenile Court. Hence the project not only aided the boys themselves but also considerably reduced the work and the costs of the government agencies that would otherwise have had to deal with them. Moreover, the Big Brothers, the families of the boys, and the schools in which they have been enrolled also have benefited from the project.[1]

THE CLEVELAND SOCIETY FOR THE BLIND: The Cleveland Society for the Blind offers casework services, recreation and group services, home industries, teaching services, retail sales, and other services for blind and partially sighted individuals. Although it employs a number of professional workers, the Society is largely staffed by about three hundred volunteers who carry out special tasks. Before engaging in service for the Society, volunteers ordinarily undergo some training by the Society's professional staff. Once trained, the volunteer may participate in any of several programs for the blind. Among these programs are those involving the teaching of good food preparation, swimming, bowling, and dancing. Other volunteers may assist at dances and provide transportation. Still others perform staff functions such as clerical assistance in the Society offices. By their work the volunteers lessen the burden of the professional employees, they bring new ideas to the organization, and they can serve as a link between the staff and the general public.[2]

THE FIVE MILE CREEK CITIZENS' COMMITTEE: The Five Mile Creek Citizens' Committee of Franklin County, Idaho, was established

---

[1] William J. Davis, "The Berkeley Big Brother Project," in Alfred de Grazia, ed., *Grass Roots Private Welfare*, New York: New York University Press, 1957, pp. 41–44.
[2] Mrs. Carrie Turner, "A Complex of Volunteer Services for the Blind," *ibid.*, pp. 104–107.

to build a dam and initiate soil conservation practices, with no aid from the government, in an area that had experienced serious soil erosion. During the 1930's and 1940's flash floods in the creek cut a canyon three miles long, in some places 600 feet wide and 100 feet deep. Each year floods stripped away from fifty to seventy-five acres of good farming land.

In 1951 the Soil Conservation Service of the Department of Agriculture made a preliminary survey of the situation, which cost $30,000. Engineers estimated that a dam to stop erosion would cost about $500,000. The 10,000 people of the county were antagonistic to the proposal, decided to take matters into their own hands, and organized a citizens' committee to deal with the problem.

An engineer developed a plan calling for one major dam, with smaller dams in the tributary gullies, and the planting of willows along the channel. The committee unanimously agreed that there would be no appeals for government aid to put the plan into effect. Farmers, local firms and banks, chambers of commerce, a railroad, and a private power company made financial contributions. Some individuals contributed their labor, material, or machinery. The machinery included a tractor, bulldozer, air hammers, and other equipment. Largely with volunteer labor the people of the county built the major and tributary dams at a cost of $39,745. At the same time soil conservation practices of various kinds were sponsored to ensure the effectiveness of the dams.[3]

THE TRUSTEES OF THE VALLEY CLINIC AND HOSPITAL, INC.: The organization formally titled the Trustees of the Valley Clinic and Hospital, Inc., of western North Carolina, was established to construct and maintain a hospital in an area almost totally lacking medical facilities. The area consists of a 500-square-mile valley system occupying parts of each of four counties, in whose gorges and mountain hamlets live some six thousand people. In the fall of 1947 a young doctor, who had recently arrived in the area, called together ten of its leading farmers and merchants. He pointed out the necessity of having a hospital in the area and suggested one with twelve beds, which would ordinarily cost $168,000.

First, with the doctor's encouragement, a local Elks club contributed $1,500 to buy an abandoned brick schoolhouse. At this point the leaders, now a group of twenty men, incorporated themselves. To raise additional support they wrote letters to persons in all four counties, made speeches before club and church groups, and actively solicited funds. Through these efforts they eventually raised $12,000 in cash contributions. The women of the community gathered an additional $4,000. An

[3] *Christian Economics*, Jan. 22, 1957.

54

architect drew up plans free of charge. A construction boss volunteered and, with the trustees, estimated the need for materials, volunteer manpower, and hard cash. Some people gave trees, logs, or nails; a local sawmill cut the lumber. Construction began early in 1948. Between fifteen and thirty men—carpenters, rock masons, electricians, sawyers, and common laborers—worked regularly on the project for the next eight months.

In October, 1948, the hospital was dedicated. The total outlay, aside from $14,600 from outside sources, consisted of funds and man-hours donated by local people. The community interest that was developed to support the project continued; some years later, half the people working for the hospital were volunteers, and on a number of occasions local contributions sufficient to meet the hospital deficit were raised.[4]

Professional

HERE TWO URBAN PROFESSIONAL WELFARE ORGANIZATIONS are described. The first has been introduced to suggest the process by which a non-professional organization may become professional.

THE COMMUNITY SERVICE SOCIETY: The Community Service Society of New York City provides an illustration of the procedure by which a non-professional organization transformed itself into a professional organization. It originated as the New York Association for Improving the Condition of the Poor (AICP). A non-professional organization founded in 1841, the AICP was primarily concerned with individual moral aid. It was established in an era of economic depression and of chaotic relief and welfare activities. There was a multitude of small relief societies, almost all of them founded since the year 1800 and serving very restricted purposes.

The AICP organized relief programs in many parts of the city, using hundreds of volunteers to give counsel and assistance to individual families. In the ensuing decades the volunteers were supplemented by paid "agents." As universities established curricula and schools of social welfare these agents were more and more drawn from the ranks of graduates of these curricula and schools. Ultimately, unpaid volunteer effort was almost entirely replaced by salaried professional service. The AICP found it necessary to raise and disburse relief funds, and expanded its activities to include job finding, friendly visiting for the sick and aged, and investigation of health and housing conditions. Subsequently

[4] Elmore M. McKee. *The People Act: Stories of How Americans Are Coming Together to Deal with Their Community Problems*. New York: Harper & Brothers, 1955, pp. 13–29.

the AICP amalgamated with the New York Charity Organization Society, to be known jointly as the Community Service Society.[5]

The AICP came into existence as certain people recognized that the welfare problems of New York City were not isolated instances, but were continuing problems, and that large numbers of individuals were being affected. These conditions required an organization to deal with them. In time came recognition of the complexity of these problems and the interrelations among poverty, unemployment, discouragement, bad health, and poor housing. With this recognition organization expanded and new techniques and areas of activity developed. These trends are present in the development of many formal community agencies, including the community service societies of other urban communities. With organization and operation come new knowledge and interest; original purposes are altered and discarded; extension and specialization of activity occur; and unpaid volunteers give way to salaried professionals.

THE VOCATIONAL GUIDANCE AND REHABILITATION SERVICES: The Vocational Guidance and Rehabilitation Services, of Cleveland, Ohio, is a small professional welfare agency designed to provide vocational counseling and to find employment for people between the ages of fifty and sixty-five. Actually, these were only the original age limits envisaged by the founders of the organization; soon after its founding in 1949 persons both well below fifty and well over sixty-five were asking the Services for aid.

The difficulties of the individual might stem from age alone, or from a physical or mental handicap or combination of handicaps. The principal undertaking of the Services has been to supply these people with counsel, to enable them to find suitable work either through their own efforts or through some other agency. Meanwhile the Services itself has gradually accumulated a list of businesses that will employ its clients. By 1956, after seven years of operation, the Services had had about 2,000 clients; of these, more than 350 had secured employment through the Services itself and over 700 others had secured employment through other means. Many clients had been referred to other agencies that might remove or alleviate their difficulties. The program is staffed primarily by a trained and salaried vocational counselor, who in 1956 was himself sixty-three years of age. There are also some volunteer workers. The cost of the agency has been about $6,000 a year, part of which is covered by fees and another part of which comes from contributions.[6]

[5] Russell H. Kurtz, ed. Social Work Yearbook 1957. New York: National Association of Social Workers, 1957, p. 23.
[6] Paul A. Wilson, "Vocational Counseling of Older Workers," in de Grazia, ed., op. cit., pp. 230–34.

The Whole Pattern of Welfare Agencies in One City: San Francisco

THIS SECTION COMPLEMENTS the previous descriptions of a number of separate community welfare organizations by portraying the entire scope of non-governmental welfare organization in a single American community: San Francisco. San Francisco is one of the larger cities in the United States, having a population of about 800,000. The per capita income is somewhat above the national average and there are not the serious slum problems in San Francisco that there are in many other large cities. Yet in 1954 there were 225 non-governmental welfare organizations serving the city and its people. These organizations were concerned with one or more of five areas of welfare service: (1) services for children (ages one to five); (2) services for youths (ages six to twenty-one); (3) services for adults; (4) services for the aging; and (5) health services for all age groups. These areas can be subdivided according to the *type* of service provided, as they are in Table 1. (In New York City, by comparison, there were over 1,000 non-governmental health and welfare organizations, according to the 1958–59 *Directory of Social and Health Agencies of New York City*.)

The figures in Table 1 indicate the range of non-governmental welfare organizations serving the people of San Francisco. Most of the 225 welfare organizations operated in only one area of service; twenty-four of them operated in two areas, and only seven were active in three or more areas. A number of organizations provided more than one type of service within a particular area of interest. About two-thirds of the organizations provided services in the city alone; the others served a larger area as well. An estimated four out of ten organizations had religious or ethnic group affiliations.

SERVICES FOR CHILDREN: Forty-four organizations provided services for children. They gave material and other assistance to the child in its home, made adoption arrangements, and gave care to unwed mothers. Nearly two-thirds of these organizations gave only one type of service (cf. Table 1). Two examples of the small agencies and groups providing such specialized services to children were the Salvation Army Lytton Home and the non-professional, volunteer group known as Saints and Sinners. The Lytton Home provided year-around care to about 120 children. The Saints and Sinners in 1954 gave above $50,000 worth of milk for 4,800 school children who were in "economic need." An organization that has provided several types of service for children is Edgewood, the San Francisco Protestant orphanage. Edgewood cared for about seventy-five children, was licensed as an adoption placement agency, and also placed children in foster homes.

57

TABLE 1

NON-GOVERNMENTAL WELFARE ORGANIZATIONS IN SAN FRANCISCO, 1954 (225 Organizations) [1]

Areas and Types of Services	No. of Organizations Providing Services	No. Providing One Type	No. Providing Two Types	No. Providing Three or More Types	No. Providing Region-wide Services[2]	No. Serving San Francisco Only	No. with Religious Affiliations (Est.)	No. with Ethnic Affiliations (Est.)[3]
Services for Children	44	29	9	6	17	27	15	6
(1) In Their Own Homes	3					3		
(2) Placement in Homes	6				1	5		
(3) Institutional Care	16				12	4		
(4) Unmarried Mothers	3				3			
(5) Adoption Services	6				2	4		
(6) Counseling	11				1	10		
(7) Homemaking Services	4					4		
(8) Well-Baby Services	1					1		
(9) Day Care Services	6					6		
(10) Other	4					4		
Services for Youths	49	32	11	6	3	46	16	9
(1) Group Work & Recreation	34				3	31		
(2) Counseling and Guidance	9					9		
(3) Living Quarters	15					15		
(4) Other	1					1		
Services for Adults	63	43	13	7	18	45	18	16
(1) Material Assistance	25				9	16		
(2) Travelers & Migrants	18				9	9		
(3) Institutional Housing	5					5		
(4) Services in Institutions	9					9		
(5) Legal Aid	6					6		
(6) Military, Vets. Services	12				5	7		
(7) Disaster Relief	1					1		
(8) Group Work and Recreation	7					7		
(9) Other								
Services for the Aging	25	17	6	2	13	12	11	5
(1) Material Assistance								
(2) Institutional Housing	15				13	2		

[1] Because many organizations provided more than one type of service in one area, and other organizations provided services in several areas, the numbers of organizations given in the vertical columns sum to more than their respective sub-totals, and the sub-totals when summed exceed the actual number of organizations.

[2] Organizations providing services for four counties or more, including San Francisco County (which is coterminous with the city of San Francisco).

[3] These are organizations such as the Jewish Community Center, the Italian Welfare Agency, the Russian Charitable Organizations of the United States, and others.

Areas and Types of Services	No. of Organizations Providing Services	No. Providing One Type	No. Providing Two Types	No. Providing Three or More Types	No. Providing Region-wide Services[2]	No. Serving San Francisco Only	No. with Religious Affiliations (Est.)	No. with Ethnic Affiliations (Est.)[3]
(3) Group Work & Recreation	8					8		
(4) Employment Services	2					2		
Health Services, All Ages	91	79	9	3	35	56	17	5
(1) Medical Services	32				4	28		
(2) Research & Education	17				15	2		
(3) Programs for Crippled	8				7	1		
(4) Mental Health Programs	7				1	6		
(5) Cerebral Palsy Programs	4				2	2		
(6) Infantile Paralysis	3				3			
(7) Tuberculosis	3				2	1		
(8) Chronically Ill	6				4	2		
(9) Dental Services	9					9		
(10) Services for Blind, Deaf	11				7	4		
(11) Rehabilitation	15				3	12		
(12) Other	2					2		

Source: Vaughn Davis Bornet. *California Social Welfare.* Englewood Cliffs, N.J.: Prentice-Hall, 1956.

In the mid-1950's there were sixteen organizations providing institutional care for children, serving either San Francisco exclusively or the Bay Area in general. In 1954 these institutions cared for over 700 San Francisco children. Three Bay Area institutions were especially concerned with the unmarried expectant mother and, after it was born, her child. These institutions, the Salvation Army Booth Memorial Home, the Florence Crittenton Home, and St. Elizabeth's Infant Hospital, admitted 650 unwed expectant mothers in 1954.

There were also a number of agencies providing casework services that benefited San Francisco children. Many of these organizations were affiliated with the Family Service Association of America. Family and adult casework service in the city were provided by eleven agencies, notably the San Francisco chapter of the Red Cross, the Catholic Social Service, and the Family and Children's Agency. The average monthly caseload over the year 1954 totaled 3,800 for the eleven agencies. In addition to casework they provided $16,000 to be used by families for their children.

Four agencies provided homemaking services for children who

would otherwise have had to be placed outside their own homes. (Home-makers are selected, trained, and usually salaried by agencies providing such services.) In 1954–55 one of these agencies, the San Francisco Family and Children's Agency, placed homemakers in 140 homes, for varying lengths of time, caring for 373 children.

SERVICES FOR YOUTHS: There were forty-nine organizations pro-viding one or more services for San Francisco youths in 1954. Thirty-four agencies supplied group work and recreation, often with the over-all purpose of reducing the likelihood of juvenile delinquency. Nine agencies offered counseling and guidance, and fifteen provided living quarters.

In San Francisco, as in most communities, the Young Men's Chris-tian Association (YMCA) was the largest organization concerned with group work and recreation. Over half the individuals participating in group activities and using facilities of such organizations did so at the nine San Francisco YMCA centers. The San Francisco Boys' Club and the Jewish Community Center each provided services for about 7 per cent of the total group of participants. The Jewish Community Center was one of twelve San Francisco community centers, all of which in 1954 expended nearly half a million dollars to provide facilities, ed-ucational and entertainment programs, and other group activities for young people, particularly the members of minority groups and the in-habitants of low-income, congested neighborhoods. Several of these centers were sponsored by religious groups, including the Presbyterian Donaldina Cameron House, serving Chinese girls; the Good Samaritan Community Center of the Episcopalians; and the Catholic Kolping So-ciety. The International Institute, which also provided services to adults, was concerned largely with the foreign-born, providing services ranging from folk dancing and singing for young people to casework and financial assistance to families, on a 1954 budget of about $25,000.

Recreational programs as provided by these agencies affect a very large number of persons. The eighteen largest agencies providing or-ganized group work and recreational services catered to an average of 325,000 persons per month in 1954. This figure is not quite so impres-sive as it appears at first glance, however. It involved a great deal of multiple counting (i.e., persons using facilities or services more than once a month were counted once for each use), and a number of adults were included in the total. Nevertheless, on the basis of a six-day week some 12,000 persons a day used the facilities and participated in the activities of these eighteen agencies. In 1954 the total income of these agencies in San Francisco and neighboring Alameda County was over $1.5 million, of which slightly less than half came from community chests.

Twenty-three San Francisco agencies offered interviews, consultation, and guidance to individuals with personality and social adjustment problems. Nine were particularly concerned with the problems of youth, notably the San Francisco Boys' Club, the "Y's," and the Jewish Community Center. In 1954 the San Francisco Boys' Club interviewed or gave consultation to 20,100 individuals. A smaller organization, the Salesian Boys' Club, listed 1,200 cases for the year.

Fifteen agencies, including many of those mentioned above, provided free or part-pay housing accommodations for youths. In San Francisco as in other American cities the YMCA's and YWCA's provided these services for many young persons. Community centers, clubs, and houses offered similar facilities. The Evangeline Residence, Harbor Light Corps, and Pinehurst Emergency Lodge, all maintained by the Salvation Army, all provided accommodations for young people, as did Donaldina Cameron House, the Emanu-el Residence Club, and the San Francisco Working Boys' Club. The San Francisco Youth Association promoted youth citizenship programs.

SERVICES FOR ADULTS: Welfare services for adults available in most communities include casework, financial assistance, travelers' aid, legal aid, recreation, and housing. In 1954 some sixty San Francisco agencies provided these services. Twenty-five organizations provided financial aid or payments in kind. Thirteen of these agencies, notably the San Francisco chapter of the American Red Cross, the Jewish Family Service Agency, the Society of St. Vincent de Paul, Catholic Social Service, and the Salvation Army Family Welfare Bureau, provided a total of $300,000 in financial assistance to 14,000 families and individuals.

Some San Francisco organizations served particular groups of adults. Among them were the Navy Relief Society, the Hebrew Free Loan Association, the American National Committee to Aid Homeless Armenians, the Russian Charitable Organizations of the United States, the Jewish Committee for Personal Service, the Lutheran Institutional Ministry, and a number of others.

Institutional housing was provided by the Salvation Army and the Y's. Visiting and rehabilitation work in institutions were the concern of Alcoholics Anonymous, Helpers of the Holy Souls, and Volunteers of America. Legal aid could be obtained either from the American Civil Liberties Union, the Legal Aid Society of San Francisco, or from any of four other agencies. Two of the latter organizations dealt primarily with the legal problems of particular groups: the National Association for the Advancement of Colored People and the Hebrew Sheltering and Immigrant Aid Society of America.

There were many sources of assistance for veterans and military personnel, among them the assistance programs of veterans' organizations such as the American Legion and its auxiliaries, and the VFW. The United Service Organizations (USO), the YMCA, the Red Shield Club Canteen, and several religious organizations were particularly concerned with the welfare of active military personnel.

Several specialized agencies made recreation and group work available for adults. The recreation programs of the Y's are cited above. Community and neighborhood centers also provided these services. In 1954 about 2,000 people each month used the facilities of the San Francisco Community Music Center, an organization that received nearly two-thirds of its financial support from the San Francisco Community Chest. The Apostleship of the Sea and Recreation for the Blind extended recreational facilities to particular groups.

SERVICES FOR THE AGED: California has a higher proportion of aged in its population that almost any other State. In 1954 there were twenty-five San Francisco agencies providing material assistance, institutional housing, recreation, or employment services for this group. There were at least fifteen institutions in San Francisco providing living quarters for the aging on either a free or a part-pay basis. There were a number of other boarding homes or institutions, licensed by either the State or the county, whose residents were supported by relatives, savings, or, more and more frequently, by OASI, the State of California's Old Age Security Program, and/or non-governmental pensions. (Individuals in private boarding homes and institutions were not eligible for social security benefits if they had entered into a life-care contract with the institution.)

A number of previously mentioned community centers and family welfare agencies also operated programs for the aged, as did Goodwill Industries and the Sunset Club of Volunteers of America. Two agencies that attempted to secure jobs for the aging were St. Benedict's Employment Service and the utility workshop of the San Francisco Committee for Service to Émigrés.

HEALTH SERVICES FOR ALL AGE GROUPS: Of the 225 non-governmental organizations providing welfare services for the people of San Francisco, 40 per cent supplied health services of some type. These organizations included hospitals with free or part-pay plans, local chapters of the national health organizations such as the Muscular Dystrophy Association, clinics, rehabilitation centers, groups with programs for the blind and deaf, and associations such as Alcoholics Anonymous and the Visiting Nurse Association of San Francisco.

At least fifteen San Francisco hospitals offered free or part-pay services. Two of the smaller ones, Arequipa Sanitorium with sixty beds (for tubercular patients) and Garden Hospital with 100 beds (for chronically ill individuals), received significant portions of their finances from community chests. There were also about fifteen clinics and out-patient service and facility organizations for individuals unable to meet medical expenses. The total income of these organizations in 1954 was somewhat over $1 million; these funds came from contributions, fees, endowments, and government sources.

In 1954 at least nine of the national health organizations operated programs that benefited San Francisco residents. The American Cancer Society, United Cerebral Palsy, National Society for Crippled Children and Adults, American Heart Association, Muscular Dystrophy Association, and the National Foundation for Infantile Paralysis all maintained San Francisco chapters. Three others, the National Multiple Sclerosis Society, the Hemophilia Foundation, and the Elizabeth Kenny Polio Foundation, did not have San Francisco chapters but had chapters extending over a somewhat larger area, usually northern California.

Most of these national health organizations sponsored research and educational programs through their local chapters; some also provided direct aid for victims. For example, in one year the San Francisco chapter of the American Cancer Society provided the Visiting Nurse Association with 50,000 surgical dressings and with funds for over 4,000 visits to indigent cancer patients. The Society also sponsored a large number of film showings, window displays, speakers, and public meetings. The national organization of the American Cancer Society made grants of $413,000 in 1954 for cancer research in California, about a third of all government and non-government cancer research expenditures in the State. Over a six-year period the Society granted $1.2 million for cancer research in the Bay Area.

Many of the smaller health agencies in San Francisco were concerned with the victims of a single disease or a single type of illness such as chronic illness. The Avery-Fuller Children's Center, for example, gave financial aid for the treatment of handicapped and crippled children. The May T. Morrison Center for Rehabilitation had a multiple program of consultation and physical and occupational therapy for people with missing limbs, speech defects, arthritis, or crippling after-effects of polio and cerebral palsy. Some of these cases were paid for by governmental and non-governmental insurance, some by other non-governmental health organizations, and still others from the funds of the Center itself.

The San Francisco Mental Health Society, Aid Retarded Children, Inc., and several other groups conducted mental health programs. There were nine organizational sources of free or part-pay dental services, and many private dentists offered similar services. There were also many schools and programs for the blind and deaf.

MULTI-PURPOSE AGENCIES: Ten of the non-governmental welfare agencies in San Francisco provided a number of services for persons of several age groups. Most of these agencies have counterparts in other American cities. They are:

American National Red Cross
Catholic Social Service
International Institute of San Francisco
Italian Welfare Agency
Jewish Family Service Agency
Salvation Army
San Francisco Center for the Blind
Travelers' Aid Society for San Francisco
Young Men's Christian Association
Young Women's Christian Association

Four of these organizations, though they did not operate on a large financial scale, attempted to provide multiple services for particular groups: the Italian Welfare Agency, the Travelers' Aid Society, and the San Francisco Center for the Blind.

The San Francisco chapter of the Red Cross, which by contrast directed its benefits to the entire population of the city, provided family and child counseling, swimming and first-aid instruction, nurse's aides, education in mother and child care and in home care of the sick, rehabilitation work in hospitals, ambulance services, classes in nursing and first aid, financial assistance to needy persons and families, services for travelers and migrants, and disaster relief; it also maintained the Grey Ladies, a subsidiary organization working chiefly in military hospitals.

The Salvation Army provided an almost equally wide range of services for the people of San Francisco. It operated the Evangeline Residence for youths; maintained a Family Welfare Bureau that provided casework services and financial assistance; organized girls' groups; supported the Harbor Light Corps Centers, which provided food and shelter for men, Pinehurst Emergency Lodge for both children and adults, the Men's Service Center, and the Red Shield Club Canteen for Servicemen; and maintained a Prison and Police Court Bureau, which carried on rehabilitation and counseling work.

The Catholic Social Service (CSS) of the Archdiocese of San Francisco coordinated Catholic services in the eight counties of the Bay Area. The CSS of San Francisco in 1954 received $400,000 from community federated campaigns. It provided a wide variety of services to Catholic children, including services in the child's home, placement of children in foster homes, adoption programs, child counseling, and homemaker services. For individuals of all age groups it provided counseling services, referrals to Catholic hospitals, and dental services. In addition it provided material assistance to needy families.[7]

Organizations with Subsidiary Welfare Programs for Non-Members

THERE IS A third type of non-governmental community welfare organization that should be mentioned. In many communities there are churches, fraternal orders, business groups, and social clubs that have developed welfare activities for non-members as an extension or addition to their original interests. For many of these organizations, such as the Junior Chamber of Commerce, the Masonic orders, certain women's groups, and many religious bodies, welfare activities for non-members are definitely secondary to the main purpose of welfare for members. For a few, however, such as the Lions, the Kiwanis, and some special religious orders, service and welfare activites for non-members have become of primary concern. The welfare activities of these various groups are considered in subsequent chapters on the church, fraternal orders and service organizations, businesses, and unions.

STAFF WELFARE ORGANIZATIONS

Types of Agencies in the Superstructure

COMMUNITY WELFARE COUNCILS: In more than 500 American cities there are community welfare councils to coordinate and plan community welfare activities. The first welfare councils were organized in Pittsburgh and Milwaukee, in 1909. They have since developed in many different forms, and now perform a variety of functions.

All councils have certain elements in common. They represent nonprofessional citizens and both non-governmental and governmental welfare agencies. Agencies are typically represented on the council by an agency board member and a professional staff member of the agency, serving as delegates. Most councils include officials from government welfare departments. Non-professional representation is customarily drawn from business, labor, religious, patriotic, nationality, occupational, and parent-teacher organizations.

Councils collect data; serve as a clearinghouse for conferences, joint planning, and coordination; and administer certain staff services for agencies. Often councils assist in the budgeting processes of federated

[7] The data for this section are from Vaughn Davis Bornet, *California Social Welfare.* Englewood Cliffs, N.J.: Prentice-Hall, 1956.

fund-raising campaigns and governmental appropriating bodies. Councils may also help promote and develop new welfare agencies and neighborhood organizations. Finally, in varying degrees, they may operate public relations programs.

The fundamental unit of the community council is its delegate body, which in large cities may number up to five hundred individuals. These include the representatives of governmental and non-governmental health, welfare, and recreation agencies, representatives of civic and occupational organizations, and in many councils a group of citizens-at-large. The type of representation on the council is generally indicative of council philosophy; the current trend has been to draw representatives from more and more groups in the community. This is done in recognition of the fact that health and welfare planning affect not only welfare agencies but many other organizations and individuals as well; broader representation also makes it easier for a council to develop new programs and obtain support for them.

When a delegate body contains several hundred individuals it is generally too large to deal directly with administrative tasks. Therefore council activities are usually supervised by a board of directors, some elected by the delegates, others *ex officio* chairmen of divisions and departments in the councils. These divisions and departments, along with project committees, are the operating units of the council. The divisions are organized along functional lines, often in the form of a miniature council. The most common functional divisions are family welfare, child welfare, health, and recreation. All the member agencies concerned with recreation are represented in the recreation division, for example. Even in smaller cities each council division is usually served by a full-time professional staff member; in larger cities divisions can become exceedingly complex, having committees, sub-committees, and subordinate sections. For example, within the family welfare division of a large council there might be a subdivision dealing solely with settlement houses, and another dealing only with community centers.

The *departments* of the council administer the common services that cut across the functional areas. Whereas the divisions deal with the coordinating, planning, and other problems that are unique to a particular type of welfare agency, the departments may extend information and referral services to the general public, operate a volunteer bureau and a social service exchange, perform research and statistical services, and conduct general public relations programs. *Project committees* are usually temporary, and, as their name suggests, are established to deal with the various problems involved in expanding or initiating certain health and welfare services.

In many communities there are both community welfare councils and community chests (described at length below). The relations between the two organizations may take any one of several forms. First, the chest and the council may be combined as two departments of a single "community welfare federation." Second, they may be separate agencies but with any of several types of interrelations. For example, they may share a common executive and common staff members, or have joint boards or committees; or the council may be a member agency of the chest. Third, the council may be a department of the chest; or, finally, the chest may be a department of the council. Among the factors influencing these relations are the scope of membership of both the chest and the council, the size of the community, the past history and operations of both organizations, and personality conflicts and affinities among the chest and council leaders.

In most cases, whatever the organizational relations between council and chest, the councils derive most of their financial support from the chests. Some support may also be provided by individual and foundation contributions, appropriations from tax funds, and fees and dues from member agencies.[8]

COMMUNITY FUND-RAISING: The success of community welfare agencies depends in large part on adequate financial support. In 1960 community chests and united funds provided the largest part of this support in some 2,000 communities in the United States. There were 2,100 federated campaigns, carried out in areas in which well over two-thirds of the population of the United States lived. These campaigns raised over $450 million for 1960 agency budgets. It has been estimated that in 1959 about one-third of the funds raised came from firms and corporations, and about 50 per cent from employees and executives, usually through on-the-job solicitations or payroll deduction plans. The remainder was donated by individuals approached in their homes. On a nation-wide average about 25 per cent of the persons living in a campaign area made contributions, either to chests or to funds.[9]

1] *Community Chests.* Membership in community chests usually consists of both welfare agencies and non-professional citizens. In addition to raising funds for affiliated agencies the chest participates in welfare planning and coordination. Planning and coordination is an outgrowth and a necessary concomitant of the budgeting process, and is often carried out in conjunction with the community welfare council.

Chests that are independent of welfare councils are usually controlled by boards of directors. There are at least two methods of choos-

[8] Arthur Dunham, *Community Welfare Organization: Principles and Practice,* New York: Thomas Y. Crowell, 1958, pp. 124–55; Kurtz, *op. cit.,* pp. 185–90.
[9] *Giving USA 1960.* New York: American Association of Fund-Raising Counsel, 1960, pp. 43–44.

ing the board members. Typically most or all of the board is chosen by the chest agencies. On the other hand a few chests are self-perpetuating, the board members themselves choosing new members. United Community Funds and Councils of America (UCFC) suggests an organization plan with two types of membership: individual members, both contributors and volunteers; and institutional members, representing the agencies affiliated with the chests. The UCFC plan also recommends the establishment of committees on campaign, publicity, and budget and admissions.

The community chest campaign itself is familiar to most Americans. The period in which funds are solicited is seldom longer than ten days; it is usually conducted in the fall and is characterized by high-pressure publicity. Although the greatest activity is centered around planning and conducting the campaign, the budgeting process and record-keeping are close to being year-around occupations. The budgeting process is crucial. The programs and policies of an agency are reflected in its budget, and those making the chest budget must decide which services shall be financed and how much they will receive. In effect the chest board surveys all chest-financed welfare activities in the community and attempts to determine which programs will best serve the community. An analysis of the budgeted distribution of chest funds for ninety community chests in the mid-1950's is given in Table 2. By 1960, the only significant changes were in health service grants, which increased to about 25 per cent, and in administrative and campaign costs, which were down.

TABLE 2

BUDGETED DISTRIBUTION OF FUNDS OF NINETY COMMUNITY CHESTS

AGENCIES		84.8%
Family-children's service and general dependency	30.1%	
Recreation services	37.5%	
Health services	14.9%	
Care of aged, community organization, miscellaneous	2.3%	
CHESTS AND COUNCILS		12.4%
SHRINKAGE ALLOWANCE (in anticipation of failure to collect all campaign pledges)		2.8%
		100%

Source: Arthur Dunham, *Community Welfare Organization: Principles and Practice*, New York: Thomas Y. Crowell, 1958, p. 178, from *Budgeting for 1957*, New York: United Community Funds and Councils (Bulletin 196), 1957, p. 1.

Chest-supported agencies do not receive all their funds from the chest. The amount of chest support varies greatly with the type of agency. Agencies providing family services as a rule receive a greater portion of their funds from the chest than any other type of agency. In 1954 in San Francisco, family service and dependency agencies received 81 per cent of their funds from the chest. Agencies caring for children and for the aged received 33 and 32 per cent, respectively, of their financing from the chest.

A study of eleven California chests covered 348 chest-affiliated agencies. These agencies had total receipts of about $26 million, of which 53 per cent came from chests and 47 per cent from other sources, including fees and payments for services, payments from tax funds, and, to a limited extent, interest on investments.[10]

Not all non-governmental community agencies are affiliated with chests. Chests generally include such organizations as the Y's, Boy Scouts, Salvation Army, family service agencies, clinics, hospitals, and homes for the aged and for children. However, they frequently do not include the American Red Cross, local chapters of the national health organizations, and some religious organizations. A count of 118 health, welfare, and welfare-related organizations in Cincinnati and the Cincinnati area listed in the *Cincinnati Report 1952* indicates that 77 per cent (ninety-one) were chest-affiliated. Of the twenty-seven agencies and organizations that were not chest-affiliated, about half were affiliated with religious groups (a number of religiously affiliated agencies *did* receive chest funds, however). The remaining non-chest-affiliated organizations were either local chapters of national organizations that conducted their own campaigns, agencies supported largely from fees, or organizations such as the Planned Parenthood Association and certain veterans' organizations that do not ordinarily solicit funds from the general public. (Organizations such as Planned Parenthood and the American Legion may solicit funds, but do so from members and interested or affected persons as a rule.)

2] *United Funds.* The united fund movement, which began in Detroit in 1949, arose from the same impulse that had led to the community chest movement: the desire to do away with uncoordinated appeals by various agencies. Such appeals had again appeared on the community scene because of the unwillingness of the national health organizations to allow their local chapters to join community chests, and because of the large number of capital-fund campaigns that took place immediately after World War II. The first united fund drive was limited to on-the-job solicitation in Detroit area automobile factories. Contributions were solicited for the local chapters of certain national health agencies and also for agencies customarily associated with a community chest.

The first ten years of the united fund movement were marked by

[10] Bornet, *op. cit.*, pp. 186–87.

conflict, largely over which agencies and local chapters of national organizations should participate. In the 1959 campaign year there were 1,217 united funds, which raised 81.9 per cent of all funds collected by federated campaigns, including community chests. Nevertheless, a number of national organizations have forced their local chapters to withdraw from united funds, arguing that when the chapters undertook their own campaigns they received greater contributions. In the late 1950's, both the American Cancer Society and the American Heart Association prohibited their affiliates from participation in federated financing. In early 1958 the former organization ordered local units to sever their ties with united fund organizations or face expulsion from the Society.

In contrast to the arguments of these national organizations, the American Red Cross, at its thirty-third annual convention in May, 1958, cited statistics indicating that chapters associated with federated drives had been financially more successful than those having their own drives. There were seventy-nine large chapters participating in federated fund drives, and of these 24 per cent achieved their budgetary goals. Of the twenty-eight large chapters outside federations only 18 per cent met their goals. The difference was more apparent among the 3,500 smaller chapters of the Red Cross. Of 1,068 participating in federated drives 26 per cent made their goals, compared with 15 per cent of the chapters conducting their own drives.[11]

More than three-fourths of the 1957 united campaigns included participating Red Cross chapters. United funds also included some 450 local chapters of both the cancer and heart organizations, as well as 147 crippled children chapters, 112 polio chapters, and 53 tuberculosis chapters.[12] By the 1959 campaign year, all but 140 of the 1,217 united funds included the Red Cross.

In many cities and campaign areas united funds are assimilating the community chests, or with the chests are being used to form single, overall fund-raising organizations. These campaign under a variety of titles: "United Bay Area Crusade," "United Community Chest," "San Francisco Federated Fund," "United Appeal," and "United Givers Fund" are some examples. Their primary differences from community chests, in the communities where they are still separate, are that they are designed to provide for national services as well as local, and that in general they are more interested in health programs. In some areas they are being formed into United Health Funds in an attempt to combine the finances of all the community health agencies and the chapters of national organizations. By 1960, little emphasis was being placed on the distinction between united funds and community chests; their

[11] *New York Times*, May 5, 1958.
[12] Dunham, *op. cit.*, p. 188.

fund-raising activities were becoming generically known as "united campaigns," and the slogan "Give the United Way" was common to both.

A number of individuals and organizations have demanded a national united health research fund to replace the competing national agencies. At the local level there have been indications that national agencies are resisting a trend in continuing their multiple appeals. Organizations of volunteers, most of them women, who provide the canvassers for funds, have in many communities expressed hostility to new campaigns. In Norwalk, Connecticut, for example, the Council of Community Associations has considered boycotting the organizations making individual appeals by refusing to cooperate or participate if the appeals do not combine.[13]

3] *Other Fund-Raising Bodies.* In some urban areas there are specialized fund-raising organizations that finance functional or religious groups of agencies. The Federation of Jewish Philanthropies in New York City is perhaps the largest of this type. Its 1958 campaign goal was $20.9 million, to be distributed among 116 Jewish hospitals and service agencies. The Federation estimated that these welfare organizations aided almost 700,000 persons each year, most but not all of them members of the Jewish faiths.[14] The Council of Jewish Federations and Welfare Funds, representing Jewish fund-raising organizations in nearly 800 communities, has estimated that 1957 Jewish campaigns raised over $140 million for Jewish community welfare, 1958 campaigns $125 million, and 1959 campaigns over $130 million.[15]

It should be emphasized in conclusion that not all fund-raising for community welfare organizations is done in large campaigns. A sizable minority of organizations do part or all of their own fund-raising by individual solicitations, in person or by mail, unconnected with any community or national campaigns. Some, particularly in small communities, do so because there are no community chests or other federated campaigns in their areas. For example, ambulance and rescue squads in small communities or rural areas usually raise their own funds, resorting to means such as mail solicitation, community fairs, dinners, and dances, and solicitation from travelers on highways in the area. Other organizations, such as Patrolmen's Benevolent Associations and Planned Parenthood Associations, may be considered to lie outside the interests of a community campaign because of their specialized nature or because some contributors might not be willing to donate to a campaign that included them. Finally, some community welfare organiza-

---

[13] *New York Times*, May 28, 1959.
[14] *Ibid.*, Oct. 4, 1957.
[15] *Giving USA 1960*, pp. 31–32. Also see the section "Jewish Communal and Social Services," in Chapter 6 of this book.

tions may not join campaigns or may rely on campaigns only in part because they have what they believe to be more effective means of raising funds. For example, some welfare agencies and institutions may have a relatively short list of benefactors each of whom regularly contributes a sizable amount of money, often following a personal request by the director or an officer of the organization. Not infrequently the major benefactors of welfare organizations that raise their funds in this manner are to be found on the governing board of the organization.

Functions

APART FROM FUND-RAISING, community staff agencies have five major functions:

(1) Fact-finding
(2) Program development
(3) Establishment of standards
(4) Coordination
(5) Education

FACT-FINDING: Fact-finding gives an agency the basis of fact it needs for its assumptions about the welfare of the community. An agency often needs information about the social and economic structure of the community. It must be familiar with the cost and nature of services necessary for fulfilling a function. If it is concerned with health it must know the incidence of various diseases in its area. It may want a measure of the effectiveness of a given operating program.

If an agency is unable to gain information itself it may turn to the welfare council, which in some communities supplies fact-finding services. Councils in larger cities usually have research departments, which may collect service statistics, conduct surveys, and prepare demographic data. In some communities there are service agencies that are primarily concerned with fact-finding and research. As an illustration, the Institute of Welfare Research of the Community Service Society of New York City makes evaluative studies of social casework.[16]

Authorities have suggested a five-category classification of social work research:

(1) Studies establishing and measuring the need for service.
(2) Studies measuring the relation of service to need.
(3) Studies evaluating the results of social work practice.
(4) Studies testing the effectiveness of various techniques.
(5) Studies in research methodology.[17]

[16] Mary E. Macdonald, "Research in Social Work," in Kurtz, *op. cit.*, pp. 489–500.
[17] Philip Klein and I. C. Merriam. *The Contribution of Research to Social Work.* New York: American Association of Social Workers, 1948.

In practice, the two questions most frequently asked of the social work researcher are, "What are the needs?" and "How effective are the services?" [18]

PROGRAM DEVELOPMENT: Program development refers to almost any introduction of new service, or modification of existing service, planned for an agency or group of agencies. For example, it includes the promulgation of a new eligibility policy by a national health agency to its local and regional chapters, and planning by a welfare council for the integration of the health and welfare services of an entire community. Program development may involve the organization or reorganization of an agency, the establishment of channels of interagency communication, the planning of broad programs for recipient groups, or opposition to existing or proposed programs. It may be preventive as well as promotional.

ESTABLISHMENT OF STANDARDS: Standards are rules for operation designed to enable an agency to perform its tasks in the most efficient manner. They are also criteria by which an agency can judge its achievements and effectiveness of service, and its efficiency in the utilization of resources. Standards may be concerned with maximum caseloads, reporting procedures, training required of personnel, budgeting requirements of a particular type of program, preferable types of relations with clients, and many other operating conditions.

Standards may be established in many ways. Agencies themselves may establish their own sets of standards, often in terms of the expectations of their professional workers. Associations of social workers often suggest standards of various types. In the community the welfare council may often strongly recommend certain standards to its member agencies for the purpose of achieving what the council believes to be an adequate level of service. In such cases the representatives of the agencies concerned usually assist in the determination of standards, which may increase the likelihood that the standards will be acceptable to the agency itself.

COORDINATION: Coordination is ordinarily the chief purpose of staff welfare organizations. Overhead supervision of voluntary welfare organizations permits specialization in operation, division of territory, joint use of services and equipment, pooling of information, and the organization necessary to undertake large-scale operations.[19]

Community welfare councils are typically the focus of welfare coordination. Although they have a great variety of forms they have cer-

---

[18] Macdonald, *op. cit.*, p. 491.
[19] Dunham, *op. cit.*, pp. 47–48.

tain activities in common. They provide common services for all community health and welfare organizations, including preparation of agency directories, information and referral services, collection of statistical data, volunteer bureaus, and social service exchanges. Some of these have been discussed under previous headings. Volunteer bureaus and social service exchanges require separate comment.

The original purpose of volunteer bureaus was to recruit individuals for volunteer service and refer them to the agencies and organizations in need of volunteer assistance. This function has been elaborated in many ways. Volunteer bureaus offer consultation services to agencies to help them organize for volunteer services, to train and supervise the volunteers referred to them, and to maintain standards for volunteer service. The bureaus may engage in extensive recruiting campaigns, sponsor educational programs to heighten citizen participation, and promote the recognition of volunteers in community services. Often they counsel civic organizations on providing volunteer opportunities for individual members, selection of group projects, and organization of the volunteer programs of the civic groups. They also may directly coordinate the activities of several agencies as they relate to recruiting and training volunteers.[20]

The social service exchanges keep central confidential files on families and individuals being served by the member agencies of the exchange. This undertaking is desirable because most welfare services in a community tend to be consumed by the same group of people, any one of whom may be receiving services from as many as a half dozen agencies. In 1959 there were 168 social service exchanges in operation in the United States. Most of them (108) were units or departments of central community agencies, 39 were under public welfare departments, and a few (14) were independent. In successful operation, the exchange ensures that agencies will not duplicate one another's efforts in a given case and will know where to obtain all relevant information on a case. During the 1950's however, the number of exchanges in operation steadily declined. This trend is believed to reflect a shift in the philosophy of casework. Member agencies had begun to doubt the value of registering all their cases and to question the propriety of revealing the identity of clients. In some instances specialization of services was such that agencies felt there was little value in determining the nature of other services provided the client, especially in the face of rising costs of maintaining the exchange.[21]

[20] Robert F. Fenley, "Volunteers in Social Welfare," in Kurtz, *op. cit.*, pp. 592–98.
[21] Kenneth I. Williams, "Social Service Exchanges," in Russell H. Kurtz, ed., *Social Work Year Book 1960*, New York: National Association of Social Workers, 1960, pp. 559–63.

74

In addition to coordinating service facilities, community councils are extensively concerned with developing rapport and understanding among community welfare organizations, both governmental and non-governmental. Broad welfare problems are frequently examined by committees representing a large number of agencies. Through the council member agencies are informed of changes and developments of service, and the ultimate result is both inter-agency understanding and an awareness of problems outside the scope of a single agency. The councils also perform an extensive planning function, coordinating and sponsoring the modification of existing activities and the development of new services.[22]

EDUCATION: Education for public understanding and acceptance has become increasingly important among the functions of the staff welfare organizations. Much of the demand for this educational function rises from the newness and constant change that characterize most welfare activities. There are a number of objectives of this education; the most important are:

(1) Strengthening public acceptance of the claim of social work to professional status.
(2) Strengthening acceptance of professional statements of welfare needs.
(3) Developing acceptance and understanding of specific governmental and non-governmental welfare programs.
(4) Developing individual and organizational support for welfare programs, especially financial support.
(5) Counteracting criticisms of both professionalism and particular programs.
(6) Informing the public of the nature and extent of services available.

An educational program instituted by a welfare organization may be directed at several of these objectives. It usually concentrates on certain audiences: all residents of a geographic area, a particular elite group, or certain types of organizations. In each case the audience is selected in terms of the purpose of the educational program. A welfare council seeking support for an area rehabilitation program attempts to develop general public awareness of conditions and public interest in changing these conditions. It directs educational material with a more sophisticated content at community leaders. The success of an area rehabilitation program depends in part on the degree of financial support received, the cooperation of various agencies, and perhaps most impor-

---

[22] Howard F. Gustafson, "Community Welfare Councils," in *Social Work Year Book* 1960, pp. 191–98.

tantly, the active interest of volunteers and citizens in the area to be rehabilitated. An appropriate educational program can be of great value in achieving these conditions.

CONCLUDING REMARKS

EVERY SIZABLE COMMUNITY has a multitude of non-governmental welfare agencies performing a wide variety of functions. Some such agencies and organizations are staffed by professional social workers, counselors, and other trained personnel; many others, most of them relatively small, carry out their work almost solely with the help of volunteers. Even agencies with professional staff and supervision generally rely on volunteers as well.

Operating community welfare organizations may be concerned with dependent children, "problem families," the aged, or health conditions; some may provide counseling services and financial and material assistance, others may give institutional care. Some may restrict their services to members of particular religious or nationality groups, others may attempt to help all those who ask for assistance within the limits of their resources. In the mid-1950's there were 225 community welfare organizations of all types in San Francisco, providing a comprehensive net of services for its 800,000 residents.

There are a number of community welfare organizations whose primary interest is providing staff assistance to other welfare bodies. The most notable of these are the community welfare councils, whose purpose is to coordinate all community welfare activity, often governmental programs along with non-governmental welfare operations. Most communities also have federated fund-raising bodies, which more and more frequently are associated with the welfare councils. Community chests and united funds raise nearly half a billion dollars annually, most of it for the support of community agencies, some of it for the national programs of the non-governmental health agencies.

The dominant characteristic of contemporary urban community welfare is the trend toward coordination, carried out under the aegis of the welfare councils and federated campaigns. These bodies review the activities of local agencies, prepare over-all plans for community welfare, and often allocate funds to the agencies on the basis of what the council members or the campaign board consider to be the welfare needs of the community. Both the agencies themselves and the community at large are represented on the councils and boards, and the community welfare plans and distribution of funds almost always meet the satisfaction of all parties concerned. The trend toward coordination

76

is likely to continue and to involve local governmental agencies to an increasing extent. It will be more and more common in the coming decades to see urban communities with a comprehensive, integrated system of social welfare services of all types, available to all citizens, operated by citizens, professional personnel, and government officials alike. It is more doubtful that similar coordinated services will be provided for rural communities, which have neither the concentrations of needy persons nor the resources to support extensive services, as a rule. For some years to come welfare in rural and small-town America will be provided in large part by groups organized to solve a particular problem, such as the Trustees of the Valley Clinic and Hospital, described above, and by a variety of *ad hoc*, temporary bodies, inspired by the earlier American tradition of mutual assistance. The same tradition is present in urban neighborhoods but there must be merged with it the organization and professionalism required to deal with widespread and complex welfare problems.

Chapter Five

STATE-WIDE AND NATION-WIDE

ORGANIZATIONS

THE STATE-WIDE AND NATION-WIDE WELFARE ORGANIZATIONS cap the structure of welfare organizations in the United States. Such organizations can be classified in at least two ways. First, as in the case of community organizations, State-wide and nation-wide welfare bodies may be classified according to whether the majority of their functions are *line* or *staff*. Second, they may be classified according to whether or not they have local chapters or affiliates. If the organization does have such local groups, its primary purpose is usually to carry out staff functions for them. On the other hand, if it does not have local chapters or affiliates, depending on the organization it may conduct either line functions for the public or staff functions for other agencies. One important characteristic of State-wide and nation-wide welfare organizations is that to an even greater degree than community organizations they cooperate with governmental welfare bodies. This chapter deals first with State-wide line and staff agencies and then with nation-wide line and staff agencies.

STATE-WIDE WELFARE ORGANIZATIONS

THERE IS A great variety of State welfare organizations. It has been estimated that there are more than three hundred State-wide line agencies and, as of 1949, about two hundred State-wide planning and coordinating agencies whose primary interest has been social welfare.[1]

State-Wide Line Agencies

NON-GOVERNMENTAL STATE-WIDE LINE AGENCIES are usually concerned with specialized problems. They may provide treatment and facilities for victims of diseases such as tuberculosis, mental illness, infantile paralysis, and cancer. They may extend services for the crippled or for persons on probation or parole from State institutions. Some provide State-wide services to families or State-wide child placement. This section includes accounts of two such State-wide organizations.

THE SENIOR CRAFTSMEN OF OREGON: The Senior Craftsmen of Oregon is a non-profit cooperative organization created to help craftsmen over fifty years of age to make and sell products and thus provide for their own financial support and well-being. Although it is not a welfare agency in the ordinary usage of the term, by assisting its members, who are predominantly women, to produce and retail salable goods it helps them avoid becoming wards of other welfare agencies.

The Craftsmen was initiated by eight Oregon women, all active in community affairs. The Portland chapter of the American Red Cross donated space for the organization and its Portland area members. Other members throughout the State work in their homes. Donations to provide raw materials for the members have come from many sources, including business firms, a Eugene teen-agers' club, and the Portland Altrusa Club. Volunteers have provided most of the administrative work of the organization, such as bookkeeping and legal assistance.

Goods produced by the members were originally sold by church groups and at annual sales. The Senior Craftsmen now have their own store, and often sell goods in quantity to other stores. Three-fourths of the selling price is paid to the producers, thus providing them with financial support. It also helps them make satisfying and productive use of their time and abilities, thus avoiding the feelings of despondency and inadequacy that often accompany old age.[2]

FOUNTAIN HOUSE: Fountain House, in Philadelphia, is an agency to supervise and rehabilitate people in Pennsylvania who have just been discharged from mental hospitals. It is incorporated under State law and is administered by a board of directors. It secures all its funds from non-governmental sources, for example individual contributions and returns from benefit concerts. Fountain House also receives funds and

[1] Arthur Dunham, *Community Welfare Organization: Principles and Practice.* New York: Thomas Y. Crowell, 1958, pp. 195–99.
[2] Lola R. Ballinger, "The Senior Craftsmen of Oregon," in T. H. Stevenson, ed., *Building Better Volunteer Programs,* Princeton, N.J.: Foundation for Voluntary Welfare, n.d. (1958), pp. 55–67.

79

services from a variety of other non-governmental welfare organizations. It has an annual fund-raising campaign and conducts year-around public relations activities through such media as donated car-card space in public transportation vehicles and free spot announcements on radio stations. Fountain House employs trained psychiatric social workers to counsel former patients, but relies to a considerable extent on volunteers.

Fountain House carries out its rehabilitation function through its Fellowship program. Participants in this program include a professional employee of the House, non-professional individuals who have volunteered their assistance, and recently discharged patients from mental hospitals who feel that they need help in readjusting to the outside world. At meetings of such groups, which take place once or several times a week, clients may obtain counseling services or share in games and dramatics. Fountain House has the additional goal of educating the public respecting the problems of recently discharged mental patients.[3] The success of Fountain House has led to the establishment of related agencies, having the same name, elsewhere—in New York, for example.

State-Wide Staff Agencies

CONFERENCES OF SOCIAL WORK: The most widespread State-wide staff agencies are the State conferences of social work, which exist in almost every State. Their functions, however, are rather limited. Most of them hold an annual forum and occasional regional conferences and through these meetings most of them initiate, endorse, and promote social legislation, with varying effects on State legislatures. Aside from this, most State conferences have few or no year-around activities. The conferences are usually barred from further activity in planning for health and welfare on a State-wide basis by both lack of financial support for the conference itself and the distances and variations among communities. In 1956 only eighteen had full-time executives and few had additional staffs. In a few States, however, notably Michigan, Missouri, Wisconsin, and several others, they have made serious efforts to encourage and to assist the establishment of welfare organizations at the community level.

OTHER AGENCIES: Table 1 enumerates some of the other types of State-wide staff agencies (excluding certain government commissions and planning boards of similar nature).

Among the agencies listed above, citizens' welfare associations per-

[3] Marcella I. Schmoeger, "Pennsylvania's Fountain House," in Alfred de Grazia, ed., *Grass Roots Private Welfare*. New York: New York University Press, 1957, pp. 14–19.

form one or more of the following activities: social planning; social action (*i.e.*, demands for local and state legislation); fact-finding; and education. The New York State Charities Aid Association, founded in 1872, is the largest of the associations, and in recent years has had an annual budget of about $1 million. The Pennsylvania Citizens' Association for Health and Welfare (PCA) was organized in 1912. With some 3,000 individual members and an annual budget of about $135,000, the PCA has undertaken research and education programs, lobbied for legislative programs, and sponsored extensive planning programs. Typical of its activities have been its efforts to establish adequate institutional facilities for children, the mentally retarded, and penal offenders. It maintains liaison with State and federal agencies and has promoted reorganization of State and local welfare services.

TABLE 1

STATE-WIDE NON-GOVERNMENTAL STAFF ORGANIZATIONS (1949)

Health Councils and Associations	19
Planning Boards	16
Associations of Chests and Councils	9
Recreation Commissions and Associations	9
Legislative Councils	6
State Chests and Review Boards	6
State Citizens' Councils	5
State-Wide Citizens' Welfare Associations	5
Community Organization Service (Massachusetts)	1
Total State-Wide Bodies	76

Source: *Directory of State-Wide Agencies.* New York: Community Chests and Councils of America, 1949.

In 1959 there was State-wide joint fund-raising or staff assistance to local community campaigns in twelve States. In some instances these programs were in the stages of development, and hence were concerned primarily with conferences, joint study, the establishment of quota and budget systems, and consultation services. The Michigan fund has been the largest; in 1956 it raised $2.5 million. The total funds raised in other States varied from $960,000 in Pennsylvania to $124,000 in Virginia.[4]

In several States having a number of community chests and councils, State-wide associations of chests and councils have been formed; however, their purposes are not fund-raising. Instead, they promote legislation, sometimes support research, and perform budget review

[4] Dunham, *op. cit.*, pp. 196–210.

services for their member organizations. For example, the Ohio Community Chest Association in conjunction with the Ohio Citizens' Council has developed a quota plan for local support of State and national fund-raising appeals. In New York State the association of chests and councils has joined with a national non-governmental agency to co-sponsor a study of welfare services by national organizations in a particular city.[5]

There are also State chapters of most of the larger national health organizations. These State chapters provide staff assistance to local chapters, in connection both with fund-raising campaigns and with local operating programs. State chapters may also conduct educational programs, make grants for research to be conducted in the State, and sometimes provide direct payments for services to individuals.

NATION-WIDE WELFARE ORGANIZATIONS

ACCORDING TO THE *Social Work Year Book 1960*, there then were 337 voluntary national organizations directly or peripherally concerned with social welfare. More than half of these organizations, some 200 of them, were *primarily* concerned with social welfare. Most of the latter were devoted to providing staff services for State and community agencies and their personnel. A few were line agencies, offering services directly to individuals.

Nation-Wide Line Agencies

A NATION-WIDE LINE AGENCY is generally a small organization operating out of a single office or establishment. It may provide its services to clients through members scattered across the country, as does the John Howard Association. Or, it may provide its services partly through the mails, the method used by the Hadley School for the Blind. A third type of nation-wide line agency operates an establishment to provide facilities and services for clients who come from all over the country, as do some homes for the aged and hospitals such as the City of Hope at Duarte, California.

THE JOHN HOWARD ASSOCIATION: The John Howard Association, of Chicago, is governed by a board of directors, and in 1960 had one thousand members in sixteen States. The Association attempts to assist men who either are in or have just been released from State and federal

[5] Richard S. Bachman, "State and Regional Welfare Organization," in Russell H. Kurtz, ed., *Social Work Yearbook 1960*, New York: National Association of Social Workers, 1960, p. 576.

prisons. Its members furnish these men with casework services, lend them money, and try to find jobs for them. Also, the members seek through research and education to increase community understanding of the prisoner and the former prisoner, and their needs. Finally, the members urge the passage of laws to reform the present penal system.

THE HADLEY SCHOOL FOR THE BLIND: The Hadley School for the Blind, in Winnetka, Illinois, is devoted to the education of adult blind persons throughout the United States. To carry out this purpose it provides, free of charge, home-study courses printed in Braille. These courses range from the reading of Braille through elementary and secondary school subjects to courses at college level—the last furnished through an arrangement with the Home Study Department of the University of Chicago. The School also provides, free of charge, the textbooks for the courses, counseling, and guidance.

Nation-Wide Staff Organizations

THE NATION-WIDE STAFF WELFARE ORGANIZATIONS include the largest, best-known, and most influential non-governmental welfare bodies in the United States. There are four general types of such organizations: those that are primarily concerned with raising funds (usually for the use of local chapters and for research and education), such as the National Society for Crippled Children and Adults; national service organizations, such as the National Federation of Settlements and Neighborhood Centers; vocational associations and conferences, such as the National Association of Social Workers; and federations of national bodies, such as United Service Organizations (USO). There may be some overlapping in the functions carried out by these groups. National fund-raising organizations, for example, may also provide services and planning for their subordinate bodies.

FUND-RAISING ORGANIZATIONS: The largest of the fund-raising bodies are the national health organizations. They may carry out their fund-raising function in any of several ways. Although all of them conduct national campaigns, involving a variety of publicity techniques, the actual solicitation of funds for most of them is done by their subordinate chapters or affiliates. These local units may conduct the campaign in their area in coordination with the national publicity campaign of their parent organization, a practice that is considered desirable or is required by most national health organizations, or the local units may join the federated campaigns of their communities. In either case the local units may be required to turn a certain part of their proceeds over to the national organization.

83

TABLE 2

THE MAJOR NATIONAL FUND-RAISING ORGANIZATIONS, 1959

Organization	Year Founded	National and Local Income, 1959 [1]
American National Red Cross	1881	$ 94,101,000
National Foundation (March of Dimes)	1938	39,268,000 (1958)
American Cancer Society	1913	35,380,000
National Tuberculosis Association	1904	28,776,000
American Heart Association	1948	24,917,000
National Society for Crippled Children and Adults	1921	16,841,000 (est.)
United Cerebral Palsy Associations	1948	12,008,000 (est.)
National Association for Mental Health	1950	5,511,000
Muscular Dystrophy Associations of America	1950	5,509,000
Sister Elizabeth Kenny Foundation	1942	4,667,000 (1958)
Arthritis and Rheumatism Foundation	1948	3,606,000
National Fund for Medical Education	1949	3,249,000
National Multiple Sclerosis Society	1946	3,000,000 (est.)
American Foundation for the Blind	1921	2,730,000
National League for Nursing	1952	2,613,000
National Association for Retarded Children	1953	2,500,000 (est.)
Planned Parenthood Federation of America	1922	2,250,000 (est.)
Seeing Eye	1919	1,877,000
National Council on Alcoholism	1944	1,375,000 (est.)
Damon Runyon Memorial Fund for Cancer	1946	1,264,000
National Kidney Disease Foundation	1950	940,000
National Foundation for Muscular Dystrophy	1953	783,000
National Society for the Prevention of Blindness	1908	551,000 (est.)
American Social Health Association	1912	535,000
Seventeen other organizations [2]		3,440,000 (est.)
Total		$297,700,000 (est.)

Source: *Wise Giving Bulletin* (Spring, 1960 edition). New York: National Information Bureau, 1960.

Note: The forty-one organizations indicated in this table include most but not all the non-governmental health-related organizations that undertake campaigns and attempt to provide services on the nation-wide level. Varying portions of their income derive from local united funds and community chests (though certainly less than half the total), and varying portions are spent at the local level, by local chapters.

[1] Including bequests, interest, sales, etc., as well as campaign income. Figures are not necessarily comparable, in several places include 1958 data in lieu of more recent information, and include a number of estimates.
[2] These "other organizations" had incomes ranging from $47,000 to $492,000, some of them reporting national income only. They include such groups as the Leukemia Society, Recording for the Blind, the Parkinsons Disease Foundation, and the National Association for Practical Nurse Education and Service.

There are at least forty fund-raising organizations on the national level. From 1955 to 1959 the national and local campaign incomes of these organizations averaged over $250 million a year, about 30 per cent less than the total income of local federated campaigns for the same years. The figures are by no means comparable since many of the receipts of the national fund-raising organizations derive from federated community campaigns, as noted above.

Some of the major non-governmental organizations that mount wide-spread campaigns for health and health-related purposes are given in Table 2. The listing is not complete, though it includes all the major national agencies in existence in the late 1950's. As much as $200 million of their income in 1959 was raised through their independent local, regional, and national campaigns, which are conducted at various times during the year—usually between October and April. Other portions came from local united funds and community chests, in which some local chapters choose or are allowed to participate. With the exception of the American National Red Cross, these national bodies are mainly concerned with particular types of diseases. Four of these diseases are among the fields of interest of the National Health Institutes of the federal government: National Cancer Institute, Mental Health Activities, National Heart Institute, and Arthritis and Metabolic Disease Activities.

Policies governing expenditures for functions apart from that of fund-raising vary considerably from organization to organization. The most frequent expenditures on the local level are research grants and grants to clinics. Public information and education programs also take large amounts of funds. Most health organizations do not make significant expenditures for direct patient care. The National Foundation, formerly known as the National Foundation for Infantile Paralysis, is an exception. Under its former name this organization spent about 60 per cent of its income for patient care, a practice made possible by the small number of poliomyelitis cases in the population. Its present interests include other crippling diseases as well, and it continues to provide direct patient care. By contrast, the heart and cancer organizations, concerned with relatively high-incidence diseases, emphasize research and education.[6]

The activities of a local chapter of the National Foundation are suggested by this summary of services provided by the Somerset County, New Jersey, chapter in 1959. The county had a population of some 100,000. The county chapter was providing care in one form or another for 193 victims of polio and similar diseases, and gave about 5,000 Salk Vaccine shots. Total expenses were about $10,000, including $2,700 to hospitals, $1,140 for physical therapy, $1,470 for braces, $700 for medical care, and $3,600 for nursing services.

The American Red Cross is the largest of the national health or-

[6] Vaughn Davis Bornet, *California Social Welfare*, Englewood Cliffs, N.J.: Prentice-Hall, 1956, pp. 319–22.

ganizations in terms of expenditures and is one of the largest in terms of staff and membership. Its 1959 national campaign netted it and its affiliated chapters $85 million, while other contributions and sources of income added $9 million to this. Its total membership was 44.0 million, including both adults and young people, and its operations were staffed by an estimated two million volunteers and 13,400 career staff members. Its major services in the late 1950's were provided to members of the armed forces, veterans, and their families; to disaster victims throughout the world; and to those benefiting from its blood program. It also provided extensive health, nursing, and safety services, and a variety of other community services. Its total 1959 expenses for its public information programs, general management, and membership enrollment and fund-raising campaigns were $17.2 million, one-fifth of its total operating expenditures. Enrollment and fund-raising costs together were only $3.2 million, less than 5 per cent of total campaign fund contributions.

The USO is a different type of national fund-raising organization. Established by six national non-governmental agencies in 1941, it was to finance and coordinate the war-connected programs of the national YMCA and YWCA, the National Catholic Community Service, the Salvation Army, the National Jewish Welfare Board, and the National Travelers Aid Association. These programs were primarily for the benefit of the men and women in the armed services. The USO passed out of existence after World War II but was reestablished at the beginning of the Korean conflict.

Among other national fund-raising organizations is the United Negro College Fund, a fund-raising agency for thirty-three private colleges. It makes an annual drive in some 120 communities across the nation. The United Jewish Appeal for Refugees, Overseas Needs and Palestine is a national organization raising funds through local campaigns for three other national agencies. In 1958 it raised over $14 million for the American Jewish Joint Distribution Committee, largely for overseas expenditures. It also financed the United Israel Appeal and the New York Association for New Americans.

SERVICE AGENCIES: National service agencies provide research, planning, and promotional services to community and regional welfare organizations. They are the most common type of national welfare organization. They may be concerned with a specific group of recipients or a particular problem, as are the National Council of the Boy Scouts of America, the National Council of the YMCA, the National Industries for the Blind, and the American Council to Improve Our Neighborhoods (ACTION). Other national service organizations, such as the American Public Welfare Association, have a broad scope of interest. The Association is active in "the development and maintenance of sound principles and effective administration of public welfare services." To accomplish this, it provides technical and advisory services to legislatures and administrators, serves as a clearinghouse for information in the field of government welfare, and promotes training programs for governmental welfare personnel. In 1960 it had an individual membership of 4,800, and 1,600 associated organizations.[7]

Another service organization is the National Planning Association, with some two thousand individual members. This agency undertakes studies and recommends policies for dealing with social and economic problems, maintaining a professional staff and a number of special committees. Not all its activities are directly related to social welfare narrowly defined; rather, it is a meeting ground for individuals with a variety of interests and backgrounds, including professional people and farm, business, and union leaders, allowing them to discuss and study broad problems of national welfare.

National agencies have been particularly concerned with research, though few of them have maintained continuing research programs. The United Community Funds and Councils of America is an exception; its Department of Research and Statistics has been collecting uniform welfare statistics since the early 1930's. Another national organization, Community Research Associates, has been formed for the specific purpose of conducting research programs in social welfare.

There are four ways of differentiating among the structures of nation-wide service organizations:

First, whether the organization has affiliated local bodies, individual members, or both. United Community Funds and Councils of America has only organizational members. The American Cancer Society has sixty local affiliates, termed divisions. By contrast, the National Association of the Deaf includes both individuals and State and local associations of the deaf among its members.

Second, the group in ultimate control. The board of control may be comprised of agency representatives, non-agency-connected individuals, or both. Some national agencies have self-perpetuating boards; others, according to their constitutions, permit board members only limited tenure.

Third, the degree of central authority of the national organization over its local affiliates. This is the most crucial differentiation, in terms of the influence of the national organization over local welfare activity. Some local organizations—Red Cross, Girl Scouts, YMCA's—receive charters only from the national organization. Others, such as the Family

---

[7] Kurtz, *op. cit.*, p. 668.

Service Association of America (FSAA), require certain high standards of local agencies wishing to affiliate with the national body. The 284 agencies affiliated with FSAA must be primarily concerned with providing family social work. They must have a responsible board comprised of non-professionals, which participates with the staff and executive in planning; they must have a paid staff, receive the majority of their support from non-governmental sources, and have "a lay constituency that understands and supports the work of the agency." [8]

Fourth, the nature of the controls (if any) imposed by the national organization on the policies and programs of the organizations affiliated with it. A national organization may control:

(1) fund-raising practices;
(2) distribution of funds;
(3) operating practices;
(4) personnel practices;
(5) determination of clients served.

Controls may be implemented by the issuance of codes and manuals, statements of regulations, the requirement of periodical reports, visits of inspection by representatives from the national organization, or by less direct means such as the promulgation of "suggested practices."

Controls are not effective, however, unless a national organization can impose sanctions on the affiliates or units that fail to follow its policies. The most effective sanction is available to the national organizations, notably the national health groups, that charter local units. If they feel it necessary, they can revoke the charter of a recalcitrant unit, thus cutting it off from participation in the national campaign and from various staff services. National organizations such as the FSAA, which have specific requirements for membership, may also be able to suspend their affiliated organizations. In actuality these sanctions are seldom imposed, since local agencies usually find it to their definite advantage to retain their affiliations with such national organizations.

The majority of national organizations, however, do not have sanctions that can be applied to member organizations even in theory. They are not so much interested in *controlling* the policies and programs of affiliated organizations as they are in providing whatever staff assistance local organizations may find useful. When national organizations such as the National Advisory Council on State and Local Action for Children and Youth and the Cooperative Health Federation of America make policy suggestions to member organizations they are only sugges-

[8] Rae C. Weil, "Family Social Work," in Kurtz, *op. cit.*, pp. 251–57; Dunham, *op. cit.*, pp. 222–23.

tions, though almost certainly they will be given serious consideration by the members.

The financing of nation-wide service organizations varies with the type of organization. The national health organizations, as noted above, are financed chiefly through national fund-raising campaigns, in conjunction with their local affiliates. Other national bodies receive their financial support from a variety of sources. Thirty-two national organizations reporting to the National Budget Committee in 1955 stated that they raised $23.4 million for their national programs, an average of about $700,000 per organization. Some of these funds were raised in small-scale campaigns, others were fees from local affiliates, often paid from funds raised in local federated campaigns. Individuals and corporations may make direct contributions or pay membership fees. Foundations occasionally make grants for special projects: for instance, between 1955 and 1958 the Rockefeller Brothers Fund gave the Council on Social Work Education about $75,000 for a study of curriculum offerings in social work education. A study of the social welfare agencies in Utica, New York, indicated that nationally affiliated local service agencies gave an average of 5 per cent of their locally raised funds to their various national organizations in membership fees. Local recreation agencies gave about 3 per cent to their national organizations.[9]

Financial support has recently become a more serious problem for the older, local-agency-centered national organizations. Few of them are satisfied with their present programs, yet funds are not always available for expansion. Most of them have accepted federated financing and receive much of their support from federated campaigns, either directly or through their local affiliates. The directors of federated community campaigns, however, are as a rule unwilling to increase allocations to national organizations, arguing that the funds were donoted with the expectation that they would be *used* locally. In the face of these circumstances, certain national agencies have considered "packaged" fund-raising, in one form or another, with the expectation that such campaigns could generate the emotional appeal and some of the financial success of the Red Feather and similar campaigns.

NATION-WIDE VOCATIONAL ASSOCIATIONS AND CONFERENCES: Vocational associations bring together the professional workers and personnel of various sectors of the welfare field, for the exchange of information, improvement of techniques, maintenance of standards, and evaluation of services. There are several types of vocational associations. Some service organizations, discussed in the previous section,

[9] George W. Rabinoff, "National Organizations in Social Welfare," in Russell H. Kurtz, ed., *Social Work Year Book 1957*, p. 386.

resemble vocational associations in that they have individual members
who may share vocational interests.

Some vocational associations cut across the entire professional field,
as does the National Association of Social Workers. Formed in 1955
from seven older professional associations, in 1960 it had approximately
26,500 members; requirements regarding professional education must be
met for a social worker to become eligible for membership. These are
the objectives of the Association, as defined in the 1960 edition of its
publication, the *Social Work Year Book*:

(1) To improve and extend social work practice through setting
standards. . . .

(2) To establish principles and procedures for determining and
certifying competence to practice. . . .

(3) To define and help to bring about the working conditions
necessary for the best practice. . . .

(4) To define each specialty's area of concern within the practice
of social work. . . .

(5) To delineate the nature of new, evolving areas of social work
practice, and to provide or to seek opportunity for their development.

(6) To collaborate with other professional groups. . . .

(7) To interpret to the community the contribution of the professional social worker. . . .

(8) To make studies and to take action in relation to social conditions.

(9) To recruit new workers. . . .[10]

Other vocational organizations are associations of personnel of particular types of agencies. The American Recreation Society in 1960
had over 5,100 members among recreation workers, as well as thirty-
five State and local organizations. Still other vocational organizations
are the American Industrial Hygiene Association, the National Association of Jewish Center Workers, and the Association of Girl Scout Professional Workers. Such organizations are frequently quite small and
their activities restricted to annual conventions and small projects. There
are a few organizations, such as the Social Work Vocational Bureau
and the National Health and Welfare Retirement Association, that
provide specific services for welfare professionals.

The American Women's Voluntary Services (AWVS) is representative of still another type of vocational association, the associations
of volunteers. With 5,000 members, AWVS is concerned with offering
"an opportunity for every woman to serve her country and her community. . . . It recruits, mobilizes, and trains women for all types of

[10] *Social Work Year Book* 1960, pp. 697–98.

community service and places them where they may be of maximum assistance to give service to recognized local agencies." [11] The AWVS provides volunteers to work for agencies dealing with disabled and hospitalized veterans and civilians; to staff and maintain child-care centers and information centers; and to assist in workshops that recondition and make clothes for local and overseas use. The Association of the Junior Leagues of America, Inc., is a larger organization (68,000 individual members in 1957) that might be considered either a service organization or a vocational organization. Its members are organized in 186 local leagues concerned with providing volunteer services to community agencies; the national organization serves the local leagues by providing them education, arts, welfare, and other program information and assistance, on a consultant or advisory basis. Organizations such as the Catholic Daughters of America are at least peripherally interested in providing volunteer services. The 210,000 members of this organization are primarily devoted to "the material, moral, and intellectual development of Catholic womanhood. . . . Among its activities are dispensing of charity and assisting Catholic charitable and educational projects." [12]

There are also a handful of national organizations that exist primarily to plan and conduct periodical conferences on welfare topics. Largest is the National Conference on Social Welfare, with 5,500 individual members and 1,200 organization members (1960). In addition to its annual forum it issues certain publications and extends organizational services to State conferences. Other conferences are the National Conference of Jewish Communal Service, the National Conference of Catholic Charities, and the Church Conference of Social Work. Many of the other national service and vocational organizations conduct annual or biennial conferences, as integral but secondary parts of their programs.[13]

FEDERATIONS OF NATION-WIDE ORGANIZATIONS: At the top of the complex hierarchy of nation-wide welfare bodies are half a dozen organizations providing coordination and services for the entire field. Broadest in scope is the National Social Welfare Assembly (NSWA), the central federated group of sixty-nine nation-wide organizations, fourteen of which are units of the federal government. This is the NSWA's statement of purpose:

The National Social Welfare Assembly believes that social welfare means the well-being of all people. All parts of social welfare

[11] *Ibid.*, p. 671.
[12] *Ibid.*, p. 677.
[13] Dunham, *op. cit.*, pp. 218–19.

are interrelated. The Assembly's purpose is to further these concepts through a three-fold partnership of government and voluntary, national and local, lay and professional interests. To these ends, the Assembly undertakes: to study and define social welfare problems, and plan action to meet them; to serve as an agency for consultation and conference on social welfare needs and problems; to facilitate more effective operation of organized social welfare; to provide leadership and facilities for affiliate organizations, associate groups, and individual members so they may plan and act together voluntarily in matters of common interest; to encourage and strengthen voluntary joint action of all agencies and individuals in behalf of social welfare; and to act in behalf of social welfare on national and international issues, where representation of its interests is desired.[14]

The Assembly considers itself "the national planning body for social welfare." These were its members in 1960: 133 individuals nominated by its fifty-five affiliated national non-governmental organizations, fourteen federal government agencies, and four associate groups; and eighty-eight elected members-at-large. In 1956 the staff consisted of seven technical and professional personnel and some part-time workers. Its total expenditures for the year were $264,000. Its activities are conducted through more than twenty conferences and committees, as diverse as the National Committee on the Aging and the Committee on Comics. The published work of its committees is often widely circulated. With United Community Funds and Councils of America, the Assembly jointly sponsors three committees, an institute, and a workshop; with the National Association of Housing and Redevelopment Officials it co-sponsors a Committee on Housing.

There are several other nation-wide federations. Four of these are independent councils associated with the NSWA. They are the Council on Social Work Education, whose membership includes schools of social work, vocational associations, individuals, and certain line agencies; the National Council on Agricultural Life and Labor, a federation of farm, labor, civic, and religious groups; the National Health Council, with sixty-five member organizations, most of them national health agencies and professional societies, others government and business organizations; and the United States Committee of the International Conference of Social Work.

There are, finally, several organizations that provide specialized services for many nation-wide agencies. One, the Social Work Vocational Bureau, has already been mentioned; in effect it provides an em-

[14] Russell H. Kurtz, ed. *Social Work Year Book 1957.* New York: National Association of Social Workers, 1957, p. 700.

ployment service and maintains professional records for agencies and individuals. The National Publicity Council for Health and Welfare Services serves some 1,800 nation-wide and local organizations as a distributing center for information on publicity techniques and as a consultant on public relations problems.

There are two national agencies that perform an evaluative, occasionally critical, function for the nation-wide agencies they serve. One, the National Budget and Consultation Committee, examines and reports on the programs and budgets of thirty-two nation-wide health and welfare agencies, "a service to the agency and to communities which cannot examine national agency budgets adequately for themselves." [15] Although the Committee is supported at present by the NSWA and United Community Funds and Councils, neither organization has the right of review over the Committee's findings. There is no compulsion for nation-wide organizations to subscribe to the services of the Committee, and those that do are organizations with relatively small budgets.

The other, the National Information Bureau, provides what amounts to an endorsement service for individuals, corporations, foundations, welfare councils and chests, and chambers of commerce. It evaluates the activities of about six hundred organizations that solicit contributions on a national or international level and provides this information primarily to those concerned with contributing to campaigns. The Bureau is designed to protect givers from fraudulent and questionable appeals.

CONCLUDING REMARKS

SINCE THE BEGINNING of the twentieth century, a large number of State-wide and nation-wide non-governmental welfare organizations have been developed. A few, such as the John Howard Association, provide special types of services for individuals throughout the nation. Others, such as the Family Service Association of America, provide planning, research, and information services for affiliated community agencies. A number of them bring together personnel interested in various aspects of social welfare; these are the vocational associations, among them the State conferences of social work and many national bodies such as the National Association of Social Workers. The most publicized and dynamic of the national agencies are the national health organizations, which charter local chapters and through them conduct nation-wide fund-raising campaigns; varying proportions of the funds are used by the national organization to finance research and educational programs. Many of these national bodies lay claim to considerable influence

[15] *Ibid.*, p. 684.

over the shape of American welfare; this is particularly true of the vocational associations. They set suggested standards of professional social work practice, propose welfare programs and types of services, and sponsor various kinds of State and national welfare legislation. They are often looked to as the source of authoritative opinion on matters of welfare concern. The most clear accomplishments of the vocational associations have been the promotion of professionalism in social work and related fields, and the exchange of information among members.

The national staff service agencies generally have a more definite impact on the actual provision of welfare services. Their members are usually community organizations of a specific type, and they can concentrate their efforts on the problems and requirements of one type of agency, such as family service agencies, neighborhood improvement groups, or settlement houses. Depending on the closeness of their ties with their local members, they may have considerable influence on the personnel and services of local agencies. In the case of groups like the YMCA and the Family Service Association of America, local organizations adhere quite closely to the standards set forth as desirable by the national agency.

National health agencies generally determine the activities of their local chapters quite closely, in regard to both fund-raising practices and permissible uses of funds. The national health agencies and, to a lesser extent, the national staff service agencies thus have come more and more in conflict with community coordinating bodies, and this conflict may be expected to continue. Community welfare fund-raisers often object to competition from national fund-raising campaigns and point out that national campaign expenses are too high. More importantly, community welfare councils sometimes find that local chapters and affiliates of national agencies resist integration with other community welfare activities, and thus impede coordination.

Chapter Six

CHURCHES

T HE MORE THAN 110 MILLION AMERICANS who were members of religious bodies in 1959 formed the largest mutual-aid group in the nation. In that year individuals and organizations gave nearly eight billion dollars for philanthropic purposes. The churches received slightly over half this sum, largely from churchgoers. Religious bodies have a long tradition of welfare undertakings. For centuries the Roman Catholic, Protestant, and Jewish organizations have been performing charitable works. The express motives behind the establishment of many, or even most, welfare programs have been essentially religious. Churches themselves do not confine their welfare endeavors to the pulpit and the altar. To the contrary, they have instituted social services and social action movements; expanded religious education activities; and developed parishes resembling community centers, offering social events, recreation throughout the week, and educational and cultural programs and discussions.

The development of lay concern and activity in the welfare field, often instigated by the churches, has led to some shifts in the nature of religious welfare activity. In certain areas the concern of the churches has changed from one of direct involvement through their members and as agents themselves to one that is more impersonal or one of narrower scope so as to deal with particular welfare problems. Nevertheless, much religious activity still parallels secular professional welfare activity. The consultation extended to parishioners under the name of "pastoral psychology" resembles social casework and shares many of its techniques and practices. The Roman Catholic Church in particular has sponsored a trend toward social casework and group work under the direct guidance of local parishes.

Less directly connected with local parishes and congregations are the multitude of "church-related" welfare agencies. These are hospitals, family and child service agencies, shelters, recreation centers, community centers, and homes for the aged, which exhibit many types of relations to their sponsoring churches. Both the Roman Catholic and Episcopal churches have religious orders devoted to operating and staffing welfare services, notably hospitals and homes. In an intermediate position are certain other hospitals, service agencies, and centers that receive part of their financial support from church bodies and are administered or partially controlled by churches. Finally, there are organizations such as the Young Men's Christian Association (YMCA), the Young Women's Christian Association (YWCA), and some service agencies that have only the most tenuous connections with organized religion. These last may be subject only to requirements that they operate in accordance with Christian principles and have religious representation on their controlling or advisory bodies.

The clientele or recipient groups of church-related agencies are equally varied. Homes for the aged operating under the auspices of organized religions are frequently restricted to members of a particular denomination. Religiously affiliated hospitals, on the other hand, usually extend their facilities to individuals of all denominations, a practice justified by the fact that most of their income is from fees. However, the nation's sixty-four Jewish hospitals (1956) drew nearly a third of their patients from the Jewish population, which comprised little more than 3 per cent of the total population.

This chapter first discusses church membership and religious giving and then outlines the principal welfare activities of the Protestant, Catholic, and Jewish religious bodies.

CHURCH MEMBERSHIP AND RELIGIOUS GIVING

Membership

BY THE BEST available estimates, in 1958 there were 107.3 million Americans of all ages on church membership rolls. They comprised 61 per cent of the population of the United States and were served by a third of a million men of the cloth—ministers, priests, and rabbis. The various Protestant denominations reported having 61,505,000 members,[1] the Roman Catholic Church 39,510,000 members. It is roughly

[1] Data on the Latter-Day Saints (Mormons) are included in Protestant statistics, though strictly speaking the 1.5 million Mormons in the United States do not consider themselves Protestants.

estimated that 3,200,000 American Jews had formal affiliations with synagogues of one of the three Jewish bodies. The Eastern churches counted 2,545,000 members, and other religious groups had 488,000 members.[2]

There is another source of information on church membership besides church membership rolls—the American people themselves. In March, 1957, the United States Bureau of the Census conducted a sample survey, asking "What is your religion?" More than 97 per cent of persons fourteen or older reported a religion in response to this question. Some relevant data are given in Table 1. Clearly, many more Americans consider themselves religious, or at least would like others to consider them religious, than are formally attached to churches.

TABLE 1

RELIGIOUS AFFILIATIONS OF PERSONS FOURTEEN OR OLDER, 1957

FAITH	PERSONS REPORTING RELIGIOUS AFFILIATION (*Based on Sample Survey Data*)		PERSONS ACTUALLY ON CHURCH ROLLS[1]	
	Number	Per Cent	Number	Per Cent[1]
Protestant	79,000,000	66.2%	42,420,000	35.6%
Roman Catholic	30,700,000	25.7	25,320,000	21.2
Jewish	3,900,000	3.2	2,270,000	1.9
Other Religions	2,500,000	2.2	2,140,000	1.8
No Religion	3,200,000	2.7	47,150,000[2]	39.5
Total	119,300,000	100%	72,150,000	100%

Source of survey data: *Current Population Reports*, Series P-20, No. 79. Bureau of the Census. Washington, D.C.: USGPO, 1957.

[1] The numbers of persons aged fourteen or over on church roles were approximated by multiplying their reported membership figures, given in 1958 religious yearbooks, by .709, that fraction of the total population which was fourteen or older at the time of the 1950 census. The percentages are calculated on the basis of the total population aged fourteen or older (119,300,000 in 1957).
[2] The difference between persons aged fourteen or above on church rolls (est. 72,150,000) and the total number of persons in the population aged fourteen or older. This figure is not included in the total.

There appear to be some thirty-six million would-be Protestants and five million would-be Catholics. The difference between the two figures for Jews probably results from the fact that many persons not affiliated formally with synagogues nevertheless identify themselves with Judaism

[2] Benson Y. Landis, ed., *Yearbook of American Churches 1960*, New York: National Council of the Churches of Christ in the U.S.A., 1959, p. 252; *American Jewish Year Book 1958*, New York and Philadelphia: The American Jewish Committee and the Jewish Publication Society of America, 1958, pp. 114–15. The "other religious groups" are Buddhist, Old Catholic, Polish National Catholic, and the Armenian Church of North America.

as a cultural group.[3] Few persons indeed will publicly state that they have no religious affiliations.

Neither a person's avowed religious affiliation nor his presence on a church membership roll proves that he is actually involved in church affairs. One possible measure of involvement is church attendance. The American Institute of Public Opinion since 1939 has occasionally polled samples of civilian adults (twenty-one or older), asking whether they had attended church during the week preceding the interview. Some of their data are summarized in Table 2. In 1955 the poll was repeated several times (not indicated in Table 2) and little difference was found in attendance by season of the year.

TABLE 2

CHURCH ATTENDANCE AND CHURCH MEMBERSHIP, 1939–1958

ADULTS ATTENDING CHURCH ACCORDING TO SAMPLE SURVEY DATA		CHURCH MEMBERSHIP AS A PERCENTAGE OF POPULATION ACCORDING TO CHURCH MEMBERSHIP ROLLS	
Date	Per Cent	Date	Per Cent [1]
February, 1939	41%	1940	49%
November, 1940	37		
May, 1942	36		
May, 1947	45		
April, 1950	39	1950	57
July, 1954	46		
December, 1955	49	1955	60.9
April, 1957	51		
December, 1957	47	1957	61.0
December, 1958	49	1958	62.4

Source: Landis, *op. cit.,* pp. 293, 297.

[1] These percentages do not take into account the fact that not all American Jews are formally affiliated with synagogues. Data for 1958 include 2,000,000 Catholics, with their families, on military duty and not counted in previous years, hence the sharp rise in 1958 over the 1957 percentage.

The figures on attendance probably cannot be taken at face value. It is generally true that in an interview situation people tend to exaggerate what they believe to be desirable information. Many more persons claim religious affiliation than are actually church members, and presumably more persons would claim to have attended church recently than had actually done so. Nevertheless, there are no better data available.

The same surveys also produced data on the numbers of persons attending church classified by religion. This information for 1957 is

[3] See *The American Jewish Year Book 1958*, p. 115.

given in Table 3. It is doubtful if church attendance was as high as these figures indicate. Few organizations of any kind can claim 90 per cent or even 75 per cent at their gatherings. Apparently, however, Roman Catholics were more faithful in their attendance than Protestants, and Protestants attended church services much more faithfully than Jews.

TABLE 3

ADULTS ATTENDING CHURCH, BY FAITH, DECEMBER, 1957

Faith	Number Attending According to Survey Data	Percentage of Persons Claiming Religious Affiliation [1]	Percentage of Persons Actually on Church Rolls [2]
Protestant	27,100,000	40	74
Roman Catholic	19,500,000	74	89
Jewish	600,000	18	31
Total	47,200,000		

Source: Landis, *op. cit.*, pp. 293, 297.

[1] Based on 1957 Bureau of Census survey data.
[2] Derived by multiplying membership figures as reported by churches by .611, that fraction of the total population which was twenty-one years of age or older at the time of the 1950 census, to arrive at an estimate of adults on church rolls, and dividing the American Institute of Public Opinion figures by these estimates.

Religious Giving

AN ESTIMATED $3.96 billion were contributed to religious groups in 1959 (cf. Table 4), but not all denominations received equally from their parishioners. Most Protestant and Eastern churches have maintained fairly accurate records of their receipts, which totaled $2.21 billion in 1957. Their average church member (thirteen years of age or older) contributed about sixty-three dollars. The Seventh-Day Adventist and Wesleyan Methodist churches were farthest above this average, receiving about $200 per capita. The Methodist Church, only one of a number of Methodist groups but the largest single Protestant church (nine and a half million members of all ages) received forty-nine dollars per capita. The Southern Baptist Convention, second largest Protestant body, received fifty dollars per capita. Members of smaller religious bodies as a rule were more generous in their contributions than those of larger churches.[4] In 1958, forty-nine Protestant and Eastern Orthodox denominations reported contributions of $2.35 billion.

It is estimated in Table 13 of this chapter that Jewish donations to social and communal services were about fifty-four dollars per capita

[4] Landis, *op. cit.*, pp. 277–78. Per capita figures are based on members thirteen years of age or older.

in the late 1950's. This figure is admittedly low, perhaps no more than two-thirds the true figure, for it does not include contributions made directly to synagogues or for congregational activities. There are no direct data available on per capita Roman Catholic contributions, but Catholics traditionally give very generously to the Church.[5]

TABLE 4

ESTIMATES OF EXPENDITURES BY RELIGIOUS ORGANIZATIONS, 1950, 1955, 1959 (*In Millions of Dollars*)

	1950		1955		1959	
Purpose	Amount	Per Cent	Amount	Per Cent	Amount	Per Cent
Current Operating Expenditures	$1,176[1]	60%	$1,836[1]	59%	$2,262[1]	57%
Church Construction	409	21	734	24	925	23
Church-supported Welfare	200	10	290	9	468	12
Church-supported Hospitals, Clinics, Other Medical Services	60	3	90	3	118	3
Foreign Relief and Foreign Missions	118	6	150	5	185	5
Totals	$1,963	100%	$3,100	100%	$3,958	100%

Source: *Giving USA* 1960, New York: American Association of Fund-Raising Counsel, 1960, p. 27. Estimates for 1950 and 1955 prepared by Thomas Karter, U.S. Department of Health, Education and Welfare, Division of Program Research; 1959 estimates by AAFRC.

[1] Includes salaries, maintenance, and expenditures for church-supported educational programs.

Despite the large amount of money donated to religious bodies, most church-related welfare organizations have ceased to rely on their parent churches for more than a small part of their financial support. Most of the $3.96 billion donated in 1959 by the members of organized religion to their churches was devoted to other purposes. Over 80 per cent of the receipts of religious organizations for each year of the 1950's was used to meet operating expenses and the costs of church construc-

[5] There is reason to believe that the $3.9 billion estimate of 1959 religious giving is low, perhaps by a considerable extent. On the basis of known data, Protestant, Eastern, and Jewish bodies almost certainly received no less than $2.7 billion and perhaps as much as $3 billion from their members in 1959. Even given the lesser of these estimates, and accepting the estimate of $3.9 billion total religious giving, the Roman Catholic per capita contribution can be computed as no more than $35, a figure contradicted by observation. Probably the average contribution by Catholics thirteen years old or older would be at least twice this amount. If $70 were the Catholic per capita contribution, and other estimates are accurate, religious giving in 1959 was about $5.0 billion. Although the remainder of this chapter relies on the American Association of Fund-Raising Counsel estimate of $3.9 billion, the possibility that it is low should be kept in mind.

tion. Table 4 gives rough estimates of church expenditures for 1950, 1955, and 1959. It is assumed that expenditures are generally comparable to contributions, since virtually all the income of religious bodies derives from their parishioners.

PROTESTANTISM AND SOCIAL SERVICE

PROTESTANT SOCIAL SERVICES are not nearly so well integrated as the welfare activities of the Roman Catholic and Jewish faiths. This lack of integration is the result of several conflicting philosophical points of view that cut across all Protestantism. Protestants are fundamentally uncertain as to their role in welfare, especially where their activities overlap those of secular organizations.

In 1958 the Protestant and Eastern churches had 57 per cent of United States church membership, compared with 36 per cent for Roman Catholicism and 3 per cent for Jewish congregations. The Protestant churches had 61,505,000 members; the Eastern churches (notably the Greek and Russian Orthodox), 2,545,000 members. Protestant and Eastern church members comprised 36 per cent of the population of the United States. Membership figures for the major Protestant and Eastern Church bodies are given in Table 5, for 1957.

Protestant Social Concern

The Protestant churches of America, including more than a third of the population, are among the largest of non-governmental welfare organizations. In the past half century there has been a growing self-conscious effort on their part "to influence the social atmosphere of society," through social pronouncements, social education, social action, and social services. However, a comprehensive 1955 survey of Protestant welfare interests by the National Council of the Churches of Christ in the U.S.A. (NCCC) noted that

the most striking fact of the Protestant churches' involvement in social welfare today is its seemingly indefinite variation of expression. No matter what dimension is taken, there does not appear readily a pattern of what might be typical or of what might be generally true for Protestantism, except for the fact of great range.[6]

One reason for this lack of pattern is that Protestant concern with social welfare has been largely secondary to more fundamental religious

[6] Horace Cayton and Setsuko M. Nishi. *The Changing Scene: Churches and Social Welfare*, Vol. II. New York: National Council of Churches of Christ in the U.S.A., 1955, p. 8.

TABLE 5

PROTESTANT AND EASTERN CHURCHES IN THE UNITED STATES, 1957 [1]

Religious Group	Congregations (to Nearest 10)	Membership (to Nearest 1,000)	Membership Rank
Adventist Bodies (5) [2]	3,460	323,000	18
Assemblies of God	8,100	482,000	13
Baptist Bodies (27)	89,610	19,766,000	1
Brethren (German Baptist; 5 bodies)	1,400	247,000	21
Christian Churches (Disciples of Christ), International Convention	8,000	1,944,000	7
Churches of God (9 bodies)	8,430	400,000	15
Church of God in Christ	3,600	360,000	17
Church of the Nazarene	4,230	282,000	19
Churches of Christ	16,500	1,750,000	8
Congregational Christian Church	5,540	1,393,000	10
Eastern Churches (21 bodies)	1,360	2,540,000	6
Evangelical and Reformed Church	2,730	800,000	11
Evangelical United Brethren Church	4,160	746,000	12
Friends (9 bodies)	980	120,000	25
Independent Church of the Four-Square Gospel	680	113,000	26
Jehovah's Witnesses	3,720	208,000	22
Latter-Day Saints (6 bodies) [1]	3,930	1,491,000	9
Lutheran (19 bodies)	16,780	7,530,000	3
Mennonite Bodies (13)	1,600	160,000	24
Methodist Bodies (22)	54,020	11,940,000	2
Pentecostal Assemblies (9)	4,480	366,000	16
Presbyterian Bodies (10)	14,550	4,043,000	4
Protestant Episcopal Church	6,840	2,965,000	5
Reformed Bodies (5)	1,410	450,000	14
Salvation Army [3]	1,280	250,000	20
Spiritualists (3 bodies)	490	176,000	23
Unitarian Churches	370	105,000	27
Other Protestant Churches	12,850	1,409,000	
Totals	281,100	62,364,000	

[1] See footnote 1, this chapter.
[2] The term "bodies" and the numbers in parentheses refer to the regional, schismatic, or other groupings within a major religious group.
[3] The Salvation Army is listed as a religious body by both the *Year Book of American Churches* 1959 (Benson Landis, ed.) and the *Statistical Abstract of the United States* 1958 (U.S. Bureau of the Census), the sources of the above statistics. The former source also cites the Volunteers of America as a religious group, with a membership of 28,000; this statistic is included in the "Other Protestant Churches" figures, above.

concerns. The social programs have been developed to supplement the traditional religious institutional functions of religious education, missionary endeavor, and pastoral care of the congregations. These traditional functions still make up the largest portion of present-day Protestant welfare activities.

By far the most numerous Protestant social welfare agencies, either in country or in city, are the local churches themselves. Even the more conventional ones make important contributions to this field. Their pastoral and fraternal assistance to constituents has both a preventive and remedial aspect. They render material aid, help in sickness, exercise vocational guidance and contribute to employment all as a matter of course, without much consciousness that these are social ministries. The church's contribution to social morale is essentially beyond measurement. It is entirely demonstrable, however, that in the pre-depression era a full third of all the social welfare funds, both public and private, expended in typical American cities were expended for the support of leisure-time and character-building activities, entirely paralleling the normal activities of organized groups in the church, often sponsored by churches and generally supported by church people. The share of the church in welfare work, as a by-product of its religious value, is accordingly enormous. Its more highly organized groups for women, young people, boys and girls, realize many, if not most, of the values found in the organizations undertaken for similar age groups in the name of social work.[7]

The church is a primary social institution particularly in rural areas:

The social welfare work of the rural churches . . . professionally judged, is almost nonexistent. That, however, is not to say that there is none of a sort. Few are the rural churches that have not aided the poor or unfortunate among their own number. But the average rural church member would be surprised to hear that having the Boy Scouts take care of Widow Jones' fires or that sending garments to tenant Smith's children after they are burned out, classified as social welfare work. *Rural people are neighborly and they are chiefly neighborly within the social groupings to which they acknowledge allegiance.* It is in such a way that a rural church moves to relieve distress when confronted with it.[8]

However, in rural as well as urban churches traditional social functions have experienced change. The internal structure of a typical parish or congregation has been greatly elaborated, to fulfill these functions in more specialized ways for particular age groups and interest groups. There have been modifications in church organization, methods, and

[7] H. Paul Douglass and Edmund de S. Brunner. *The Protestant Church as a Social Institution.* New York: Harper & Brothers, 1935, pp. 188–89. Cited in Cayton and Nishi, *op. cit.,* p. 12.
[8] Douglass and Brunner, *op. cit.,* p. 187. Cited in Cayton and Nishi, *op. cit.,* p. 12. Our italics—A. de G. and T. G.

administration; a widening range of training, interests, and abilities on the part of pastors; and additions to staff, plant, and expenditures.

Also contributing to the lack of pattern in the Protestant social ministry have been great inter-denominational differences in its forms and objectives. Within Protestantism are groups differing in religious and social tradition, in geographic concentration, in income levels, and in education. For instance, some are strongly evangelical, whereas others are rationalistic; some are primarily urban middle-class, but others draw their strength from low-income rural folk. Some of the confusion in Protestant social services is inherent in the differences in these people's religious needs; on the other side of the coin, Protestantism has not developed welfare principles broad enough to embrace these differences.

Confusion and lack of clear purpose are most apparent in the church-related agencies of the Protestant denominations, those agencies that deal with welfare activity in ways similar to those of the social work profession. The confusion is linked in part with the development of the welfare profession. With the growth of social work outside the churches, many of the inter-personal problems that were once the province of the minister and the church worker were assumed by the social worker. The churches on the one hand "felt themselves infringed upon by a new 'scientific' approach to human relations"; meanwhile the non-church-connected agencies and their professional staffs believed that their scientifically based techniques gave them the competence to deal more adequately with these problems.

In theory, both from the broader social standpoint and from the statements of both religious writers and social workers, many of the goals and means of religion and social work are the same. Social work and religion share the same motivating impulse: to improve the welfare of man. Social work, however, tends to emphasize the material aspects of man's welfare, whereas the church has traditionally been concerned with his spiritual welfare. Social workers, unless directly connected with church welfare work, tend to shy away from including any religious or spiritual content in their practice and may view religious welfare interests as undesirable.

Almon Pepper, one-time director of the Episcopal Churches Department of Christian Social Relations, suggested four of the many rationalized motives for Christian social work:

(1) Christian charity, and the pastoral concern of the church for its own people.

(2) An evangelistic hope that the religious life of the individual cared for will be nurtured and strengthened and that he may be encouraged to join the church if not already a member.

(3) A broadly humanitarian and democratic concern for the

needs of people and the improvement of society, which provides service purely in terms of need.

(4) The professional attitude of performing a given service or function in the way most satisfactory and beneficial to the client and the community.[9]

There are at least five sets of principles in Protestantism guiding these motives in practice.

First, there are some Protestants, though not necessarily Protestant denominations, who maintain that Protestants should emulate the Roman Catholic pattern of relatively complete church handling of social welfare needs. In theory, this would involve extensive welfare organization, including specialized institutions and agencies, welfare organization at the diocesan level or its Protestant equivalent, and specialized services by the individual church. Although some Protestants have advocated this approach, others have argued that it "leads straight to the absorption of function after function by the Church," thus denying the strong threads of individualism and voluntarism [10] shot through Protestant theology.

Another Protestant pattern calls for the devolvement of social work on secular agencies and the exclusion of the churches from organizational participation. Proponents of this point of view support it by arguing that secular agencies are already characterized by a Protestant Christian pattern. They also urge that Protestants should participate, on a voluntary basis, in these agencies. "These agencies furnish a channel of Christian benevolence and also a vocational outlet for the ideals of a service that Christianity has fostered." [11]

These are largely opposed points of view. There are at least three others occupying intermediate positions. One might be termed the "whole man" philosophy. "The churches should cooperate with an institution even if independent, if it gives evidence of meeting the needs of, or of ministering to 'the whole man.' If an agency denies the need of such a comprehensive service and ministry, then the churches would be justified in setting up their own organization." [12] What constitutes service to the whole man is presumably the decision of a given denomination, which seems to leave the question with no definite answer.

A good number of Protestants, and some Protestant denominations,

[9] Almon Pepper, "Protestant Social Work," in Russell H. Kurtz, ed., *Social Work Year Book 1945*, New York: Russell Sage Foundation, 1946, pp. 304–305.
[10] The dictionary prefers "voluntaryism" where this book uses "voluntarism." It is felt that the former is unmanageable and the latter popular enough to warrant its use.
[11] F. Ernest Johnson, "Protestant Social Work," in Russell H. Kurtz, ed., *Social Work Year Book 1954*, New York: American Association of Social Workers, 1954, pp. 378–79.
[12] Cayton and Nishi, *op. cit.*, p. 74.

4- hold the "impetus theory" of the church's role in social welfare. According to this theory, when a welfare problem becomes apparent the church acts as the conscience of the community, urging it to take action. Through preachments and social action the local churches develop community awareness of the problem. Once adequate programs are developed and under way, the responsibility of the church has largely been fulfilled. Only if other community organizations fail to develop programs is the church justified in establishing its own agencies. It might be noted that this approach to social service by some churches is quite similar to that of some secular non-governmental agencies in respect to governmental bodies: these secular agencies feel that their role is to begin pilot programs, with the expectation that the local, State, or federal government will ultimately assume the responsibility.

These four Protestant approaches have one element in common. They all attempt to cope with the challenge of professional social work on the professional social worker's own ground: they all seem to assume that Protestant participation in organized social welfare is an either-or proposition. Either the churches take on social work, with all its professional techniques and complexities, or they wash their hands of it, at least in its operational aspects.

The final Protestant approach largely avoids this by viewing social welfare services as an extension of traditional Protestant church functions. For the advocates of this point of view, Protestantism has definite contributions to make to any welfare service: the concern with spiritual welfare, the possibilities of more intense personal interest and contact with recipients, willingness to give unusual service, and a quality of devotion and love. Government agencies and secular non-governmental agencies are often unable or unwilling to include these elements in their welfare services. Thus, the role of Protestantism is neither to absorb all welfare functions—which is beyond its potential—nor to absolve itself

5 of responsibility. Its role is to infuse welfare services with some sense of Christian charity and spiritual concern, working through both existing secular agencies, and its own agencies, where it has had the resources to establish them. These sentiments and their Christian rationale have been expressed in this way:

> Charity and welfare work are not synonymous. It is possible to have either without the other. A charitable intent expressed in a charitable deed does not necessarily result in a contribution to welfare. . . . On the other hand, social welfare may be promoted by means which are provided without a charitable intent. . . . Charity needs guidance in its expression lest it be wasted or worse, and . . . social welfare work needs the spirit and quality of charity lest it degenerate into mere professionalism or into a factor of

group conflict. . . . The resources are found in our Christian faith and experience. First of all, the Christian knows that he is not alone in caring. . . . Second, the Christian knows that there are limitless resources of inner strength and security.[13]

TABLE 6

SERVICES OF PROTESTANT CHURCH-RELATED HEALTH AND
WELFARE ORGANIZATIONS, 1954

Services		Estimated Number of Organizations
Services to Children		800 [1]
Institutional care	400	
Child-placement services	300	
Day nursing service	300	
Miscellaneous services	600	
Homes for the Aged		700
Hospitals		600
Neighborhood Houses and Settlements		550
Residences, Hospices, Temporary Shelters		475
Camps Operated by Church Welfare Agencies		170
Rehabilitation Services		140
Group Work and Recreation (Agencies other than Houses and Settlements)		135
Family Welfare Services		120 [2]
Chaplaincy Services		90
Clinics, Dispensaries, Convalescent Homes, etc.		65
Maternity Homes		60
Protective Services		15
Other Services		80
Total		4,000

Source: C. G. Chakernian and W. J. Villaume. *Health and Welfare Estimates, Based Upon Recent Research* (bulletin). Hartford, Conn.: Hartford Seminary Foundation (n.d.). Estimates were based on "mathematical projections of statistical reports from church bodies constituting 70 per cent of the total membership of Protestant and Eastern Orthodox churches, and detailed questionnaires returned by about 30 per cent of the agencies and institutions reported by these bodies." The statistical reports were obtained in the NCCC's 1954 national inventory of such organizations. It should be emphasized that these figures are *estimates* and may well err in either direction; also, definitions of "church-relatedness" vary widely.

[1] Many organizations serving children provided more than one type of service.
[2] About 380 organizations listed under other categories also offered family welfare services.

Church-Related Agencies, 1954

DESPITE THE CONFUSION of Protestantism concerning its welfare role, in 1954 there were estimated to be 4,000 Protestant church-related agencies

[13] Roswell Barnes, "Charity and Welfare Work," *Christian Social Welfare*, I, No. 1, 1953 (New York: National Council of the Churches of Christ in the U.S.A.).

and institutions whose primary functions were health or welfare service. (This does not include the various Protestant church-related schools.) These organizations served approximately seventeen million persons that year, and at least one out of three of these persons was of some faith other than Protestant or Eastern Orthodox. Table 6 lists these agencies and institutions according to the types of services provided.

These organizations employed about 250,000 full- and part-time salaried personnel, who were assisted by an estimated 150,000 volunteers. Capital assets were estimated at $3.3 billion, more than half in buildings, land, and equipment; 46 per cent was held in endowments and investments. These figures are based on projections made from data supplied by about one thousand agencies, in a 1954 study by the NCCC, the only such study to appear in recent years. Among the personnel reported *by the thousand agencies* were 1,641 social workers, 675 of whom had accredited degrees in social work. There were also 874 ordained persons on the staffs of these agencies and hospitals.

TABLE 7

SOURCES OF INCOME OF CHURCH-RELATED HOSPITALS AND
AGENCIES, 1954
(*Based on a Sample of Protestant Church Agencies*)

SOURCE	HOSPITALS (600)		AGENCIES (3,400)	
	Per Cent	Amount	*Per Cent*	Amount
Religious Groups	0.7%	$ 4,200,000	15.1%	$ 45,300,000
Individuals	0.8	4,800,000	17.9	53,700,000
Community Chests	4.8	29,000,000	5.1	15,300,000
Other Contributions	1.5	9,000,000	26.5	79,500,000
Earned Income [1]	92.2	553,000,000	34.3	102,900,000
Public Funds			1.1	3,300,000
Totals	100%	$600,000,000	100%	$300,000,000

Source: Cayton and Nishi, *op. cit.*, pp. 126–28; Chakernian and Villaume, *op. cit.*

[1] Service fees and investments. When both groups are combined, about 77 per cent of operating income was *earned* income. This can be broken down as follows: 66 per cent from individual fees; 2 per cent in service fees from public funds; 4.5 per cent income from investments; and 4.5 per cent other earned income.

The term "church-related agency" does not necessarily imply extensive church financial support, at least not among Protestant health and welfare organizations. Church-related hospitals, for example, received less than one per cent of their total operating expenses from religious bodies; all other church-related welfare organizations received 15 per cent of their support from churches. Percentages of income from various sources, as obtained from the NCCC sample, are given in Table

7; estimated expenditures are based on projections. An analysis of the actual sources of the religious contributions is given in Table 8.

The nature of "church-relatedness" was not financial; nearly a quarter of the agencies in the NCCC sample reported no religious financial support of any kind, a situation that was sharply criticized by many agency directors. The religious involvement was more likely to be one of control and character of service.

TABLE 8

SOURCES OF RELIGIOUS CONTRIBUTIONS TO CHURCH-RELATED
WELFARE ORGANIZATIONS

Source	Per Cent
Local churches	53%
Other local religious organizations	5
State and regional religious organizations	16
National religious organizations	18
Other religious sources	8
Total	100%

Source: Cayton and Nishi, *op. cit.*, p. 127.

Nine out of ten of the organizations reported that they were "officially recognized" by their related religious bodies. Eight per cent of all organizations were directly responsible to a religious organization and had no governing bodies of their own; most of these were hospitals. More than a third of the organizations had their governing boards elected, appointed, or nominated by religious organizations. All board members of 57 per cent of the church-related organizations were required to have specific religious affiliations. Other agencies and hospitals had religious requirements of at least some of their board members, and eight out of ten required that their directors have a specified religious affiliation.

There was a religious content in the welfare services of some of the church-affiliated organizations, and a number of them limited their services to individuals of certain religious affiliations. Almost nine out of ten of the organizations claimed religious objectives, most often expressed in the form of worship services. Chapel facilities, religious instruction, and pastoral services also were sometimes extended to recipients.

Limitations of service to persons of particular religious conviction varied with the type of organization. Nearly 30 per cent of them made a practice of restricting their services on religious grounds, although only about two-thirds of them did so because of stated requirements. The organizations that most typically limited their services along religious lines were child placement agencies (67 per cent) and homes for the aged (57 per cent). Least restrictive were neighborhood houses and settlements (6 per cent), and hospitals.

There were several other indices of religious affiliation. Seventy-eight per cent of the welfare organizations in the study had originated under religious auspices. One in five had been established in the nineteenth century, another 40 per cent in the first three decades of this century. Those that did not originate under religious auspices presumably affiliated with religious bodies some time after their origin, which suggests an extension of Protestantism into established welfare organizations, on a small scale.

A full half of the organizations reported that they used buildings owned by religious organizations, most of these being provided rent-free. Homes and residences for various age groups were most frequently owned by religious bodies. Nearly two-thirds of all the church-related agencies and hospitals reported that they received non-monetary assistance from religious sources: gifts in kind, such as food and clothing; promotional and fund-raising assistance; ministerial or pastoral services; consultation services; and recruitment, training, or referral or volunteers.

The executives of a number of church-related agencies and hospitals reported that they had difficulty in obtaining funds from outside sources *because* they were church-related. This was the case particularly with the larger church-related agencies. By contrast, many small church-related agencies received *all* their income from the churches. Although less than 6 per cent of *total* financial support for church-related organizations came from churches, 22 per cent of all such organizations reported that they received their total incomes from their respective churches, and another 24 per cent received over half.

There were some data indicating that the more tenuous an organization's ties with the churches the more likely it was to receive funds from community chests. Those that received chest funds had less religious control, required fewer religiously affiliated or chosen board members, and offered fewer "distinctly religious services." This was particularly true of the larger church-related agencies; this may have reflected a gradual drift from Protestantism among them, or it may be that from their origins they have had only tenuous ties with Protestantism.

There is one final set of data from the NCCC study bearing on the relations between church-related welfare organizations and professional social work. As stated above, the thousand reporting organizations employed 1,641 social workers, some forty per cent of whom had degrees accredited by the Council on Social Work Education. The stronger an agency's religious affiliation, however, the less likely it was to employ social workers with accredited degrees. In the employing agencies with the least religious control, over 60 per cent of the social workers had accredited degrees; only about 20 per cent employed by the agencies with the highest level of religious control were accredited.[14]

The New York Federation of Protestant Welfare Agencies, 1959

IN THE Greater New York area, as well as in some other regions, Protestant-related welfare agencies have established their own welfare federations. The New York Federation of Protestant Welfare Agencies, which dates from about 1920, had 221 member agencies in 1959. These agencies provided welfare services in sixty-three day care centers for children; fifty-four homes for the aged and blind; eighteen Golden Age clubs; twenty hospitals, maternity shelters, and nursing homes; fifty-two neighborhood centers and youth programs; forty-four foster care services for children; and fifty-one camps. All told, more than 525,000 persons were given assistance.

The Federation itself had a budget of $1 million, some of which financed its staff services for member agencies, some of which ($152,000) was distributed to the agencies for special projects. These projects included work with narcotics addicts, diagnosis of deviant behavior of individuals at a community center, employment of a group worker at a settlement house to help pre-delinquent teen-age girls, and employment of a Spanish-speaking person to counsel newly arrived residents. In 1960 the Federation established a new homemaker service agency, "to care for children in their own homes in emergency situations which formerly would have necessitated their being placed in children's shelters." The Federation also has been interested in placing children in foster homes. Between 1950 and 1959 it placed 2,000 children, and was especially concerned with Negro children, "since seven out of eight youngsters awaiting placement in foster homes were Negro children." [15]

Non-Denominational Protestant Activities

AT THE LOCAL, State, and national levels there are Protestant welfare activities that cut across denominational lines. In addition to the church-related welfare organizations discussed in the preceding sections, three non-denominational Protestant-related welfare bodies have units in communities throughout the United States: the YMCA, YWCA, and the Salvation Army. There are nearly one thousand State and local inter-

---

[14] The data in this section are from Cayton and Nishi, *op. cit.*, pp. 128–31, 143–49, and from Chakernian and Villaume, *op. cit.*
[15] "Protestant Aid Given to 525,000." *New York Times*, February 15, 1960.

denominational church councils, which at least in theory concern themselves with Protestant welfare. There are also about 2,000 State and local councils of church women, whose three-quarters of a million members may perform volunteer social services or participate in social action and education programs. Finally, the National Council of the Churches of Christ in the U.S.A. (NCCC), formed in 1950, has three departments concerned with social services.

THE YMCA, YWCA, AND THE SALVATION ARMY: In 1960 there were about 1,850 local YMCA's in the United States, representing two and a half million members. Their major interests were maintaining residences, camps, group work and education programs, employment services, social and citizenship education programs, and counseling services. In 1954, 166,000 different persons served on the committees, boards, and councils of these Y's, and another 118,000 served as volunteer leaders of Y activities. Ordinarily, local Y's are affiliated with the local inter-denominational council of churches, and the National Council of the Young Men's Christian Association of the United States of America is a related agency of the NCCC. This is almost the entire extent of the YMCA's affiliation with Protestantism. About two-thirds of its membership has been Protestant, and about 30 per cent Roman Catholic. The total annual income of YMCA's has been approaching $150 million and has been derived largely from community chests and membership and service fees.

The YWCA is comparable to the YMCA in structure but emphasizes somewhat different programs. In 1959 it had 721 local associations working in some 1,800 communities as well as 500 college and university associations. There were more than three million members in community YWCA's. Three thousand professional employees, supplemented by 100,000 volunteer leaders, provided group work with young adults and teen-agers, educational programs, residences, camps, health education, and recreation in other forms. The YWCA's national organization is a related agency of the NCCC, but local Y's have received practically no financial support from organized Protestantism. Of the $33 million spent by YWCA's in 1954, 68 per cent was raised by the local units themselves, from fees as well as contributions, and the remainder was received from community chests and united funds.

The Salvation Army is a religious and social welfare organization operating throughout the world, devoted to providing both informal and professional social services to anyone in need. In the mid-1950's it maintained 1,900 centers of operation in the United States. Staffed by nearly a quarter million volunteers, in addition to paid staff, the Army provided direct relief, medical care, child care, shelters, camps, recreation, and employment. In 1954 the Army's three hospitals, two clinics, and thirty-four maternity homes in the United States cared for nearly 30,000 patients. Seven children's homes and foster care services helped 200,000 children; another 150,000 children were served in settlements and nurseries. Homes, shelters, and social service centers gave nearly three million nights' lodgings, and nearly five and a half million meals, largely to transients. Forty-five thousand jobs were obtained through the Army's employment services. Those reached through the Army's other services, including summer camps, community centers, prison work, disaster assistance, and others numbered in the hundreds of thousands. Support for the Salvation Army has to a great extent come from federated campaigns. The San Francisco units of the Army, for example, received about two-thirds of their funds from the Community Chest in 1955. The Army also receives a number of individual contributions of funds, as well as of goods and services.[16]

STATE AND LOCAL CHURCH COUNCILS: Church councils, representing the Protestant denominations of a community or State, concern themselves with social welfare, social education, and social action. In the mid-1950's there were over 900 such councils; there was a local church council in almost every community in the United States with more than 25,000 inhabitants, and there were State-wide councils in forty States. Of these councils, 212 had paid staff members and/or directors; more than 700 were directed and staffed entirely by volunteers. Seventy-five councils employed individuals with social work degrees.

The social service interests of councils may take a number of forms. They may supervise direct council social service activities, coordinate denominational social service activities, provide professional social work assistance to denominations and Protestant-related welfare agencies, and help liaison between Protestant churches and governmental and nongovernmental welfare organizations. The following data on the social service activities of 107 church councils, all with paid staffs, was obtained in a study covering a two-year period in the mid-1950's:

> Thirty-six councils gave direct aid such as food, clothing, and money to persons or groups as an emergency service.
> Eighty-three provided ministerial or chaplaincy services in institutions, particularly in hospitals, homes, and prisons.
> Forty-six gave organized assistance to community fund-raising drives, notably to federated campaigns.

[16] Cayton and Nishi, *op. cit.*, pp. 131–33; Russell Kurtz, ed., *Social Work Yearbook 1960*, New York: National Association of Social Workers, 1960, pp. 616, 729; Vaughn Davis Bornet, *California Social Welfare*, Englewood Cliffs, N.J.: Prentice-Hall, 1956, p. 247.

Forty-four sponsored visiting and entertaining by laymen in institutions.

Thirty-eight recruited, trained, or referred volunteers for health and welfare agencies.

Thirty-seven counseled local church groups on health and welfare matters.

Fifty-two organized discussion and cooperative planning of church and social welfare interests.

Seventy-five represented church social welfare interests on community planning and financing boards.

In addition, fifty councils reported that they used a total of 10,000 volunteers in providing their regular, organized direct social services.[17]

LOCAL COUNCILS OF CHURCH WOMEN: Local councils of church women have much the same interests as the local and State church councils: social service, social education, and social action. There are about 2,000 such councils, whose over-all coordination is provided by the NCCC General Department of United Church Women. On the basis of a sample study the average council represents about 400 women; about half the councils engage directly in social services.

The councils that participate in social service undertake a variety of activities. Most frequently, they have provided people in need with direct aid in the form of food, clothing, home furnishings, facilities, and money. They have been a source of organized assistance to community fund-raising campaigns as well, and have provided visiting services in hospitals and other institutions. In 1954, 132 councils engaged in social service activities reported on their volunteer strength. An average of 130 women of each council had done volunteer work, a total of nearly 11,000 volunteers.

Distinct differences have been noted between the services of women's church councils in large urban areas and their services in smaller cities. In the largest cities their most important service has been organized assistance to fund drives, a formalized and indirect contribution to welfare. In somewhat smaller cities some of their reported activities have been Golden Age clubs, gifts of supplies to welfare organizations and to migrants, special schools and clinics, and a Negro child-care center. Generally, the smaller the community the more often do women's church councils provide direct services to needy persons.[18]

WELFARE PROGRAMS OF THE NATIONAL COUNCIL OF THE CHURCHES OF CHRIST: The NCCC has a number of departments concerned with

[17] Cayton and Nishi, op. cit., p. 108; The Social Welfare Department in a Local Council of Churches, New York: Intercouncil Field Department, 1950, p. 2 (pamphlet).
[18] Cayton and Nishi, op. cit., pp. 108–10.

social welfare. Among them is the Department of Social Welfare, which fulfills a primarily advisory function for the Protestant churches, comparable to the National Social Welfare Assembly but on a smaller scale. The Department is concerned with establishing cooperation in welfare matters among the Protestant denominations, developing standards, and serving as a liaison agent between Protestant and secular welfare organizations.

The Division of Home Missions and its various committees have a number of operating welfare programs, notably for migrants and American Indians. These programs are "closely interwoven within the churches' spiritual ministry and generally fall outside the usual concern of the professional social work structure."

The Division has various programs for migrant farm workers, of whom there are perhaps two million in the United States. The Division's Migrant Committee conducts a field service, in conjunction with local church groups. A field report for a region including ten central States suggests the extent of one year's work:

> Work was carried on in 52 different communities each having its own local committee with a combined membership of 689 people. Eight of these projects were new. Helping them and the staff were 1,116 volunteers who gave time and energy to direct work with the migrants. The combined expenses of the work in these local communities was $41,000. Added to this were duplicated expenditures by the Division of Home Missions of nearly $39,000, making a total of $80,000 expended. There are nine active state committees with a membership of 80 people. Used in this region were five Harvesters, one staff car, and twenty-nine additional temporary Harvesters owned and operated by local projects.[19]

The Division has noted that even with a tenfold expansion of its activities and volunteers it could reach no more than a small proportion of all migrants. Thus its policy was described as "encouragement by example." Its workers have established child-care centers, schools, and housing improvement programs as pilot projects, many of which have subsequently been turned over to employers, local non-governmental groups, and State and local government authorities.

The Division has devoted considerable effort to instigating government activity on behalf of migrants. Among its results it claims the extension of social security benefits to migrants, a special Farm Placement Service program, stronger child labor laws in some States, and State inspection of migrant camps.

[19] *Ibid.*, p. 83. A Harvester is a station wagon containing equipment for religious services, craft materials, books, first-aid supplies, sports equipment, motion-picture projector and movies, and record player, used for visiting and helping migrant families and camps. In 1955 the Division operated twenty-two regular Harvesters.

The Division of Home Missions also works with the 350,000 Indians in the United States. Because the Indians are a smaller group and because there are extensive government programs for them, the Protestant churches have been mainly interested in providing supplementary services to as many Indians as possible, rather than in stimulating further outside services. In 1950 there were some three hundred church "projects" under the auspices or guidance of the Division, including parish halls, Sunday schools, and sanctuaries. There were also hospitals, clinics, schools and educational programs, and homes for Indians. It was estimated that through these various services the Protestant churches were in contact with more than half the American Indian population.

The largest-scale welfare activities of the NCCC have been carried out through the Church World Service (CWS), which extends material relief and technical assistance throughout much of the world. In 1954 nearly $2 million in relief and reconstruction funds were channeled through the CWS, and between 1954 and 1957 the CWS and several other relief organizations together shipped $150 million worth of government surplus commodities overseas. In 1954 the CWS shipments of relief materials obtained from its own sources included 15,324 tons of clothing, bedding, medicines, vitamins, and other goods. In 1958, the CWS spent $510,000 for technical assistance, for example, to establish self-help industries and to introduce new farming methods in Asia and Africa.

The CWS conducts an extensive immigration service, providing medical, rehabilitation, or other assistance to persons already resettled in this country, resettlement of persons eligible to come to the United States, services to orphans immigrating under CWS sponsorship, and other types of assistance. It also cooperates with other non-governmental agencies that are concerned with migration and refugees, and participates in their programs. In 1954, the CWS assisted some 20,000 immigrants and refugees, by initiating applications for their coming to the United States or by providing them with transportation and other assistance on their arrival. The CWS has also maintained some overseas projects in medical care and provides scholarships and expenses for theological students from all parts of the world.

The NCCC Department of Pastoral Services fulfills an advisory and educative function to assist ministers professionally. It circulates information on pastoral counseling, specific social problems, and available social welfare services. The Department includes the Commission on Religion and Health and the Commission on Ministry and Institutions, the latter promoting chaplaincy services in hospitals, homes for children and the aged, prisons, and reform schools.[20]

[20] Ibid., pp. 76–90.

Protestant Schools

SOME PROTESTANT DENOMINATIONS, for example the Protestant Episcopal Church, the Lutheran Churches, and a number of others, sponsor and in part finance a few elementary and secondary schools, predominantly the latter. The number of students attending such schools is quite small compared to those attending Roman Catholic and Jewish schools. (Cf. the section on "Private Elementary and Secondary Schools" in Chapter 8.)

There are a number of Protestant seminaries and similar institutions providing college-level training for Protestant ministers, missionaries, and other church personnel. Most of these institutions are sponsored by a specific denomination and may receive a significant part of their income from it. However, the most important connection between Protestantism and higher education is largely an indirect one. A large number of the private colleges and universities in the United States were founded by Protestant churches and were operated under their auspices. The majority of such institutions now have only tenuous connections with Protestantism, *e.g.*, there may be religious requirements of some members of the board of trustees, attendance at religious services may be required of students, there may be scholarship and perhaps other funds from religious sources, and there may be Protestant theologians and ministers of a particular denomination on the staff. There are also, however, some Protestant-founded colleges and universities (other than seminaries) that are operated directly by certain denominations, and now and then new institutions of this type are founded.

CATHOLIC WELFARE [21]

THE WELFARE CONCERN of the Roman Catholic Church is probably as intense as that of any other organized religious body in the United States, with the possible exception of Judaism. It is difficult to portray Catholic welfare accurately, for Catholic organizations seldom prepare or publicize comprehensive descriptions of their activities comparable to those on Protestant and Jewish welfare services. The following sections demonstrate, however, that Christian charity is given extensive expression in Catholic parish activities, diocesan agencies, service programs, volunteer organizations, and religious orders.

[21] The terms "Catholic" and "Catholicism" in this section refer to the Roman Catholic Church.

The Parish

THE CATHOLIC PARISH undertakes primary responsibility for the spiritual and physical needs of its own people. In 1959, there were 16,753 Catholic parishes in the fifty States and 4,867 home missions, served by some 50,000 priests. Within these parishes and missions were 39,505,000 Catholics, an average of about 750 parishioners per priest.[22] There also were 10,000 brothers and 165,000 sisters enrolled in Catholic orders, many of whom served in parochial schools, diocesan hospitals, and welfare agencies.

Most ecclesiastical functions of the Catholic Church are carried out in the parish. Six of the seven sacraments are performed by the parish priest: baptism, confirmation, holy communion, matrimony, confession, and extreme unction. In addition to ecclesiastical functions the priest may visit the sick, counsel those with problems, and instruct those who are about to be confirmed or married. He may initiate children's recreation programs; organize social action, educational, or charitable groups among his parishioners; send goods and money to the needy of the parish; and solicit funds for many purposes, from building new parish facilities to supporting overseas missions. In effect the parish priest is a full-time, all-purpose social worker: he counsels, consoles, and assists to the best of his abilities, and organizes and directs welfare work within the parish.

In Spotswood, New Jersey, a parish priest conducted a campaign for new parish facilities. In early 1958 the parish made plans to raise part of the costs of a new school, church, and auditorium on a fourteen-acre tract. Father Charles Poltorak and local parishioners led a seven-week campaign during which volunteers solicited $250,000 in subscriptions from other parishioners. In summing up the campaign for parish leaders, Fr. Poltorak commented, "If I ever needed proof of the Catholic spirit of my parishioners it has now been given me in abundance. You have clearly demonstrated that when you are presented with a problem and a need you accept the challenge and provide the solution." [23] This campaign was not exceptional; in hundreds of Catholic parishes across the United States similar campaigns take place each year.

---

[22] Rev. F. A. Foy, O.F.M., ed. *The 1960 National Catholic Almanac*, Paterson, N.J.: St. Anthony's Guild, p. 435. According to another Catholic source, *The National Council of Catholic Men* (Federation of Catholic Action, n.d.), p. 1, there are over 1,200 American Catholics for each parish priest.
[23] *The Trenton Monitor*, June 20, 1958.

The Diocese and the Archdiocese

THE DIOCESE AND THE ARCHDIOCESE, the second level in the Roman Catholic hierarchy, supplement parish concern with Catholic welfare and Catholic charity. In 1960 there were about 140 dioceses and archdioceses in the United States, each presided over by a bishop or archbishop. They ranged in size from the Juneau, Alaska, diocese, with 14,000 Catholics, to the Chicago archdiocese, with 2,027,000 Catholics.[24]

In the diocese, Catholic social service is centered in Catholic Charities, one of the agencies of the bishop. The functions of diocesan Catholic Charities, sponsored by the National Conference of Catholic Charities (CC), include the planning, coordination, supervision, and financing of social work under Catholic auspices. The diocesan CC agency also "exercises leadership within the community, surveys needs, measures resources, and establishes services. It coordinates the social work activities of its affiliated agencies with one another and with related services in the general community. . . . A continuing program of public relations is carried on by the central agency."[25]

In 1959, there were 340 diocesan and branch agencies of Catholic Charities in the United States, located in 115 dioceses. The diocesan CC agency is ordinarily administered by a specially trained priest, and in the larger dioceses he is assisted by a professional staff. The relation between the diocesan agency and the actual operating programs may take several forms. In many dioceses the CC agency has direct jurisdiction over service and assistance programs. In others it is limited to planning and coordination. In a number of dioceses, among them some of the largest, the CC agency undertakes fund-raising campaigns that solicit primarily from the Catholic community.

The Catholic diocesan welfare programs provide the same types of services that the church-related welfare organizations of Protestantism and Judaism provide. The primary diocesan concerns are children's and young people's welfare, family services, care for the aged, and health and hospital care.

CHILDREN'S AND YOUNG PEOPLE'S WELFARE: The Catholic emphasis at present is on foster care of needy children rather than institutional care. Whenever possible the child is maintained in his own family

---

[24] One of the dioceses and archdioceses is an *abbacy nullius*, Belmont Abbey in North Carolina, which has jurisdiction over only 1,000 priests, monks, and people of local churches, and is subject directly to the Holy See. The archdiocese is so similar to the diocese in its charitable work that for convenience in this discussion the term "diocese" has been used to denote archdioceses as well.

[25] John Lennon, "Catholic Social Service," in Russell H. Kurtz, ed., *Social Work Year Book 1957*, New York: National Association of Social Workers, 1957, p. 140.

or that of a relative; when it is necessary to resort to other institutions, Catholic leaders prefer that these institutions be of the child's own religious background. In the 1950's there were about 650 Catholic child-care institutions in the United States. They included 153 settlement and day-care centers, 35 (1959) institutions for physically handicapped children, 93 (1959) residential schools for socially maladjusted boys and girls, 61 maternity hospitals and infant homes, 24 (1959) institutions for mentally handicapped children, and 288 institutions for the care of other dependent children.[26] Under the category of "Orphanages and Infant Asylums," the 1960 *National Catholic Almanac* listed 286 institutions (these are among the 650 institutions listed above), which in 1958 cared for 26,766 children. In comparison, 21,855 children were being maintained in foster homes.

Programs and institutions for teen-agers also are part of diocesan welfare concern. The St. Euphrasia School in Columbus, Ohio, is representative of one type of Catholic institution for young people. Since 1945 the School has conducted a program for teen-age delinquent girls that has been praised by welfare workers as a model in its field. The home has ordinarily housed about seventy girls, referred to it by juvenile courts in central Ohio, for whom it provides a vocational curriculum emphasizing courses in elementary nursing, home economics, typewriting, and budgeting. The institution is highly regarded because of the warmth and kindness with which the girls are treated, qualities often lacking in institutional correctional work. The School is staffed by eighteen sisters of the order of Sisters of the Good Shepherd and two lay workers.[27]

Most dioceses have youth directors, who coordinate parish and diocesan chapters of national Catholic youth organizations such as the National Catholic Camping Association. Programs are devoted to spiritual, cultural, social, and athletic activities, for the benefit of all Catholic youths who wish to participate. Summer camps, hobby and craft groups, study programs, and occupational training may all be provided for them.

There are few available data on the financing of Catholic child-care and youth programs. Funds are believed to be derived from individual contributions, community chests, and government sources. In one recent year the Catholic Social Services of the archdiocese of San Francisco received nearly half its operating funds from local, State, and federal government sources, as well as $400,000 from federated community campaigns. Concerning the acceptance of government funds by Cath-

[26] Lennon, *op. cit.*, p. 141; R. J. Gallagher, "Catholic Social Services," in *Social Work Year Book 1960*, p. 137.
[27] "Ohio Charity Aids Delinquent Girls," *New York Times*, Sept. 23, 1958.

olic welfare organizations, one authority on Catholic social welfare has written: "Catholic leaders have taken the position that, in line with American tradition, government should encourage and facilitate the work of the voluntary and religious associations and agencies before acting directly to bring public aid." [28]

FAMILY SERVICES: The family casework agency is an essential part of Catholic family services. In addition to such agencies most dioceses also have representatives of other Catholic agencies that deal with the family, the most important among them being the Family Life Bureau, a member of the National Catholic Welfare Conference. The Bureau was organized to develop and coordinate family life programs, such as the Family Retreat Movement, Pre-Cana and Cana Conferences, and the Holy Family Guilds. Bishops have appointed priests as family life directors in almost all dioceses in the United States. The Christian Family Movement, devoted to the creation of communities conducive to Christian living, also is active in a number of parishes and dioceses.

CARE FOR THE AGING: Catholic institutional facilities and service programs for the aging have been expanding. In 1959 there were 332 Catholic homes for the aged in the United States, with some 29,000 people in residence. Diocesan programs for Catholic aged, primarily for those who are not institutionalized, provide social casework, group work, counseling, homemaker service, residence clubs, apartment projects, day activity centers, retreats, employment counseling, and facilities for the care and treatment of chronic illness. Extensive programs for these purposes have been established in a few dioceses; they are beyond the financial means of many other dioceses.

In Catholic opinion, however, institutional care and non-institutional programs for the aged are not necessarily desirable. Wherever possible the Catholic Church encourages families to care for their older members within the family group, on the theory that no organization, however complex, can compete with the family in providing for the psychological welfare of the older person. The National Conference of Catholic Charities has sponsored four studies of the aging in four urban parishes, in Cleveland, St. Louis, Milwaukee, and Buffalo. The findings contradicted many widespread beliefs about the status of older people. These are some of the conclusions of the study of the aging in St. Louis' St. Philip Neri parish, which is located in a low-income area: families were large and self-contained; the aged did a great deal to provide for their own security; they expressed intense desires to continue useful employment; 74 per cent of the aging owned their own homes

[28] Lennon, *op. cit.*, p. 141.

and an additional 13 per cent lived in homes owned by their relatives or friends; many chronically ill aged were taken care of in their own homes by their relatives; the Catholic Church occupied a prominent place in their lives, expressed by their feeling that they belonged to a "truly vital institution that meant a great deal in their lives."

> The aging in St. Philip Neri parish do not present many problems that they themselves and their families cannot solve through their own efforts, or with the ordinary aids that are at their disposal through the growing Social Security program, through private pensions . . . , and through the various health and hospital benefits that are available in the community.[29]

A similar picture was presented by the other studies, suggesting that Catholic aged, at least, are well-equipped both physically and spiritually to pass their later life in a satisfying manner.

HEALTH AND MEDICAL CARE: The most extensive diocesan welfare programs are carried out by about 1,150 Catholic medical care institutions in the United States. In 1958 there were 895 general hospitals and 252 related agencies under Catholic auspices in the United States; the hospitals alone treated over eleven million patients. There were also 346 Catholic nursing schools, in which 35,000 students were enrolled. The most exceptional feature of Catholic hospitals is the method by which most of them are staffed on the non-professional and semi-professional levels. To a large extent they draw their staffs from 25,000 members of more than 250 religious orders, some dating back as far as the fifth century A.D. Most hospitals are served by orders of sisters, notably the various orders of the Franciscan Sisters, the Benedictine Sisters, the Sisters of St. Joseph, and the Sisters of Mercy. The Alexian Brothers, an order of male nurses, do smiliar work.

OTHER DIOCESAN WELFARE-RELATED ACTIVITIES: In addition to Catholic Charities activities on the diocesan level there are diocesan recreational programs, Catholic men's and women's organizations, rural life programs, and home missions. The National Council of Catholic Men has nearly 10,000 affiliated parish and diocesan men's groups, with a total membership of about nine million. The National Council of Catholic Women is a similar body, with about nine million members. Local Catholic men's and women's clubs stimulate the study of Chris-

[29] Older People in the Family, the Parish, and the Neighborhood, A Study of St. Philip Neri Parish, St. Louis, Missouri, St. Louis: Catholic Charities of St. Louis, 1955, p. 11; also Sister Mary Therese, A Study of the Aging in a Cleveland Parish, Washington, D.C.: National Conference of Catholic Charities, 1954; and Janet Bower, Older People of St. Boniface Parish, "The Fruit Belt," Buffalo, N.Y., Buffalo: Catholic Charites of Buffalo, N.Y., 1957.

tian principles and put them into practice in their charitable and mission activity, fund-raising projects, and volunteer services.

Rural life directors in 117 parishes are particularly concerned with the welfare of the rural population, non-Catholics as well as Catholics. There are hundreds of counties and thousands of towns in the United States with no Catholic church or priest. To serve Catholics in these areas about fifty dioceses carry out home mission work. More than a thousand priests, nearly half of them members of special religious orders, carry out full- and part-time missionary work, primarily in rural areas.

There are also special missions to Negroes and American Indians. There are about 500 predominantly Negro Catholic churches, containing over half a million American Negroes. These churches are served by 720 priests, and some 91,000 Negro children attend 340 Negro Catholic schools. These arrangements have been necessary in the southern States in particular, where many Catholic parishes have been unwilling to integrate Negro and white parishioners, sometimes in the face of diocesan pressures to the contrary. In some southern dioceses, though, the Catholic Church has taken the lead in integration, notably in schools. In 1959 there were 120,000 Catholic Indians in the United States, served by 230 priests. Catholic missions to Indians include 415 missionary churches, two hospitals, and twelve clinics. In fifty-seven day schools and boarding schools there were 8,000 Indian pupils.

Catholic Education

THE CATHOLIC EDUCATIONAL SYSTEM extends from primary school through the highest level of university training. The Code of Canon Law of the Catholic Church states:

> From childhood all the faithful must be so educated that not only are they taught nothing contrary to faith and morals, but that religious and moral training takes the chief place.
> In every elementary school religious instruction adapted to the age of the children must be given. . . .
> Catholic children must not attend non-Catholic, neutral or mixed schools. . . . The Church has the right to establish schools of every grade, not only elementary schools, but also high schools and colleges.[30]

Statistics on Roman Catholic schools and their students are given in Table 9. If the Catholic population in the United States has approximately the same age distribution as the total population, there were about 7.9 million Catholic children of elementary and high school

---

[30] *Canons*, 1372–75.

age (five to seventeen) in 1957. About fifty-five per cent were enrolled in Catholic elementary and high schools (cf. Table 9). As many as 25 per cent of the others were given released time from public schools to attend religious instruction classes at their churches. There are also probably a number of Catholic children who live beyond the geographic reach of the Catholic school system.

TABLE 9

CATHOLIC SCHOOLS AND STUDENTS IN THE UNITED STATES, 1957

Type of School	Number	Students
Elementary Schools	10,287	4,083,860
High Schools	2,428	810,768
Colleges and Universities	258	290,867
Seminaries and Scholasticates [1]	518	38,105
Totals	13,485	5,223,600

Source: *The Official Catholic Directory* 1959. New York: P. J. Kennedy and Sons, 1959, Statistical Insert.

[1] Includes data on students for the priesthood in diocesan seminaries and in schools of various orders.

There are special Catholic educational programs for blind, deaf, and retarded children. There are a handful of residential and day schools for blind children, as well as fourteen Catholic guilds and five homes for the blind. In a few cities there are special classes in parochial schools for blind children, and some are integrated in regular classes. For deaf children, Catholics maintain six resident and seven day schools. There were seventy-eight day and resident schools for mentally retarded children in 1959, having about 4,500 students. There were also nineteen cerebral palsy clinics and schools under Catholic auspices, about half of them connected with Catholic hospitals.

National and International Catholic Welfare

NATIONAL ORGANIZATIONS: There are several Catholic national organizations that do most of their work outside the parishes and dioceses. One is the National Catholic Community Service (NCCS), a member agency of the United Service Organizations (USO). NCCS devotes itself to the religious and physical welfare of military personnel and veterans. It has programs in the Veterans Administration hospitals, and in 1956 provided staffing and 9,000 volunteers for USO clubs.

The National Catholic Apostleship of the Sea Conference in 1959 maintained maritime clubs in seven major American ports and in some sixty overseas cities. These clubs provided a social program, rest facilities, and religious services for seamen.

There are fourteen Catholic guilds for the assistance of the blind of all ages, united in the American Federation of Catholic Workers for the Blind. The Xavier Society for the Blind is a publication center and library for the blind, located in New York City. There is also an International Catholic Deaf Association, active in the United States.

The National Catholic Welfare Conference (NCWC) is the national clearinghouse and service center for Catholic works and programs in social welfare and related fields. It has eight regularly constituted departments: the Executive Department; the Department of Education; Press, Immigration, Social Action, Legal, and Youth Departments; and the Department of Lay Organizations. These departments, in conjunction with fourteen bishops' special committees, supervise in varying degrees the various national Catholic organizations, including those cited above. For example, among the constituent bodies of the Department of Lay Organizations are the National Councils for Catholic Men and Catholic Women, and the National Council of Catholic Nurses. Among the bishops' committees are the American Board of Catholic Missions, the Committee on Motion Pictures (which directs the National Legion of Decency), and the Committee on the Propagation of the Faith.

VOLUNTEER ORGANIZATIONS: There are innumerable Catholic volunteer organizations. The largest of these in the United States is the Society of St. Vincent de Paul, whose 35,000 lay members practice "spiritual and corporal works of mercy." These take the form of spiritual counseling, promotion of religious education, visiting the sick and the imprisoned, helping handicapped and foster children, working in boys' clubs and summer camps, and supplying financial assistance and goods in emergencies. The Superior Council of the Vincentians in the United States oversees the work of the 4,000 parish conferences in which Vincentians are organized. Among other Catholic volunteer groups are the Knights of Columbus (a fraternal organization, discussed in Chapter 7), Catholic Daughters of America, and Catholic Big Brothers. Some but not all of these volunteer groups are organized along parish lines, as are the Vincentians, and most of their actual projects may thus be considered parish activities, though following forms prescribed by their national organizations.

INTERNATIONAL CATHOLIC WELFARE: Most of the extensive international welfare activity of American Catholicism has been directed by Catholic Relief Services, which is associated with the NCWC. Created in 1943, Catholic Relief Services shipped overseas 2.1 million

tons of food, clothing, medicines, and other relief supplies, valued at
$723 million, in its first fifteen years. Many of these goods were govern-
ment surplus; some were donated by Catholic parishes throughout the
country. Catholic Relief Services gives help to refugees from the Communist countries; it assisted in the resettlement of 10,000 European
refugees in 1956, and in the resettlement of 850,000 Vietnamese, most
of them Catholic, who fled North Vietnamese communism.

Another international welfare program is the maintenance of foreign
missionaries. In the late 1950's there were about 3,500 American Catholic priests and brothers and about 2,500 Catholic sisters in active
service outside the United States, providing educational, medical, and
material as well as spiritual assistance. Some 2,100 of them served in
Central and South America, another 1,900 in Asia, and the others
throughout the rest of the world, from Ghana to New Zealand.

JEWISH COMMUNAL AND SOCIAL SERVICES

THE 5,367,000 JEWS in the United States [31] have a highly organized,
integrated, well-supported system providing for spiritual and physical
welfare. It is based on religious injunction and religious law, and rooted
in long practice.

In the ghettos of Eastern Europe, charity, organized around
the synagogue, included programs to feed and clothe the poor,
visit the sick, assist in burial of the dead, provide dowries for poor
maidens, grant interest-free loans, shelter the homeless, and educate the parentless child. "Tzdoka," the giving of charity, was second in prestige only to education, and there were many occasions
for making contributions. The birth of a child called for a gift
to the poor, as did a death in the family, recovery from illness, and
celebration of a birthday or anniversary. The Jews who came to
the United States brought these traditional practices with them.[32]

Because of the geographic distribution of the Jewish population in
the United States, these traditions have readily been put into practice.
Over three million Jews live in the four largest urban areas: 2,018,000
in New York City, 390,000 in Los Angeles, 282,000 in Chicago, and
331,000 in Philadelphia. There are ninety-four urban areas in the United

[31] Estimates of the Jewish population in the United States vary. This figure, for
1959, is taken from the American Jewish Year Book 1960, p. 3. If this figure is
accurate, 3.1 per cent of the United States population is Jewish. An independent
study mentioned in the World Almanac 1958 (New York: World-Telegram Corp.,
1958), p. 270, places the percentage at 3.69, or 6,290,000 (in 1958). A third
estimate of 5,030,000 (in March, 1957) has been obtained on the basis of a U.S.
Bureau of the Census sample survey. These differences may be ascribed partly to
statistical inaccuracies, partly to different definitions of what constitutes Jewishness.
[32] William Avrunin, "Jewish Social Services," in Kurtz, op. cit., p. 324.

States having 5,000 or more Jewish inhabitants, and in these areas live about 90 per cent of American Jews. Concentrated in urban areas, they can be readily reached by Jewish social and communal services. With few exceptions each of these urban areas has at least one, and usually several, Jewish social service organizations.

The religious welfare functions of Judaism in the United States are carried out through the local congregation and the local synagogue. The three major denominations—Orthodox, Conservative, and Reform—each claim a membership of about one million individuals. In smaller communities, some of these individuals attend "independent" synagogues (judging from usage in the *American Jewish Year Book*, the phrase "independent synagogue" is a category that includes a variety of congregational and denominational forms). In addition to the three million Jews who are formally affiliated with synagogues, the synagogue is a matter of some concern to most other Jews. It is highly exceptional for those who consider themselves Jewish in terms of family and cultural background not to turn to the service of the Judaic religion for the "sacramental events in life," especially marriage and death.

The Orthodox body claimed 1,500 congregations in 1959; the Reform body claimed 575 congregations; the Conservative body claimed 660. All denominations are represented on the Synagogue Council of America. There were some 5,000 ordained rabbis in 1957, about half of them having congregations. The others were in seminaries or otherwise connected with Jewish education, or retired.[33]

In addition to the welfare activities directly associated with the synagogues and temples, a Jewish community may have educational and recreational programs, refugee programs, hospitals, family and child-care agencies, homes for the aged, and employment and vocational guidance services. There are a number of national Jewish bodies as well as organizations channeling aid to overseas Jewish communities.

Local Jewish Communal and Social Services

THE FUNDAMENTAL UNITS in American Jewish communal service are the local Jewish federations, welfare funds, and community councils. In 1958 there were about 290 such organizations associated with the Council of Jewish Federations and Welfare Funds. They covered 800 communities, in which lived 95 per cent of the American Jewish community. These organizations are autonomous, and themselves determine the scope of activity and the organizations for which they request financial support. In 1958, these funds raised an estimated $123.3 mil-

[33] Arthur Hertzberg, "Religion," in *American Jewish Year Book 1958, op. cit.*, pp. 113–15; Jacob Neusner, "Religion," in *American Jewish Year Book 1960*, p. 52.

lion, of which about $33 million was for local services. (Nearly two-thirds of the total was given to the United Jewish Appeal for overseas use and the remainder went to a number of national service, health, welfare, and cultural agencies. These are discussed below.) [34]

TABLE 10

LOCAL JEWISH HEALTH AND WELFARE SERVICES, 1956

Type of Service	Number of Organizations Known [1]	Estimated Number of Recipients	Estimated Total Expenditures [2]
Family Service	106 [3]	64,000	$ 12,000,000
Child Care	25	7,000	10,000,000
Homes for the Aged	71	13,000	17,000,000
Hospitals [4]	58	500,000	130,000,000 [5]
Clinics	60 [6]	270,000	
Vocational Services	22	170,000 [7]	1,000,000
Totals	285	1,024,000	$170,000,000

Sources: *American Jewish Year Book 1958*, New York and Philadelphia: The American Jewish Committee and the Jewish Publication Society of America, 1958, pp. 140–85; *Yearbook of Jewish Social Services 1956*, New York: Council of Jewish Federations and Welfare Funds, 1956, "Appendix" (no page numbers).

[1] Estimates on the number of organizations vary, some being based on "reporting agencies," others including non-reporting agencies. All estimates given are the highest available, with the exception of homes for the aged. The *Yearbook of Jewish Social Service 1956* asserts that eighty-four such homes existed in 1955.
[2] These are estimates only, based on projections of known data for about two-thirds of the organizations listed.
[3] About fifty of the Family Service agencies also provided child care.
[4] Six nationally supported Jewish hospitals are not included in these statistics.
[5] Based on 1955 data, and includes expenditures of all but three clinics.
[6] Based on 1955 data. All but three clinics were affiliated with hospitals, either as out-patient clinics or as departments. There is probably considerable double counting in the recipient figures for hospitals and clinics.
[7] About 100,000 of these were reached through group guidance programs. The others were new or old job applicants, 15,000 of whom received direct, individual service. Direct placements were made for 16,000 individuals.

HEALTH AND WELFARE SERVICES: Health and welfare services under Jewish auspices are available in almost every community having more than 5,000 Jews. Over one million persons were assisted by about 285 Jewish health and welfare organizations in 1956 (cf. Table 10). The estimated incomes of these organizations, by source, are given in Table 11.

Care given the recipients of Jewish social services varies greatly. The family service agencies serve immigrants, local families, and transients.

[34] *American Jewish Year Book 1960*, pp. 76–79.

Between 20 and 25 per cent of the 1956 expenditures of these agencies were for direct financial assistance for these people, often to supplement public assistance funds. At one time the bulk of direct financial assistance was to immigrants; as the number of Jewish immigrants has declined, the volume and cost of service for them has fallen.

TABLE 11

SOURCES OF OPERATING EXPENDITURES OF JEWISH HEALTH
AND WELFARE ORGANIZATIONS, 1956

SOURCES	ALL ORGANIZATIONS		ALL ORGANIZATIONS EXCLUDING HOSPITALS	
	Amount	Per Cent	Amount	Per Cent
Jewish Philanthropy [1]	$ 31,400,000	18.5%	$15,800,000	39.5%
Other Philanthropy [2]	8,870,000	5.2	5,620,000	14.0
Payments for Service	110,380,000	64.9	12,880,000	32.2
Public Funds	12,770,000	7.5	3,670,000	9.2
Others	6,580,000	3.9	2,030,000	5.1
Totals	$170,000,000	100%	$40,000,000	100%

Source: Derived by applying 1955 percentages (from *Yearbook of Jewish Social Services 1956*) to 1956 estimates given in Table 10.

[1] Funds from Jewish federations and funds, direct contributions, and dues.
[2] Funds donated directly to Jewish welfare and health organizations by non-Jewish community chests, and community chest funds channeled to Jewish social services through Jewish federations.

Children received the largest per capita expenditures among the recipients of Jewish social services in 1956. About one-third of the children served were living in Jewish institutions. Nearly half were living in foster homes, under direct supervision of Jewish child welfare agencies. The others were assisted in the homes of their parents or relatives.

Not all the recipients of Jewish health and welfare services are Jewish. The Jews have traditionally extended assistance to non-Jewish individuals in their midst when these people have been in need. Hospitals are the only institutions for which statistics on the religious affiliations of recipients are available: 47 per cent of the patients admitted to Jewish hospitals in 1956 were Jewish, and 40 per cent of those admitted in 1958 were Jewish. It is likely that recipients of other Jewish welfare services included a much higher proportion of Jews.

RECREATION PROGRAMS: In 1959 there were 337 Jewish community centers and YM and YWHAs, serving more than 200 communities. They included 181 centers and Y's and nearly 100 country camps, as well as branch centers and synagogue centers. Community center programs have two common aims:

> to serve as the common meeting ground for all individuals and groups in the Jewish community . . . and to provide a guided program of services designed to aid Jewish individuals and groups in the constructive use of leisure time, for the purpose of personality growth, enriched Jewish group living, and active participation in the general community.[35]

Over 600,000 persons participated in center activities in 1958. About one-third were children under fourteen; nearly half were adults over twenty-five years of age. Fifteen hundred professional staff workers provided an array of programs from athletics, camping, and dancing to dramatics and special classes.

The estimated aggregate budgets of the 337 community centers in 1959 were $22 million, derived from membership dues, program fees, and allocations from both Jewish and non-Jewish federated campaigns. Federation allocations for "recreation and culture" in eighty-three communities totaled $6.0 million in 1956 and $6.3 million in 1957, more than a fifth of all federation allocations for local Jewish services in each year. About 60 per cent of these allocations from federated campaigns were raised in Jewish campaigns; the remainder was given to Jewish agencies by local community chests and funds.[36]

Jewish Education

IN 1958, 554,000 young people attended Jewish schools, 250,000 of them in one-day-a-week (Sunday) schools, 261,000 in weekday afternoon schools, and 43,000 in all-day schools. Students in all-day Jewish schools are almost exclusively Orthodox. Among Conservative and Reform congregations, the usual practice has been to send the child to a weekday school for two hours each afternoon (following public school), between the ages of ten and thirteen. Enrollment in Jewish schools has been growing rapidly. Between 1951 and 1956 it rose more than 100 per cent in Jewish high schools, and in all Jewish schools, elementary and secondary, it increased 70 per cent.

The fundamental purpose of all Jewish schools is to inculcate in Jewish young people a knowledge and appreciation of Jewish traditions and the Jewish religion. They vary in their approach, however. The

[35] Herbert Millman, "Jewish Community Centers," in *American Jewish Year Book 1958, op. cit.*, pp. 190–91.
[36] Herbert Millman, "Jewish Community Centers," in *American Jewish Year Book 1960*, pp. 92–100.

Sunday schools concern themselves primarily with the history, customs, and ceremony of the Jewish people and the Jewish religion. Day schools, which for the most part are afternoon schools only, emphasize the teaching of Hebrew and of Hebraic writings. Schools also vary in auspices: some are under the direct auspices of one of the three major congregations, Orthodox, Conservative, or Reform; others are non-denominational.

In 1958 the operating costs of Jewish schools in the United States totaled about $60 million. This excludes the budgets of the independent Jewish teachers' seminaries. (In 1956 there were ten Jewish teachers' colleges in the United States, five of them in New York. In recent years they have graduated about one hundred teachers annually.) Most of the costs of Jewish education have been met by student fees.[37]

National and International Jewish Programs

AMERICAN JEWS PROVIDE considerably more financial support for national and international Jewish programs than they do for local services. In 1958 they donated about $33 million for local health and welfare organizations, $35 million for various national programs, and $79 million for overseas programs. The receipts of national and international Jewish organizations from various United States sources for 1956 are given in Table 12.

NATIONAL PROGRAMS: National Jewish programs fall into five categories: community relations agencies, national health and welfare agencies, national service agencies, cultural agencies, and religious agencies.

There are five major national Jewish community relations agencies. The Anti-Defamation League of B'nai B'rith is the most notable; B'nai B'rith "seeks to unite Jews through civic, educational, cultural, philanthropic, and patriotic activities." [38] Others are the Jewish Labor Committee, the Jewish War Veterans of America, the American Jewish Committee, and the American Jewish Congress. The American Jewish Committee and the Anti-Defamation League have national and local programs that operate through the mass media and present specialized programs to various non-Jewish interest groups.

There are six national Jewish hospitals, three of which have been predominantly concerned with tuberculosis victims. The others have also provided care for victims of that disease, and for victims of cancer

[37] Uriah Zevi Engelman, "Jewish Education," in *American Jewish Year Book 1960*, pp. 127–49.
[38] *American Jewish Year Book 1958, op. cit.*, p. 434. Also see Chapter 7.

131

and heart diseases as well. The 1958 income of these hospitals was $9.8 million, most of which was raised in their own fund drives. Four-fifths of the patients at the three tuberculosis hospitals were non-Jewish.

TABLE 12

RECEIPTS OF NATIONAL AND INTERNATIONAL JEWISH ORGANIZATIONS FROM UNITED STATES SOURCES, 1956

	Jewish Federation & Funds	Other Contri- butions	Other Income	Total
DOMESTIC PROGRAMS				
Community Relations Agencies (5)	$ 2,928,000	$ 2,663,000	$ 672,000	$ 6,263,000
National Health Agencies (6)	184,000	6,229,000	1,634,000	8,047,000
National Service Agencies (5)	1,220,000	56,000	211,000	1,487,000
Cultural Agencies (18)	616,000	6,402,000	3,195,000	10,213,000
Religious Agencies (22)	445,000	9,539,000	3,328,000	13,312,000
Sub-totals	$ 5,393,000	$24,889,000	$ 9,040,000	$ 39,322,000
OVERSEAS PROGRAMS				
United Jewish Appeal and Beneficiary Agencies (5)	$70,589,000	$ 3,010,000	$ 299,000	$ 73,898,000
Other Overseas Agencies (14)	2,447,000	14,168,000	2,159,000	18,774,000
Sub-totals	$73,036,000	$17,178,000	$ 2,458,000	$ 92,672,000
Total All Programs	$78,429,000	$42,067,000	$11,498,000	$131,994,000

Source: S. P. Goldberg, "Jewish Communal Services." In *American Jewish Year Book 1958*, pp. 174–79.

There are five national service agencies acting as coordinating and consultative bodies for Jewish organizations and activities. The oldest and largest is the National Jewish Welfare Board, one of the participants in the United Service Organizations (USO). Among the others are the American Association for Jewish Education and the National Conference of Jewish Communal Service. Their income has been derived primarily from local Jewish federations and welfare funds.

Cultural and religious agencies are perhaps the most important of the national Jewish organizations. There were fifteen cultural agencies in the United States in 1958, one of them, Brandeis University, accounting for more than half of their $12.8 million in income. Three of the others also were institutions of higher education, although much smaller than Brandeis. The most important cultural agency other than the colleges was B'nai B'rith National Youth Service. Most of the

smaller organizations were concerned with research and scholarly publication programs: *e.g.*, the American Academy for Jewish Research,
the Jewish Publication Society, and the American Jewish Historical
Society.

Twenty-one national religious agencies were devoted primarily to
elementary Jewish education, rabbinical training, general religious programs, and the training of cantors, Jewish educators, *schochtim*, and
other religious functionaries. Some of these agencies were seminaries,
affiliated with the Reform, Conservative, or Orthodox groups. The religious agencies received $18.9 million in 1958, two-thirds of this in con-
tributions. Perhaps the best known of these institutions are Yeshiva
University and its associated Einstein Medical School, and the Jewish
Theological Seminary.[39]

INTERNATIONAL JEWISH PROGRAMS: The international Jewish programs have a variety of purposes, most of them being to aid Jewish
people in Israel. Most overseas Jewish aid has been channeled through
the United Jewish Appeal (UJA), which has received most of its funds
from local Jewish federations and funds. In 1957 the UJA raised a total
$73 million. This included a special fund estimated at $30 million to
aid Hungarian, Polish, Egyptian, and North African Jews, many of
whom were being forced to migrate to Israel. UJA also has several
major beneficiary agencies that expend their funds for a variety of purposes, largely in Israel. The most extensive program has been the agricultural settlement of immigrants, with the objective of eventually making the newcomers self-supporting. Settlers have received funds and
equipment for houses, irrigation and farm equipment, seeds, instruction,
and long-term loans. There have also been programs for the training
and maintenance of immigrant youths. The Malben program of the
American Jewish Joint Distribution Committee (AJJDC, an affiliate
of UJA) has served the sick, aged, and handicapped immigrants in
Israel.

Overseas programs also aid the Jewish populations of nations other
than Israel. ORT, the Organization for Rehabilitation through Training, has provided vocational training in Israel, the Moslem countries,
and Western Europe. In 1958 there were 34,000 ORT trainees. The
Jewish populations of the Moslem countries have also benefited from
AJJDC relief, health, and educational programs. Jewish immigrants to
the United States receive financial aid from the New York Association
for New Americans, another affiliate of UJA.

[39] Information and data on national Jewish activities and on the following overseas
Jewish activities are from S. P. Goldberg, "Jewish Communal Services," in *American
Jewish Year Book 1958*, pp. 140–79, and his articles of the same title in *American
Jewish Year Book 1959*, pp. 67–99, and *American Jewish Year Book 1960*, pp. 61–91.

Thirteen overseas agencies unaffiliated with the UJA received $22.8 million from American sources in 1958, most of it through their own campaigns. By far the largest was Hadassah, which provided medical and youth services, especially in Israel. Some of the other important overseas Jewish agencies are the National Council of Jewish Women, United Hias Service, and the America-Israel Cultural Foundation. In November, 1959, another such agency, the National Committee for Labor Israel, reported that it had raised $16.7 for Histadrut, Israel's labor federation, over a five-year period. Most of the funds had come from the United States and had financed extensive medical and social welfare projects in Israel. Part of it had been used in the construction of medical centers, which Histadrut maintains throughout Israel and which serve 1.3 million men, women, and children, both Jews and Arabs.[40]

Jewish Philanthropic Contributions

THE DATA on Jewish social and communal services are sufficiently complete to permit a reasonably accurate estimate of the extent of Jewish financial giving *in these areas*. These data are summarized in Table 13.

TABLE 13

JEWISH PHILANTHROPIC CONTRIBUTIONS TO JEWISH SOCIAL AND COMMUNAL SERVICES FOR A TYPICAL YEAR IN THE LATE 1950's [1]

Service	Amount	Per Cent
Jewish Education	$ 46,500,000	21.0%
Community Centers [2]	15,000,000	6.8
Local Health and Welfare Agencies [2]	32,100,000	14.5
National Programs	34,000,000	15.2
Overseas Programs	94,100,000	42.5
Totals	$221,700,000	100%
Per Capita Jewish Donations [3]	$54.50	

[1] Data is for 1956 or 1957.
[2] Contributions to Jewish welfare organizations from non-sectarian campaigns have been deducted.
[3] Based on an estimate of 4,070,000 Jews aged thirteen or older in the United States in 1957.

It should be emphasized that these figures do not include the funds that supported the more than 4,000 congregations reported by the Synagogue Council for 1957. Data on the funds that support the synagogues, salary their functionaries, and finance direct congregational activities are not

[40] "$16,711,847 Given to Labor Israel," *New York Times*, Nov. 27, 1959.

available. Assuming that congregations contribute an average of $20,000 a year to the support of each synagogue, the total is about $80 million. Of course, none of these estimates account for the time, effort, and goods contributed to local congregations and to the local and national Jewish agencies. Jewish fund-raising campaigns make extensive use of volunteers. It is probable that the boards and committees of most local and many national Jewish organizations consist largely of individuals serving without pay, and the staffs of local health and welfare agencies under Jewish auspices undoubtedly include many volunteers. Judaism in the United States is characterized by strong motivation and interest and a high level of financial support.

CONCLUDING REMARKS

THE PROTESTANT, Roman Catholic, Jewish, and other churches of America lend a blaze of color to the American welfare scene. Without them, the American welfare process would be fundamentally different. The facts and figures in this survey show how broad and intensive are the welfare activities related to religion in gross accounting terms, but they may be insufficient to demonstrate the great dependence of the welfare system upon the churches and synagogues for imagination, spirit, and energy. It should be remembered that a great many of the goads of conscience and concern that stimulate welfare activity in business firms, labor unions, governmental agencies, and educational institutions originate historically and currently from religious opinion.

Each religious group has its nuclear unit, the church or synagogue itself, around which are ordered a number of secondary groups. These auxiliary groups are in some cases very closely tied to the church, but in other cases venture so far from church control of their ideas, finances, membership, and activities as to be religious in name only. Catholic schools, for instance, are invariably close to the thought and leadership of their sponsoring hierarchy; many Protestant schools bear only a historical and social connection to a Protestant church and serve members of all denominations and non-sectarians without distinction. Most churches also maintain or are affiliated with local, national, and international welfare agencies. All major denominations have what may be called line and staff agencies on the national level. The line agencies furnish direction, financing, coordination, and control, while the staff agencies provide information, advice, and some cooperative services. The distinction between the two types is rarely precise.

Differences in theology are apparent in the overlapping of services and agencies, sometimes within the same denomination. This is true particularly of Protestant churches on the national and international level. However, there are also numerous religious orders and overlapping jurisdictions of different organizations within the Catholic Church that produce organizational conflict. The Protestant churches are ordinarily more restrained by local conditions than the Catholic parish churches, because the source of ultimate power in the latter case is rarely in doubt. The parish powers in welfare matters, as in religious matters, are delegated and therefore subject to recall at any time, even though they are very large and uninterrupted in practice. The local Protestant church is usually dependent on local support and independent of higher controls on many important questions of organization, finance, personnel, and welfare activities. Consequently, one finds among Protestant churches much more than among Catholic churches that church activities merge with those of the general community. Protestant churches take part in more of the thousands of councils, committees, and secular welfare agencies of the American scene. Great welfare agencies such as the YMCA and YWCA are scarcely religious except in so far as some of their leaders may be active Protestants as well.

The welfare and service organizations maintained and richly financed by American Jews are quite secular in nature, largely because the American Jewish community is as much a social and cultural community as it is a religious one. This does not mean that the services of Jewish welfare organizations are lacking in religious content, but that they are expressions of Jewish culture, in which religion has played a large and inseparable part.

There is much debate over the social mission of the churches. Protestants are most divided and vocal on the issue, but the Catholics also are perturbed by it. Some claim that the welfare of the distressed and handicapped should be the concern largely of religious groups, leaving a minimum of such work to other institutions. Others welcome government action in many areas and see their mission as an agitational and pioneering one, an attitude similar to that prevailing in the social work profession. Despite a large area of agreement among many church people and most social agencies, the connections between churches and governmental and non-governmental agencies are far fewer than they might be. One of the obstacles to greater coordination of religious groups with the others is the doctrine of separation of church and state, embodied in federal and State constitutions and given a strongly separatistic meaning by a large body of public opinion. The important possibilities of bringing some of the devotional and self-sacrificing spirit liberally present in church groups into governmental operations and also into the sometimes mechanistic operations of non-governmental professional welfare groups need to be explored.

Chapter Seven

FRATERNAL AND SERVICE
ORGANIZATIONS

T HE MASONIC LODGE, the Lions Club, the American Legion Post, and
their kindred fraternal and service organizations are part of the life of
almost every American community. They are a distinctly American expression of a desire to combine good-fellowship with the concerns for
mutual welfare and community welfare. For their members, who may
number more than thirty millions, they may offer insurance benefits
and, when necessary, physical and financial assistance. For their communities they provide services and facilities ranging from volunteer welfare work to children's hospitals. They are a distinct and important
variety of community organization; they have been given little attention in the study of community welfare, however.

Few of them were originally motivated by desires to contribute to
community welfare. Characteristically, they were inspired by the American tradition of mutual assistance, often supplemented by the desire to
"have a good time" that is still expressed in the elaborate ceremonials
and regalia of traditional fraternalism and in the informal joviality of
the businessmen's luncheon club.

In time most of these organizations have come to identify their
activities with the public interest, an identification common to most
publicly conscious organizations in contemporary American society.
This is evident from statements of their purposes and is given expression in the "community service activities" that are pridefully pointed
out by almost every club, lodge, post, and aerie, though these com-

munity services may be no more complicated than erecting billboards saying "Welcome to Friendly Oleanna" at the city limits.

Most fraternal orders, service organizations, labor unions, farmers' associations, professional bodies, and similar groups began as mutual-assistance organizations. They have developed along different lines, however. Fraternal orders, with a few notable exceptions, have been largely content to elaborate their mutual-assistance activities, whereas service organizations, as the term implies, have supplemented mutual assistance with community assistance.

Labor unions, the Grange, the National Association of Manufacturers, and, to some extent, the American Legion have in varying degrees become pressure groups devoted to attaining benefits for their members from other sources, particularly government bodies. They have found this to be their most effective means of operation, though they may still concern themselves to some extent with mutual assistance and community welfare. (The community welfare interests of labor unions are discussed at length in Chapter 10.) As pressure groups they nevertheless retain points of similarity with fraternal and service organizations. They are internally motivated by common interests and fellowship, and justify their activities in terms of the public interest. The Elks and the Eagles, chambers of commerce, and the American Legion follow the pressure group practice of sponsoring or opposing government action. Because of these indistinct boundaries between service and fraternal organizations on the one hand and pressure groups on the other, pressure groups and pressure activities receive some attention in this chapter.

ORIGINS AND CHARACTERISTICS

ALL THE NON-GOVERNMENTAL ASSOCIATIONS and societies in the United States are interest groups, in that they are organized on the basis of interests held in common by their members. There are three criteria that distinguish fraternal and service organizations from the thousands of other associations and societies for inclusion in this chapter. These criteria are: (1) organization on a national scale; (2) no present restriction to members of a particular profession or occupation; (3) significant involvement in welfare activity, at least some of which benefits non-members.

There are three somewhat distinct yet overlapping sub-species of organizations meeting these criteria: fraternal orders, service clubs, and veterans' organizations. Some of the larger of these groups are listed in Table 1. There are several types of non-governmental associations that in certain respects resemble fraternal and service organizations but do not entirely meet the above criteria. Interest groups such as the National Grange and the American Medical Association are excluded because they are organized along professional and occupational lines. Many pressure groups, that particular variety of interest groups that attempts to attain its ends by winning assistance from external bodies, also are excluded. Two of the more influential pressure groups are the National Association of Manufacturers and the American Farm Bureau Federation. B'nai B'rith and the National Association for the Advancement of Colored People, though partly pressure groups, also perform considerable mutual assistance such as providing legal aid in civil rights cases; B'nai B'rith conducts community assistance projects. It might be

TABLE 1

Some Fraternal, Service, and Veterans' Organizations in the United States with More Than 50,000 Members [1]

Organization	Membership [2] (To Nearest Thousand)
General Federation of Women's Clubs	11,000,000 [3]
Masonic Order (Inc. the Mystic Shrine)	4,000,000 (est.)
Order of the Eastern Star	3,000,000
American Legion	2,694,000
American Legion Auxiliary	1,000,000
Veterans of Foreign Wars of the U.S.	1,700,000
Ladies Auxiliary to the VFW	350,000
Independent Order of Odd Fellows	1,346,000
Benevolent and Protective Order of Elks	1,300,000
Chambers of Commerce in the U.S.	1,250,000 (est.)
Knights of Columbus	1,087,000 [3,4]
Loyal Order of Moose	1,025,000
Fraternal Order of Eagles	850,000
Lions International	578,000
Rotary International	472,000 [3]
B'nai B'rith (incl. womens and youth groups)	469,000
Modern Woodmen of America	456,000
National Association for the Advancement of Colored People	335,000
National Audubon Society	330,000
Companions of the Forest of America	300,000
The Maccabees	297,000 [3]
Kiwanis International	256,000 [3]
Knights of Pythias	255,000
Alcoholics Anonymous	250,000
Catholic Daughters of America	210,000 [4]
Junior Chambers of Commerce in the U.S.	180,000
Supreme Forest Woodmen Circle	152,000
P.E.O. Sisterhood	133,000 [3]
Improved Order of Red Men	128,000
League of Women Voters	127,000

TABLE 1 (*continued*)

Organization	Membership [2] (*To Nearest Thousand*)
American Veterans of World War II and Korea	125,000
Daughters of Isabella	116,000 [4]
Walther League	89,000
William Penn Fraternal Association	88,000
Exchange Club	85,000
Women World War Veterans	80,000
National Urban League	75,000
Association of the Junior League of America	73,000
Optimist International	66,000
Order of the King's Daughters and Sons	58,000
Greater Beneficial Union of Pittsburgh	53,000
Total	36,448,000 [5]

[1] This listing is not authoritative. It includes organizations such as the League of Women Voters and Alcoholics Anonymous that are not, in the strict sense, fraternal or service groups. (In the strict sense, "service clubs" refers to businessmen's organizations such as the Lions and Kiwanis.) Other groups having welfare interests that possibly could have been included are the Daughters of the American Revolution; "Greek letter societies" such as Beta Sigma Phi; the Hibernians; the Workmen's Circle; and even groups such as the American Automobile Association, which provides a number of travel services for non-members as well as members.

[2] Most membership figures from Harry Hansen, ed., *The World Almanac 1960*, New York: World-Telegram Corp., 1960, pp. 502–17 and other editions. A few membership figures are from current literature of the organizations concerned.

[3] These figures are known to include members in chapters outside the United States and its territories and possessions. The Knights of Columbus, for example, have 949,000 members in the United States, 116,000 in Canada, and 22,000 in other countries; an estimated 200,000 Rotarians are enrolled in clubs outside the United States. Several of the larger fraternal orders, as well as some of the smaller ones, include a number of Canadian members.

[4] These organizations are known to have religious origins or affiliations. In structure and purpose, however, they are primarily fraternal or service organizations.

[5] This total is an artificial one: many of the membership figures are estimates and probably high; there are many smaller organizations of this type whose membership figures are not included; and, most important, many Americans belong to more than one such organization and sometimes as many as ten.

objected that there is no clear reason for excluding the Parent-Teacher Association (PTA) from a discussion of fraternal and service organizations. The PTA, however, because of its close relation to the public school system, is more appropriately considered in connection with education (cf. Chapter 8).

The remainder of this chapter is divided into four sections, on fraternal orders, service organizations, veterans' organizations, and related groups. General commentaries on each type are followed by descriptions of some specific organizations and their activities.

FRATERNAL ORDERS

FRATERNAL ORDERS DEVELOPED from the same impulses that led to the rise of labor unions—the desires of men of similar occupations or social standing for mutual help and protection. The major difference that has developed between the unions and fraternal organizations is that unions seek collective benefits for their members from outside sources, whereas the fraternal orders have largely adhered to the principle of mutual assistance and have elaborated their own insurance programs. The first distinct fraternal insurance plan in the United States was developed in 1868 by the original lodge of the Ancient Order of United Workmen, a fraternal organization of craftsmen. Fraternal insurance became hugely popular in late nineteenth- and early twentieth-century America, first life insurance and shortly thereafter health insurance. Members of fraternal orders presently can take out a wide variety of coverage for themselves and their dependents, including life, burial, accident, sickness, old-age, and even maternity insurance, at reasonable rates.

Early in 1957 there were 9,748,000 insured members under the fraternal benefit system in the United States and Canada, over two million of whom were children and young people, or "junior members." Insurance is not compulsory for the members of fraternal orders offering insurance plans; in the 81,100 local lodges surveyed by the publication *Fraternal Monitor* to obtain these data there were over 900,000 social, or associate, members who were not covered by fraternal insurance.

Insurance obtained under fraternal benefit plans has been increasing in popularity and rivals in scope the insurance plans of other institutions and organizations. In 1955, an estimated 3.2 per cent of the life insurance policies in the United States were held through fraternal benefit systems. By contrast, collectively bargained insurance policies for labor union members accounted for about 3.7 per cent. Between 1955 and 1956 there was an increase of about 8 per cent in the number of policies in force under fraternal systems; in 1957 the value of fraternal insurance in force was $10.5 billion.[1]

The typical fraternal benefit society operates under a representative form of government as a non-profit system for the benefit of its members. Local or subordinate lodges are established by and operated under the auspices of a supreme lodge, which is composed of delegates elected by members of local lodges. Conventions are held by the supreme

[1] "Insurance Takes Fraternal Turn," *New York Times*, Aug. 4, 1957.

lodge, usually annually, to enact regulations for the order and to elect officers and a board of directors. For most delegates to a convention, though, the business aspects of the convention are subordinate to its play aspects.

The play, or fellowship, elements in fraternalism are common to service and veterans' organizations as well, although they may be assigned roles of varied importance by different groups, both in theory and in practice. Their importance also varies among the locals of the same fraternity or service organization, depending on the personalities of the members of the group. The play elements in fraternalism have been subjected to various interpretations; proponents of fraternalism have tended to evaluate them favorably, as did Walter Bayse, writing in 1919 when fraternalism was in a period of rapid growth:

> The privilege of attending lodge and enjoying the fellowship of others is a feature of membership in benefit societies that should not be valued lightly. The lodge is the people's forum and club. Questions of importance to the community are discussed there, and the social affairs are events that call together those who desire entertainment and recreation. The ritual gives an opportunity for those with dramatic ability to express their talents. A lodge composes a group of people with mutual interests who are bent on co-operating for the good of all, enjoying the society of each other and extending encouragement and relief to those who have been overtaken by misfortune.[2]

Other writers have been more critical in their evaluations. To outsiders fraternal rituals frequently appear highly amusing, and the activities of fraternal brothers and sisters at conventions often bring about reactions that sometimes shade into irritation. Fellowship can be an end in itself and a definite contribution to the welfare of individual members, however, and from a broader standpoint these highly visible features of fraternalism are only one part of fraternal activity.

Most important, fraternal orders as well as service and veterans' organizations embody the spirit of mutual assistance and cooperation that is frequently lacking in other institutions of contemporary society. Fraternalism has considerable potential as a source of welfare, both for members and for others in the community, and to note that this potential is frequently unused or obscured is not to deny its existence.

Fraternal organizations in the United States vary greatly in size, ranging from those containing more than a million members, such as the Masonic orders, to a number of smaller orders, such as the Royal

[2] Walter Bayse. *History and Operation of Fraternal Insurance.* Rochester, N.Y.: Fraternal Monitor, 1919, pp. 19–20.

Arcanum, with 45,000 members.[3] There are many regional fraternal orders and some national and international orders that have still fewer members, *e.g.*, the Royal Neighbors of America, the Union of Czech Catholic Women of Texas, and the International Concatenated Order of Hoo Hoo.

Many fraternal orders have developed extensive service and welfare programs in addition to or in lieu of insurance plans. The welfare activities of several of the larger fraternal groups—the Freemasons, the Eagles, the Elks, the Knights of Columbus, the Daughters of Isabella, and B'nai B'rith—are outlined in the following sketches, on the basis of information derived from the literature of these organizations.

Freemasonry

FREEMASONRY WITH its many appendant bodies is the oldest and largest fraternal grouping in the United States. The Masonic Fraternity as it is known includes among others the Knights Templar, the Royal Arch Masons, the Order of the Mystic Shrine, and two Supreme Councils of the 33° Scottish Rite, a Northern and a Southern Jurisdiction. Membership in the entire Masonic Fraternity in the United States is about four million. In addition the Order of the Eastern Star, an offshoot of the Masonic movement, has a membership of three million women. Organized Freemasonry in the United States dates back at least to 1781, the founding date of the Grand Lodge of the State of New York.

Masonic orders embody many elements of fraternal ritualism, which some people charge are reflections of anti-Roman Catholic and anti-religious biases. Current Masonic literature expressly disavows such biases, however, and states the purposes of the Masons as "charity and the building of character."[4] In the name of charity the Masonic orders sponsor and support many benevolent activities for members and non-members. In the Northern Jurisdiction of 33° Masons, which has close to half a million members, "each of the local bodies . . . has an Almoner, who is provided with substantial funds to administer to the needy, without regard to Masonic membership. This long-time contribution of the Rite to public welfare is never publicized; its extent and importance are rarely known."[5]

There are few current statistics on the charitable activities of Free-

[3] Membership statistics on fraternal and service organizations, unless otherwise specified, are from Harry Hansen, ed., *The World Almanac*, New York: World-Telegram Corp., 1960, pp. 502–17.
[4] "Some Misconceptions About Freemasonry," *The Short Talk Bulletin*, XXXVI (August, 1958), p. 4. Washington, D.C.: The Masonic Service Association of the United States.
[5] *Ibid.*, p. 9.

masonry's many coordinate bodies. It is known, however, that in one recent year thirty-eight out of forty-nine of the Masonic Grand Lodges allotted a fixed portion of their membership fees to charity.[6] It can be roughly estimated that Masonic contributions to charitable purposes from this source have been between $2.5 and $3 million annually. In twenty-seven State Grand Lodges part of the fee for each Masonic degree also is prorated to charity, the source of an additional $1–$1.5 million each year. These estimates cover only part of the charitable contributions of Masonic lodges, for other portions of the fees and dues may eventually be used for charitable purposes, and individual lodges may contribute funds for particular local projects. Masons also carry out many welfare and service activities such as providing time and materials for community welfare projects that either have not been or cannot be evaluated in monetary terms.

Masonic organizations have donated large sums to education. The George Washington University School of Government was founded by the Southern Jurisdiction of 33° Masons with a grant of a million dollars, which has been supplemented with further gifts and scholarships. The Southern Jurisdiction has recently given $20,000 to American University in Washington, D.C., and $10,000 to Baylor University. The Knights Templar have maintained a trust fund for student loans since the 1920's, and currently lend about half a million dollars a year to college students. Grand Lodges have maintained vocational schools (six in 1946) and high schools (four in 1946), usually in connection with a Masonic home.[7]

There is an extensive system of Masonic homes, orphanages, and hospitals, many of which are open to both members and non-members of Masonic orders. A 1946 survey disclosed that thirty-six Masonic jurisdictions maintained homes for either adults (usually the aged), children, or both; 4,500 adults were in residence, most of them Masons and their wives. Thirteen jurisdictions operated hospitals, nineteen operated infirmaries, and four others operated both, most of them presumably in connection with the homes.[8] The Masonic Home for the Aged, with 310 people in residence in 1955, was the largest home for the aged in Alameda County, California; a Masonic Home for Children serves four counties in the San Francisco Bay area.[9]

[6] *Grand Lodge Facts and Figures* (rev. ed.). Washington, D.C.: The Masonic Service Association of the United States, 1955, p. 18.
[7] *Ibid.*, pp. 8–9.
[8] *Masonic Homes, Orphanages, Hospitals, Infirmaries, Sanitariums and Charity Foundations of the Forty-Nine Grand Jurisdictions of the United States* (2nd ed.). Washington, D.C.: The Masonic Service Association, September, 1946.
[9] Vaughn Davis Bornet. *California Social Welfare.* Englewood Cliffs, N.J.: Prentice-Hall, 1956, pp. 268, 366.

Hospitals and agencies for crippled children have long been of interest to Masonic orders. One author has stated that: "Private crippled children's agencies, established and supported by such fraternal orders as the Shriners, the Elks, and the Rotary Clubs . . . have been pioneers in this field. They built the first orthopedic hospitals and clinics and encouraged State legislation for crippled children preceding the Social Security Act of 1935." [10]

The Order of the Shrine's activities on behalf of crippled children have been particularly well-publicized. In 1958 there were seventeen Shriner hospitals for crippled children in operation, fifteen of them having been in existence since the 1920's, and in that year the Imperial Council of the Shriners approved plans for the construction of two new hospitals in St. Louis and Mexico City, to replace Shriner hospitals already in use in those cities. The St. Louis hospital was to cost $3.5 million and the Mexico City hospital $600,000. In addition to construction expenditures the Shriners must also bear the costs of maintenance, salaries, and treatment; more than 250,000 crippled children have been treated in these hospitals over a thirty-year period. The sources of funds have been gifts, bequests, voluntary contributing memberships, and the rather unusual practice of life insurance policies naming Shriner hospitals as beneficiaries.[11]

The Masonic Service Association, which acts as a clearinghouse for a number of Masonic Grand Lodges, operates a veterans' service program out of funds received from Grand Lodges. In 1957 these amounted to $200,000 and financed the operations of fifty-one centers whose primary activity has been visiting and providing special services for men in veterans' hospitals.[12]

The Fraternal Order of Eagles

The Order of Eagles is one of several large fraternal organizations that have developed service programs specifically for the welfare of groups outside the order. Local aeries (lodges) and their women's auxiliaries contribute time, money, and energy to small-scale civic and community projects, and the national organization has several overseas projects in the "world service field."

Fund-raising for health and welfare purposes attracts the attention of most local lodges. In 1958, for example, Eagle Auxiliaries raised

[10] Walter Freidlander. *Introduction to Social Welfare.* Englewood Cliffs, N.J.: Prentice-Hall, 1955, p. 336.
[11] *Official Souvenir Program, 84th Imperial Council Session,* 1958, pp. 26–27; "Shriners to Build," *New York Times,* July 18, 1958.
[12] *Report of the Executive Commission of the Masonic Service Association of the United States.* Washington, D.C., 1958.

$65,000 for muscular dystrophy, giving the funds to the Muscular Dystrophy Foundation. Over a ten-year period local lodges have donated about $850,000 to the Damon Runyon Fund for cancer research. Other fund-raising drives are conducted among Eagles for overseas programs. Three European youth training centers are currently sponsored and partly or completely financed by the Eagles. For many years Eagles also have made sizable contributions to several children's institutions, notably Boys Town, Nebraska, and Home on the Range for Boys, in North Dakota.

A summary listing of the community activities of local aeries includes "thousands of service projects: youth guidance activities, accident prevention programs, fire prevention week, community betterment projects, presentation of civic awards, support for welfare drives, undertakings that range from a single act of charity to community-wide campaigns to build better communities." [13] In many aeries, however, such programs are of minimal importance, being overshadowed by pro-membership social and recreational activities.

In annual conventions the Eagles, like most other fraternal and service organizations, adopt resolutions in favor of government programs such as old-age security, health insurance, and full employment; the impact of such resolutions on legislative and administrative bodies is problematical. There is a tendency for such organizations to overstate their influence in community and national affairs; the Eagles, for example, claim to be "the Order that pioneered the fight for old age pensions and social security." [14]

One type of pro-membership activity of the Eagles that merits special mention is conducted by the Eagles Memorial Foundation. Founded in 1944, in its first thirteen years the Foundation amassed assets of almost four million dollars, largely from membership contributions. The income, which totaled $110,000 in one recent year, provides educational grants and medical services for children of members of the order who died during wartime military service.[15] Similar foundations have been established by other fraternal and service organizations to provide funds for welfare purposes.

The Benevolent and Protective Order of Elks

THE ORDER OF ELKS is larger and more active than the Order of Eagles. It had about one and a quarter million members in 1959, compared

[13] Bob Hansen, "The Eagles," in *The Fraternal Order of Eagles* (booklet), 1954, p. 38; *Eagle Digest*, VI (Sept. 15, 1958), p. 1.
[14] *Eagle Digest*, VI (Aug. 25, 1958), p. 1.
[15] Hansen, *op. cit.*, p. 487.

with about three-quarters of a million in the Eagles. The welfare and service interests of the Elks are wider than those of the Eagles and are given greater financial support (cf. Table 2). The only major activity sponsored by the Eagles that is not of current interest to the Elks is overseas service. A survey of the publications of these two orders suggests that the membership of the Elks is drawn from a higher socio-economic level than that of the Eagles, which may account for some of these differences.

Almost all the activities listed in Table 2 are for the welfare of those outside the order. The only exception is relief of needy members,

TABLE 2

Expenditures for Health, Welfare, and Related Activities
by Elk Lodges, April, 1957, to March, 1958

Purpose	Amount (To Nearest Thousand)
Care of Needy Families (Including Thanksgiving and Christmas Baskets)	$1,044,000
Youth Work	949,000
Relief of Members, Widows, Dependents	700,000
Crippled Children	825,000
Cerebral Palsy	545,000
Medical Aid and Hospitals	426,000
Scholarships, Free Textbooks, etc.	303,000
Red Cross, Salvation Army, etc.	314,000
Summer Outings, Camps, Health Resorts	289,000
Elks National Foundation	201,000
Veterans' Relief	186,000
Miscellaneous (Including Patriotic Activities)	839,000
Total	$6,621,000

Source: "Digest of Annual Reports," *The Elks Magazine,* XXXVII (August, 1958), pp. 36–39.

widows, and dependents, amounting to little more than 10 per cent of the $6,620,000 spent by the Elks for welfare purposes in 1958. The Elks National Foundation (Table 2) is a philanthropic fund that has received $5 million in donations since its founding in 1928. (The market value of the securities in its investment portfolio was more than $7 million in 1958.) Donations to the Foundation in the Elks' 1958 fiscal year were about $400,000, of which half came from subordinate lodges (the $201,000 noted in Table 2); individual members donated the rest. Annual income from investments has been about $250,000, which has been spent for charitable and educational purposes, notably grants for doctors, technicians, and teachers working with cerebral palsy victims, and the "Most Valuable Student" awards, which totaled $40,000 in 1958 and $70,000 in 1959.[16]

The Elks National Service Commission spent about $400,000 in 1958 to maintain six fraternal centers for servicemen and to provide volunteer services in the 172 hospitals of the Veterans Administration. The latter services include providing professional talent, sports nights, carnivals, and trips outside the hospital for patients, as well as ward visits, wheel-chair patient escorts, occupational therapy instructions, letter writing, and so forth. These are the same types of voluntary services provided by the United Service Organizations (USO) and other non-governmental bodies that supplement the veterans' programs of the national government.[17]

As with many other fraternal and service organizations the Elks have placed primary emphasis on youth programs, however. In Georgia, Florida, Colorado, Idaho, and Texas, Elks own and operate hospitals for crippled and handicapped children. In at least six other States they operate clinics and camps for physically handicapped children and in five States they have specific programs for cerebral palsy victims. The California State Elks Association in 1958 had twenty-three mobile units handling a caseload of about 600 children throughout the State. Elks lodges have sponsored some 700 Boy Scout troops, nearly a thousand Little League baseball teams, and many other youth organizations. In 1958 at least seven State lodges also operated summer camps, primarily for underprivileged youngsters.[18]

Finally, the Elks operate a well-equipped home for the aged in Bedford, Virginia, which in 1958 had 265 residents.[19]

Catholic Fraternal Orders

AMONG THE LARGER fraternal organizations are several Roman Catholic orders, including the Knights of Columbus, the Daughters of Isabella, and the Catholic Daughters of America.

The Knights of Columbus is a fraternal society of Catholic men, organized in 1882 by a parish priest. Its objectives, typical of the fraternal orders of its day, were "to provide a system of fraternal insurance to care for the widows and orphans of members; to provide fellowship

[16] "Digest of Annual Reports," The Elks Magazine, XXXVII (September, 1958), pp. 19–21.
[17] Ibid., p. 21.
[18] $7 Million Elk Benevolences Put Major Emphasis on Youth Program (pamphlet). New York: National Memorial and Publication Commission, Benevolent and Protective Order of Elks of the U.S.A., 1958
[19] "Digest of Annual Reports," The Elks Magazine, XXXVII (August, 1958), p. 37.

among the members, to aid the cause of religion, and to perform charitable, educational and patriotic works for the benefit for their fellow men and their nation." [20] In 1958 the Knights of Columbus had well over a million members. Insurance in force was over $780 million, plus $45 million in juvenile insurance. Expenditures for charitable and educational purposes in particular have been quite large, although for any given year there are no estimates available for the entire organization.

Many of the charitable activities of the Knights of Columbus have taken place at the State council level. A number of homes for children, youth camps, and other facilities for young people—customarily for Catholic youth—have been financed by the order. Since 1923 the Indiana State Council has contributed more than $600,000 to establish and maintain a boys' home near Terre Haute; during the 1950's it made annual contributions of $25,000 to the institution. There have also been gifts for educational purposes. The New York State Council has annually awarded about $35,000 in the form of scholarships, and at one time granted $300,000 to Canisius College. The Iowa State Council has contributed $55,000 to Catholic bishops in the State to assist the education of candidates for the priesthood and $50,000 for the maintenance of student pastors at educational institutions in the State. Similar contributions could be cited at length.

The national Supreme Council directs several funds, primarily for educational purposes. One of these provides approximately thirty fellowships a year for graduate students at the Catholic University of America, with preference to members of the Knights of Columbus and their sons. The Educational Trust Fund in 1958 granted $40,000 in scholarships to the children of members of the order who had been killed or disabled during military service. The Italian Welfare Fund of the order disbursed about $70,000 in 1958 for the maintenance of seven recreation grounds operated by the Knights of Columbus in Rome.[21]

The Daughters of Isabella is an association of Catholic women, having 115,000 members in 1957. Although some of the charitable work of the order has taken the form of financial contributions (about $8 million were donated to churches, hospitals, schools, missions, and other institutions between 1921 and 1956), most of the charitable activity of local circles, or chapters, has been non-monetary. The association is unique in that it has maintained records on the number

[20] *These Men They Call Knights* (No. 9 in a series of pamphlets). New Haven: Knights of Columbus (n.d.), p. 1.
[21] *Ibid.*, pp. 20–26; *Annual Report of the Supreme Secretary*, New Haven: Knights of Columbus, 1958.

of hours of service its members have devoted to various welfare purposes. Figures for two years' service are given in Table 3. During this peacetime period members averaged about one and one-half hours per year of welfare work. During the four years of World War II, however, members of the order contributed 4.4 million hours of service for various purposes, an average of about ten hours per member per year. If these figures appear low it should be remembered that they do not include all activities of the members as members. Pro-membership

TABLE 3

HOURS OF NON-MONETARY WELFARE SERVICE PROVIDED BY THE
DAUGHTERS OF ISABELLA, 1954–55 AND 1955–56

Type of Service	Hours (To Nearest Hundred)
Church, School, and Community Projects	168,300
Hospitals	52,700
Missions	30,900
Chaplains' Aid	23,800
Red Cross and Grey Ladies	21,500
United Service Organizations (USO)	13,200
Civil Defense	4,100
Blind and Shut-ins	3,000
Boy and Girl Scouts	2,700
Visiting Sick and Aged	800
Catholic Youth Organization (CYO)	500
Miscellaneous Services	2,300
Total Hours of Service	323,800
Membership: 110,000 (est.)	
Average Hours Service per Year per Member	1.47+

Source: *National Circle, Daughters of Isabella: Survey: Contributions—Activities* (pamphlet, n.d.).

activities, such as meetings and social gatherings, are not included, and it may be that some welfare work, for local parishes for example, also is excluded.

The Catholic Daughters of America, with 200,000 members, is devoted to the well-being of Catholic girls; it is discussed briefly in Chapter 6.

B'nai B'rith

B'NAI B'RITH (Sons of the Covenant) was founded in 1843 with the avowed mission of "Uniting Israelites in the work of promoting their highest interests and those of humanity." It was essentially a mutual-assistance organization, similar to many fraternal orders but including in its interests all members of the American Jewish community. It is now closely associated with many of the other Jewish philanthropic and social service bodies, and indeed was responsible for the establishment of some of them, but still undertakes many activities of its own.

B'nai B'rith is actually composed of three bodies: B'nai B'rith Men, with about 200,000 members in 1960; B'nai B'rith Women, 135,000 members; and B'nai B'rith Youth, 37,000 members. Expenditures of all three bodies together in 1958 were $5.9 million, about two-fifths of which was for the Anti-Defamation League, whose purpose is the elimination of discrimination through fact-finding and information campaigns. Other major B'nai B'rith programs are the Hillel Foundations, serving Jewish students on several hundred campuses in the United States and Canada; the Vocational Service, with nineteen regional offices (1959), which provided some 200,000 persons with career guidance and job counseling between 1956 and 1959; a youth encampment program; and a number of others. B'nai B'rith undertakes fund-raising campaigns as well; it raised $1.5 million for its youth services in 1958 (not included in the figures above), provides funds and volunteers for local Jewish welfare campaigns, and has given extensive funds and material assistance to refugees, disaster victims overseas, and to groups in Israel.[22]

SERVICE CLUBS

The characteristic that most distinguishes service clubs from fraternal orders is their primary emphasis on community service. Service clubs are typically composed of businessmen, and interpersonal relations are less formal than they are in fraternal orders. These comments, written by a Princeton University sociologist in the 1930's, are still largely valid:

> In terms of the activities centered within the group itself, these respective types of organizations overlap in their functions albeit there are conspicuous differences in the tone and atmosphere. Fellowship, the prestige coming from membership in a select group, character-forming influences, all these are felt to be individual values accruing from membership in both. Yet it is in perhaps the differences which these two types of organizations exhibit which explain the popularity of the service club. . . . The fraternal organizations are formal and esoteric. The service club is highly informal and extremely open to public view. Visitors constantly are invited to service club luncheons and sit through their

[22] *The President's Message.* Twenty Second General Convention of the Supreme Lodge. Jerusalem: B'nai B'rith, 1959, pp. 28–42.

business proceedings. This informality and cordial openness of the service club is, perhaps, more in tune with modern small city American life than the formality and ritual of the fraternal organization.[23]

The three largest businessmen's service clubs (excluding chambers of commerce, which are a slightly different type of organization) are: Lions International, with over half a million members; Rotary International, with close to half a million members; and Kiwanis International, with a quarter million members. Lions and Rotary have affiliated clubs throughout the world, and their service interests have a distinct international flavor. Aside from these two clubs, the appellation "international" has little meaning; it usually refers to a handful of Canadian clubs.

TABLE 4

BUSINESSMEN'S AND BUSINESSWOMEN'S SERVICE CLUBS, 1958

Organization	No. of Clubs	Membership (To Nearest Hundred)
Lions International	13,617	574,300
Rotary International	9,682	454,000
Kiwanis International	4,440	252,000
National Exchange Club	1,400	80,000
Optimist International	1,505	60,400
Civitan International	725	26,500
Ruritan National	670	25,000
Sertoma International	267	13,500
Twenty-Thirty Club	342	7,000
Gyro	123	5,500
Cosmopolitan International	79	4,000
Loyal Knights of the Round Table	44	1,700
American Federation of Soroptomist Clubs (women)	(n.a.)	20,000
Altrusa International (women)	(n.a.)	15,500
Zonta International (women)	(n.a.)	13,700

Sources: Hansen, op. cit., pp. 502–17; "Major Service Club Organization Statistics," Chicago: Lions International, 1958.

The businessmen's service club is of distinctively American origin. During the first two decades of the twentieth century, group solidarity developed among the owners and managers of small- and medium-sized businesses, one result being the development of large numbers of businessmen's luncheon clubs. Rotary and Kiwanis began as single

[23] Charles F. Marden. Rotary and Its Brothers. Princeton, N.J.: Princeton University Press, 1935, p. 151.

clubs in two midwestern cities, each of them subsequently sponsoring other clubs under their names in other communities. Rotary International is the oldest of the three, dating itself from 1905. Kiwanis began in 1915, the Lions in 1919. Lions International resulted from the amalgamation of a number of clubs already in existence, under the leadership of a Chicago club.

Through time these clubs have gradually drawn away from the self-interest and business boosting that initially brought their members together. Their currently-avowed purposes include both service to their communities and maintenance of business ethics. For example, Rotary International seeks:

> To encourage and foster the ideal of service as a basis of worthy enterprise and, in particular, to encourage and foster:
>
> (1) The development of acquaintance as an opportunity for service;
>
> (2) High ethical standards in business and professions; the recognition of the worthiness of all useful occupations; and the dignifying by each Rotarian of his occupation as an opportunity to serve society;
>
> (3) The application of the ideal of service by every Rotarian to his personal, business, and community life;
>
> (4) The advancement of international understanding, good will, and peace through a world fellowship of business and professional men united in the ideal of service.[24]

These purposes were phrased more succinctly by Melvin Jones, the founder of Lions International: "You can't get very far without doing something for somebody else." [25]

The actual impact of these ideals on the members of businessmen's clubs is a matter of dispute. It is apparent that the clubs and their leaders believe sincerely in the ideal of "service," and their literature contains innumerable references to welfare work carried out in the name of community service. However, in one of the very few analytical studies of men's service clubs, Charles F. Marden has asserted that comradeship and like-mindedness are the primary bonds among members, and that the practice of the above-mentioned ethical ideals is usually secondary.[26]

The theme of helping oneself by helping others is apparent in many service club projects. In San Gabriel, California, for example, the local

[24] *Service Is My Business*. Chicago, London, Zurich: Rotary International, 1948, p. 8.
[25] Robert Casey and W. A. S. Douglas. *The World's Biggest Doers: The Story of the Lions*. Chicago: Wilcox and Follett, 1949, p. 237.
[26] Marden, *op. cit.*, p. 133.

Rotary and Kiwanis clubs have jointly sponsored a youth employment service. The two clubs have paid the director's salary and all expenses of the operation, and provide free publicity for the service. The clubs have benefited the youth of the community; they have also, perhaps incidentally, kept their members in contact with prospective employees.[27]

The fixed point of club activity of the service club member is the weekly luncheon meeting of his club. This luncheon is an informal affair that includes a brief business meeting, a speaker, perhaps the singing of club songs, and a great deal of informal discussion that may or may not have bearing on current service projects. Considerable social pressure is brought to bear on members both for attendance at these meetings and for participation in projects. These projects may include not only welfare undertakings but also civic, political, and patriotic activities, and, not infrequently, activities in support of local business. Few projects are carried on within the framework of the luncheon meeting, of course, but it is here that they are suggested, planned, and evaluated, and it is here that club membership is enlisted in their support and financial contributions are raised.

Chambers of commerce and junior chambers of commerce are organizations of businessmen that differ from the service clubs in some respects. In almost every case they represent the leading businessmen of their communities, which is not necessarily the case with service clubs, and their primary interests are business affairs. Such service activities as they undertake generally have definite aspects of business promotion. There are 2,500 chambers of commerce in the United States, estimated to have over a million members. Junior chambers of commerce have about a quarter million members.

Sketches of four service organizations are given below. The Kiwanis, Rotary, and Lions have sufficiently diverse characteristics that all are described; one of the smaller service clubs, Optimist International, also is discussed. Finally, a description of the work of chambers of commerce is given.

Rotary International

ROTARY INTERNATIONAL is the second largest businessmen's service club and is the most international in scope. In 1958 Rotary had 460,000 members in nearly 10,000 clubs throughout the world, in cities as far apart as Mandalay, Helsinki, Honolulu, and Sydney, Australia. Little more than half the membership and fewer than half the local clubs are in the United States (cf. Table 5).

[27] "Family Answers: Service Clubs Sponsor Youth Jobs Agency in San Gabriel," *Los Angeles Times*, April 21, 1958.

The objects of Rotary International are summarized in the mottoes "Service Above Self" and "He Profits Most Who Serves Best." Service activities take many forms and vary both with the conditions of a community in which a Rotary club is active and with the part of the world in which the community is located. In foreign countries there are some particularly notable examples of Rotary Club projects. One of these was initiated in 1954 by the 163 members of the Calcutta club, which established, equipped, maintained, and managed a complete crippled children's clinic, giving some 35,000 treatments in a four-year period. In 1958, however, the clinic was turned over to the government of West Bengal, to permit the club to devote its time and energy "to some other field of Community Service where it can successfully be applied and where it is badly needed." [28]

TABLE 5

ROTARY CLUBS AND MEMBERSHIP BY REGION, 1958

Region	Number of Clubs [1]	Membership [2]
U.S.A. and Canada	5,095 [3]	287,000
Continental Europe, North Africa, Eastern Mediterranean	1,440	53,400
Great Britain and Ireland	852	38,500
Latin America (including Mexico and the West Indies)	1,322	37,300
Asia	568	21,800
Australia, New Zealand, southern Africa, and Areas Not Listed Elsewhere	574	22,300
Totals	9,851	460,300
Membership of Average Rotary Club		47

Sources: "Brief Facts About Rotary," Rotary International, 1958, p. 10; *1958 Proceedings: Forty-Ninth Annual Rotary Convention*, Rotary International, 1958, p. 306.

[1] These figures are complete to June 18, 1958.
[2] These figures are complete to April 15, 1958.
[3] Of these, 342 were in Canada.

In 1958 the Aguascalientes, Mexico, Rotary raised $95,000 to build a school, and in addition provided all furniture and materials. The Rotary Club of Singapore has established and furnished a school in a poverty-stricken outlying area. In Jamshedpur, India, a city of about 150,000, the Rotary Club during 1957 maintained a ward in a leprosy asylum, operated four clinics, and examined 42,000 persons in the course of a continuing health survey.

[28] "Rotary Reporter," *The Rotarian Magazine*, XCIII (October, 1958), p. 44.

For the most part, Rotary clubs in the United States undertake less ambitious activities and more frequently are involved in publicity and community boosting. These are some typical service projects: the Tarkio, Missouri, Rotary sponsored a fund-raising campaign to build a community park; in a small Texas city Rotary makes an annual award to the "teacher of the year"; the Rotary Club of Dallas, Texas, "has given assistance to the Dallas Lighthouse for the Blind, including tools as well as financial contributions and promotional activity." [29]

It is impossible to make accurate comparisons without a complete picture of a given club's yearly activities; the evidence suggests, however, that Rotary clubs outside the United States make more significant contributions to community welfare than those in the United States. One possible explanation is that Rotary clubs in many foreign communities may occupy a relatively more important place among the voluntary associations of their communities than do Rotary clubs in the United States, which are usually but one of a large number of community-conscious groups.

In addition to local projects, Rotary clubs throughout the world support the Rotary Foundation, which grants fellowships for graduate study. Between a quarter and a half million dollars has been donated to the Foundation each year since 1950, and in 1958 the Foundation had assets of $5.5 million. It began granting fellowships in 1947, and in its first twelve years gave well over $2.5 million to nearly 1,100 students for foreign study. About half the fellows, both men and women, have come from sixty other countries; the fellows have elected to study in forty-two different countries. The major fields of study of these fellows indicate that there is no bias in the direction of business interests. Through 1958, International Relations and Political Science (a single category) had been most strongly represented, being the interest of some 16 per cent of the fellows. Following it in order of frequency were Engineering, Literature, Education, Medicine, and History. Business Administration, Industrial Relations, and Economics combined accounted for 10 per cent of the fellows.[30] The type of international fellowship program sponsored by the Rotary Foundation appears well-designed to meet Rotary's object of advancing "international understanding, good will, and peace."

Kiwanis International

WITH A QUARTER MILLION MEMBERS, Kiwanis is the third largest businessmen's service club in the United States, and in many respects its

[29] *Proceedings,* pp. 315–17.
[30] *Facts and Figures: The Rotary Foundation of Rotary International.* The Rotary Foundation, March, 1957 (pamphlet).

Fraternal and Service Organizations

activities parallel those of the Lions and Rotary: community service, business affairs, and youth service. Each of these clubs, however, has traditionally emphasized one particular welfare interest over others. The interest of Rotary in international service is noted above; the Lions since the 1920's have provided aid and services to the blind; the heart of Kiwanis has been a concern for youth.

This is an outline of Kiwanis youth services undertaken during 1957: [31]

Children visiting Kiwanis-sponsored recreational facilities:	1,382,000
Children provided entertainment on Kids' Day:	1,569,000
Youth groups sponsored and supported by Kiwanis (Scouts, Boys' and Girls' Clubs, 4-H, etc.):	2,812
Youths provided vocational counseling:	616,000
Children contacted in clinics and projects for sight-saving, conservation of hearing, and mentally retarded:	453,000
Scholarships, loans, and awards relating to education:	122,000
Young people provided religious education in day camps:	69,000
Free school lunches and quarts of milk provided:	707,000
Funds raised on Kids' Day:	$1,082,000
Value of scholarships and loans:	$ 794,000

Kiwanis has organized nearly 1,700 Key Clubs, which in effect are high school service clubs, with about 40,000 members in 1957. The young men in Key Clubs operate programs similar to those of local Kiwanis clubs: for example, they have carried out charity drives, established a community youth center (in Union City, Indiana), and assisted in the programs of their Kiwanis sponsors. These activities are paralleled by 180 Circle K clubs at the college level, which are also under the guidance of local Kiwanians.

Not all Kiwanis welfare services are directed to youth. Other areas of activities listed in the 1957 annual report are "Agriculture and Conservation," in which Kiwanis clubs sponsored several thousand soil conservation and drainage projects, planted some two and a half million trees on their 1957 annual tree planting days, and did many hours of work for and with rural youths; "Public and Business Affairs," including typical business and community-boosting activities, surveys, safety campaigns, and get-out-the-vote drives; and "Support of Churches in Their

[31] *Kiwanis in Action* (1958 Edition). Chicago: Kiwanis International, 1958 (booklet).

Spiritual Aims." In 1957 Kiwanians collected and/or contributed over $20 million for national health campaigns, community chests, and other local fund drives; the particular value of using business club members in community campaigns is that they can most readily contact other businessmen. In some communities Kiwanis clubs have undertaken entire fund-raising campaigns by themselves, with some notable successes. In The Hamptons, New Hampshire (population 3,000), the local Kiwanis club raised $10,000 for a local hospital, for example.[32]

Lions International

LIKE ROTARY, "Lionism" is distinctly international: in 1958 there were 13,771 Lions clubs in ninety-one countries and territories, with nearly 580,000 members. During the year 760 new clubs were established (included in the above total), about half of them in the United States; others were located in such widely separated places as Costa Rica (with six new clubs), Northern Ireland, and Ruanda-Urundi (Belgian East Africa).[33] It is estimated that somewhat over half of Lions International membership is in the United States.

Like Kiwanis, the Lions list their projects by number and by area of interest, including the following in their 1958 annual report: [34]

Soil conservation and agricultural pest eradication programs, and financial and physical assistance to farmers and farm organizations:	1,564
Sponsorship of youth organizations; provision of parties, field days, educational tours, and athletic events for boys and girls; maintenance of youth camps:	32,164
Observations of civic holidays, classes for new citizens, and financial aid for displaced persons and exchange students:	3,064
Urban clean-up projects, and establishment and construction of community recreation centers and areas:	10,084
Sponsorship of community musical and theatrical organizations, social activities of all types, and outings; contributions of money and time to community projects and surveys; and initiation of, and participation in, community-boosting projects:	53,994
Provision of transportation for school children; assistance to vocational schools; and sponsorship of contests, presentation of awards, and observation of Education Week:	15,523

[32] Ibid.
[33] The International President Reports (41st Annual Convention). Chicago: Lions International, July, 1958.
[34] Ibid.

Provision of equipment, goods, and funds, to families, schools, hospitals, clinics, and children's centers; sponsorship of, and donations to, campaigns; and repair and construction of homes for the needy and disaster victims: 24,554

Children's safety, fire prevention, and first aid: 3,886

Provision of sight-saving equipment, guide dogs, Braille books and typewriters, and other equipment, to the blind and partially sighted; provision of, and payment of salaries of, instructors and caseworkers for the blind; financing of hospital care; establishment of clinics; and other aid for the blind: 33,887

Publicity programs and other activities for the United Nations: 2,141

Who belongs to a businessmen's service club? Some answers to this question were obtained in 1957 by an independent market research organization that made a study of subscribers to *The Lions Magazine*. The data in Table 6 were obtained in personal interviews of a weighted sample of some 1,000 Lions. Lions clubs in the United States clearly represent the upper-middle economic and social level—the proprietors of small and medium-sized businesses and the managerial group. In this respect Lions are probably typical of the other businessmen's service club members (though not necessarily of chambers of commerce members). Their service, or welfare, activities are partially determined by their economic interests, as is manifest in their community-boosting projects. At the same time, however, their backgrounds as independent businessmen reinforce a political, social, and economic outlook that underlies the non-governmental, localized, and primarily charitable nature of their service work.

Optimist International

THESE ARE THE OBJECTIVES of the Optimists, one of the smaller men's service clubs: [35]

(1) To internationally develop Optimism as a philosophy of life.

(2) To promote an active interest in good government and civic affairs, to inspire respect for law, to promote patriotism and work for international accord and friendship among all people.

(3) To aid and encourage the development of youth throughout the world.

Like Kiwanians, Optimists are primarily concerned with youths; the Optimist slogan is "Friend of the Boy." The international aspects of

[35] *Symbol of Service: Optimist International*. St. Louis: Optimist International, 1958, p. 5 (booklet).

TABLE 6

BUSINESS AND PROFESSIONAL CHARACTERISTICS OF LIONS
CLUB MEMBERS, 1957

Business or Profession	Per Cent	
Industry		
Building, Contracting, and Engineering	13	
Manufacturing	11	
Transportation, Shipping, and Communications	5	
Mining and Chemicals	3	
Public Utilities	3	
Printing and Publishing	2	
		35%
Trade		
Retail Distribution	19	
Finance, Insurance, and Real Estate	15	
Wholesale Distribution	10	
		44
Professions		
Medical	5	
Teaching and School Administration	3	
Government	2	
Law	2	
		12
Agriculture	8	
Retired	1	
		9

Positions Held	Per Cent
Owner	32%
Partner	14
President	9
Vice President	6
Other Corporate Officers	13
Branch Manager or Department Head	22
Non-Executive Worker	3
Retired	1

Source: *Captive but not Caged: A Market Study of Lion Magazine Subscribers.* Chicago: The Lions Magazine (n.d.), pp. 3–7 (booklet).

Note: Totals do not necessarily add because of rounding.

the Optimist program are relatively unimportant; in mid-1958 there were about 1,600 Optimist clubs with 63,000 members, almost all of them in the United States. There were a very few others in Canada, Great Britain, and Australia.

Some typical year-round projects of Optimists (cf. Table 7) include Boys Club of America, Junior Optimist Clubs, Air Cadets, and others. Among short-term projects sponsored by local Optimist clubs are athletic programs, citizenship projects, and Christmas parties. More than a third of the expenditures for individual assistance went for scholarships, and $30,000 was used for Christmas gifts.

Funds for various boys' projects are raised through locally sponsored drives, which netted about $3.2 million in 1957. Fund-raising dances, carnivals, barbecues, and athletic events are the usual means of raising this money; they are supplemented by contributions from individual members. Optimists own and operate nine homes for boys. Included in the programs of many local Optimist clubs are camps, clubhouses, shops, and playgrounds. Through Big Brother organizations, juvenile courts, and clinics, counseling services are extended to young people. Although Optimist International has its unique aspects, it is generally

TABLE 7

Youth Services of Optimist International, 1957

Type of Activity	Number of Boys	Expenditures
Regular Projects (3,277 Clubs and Groups with Year-round Activities)	205,200	$1,058,000
Short-Term Projects	1,271,900	1,385,000
Individual Assistance	40,000	145,000
Contributions to Youth Agencies		406,000
Totals	1,517,100 [1]	$2,994,000

Source: *Symbol of Service: Optimist International*, p. 5.

[1] This figure probably includes some double counting.

typical of a number of smaller service organizations. These groups undertake community projects on a relatively small scale without being subjected to a great deal of publicity, yet in sum they contribute considerably to community welfare.

Chambers of Commerce

The following statement, or one similar to it, appears in the bylaws of each of the 2,500 chambers of commerce in the United States: "To promote the industrial, commercial, and civic welfare of the community." These chambers have over a million members, the leading business and professional men of their communities. Their objectives, however, are not identical with those of the members of service clubs. Chambers of commerce emphasize promotion of local business, planning for their communities, and a general overseeing of community activity. Such programs as local chambers undertake are seldom for the direct benefit of any particular underprivileged group, but rather are directed at improving the general welfare of the community and the welfare of its business elements in particular.

The Chamber of Commerce of the United States suggests eighteen types of activities to local chambers of commerce: [36]

Advertising and Publicity	Economic Understanding
Agriculture	Fire Prevention
Congressional Action	General Civic Activities
Convention Promotion	Health
Education	Housing
Industrial Development	Taxation
Information Service	Tourist Promotion
Recreation	Trade Promotion
Safety	Transportation

Some sample activities suggested under these headings are: conducting a survey of community hospital and clinical facilities; providing vocational counseling and part-time work for high school students; sponsoring agricultural fairs, athletic events, and traffic surveys; and developing policy and proposals on matters of government and legislative concern.

Examples from local chambers of commerce give substance to these suggestions. The Schools and Education Committee of the San Pedro, California, Chamber of Commerce organized counseling for more than 450 high school students; its Highways and Transportation Committee successfully lobbied for $8 million for local highway construction; and the Industrial Committee stated that its most important achievement had been to obtain the release of "San Pedro's greatest potential light manufacturing area . . . from government ownership to private." [37]

The Danbury, Connecticut, Chamber of Commerce "actively participated in the location of three new plants in the Danbury area," "helped to effect creation of the Danbury Parking Authority," "extended the Community Service Fund plan of charitable giving to eight companies," "prepared plans for a Loan Scholarship Fund," and "helped secure adoption of Town planning and zoning." [38]

Both San Pedro and Danbury have well under 100,000 residents; in a city such as Richmond, Virginia, with a population approaching a quarter million, Chamber of Commerce activities are more extensive. In 1957, they included the preparation and distribution of an extensive series of statistical studies of the business and economic life in Richmond; sponsoring and participating in dozens of area activities, includ-

[36] *Mesh the Gears with a Program of Work.* Washington, D.C.: Chamber of Commerce Service Department (n.d., booklet).
[37] *San Pedro: The Scenic City,* 1957–58 annual report of the San Pedro Chamber of Commerce.
[38] *The Year's Record: '58,* annual report of the Danbury Chamber of Commerce.

ing the Community Chest drive; and the successful promotion of municipal and State legislation.³⁹

The significance of local chambers of commerce is not that they include among their activities a few projects for the welfare of under-privileged groups. Their importance and their potential lies in the fact that they are one of the major sources of leadership in the community and that they are in a position to assume social responsibility for community welfare.

VETERANS' ORGANIZATIONS

NEARLY FOUR MILLION VETERANS of the two world wars and the Korean War have joined veterans' organizations. More than half of them have joined the American Legion, helping to make it one of the more powerful and influential non-governmental associations in the United States. Veterans have had different motives for joining veterans' organizations: a desire to perpetuate the comradeship experienced during military service; a desire to obtain the benefits they felt were due them because of their military service; and in some cases a desire to achieve through organization a peaceful society, military preparedness, or other ideals. In practice the veterans' organizations have become both effective pressure groups in obtaining government benefits for their members and a source of mutual assistance and community service.

The four largest veterans' organizations in the United States are the Legion, with close to two and three-quarter million members, plus one million members in its women's auxiliary; the Veterans of Foreign Wars of the United States (VFW), with 1,200,000 members and a ladies' auxiliary of 375,000; the Disabled American Veterans (DAV), 194,000 members; and the American Veterans of World War II and Korea (AMVETS), 125,000 members. The American Legion, although by far the largest of the four organizations, is not the oldest. The Legion was formally organized in 1919 by Lieutenant Colonel Theodore Roosevelt, Jr., and a number of other officers, meeting in Paris; the VFW was organized in 1899.

These four organizations, and three others, are chartered by act of Congress: the others are the Military Order of the Purple Heart, 9,000 members in 1958; the Marine Corps League, 10,000 members in 1958; and the United Spanish War Veterans, nearly 30,000 members in that year. There are also a number of unchartered veterans' organizations, such as the Jewish War Veterans, the National Association of Veterans'

³⁹ *Building for a Greater Richmond: Progress Report for 1957,* annual report of the Richmond Chamber of Commerce.

Employment Councils (NAVEC), Women World War Veterans, Catholic War Veterans of the U.S.A., and the Handicapped War Veterans' National Organization (HWV). Some of the latter have engaged in national or local fund-raising—the NAVEC for example. The AMVETS and the DAV have also conducted campaigns to raise funds for welfare programs for members. Their usual method has been to mail merchandise throughout the country, for which donations are requested; campaign expenses have been quite high. In 1955, 1956, and 1957, the DAV grossed $12.1 million through its campaigns, of which $9.9 million, about 82 per cent, went for campaign expenses. In about the same period the AMVETS and the commercial firms that have used AMVETS stationery (by arrangement with AMVETS) raised $8.9 million, 85 per cent of which was absorbed in the fund-raising.[40]

The American Legion is the only veterans' organization discussed in detail in this chapter. It has retained some of the aspects of the military command hierarchy in its organization. In the early 1950's the Legion had well over 17,000 local posts, organized in fifty-eight departments, all of them ultimately responsible to the National Headquarters at Indianapolis.[41] At the department level policies are established by elected delegates from the local posts. National policies are supposedly formulated by delegates from the departments, meeting in annual conventions, though in fact major policy decisions are most often made by the National Executive Committee, which meets twice a year, operating in close conjunction with the staff of the National Headquarters. There have been allegations that some of the policies laid down at the national level, and the publicity and lobbying activities that have been undertaken in the name of these policies, have been too far removed from the desires of the Legion rank and file.[42]

Two of the primary welfare interests of the Legion have been children's welfare and veterans' rehabilitation. On the Legion's national level many of these activities are directed by the Child Welfare Division and the Rehabilitation Division. There are many other phases of Legion interest, represented by the National Americanism Commission, the National Security Division, the Economic Commission, the Foreign Relations Commission, the National Legislative Division, and the Public Relations Division, among others.

[40] Ralph Lee Smith, "Waving the Flag and Passing the Hat." *The Reporter*, XIX (Oct. 2, 1958), pp. 33–36.
[41] *The American Legion: A Brief History*. Indianapolis: National Public Relations Division, The American Legion (n.d., booklet).
[42] For example, cf. Mark Duffield, *King Legion*, and Justin Gray, *The Inside Story of the Legion* (New York: Boni and Gaer, 1948). Both are critical, sometimes sharply so, of Legion policies and practices; the latter was written by a one-time staff member at the National Headquarters of the Legion.

Financial assistance and service for children was valued at $8.6 million in 1958 (cf. Table 8). Nearly 370,000 dependent children received direct aid and services; over 110,000 families received service work without financial aid. Most of this aid was given to the children and families of veterans, not necessarily veterans who were members of the Legion, however. "Among the 6,600,000 families which change residence every year, there are an estimated 1,000,000 veterans with 2,500,000 children," states a Legion publication. "Most of these moves are accomplished without need for outside help. But some families encounter emergencies . . . cutting them off from all the normal sources of help. These families account for a large portion of the direct help given by American Legion Posts and the National Child Welfare Division." [43]

TABLE 8

AID GIVEN CHILDREN BY THE AMERICAN LEGION AND ITS
AFFILIATES, 1958

Source	Expenditures (To Nearest Thousand)
Aid Granted by National Child Welfare Division	$ 58,000
Direct Aid from Posts for Food, Clothing, etc.[1]	809,000
Direct Aid from Legion Departments	185,000
Direct Aid from Auxiliary Units	1,054,000
Direct Aid from Auxiliary Departments	116,000
Contributions to Child Welfare Agencies by Legion Posts and Departments	794,000
Contributions to Child Welfare Agencies by Auxiliary Units and Departments	387,000
Other Child Welfare Expenditures by Legion and Auxiliary	3,070,000
Administrative Expenses, Legion and Auxiliary Departments (Assigned to Child Welfare)	93,000
Aid from 40 and 8 Voitures	1,746,000
Aid from 8 and 40 Salons	338,000
Total	$8,650,000

Source: *1958 Child Welfare Report*. Indianapolis: National Child Welfare Commission, The American Legion, 1958, pp. 10–11.

[1] This figure was compiled from reports from 45 per cent of all Legion posts. Other figures are more nearly complete.

In 1954 the Legion created the American Legion Child Welfare Foundation, which in its first four years built up assets of about $150,000 from unsolicited gifts. During the period, grants of $67,000 were made

[43] *After 40 Years: 40th Annual Report*. Indianapolis: The American Legion, 1958, p. 13.

to research projects in the fields of mental retardation, juvenile delinquency prevention, mental health, and related areas.[44]

The major programs of the National Americanism Division have also been directed toward children and young people. Each year the Division sponsors the National High School Oratorical Contest, with the purpose of "deepening understanding and appreciation of the Constitution." [45] The national winners receive scholarships. Many more young people are reached through Legion-sponsored Boy Scout troops and the American Legion Junior Baseball program. In 1958 there were 4,244 Boy Scout troops sponsored by posts and their auxiliaries, and under the latter program there were 18,000 teams at the close of the 1958 playing season.

In rehabilitation, as in other areas affecting veterans' welfare, the American Legion has a close working relation with the Veterans Administration (VA). The VA was organized in 1931 from all federal agencies dealing with veterans, largely at the instigation of the Legion, and the Legion has always attempted to keep a guiding hand on VA legislative and administrative policies, as it did with the predecessors of the VA. The National Rehabilitation Division of the Legion maintains a large staff to review veterans' cases and plead them before the VA, and thousands of Legion and Legion Auxiliary volunteers work in VA hospitals.

The primary source of funds for the national organization of the Legion is membership dues. Of each Legionnaire's annual dues, which may vary from place to place, $1.50 must be transmitted to National Headquarters. Half of this pays for the member's subscription to the *American Legion Magazine*, $.25 is allocated to the rehabilitation program, and $.50 meets the cost of other national programs.[46] Another source of income for both the rehabilitation and child welfare programs is the American Legion Endowment Fund Corporation, which held assets of some $7 million in 1957. Earnings in that year were $181,000, which were divided equally between the child welfare and rehabilitation programs.

The Legion has been criticized for its activities as a pressure group, which it has carried on both on behalf of veterans and for what the

[44] *Ibid.*, p. 28.
[45] *Ibid.*, p. 10.
[46] *Ibid.*, p. 27. In 1957, only $54,453 was actually allocated to rehabilitation, far less than would be expected on the basis of the stipulated distribution (income from dues was $921,000). About half a million dollars were being held in a reserve rehabilitation fund. Total assets of the American Legion National Headquarters at the end of 1957 were $6,791,000, exclusive of the Legion Endowment Fund Corporation and the Child Welfare Foundation funds. Assets included $2,667,000 in trust funds, other than those mentioned, $819,000 in real estate, and $695,000 in investments. (*Ibid.*, pp. 29–31.)

Legion has believed to be the welfare of the nation as a whole. (However, the constitution of the Legion prohibits it from supporting the candidacy of any person for government office.) The Economic and Rehabilitation commissions have been most concerned about achieving favorable legislation on behalf of veterans. The former commission was active in the mid-1950's in securing housing legislation favorable to veterans; it also has acted as an intermediary between Legionnaires and the federal government's Bureau of Employee Compensation and related agencies, as they affect veterans. Three other commissions of the Legion, Legislative, Foreign Relations, and National Defense, have either backed or opposed a number of proposed bills in Congress, not necessarily relevant to veterans. During 1957–58 the Legislative Commission and Division were made responsible for 336 resolutions relating to national legislation. Of these, 220 were adopted in national conventions, the others by the National Executive Committee. The Legion claimed that by June 11, 1958, 118 of these resolutions recommending national legislative action had been heeded, including those regarding adoption of a new military pay scale, asking a rejection of a provision in the postal rate increase bill that would have raised postal rates for publications of non-profit organizations, and pleading against any action to weaken the Immigration and Nationality Act.[47]

Legion claims to influence over legislative action affecting the national welfare bear more attention than similar claims by fraternal and service organizations. The Legion, as the largest veterans' organization, because of the social and economic groups it represents and because of the skills of its Washington representatives, has come to be accepted as the non-governmental authority on veterans' matters, and its weight is so felt in this sphere that it sometimes can bring influence to bear on other legislative issues. Staff members of the Legion's national divisions and commissions regularly appear before Congressional committees or file statements concerning proposed legislation with appropriate committees. Such statements usually receive an attentive hearing, for they can be and frequently are backed up with grass-roots support, in the form of resolutions and letters from Legion posts and departments directed to individual congressmen. Using more informal methods, Legion posts also make themselves felt as pressure groups in their communities. The practice and methods of influencing politics both locally and nationally are not unique with the Legion, of course. The Legion merely utilizes them more effectively than most other non-governmental associations.

[47] *Ibid.*, p. 20.

OTHER ORGANIZATIONS WITH FRATERNAL AND SERVICE CHARACTERISTICS

A NUMBER OF THE LARGER associations and societies listed in Table 1 of this chapter are not treated specifically in the foregoing discussion. Some of them closely resemble organizations described at length above. The Loyal Order of Moose is a fraternal order that has a number of programs for children. Among the organizations providing fraternal insurance are the Independent Order of Odd Fellows, the Modern Woodmen of America, the Knights of Pythias, the Supreme Forest Woodmen Circle, and the Improved Order of Red Men, all of which in this respect resemble the Eagles and the Knights of Columbus. Most of them, however, do not have other important welfare or service programs. Typical of this group are the Maccabees, a fraternal life insurance society with some 297,000 members in the United States and Canada (1958). In 1957 members of the society and their families were covered by life, sickness, accident, disability, and hospitalization policies with a value of $438 million. The society maintains several fully equipped homes for the aged as well, for its members.[48]

The Order of the King's Daughters and Sons is a religiously oriented organization of a fraternal nature whose objects are "the development of spiritual life and the stimulation of Christian activities." [49] The Order participates in community projects, usually on a small scale, and contributes to various charitable purposes. The Order also operates a few institutions. In the San Francisco Bay area the King's Daughters of California has conducted its own annual fund-raising campaign, provided financial support and volunteer workers for a non-governmental children's agency, and operates the King's Daughters Girls' Residence and the King's Daughters of California Home for Incurables.[50]

Finally, there are some associations performing welfare services that, strictly speaking, are neither service clubs nor fraternal orders, though they may partake of some of their characteristics. One of them, the Junior Leagues of America, is discussed in Chapter 5 as a national vocational association, though it equally well could have been discussed here. Among the others are the General Federation of Women's Clubs, the National Audubon Society, the International Federation of Catholic Alumnae, Alcoholics Anonymous, the P.E.O. Sisterhood, the League of Women Voters, and the National Urban League.

[48] *Mutual Aid in Time of Need.* Detroit: The Maccabees, 1958, pp. 3–4 (pamphlet).
[49] Mary Lowe Dickinson, *The Significance of the Order.* New York: International Order of the King's Daughters and Sons, 1956 (pamphlet).
[50] Bornet, *op. cit.*

Fraternal and Service Organizations

The largest of all associations listed in Table 1 is the General Federation of Women's Clubs, "a national and international organization comprising an over-all membership of approximately 11,000,000 in 55 countries, territories, and possessions, including 875,000 per capita members in 15,500 clubs and state, national, and international organizations affiliated with the General Federation." [51] The Federation, which is largely an advisory body for groups having programs of their own (including some women's groups cited elsewhere in this chapter), carries on its work through a number of departments, among which are departments on Community Affairs, Education, Conservation of Natural Resources, International Affairs, and Public Affairs.

The activities of the more than six thousand local groups of Alcoholics Anonymous are well-known; they offer every type of assistance to the sick alcoholic who asks for help. The League of Women Voters, with 126,000 members in all fifty States, is a non-partisan group that promotes active and informed citizen participation in government. Among its many activities are "the study of state and local administration and financing of education, public health, and welfare, including institutional and non-institutional care, public assistance, planning and housing." [52] The 75,000 members of the National Urban League promote interracial cooperation in improving Negro welfare and race relations, engaging in social research and planning, vocational guidance, community organization, and neighborhood activities.

The P.E.O. Sisterhood is an international women's organization primarily interested in furthering opportunities for higher education for women. The Sisterhood maintains an educational loan fund for girls; in 1958 more than two-thirds of the $900,000 fund was on loan. International Peace scholarships have been provided for foreign students wishing to study in the United States; about $70,000 was donated for this purpose by members in 1958. The most ambitious undertaking of the Sisterhood has been the establishment and operation of Cottey Junior College for Women, at Nevada, Missouri. The Sisterhood is the primary source of funds for the college, which receives contributions of at least one dollar annually from each of the 133,000 members of the society. Local chapters often provide scholarships, work in veterans' hospitals, and assist in carrying out community projects.[53]

[51] Russell H. Kurtz, ed. *Social Work Year Book 1957*. New York: National Association of Social Workers, 1957, p. 672.
[52] *Ibid.*, p. 676.
[53] Correspondence with Alice Spensley Rinehard, President, Supreme Chapter P.E.O. Sisterhood, September, 1958.

169

CONCLUDING REMARKS

VOLUNTARY ASSOCIATIONS ARE a widespread phenomenon in American society. This chapter touches only on some of the larger ones, and of these only the ones that are organized nationally and provide services of a welfare character for those other than their members as well as for their members. Taken as a whole, however, the welfare services of other associations are of considerable magnitude, though as individual instances they may attract little attention. In general, it can be said of voluntary associations that they provide an organizational context, a philosophy, and a tradition that greatly implement welfare activities. As established organizations they may be able to focus interest and effort on existing problems, and they can deal with larger problems than can the individual. At the same time they maintain a tradition of mutual assistance and service and can lend a personal quality to much of community welfare. Finally, they may provide a source of largely informal fellowship in communities that may have few other centers of informality and friendship, and through their national organizations they may foster a sense of national and sometimes international unity.

Chapter Eight

THE EDUCATIONAL SYSTEM

A

LTHOUGH AMERICAN SCHOOLS HAVE COME to be considered largely
as institutions for the general welfare of society, open to all who qualify
in terms of age and intelligence, they still provide welfare services for
special groups. American school systems not only provide education
for normal students; they have developed programs for the blind, the
retarded, and the gifted, among others, and have become the locus
of welfare activity not directly related to the educational process as
such, *e.g.*, school lunch programs, health programs, social casework, and
psychiatric counseling. This chapter describes briefly the organization
and welfare characteristics of governmental and non-governmental educational institutions in the United States.

PUBLIC ELEMENTARY AND SECONDARY SCHOOLS

PUBLIC ELEMENTARY and secondary schools—that is, governmental, tax-
supported schools—comprise the largest part of the educational system
of the United States. In October, 1959, there were 35.3 million students
enrolled in the public schools of the fifty States, including students at
the kindergarten, elementary, and secondary levels. This section discusses the administration and personnel, financing, and functions of the
public schools, with particular emphasis on services extended to young
people needing special attention. It also describes briefly the problems of
education for Negroes.

Administration and Personnel

THE FUNDAMENTAL ADMINISTRATIVE UNIT of the school system is the school district. Most school districts are organized as quasi-corporations that are actual local governments, under the jurisdiction of local boards of education. By contrast, a considerable number of school districts (about 2,500 in 1958) are instead administrative subdivisions of State, county, municipal, or township governments. The first type are called *independent*; the second, *dependent*. These districts, in varying degree from State to State, determine the location and size of schools, the kinds of educational programs and services offered, and the amount of financial support to be provided locally.

Most districts are directed by a superintendent, subject to the policy-making and supervisory authority of the local school board (which usually has between three and nine members). Dependent districts are under the authority of other government officials as well. The total number of independent districts in the United States has been dropping steadily—from 103,000 in 1945–46 to about 45,400 at the beginning of the 1959–60 school year.[1] Nevertheless most independent districts are still small. In 1953–54 forty States provided information on the number of students in their independent school districts, and in 46,000 independent districts reported, 55 per cent had fewer than twenty-five students in average daily attendance. Only 8 per cent had more than one thousand. On the average, dependent districts are several times as large.[2] By 1960, more than 20,000 school districts still had enrollments of fewer than fifty pupils each.

In most States local school board members are popularly elected; in a few they are appointed by any one of various government officials. In 1953–54 there were an estimated 230,000 school board members, most of them serving without salary.[3] In 1957 there were 189,000 elective school district officials, one per cent of whom were paid for full-time employment, 11 per cent for part-time employment. The others were unpaid.[4] In the mid-1950's there were also about 300,000 "non-instructional" employees of school districts; they included superintendents and their aides, attendance enforcement officers, and persons involved in school health and recreation, student transportation, the school lunch

[1] *The Book of the States 1960–1961.* Chicago: Council of State Governments, 1960, p. 286.
[2] "Statistics of State School Systems: Organization, Staff, Pupils, and Finances: 1953–54" (Chapter 2, *Biennial Survey of Education in the United States, 1952–54*). U.S. Office of Education. Washington, D.C.: USGPO, 1956, p. 4.
[3] *Ibid.,* p. 4.
[4] *Statistical Abstract of the United States 1960.* U.S. Bureau of the Census. Washington, D.C.: USGPO, 1960, p. 359.

program, and the operation and maintenance of the school plant.[5]

Instructional personnel, including principals and certain other staff members but excluding 87,000 emergency teachers, numbered about 1.3 million in 1956–57. Ninety-four per cent of them were classroom teachers. The number of instructional personnel has been rising steadily in the public schools and has been more than keeping pace with increased enrollment. The ratio between instructional staff and students declined slightly from 1 : 26.1 in 1949–50 to 1 : 25.6 in 1955–56. These statistics are somewhat misleading, however, since "instructional personnel" include principals and others who are not actually engaged in teaching. The average class size in all urban public school systems in November, 1957, was 30.1. A 1957 study by the National Education Association (NEA) showed that the median class size reported by public school teachers was 29.4. About 8 per cent of teachers had forty or more students; 16 per cent had nineteen or fewer students.[6]

Teachers have been increasing in number in the United States. In 1948 there were 823,000 certificated teachers in the public schools and in 1957 there were 1,242,000, an increase of more than 50 per cent. In 1956–57, 27 per cent of all degrees conferred in the United States were in education; between 1950 and 1957 education degrees increased by 33 per cent while degrees granted in all other academic fields declined 28 per cent.[7] By the Fall of 1959 there were 1,367,000 classroom teachers in public elementary and secondary schools.

In most States over-all policy for all public elementary and secondary schools in the State is set by a State board of education. In 1960 there were general boards in forty-seven States; the other three States had special-purpose boards. The number of board members ranged from three to twenty-one. Complementing the State boards are State departments of education, each headed by a chief State school officer, who may be either elected or appointed to his post depending on the State. These departments, found in each State, are the *operating* units of the State educational system. In 1953–54 they employed nearly 9,000 individuals, about 3,400 of whom were supervisory and professional staff members. In the same school year thirty States, particularly those with many small school districts, had administrative units coterminous with counties, for example intermediate between the State level and the district. These units have seldom been involved in direct operation of schools but have provided consultative, advisory, and statistical services, as well as regulating and inspecting local districts. Some of these

[5] "Statistics of State School Systems," p. 4.
[6] Roger A. Freeman. *Financing the Public Schools, Volume I: School Needs in the Decade Ahead.* Washington, D.C.: Institute for Social Science Research, 1958, pp. 34, 53, 77–80.
[7] *Ibid.*, pp. 57–64.

intermediate units provided health supervision, attendance service, and student transportation; about a third of them had policy-making boards of education.

Financing

IN 1953 expenditures for all public schools, elementary, secondary, and higher, in the United States were 3.42 per cent of the national income, a higher percentage than that in any other country except Japan (and perhaps the U.S.S.R., for which figures were not available). By 1958 expenditures had risen to 4.64 per cent of the national income, a total of $16.5 billion.[8] The expenditures by all levels of government on education were greater than any other category of government expenditure

TABLE 1

ELEMENTARY AND SECONDARY SCHOOL RECEIPTS FOR THE SCHOOL YEAR 1955–56

Type and Source	Amount	Per Cent
Revenue Receipts [1]		
Federal Government	$ 406,312,000	3.4%
State Governments	3,870,071,000	32.1
Intermediate Units	164,514,000	1.4
Local Governments	5,253,404,000	43.5
Non-revenue Receipts [2]	2,361,868,000	19.6
Totals	$12,056,169,000	100%

Source: Same as Table 2.

[1] Include income from taxes, appropriations, permanent funds, school land leases, etc.
[2] Include income from bond sales, loans, sale of property, and related transactions. These funds are devoted to capital outlay (construction) programs.

except national defense. In 1956, 40.4 per cent of all expenditures by all governments in the United States were for national defense and 14.2 per cent for education; next were interest on the national debt and highway expenditures, each slightly over 7 per cent.[9] In terms of *constant dollars*, public school expenditures nearly doubled between 1922 and 1946 although public school enrollment remained almost constant, doubled again between 1946 and 1950, doubled yet again between 1950 and 1956, and are still rising rapidly, whereas total enrollment between 1946 and 1956 increased by about a third.[10]

[8] Expenditures on non-public education (1958), at all levels, were about $3.9 billion, giving a grand total of $20.4 billion, 5.75 per cent of national income, spent for education.
[9] Freeman, *op. cit.*, pp. xxviii, 5, 7.
[10] *Ibid.*, p. 18.

With respect to public elementary and secondary schools alone, Tables 1 and 2 show the types and sources of their receipts, and their expenditures classified by purpose. These tables show that public elementary and secondary schools are supported almost entirely by State and local funds. There were major shifts in sources of school revenue between 1929 and the 1950's, however. Over that period the State government percentage more than doubled, local government sources fell about 30 per cent, and national government contributions increased tenfold.[11]

Schools also receive varying degrees of financial support from one State to another. In 1955–56 the average expenditure per student in the United States in public elementary and secondary schools was $294. In nine southern and southeastern States, however, the annual cost per student was less than $200, Mississippi spending the least, $158. (In the Commonwealth of Puerto Rico, the figure was $90.) The State of New York spent $426 per student, the highest of any State, and the then territory of Alaska spent $419. New Jersey, Delaware, Oregon, and Illinois all spent more than $350 per student.[12]

Public elementary and secondary schools receive some of their support from other than government sources. For example, local Parent-Teacher Associations (PTA's) furnish volunteer services for public schools, ranging from promoting school bond proposals to providing direct help to supplement the professional staff. In 1960 there were over 45,000 local PTA's in the United States and its territories, with eleven and a half million members; a similar organization, the National Congress of Colored Parents and Teachers, had 3,500 local groups and 200,000 members in the late 1950's. A distinct pattern of parent participation is evolving in many school districts, in the form of attempts to establish "parent-school teams." The principal of an elementary school in New Rochelle, New York, reported that in 1956–57 parents had provided his school with 2,700 hours of service, including "helping in the lunchroom serving milk, in the library typing and processing, on class trips, class parties and programs, helping with school traffic safety, working in health and welfare on Salk shots, check-ups and kindergarten registration, taking pre-school census, raising funds for school equipment and developing school organization." [13]

There are other sources of non-governmental assistance for public

[11] *Trends in Significant Facts on School Financing.* U.S. Office of Education, Washington, D.C.: USGPO, 1958, p. 24. These percentages are based on "current dollars" figures, *i.e.*, figures as reported for those years, not adjusted in terms of purchasing power or consumer price index.
[12] *Statistical Abstract* 1960, p. 120.
[13] "Education in Review: Part Parents and Citizens Should Play in School Affairs Is Outlined by Experts," *New York Times.* Sept. 15, 1957.

TABLE 2

PUBLIC ELEMENTARY AND SECONDARY SCHOOL EXPENDITURES,
FOR THE SCHOOL YEAR 1955–56

Purpose	Amount (est.)	Per Cent
CURRENT EXPENDITURES [1]		
Administration:		
Professional and Technical [2]	$ 164,000,000	1.4%
Clerical [2]	131,000,000	1.2
Supplies and Expenses	49,000,000	0.4
Instruction:		
Supervisors and Principals [2]	476,000,000	4.3
Teachers [2]	4,911,000,000	44.0
Clerks [2]	98,000,000	0.9
Books, Supplies, Expenses	353,000,000	3.2
Fixed Charges:		
Pension and Retirement Funds	312,000,000	2.8
Insurance, Rent, Taxes, etc.	115,000,000	1.0
Operation of Plant:		
Salaries, Wages [2]	484,000,000	4.3
Supplies, Fuel, Gas, Water, etc.	361,000,000	3.2
Maintenance of Plant:		
Grounds	66,000,000	0.6
Equipment, Other	255,000,000	2.3
Other School Services:		
Health Program (Medical, Dental, Nurse)	115,000,000	1.0
Transportation	172,000,000	1.5
Miscellaneous	131,000,000	1.2
Community Programs [3]	172,000,000	1.5
CAPITAL OUTLAY (NEW CONSTRUCTION)	2,581,000,000	23.1
DEBT SERVICE (INTEREST, ETC.)	209,000,000	1.9
Totals	$11,155,000,000	100% [4]

Sources: "Preliminary Statistics of State School Systems 1955–56" (Circular No.
508), U. S. Office of Education, Washington, D.C.: USGPO, 1957; *Current Expenditures Per Pupil in Public chool Systems: Small and Medium-Sized Cities, 1955–56*, U.S. Office of Education, Washington, D.C.: USGPO, 1957.

[1] These figures were derived from the average expenditure figures of school systems in 157 cities in the 10,000–25,000 population range. The expenditures of these school systems, by purpose, were given in percentages, and these percentages were applied to the known total "Current Pupil Expenditure" figure. As a result, some biases may have been introduced, but it is believed that most of these are insignificant. For example, transportation costs are higher in rural areas than in small cities, but lower in large urban areas. Expenditures for special services (health and counseling) are less in rural school systems than in small cities, as a rule, but higher in most large cities. Such differences would tend to cancel each other out.
[2] These are salary items. Other items also include salaries, but actual breakdowns are not available; e.g., the figure for the school health program is believed to be largely for salaries.
[3] Some public school systems provide public recreational facilities, public forums, summer schools, community colleges, adult education, and similar general services.
[4] Percentages do not add because of rounding.

176

schools. With increasing frequency, foundations and businessmen have been contributing to elementary and secondary schools. The following examples are somewhat exceptional, yet they may foreshadow future developments.

In 1956 the Fund for the Advancement of Education and the New York Fund for Children began a pilot project to provide volunteer workers for non-teaching duties in public schools, to relieve teachers of non-teaching duties, "to utilize the human resources of the community . . . and provide service for which adequate personnel is not available," and to develop greater understanding of the schools among citizens. Volunteer tasks have included clerical work—attendance reports, preparing teaching materials, and so forth—reading stories, going on class trips, and organizing libraries. During the first year of operation in a Manhattan school, sixty-two volunteers served under the program, working 176 days. Plans were made to include in the program "operation of audio-visual machines, handicrafts, library procedures, basic Spanish and the three R's." [14]

Monroe, Louisiana, is the site of an innovation in public secondary school teaching financed by industry. On three grants from the Forest Products Division of the Olin Mathieson Chemical Corporation, totaling $24,000, rigorous special courses in chemistry and physics were established at two high schools in the Monroe area. The classes were open to interested students who passed competitive examinations and were taught by carefully selected teachers obtained especially for the program.[15]

Functions

WITH RESPECT to their function of teaching the student in the average range, American public elementary and secondary schools have an enormously broad curriculum. Schools no longer offer simply the three R's. Today the schools give courses intended to prepare the student to enter college; courses designed to ready the student to earn his living upon graduation from high school; and courses whose asserted purpose is to help the student to adjust to problems he will encounter as an adult.

In the typical high school there are certain course requirements, such as three or four years of English, one year of mathematics, one year of science, and several years of social studies, including American

[14] "School Volunteers: Successful Effort to Relieve Overburdened Teachers," *New York Times,* June 30, 1957.
[15] "Olin Mathieson Provides Funds for Class at Louisiana School," *New York Times,* Aug. 24, 1958.

history.[16] Beyond this the student is usually free to choose among "electives," including academic courses such as sciences, languages, history, and so forth, as well as driver education, woodworking and metalworking, buying, typing, bookkeeping, home economics, music, and art.

Apart from teaching the schools provide a host of special services, whose range is suggested by the 1953–54 personnel statistics in Table 3. Teachers themselves engage in a great deal of non-teaching activity both in the classroom and out of it. They may lead recreation programs, be expected to participate in projects of the PTA and other civic groups, and act as advisers of student groups.

TABLE 3

SELECTED NON-TEACHING PERSONNEL IN PUBLIC ELEMENTARY AND SECONDARY SCHOOLS, 1953–54 [1]

Type of Personnel	Number of States Reporting [1]	Number Employed [2]	Average Per State
Guidance Personnel	24	4,684	195
Psychological Personnel	8	563	70
Physicians and Psychiatrists [3]	26	4,654	179
Dentists [3]	20	1,663	83
Nurses [3]	33	9,048	274
Other Professional and Technical Health Personnel [3]	7	130	19
Recreation Personnel	14	3,747	268
Food Services Personnel [3]	27	49,443	1,831
Attendance Officers and Home School Counselors [3]	25	4,167	167

Source: "Statistics of State School Systems: Organization, Staff, Pupils, and Finances 1953–54" (Chapter 2, *Biennial Survey of Education in the United States, 1952–54*). U.S. Office of Education. Washington, D.C.: USGPO, 1956, pp. 42–49.

[1] Many States, in some cases most States, have not maintained separate statistics for these various categories.
[2] Some of these figures include both part-time and full-time personnel. The only categories in which part-time personnel outnumber full-time personnel are physicians and psychiatrists, dentists, and recreation personnel.
[3] As a rule, these personnel are employed by school districts, rather than by individual schools, and in many cases serve more than one school.

Most special services are designed for students outside the normal range. These services fall into two categories: those that directly pertain to education, and those that in large part are unrelated to the teach-

[16] *The Pursuit of Excellence: Education and the Future of America, Panel Report V of the Special Studies Project* (the "Rockefeller Report"). New York: Doubleday, 1958, p. 26.

ing function. In the first group are education for the "exceptional child" —the blind, the deaf, the handicapped, the retarded, the gifted. In the second group are health programs, subsistence programs (notably the school lunch program), school social work, and psychological counseling and guidance.

SPECIAL EDUCATION: Some though by no means all public schools have programs for one or more of eight groups of exceptional children. The children in seven of these groups have characteristics that are socially defined as non-desirable: they are the visually handicapped, the deaf and hard-of-hearing, the speech handicapped, the crippled, those with special health problems, the socially maladjusted, and the mentally retarded. A relatively small but growing interest has been expressed in special education for an eighth group, the gifted children. Some of the available statistics on education for exceptional children are given in Table 4.

TABLE 4

SPECIAL SCHOOLS AND CLASSES FOR EXCEPTIONAL CHILDREN, 1953 [1]

GROUP	STATES REPORTING	PLACES REPORTING	TEACHERS	ENROLLMENT Elem.	Second
Speech-Defective	49	1,087	2,256	254,179	52,568
Mentally Retarded	48	1,244	7,067	84,878	28,687
Crippled	45	596	1,498	15,924	1,889
Hard-of-Hearing	46	497	480	9,680	2,252
Special Health Problems [2]	40	330	868	10,166	1,289
Partially Seeing	39	408	647	6,544	1,470
Deaf	34	185	479	3,446	489
Blind	19	67	95	658	181
Mentally Gifted [3]	15	27	926	3,683	19,233
Totals	49 [4]	1,785 [5]	14,316 [6]	389,158	108,058

Source: *Statistical Abstract* 1960, p. 130.

[1] Covers public elementary and secondary day schools. Excludes data for truant, delinquent, and maladjusted children; and exceptional children in residential schools.
[2] Includes epileptic children, children with "delicate" health, etc.
[3] Since 1953, special attention for this group is believed to have grown more than for any other group listed.
[4] Includes District of Columbia.
[5] Total number of places reporting one or more special programs.
[6] Includes both full-time and part-time teachers.

In 1953 nearly half a million students in public elementary and secondary schools were benefiting from special education programs; they were taught by more than 14,000 teachers. Attention to all groups of exceptional children has increased since 1953, most especially to mentally gifted children.

The teaching approaches to exceptional children vary considerably. Classes utilizing special equipment and taught by teachers with specialized training may be set up for them; in some large cities, separate public schools have been established for exceptional children. Such programs may be sponsored by the State as they are in Massachusetts, which has a State-subsidized special-class program for the mentally retarded. In June, 1956, there were 600 such classes in 131 communities in the State, enrolling over 8,000 children who were being taught by nearly 600 special teachers. In other school systems throughout the country some exceptional children attend regular classes and only occasionally are provided with special instruction or equipment. Finally there are special programs not included in Table 4: for example, special schools for the socially maladjusted and for young people who present disciplinary problems, which have been established in some cities, among them New York; and special programs for children who must remain at home or in hospitals, in a few areas.

SCHOOL SOCIAL SERVICES: Concern for the emotional and social adjustment and physical well-being of the child has made the school social services a rapidly growing sphere of school activity. Schools may provide their students with dental and medical examinations, some medical treatment, social casework, psychiatric counseling, vocational guidance, transportation, subsidized hot lunches, social clubs, and after-school and weekend recreation. A few schools have provided shoes and clothing for their students. Mrs. Katherine Oettinger, Chief of the U.S. Children's Bureau, said late in 1958 that she was working with the Commissioner of Education to develop a combined service to help the unmarried mother in the school system.[17]

The following statement, written for a high school audience, describes some of these school services:

Good schools . . . provide a remarkable range of personal service. From the time you enter the first grade the check-ups begin: Hearing, eyesight, teeth, general health, intelligence, etc. Your chassis isn't standardized, so the school finds plenty to be done for you.

If your eyesight is poor you go into special sight-saving classes. If your hearing is deficient special teachers take over. For the crippled there are special exercises and sometimes special schools. Those slow to read receive attention from reading experts. Programs of instruction adjust learning to *your* rate of progress. . . .

[17] "More Aid Is Urged for Child Mother," *New York Times*, Oct. 19, 1958.

Consider what modern schools do for students: Clubs and committees help the shy to lose their shyness. Speech classes, discussions, and student government teach you to speak on your feet. Sports, physical education, and dancing help the awkward. In general shop, homemaking, art, music, and other activities, students discover what they can do best. In vocational and business education they can turn their aptitudes into skills which pave the way to jobs. In family living and other courses and activities boys and girls learn lessons in personal living: how to budget, how to buy intelligently, how to groom oneself and dress attractively, how to decorate a home, feed a husband, and care for a baby.

While you count the blessings modern education affords you, add these if they come your way: Transportation to and from school in a bus; a nutritious lunch at low cost; a free library service; free textbooks and supplies; enjoyable recreation; newspaper and yearbook, and a personal counseling service.[18]

Health care is the oldest of the school health and welfare programs. Originally intended primarily as a protective service to prevent the spread of infectious diseases among school children, it is today based on the principle that every child is entitled to periodic physical examinations. In some school districts health care is advocated on the grounds that underprivileged children need medical care, to which ordinarily they have no access, and that the schools are an efficient medium for reaching them. There is great diversity among school health programs. There are variations in the distribution of responsibilities between the local school system and local health authorities, the responsibilities assumed for children under the care of private physicians, the extent of treatment provided, and the quality and frequency of student health examinations.[19]

Statistics on school health services are incomplete. The most recent comprehensive study of physicians and nurses in elementary schools was made in 1946, and indicated that there were forty-four physicians and sixty-five nurses per 100,000 public elementary school children. Most of the physicians and nearly two-thirds of the nurses were part-time. A 1955 Public Health Service report stated that 7,730 nurses were employed by school boards, the great majority of them full-time employees. Furthermore, nurses employed by non-school health agencies also serve school children in some districts.[20] The physicians are primarily involved

[18] "Our American Schools," *Senior Scholastic*, LIX (Nov. 7, 1951), part 2, p. 7, cited in Sturges F. Cary, *New Challenges to Our Schools*, New York: Wilson, 1953, pp. 28–29. Copyright 1951 by Scholastic Magazines Inc. Reprinted by permission.
[19] *School Health Services: A Selective Review of Evaluative Studies*. U.S. Children's Bureau. Washington, D.C.: Social Security Administration, 1957, p. v.
[20] *Ibid.*, pp. 26–30.

in examination of children; whether they provide treatment (and the extent of that treatment) depends on local or State policy. They frequently make referrals to family physicians or to local health agencies. In addition to providing first aid the school nurse is held to function as "interpreter to the school staff of health information about specific children and liaison between school and community health resources." [21]

Expenditures for school health programs have not been great in comparison with total school expenditures. The average expenditure per student in the school health programs of cities in the 10,000–25,000 population range was $2.42 in 1955–56, about one per cent of the average total expenditure per student of $251. This $2.42 was distributed among nursing, medical, and dental programs in a ratio of about 2:1:1.[22] If this average held for all the 31.5 million public school students enrolled in 1955–56, it represented a total investment of about $80 million in the health of American children.

The child's mental health not only is the concern of the teaching and recreation staff, but receives the attention of psychiatrists, psychologists, psychometrists, and counselors. One prominent authority on mental health services has stated:

> Mental health suffers more than any other aspect of health from lack of support, for it must be considered in the whole of the school's work. In fact, mental health and education are so inseparable as often to be considered one and the same. Mental hygienists, including educators, are concerned with this one objective—to develop potentialities of the child for meeting life's situations satisfactorily. . . .
>
> Since mental health is the goal of education, there is no one aspect of education which can be properly termed the mental health aspect.[23]

School districts may hire psychiatrists either full- or part-time, sometimes to help children, sometimes to advise parents or teachers. In a few cities the board of education maintains a child guidance clinic, but with increasing frequency schools are using the services of community psychiatric clinics. Psychological testing is widely used in the public schools; IQ, comprehension, reading speed, manipulative skills, personality, and social adjustment may be tested, and results are usually made available to the teaching staff.

[21] Florence Poole, "School Social Services," in Russell H. Kurtz, ed., Social Work Year Book 1957, New York: National Association of Social Workers, 1957, p. 505.
[22] Current Expenditures Per Pupil in Public School Systems: Small and Medium-Sized Cities, 1955–56. U.S. Office of Education. Washington, D.C.: USGPO, 1957, pp. 6, 15.
[23] George S. Stevenson. Mental Health Planning for Social Action. New York: McGraw-Hill, 1956, pp. 237–38.

If a public school student's problems seem to originate outside the school, particularly in his family, another specialist may be called in: the school social worker, who first appeared on the educational scene in 1906 as the "visiting teacher." A statement of his or her functions appears in the 1957 *Social Work Year Book*:

> The school social worker, as a member of the school staff, is identified with the school's aims and purposes and works within the school's regulations and authority. Teachers and other school personnel seek from the social worker help with those children who show problems of maladjustment. . . . The causes for these problems may be many. They may be related to financial, emotional, or social problems or a combination of these which affect both the child and his family.
>
> The social worker offers individual casework help to the child and to his family. If there is need for other specialized service, the social worker interprets the services of community resources and assists the parents in making an application for them. In all of his work with children and parents, the school social worker maintains a close working relationship with the teacher, the principal, and other specialized services in the school, helping to integrate the contribution of all the services for the benefit of the child.[24]

School social work, despite its relatively long history, has only recently entered a period of rapid growth. By 1956, in seven States school social work was carried out on a State-wide basis. The program in Illinois in that year employed about 160 social workers in over 100 school districts. The School Social Work Section of the National Association of Social Workers had over 1,000 members in 1959, one index of the extent of school social work in the United States.[25]

Another group of school programs provides subsistence for school children. The most important of these is the school lunch program, which is partially subsidized by the national government in the form of cash grants and donations of surplus food. In 1959, 26.2 million children in public and non-public schools participated in these school lunch programs, nearly two-thirds of all children in elementary and secondary schools. To one group of participating schools the national government distributed 453 million pounds of food, valued at about $110 million dollars. To another group of schools $94 million was distributed in reimbursement for local purchases of food. In addition about two million half-pints of milk were distributed to various schools, at a cost of about $74 million.

[24] Poole, *op. cit.*, pp. 511–12.
[25] *Ibid.*, pp. 509–12.

The federal program is administered by the Department of Agriculture, acting in most cases through State educational agencies. The States are required to match the federal contribution in a ratio of 1:3; in 1958 the national government expenditures under the program were $241 million, State and local contributions $84 million. In 1955 the Department of Agriculture also made direct cash payments to non-profit private schools in twenty-seven States in which legal barriers prevented a State agency from doing so. Some of the complexity of the lunch program is indicated by the following description of the program in San Francisco:

> The San Francisco Unified School district in 1954–55 expended $22,000 for free lunches to 450 children on each of the 177 school days, receiving $3,186 in subsidy. In addition, $45,276 was received as subsidy for the "best quality" lunch purchased by "the other children" in the schools, since a daily average of 8,400 children purchased that lunch. In addition, the federal government made available 6,475 cases of surplus food products, fair market value of $82,313, charging the district only $6,475.
> The supplying of free and part-pay milk is another service in which the federal government plays a part. Under the Agricultural Act of 1954, in an effort to encourage the consumption of whole milk by children, the federal government subsidized the San Francisco district with $27,290. The District used this to increase individual servings of milk to every child from the ½ pint being purchased to ⅓ of a quart, not increasing the price. Another milk program is that of the city's Board of Health, which supplied 148,237 bottles of mid-morning milk free to 925 elementary school children in 1954–55, at a cost of $6,000, distribution being on the certifications of school nurses that a child was undernourished. A private organization with no paid staff, Saints and Sinners, furnished 4,800 children with 766,114 bottles of milk by paying the District $45,967 in 1954–55, these children being certified as in "economic need" by school principals.[26]

Even in public schools having lunch programs that are subsidized from several sources, however, the parents of most children make some contribution; on the average they pay about half the cost of a given meal.

Some school systems provide children with shoes and clothing. The superintendent of the Washington, D.C., public school reported that in 1957–58 the schools received approximately 700 requests a month for clothing and 650 a month for shoes, from school personnel concerned about the well-being of some of their students. Of the schools

[26] Vaughn D. Bornet. *California Social Welfare*. Englewood Cliffs, N.J.: Prentice-Hall, 1956, p. 265. Copyright 1956 by Commonwealth Club of California, San Francisco, California.

in the district 113 had received such requests, and he estimated that at least 1,300 school children had missed varying periods of school because they lacked shoes or clothes. Requests were handled by school officials, ranging from principals to nurses, and referred to welfare agencies when the schools could not meet the demand.[27]

There are some school programs such as vocational guidance and recreation that should be termed special services yet that may have value for any student. Vocational guidance shares with the mental health program the intent of helping the child to adjust to himself and to his social environment. The psychological services of the mental health program are intended to smooth the student's adjustment to the school pattern, however, whereas vocational guidance is provided primarily on the secondary level to help the high school student relate his education to some future occupation. Guidance actually begins in the elementary grades, where the curriculum contains information about various careers. In secondary schools practice varies. Special full-time counselors may be provided and all students may be required to visit these counselors at least once during their three or four years in high school. Often there is special testing in connection with the guidance program, and in some areas there are cooperative arrangements with State employment services. Some schools having no full-time counselors may require teachers to devote some of their time to guidance; special classes dealing with occupational opportunities may be provided and sometimes required. In other secondary schools speakers on various occupations are brought to the schools to talk to student groups as a regular part of the academic program. In a few schools having elaborate vocational guidance systems, the school system or the school itself operates a placement service.[28]

Growing emphasis has been placed on recreation in the public schools. Compulsory physical education courses tend more and more to include recreational activities, *e.g.*, swimming, dancing, skiing, and camping. There has also been increasing interest in providing recreation for the public. In a number of communities, school facilities have been turned over to recreational purposes after school hours for the benefit of adults, children, or both. Another contributing factor to the growth of school recreation programs has been that in many urban areas public authorities have turned to the school system to provide a solution for the juvenile delinquency problem. The presumption has been that youths who were furnished recreational facilities would not become delinquent.

[27] "Lack of Shoes Blamed for 1300 Cutting Schools," *Washington Post*, July 18, 1958.
[28] Poole, *op. cit.*, pp. 508–509.

The school board of New York City has developed extensive after-school and summer recreation programs under the direction of its Division of Community Education. During the 1957–58 school year, 374 of the 900 school buildings in the city were kept open in the afternoons and evenings to provide recreation and adult education programs. During the summer of 1957 the board operated 443 summer playgrounds, forty-three swimming pools, and thirty-one athletic fields; at that time the president of the school board proposed that the schools remain open seven days a week throughout the year to provide supervised recreation.[29] In 1958 the school board announced that it intended to increase its special projects "to raise the cultural horizons and educational performances of underprivileged youngsters," particularly in predominately Negro areas. The program included "not only intensive counseling and guidance and specialized school programs, but enrichment activities, such as visits to concerts, operas, museums, and colleges, that are designed to offset the cultural deprivation experienced by the students." [30]

Another development in recreation is the school camp program. In Michigan, for example, in the early 1950's there were some fifty elementary and secondary schools providing some camping experience as part of their programs. This "education in the out-of-doors" sometimes involved occasional trips, sometimes camping periods of one or more weeks for students and their teachers. The longer camping periods gave students an opportunity "to participate in direct learning experiences that cannot be carried on in the classroom. The instruction is provided by boards of education, and the cost of maintenance is assumed by the home." Most of the school camping in Michigan was done on school time.[31]

Negroes and Public Education

ADEQUATE, NON-DISCRIMINATORY EDUCATION for Negro Americans is perhaps the most serious welfare problem, in the broadest sense of the word, facing public education in the United States. When the Supreme Court in May, 1954, ruled that segregated public education was no longer constitutional, seventeen southern and border States had 8.3 million white children in one set of schools and 2.4 million Negro children in another. In 1960 the enrollment of white children was 9.9 million and Negro enrollment was slightly over three million; only 181,000 Negroes, 6 per cent of the total, were actually enrolled in integrated elementary and

[29] "Wider Play Role Urged on Schools," New York Times, July 17, 1957.
[30] "School Projects to Aid Deprived," New York Times, Sept. 30, 1958.
[31] Julian W. Smith, "Community-School Camping—a New Frontier in Education," School Activities, XXI (April, 1950), pp. 254–55, cited in Cary, op. cit., pp. 35–36.

secondary schools. Almost all the Negro children in integrated schools were in the District of Columbia and the six border States of West Virginia, Delaware, Missouri, Kentucky, Oklahoma, and Maryland. A total of 4,200 Negro children were in schools with white children in the States of Texas (3,300), Florida (512), Tennessee (169), Arkansas (98), Virginia (103), and North Carolina (34). There was not a single integrated public school in Alabama, Georgia, Louisiana, Mississippi, or South Carolina, though these States had 1.4 million Negro students.

School segregation is a welfare problem in several respects. For the Negro it is one more mark of his status as a "second-class citizen," and a particularly painful and depressing one. It is not only evidence of an invidious social distinction but also the first of many barriers that keep the young Negro from full participation in the life of the larger community. A more immediate aspect of school segregation is that it generally means poorer quality education, especially for the Negro but also to some extent for white students. In the southern States in general, less is spent per student than elsewhere in the nation, and within most southern States less is spent per Negro student than per white student. In four States in 1956–57 expenditures for Negro instruction fell below 90 cents for every white student's dollar: Mississippi (63 cents), Arkansas (75), South Carolina (77) and Louisiana (79). Even in southern States where per-student expenditures approach equality, counties must bear the expense of maintaining two sets of facilities and personnel, which means that, for money spent, neither Negro children nor white have as good an educational system as they would with a single socially and administratively integrated system.[32]

Segregation has still other welfare aspects. In the southern States generally, thanks to the lack of adequate education, a large segment of the population cannot develop its skills to their fullest, which means fewer scientists, educators, physicians, technicians, and administrators both for the South and for the nation as a whole. Nor can the anguish— and perhaps guilt—felt by southern whites in their attempts to prevent integration be discounted in considering the welfare consequences of segregation.

PRIVATE ELEMENTARY AND SECONDARY SCHOOLS

PRIVATE ELEMENTARY and secondary schools—that is, non-governmental schools that receive little if any support from taxes—constitute an

[32] "Negro Education in the United States," *Harvard Educational Review*, XXX (Summer, 1960), pp. 177–305, especially Marvin Wall's article, "Events in Southern Education Since 1954" (pp. 209–15).

important and growing part of the educational system of the United States. Private schools are subject to State regulatory controls of various kinds, but are under the immediate operational control of a private individual or organization. They may be church-related or non-sectarian; they may be operated for profit or as non-profit institutions.

Enrollment in private elementary and secondary schools has been increasing more rapidly than public school enrollment. In October, 1959, 6.1 million students, 15 per cent of all elementary and secondary school enrollment, were in private schools. Between 1940 and 1956 private school enrollment increased by nearly 90 per cent but public school enrollment increased only 22 per cent, i.e., private schools grew four times as rapidly as public schools. Private school enrollment accelerated even more rapidly from 1956 to 1957; of the increase in enrollment between the two school years, 42 per cent went to the private schools. The rate of increase slackened between 1957 and 1959, however; it also should be noted that the largest proportional increase in private school enrollment during the 1950's was at the kindergarten level, which is included in most data on public and private elementary schools.

There were 12,500 private elementary schools in 1956, excluding kindergartens, and 3,900 private secondary schools. (By comparison, there were 105,000 public elementary and 26,000 public secondary schools.) The instructional staff of all the private schools in 1956 numbered about 145,000.

There is no comprehensive information on the financing of private elementary and secondary schools, but their fiscal operations are known to be of two somewhat distinct types. The Roman Catholic schools have relatively low operating costs, partly because their teaching staffs are usually comprised of members of religious orders who are not salaried in the ordinary sense of the word. Most operating costs thus can be met from student tuition fees. New facilities generally are financed by contributions directly from parishioners and from general church funds. Private kindergartens also subsist largely on tuition fees. Other secular private schools, by contrast, resemble private colleges and universities in their fiscal operations. Tuition payments meet only part of their operating expenses; for other operating expenses and new construction they generally must rely on philanthropic contributions and endowment income. In 1957–58, 117 such independent schools reported gifts of $22.4 million, and thirty-nine of the same schools received an additional $24.4 million in capital fund drives. In 1959 the National Council of Independent Schools reported that 65 per cent of 364 schools it contacted had annual alumni giving programs. Corporations increasingly are contributing to secular private schools, and the

Council for Independent School Aid reported in 1959 that 123 such schools had joined in establishing nine metropolitan or State-wide funds for cooperative solicitation from business and industry.[33] The private elementary and secondary schools operated by religious groups other than the Roman Catholic Church may follow either fiscal pattern; generally they receive substantial support from both sponsoring church groups and philanthropic individuals.

Why do parents send their children to private schools? It is generally not immediately financially advantageous, for these parents must pay their share of public school taxes plus tuition fees for their own children. The primary motive is a religious one. In 1953–54 over 80 per cent of the private school enrollment was in denominational schools, usually Roman Catholic. There are other motives that may be relevant, however, even in denominational school attendance. Group pressures, especially in Catholic circles, may impel parochial school attendance. Private school attendance may be a mark of social status, as a means either of attaining it or of maintaining it. Also some parents wish to shield their children from association with children of certain racial and religious groups. For some parents it is merely a matter of convenience or a way of rejecting family responsibility to send a child to a private boarding school. One other frequent reason for private school attendance involves academic standards: that is, some private schools offer better education than many public schools, especially in preparing students to enter college.

Roman Catholic elementary and secondary schools enrolled an estimated 4,900,000 students in 1959, about 80 per cent of total private school enrollment.[34] There were about 400,000 students in 4,800 church-related schools of other religious denominations, notably Lutheran, Protestant Episcopal, and Seventh-Day Adventist schools, and including the 42,700 students in Jewish all-day schools in 1959. There were an estimated 800,000 students in non-sectarian private schools.[35] There are great differences in private school enrollment among the States. In Georgia and the Carolinas, in 1953–54, less than 2 per cent of school enrollment was in private schools, whereas in eight States more than 20 per cent was in private schools. These States, in order of increasing percentage of private school enrollment, were Pennsylvania, Illinois, New Jersey, Massachusetts, Wisconsin, New York, New Hampshire, and

[33] *Giving USA 1960.* New York: American Association of Fund-Raising Counsel, 1960, pp. 14–15.
[34] Rev. F. A. Foy, O.F.M., ed. *The 1960 National Catholic Almanac.* Paterson, N.J.: St. Anthony's Guild, 1960, p. 496.
[35] Benson Landis, ed. *Yearbook of American Churches for 1960.* New York: National Council of the Churches of Christ in the U.S.A., 1959, p. 283.

Rhode Island. In Rhode Island, private school enrollment was nearly 30 per cent.[36]

There are other private schools of less than college grade, usually operated for profit, that can be considered neither elementary nor secondary; rather, they offer special training. They include business colleges, commercial schools, and secretarial schools; schools of art, design, drafting, interior decorating, beauty culture, and cosmetology; broadcasting and dramatic schools; trade, industrial, and vocational schools; and jewelry and watch-repairing schools, among others. It has been estimated that in 1956–57 there were half a million students enrolled in private commercial schools alone, which suggests that enrollment in all private vocational schools may total several millions.[37]

In every State the private schools are in some way responsible to the State government. They are subject to a variety of State regulations and often are recipients of State assistance. At the same time the private schools have by law and practice certain fundamental rights. The outlines of State-private school relations were stated in the United States Supreme Court decision that found the Oregon Compulsory Education Act unconstitutional (1925).

> The fundamental theory of liberty upon which all governments in this Union repose excluded any general power of the State to standardize its children by forcing them to accept instruction from public teachers only. The child is not the mere creature of the State; those who nurture him and direct his destiny have the right, coupled with the high duty, to recognize and prepare him for additional obligations.
>
> No question is raised concerning the power of the State reasonably to regulate all schools, to inspect, supervise and examine them, their teachers and pupils; to require that all children of proper age attend some school, that teachers shall be of good moral character and patriotic disposition, that certain studies plainly essential to good citizenship must be taught, and that nothing be taught which is manifestly inimical to the public welfare.[38]

The most general regulations affecting the private schools are the laws that apply to general business and charitable activities. Schools operated for profit are subject to business regulations; non-profit schools, as all non-profit organizations, are also subject to general laws. Aside from general regulations there are at least six classes of legislation that apply explicity to private schools *as educational institutions*. There may

[36] *The State and Nonpublic Schools.* U.S. Office of Education. Washington, D.C.: USGPO, 1957, p. 2.
[37] *Ibid.*, p. 5.
[38] *Pierce v. Hill Military Academy* and *Pierce v. Society of Sisters. United States Reports*, Vol. 269, pp. 534–35.

be laws pertaining to the incorporation of private schools. A State agency such as the State board of education may be required or allowed to evaluate and approve (or disapprove) the educational program, facilities, and/or faculty of a private school. Third, State compulsory education legislation may make explicit provisions for private schools, and require that certain subjects be taught. Tax exemptions are granted by law to certain private schools in every State, particularly to non-profit schools. Fifth, the various State governments require the licensing of at least eighty occupations, and through this requirement the State licensing boards exert formal and informal controls over private voca-tional schools; they may be required to approve such schools, for example.[39]

Finally, State legislation may be concerned with governmental sup-port for private schools. Such support has taken many forms and is quite widespread. In sixteen States (1957) there was statutory au-thority permitting tax-supported transportation for children attending private schools. In New Hampshire, New York, Pennsylvania, and Rhode Island the law provides for the physical examination of children attending private schools.[40] In Connecticut there is no such State leg-islation, yet in thirty-six public school districts in 1957 health services were being provided to private school students, and in twenty-eight towns and cities tax-supported transportation was being supplied, all of these services being provided by rulings of town councils and local boards of education.[41]

In some southern States textbooks are provided to students at private schools out of tax funds, although the schools receiving use of these textbooks must submit to specific State regulations. In a number of States departments of education are authorized to allocate school-lunch funds and food to non-profit private schools. Some State governments make payments to private schools for certain services. The most fre-quent arrangement is for a government body to contract with a private school to provide instruction or care for exceptional children for whom public facilities are not available. In a few States private schools, mainly at the college level, request and receive financial assistance from the State legislature.[42]

The total extent of State regulation of private schools suggests one important conclusion: whatever special benefits the private school stu-dent may receive, such as religious instruction and intensive or spe-cialized education, he has the opportunity to receive at least as good

---

[39] *The State and Nonpublic Schools*, pp. 10–13, 25.
[40] *Ibid.*, p. 27.
[41] "Stamford Raises School Aid Query," *New York Times*, July 4, 1957.
[42] *The State and Nonpublic Schools*, pp. 12, 27–28.

an education as that provided by the public school system. This is the specific intent of much State legislation regulating the private schools.

HIGHER EDUCATION

THE HIGHLY DIVERSE colleges and universities of the United States are relevant to a discussion of welfare in a number of respects. Their most general contribution to welfare is to provide young men and women with the knowledge and skills to live satisfying, productive lives. In addition the study and research of their faculty members and graduate students are the major sources of new knowledge in American society. They may also provide specific community services, and usually provide special assistance to at least some of their students, through scholarships and fellowships for example.

TABLE 5

STUDENTS IN INSTITUTIONS OF HIGHER EDUCATION, 1959

Type of Institution	Number of Students
Universities	1,465,000
Liberal Arts Colleges	966,000
Independent Professional Schools:	
Teachers Colleges	352,000
Technological Schools	104,000
Theological Schools	42,000
Other	62,000
Junior Colleges	411,000
Total	3,402,000

Source: *Opening Enrollment in Higher Educational Institutions, Fall.* U.S. Office of Education. Washington, D.C.: USGPO, 1959.

Students, Faculty, and Administration

IN 1959 there were about 2,010 institutions of higher education in the United States. More than 3.4 million students were in attendance, nearly two-thirds of them men, and they were being instructed by more than 300,000 faculty members. The number of students by type of institution is given in Table 5. In Fall, 1960, total enrollment was estimated at 3,980,000, including both students working for degrees and non-degree-credit students.

On the basis of 1956 data, 56 per cent of the students were attending publicly controlled institutions; the others were in privately controlled institutions.[43] About 52 per cent of faculty members were teaching in publicly controlled colleges and universities in 1954.[44]

There are four State bodies or authorities involved in the administration of most publicly controlled institutions of higher education: the legislatures, the governors, central State administrative agencies, and the boards that directly govern the State institutions. (There are a few publicly controlled institutions that are controlled by other than State governments, among them the five United States military service academies and institutions such as the University of Omaha that are under the auspices of local governments.) The legislatures are usually involved in the appropriation of funds; along with the governors they may have reservations of power to deal with the determination of educational programs and activities, fiscal management, and personnel management. The central State agencies involved in higher public education perform specialized management functions, in particular budgeting, auditing, purchasing, and legal services.

The institutional governing boards are the actual points of contact between the State government and the institutions. In some States the State board of education governs some or all of the State institutions of higher education, as well as public elementary and secondary schools. In others some or all of the State colleges and universities are each administered by a single governing board. In still others a single governing board administers some or all of the State institutions of higher education. The boards in Oklahoma, New York, Montana, and New Mexico operate on a State-wide basis as coordinating agencies for all publicly controlled higher education, for example. Most of their members are appointed by the governors.[45]

In 1952 a study was made of 164 boards governing 367 State colleges and universities to determine their relations with other State government bodies. Two-thirds of the boards, governing three-quarters of the institutions, had full authority over the determination of the educational program, *i.e.*, over courses and degrees to be offered; admission and graduation requirements; and extension, adult education, and other programs to be offered. However, 15 per cent of the boards, governing 10 per cent of the public institutions, exercised final authority over none of these concerns. If a board administered only one school, the likelihood that it had full authority was less than if it administered two or more schools. Where the board lacked full authority the legislature

---

[43] *Statistical Abstract 1960*, p. 121.

[44] "Statistical Summary of Education 1953–54" (Chapter 1, *Biennial Survey of Education in the United States 1952–54*). U.S. Office of Education. Washington, D.C.: USGPO, 1956, pp. 51–53.

[45] *Higher Education in the Forty-Eight States: A Report to the Governors' Conference.* Chicago: The Council of State Governments, 1952, pp. 2–3, 125–26.

decided the matters by law. Legislatures also exercised considerable direction over the budgeting and appropriation process. The legislatures, in conjunction with State administrative agencies, reviewed and often revised budgets submitted by the boards. Two-thirds of the boards reported that some or all institutional income from fees, endowment earnings, private gifts and grants, and/or auxiliary enterprises could not be expended without the specific authorization of the legislature at each session.[46]

Privately controlled institutions may be governed by a variety of means. The body with ultimate responsibility is generally the board of trustees. In the case of religiously affiliated colleges and universities the board may consist partly or entirely of officials and functionaries of the church, or the institution may be controlled by a body within the formal structure of the church. In the case of the non-sectarian private institutions the trustees are usually prominent citizens; often they may play a minor role in the affairs of the institutions, leaving considerable freedom of action to the president. In most cases the president and the trustees act with the advice and consent—either formal or informal—of alumni groups, faculty bodies, and, occasionally, student organizations. Finally, privately controlled colleges and universities may be subject to a number of State regulations similar to those regarding private elementary and secondary schools.

Financing

BOTH PUBLIC AND PRIVATE COLLEGES and universities are supported by business operations, government, and philanthropic giving. They function as business organizations, receive government funds, and appeal to foundations, churches, businesses, and individuals for contributions to meet their budgets. In 1953–54 the income of institutions of higher education in the United States totaled $3.6 billion; current income, receipts for plant expansion, and receipts for endowment and related funds are given in Table 5 for publicly and privately controlled institutions. Income by source is given in Table 6. There were sharp increases in income in 1955–56; current income alone totaled $3.6 billion, of which $722 million was from student fees, $1,475 million from government sources, and $245 million from private gifts and grants. The greatest relative increase was in private gifts and grants. Receipts for plant expansion in 1956 were $821 million, nearly double the 1953–54 amount; receipts for endowment and similar funds were $350 million, 80 per cent increase over 1953–54. Private colleges and universities

[46] *Ibid.*, pp. 135–43.

INCOME OF PUBLICLY AND PRIVATELY CONTROLLED INSTITUTIONS OF HIGHER EDUCATION IN THE UNITED STATES, 1953–54
(In Thousands of Dollars)

Source or Type of Income	Publicly Controlled Institutions		Privately Controlled Institutions		All Institutions	
	Amount	Per Cent	Amount	Per Cent	Amount	Per Cent
Current Income						
Student Fees	$ 145,730	7.5%	$ 405,694	25.1%	$ 551,424	15.5%
Federal Governments	214,620	12.1	202,476	12.5	417,097	11.7
State and Local Govts.	804,607	41.5	23,633	1.4	828,240	23.3
Endowment Earnings	14,668	0.8	112,808	6.9	127,475	3.6
Private Gifts	38,392	2.0	152,507	9.4	190,899	5.4
Sales and Services	93,194	4.8	71,687	4.4	164,880	4.6
Auxiliary Enterprises [1]	284,511	14.7	290,258	17.9	574,770	16.1
Other	36,066	1.9	54,698	3.4	90,765	2.6
Total	$1,631,789	84.2%	$1,313,762	81.0%	$2,945,550	82.7%
For Plant Expansion						
Federal Government	$ 6,282	0.3	$ 2,098	0.2	$ 8,380	0.2
State and Local Govts.	144,757	7.6	1,311		146,069	4.1
Gifts and Grants	7,466	0.4	96,310	5.9	103,776	2.9
Loans and Bond Sales	69,345	3.6	63,491	3.9	132,837	3.7
Other	20,024	1.0	12,871	0.8	32,895	0.9
Total	$ 247,876	12.8%	$ 176,082	10.9%	$ 423,957	11.9%
For Nonexpendable Funds [2]						
Endowment Funds	$ 56,559	2.9	$ 125,368	7.7	$ 181,927	5.1
Student Loan Funds	1,362	0.1	1,678	0.1	3,040	0.1
Annuity Fund	482		5,454	0.3	5,936	0.2
Total	$ 58,403	3.0%	$ 132,499	8.1%	$ 190,903	5.4%
Final Totals	$1,938,068	100%	$1,622,343	100%	$3,560,410	100%

Note: Detail does not necessarily add because of rounding.
Source: *Biennial Survey of Education in the United States 1952–54*. U.S. Office of Education. Washington, D.C.: USGPO, 1956, Chapter 1, "Statistical Summary of Education 1953–54," p. 64; Chapter 4, "Statistics of Higher Education, Part II, Receipts, Expenditures, and Property, 1953–54," pp. 28, 47–48, 97–99.

[1] Includes income from residence and dining accommodations (including students' room and board payments), bookstores, intercollegiate athletics, and so forth.
[2] These figures include profits on investment transactions and investments earnings that were added to the principals of the funds, as well ᵃˢ private gifts; private gifts comprised somewhat over half of all these funds.

benefited somewhat more from the increases than did public institutions.[47]

TABLE 7

INCOME OF HIGHER EDUCATION BY SOURCE, 1953–54
(*In Thousands of Dollars*)

SOURCE	PUBLICLY CONTROLLED INSTITUTIONS		PRIVATELY CONTROLLED INSTITUTIONS		ALL INSTITUTIONS	
	Amount	*Per Cent*	Amount	*Per Cent*	Amount	*Per Cent*
Business Operations [1]	$ 685,900	35.3%	$ 946,100	57.9%	$1,632,000	45.6%
Government	$1,170,300	60.2	$ 229,500	14.0	$1,399,800	39.1
Federal	220,900	11.4	204,600	12.5	425,500	11.9
State	849,200	43.7	22,900	1.4	872,100	24.4
Local	100,200	5.2	2,000	0.1	102,200	2.9
Philanthropy [2]	$ 87,800	4.5	$ 458,100	28.0	$ 545,900	15.3
Totals [3]	$1,944,000	100%	$1,633,700	100%	$3,577,700	100%

Source: Table 6; also "Statistics of Higher Education, Part II, Receipts, Expenditures, and Property, 1953–54" (Chapter 4, *Biennial Survey of Education in the United States 1952–54*), U.S. Office of Education, Washington, D.C.: USGPO, 1956, pp. 20–21.

[1] Includes fees, auxiliary enterprises, sales and services, profits on investments, and income not allocable to other sources.
[2] Includes income from endowment applied to current expenses, but not income from endowment and other nonexpendable funds added to principals.
[3] These totals are slightly higher than those in Table 5 because figures for *Philanthropy* include contributions to colleges and universities outside the continental United States, and because there is a small amount of duplication between *Business Operations* and *Philanthropy* figures.

BUSINESS OPERATIONS: The business operations of colleges and universities are activities that resemble the activities of conventional business enterprises. Income from these operations include tuition and fees from students; the income from endowments and investments; returns from auxiliary enterprises such as dormitories, dining halls, and bookstores; payments for services such as research done under contract for outside organizations; and rents from non-academic buildings and land. In 1953–54 business operations income provided 35 per cent of the income of publicly controlled institutions, and 58 per cent of the income of privately controlled institutions.

GOVERNMENT: Government as a source of financial support has been extremely important to the publicly controlled schools; in 1953–54,

[47] *Statistical Abstract 1959*, pp. 122–23.

they received 60 per cent of their income from government, more than two-thirds of it from State governments. In comparison only 14 per cent of the total income of private colleges and universities was government-provided, and this came almost entirely from the national government. The role of the national government in higher education is somewhat different from that of the States. In 1953–54 the national government was the source of about 12 per cent of the income of higher education, $428 million (see Table 7). More than three-quarters of this was for research and veterans' tuition and fees. Of the federal funds received by privately controlled institutions, 95.5 per cent was for these two purposes.

TABLE 8

INCOME OF HIGHER EDUCATION FROM THE NATIONAL GOVERNMENT,
1953–54
(*In Thousands of Dollars*)

TYPE OF INCOME	PUBLICLY CONTROLLED INSTITUTIONS		PRIVATELY CONTROLLED INSTITUTIONS		ALL INSTITUTIONS	
	Amount	*Per Cent*	Amount	*Per Cent*	Amount	*Per Cent*
Veterans' Tuition and Fees	$ 17,400	7.8%	$ 26,900	13.1%	$ 44,400	10.4%
Research Grants and Contracts	113,800	51.0	168,500	82.4	282,400	66.0
Land-Grant Appropriations	49,900	22.3	700	0.3	50,600	11.8
Plant Fund Additions	6,300	2.8	2,100	1.0	8,400	2.0
Other Receipts [1]	35,900	16.1	6,400	3.2	42,200	9.9
Totals [2]	$223,300	100%	$204,600	100%	$427,900	100%

Note: Detail does not necessarily add because of rounding.
Source: "Statistics of Higher Education, Part II, Receipts, Expenditures, and Property, 1953–54" (Chapter 4, *Biennial Survey of Education in the United States 1952–54*). U.S. Office of Education. Washington, D.C.: USGPO, 1956, pp. 16–17.

[1] Includes payments for maintenance of records on students under Public Law 550, tuition and costs paid for training programs under the Department of Defense, and other items.
[2] Totals do not agree with those given in Tables 6 and 7 because figures above include grants to educational institutions in outlying territories of the United States.

In general, governmental expenditures for higher education have been increasing. In 1940, 30 per cent of current income of colleges and universities was from government; in 1956, 41 per cent. Local government contributions remained about the same—3 per cent. State government expenditures for higher education increased from 21 to 24 per cent of current income. National government contributions rose from

5.5 per cent to 13 per cent, most of the increase being for research. In 1958 the national government enacted the National Defense Education Act, which made $295 million available for loans to college students from government funds; the colleges and universities that have accepted the loan funds apply to the national government for them and themselves administer the loans in keeping with government regulations. In 1959–60 about 120,000 students at 1,372 institutions applied for $30 million in such loans.

PHILANTHROPIC GIVING: Philanthropic giving for higher education, particularly for the private institutions, has been steadily rising, though how long it will continue to do so is a matter of some concern. Many college administrators are interested in expanded programs, which, they believe, are of such scope that philanthropic donations cannot meet their costs. Some of them have expressed this concern in requesting new national aid programs. Of all private gifts and grants made to colleges and universities in 1953–54, alumni and other individual donors provided roughly 50 per cent, churches 30 per cent, and foundations and corporations 20 per cent. An annual survey of philanthropic giving for higher education made by a private organization suggests that since that time foundations have been playing a larger role. In fifty large private colleges and universities surveyed each year, gifts and bequests totaled $132 million in 1953–54 and increased to $272 million in 1956–57. Of the latter, $53 million was part of the exceptional Ford Foundation grants to higher education made between 1955 and 1957.[48]

There are several estimates of 1958–59 philanthropy for education. A survey of 1,071 colleges and universities by the Council for Financial Aid to Education showed contributions of $626.6 million, which came from:

Alumni	$152.6 million	24%
Other individual donors	$129.3 million	21%
Corporations	$ 98.5 million	16%
General-purpose foundations	$ 88.3 million	14%
Religious bodies	$ 64.2 million	10%
Non-alumni, non-church groups	$ 52.4 million	8%
Governing boards	$ 24.4 million	4%
Other sources	$ 16.9 million	3%

This did not include corporate contributions for fellowships and scholarships; all corporate contributions to higher education, other than those

[48] *American Philanthropy for Higher Education Sets New Record, Report for 1956–57, Gifts and Bequests to Fifty Selected Colleges and Universities.* New York: John Price Jones, 1958.

given through corporate foundations, were an estimated $150 million. Another survey of 1958–59 giving to higher education, conducted by the American Alumni Council and covering 1,142 colleges and uni-versities, showed total contributions of $813.2 million of which $185.9 million came from alumni.[49] On the basis of these figures total giving to the 1,850 colleges and universities in the United States in 1958–59 was about $1 billion, some 20 per cent of their total expenditures for opera-tion and new construction; by comparison, in 1953–54 giving was about $550 million, the equivalent of about 15 per cent of their total ex-penditures.

Functions of Colleges and Universities

THERE ARE FOUR FUNCTIONS of colleges and universities that warrant attention here: teaching; in conjunction with teaching, the provision of financial assistance for students; research; and community services.

TEACHING: Teaching subject matter of one sort or another is the most evident function of colleges and universities, and one that is com-mon to all of them. Once designed to train young men in theology, medicine, and law, colleges and universities now can prepare students for a host of professions and occupations, ranging from animal hus-bandry to newscasting. Numerous professions, such as teaching, med-icine, the law, and engineering, are closed or practically closed to all save those with one or more college or university degrees. In 1958 there were 440,300 degrees conferred on students at American colleges and universities. Of them, 365,700 were bachelor's and first professional degrees, 65,600 were second-level degrees, and 9,000 were doctorates. In Table 8 they are listed by major field of study for 1957. Of these degrees two-thirds were conferred on men.

As an adjunct to teaching *per se*, colleges and universities give other services to their students. Among them are medical insurance and care, which are usually provided to all resident students; recreational facilities; and entertainment, in the form of plays, films, and athletic events. Stu-dents also receive many intangible benefits from the college environ-ment, benefits whose nature is conveyed in such phrases as "liberal education" and "broadening of interests."

FINANCIAL ASSISTANCE FOR STUDENTS: Colleges and universities in one way or another provide financial assistance for thousands of students who are mentally and physically qualified to undertake higher education but lack the financial resources to do so. For example in 1953–54 private colleges and universities gave $50 million in scholar-

[49] *Giving USA 1960*, pp. 16–17, 37–38.

ships, fellowships, and prizes. The U.S. Office of Education has estimated that in 1955–56, $66 million in scholarships and $18 million in fellowships were granted to students in all American colleges and universities.

Another form of aid available for college students is the student loan. A recent U.S. Office of Education study estimated that about $27

TABLE 9

DEGREES GIVEN BY AMERICAN COLLEGES AND UNIVERSITIES, 1957

Major Field of Study	Bachelor's Degrees [3]	Second-Level Degrees	Doctorates
Education	77,722	30,972	1,533
Business and Commerce	46,760	3,270	93
Social Sciences [1]	44,165	4,552	1,098
Engineering	31,211	5,233	596
Health Professions [2]	23,075	1,385	150
English and Journalism	17,998	2,255	354
Biological Sciences	13,868	1,432	1,103
Physical Sciences	12,934	2,704	1,674
Fine and Applied Arts	11,785	2,387	246
Law	8,832	456	31
Religion	8,289	1,114	246
Psychology	6,191	1,095	550
Mathematical Subjects	5,546	965	249
Agriculture	5,490	953	289
Home Economics	4,614	481	46
Foreign Languages and Literature	4,322	880	215
Philosophy	2,833	292	85
All Others [4]	14,713	1,160	198
Totals	340,347	61,955	8,756

Source: *Statistical Abstract* 1959, p. 129.

[1] Includes social work (1,901 degrees) and history (11,692 degrees); excludes psychology.
[2] Includes pharmacy, nursing, dentistry, and medicine; all M.D., D.D.S., and D.M.D. degrees listed under bachelor's degrees.
[3] Includes first professional degrees (law, medicine, engineering, etc.).
[4] Includes military science, trade and industrial training, architecture, forestry, library science, geography, and other degrees.

million was available for student loans in funds held by colleges and universities. In 1955–56, however, only half of these funds were borrowed. On the whole, loans have been a relatively unpopular means of financing higher education, largely because students do not like to leave college in a state of indebtedness.

At endowed institutions students paying tuition as well as those receiving scholarships and loans are usually receiving indirect benefits as well. That is, the actual cost of educating the student may be far greater than the tuition he pays; the difference is made up partly by income from endowments. There have been various practices among privately controlled institutions. A few have expected the tuition-paying student to meet the full cost of his education; others, and not necessarily those that are well-endowed, have expected him to meet only a fraction of the costs. At publicly controlled institutions this difference between costs and tuition is made up mainly by State government appropriations. State colleges and universities, however, may also have endowments and many receive grants and gifts from non-governmental sources. Tuition fees at State colleges and universities are generally nominal, and in a few States such institutions may be required by law to accept any graduates of the high schools of the State who wish to apply and can meet the costs of room and board.

RESEARCH: Colleges and universities are the centers of vast research projects, conducted for both governmental and non-governmental agencies. Universities also finance considerable research from their own general funds and receive foundation grants for research programs. In 1953–54 universities spent an estimated $420 million for research, about $80 million of which was from their own funds; another $282 million was from the national government. Foundations provided about $12 million (see Chapter 11). The remainder, about $45 million, presumably was from business organizations. In 1958 university research expenditures were estimated at $750 million, of which about $200 million was from university funds and $500 million from the national government.[50] In 1960, colleges and universities performed an estimated one billion dollars worth of research. (Some university research is financed by State governments as well.)

The 1958 government-provided research funds for universities were of three types. They included $175 million for research centers managed by educational institutions for the government, $265 million for research and development conducted in regular academic departments, and an estimated $60 million for the construction and operation of research facilities and equipment at educational institutions.[51]

The responsibilities assumed by the colleges and universities are varied, resulting from the different requirements and interests of the federal departments and agencies that contract for extramural research. (Of the $3 billion in federal research funds appropriated in fiscal 1958, nearly half was used in government laboratories, and another $1 billion was contracted to non-educational profit and non-profit organizations.) The agencies that provided the largest portions of research funds for educational institutions were the Department of Defense (32 per cent),

[50] *Statistical Abstract 1959*, p. 538.
[51] *Government-University Relationships in Federally Sponsored Research and Development*. National Science Foundation. Washington, D.C.: USGPO, 1958, p. 4.

the Atomic Energy Commission (AEC) (35 per cent), the Department of Agriculture (8 per cent), and the National Science Foundation (NSF) (7 per cent). Nine other departments and agencies provided the remaining one per cent.[52]

About one-third of the $265 million for research in the regular academic departments was for "programs in which university scientists are financed to conduct research of their own choice." This was primarily fundamental research; all the grants of the NSF, for example, were of this type. In the case of fundamental research grants and contracts, responsibilities to the granting agency are at a minimum. The remainder of the $265 million was spent for programs "in which the government departments, on their own initiative, contract with universities for applied research necessary to the development of products, systems, and processes, as well as for fundamental research related to the practical mission of the department."[53] Universities managed twenty-four government-owned research centers for the Department of Defense and the AEC on grants of $175 million.

COMMUNITY SERVICES: A comparatively new trend in publicly and privately controlled higher education is the provision of community services. In the broadest sense, of course, almost all the activities of the college and university are for the ultimate good of the community. In a 1952 report to the Council of State Governments several trends were noted, with particular reference to the publicly controlled universities and colleges:

(1) it is now generally agreed that higher education should be made available to broad segments of the population; (2) education in the applied sciences—technical and vocational education generally—now has wide recognition and status; and (3) the performance of broad public services and participation in activities designed to serve both immediate and long-range needs of society are generally accepted as proper and important functions of institutions of higher education.[54]

One program of a community service nature is the cooperative agricultural extension program, carried on by sixty-eight land-grant institutions. The program is actually a form of adult education directed toward improving agriculture and rural life; in the early 1950's expenditures for the program averaged about $75 million a year, shared between the national and State governments. In 1960 the federal contribution was $62 million.

[52] *Ibid.*, p. 5.
[53] *Ibid.*, p. 11.
[54] *Higher Education in the Forty-Eight States*, p. 2.

Other community services are forums, special conferences, lectures, seminars, workshops, and clinics, which are being sponsored in increasing numbers by many colleges and universities. Many special library services are available for public use, including "package libraries," audio-visual aids, discussion guides, and suggested bibliographies. Almost all institutions of higher education make some provision for public use of their library facilities. Publicly controlled institutions conduct a number of extension and adult education programs, and a variety of informational and cultural programs are presented by college and university radio and television stations.[55] A new development, not confined to public institutions, is the presentation of college-level courses by television.

A recent publication of the National Science Foundation states that the principal objectives of an educational institution are teaching, the expansion of knowledge, and service to the community. It goes on to relate community service to the other two objectives:

Service to the community may be only indirectly associated with the first two objectives. It may be considered obligatory or voluntary. Service to the community may include a community theater, a series of musical concerts, the eradication of wheat rust, the synthesis of a miracle drug, or the design of an antenna for a guided missile. If an institution is devoted largely to community service, many will contend that it can no longer properly be called an educational institution. In fact, if its activities and interests are restricted entirely to research and community service functions, it ceases to be a college or university. The unique and distinctive characteristic of the educational institution is the teaching function.[56]

Perhaps another way of stating this is to say that teaching is the most important community service that American colleges and universities can perform.

CONCLUDING REMARKS

ONE STRIKING FEATURE of the American educational system is the extent to which it involves social welfare and philanthropy. By 1960 some thirty-five million students were enrolled in the public elementary and secondary schools of the United States; many of them, in some cases most of them, were being provided with a wide range of welfare services, including health services, psychological and social casework services,

[55] *Ibid.*, pp. 53–55.
[56] *Government University Relationships*, pp. 15–16.

subsidized lunches, special classes for exceptional students (including the handicapped and the retarded), recreation, and a number of others. The colleges and universities of the United States, public as well as private, receive more than one-fifth of their expenses from philanthropic sources.

The role of the public school systems in providing special services as a supplement to their educative function has been a growing one. To a considerable extent this growth has been at the expense of the family and the church, which at an earlier time were almost solely responsible for the emotional and physical well-being of children. In some cases the family and the church have been unable to fulfill these responsibilities completely; more often, though, it has simply been held more convenient and efficient to provide a consistent level of special services in the school setting than to leave them to institutions that formerly had provided them in markedly varying degrees. And it is still true that the family and the church, to a lesser extent, have the primary responsibility for the well-being of children.

It is not likely that the public schools will greatly increase their special services, however, for several reasons. First, most school teachers and administrators believe that the present level of such services is adequate, if not more than adequate. Second, there is increasing reluctance on the part of local taxpayers to raise school expenditures, as demonstrated by the defeat of an increasing number of school-bond proposals in 1959 and 1960. Finally, more and more concern has been expressed throughout the nation over the quality of the actual education provided in American public schools, and it has often been charged that it is declining because too much emphasis is placed on "frills," i.e., on special services; if these charges are taken seriously, as they have been by many people, school board members will become increasingly reluctant to add to special services.

Colleges and universities, on the other hand, may expect still further involvement with other institutions as sources of support. The Council for Financial Aid to Education anticipates a doubling of philanthropy for higher education between 1960 and 1970, to about $2 billion in the latter year. More and more requests are being made for national government aid to higher education, and it is likely that increases in such aid will be forthcoming. Extensive government and business research is currently being carried out by American universities, and this too may increase, particularly as expenditures for fundamental research go up. For the college student, this means that more and more of his education is being subsidized from outside sources, either directly through scholarships, fellowships, and loan funds or indirectly through donations and tax appropriations to his college or university.

Chapter Nine

BUSINESS OPERATIONS

BUSINESS OPERATIONS, including commercial farms, self-employed individuals, and professional service agencies along with business firms, comprise one of the more important sources of welfare benefits in the United States. Indeed, using the term "welfare" in the broad sense of "well-being," business operations are more responsible than any other group of organizations for the *physical* welfare of the American people: they produce and distribute the largest part of the goods and services that Americans need and want, and provide most of the working population with its livelihood. However, most of this activity occurs in the marketplace, in transactions between employees and employers, consumers and producers, and thus lies outside the more restricted definition of welfare as *special* benefits and services provided for particular groups. The monetary transactions of the marketplace receive only passing mention here, with the exception of non-governmental insurance activities, included for reasons that appear in connection with its discussion.

Business operations also involve a number of activities that conventionally are placed in the field of welfare. These include special benefits for persons directly associated with a particular business operation, both managers and employees, and their families; and benefits ("corporate philanthropy") for persons and organizations not directly associated with business. After a brief discussion of the nature of business operations, this chapter deals with these internal and external welfare activities of business; the final section describes some of the insurance benefits provided by the business system.

THE NATURE OF AMERICAN BUSINESS OPERATIONS

A BUSINESS OPERATION may be defined simply as "the activity of one or more persons designed to enable them to earn money by selling something." The smallest business operations are conducted by one person, the largest by hundreds of thousands of individuals. The American Telephone and Telegraph Company and the General Motors Corporation are the largest non-governmental employers in the United States; in 1958 AT&T employed 725,000 people, GM employed 520,900.

TABLE 1

BUSINESS OPERATIONS AND THEIR EMPLOYEES IN THE
UNITED STATES, 1960

Business Firms	4,660,000
Professional Service Operations and Independent Professional and Technical Workers	500,000 (est.)
Commercial Farms	3,000,000 (est.)
Household Employees	2,340,000
Non-Professional Self-Employed Persons	700,000 (est.) [1]
Estimated No. of Business Operations	11,200,000
Professional and Technical Workers	4,800,000 [2]
Managers, Officials, and Proprietors	6,500,000 [2]
Clerical and Sales Workers	9,900,000 [2]
Foremen, Craftsmen, and Operators	19,600,000 [2]
Service Workers	4,900,000 [2]
Laborers (other than farm and mine)	3,600,000 [2]
Farm Operators and Laborers	4,000,000 [3]
Paid Household Workers	2,340,000 [3]
Estimated No. of Employees of Business Operations	55,600,000 [3]
Other Sectors of the Civilian Labor Force	
Government Employees	7,830,000 [3]
Unpaid Family Workers, Farm and Household	1,165,000 [3]
Unemployed	4,206,000 [3]

Source: Same as footnote 1, this chapter.

[1] Excludes managers, officials, and proprietors of business firms of all sizes, and farm owners and operators.
[2] Estimates only, based on known number of workers in each category minus estimated government employees in each.
[3] As of March, 1960.

In 1960 there were about 4,660,000 business firms in the United States and an estimated 3,000,000 commercial farms. Though precise data are lacking, there are believed to be about one million self-employed physicians, lawyers, writers, artists, accountants, architects, and other professional and technical workers, including those in business jointly with fellow practitioners (professional service firms are not included in "business firms" statistics). In 1960 there were also 2,340,000 paid household employees and an estimated 700,000 non-professional self-employed persons, who may be considered to have been conducting business operations in terms of the above definition.[1] Data on business operations and employed persons are given in Table 1.

The number of workers in the average business operation is small (cf. Table 2). In 1956 there were some eight million commercial farms, professional service operations, and business firms in the United States. Their workers, including managers, proprietors, and wage and salary employees, numbered over fifty-two millions, four-fifths of the employed civilian labor force. The average of these operations thus employed six or seven persons, including the owner or owners. The average industrial or commerical firm employed about eleven persons.

However, a relatively small number of large firms employ a large percentage of individuals and conduct a large part of business operations in the United States. Table 2 lists the number of firms having various numbers of workers, based in part on data from three million employers reporting under the Social Security Act in 1956. Of persons employed in business nearly a third worked for only 6,400 firms, each of which employed over 500 persons. At the opposite end of the scale, some eleven million individuals owned or worked for about seven million small businesses, farms, and professional service enterprises; the great majority of these operations involved fewer than five persons, most of them only one or two.

The variety of business purposes and systems of organization precludes a discussion of the general operations of American businesses. It should be pointed out, however, that as a *general welfare system* business provides most of the goods and services used each year by individual Americans and their families; it also provides most of their personal income. The data in Table 3 serve both to outline the goods and services provided by business and to suggest the relationship between the business system and the various governmental and non-governmental welfare systems with which this book is primarily concerned.

About one dollar in twenty of the income of the American people comes from social insurance, veterans' pension funds, public assistance payments, and so forth; in 1958 about $230 million of this was supplied by philanthropic sources, nearly $9 billion by government. These transactions take place entirely outside the business system; that is, they are

[1] *Statistical Abstract of the United States 1960.* U.S. Bureau of the Census. Washington, D.C.: USGPO, 1960, pp. 216–21, 484, 615. There were an estimated 1,600,-000 non-commercial farms, *i.e.*, farms operated by families and individuals who received more than half their income from non-farm sources.

not part of the producer-employer-consumer-producer cycle. On the "expenditure" side the sources of this income are social insurance contributions, taxes, and contributions to religious and non-governmental welfare organizations; here again, as far as the individual is concerned, the transactions occur outside the business system.

TABLE 2

BUSINESS OPERATIONS, BY NUMBER OF WORKERS, 1956 [1]

Worker Size	No. of Operations	Per Cent	No. of Workers	Per Cent
Commercial Farms:				
(n.a.)	3,200,000 (est.)	39.6%	4,900,000 [2]	9.4%
Professional Service Operations:				
(n.a.)	500,000 (est.)	6.2%	1,000,000 (est.) [2]	1.9%
Business Firms Not Reporting under the Social Security Act: [3]				
(n.a.)	1,375,000	17.0%	2,400,000 (est.) [2]	4.6%
Business Firms Reporting under the Social Security Act: [3]				
1–3	1,834,000	22.7%	3,095,000	5.9%
4–7	563,900	7.0	2,909,000	5.6
8–19	381,500	4.7	4,555,000	8.7
20–49	142,300	1.75	4,297,000	8.2
50–99	46,000	0.57	3,139,000	6.0
100–499	32,300	0.40	6,349,000	12.2
500–999	3,400	0.042	2,304,000	4.4
1,000–9,999	2,800	0.035	7,207,000	13.8
10,000 and up	200	0.002	7,124,000	13.6
Managers and Proprietors Not Included Above: [4]			3,000,000 (est.)	5.7
Totals:	8,080,000 (est.) [1]	100%	52,200,000 (est.) [1]	100%

Note: Totals do not necessarily add because of rounding.
Source: *Statistical Abstract of the United States 1959.* U.S. Bureau of the Census. Washington, D.C.: USGPO, 1959, pp. 218, 485, 487.

[1] Excludes household employees and non-professional self-employed persons who were not operating a firm or commercial farm.
[2] Includes self-employed owners, managers, and proprietors.
[3] A total of 3,006,500 commercial and industrial employers with 40,979,000 employees reported under the old-age and survivors insurance provisions of the Social Security Act in 1956. According to the U.S. Office of Business Economics, there were 4,381,000 business firms in that year, other than firms in agriculture and professional services. Many had no workers other than the proprietor; most others had very few employees.
[4] Managers and proprietors of reporting firms are generally considered "self-employed."

The business system itself provides voluntary social insurance schemes. One dollar in forty of personal income is paid into pension funds and medical and other non-governmental insurance plans by employers on behalf of their workers. Americans also spend part of their other income for individual insurance policies of various kinds. These practices are discussed in detail below; they have some but not all the characteristics of business transactions.

The business system provides most of the other goods and services consumed by the American people. It provides almost all food, cloth-

TABLE 3

PERSONAL INCOME AND ITS USES, 1958 [1]
(*In Millions of Dollars*)

Income:		
Direct Income from Work, Rentals, and Investment	$326,200	90.3%
Employer Contributions to Pension and Medical Plans, Injury Compensation Payments, etc. (non-Govt.)	9,100	2.5
Social Insurance and Veterans Payments, Direct Relief Payments, etc.	19,100 (est.)	5.3
Miscellaneous Transfer Payments	6,800 (est.)	1.9
Total Individual Income:	$361,100	100%
Consumption Spending: [2]		
Food, Beverages, Tobacco	$ 83,400	23.1%
Clothing and Accessories	30,500	8.4
Personal Care	4,100	1.1
Housing Rentals	36,000	10.0
Household Operations	40,700	11.3
Medical Care and Death Expenses (Incl. Insurance Payments)	16,900	4.7
Transportation	37,200	10.3
Recreation	16,300	4.5
Private Education [2]	3,200	0.9
Foreign Travel and Remittances, Net	2,600	0.7
Other Spending, Saving, and Taxes:		
Personal Business	16,000	4.4
Contributions for Religious and Welfare Purposes	3,700	1.0
Savings (Incl. Home Purchases)	21,000	5.8
Personal Contributions for Social Insurance	6,700	1.9
National Taxes	37,000	10.3
State and Local Taxes	5,800	1.6
Total Outgo:	$361,100	100%

Source: *Statistical Abstract* 1959, pp. 268, 305–308.

[1] Following U.S. Department of Commerce practice, includes receipts of unincorporated business and non-profit institutions as well as individuals, plus some non-monetary income, *e.g.*, food consumed on farms.
[2] Includes purchases by non-profit institutions; "private education" includes research expenditures of such organizations. Consumption figures obtained by applying 1957 percentages to 1958 totals.

ing, housing, and transportation (other than the construction of transportation facilities), for example. One major exception is public defense and safety, of course; public defense and safety are not "consumed" in the ordinary sense of the word, and their nature is such that business generally cannot provide them.

Still other types of services are provided in part by the business system and in part by other welfare systems. One is medical care. In 1958 Americans paid some $17 billion for medical services in what were essentially business transactions: payments to physicians, hospitals, medical insurance plans, and so forth. Governments spent about $5 billion for various medical and health services, while philanthropic organizations spent about $640 million for health care. Another is recreation. In 1958 Americans spent about $16.3 billion for recreational purposes, in purchases of goods and services provided by business. Governments spent about $600 million in providing recreational facilities and services; non-governmental recreational, leisure-time, and character-building agencies such as the YMCA and the Scouts spent about $400 million. Finally, private schools and colleges, which are essentially part of the business system, complement governmental educational systems. In 1958 Americans paid out some $3 billion for tuition and other educational services, while individuals and philanthropic groups contributed about $800 million for education; government expenditures for education exceeded $16 billion.[2]

INTERNAL WELFARE ACTIVITIES OF BUSINESSES

THE PRODUCTION of marketable goods and services is the *raison d'être* of the business system, so far as society in general is concerned. The extent to which it does so was suggested in the previous section. At the same time many businesses carry on internal welfare activities—that is, activities for the benefit of managers and employees, and their families, over and above their salaries and wages. These activities include both fringe benefits and special services. Some of these, fringe benefits in particular, are often considered simply as pay supplements, rather than "welfare." Nevertheless there is a fairly strong argument for calling them welfare, in the more restricted sense. In general they are provided for the worker instead of extra pay because it is felt that the worker will benefit more from them than he would from having the actual cash. In other words they are intended to fulfill particular and deserving "needs" on the part of the worker. Also, many fringe benefits such as health insurance coverage are provided equally to all workers, and not in relation to their respective pay. This is another characteristic of many

[2] *Giving USA 1959*. New York: American Association of Fund-Raising Counsel, 1959, various pages. Other data from Table 3 and from *Statistical Abstract 1959*, various pages.

special welfare services; everyone's need is held to be equal, independent of how much he could pay for it. The point will not be belabored; it is, however, another example of the overlapping between business and welfare.

Managers

IN ALMOST every manufacturing or service firm, managers receive welfare benefits; fringe benefits or pay supplements are not restricted to employees alone. Particularly in the case of the managers, fringe benefits are inextricably tied up with wage payments. Some indication of the pay supplements available to them is given in Table 4, which lists the percentages of manufacturing companies extending various fringe benefits to their salaried and hourly employees. The benefits available to salaried employees may be considered roughly equivalent to the benefits of the managers, who make up part of the salaried employees' group.

Other forms of managerial compensation and special benefit are not covered by such a listing, including the use of company facilities and, occasionally, personnel for personal purposes. For instance, managers may be able to use company cars for private transportation, assign personal matters to secretaries, and exploit company contacts and the prestige of the firm for private ends. Such practices are seldom formalized, but they exist to some extent in almost every firm and corporation of any size. One major benefit that is likely to be formalized and that usually applies only to the highest level of management is the "stock-option" plan whereby managers may buy company stock at a price below that on the market.

On the managerial level, of course, one major motive in providing such non-pay benefits is to avoid or ease taxation. Fringe benefits for both managers and employees generally are not taxable. There are other reasons, notably the desire to bind managers to a company. Young managers may be offered "package deals" that encourage them to stay with a company until their retirement.

Employees

FRINGE BENEFITS: There was a notable increase in fringe benefits for employees in the decade following World War II (cf. Chapter 10). This was not a complete break with past business practices, of course. For decades many businesses had regularly or irregularly provided bonuses, care for sick or injured employees, camps and recreational facilities, pensions, and assistance to the families of deceased employees. Since the war, however, there has been a systematization of fringe benefits and an increase of their value in proportion to wage payments. The

TABLE 4

PAY SUPPLEMENTS FOR SALARIED AND HOURLY EMPLOYEES, 1953, 1958

Benefit	Salaried Employees, 1953 [1]	Hourly Employees 1953 [2]	Hourly Employees 1959 [3]
Health and Security [4]			
Pensions	71%	64%	66%
Life Insurance	87	87	92
Accidental Death, Dismemberment	54	59	
Accident and Sickness	68	80	66
Hospitalization Coverage	79	83	86
Surgical Coverage	76	80	85
Maternity Coverage	61	64	
Medical Coverage	41	44	61
Catastrophe Coverage	3	3	
Polio Coverage	13	12	
Workmen's Compensation Supplements	45	39	
Sick Leave	80	14	
Bonuses			
Profit Sharing	17	10	
Year-End Bonus	42	33	
Military Leave Bonus	30	30	
Long Service Bonus	8	7	
Subsidized Savings Plans	6	5	
Time Off with Pay Practices			
Vacations	99	99	
Holidays	95	97	
Summer Military Training	40	32	
Election Day (sometimes required by law)	45	34	
Jury Duty	73	30	
Death in Family	84	20	
Illness in Family	66	4	
Marriage	56	4	
Severance Pay	39	11	
Rest Periods	31	38	
Wash Time	12	45	
Premium Pay Practices [5]			
Holidays Worked	67	95	
Saturday as Such	36	57	
Sunday as Such	42	73	

Sources: "Pay Supplements: The Fringe Benefits Package" (No. 964 in *Road Maps of Industry* series), New York: The Conference Board, 1954; *Statistical Abstract* 1960, p. 228.

[1] 100% = 375 companies.
[2] 100% = 384 companies.
[3] From a U.S. Bureau of Labor Statistics sample survey of industrial establishments. Other data not available or not comparable.
[4] Includes only companies paying all or part of the benefit costs for employee coverage.
[5] Premium pay when Saturdays and Sundays are not regularly part of the individual's work week.

value and extent of such practices prior to the 1940's was relatively small compared to their value and extent in the 1950's.

Even now not all employees in industry and commerce receive extensive fringe benefits, though. Of some seventeen million union members in the mid-1950's about a third did not have job-connected health and insurance coverage. The percentage of non-union workers not covered by such plans was slightly greater—about 40 per cent. The significant difference between union and non-union business employees in respect to such plans was in who footed the bill. About four in ten union members contributed directly all or part of the cost of coverage; six in ten non-union workers contributed directly all or part of the costs (these figures refer only to those who were covered). Part of this difference may be an apparent one only; non-union workers include the self-employed, most of whom, if they are covered under such plans, pay for the coverage themselves.

In 1957 the business system paid $198 billion in wages and salaries. Seventeen per cent of this, or $33.5 billion, was estimated to have been in the form of fringe benefits. Besides the studies referred to in Table 4, the U.S. Department of Commerce and the Chamber of Commerce of the United States have compiled extensive data on the types of fringe benefits being paid. A Chamber of Commerce survey of 1,020 manufacturing and non-manufacturing firms provided the data in Table 5. Fringe benefits comprised an average of about 22 per cent of the payrolls of these concerns, almost $1,000 per year per employee. The second part of Table 5 gives the distribution of benefits by type. In monetary value, pension and other agreed-upon payments were about equal to payments for time not worked; together these comprised nearly two-thirds of all fringe payments in the companies surveyed. In addition to old-age and survivors' insurance taxes, legally required payments included unemployment compensation taxes, workmen's compensation taxes, and so forth.

In the Chamber of Commerce survey manufacturing companies were found to pay smaller benefits, on the average, than non-manufacturing companies. There is historical basis for the contention that industrial workers' wages on the average have surpassed white-collar workers' wages because, in part, white-collar workers have been more likely to have certain benefits, notably sick leave. Yet it is far from generally true that white-collar fringe benefits exceed those of manufacturing workers; the average is belied by a number of specific cases to the contrary. The highest fringe payments for any type of business were made to workers in the petroleum industries, $1,650 per employee per year, according to the survey. Workers in coal mining, warehousing, and laundries received the second highest level of benefits, $1,329 per year. Employees

TABLE 5

FRINGE BENEFIT COSTS, 1957 [1]

LEVELS OF FRINGE PAYMENT

	Per Cent of Payroll	Cents per Payroll Hour	Dollars per Year per Employee
10% of Firms Paid More Than	31.0%	72.0¢	$1,478
25% of Firms Paid More Than	25.6	58.3	1,188
50% of Firms Paid More Than	21.0	45.8	956
75% of Firms Paid More Than	16.6	34.8	729
90% of Firms Paid More Than	13.3	22.8	478
Average Payment:	21.8%	47.4¢	$ 981

TYPE OF FRINGE PAYMENT

Type of Payment	Manufacturing Companies	Non-Manufacturing Companies	All Companies
Legally Required Payments [2]	4.1%	3.5%	3.9%
Old-Age and Survivors Insurance	2.0	2.1	2.1
Other	2.1	1.4	1.8
Pension and Other Agreed-Upon Payments [2]	5.8	8.6	6.8
Pension Premiums and Payments	3.1	5.9	4.1
Life, Health, Other Insurance	2.3	1.9	2.2
Non-Govt. Unemployment Benefit Funds	0.2		0.1
Discounts for Employee Purchases		0.3	0.1
Savings Plans, Free Meals, etc.	0.2	0.5	0.3
Paid Rest and Lunch Periods, etc.	2.4	2.0	2.3
Paid Vacations, Holidays, Sick Leave, etc.	6.5	7.7	6.9
Other (Profit-Sharing, Special Bonuses, etc.)	1.5	2.4	1.9
Total Fringe Payments As:			
Percentage of Payroll	20.3%	24.2%	21.8%
Cents per Payroll Hour	44.9¢	50.8¢	47.4¢
Dollars per Year per Employee	$940	$1,035	$981

Source: *Fringe Benefits 1957*. Economic Research Dept., Chamber of Commerce of the United States. Washington, D.C.: Chamber of Commerce of the United States, 1958, pp. 7–9.

[1] Based on a survey of 656 manufacturing companies and 364 non-manufacturing companies, 1,020 in all.
[2] Employer's share only.

of banks, finance companies, and trust companies received $1,294. The lowest level of benefits was received by hotel employees, an average of $354 per employee per year, the second lowest by workers in the textile products and apparel industries, $626.

It appears that different sets of factors in each industry determine fringe payments. In the petroleum and coal-mining industries higher payments are made largely because of the relative dangers involved and the prospectively shorter work-span of the employee; pension plan payments in the petroleum industry, for example, are far higher than similar payments in any other occupational category. Why low fringe benefits occur is a more difficult question. Some hotel employees receive "fringe benefits" in the form of tips, hence may make fewer demands for increased remuneration in the form of fringe benefits, and most are non-union, menial workers who have few effective means of demanding fringe benefits should they want them. Many textile industries are located in the deep South and still employ non-union "poor white" and Negro workers; apparently they have not found it necessary to pay fringe benefits to retain their employees. Income is relatively low and newcomers from rural areas provide a constant supply of new labor.

Although fringe benefits have many of the characteristics of "special benefits," as pointed out above, the workers themselves pay for them, though indirectly. From the point of view of the business the fringe benefits are part of the wage-and-salary package; in terms of money alone it matters little to business whether it pays entirely in cash or part in cash and part in benefits. Fringe benefits are "welfare" primarily because of their form and underlying motives. They have one other special advantage for the employee, however. The fringe benefit package is tax-free and thus is more valuable to him than an equivalent salary or wage increase. Payments for various insurance plans—health, life, accident, pension—are exempt from direct taxation; in effect, they represent a special benefit conferred upon the worker by the government.

It has been estimated that fringe payments jumped from 3 per cent of total wages and salaries in 1929 to about 25 per cent in 1960. Most benefits in 1929 were rest periods and vacations, and holiday pay; at present, a large part of them are pension and insurance benefits. This has raised a new set of problems: the control of non-governmental pension and welfare funds. Such funds are sometimes controlled solely by management, solely by unions or other employee groups, or jointly. Pension funds have the largest block of assets; most are relatively new and have been building up reserves. Trusteed and insured pension funds had assets of $33.3 billion at the beginning of 1958 and covered some thirteen million employees. Other corporate funds for employees were estimated at over $7 billion. These funds are customarily invested so as to yield income. For example, the trusteed funds, amounting to more than $19 billion of the pension funds, can be invested in common stocks. However, in 1957 half these fund were invested in corporate bond holdings and about 10 per cent in government securities; slightly over 30 per cent was in common stock.[3] In the case of some union-controlled funds the investment portfolio is comprised of stocks and bonds of the companies by which the union members are employed. Both business and labor spokesmen have charged that pension and welfare funds are often mismanaged. In 1957 an actuary and pension fund expert testifying before a United States Senate committee said that he believed there was about as much waste and corruption in employer-administered funds as in union-operated funds, but that, in general, "a lot more money was being wasted in health and welfare plans than was being stolen."[4] The sources of waste may be inadequate or badly planned assessments, the hiring of highly paid financial consultants for relatively small funds, or simply poor investment. Nevertheless such wastage is probably not a serious drain on the majority of pension and welfare funds, and as experience with such funds increases wastage will probably decrease.

THE HUMAN RELATIONS MOVEMENT: The human relations movement, particularly in industry, has been the source of considerable benefit to workers over and above their wages and salaries. It has also provided the broader context in which interest in fringe benefits has developed. The underlying premise of the movement is that the welfare and the satisfaction of employees is not solely a function of wage but a total function of a number of factors, including the suitability of the job to the worker, relations among workers and to their superiors, the opportunity to have some say in decisions affecting them, and so forth. Managers and owners have adopted the management techniques of human relations both to increase worker productivity and to satisfy a sincere and growing interest in employee welfare; the techniques themselves have developed from many studies in applied social science.

The first industrial relations approach of widespread acceptance was scientific management, or "Taylorism," which developed in the second decade of the twentieth century. It was based on systematic job analysis, time studies, and standardization of job operations; "its mechanistic bias seemed suited to the current attitude toward and treatment of plant employees, many of whom were recent immigrants." In the 1920's personnel management and "welfare capitalism" came into vogue; they stressed employee representation, profit-sharing and stock-ownership plans, suggestion systems, company magazines, and the first widespread use of the benefit programs outlined in the previous section. "In this

[3] "Growth in Pension Plans Aid to Market," Los Angeles Times, June 13, 1958; "New Rules Urged in Pension Plans," New York Times, July 9, 1957.
[4] "Employer Funds Scored on Waste," New York Times, May 30, 1957.

approach, management concern for the individual welfare and loyalty of plant employees becomes evident. That concern is given additional emphasis in the 'human relations' approach that began to capture management thinking in the 1930's." The impetus of this movement was provided by applied psychological studies at the Hawthorne plant of Western Electric and subsequent studies. Individual interviewing, employee counseling, and small-group communication were emphasized at first; there was a "new image of the worker" as a personality whose inner feelings needed expression and respectful treatment. This led to the present broad range of company activities "designed to improve employee satisfaction on and off the job."[5]

The greatest impact of the human relations movement has been in those companies that employ consultants in public relations, psychology, sociology, family casework, and so forth. Direct and indirect effects have been felt throughout the business system. Many techniques have been developed to measure the employee's levels of aspiration and satisfaction in many situations; it has been found that these do not necessarily vary with wage payment. Three of the most general findings, which are being taken more and more into account in employment practices, are these: the worker has a fairly definite idea of the job he is best suited for, and the closer his actual job is to that idea the better he likes it; the more predictable the work routine, up to a fairly high level, the better the worker likes his job; and the more compatible work requirements are with social, family, and other role requirements the higher the level of worker satisfaction. Another very important factor is the consistency of supervisory practices with employee independence. The most frequently expressed reason for job dissatisfaction is what the worker considers a bad balance between control and independence. "So long as an individual desires independence in decision-making, the more authoritarian the supervisory practices, the greater the dissatisfaction aroused and the greater the pressure to withdraw."[6]

Modern business is becoming what might be termed "welfare business"; ideally it conceives of itself as being conducted by principles of maximizing the welfare of its employees, depending upon the creation of an atmosphere of work that gives dignity, meaning, and voice to the individual worker and small groups of workers throughout the structure of the firm. The new employee may be tested to determine his abilities, interviewed to determine his interests, and given solicitous

[5] Discussion and quotes from Richard A. Lester, *As Unions Mature: An Analysis of American Unionism*. Princeton: Princeton University Press, 1958, pp. 37–38.
[6] James G. March and Herbert A. Simon. *Organizations*. New York: Wiley and Sons, 1958, pp. 94–96.

attention to ensure his "job adjustment." Supervisory personnel may discuss new policies and procedures with work groups, and ask their objections, suggested alternatives, and suggested means of making the changes. Employees may also be encouraged to initiate changes. Whether these human relations practices are truly effective or merely formal varies from worker to worker and from firm to firm. There is no doubt, however, that they have led to a general increase in employee welfare. Any statement about the state of worker welfare in the United States that relies solely on crude figures of fringe benefits and wages is inadequate in light of present knowledge concerning employment practices and worker satisfaction.

Thus far the human relations practices discussed are of the sort intended to benefit all or most of the employees of a firm equally. In addition the human relations movement has resulted in a certain number of special services for particular employees. Often, poor job performance or job dissatisfaction arises from conditions outside the plant or office. The worker may have severe family problems, he may be an alcoholic, or he may have had inadequate education. Thus a small but increasing number of concerns employ consulting psychologists, psychiatrists, and family caseworkers, and provide free, voluntary educational programs. An employee with a particular problem may choose to see one of these consultants, or be sent to them by his supervisor; sometimes, considerable effort is spent to "rehabilitate" the worker or to help his family. In other cases the worker may be referred to outside welfare agencies for help.

OTHER INTERNAL WELFARE BENEFITS: Aside from the formal and systematic fringe benefit and human relations practices, many businesses make other contributions to the welfare of their employees and their families. These include recreational facilities and events, free or "at cost" meals, housing, utilities, scholarships for employees' children, special gifts, and so forth; their extent is not known.

For the recreation of employees, often of their families as well, businesses may provide the traditional "company picnic" or "outing"; gymnasiums and athletic equipment; sports grounds and even parks; recreation and reading rooms; and so forth. Company facilities are sometimes used as hobby shops or for workers to repair cars and household equipment. Company cafeterias are usually operated on a non-profit basis and sometimes free meals are provided employees, especially workers on overtime or extra shifts. Managers and proprietors of smaller concerns in particular often provide employees and their families with goods or even money, sometimes as "special bonuses," sometimes because of the particular need of the person or family concerned; these may or may not be considered part of the fringe benefit package. A number of larger businesses and some smaller ones have instituted scholarship plans for children of employees; sometimes the company itself administers the plan but more often it turns it over to a college or university, or to one of the several non-profit organizations specializing in the administration of scholarship programs.

Some businesses also provide living facilities for their workers. "Company housing" and "company towns" have had a checkered history. Traditionally they were often associated with the worst kind of working conditions; immigrants and new workers from rural areas were provided miserable housing and were forced to pay excessively for it from their wages, and were often required to buy overpriced goods at company stores. In these circumstances the company town was often a highly profitable enterprise in its own right. These practices, only slightly improved, are still followed in some areas, particularly in the South and in some mining regions. In many more cases, however, company housing and towns are of decided benefit to workers. Generally, such housing ranges from adequate to excellent and is available at nominal rentals. In some copper-mining towns of upper Michigan, for example, large and well-built company houses are rented to mine workers and to others at rates as low as $1 or $2 per room per month, while water may be supplied free of charge (at Painesdale, Michigan, for example). A relatively new practice on the part of some of the largest corporations is the financing and construction of entire suburban developments in the vicinity of their plants, for rental or sale at nominal prices to their employees.

EXTERNAL WELFARE ACTIVITIES OF BUSINESSES

The owners and managers of American corporations annually contribute a half billion dollars or more of business funds to social welfare agencies, colleges and universities, hospitals, and similar organizations. These contributions are generally called "corporate giving," and their amounts are estimated on the basis of analysis of income tax returns of the 900,000 corporations in the United States. They do not include all monetary contributions of American businesses by any means, though. There are at least three and a half million unincorporated firms, as well as other business operations such as professional service operations, whose contributions cannot be estimated in this way; though most of these businesses are small their total contributions are probably on the order of tens if not hundreds of millions of dollars. In addition to monetary contributions businessmen make many donations of time, energy, and facilities and equipment for community purposes. Businesses and their employees may or may not get some direct benefits in return from these various contributions; the greatest and most direct benefits are felt by persons not directly connected with the businesses, and hence these activities are considered "external welfare."

Corporate Contributions

THERE IS LITTLE DOUBT that corporate giving makes up the bulk of the external welfare benefits provided by business. Federal law on the subject has become increasingly favorable to such contributions. The relevant provisions of the Internal Revenue Code appear in Chapter I of the Internal Revenue Code of 1954, under Section 170: "Charitable, Etc., Contributions and Gifts."

   a (1) General Rule.—There shall be allowed as a deduction any charitable contribution (as defined in subsection [c]) payment of which is made within the taxable year. A charitable contribution shall be allowable as a deduction only if verified under regulations prescribed by the Secretary or his delegate. . . .

   b (2) Corporations.—In the case of a corporation, the total deductions under subsection (*a*) for any taxable year shall not exceed 5 percent of the taxpayer's taxable income. . . .

   c Charitable Contribution Defined.—For purposes of this section, the term "charitable contribution" means a contribution or gift to or for the use of—

   (1) a State, a Territory, a possession of the United States, or any political subdivision of any of the foregoing, or the United States or the District of Columbia, but only if the contribution or gift is made for exclusively public purposes.

   (2) A corporation, trust, or community chest, fund, or foundation—

   (A) created or organized in the United States . . . ;

   (B) organized and operated exclusively for religious, charitable, scientific, literary, or educational purposes or for the prevention of cruelty to children or animals;

   (C) no part of the net earnings of which inures to the benefit of any private shareholder or individual; and

   (D) no substantial part of the activities of which is carrying on propaganda, or otherwise attempting, to influence legislation.

   (3) A post or organization of war veterans, or an auxiliary unit or society of, or trust or foundation for, any such post or organization. . . .

Under these provisions a corporation can make a very wide range of contributions, and because of the tax structure it can ordinarily do so at relatively little cost to itself or its stockholders, at least up to 5 per cent of its taxable income. If a corporation's profits are taxable at 52 per cent and it makes a charitable donation of $10,000 that is deductible, the actual cost to the corporation and its stockholders is only $4,800.[7]

TABLE 6

CORPORATE GIVING, 1942–1958
(*In Millions of Dollars*)

Year	Net Income Before Deductions	Five Per Cent Allowable Deductions	Contributions Deducted	Per Cent of Contributions to Net Income
1942	$23,139.9	$1,157.0	$ 98.3	0.42%
1945	21,405.6	1,070.3	265.7	1.24
1948	34,664.4	1,733.2	239.3	0.69
1951	43,888.6	2,194.4	343.0	0.78
1953	39,979.2	1,999.0	494.5	1.24 [1]
1954	36,642.2	1,832.1	313.7	0.86
1955	47,949.3	2,397.5	414.8	0.87
1956	46,884.9	2,344.2	418.0	0.89
1957	45,073.4	2,253.7	418.9	0.92
1958	39,224.1	1,961.2	395.4	1.08

Sources: *Giving USA 1958*, *Giving USA 1960*. New York: American Association of Fund-Raising Counsel, 1958, 1960, various pages.

[1] Excess profits taxes were in effect in 1953.

By the early 1950's sixteen State legislatures also had passed laws that in effect extended the powers of corporate managers to make charitable donations. It should be pointed out that managers have not always had such power, but until fairly recently were required to demonstrate how a particular donation served the purposes of the corporation, if its stockholders so requested.

Taking advantage of enabling legislation, a great many corporations have established foundations to take charge of their giving, and the general pace of such giving has increased from year to year. Some of the data on total corporate giving for various years are given in Table 6.

[7] The favorable effect on corporate giving of tax deduction provisions is substantiated by West Germany's experience. Between 1950 and 1958, West German corporate giving quintupled, partly because of the country's economic recovery but more particularly because of new provisions that up to 10 per cent of taxable corporate and individual income could be deducted for philanthropy.

There has been some fluctuation in such giving, partly because of general economic conditions, partly because of changes in the tax structure (*e.g.,* the excess profits tax imposed in the early 1950's), but there is a definite long-term increase. The popularity of corporation foundations as a channel for part of this giving is indicated by the fact that there were an estimated 1,500 corporate foundations in the mid-1950's (cf. Chapter 11), while new ones are continually being created.

The distribution of corporate giving by purpose is estimated in Table 7. The percentages are based on a survey by the National Industrial Conference Board of a number of large concerns; smaller corporations may or may not contribute for the same purposes and in approxi-

TABLE 7

ESTIMATED DISTRIBUTION OF CORPORATE GIVING IN 1958

Purpose	Per Cent [1]	Amount [1]
Social Welfare (Primarily Community Chests and United Funds)	39%	$205,000,000
Education	34	178,000,000
Medicine and Health	11	58,000,000
Civic and Cultural	4	21,000,000
Religion	.5	3,000,000
Other	11.5	60,000,000
Totals	100%	$525,000,000

Source: *Giving USA 1959.* New York: American Association of Fund-Raising Counsel, 1959, p. 36.

[1] Percentages from a National Industrial Conference Board survey of contributions by a small number of large corporations, applied to estimated total contributions by corporations in 1958.

mately the same proportions as do the largest corporations. Almost three-quarters of the contributions in the late 1950's were for federated welfare campaigns, local welfare agencies, and education; most contributions to education were made to colleges and universities. (Also see Chapter 8, the section on "Higher Education.")

Attitudes toward corporate giving are varied, although on the whole the general public and stockholders have favored corporate giving. In the late 1940's Opinion Research Corporation surveyed attitudes toward such giving, and, though detailed findings were held confidential, the following general conclusions were stated:

> Of the general public, 80 per cent approve corporation giving to charitable causes; only 5 per cent definitely disapprove. When the same question was asked a group of community leaders—

teachers, clergymen, lawyer, editors—a slightly smaller percentage favored: 78 per cent for, and 7 per cent against, with 5 per cent qualified support and 10 per cent no opinion. When the question was narrowed to those community leaders who hold stocks, substantially no difference was shown: 76 per cent for, and 8 per cent opposed. Under the still more searching question, "Should officers in the company in which you own stock give company money to charitable causes?" the favorable votes declined to 62 per cent, the negative rose to 12 per cent—still a strong approving sentiment.[8]

Some information on the motives of corporate giving and the means of determining the amount of corporate contributions has been obtained in a survey of corporate contributions to national health agencies, conducted by the National Better Business Bureau. Data from 158 companies were obtained; most of the companies had more than one thousand employees. In 1956 all but six of the companies had contributed to national health agencies. Their total contributions to such agencies were nearly $5 million, most of which was given to the American Red Cross.

The executives of 115 companies said that they were motivated by the health agencies' relation to "the need of society." A number of executives (twenty-one) thought that such contributions by business were not so much a corporation *obligation* as a social function. Ten executives believed that it *was* the responsibility or obligation of their corporations to make such contributions. Personal interest on the part of company executives was cited as a motive in sixty-three instances, and forty-one executives said that "the effect of a disease on the economy" was an influential consideration. Some men also mentioned pressures of various kinds, such as the interest of important customers and the pressure of "big names." Some executives had contributed because of the emotional appeal of the drives and, on the other side of the same coin, to promote public relations. Various means were used to determine the amount of a corporation's contribution; the most frequently used bases were a percentage of a local or regional campaign goal, a per-employee contribution, or a donation in keeping with the firm's own budget allowance for contributions (cf. Table 8).[9]

No doubt a good measure of the increase in corporate giving is due to a new attitude among the managerial component of business. Despite the objections of some owners, managers are often ready to make the decision to give, for one thing believing in a new image of business

[8] *Meeting the Problem of Charitable Contributions*, Princeton, N.J.: Opinion Research Corporation, 1948, cited in F. Emerson Andrews, *Corporation Giving*. New York: Russell Sage Foundation, 1952, p. 18.
[9] *Corporate Contributions to National Health Agencies*. New York: National Better Business Bureau, 1957, pp. 2–7.

that emphasizes social responsibility. They may feel that the amount to be given is small in proportion to total income and that it results in good public relations and in influence on the community and the educational system. Often they may have the unspoken hope, or may make the explicit statement, that increased business contributions to welfare and educational purposes will forestall further government activity in these fields. One prominent businessman has stated, "The question is no longer whether to give; the question is, how much and to whom?" [10]

TABLE 8

How Corporate Contribution Amounts are Determined

On a Percentage Basis of a Total Campaign Goal	23%
On a Per-Employee Basis	16
In Conformance with Budget Allowance	12
Budget Prorated According to Needs of Various Agencies	8
Matching Comparable Companies	8
On Basis of Need	5
On Basis of Previous Contributions	5
On Basis of Value to Employees and Community	4
On Basis of Matching Employee Contributions	4
On Some Other Basis	14
No Answer	1
	100%

Source: *Corporate Contributions to National Health Agencies.* New York: National Better Business Bureau, 1957, p. 8.

Other Forms of Business Philanthropy

IT WAS PREVIOUSLY MENTIONED that many businesses other than corporations make charitable contributions and that there is no accurate measure of the extent of such contributions. In addition businesses of all sizes may extend non-financial assistance to community welfare projects. These are some examples: building material donated to a church and a community recreation center; Christmas parties and gifts for underprivileged children; workers to help repair storm and flood damage; donations of land for community recreational facilities; use of managerial and staff personnel for federated campaigns and community welfare boards. The last has received special emphasis in recent years. Many businesses strongly encourage their managerial people to seek administrative and advisory positions in community welfare activity, often on company time; the prestige and community influence of the

[10] For example, cf. Howard R. Bowen, *Social Responsibilities of the Businessman.* New York: Harper & Brothers, 1953, pp. 125–27 and elsewhere.

company are thus enhanced, and the welfare organization secures the skilled direction and assistance necessary for its success.

The relationship between a business and the community in which it is located is generally a symbiotic one. The business cannot exist without a source of labor and utilities, and a certain minimum of good-will on the part of the community; the community, in turn, is often dependent on the business, particularly if the business is fairly large or the community small, for much of its income and even for the pleasantness of its physical environment. This may seem to be some-what removed from the question of philanthropy; it is quite close to the question of welfare, however. The maintenance of good relations with the community is a fundamental motive for the external welfare activities of business. Still more pertinent is the fact that quite a few businesses have been established with the express purpose of improving a community's economy and putting its unemployed to work. It was for this reason that two physicians in Milan, Michigan, organized a plastics firm in 1946 with nine employees; by 1957 the firm had over 250 employees. Similarly, under the leadership of Arthur Morgan, former chairman of the Tennessee Valley Authority, the people of the once-depressed rural community of Yellow Springs, Ohio, have developed a number of small, locally owned industries; the economy of the area has thrived as a result. There are many parallel examples elsewhere in the United States; they demonstrate that rural and semi-rural communities need not necessarily be characterized by unemployment, impoverished families, and the migration of their young people to urban areas. Such depressed conditions are certainly not characteristic of all rural America, yet they are quite common; the development of local industry may offer a solution, as Americans have demonstrated elsewhere in the world in sponsoring community development projects in underdeveloped areas.

INSURANCE

THE NON-GOVERNMENTAL INSURANCE SYSTEM is one type of business operation that has particular relevance to welfare. The outstanding trait of insurance is that it furnishes protection to people against more or less predictable future events in their lives, a protection without which they might have to resort to special-purpose welfare programs. Two types of non-governmental insurance that particularly reveal this trait are life and retirement insurance, and health and medical insurance. They are voluntary and individually financed forms of social security. Health and medical insurance protection is offered both by firms operating on a "for-profit" basis and by organizations that are non-profit, yet non-governmental. Both are operated in keeping with business principles; their major functional difference is that they usually offer different types of coverage packages. Both types are discussed in the sub-section on health insurance, below.

One further qualification of the following discussion is that it includes both individual and group insurance, and thus partly duplicates the material above and in the following chapter on insurance that is provided as fringe benefits. This duplication is necessary for the presentation of a comprehensive picture of non-governmental insurance coverage in the United States. It should be kept in mind that much, though by no means all, of the group life and health insurance coverage is partly or entirely provided by employers for employees. Industrial life insurance and retirement insurance are almost entirely employer-financed.

Life Insurance and Retirement Insurance

LIFE INSURANCE and retirement insurance are designed to protect the insured and his family against the foreseen consequences of either premature death or old age without sufficient income. Some types of policies—annuity contracts—provide for both contingencies: they pay a lump sum if the insured dies before a specified age and after that age, usually the retirement age, they pay a monthly sum until death. There is a great variety of insurance contracts and for the most part they can be discussed here only in general terms. One increasingly popular type that deserves separate mention is the family income policy, noteworthy for its similarity to the national government Old Age and Survivors Insurance (OASI). The family income policy pays a monthly sum to the insured's family—his wife and children—if he dies before a specified age; his family is thus guaranteed more long-term protection than a lump-sum payment of straight life insurance would provide.

A few statistics demonstrate the extent of life insurance holdings in the United States. At the end of 1958 seven out of ten persons, 123 million people, were covered by some form of non-governmental life insurance. Of these people 112 million were insured by the legal reserve insurance companies; the value of their insurance was about $490 billion, or $8,800 per family, nearly triple the average amount of insurance per family held in 1946. More than half of this insurance was accounted for by ordinary life insurance policies—policies purchased individually, which are of several types, including family income policies and retirement income annuity policies. The rest of it (cf. Table 9) was group life insurance, industrial insurance, and credit insurance; the last assures full payment of loans in the event of the insured's death. Life insurance on a non-profit basis is provided individuals by fraternal orders (cf. Chapter 7) and by assessment life associations; in 1957 there were 11.5 million such policies, with a value of $10 billion in force.

TABLE 9

LIFE INSURANCE IN THE UNITED STATES, 1958

Type of Insurance	Number of Policies (*Thousands*)	*Per Cent of Population Covered* [1]	Value of Policies (*Billions*)	Value per Policy
Commercial				
Ordinary Life	89,260	(*n.a.*) [1]	$287.8	$3,220
Group Life	38,716 [2]	22.1%	144.6	3,730
Industrial Life	104,246	(*n.a.*) [1]	39.6	380
Credit Life	35,004	20.0%	21.5	610
Fraternal [3]	8,669	5.0%	$ 9.2	$1,060
Assessment [3]	2,800	1.6%	$ 0.8	$ 270
Totals	278,700 [1]	70.3% [1]	$503.5	$1,810

Payments to Policyholders	Amount (*Millions*)	Per Cent
Commercial Insurance Companies		
Death Benefits	$2,972	38.3%
Policy Dividends	1,566	20.2
Surrender Values	1,457	18.6
Matured Endowments	760	9.9
Annuity Payments	578	7.4
Disability and Accidental Death Benefits	133	1.7
Fraternal Insurance Benefits [3]	167	2.2
Assessment Associations [3]		
Death Benefits	6	0.1
Other Payments to Members	133	1.7
Totals	$7,772	100%

Note: Totals do not necessarily add because of rounding.
Source: *Statistical Abstract* 1959, pp. 472–75.

[1] Many persons hold several insurance policies, hence the total number of policies in force is more than twice the actual number of persons covered (an estimated 123 million). Many persons are covered by several ordinary life policies, many are covered by several industrial life policies.
[2] Group life policy figures refer to actual numbers of persons covered.
[3] Data for 1957.

Benefits paid by life insurance companies in 1959 were some $7.7 billion. Less than half of this was in death benefits to beneficiaries; the rest was paid to living policyholders in the forms of policy dividends, surrender values, matured endowments, and annuity and disability payments. That the largest part of benefits was paid to living policyholders suggests that "life insurance" has actually become largely a form of individual savings, carrying with it some additional benefits in protection.

Insurance companies also handle some of the pension plans provided by employers for their employees. Insured pension plans covered 4.5 million persons in 1956; four-fifths of the premiums paid in were contributed directly by employers.[11] In 1958 a total of nineteen million non-governmental employees were covered under various pensions plans; insurance companies thus administered the plans covering about one quarter of them.[12]

One important problem for life insurance companies in the United States is the investment of their assets. By 1959 the assets of life insurance companies totaled nearly $114 billion. More than half these funds were placed in business and industrial securities, while a third were mortgages. Total corporation assets in 1959 were over one trillion dollars, and insurance companies held nearly 5 per cent of these in the form of stocks and bonds—primarily the latter. In addition many of the assets of fraternal orders, health insurance plans, property insurance companies, and other insurance organizations also are held in the form of bonds. As more and more consumers purchase insurance, insurance organizations will come to hold more and more dominant positions as investors in the economy; they are generally subject to State regulations as to the types of investments they may make, and are themselves interested in stable, long-term investments. It has been suggested that their conservative investment interests may have considerable influence on future economic stability.

Health Insurance

HEALTH INSURANCE, or "voluntary private illness insurance," has been one of the most rapidly growing types of insurance protection. Some of the recent data on the subject are given in Tables 10 and 11. In 1958 at least three-fourths of the population was covered by some form of health insurance; many persons were covered by several types. Because of the large degree of overlapping among types of policies, it is not possible to determine the exact number of persons who are covered by some form of health insurance at any given time. In addition, between

[11] *Life Insurance Fact Book: 1957.* New York: Institute of Life Insurance, 1957, pp. 32–39.
[12] *Statistical Abstract 1960,* p. 475. Many of the remaining pension plans were administered by corporations themselves, a few by unions. Educational, religious, and other non-profit organizations also administer pension funds for their employees.

TABLE 10

HEALTH INSURANCE COVERAGE, 1957

Type of Plan	Enrollment [1]	Enrollment as Percentage of Population [1]
Medical Care Insurance		
Hospitalization	121,161,000	72.0%
Commercial Individual Insurance	28,673,000	17.0
Commercial Group Insurance	48,439,000	27.6
Blue Cross Plans (Non-Profit)	51,857,000	30.8
Other Plans [2]	8,013,000	4.8
Surgical	108,683,000	64.6%
Commercial Individual Insurance	24,928,000	14.8
Commercial Group Insurance	48,955,000	29.1
Blue Shield Plans (Non-Profit)	38,343,000	22.8
Other Plans [2]	11,637,000	6.9
Medical Care	71,611,000	42.5%
Commercial Individual Insurance	7,371,000	4.4
Commercial Group Insurance	28,317,000	16.8
Blue Cross and Blue Shield (Non-Profit; est.)	37,000,000	22.0
Other Plans [2] (est.)	6,000,000	3.6
Major Medical Expense [3]	13,262,000	7.9%
Commercial Individual Insurance	834,000	0.5
Commercial Group Insurance	12,428,000	7.4
Loss of Income Insurance (1955 Data)		
Commercial Individual Insurance	14,238,000	8.8
Commercial Group Insurance	19,238,000	11.9
Other Plans (est.)	1,200,000	0.7
Paid Sick Leave [4]	3,100,000	1.9

Sources: *Statistical Abstract 1959*, pp. 475–78; John G. Turnbull et al., *Economic and Social Security: Public and Private Measures Against Economic Insecurity*, New York: Ronald Press, 1957, pp. 354–55.

[1] On the basis of total civilian population of the United States, 168.4 million in mid-1957, 162.3 million in mid-1955. All *totals* have been adjusted downward for duplication, which varies from 5 to 15 per cent in different categories.
[2] These include plans established by industry, local consumer groups, fraternal orders, private clinics, and universities.
[3] There is believed to be no significant duplication in this category.
[4] In addition, 4.8 million civilian government employees were covered by paid sick-leave provisions.

5 and 15 per cent of the persons with a given type of health insurance are covered by several policies.

One indication of the growth of health insurance is the fact that the total number of policies in force in 1945 was about 50 million, while in 1958 it was close to 330 million. Adjusting for duplication for specific types of health insurance, between 1955 and 1958 the percentage of the population covered by hospital insurance rose from 65.5 to 71.5 per cent; surgical insurance from 55.3 to 64.7 per cent; medical insurance (for physicians' care) from 33.8 to 43.8 per cent; and major medical expense insurance (protection against especially heavy costs) from about 3 to 12.3 per cent (in 1959).

TABLE 11

PERSONAL COSTS OF MEDICAL CARE AND HEALTH INSURANCE
BENEFITS, 1954
(*In Millions of Dollars*)

Type of Cost	Amount	Insurance Benefits	Per Cent of Loss Covered by Insurance
Medical Expenses			
Hospital Services	$ 2,970	$1,442	48.5%
Doctors' Services	2,963	737	24.8
Dentists' Services[1]	975		
Other Professional Services[1]	583		
Medicines and Appliances[1]	2,197		
Net Cost of Insurance[2]	577		
Totals	$10,264	$2,179	21.2%
Income Loss			
Disability income loss	$ 6,157	$1,361	22.2
Net cost of insurance[2]	456		
Totals	$ 6,613	$1,361	20.5%

Note: Totals do not necessarily add because of rounding.
Source: John G. Turnbull *et al. Economic and Social Security: Public and Private Measures Against Economic Insecurity.* New York: Ronald Press, 1957, p. 357.

[1] Insurance benefits negligible.
[2] Premiums paid less benefits received.

Health insurance benefits by no means pay the majority of the costs of individual illness, as the data in Table 11 suggest. In 1954 they provided slightly more than a fifth of the medical expenses incurred by individuals, and income-loss payments made up for 20.5 per cent of the salaries lost because of illness and injury. The number of policies in force may have as much as doubled between 1954 and 1960, but it is not likely that more than 30 or 35 per cent of the personal costs of medical care were met by health insurance benefits in the latter year. However, one study of the subject points out that

it should be borne in mind that dental services, medicines, appliances, and other services not usually covered by insurance are included in our concept of personal health services. It is unlikely that the most comprehensive prepayment plans in existence cover more than 50 per cent of the costs of the whole range of personal health services sought by families and individuals.[13]

Health care expenses that are most often covered by insurance plans are those that are of an emergency nature, or impose heavy financial burdens on families. These are hospital service, surgery, and obstetrics. The study cited above notes that, in the mid-1950's, 50 per cent of hospital service was paid for by insurance, 38 per cent of surgery expenses, and a quarter of obstetric expenses.[14]

A survey of health insurance coverage in 1958 found that more than 123 million Americans paid $5.9 billion for such coverage, including payments made on their behalf by employers. The organizations surveyed were 706 insurance companies, eighty-three Blue Cross and sixty-six Blue Shield plans, and some 400 other health plans. They paid out benefits totaling $4.7 billion, which was 28 per cent of total medical care expenditures, $16.7 billion.[15]

There is a certain amount of substitutability between non-governmental and governmental insurance programs. How much substitution is a matter of some dispute. Some leading insurance executives, for example Carrol Shanks, from 1946 president of the Prudential Insurance Company, have considered the governmental insurance program as providing a necessary minimum level of income protection, whereas the business system builds up a private welfare program, or series of programs, above this minimum. In 1950 Mr. Shanks was quoted as saying:

> Established social security, group annuities and other private pension programs, sickness and liability insurance, hospitalization and medical insurance—group life insurance and individual life insurance—all of these together point a way to a better and more secure way of life under our traditional American freedom. Here is the effective alternative to the demands of the welfare state with its vast load of taxation on the working generation.[16]

There are problems inherent in such a system as the following quotation from a study of health insurance in the mid-1950's indicates:

> Today approximately 100 million people, or 61 per cent of the population, carry some form of health insurance. In all likelihood, approximately 15 per cent of the population cannot or need not be covered by some type of insurance because they are recipients of public assistance, in the armed services, and in institutions. This

[13] Odin W. Anderson and Jacob J. Feldman. *Family Medical Costs and Voluntary Health Insurance: A Nationwide Survey.* New York: McGraw-Hill, 1956, p. 24.
[14] *Ibid.,* p. 25.
[15] "5.9 Billion Spent on Health Plans," *New York Times,* Dec. 21, 1959.
[16] Earl Chapin May and Will Oursler. *The Prudential: A Story of Human Security.* New York: Doubleday, 1950, pp 342–43.

does not include the undetermined number of people who would not buy health insurance as a matter of choice and inertia. Thus, approximately 72 per cent of the population that can potentially be covered now carries some type of health insurance.

This achievement, phenomenal as it is, cannot be regarded as a valid measure of achievement, since adequate benefits—even when adequacy is defined as 80 per cent of the hospital and surgical costs—is by no means spread evenly over the 100 million or so covered at the present time.

Let us assume that the remaining 28 per cent of the potential population is to be covered by the usual range of benefits now generally available, namely, hospital care and in-hospital physicians' services. It would appear that this 28 per cent—roughly 40 million people—constitutes a segment of the population that is relatively difficult to reach. This segment is characterized by either low income or self-employment and frequently by both. For the low-income group some kind of subsidy from one source or another is certainly indicated. . . .

In this survey it was revealed that over 70 per cent of the families with income over $3,000 were covered by some type of health insurance, and under $3,000 approximately 40 per cent of the families were covered. . . . It is likely that further coverage of incomes over $3,000 represents an enrollment problem of individuals and small groups, and among low-income groups there are problems of both low income and lack of a common employer. Enrollment, so far, has been predominantly through group enrollment with payroll deducations. Methods need to be found to enroll individuals and small groups at a reasonable administrative cost and with benefits at least comparable to those received by persons enrolled in groups. Previous evidence has shown that benefits under individual contracts are not so broad as those under group contracts.[17]

Regarding the total cost of medical service under a non-governmental system covering the entire population, the same study estimated that the prevailing types of insurance benefits could be provided by an increase of $1.5 billion, exclusive of administrative costs; i.e., the total costs of all private personal health services at the 1954 rate would increase from $10.2 billion to about $11.7 billion. "Speculating further, if all persons were covered by the prevailing types of hospital insurance benefits, the total hospital charges for private patients might rise from $2.0 billion to approximately $2.5, or an increase of $500 million." [18]

If these speculations are valid, comprehensive health insurance cov-

[17] Anderson and Feldman. *Family Medical Costs and Voluntary Health Insurance: A Nationwide Survey.* Copyright 1956 by McGraw-Hill Book Company, Inc., pp. 82–83.
[18] *Ibid.,* p. 84.

erage could be achieved at relatively small cost. Between 1909 and 1952 there was a sixfold increase in the percentage of personal consumption expenditures for accident and health insurance and an increase by half in percentage expenditure for medical care. The individual has apparently been more than willing to pay for medical care as it has become available and as his income has increased, and the additional expenditures for total coverage are certainly close enough to be within reach. As noted above, coverage has been expanding year by year and it is likely that by the middle 1960's no more than 10 per cent of the non-institutionalized population will lack a certain minimum of protection against unexpected medical expenses.

CONCLUDING REMARKS

THE BUSINESS SYSTEM of the United States assumes the major burden for the provision of a high material level of life to the American people. Recreation, housing, clothing, medical care, and other major items of consumption are provided for most people *via* the market's bargaining process. Whenever the price of essential goods and services goes down in relation to people's income, the business system is in effect reducing the need for other methods of aiding the poorest customer. Its success in this regard goes beyond that of any other in the world. However, those welfare activities of business that are within the particular scope of the present survey are not historically those of the marketplace. Business provides a number of programs benefiting its managers, employees, and their families. It also engages in philanthropy very much as would a non-profit corporation, a foundation, a community council, or a government.

Some of the general functions of American business are close to what are otherwise regarded as special welfare needs. Insurance is the most prominent of this category; insurance foresees a possible special need for help and enables the person or group, along with other policyholders, to meet the need. Seven-tenths of the population is covered by some form of non-governmental life insurance. Three-quarters of the population is covered by some form of health insurance. The most difficult problem remains the tenth of the people whose family wage earners are uneducated, very poorly paid, and sporadically employed.

Recent years have shown a rapid increase in the "fringe benefits" paid by business not only to its ordinary employees but also to its highest officials. Even the smallest corporations now find that the tax laws and the economies of group purchases encourage insurance and other benefit plans. A recent study of a thousand firms shows that an average of $981 per employee per year was paid by business for fringe benefits, ranging from life insurance and pensions to premium pay for holiday work. The reason why certain businesses and certain occupations give more fringe benefits than others are complex and only partly known. Besides fringe benefits measured in dollar terms, companies nowadays provide more comfortable surroundings and more pleasant activities for their employees. In addition, they have taken up in most cases a new philosophy of human relations in management that gives much more scrupulous attention to the wishes, needs, and ideas of workers than was granted a generation ago.

Outside the factory and office, businesses are increasingly active in community welfare work and civic activities. Corporate philanthropy is growing rapidly and amounts now to over half a billion dollars a year in direct giving to education and welfare. Hundreds of company foundations have sprung up and more are born daily. The law of corporate contributions has been liberalized to foster company giving. In many communities business concerns have become the dominant element in various charitable fund drives. The motives behind the recent development of the non-strictly economic side of business operations in America are several; in addition to all the motives that inspire philanthropic activity in other institutions and in personal life, a doctrine of the social responsibilities of business has gathered great force in the past twenty-five years. Its new role in welfare is both an opportunity to exert greater influence and to mobilize greater economic effort and a limitation on "business as usual."

Chapter Ten

LABOR UNIONS

AMERICAN LABOR UNIONS, involving seventeen million members in 1960,[1] have always been occupied with welfare programs directed at their members. Since their founding, the majority of unions have attempted to assure their members adequate wages, protection from abuses by employers, satisfactory working conditions, job security, and some means of support for those who suffer accidents or illnesses. Many unions in the United States today have achieved most of these purposes. To further increase union prestige and economic power, as well as to attract and hold new members, a number of unions and union leaders have adopted the policy of making new and more extensive demands of business and government, demands for both more economic goods and further security for their members. These activities for the welfare of unions and their members comprise a significant sector of the American welfare system.

At the same time, unions have also sponsored an increasing number of welfare activities for the benefit of those outside unions, not only families of union members but entire communities. There are several reasons for this trend, which has become particularly evident only since World War II. One reason, of course, is that union members and their families benefit directly and indirectly in communities in which welfare activities are extensive and well-supported. Equally important, however, may be the desires of union leaders to attain legitimacy for

[1] Excluding about one million Canadian members of unions with headquarters in the United States.

their organizations, that is, acceptance by the local community, government bodies, and business organizations. This legitimacy has been hard come by. Because of the sometimes violent and anti-individualist forms taken by the union movement in the United States, particularly during the late nineteenth and the early twentieth century, labor organizations have been suspect to many Americans. Other forms of labor protest—insubordination, absenteeism, walkouts, strikes—have generally been held unacceptable in American society. Union participation in community welfare activities, on the other hand, emphasizes union interest in the general welfare and has helped improve public evaluation of the union movement.

The labor unions have had a third, very general, and indirect welfare effect on American society. Although union membership has never exceeded one-third of the labor force of the United States, the unions have contributed to raising the status and economic benefits of most employed persons. The actual extent of this union contribution is a matter of dispute; some would argue that as far as economic goods are concerned most businesses would have granted wage increases whether unions existed or not. It cannot be denied, however, that to a considerable extent the union movement has been responsible for improved working conditions, greater fringe benefits, and increased prestige for workers in most occupations. For the most part this type of welfare contribution is beyond the scope of this chapter, which is devoted primarily to the more direct welfare benefits that unions provide or obtain from their members, families of their members, and communities. However, some relevant information is given in a discussion of the general extent of fringe benefits.

The union welfare activities discussed in this chapter are the results of two different factors. One is the worker's desire for security in the face of a sometimes hostile economic environment, expressed in union demands for higher wages, more benefits, and job security; and in the aggrandizement of the political, economic, and social power of the unions. The second factor is a corollary of the first. It is the necessity for developing and maintaining union organizations that can accomplish these purposes *and* achieve legitimacy. Labor organizations have extensive financial holdings, bureaucratic structures, and full-time, professional staffs. Their favored means of operation are the conference and the contract negotiation, and they resort to strikes only when other means appear inadequate, or, as sometimes happens, when they feel it necessary to demonstrate their economic power.

Most union welfare activities have initially been responses to the welfare interests of union members and their families. They have included funeral benefits, sickness benefits, aid to distressed union members' families, and social and recreational facilities for the membership.

A second group of activities has occupied a smaller place in the total scope of union operations. These are the welfare services directed primarily to non-union recipients and welfare organizations: volunteer services to community groups, union fund-raising for social welfare services, scholarships, disaster relief, and a few others.

It is not always easy to distinguish clearly between the union programs that are concerned primarily with union membership and those directed toward other groups. One way to do so is to arrange union welfare activities on a scale that ranges from solely internal concern to solely external concern, as is done in Figure 1.

The relative positions of union welfare activities on this scale correspond roughly to their positions on a scale of "functional importance," ranging from primary functions to incidental functions (cf. Figure 1). Several premises must be made in constructing such a scale. The primary and original function of labor organization presumably was the welfare of its members: certain welfare needs of these members have been more urgent than others. For example, the fundamental desire of the worker was for a wage sufficient to provide him with the essentials of life at any given time. Second only to this was his desire for a *continuing* source of support—his desire for job security. The provision of such services as insurance, medical and pension benefits, housing, and education have been desirable contributions to the worker's welfare, from his point of view, but they could have been readily obtained from other sources; many unions have neither negotiated nor developed programs in these areas. Union community services are relevant to the interests of the individual member in so far as they strengthen welfare services outside the union that he or his family may need. Union community services also have provided the union member with an opportunity for achieving personal satisfaction through helping his neighbors and community.

In Figure 1, seven types of union-related welfare benefits are used to illustrate the two scales mentioned above, one ranging from internal concern to external concern and the other from primary importance to incidental importance. These types of benefits and others are discussed in the remainder of this chapter. Here is can be noted that the more external and incidental activities were developed most recently in the history of labor organizations. Adequate wages and job security were original concerns of labor organizations; life and disability insurance interested unions beginning in the late 1800's, labor education services were initiated about 1915, union housing projects in the 1920's. National labor organizations did not actively sponsor participation in community chests or volunteer labor on community projects until the 1940's, though of course some workers and local labor organizations had earlier participated in such activities.

FIGURE 1

UNION WELFARE ACTIVITIES

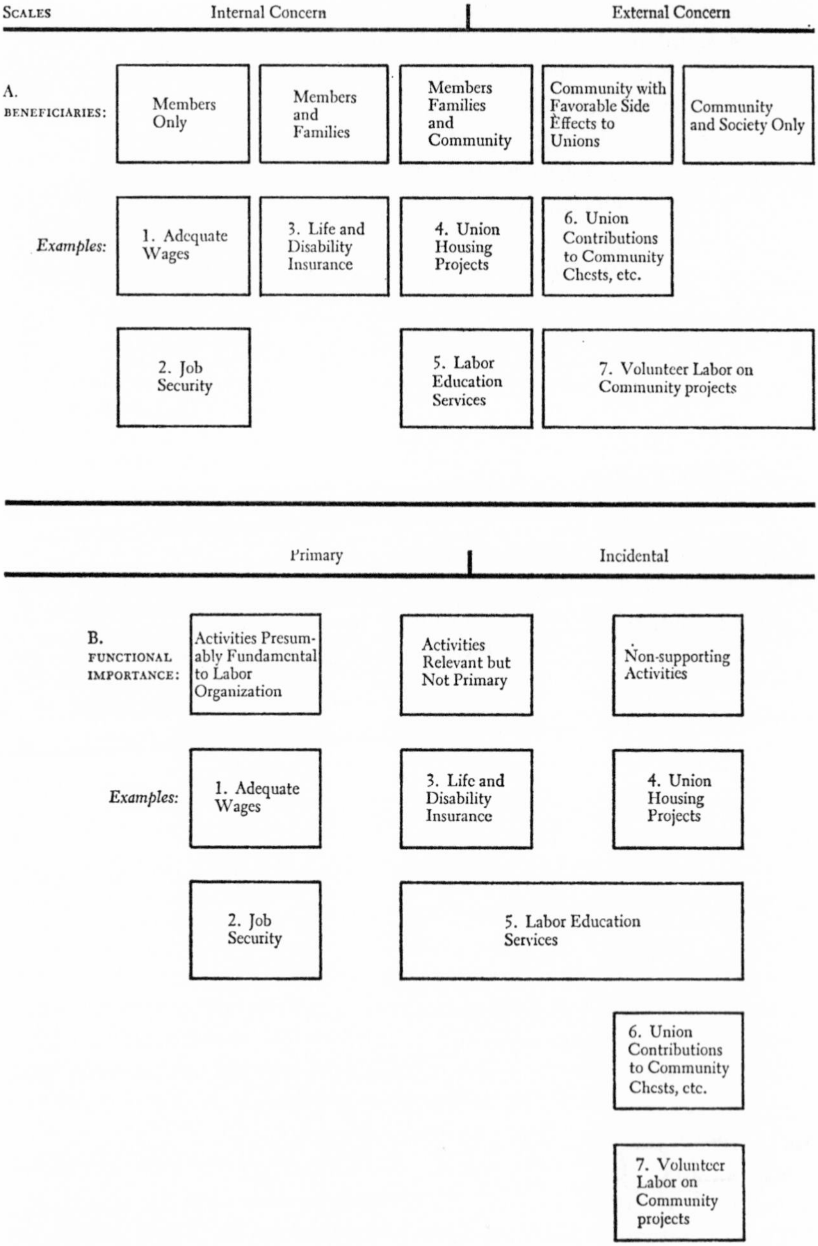

SCALES	Internal Concern			External Concern	

A.
BENEFICIARIES:

Members Only	Members and Families	Members Families and Community	Community with Favorable Side Effects to Unions	Community and Society Only

Examples:

1. Adequate Wages	3. Life and Disability Insurance	4. Union Housing Projects	6. Union Contributions to Community Chests, etc.

2. Job Security		5. Labor Education Services	7. Volunteer Labor on Community projects

	Primary		Incidental	

B.
FUNCTIONAL
IMPORTANCE:

Activities Presumably Fundamental to Labor Organization	Activities Relevant but Not Primary	Non-supporting Activities

Examples:

1. Adequate Wages	3. Life and Disability Insurance	4. Union Housing Projects

2. Job Security	5. Labor Education Services	

		6. Union Contributions to Community Chests, etc.

		7. Volunteer Labor on Community projects

UNION MEMBERSHIP AND ORGANIZATION

IN 1959 about seventeen million workers in the United States and its territories were labor union members. They comprised slightly more than one quarter of the labor force, a proportion that had been relatively constant since 1945. Four-fifths of them were men.

Most were members of some 130 AFL-CIO unions, which in 1959 had 12.7 million members. The twenty largest unions, each having 200,-000 or more members and all but two of them AFL-CIO, counted a total of nearly ten million members (cf. Table 1). In 1956 there were fifty-two independent unions organized nationally or internationally, most of them relatively small; in 1957 mergers had decreased their numbers to forty-seven. There are also many independent local unions and "company unions" that are not affiliated with national bodies; membership and other data on these unions are not known, hence most comprehensive statistics on labor organizations in the United States are somewhat inaccurate.

The AFL-CIO, formed by the merger of the American Federation of Labor and the Council of Industrial Organizations in December, 1955, is the dominant and guiding force in American unionism today. Its organization is such that its president may wield great powers. According to the AFL-CIO constitution the supreme governing body is the convention, in which all member unions are represented in proportion to their paid membership. However, this body meets only once every other year. The Executive Council, made up of the president, the secretary-treasurer, and twenty-seven vice-presidents, governs between conventions. It meets three times a year, on call of the president. At all other times the president, assisted by certain members of the Executive Council, directs the activities of the AFL-CIO. In practice, the Council is second only to the president in importance. Its duties include:

> Proposing and evaluating legislation of interest to the labor movement and keeping the federation free from corrupt or Communist influences. To achieve the latter, the Council has the right to investigate any affiliate accused of wrongdoing and, at the completion of the investigation, make recommendations or give directions to the affiliate involved. Furthermore, by a two-thirds vote, the Executive Council may suspend a union found guilty on charges of corruption or subversion.[2]

[2] *Directory of National and International Labor Unions in the United States, 1957.* U.S. Bureau of Labor Statistics. Washington, D.C.: USGPO, p. 4.

The AFL-CIO has a number of staff agencies, including six trade and industrial departments, and a department of organization. There are fourteen standing committees, many of which have staff depart-

TABLE 1

TWENTY LARGEST LABOR UNIONS, 1959 [1]

Union	Members	Change from Previous Year
International Brotherhood of Teamsters, Chauffeurs, Warehousemen and Helpers of America [2]	1,600,000	+244,000
United Automobile, Aircraft and Agricultural Implement Workers of America	1,060,000	−64,000
United Steelworkers of America	892,000	−39,000
United Brotherhood of Carpenters and Joiners of America	750,000	
International Association of Machinists	691,000	−26,000
United Mine Workers of America [2]	600,000 (1957)	
International Brotherhood of Electrical Workers	514,000	+21,500
International Hod Carriers, Building and Common Laborers Union of America	403,000	
International Ladies' Garment Workers Union	368,000	−5,500
Amalgamated Meat Cutters and Butcher Workmen of North America	329,000	+5,000
Retail Clerks International Association	315,000	+4,000
Hotel and Restaurant Employees' and Bartenders' International Union	300,000	
Amalgamated Clothing Workers of America	288,000	
International Union of Electrical, Radio and Machine Workers	280,000	−13,000
Communications Workers of America	261,000	+11,000
American Federation of Musicians	255,000	+1,000
Brotherhood of Railway and Steamship Clerks, Freight Handlers, Express and Station Employees of America	250,000	−7,000
International Union of Operating Engineers	241,000	+29,000
Building Service Employees International Union	235,000	−5,000
United Association of Journeymen and Apprentices of the Plumbing and Pipe Fitting Industry of the United States and Canada	200,000	
Totals	9,832,000	+166,000

Source: Harry Hansen, ed. *The World Almanac 1960.* New York: World-Telegram Corp., 1960, p. 49.

[1] Figures for most unions include Canadian members.
[2] These two unions are independent of the AFL-CIO.

ments. One of the more noted of these has been the Committee on Political Education (COPE), which in 1958 spent $570,000 in direct campaign aid to favored candidates, among other expenditures for political education purposes. It has received its funds in contributions from union members.[3] The work of another committee, the Committee on Community Services, is discussed subsequently.

The organization of national unions and their 77,000 locals varies a great deal. One recent study evaluated the constitutions of seventy unions (total membership about sixteen millions) with the intent of judging the degree of democracy that unions, as political societies, permit their members.[4] It found that many unions lack formal rules of due process in large areas, permitting potential and sometimes actual undemocratic procedures. Specifically:

(1) *Admissions:* Apprenticeship rules may be a bar to a person seeking membership in the union and sometimes provide an informal means for racial or political discrimination ("fraternal" approval of the applicant by the membership has the same effect). [Fourteen unions had apprenticeship programs; four unions had constitutional provisions stating racial discrimination; nine unions, representing nearly two million workers, had "fraternal approval requirements."]

(2) *Concentration of Power:* Generally speaking, most American unions reveal a concentration of power in the hands of the international president and grant only a limited effectiveness to the executive board in its task of overseeing all policy decisions. [For example, the president of the Steelworkers appoints, directs, suspends, and removes the organizers, staff members, and other employees of the union; interprets the union constitution; issues rules and regulations for the day-to-day conduct of affairs; appoints the committees of the international convention; and performs "such other duties as pertain to his office."]

(3) *The Convention:* All the unions in the sample designate the convention as the supreme body of the organization, but here again the president's power to appoint convention committees in some cases, and to preside over the convention in others, strengthens the tendency toward a concentration of executive power. [The international president appoints the convention committees in forty-nine unions; the executive committee appoints them in eleven others.]

(4) *Discipline:* In unions like the ITU [International Typographical Union], the UAW [United Automobile Workers], and the Upholsterers, there is a sensitivity to procedural rights in disciplinary cases, but in many of the unions in the sample the disciplinary board is staffed by the local executive committee or the local president—a dangerous situation because accused members are usually in opposition to the local administration.

[3] "Aid to Candidates Listed by Unions," *New York Times,* Nov. 16, 1958.
[4] Leo Bromwich. *Union Constitutions: A Report to The Fund for the Republic.* New York: The Fund for the Republic, July, 1959.

(5) *Union Press:* In almost all of the unions, the press is under the control of the incumbent administration, so that the official newspaper tends to be monopolized by a few people at the top of the union hierarchy and excludes vigorous controversy or opposition to prevailing administration policies.[5]

The existence of these conditions does not necessarily imply that the unions concerned are entirely oligarchic and undemocratic, or that their welfare-related activities do not reflect the interests of the majority of their members. These possibilities exist, however, and some union leaders have chosen to take them, in the knowledge that their union organization to a considerable extent protects them from internal pressures. It is also true that local members' interest in the union is generally low. Union membership and dues are sometimes believed to be a necessary evil contingent on employment, more often a vaguely "good thing" that protects them from employers and provides regular wage and benefit increases. Except during times of crisis, such as wage negotiations and strikes, the rank-and-file member has little knowledge of union policy on most subjects. Local business is usually conducted by a small group of activists, who also make decisions and expect the membership to ratify them almost automatically. Such conditions are true not only of unions, of course; they are to be found in most associations. They are stressed here because there is some evidence that they are more common in union organizations, and because they may affect the types of internal union welfare activities and the nature and degree of participation by union members in community welfare.

WELFARE FOR UNION MEMBERS

IN THE PAST, improving the welfare of union members has absorbed most of the energy and interest of unions. The fundamental demands of union members, adequate wages and job security, have been satisfied through collective bargaining. (It should be kept in mind that at least in some cases increased wages, benefits, and welfare services have been granted to union members by business managers other than through negotiation; that is, not all such increases in the welfare of union members have initially been sponsored by unions or first suggested in the course of contract negotiations.) Health, insurance, and pension plans, *i.e.*, unemployment and guaranteed annual wage plans, also may be obtained across the bargaining table. Newer developments have in-

[5] *Ibid.*, pp. 38–39; illustrative material from the same source, various pages.

cluded collectively bargained education funds for children of union members, union health facilities, and even welfare funds for non-union purposes, financed directly by employers but typically operated under union auspices. Some of the latter are discussed in subsequent sections. This section is concerned primarily with the welfare services and benefits that are generally provided for union members and their families through collective bargaining.

Jobs and Wages

IN 1914 Samuel Gompers remarked: "The general object of the Federation [the AFL] is to better the condition of the workers in all fields of human activity. Economic betterment in all directions comes first." In 1955 George Meany wrote: "We . . . seek an ever-rising standard of living—by which we mean not only more money but more leisure and a richer cultural life." [6] Concern for wage increases in prosperous times; for wage maintenance during depressions; for protection from arbitrary firing policies; for protection of seniority rights—these questions have been discussed at almost every union-management conference. Most industrial disputes and strikes have arisen from failure to settle these questions. In 1959 there were 3,708 work stoppages, involving about 1.9 million workers, most of them union members. These resulted in 69.0 million man-days idle, nine-tenths of them over wage and hour issues. Union organization and working conditions were responsible for almost all other strikes.

There is some information on the extent to which union-management negotiations have contributed to raising workers' real wages. In the building trades the minimum union scale increased 70 per cent between 1948 and 1959; the consumer price index rose 25 per cent in the same period. In the same decade the union minimum wage for truck drivers and helpers jumped 81 per cent. Over the same period, of course, business managers introduced organizational and technological changes that increased output per worker and made possible the payment of these higher wage rates.[7]

One new development is the practice of tying wages to the cost-of-living index. By late 1959, about one and one-quarter million workers were receiving regular pay increases in proportion to increases in the cost of living. On the average, such increases in wages amounted to about one cent per work hour each month.

[6] John A. Fitch. *Social Responsibilities of Organized Labor.* New York: Harper & Brothers, 1957, p. 23.
[7] *Statistical Abstract of the United States 1960.* U.S. Bureau of the Census. Washington, D.C.: USGPO, 1960, pp. 231, 336.

Health, Insurance, and Pension Plans

IN 1954, of the total union membership in the United States of seventeen millions, at least eleven and a quarter millions were covered by some type of health or insurance plan obtained in collective bargaining. The plans provided one or more of these benefits: life insurance policies; benefits for natural or accidental death, dismemberment, accident, and sickness; and hospital, surgical, maternity, and medical care. Life insurance covered 93 per cent of these workers; hospitalization benefits, 88 per cent; accident and sickness benefits, 73 per cent; accidental death and dismemberment benefits, 54 per cent; and medical benefits, 47 per cent. Of the more than eleven million workers covered, 62 per cent made no direct financial contribution to their insurance protection, although their take-home pay was probably slightly lower than that of workers in comparable non-covered unions. The number of workers covered under these plans had increased by 55 per cent over those covered in mid-1950.

About seven million union members in the United States in 1954 were covered by pension plans, an increase of 40 per cent over 1950. About 85 per cent of these workers were covered by non-contributory plans, that is, plans to which they made no direct financial contribution.[8]

In general, more and more workers are being covered by health, insurance, and pension plans, and their direct contributions have been decreasing. The amount and duration of various benefits have been increasing, more and more dependents are included under the programs, and new features are being added. For example, in 1957 the International Longshoremen's and Warehousemen's Union pension fund trustees announced a new policy, to the effect that widows of pensioners were to receive full pensions for a year after the death of the pensioner. The pension fund of this union was operated jointly with an employers' group, the Pacific Maritime Association.[9]

The operation and control of collectively bargained welfare plans became a center of controversy in the mid-1950's. With the increase in the magnitude of employer direct contributions came increasing employer control. In July, 1957, the director of the Industrial Union Department of the AFL-CIO, Albert Whitehouse, told the House Education and Labor Committee that "about ninety-two per cent of all plans are unilaterally administered by management and only about eight per cent are administered either jointly by labor and management

[8] Evan Keith Rowe. *Health, Insurance, and Pension Plans in Union Contracts* (U.S. Department of Labor Bulletin 1187). Washington, D.C.: USGPO, 1955, pp. 1–5.
[9] *New York Times*, Sept. 28, 1957.

or by unions alone." [10] Union spokesmen have claimed that these plans have often been managed at excessive cost, and demands that the national government regulate the funds have been made. During the 1958–59 controversy over national regulation of union trust funds such demands were apparently dropped, probably because union leaders were afraid of the inconsistency of asking government to regulate management trust funds while claiming that their own trust fund operations should remain undisclosed.

Non-Union Benefit Plans: A Comparison

BESIDES THE BENEFIT PLANS discussed above, there are many non-union-connected plans sponsored or initiated by employers and employees. These include the many fringe benefits offered by non-union businesses, group and wholesale life insurance coverage, mutual benefit associations, and a number of other plans. Statistics on the extent of union and non-union plans provide comparisons. Figures for 1954 are given in Table 2.

TABLE 2

EMPLOYEES COVERED UNDER UNION AND NON-UNION BENEFIT
PLANS, 1954

Type of Benefit	Percentage of Non-Union Employees in Wage and Salary Labor Force Covered	Percentage of Union Members Covered
Life Insurance and Death Benefits	54 ⎫	62 ⎫
Accidental Death and Dismemberment	22 ⎪	36 ⎪
Hospitalization	59 ⎬ 40% non-contributory (est.)	60 ⎬ 60% non-contributory (est.)
Surgical	52 ⎪	55 ⎪
Medical	33 ⎭	31 ⎭
Retirement	14 60% non-contributory (est.)	41 85% non-contributory (est.)

Total Wage and Salary Labor Force [1]	Non-Union Labor Force	Union Labor Force
52.6 millions	35.6 millions	17.0 millions

Sources: Rowe, *op. cit.*; A. M. Skolnik, and J. Zisman, "Growth in Employee Benefit Plans," *Social Security Bulletin*, XXI (March, 1958), pp. 4–12.

[1] The "wage and salary labor force" excludes government workers, self-employed workers, and unpaid family workers.

[10] *New York Times*, July 12, 1957.

In almost all types of plans slightly greater percentages of union members are covered; the most significant difference between the groups is in non-contributory coverage. Employees working under union contracts receive benefits without direct contributions with about 50 per cent greater frequency than non-union employees. Since many employer-contribution plans are offered employees in lieu of wage increments, however, it may be that this difference is more apparent than real.

Between 1954 and 1956 all types of benefit plans increased, union-negotiated plans increasing at a somewhat greater rate. For example, in 1956 nearly 63 per cent of the total wage and salary labor force was covered by life insurance and death benefits, compared with 57 per cent in 1954. In the same two years surgical benefits coverage increased from 53 per cent to 59 per cent and medical benefit coverage from 32 per cent to 40 per cent.[11] Workers covered by pension plans, union and non-union, increased from 13.1 millions in 1954 to 15.2 millions in 1956. Another source states that persons covered by private pension plans numbered 9.8 millions in 1950, 14.1 millions in 1954, and 17.7 millions in 1957.[12]

Employee benefit plans involve large-scale financial operations. In 1954 estimated employer and employee contributions under the employee benefit plans totaled over $6.8 billion, about 4.1 per cent of the aggregate government and private wages and salaries paid in the United States that year. Comparable figures for 1956 were $8.7 billion and 4.3 per cent. Benefits paid under these welfare programs were $3.5 billion and $4.8 billion in those two years. Table 3 lists the contributions and benefits paid in each of the seven types of employee benefit plans in 1956, and their relative percentages of total salaries and wages paid in that year.[13]

Retirement and hospitalization plans accounted for most of both contributions and benefits. Most retirement plans, being of recent origin, cover few persons yet qualified for retirement and consequently use most of their funds to build up reserves. The medical and insurance programs require only small contingency funds and thus expend most of their annual receipts.

There has been some speculation about the economic consequences of large pension and other trust fund holdings. One argument that seems to have some validity is that funds have a possible restraining influence on labor mobility. Workers are less likely to change jobs knowing that they are giving up what amounts to an investment in a pension fund. There is also concern for the concentration of economic power

[11] Skolnik and Zisman, op. cit., p. 5.
[12] Robert Tilove. Pension Funds and Economic Freedom. New York: The Fund for the Republic, 1959, p. 13.
[13] Skolnik and Zisman, op. cit., p. 6.

that may come from the use of funds. In 1957 self-insured corporate pension funds (covering both union and non-union employees) held assets of $19.3 billion. Slightly over half of this was in corporate bonds, and a quarter was in common stocks. More and more interest has been shown on the part of pension fund trustees in acquiring common stocks, which absorbed 37 per cent of the funds' net income in 1957. Some few pension funds have acquired control of the companies by which they were established, and others have acquired control of other companies, but these cases are generally considered exceptions.[14]

TABLE 3

CONTRIBUTIONS AND BENEFITS PAID UNDER ALL EMPLOYEE-BENEFIT PLANS, 1956

Type of Plan	Amount Contributed	Per Cent of Total Wages and Salaries	Benefits Paid	Amount Going to Reserve Funds	Per Cent of Total Going to Reserve Funds
Retirement	$4,030,000,000	2.13%	$ 950,000,000	$3,080,000,000	76.4%
Hospitalization	1,603,000,000	.74	1,495,000,000	108,000,000	6.7
Life Insurance and Death Benefits	995,000,000	.46	728,000,000	267,000,000	26.8
Surgical and Medical	898,000,000	.41	758,000,000	140,000,000	15.6
Temporary Disability	897,000,000	.41	800,000,000	97,000,000	10.8
Major Medical Expense	94,000,000	.04	67,000,000	27,000,000	28.7
Accidental Death and Dismemberment	50,000,000	.02	31,000,000	19,000,000	38.0
Totals:	$8,567,000,000	4.21%	$4,829,000,000	$3,738,000,000	43.6%

Source: Skolnik and Sisman, *op. cit.*, p. 6.

Guaranteed Wage and Unemployment Plans

IN THE FIRST HALF of this century most union negotiations were concerned with wages, job security, and, later, health and insurance plans. In the early 1950's unions began requesting what was originally known as the "guaranteed annual wage," now called "supplementary unemployment benefits." These plans are presently directed at supplementing the unemployment insurance provided under State laws to workers out of jobs through no fault of their own.

Neither the concept nor the form of these plans is new. Some trade

[14] Tilove, *op. cit.*, p. 86.

unions have practiced a sort of guaranteed wage plan on the local level for several decades, by limiting union membership and distributing jobs through the business agent of the local so as to guarantee each member sufficient income to tide him over the off-season slack period. As early as the 1930's guaranteed wage plans were given to employees in some small industries, both unionized and non-unionized. In some cases these plans were offered by an employer; in others they were negotiated by union locals.

Such plans were first negotiated on a large scale in 1955 in the automobile industry, in which organized labor had been asking for a so-called guaranteed annual wage for several years. In 1956 a similar industry-wide plan was negotiated between the major steel companies and the United Steelworkers (USW). As of April, 1958, about two million workers in the steel, auto, rubber, glass, maritime, and allied industries were covered by some form of supplementary unemployment benefits programs.[15]

The auto industry plans provided that for the first four weeks of unemployment the eligible worker would receive 65 per cent of his previous wages after taxes; during the succeeding twenty-two weeks of unemployment he would receive 60 per cent. Should the worker be receiving State unemployment benefits, the company would be responsible only for the amount necessary to raise his unemployment income to 65 or 60 per cent.

The steel industry's plan offered somewhat more extensive benefits, up to fifty-two weeks. A man who was laid off after being with the company for more than two years would receive 65 per cent of his former weekly net earnings for his first six months of unemployment, with a limitation on the company's contribution of $25 per week. However, once his State insurance ran out, which in most States happens after six months, his former employer would pay him up to $47.50 a week for the following six months.[16]

These plans were put to their first extensive use in the 1957–58 recession. The automobile industry had begun building up reserves in June, 1956. In February, 1958, the market value of the reserve funds of the Big Three auto companies was $153 million; the recession was about five months old at the time, and the three companies had paid out $14,063,000 in more than a million individual checks. The four largest steel companies began paying benefits in September, 1957, after building up reserves for a year by paying three cents an hour per worker into trust funds. Between September, 1957, and April, 1958, they disbursed $14 million to out-of-work USW members, about $23 per worker

[15] Fitch, *op. cit.*, pp. 30–32; *New York Times*, April 9, 1958.
[16] Fitch, *op. cit.*, pp. 32, 215.

per week, and their combined reserves had dropped to about $45 million.[17]

Certain legal and ethical questions have been raised concerning the guaranteed wage plans, specifically, as to whether it is just that employees should be receiving State government unemployment funds at the same time that they are receiving money under a guaranteed wage plan. Some plans, as negotiated with the steel and automobile corporations, have specifically provided that the plans would not go into effect unless State legislation was passed that provided that payments received by workers from employers were not wages.

A Union Welfare Trust Fund

SOME UNION LOCALS have negotiated unusual types of programs with employers. For example in St. Louis, Missouri, Local 88 of the Amalgamated Meat Cutters has had a welfare trust fund that in 1958 provided for the construction of a sizable medical institute.

In 1953 Local 88 negotiated a collective bargaining agreement by which management was to make monthly payments into a trust to provide life insurance and broad medical benefits to union members and their dependents. At the time Local 88 had 150 members. Over the next six years the membership grew to 2,000 (with 5,500 dependents), and the income from the fund had totaled $2.5 million. Nearly a million dollars in benefits had been paid out, a benevolent society for widows and orphans of members had been established, and financial and physical support had been given not only to local welfare groups (e.g., a boys' club) and national health organizations, but to groups in Israel and Italy as well.

In 1958 the local financed the construction of a $750,000 medical institute, completely equipped for all phases of medicine including dentistry and opthalmology. The institute was open to all union members and their families, and all members were required to have an annual physical checkup.

The trust fund that provided for these welfare services, and for the institute itself, was governed not by the union alone but by a joint board, consisting of two union representatives and two representatives of management and a chairman-administrator chosen by the four representatives from outside the two groups.[18]

This trust fund is relatively elaborate in its functions and of considerable financial magnitude. As such it may be considered an ideal rather than a typical collectively bargained fund (from the union point

[17] *New York Times*, April 9, 1958.
[18] "Medical Institute of Local 88," *St. Louis Post-Dispatch* (16-page magazine supplement section), Oct. 26, 1958.

of view). More and more frequently, though, unions are negotiating similar plans with employers. One feature of this fund that has been praised is its joint governing board and non-union, non-management chairman. Such an arrangement is not usual, yet it can be one effective protection against bad feeling and misuse of funds.

INTERMEDIATE WELFARE FUNCTIONS

INTERMEDIATE WELFARE FUNCTIONS of unions are those that confer welfare benefits on union members and their families, but that involve no participation on the part of employers. They include cash benefits paid from union funds, union-sponsored housing projects, and labor education services. Cash benefits for sick, injured, unemployed, striking, and retired union members and their families are paid out of funds built up through initiation fees, dues payments, and union investments. Union housing and education services have been initiated by a number of unions, but by no means a majority of them. Although they have been primarily for the benefit of members and their families, they also may have noticeable effects on other members of the community.

Cash Benefits

UNIONS HAVE long provided for the protection of members and their families against economic hazards. In 1887 the Cigar Makers asserted that one objective of unionism was "to provide a system of benefit payments which saves the workers the humiliation and degrading influence that surrounded charity and the poorhouse." [19] Old-age benefits and pensions, death benefits, and sickness benefits have been most important in union benefit programs, on the basis of partial data. In 1954, according to their annual reports, the AFL unions paid out $30 million for old-age benefits and pensions, $28 million for death benefits, and $26 million in sickness benefits. Disability benefits amounted to about $5 million, unemployment benefits $1.3 million. These figures did not include substantial sums believed to have been paid out by local unions.[20] Some unions also provide strike benefits. In the late 1940's striking members of the Photo-Engravers, for example, received $25 a week; the same union provided many other benefits as well, including sickness benefits from $10 to $25 a week, a $1,000 life insurance policy, and special hospitalization for members who contracted tuberculosis.[21] In

[19] Jack Barbash. *Labor Unions in Action.* New York: Harper & Brothers, 1948, p. 173.
[20] Fitch, *op. cit.*, p. 217.
[21] Barbash, *op. cit.*, p. 174.

1960, striking members of the International Association of Machinists received $35 a week in strike benefits.

The railroad brotherhoods and printing trade unions initiated many life, disability, accident, and health insurance programs. The Garment Workers and other trade unions, particularly the older AFL unions, initiated others. In financial magnitude, however, these programs were relatively small. They were often established only as stopgaps, to provide care for the most disadvantaged workers and families, and have since been supplemented, if not supplanted, by collectively bargained welfare plans and benefits provided under social security legislation.

Still, both union funds earmarked for special benefit programs and general union funds have continued to grow from fees, dues, and cautious but profitable investment. In 1956 it was variously estimated that local and international union funds totaled from $500 million to $4 billion. In April, 1956, the total assets of the United Steelworkers were $34.4 million, a 400 per cent increase over 1951 assets. The International Ladies' Garment Workers general fund, including holdings of locals, was $48 million at the end of 1955. Teamster assets, early in 1956, were $36.5 million; the International Brotherhood of Electrical Workers had a $40 million pension fund, and a $36 million death benefit insurance fund. The United Mine Workers, believed to be the wealthiest union in the United States, in April, 1960, had $110.3 million net assets in its general fund plus more than $100 million in its welfare and retirement fund.[22]

There have been several consequences of this tendency toward accumulation of union welfare and general funds. In 1956 and 1957 considerable public attention was focused on the misuse of union funds by union officials. As a result there were demands that the national government regulate union-controlled welfare funds, as well as employer- and jointly-controlled funds. As passed by Congress, the 1959 Labor-Management Reporting and Disclosure Act made financial reporting compulsory. Most union leaders have opposed national legislation regarding union-controlled funds. John L. Lewis of the United Mine Workers has been among the opponents. In July, 1957, he argued before the House Education and Labor Committee that there was sufficient legislation for funds and that enforcement of existing laws was needed, along with democratic action by union members if they found their leadership inadequate or corrupt. He was challenged on the latter point by Representative Stuyvesant Wainwright (R., N.Y.), who asked: "What do you do when the by-laws prevent it, or the leader is such an imposing figure that pragmatically these rights are denied?" "Funda-

[22] *Wall Street Journal*, July 5, 1956; "Mine Union Assets Total 110 Millions," *New York Times*, April 17, 1960.

mentally," Lewis answered, "we can't admit [there is] a corrupt leader of the kind you describe. That would be to deny the ability of the people to govern themselves." [23]

Union-Sponsored Housing

BY 1960 some 40,000 union members and their families were occupying housing cooperatives sponsored by and built with the assistance of various unions. Most union cooperative housing has been located in New York City. The Amalgamated Clothing Workers' Union was among the first unions to undertake housing developments for the benefit of its members, beginning in 1926. By 1950 this union had sponsored 2,500 units, capable of housing 10,000 people, at a total cost of $20 million. In addition to arranging the mortgage financing of the cooperatives, the union arranged loans for prospective members of the cooperatives and developed a number of additional activities. One of its projects, the Amalgamated Housing Corporation, was elaborately developed. Within the project were cooperative grocery, vegetable, and fruit stores. Committees of residents supervised educational and recreational activities, including a playground, a kindergarten, and a summer day camp for children. Dancing, music, and dramatic classes for young people were conducted, and a 500-seat auditorium was available for cultural events and entertainment.[24]

The International Ladies' Garment Workers' Union (ILGWU) was a sponsor-mortgagee of a housing cooperative opened in a former lower East Side slum area in 1955. Four 21- and 22-story apartment houses were built at a cost of $19.2 million, $4.5 million representing an equity investment on the part of 1,600 tenant-owner families.[25] In April, 1958, the ILGWU announced that it would contribute $20 million to a $35 million non-profit cooperative in a southwestern Manhattan slum area. Nine 20-story buildings were planned, to house 2,520 families. Included in the project were two commercial buildings, a shopping center, parking areas, gardens, and playgrounds. "In keeping with its investment policies of recent years, the union plans to draw on its welfare and general reserve funds to finance the project. Additional financing is to come from tenant-owners and banks." [26]

Among other New York area unions interested in housing have been Local 3 of the International Brotherhood of Electrical Workers, which in 1956 completed a cooperative for 2,200 families, and a local of the Amalgamated Meat Cutters, which has sponsored housing for 288

[23] *New York Times,* July 10, 1957.
[24] Fitch, *op. cit.,* pp. 73–74.
[25] *Ibid.,* pp. 73–74.
[26] *New York Times,* Feb. 20, 1958.

families. In the fall of 1958 the New York Typographical Union Local 6 began construction of eight "towers" in Queens, to provide housing for 700 families on a cooperative basis. The working capital of $11.7 million was provided by the union; the apartments were to be sold for down payments averaging $500 a room, with monthly carrying charges of about $22 per room.[27]

The unions mentioned here are among about twenty unions that are members of the United Housing Foundation, a private non-profit organization in New York City that advises other non-profit organizations interested in undertaking cooperative housing projects. It should be noted that most of these unions do not directly *subsidize* housing; their sponsorship generally involves developing plans and providing financing. Also, they seldom sponsor *rental* housing; tenants in most of these projects buy their apartments, which are often quite expensive.

A somewhat different type of housing project has been sponsored by the American Federation of State, County and Municipal Employees in Milwaukee, Wisconsin. Over 300 apartment units were planned, sixty-four of them being opened for occupancy in November, 1959; the union acted as sponsor under the provisions of the National Housing Act. In contrast to union-sponsored housing in New York, however, the apartments were rented (at $80-$90 per month for a two-bedroom apartment) rather than sold; they were open to any persons displaced by urban renewal projects or other civic improvements, or to persons evicted from public housing because their earnings exceeded the public housing limit. The project did not follow the New York plan of construction; instead of large "high-rise" buildings the Milwaukee projects consisted of many small buildings, each containing about eight apartments.[28]

Labor Education

LABOR EDUCATION PROGRAMS have been important in many of the larger unions. A union spokesman states that their purposes have been "the improvement of the worker's individual and group competence and the advancement of his social, economic, and cultural interests, so that he can become a 'mature, wise, and responsible' citizen, able to play his part in the union and in a free society and to assume for himself a status of dignity and respect." [29]

Another writer states that "Unions may carry on workers' education activities to develop a sense of loyalty to the union, to the labor move-

[27] *New York Times*, April 14, 1958.
[28] "Union Housing Project for Displaced Shown," *Milwaukee Journal*, Oct. 11, 1959.
[29] Joseph Mire. *Labor Education*, Inter-University Labor Education Committee, 1956, p. 17, cited in Fitch, *op. cit.*, p. 77.

ment, and to progressive ideas in general." The social and economic ideologies of union leadership often determine the course of labor education. "We find this motivation for workers' education figuring prominently, for example, in the International Ladies' Garment Workers' Union with the strong Socialist traditions of its leadership, and more latterly the Auto Workers and the Textile Workers." [30]

In 1957 twenty-nine international unions were known to have major educational programs established at union headquarters and staffed by at least one full-time union employee. The ILGWU and the USW have had two of the most extensive such programs. The ILGWU pioneered in the field, establishing a labor education department in 1917; it has given courses in various aspects of the labor movement and has also emphasized history, economics, current events, and cultural interests. Early in its history the ILGWU sponsored the Brookwood Labor College, a resident labor school, which ceased operations in 1938. In 1955–56 about 12,000 members participated in educational programs offered by the union. In the year ending in May, 1953, "1,288 new members attended orientation classes, 2,178 members attended courses in labor problems and trade unionism, over 2,000 were in classes devoted to music and the drama, and nearly 1,200 studied arts and crafts. Language courses were given for some 800 members—French for English-speaking workers in Montreal, English for Puerto Ricans in New York, and Spanish for the business agents who deal with them." [31] The ILGWU also operates a training institution for prospective staff members at its New York headquarters, which between 1951 and 1956 accepted 156 students for a twelve-month training program combined with field work.

The USW since 1946 has held summer classes and seminars at various campuses. In the summer of 1953 nineteen universities throughout the country cooperated with the program. Courses were open to all interested members of the union, and dealt not only with union problems but with such broader topics as human relations, politics, and community development. Among other unions interested in labor education are the Communications Workers of America, the International Association of Machinists, and the United Textile Workers of America. Their programs have included training of shop stewards, instruction in economics, preparation of grievance cases, local union administration, and vocational training. The AFL unions with strong craft ties have been particularly interested in supporting vocational education. In the late 1940's the International Brotherhood of Electrical Workers gave an endowment to Marquette University to provide electronics courses

[30] Barbash, *op. cit.*, p. 159.
[31] Fitch, *op. cit.*, p. 80.

to IBEW members. The printing and most of the craftsmen's unions either conduct their own vocational programs or work in conjunction with trade schools.

It is also known that some unions, locals for the most part, have funds to provide financial assistance for the education of members' children. They may occasionally give money to colleges, to be used for scholarships for children of union members. The source of such funds may be either union fees and dues or, more rarely, management.

Closely associated with organized labor is the American Labor Educational Service, which advises unions on their educational programs and conducts programs of its own. In the past few years it has become increasingly interested in international affairs, and has held institutes and classes in an effort to stimulate labor interest in American foreign policy and in foreign problems. One of the fruits of this interest was the AFL-CIO foreign-aid fund of $1 million, raised over a three-year period and turned over to the international solidarity fund of the International Confederation of Free Trade Unions, to provide assistance to the victims of oppression abroad.

Finally, there are union agencies such as the AFL-CIO Committee on Political Education (COPE), which have among their purposes the education of union members concerning political issues and candidates. Political action and education programs are to be found in many, if not most, of the larger unions.

EXTERNAL WELFARE FUNCTIONS

THE EXTERNAL WELFARE FUNCTIONS of unions are those services that have been developed for the avowed purpose of improving *community* welfare; they may have the benefit of union members and their families as a secondary purpose. For many years local unions have on occasion participated in community services. For the most part they did so in times of emergency or community distress, along with many other organizations and associations that responded to severe problems. More recently union leaders have made concerted efforts to increase union participation in community welfare, motivated in part by the desire to increase union stature in the eyes of the community, in part by new awareness of the kinds of assistance unions are capable of providing. Many of these efforts have beeen successful.

The AFL-CIO and Community Services

SUSTAINED UNION INTEREST in community service developed in the late 1930's and early 1940's. During this period the AFL founded Labor's

League for Human Rights and the CIO created the National CIO War Relief Committee. Established to raise funds for the relief of war victims, these organizations were the forerunners of the AFL-CIO Community Services Committee (CSC), which was established at the AFL-CIO merger convention.

According to the AFL-CIO constitution, "the Committee on Community Services shall stimulate the active participation by members and affiliated unions in the affairs of their communities, and the development of sound relationships with social agencies in such communities." The efforts of this committee have been largely directed toward planning and sponsorship of the community services of local union chapters. Its staff operations are carried out by the AFL-CIO Community Services Activities (CSA), an organization directed by Leo Perlis, a union official who first became active in union community services on the national level in 1943.

Ten specific objectives were stated for the CSC and the CSA in the AFL-CIO convention of December, 1957:

(1) Encourage equitable labor representation on agency boards and committees, both public and voluntary.

(2) Stimulate labor participation in formulating agency policies and programs.

(3) Develop techniques and methods to interpret for union members agency programs and practices such as union counseling.

(4) Assist union members, their families and other citizens in times of need, particularly during strikes, layoffs, and unemployment.

(5) Plan for union participation in civil defense and disaster relief programs and operations.

(6) Help in the development of health and welfare services, such as programs for community health education, blood banks, mental health, alcoholism, retired workers, youth, recreation and multiple screening.

(7) Coordinate fund-raising drives, through voluntary federation wherever possible, for voluntary health and welfare services, including the promotion of a national Health Fund.

(8) Cooperate with other agencies in dealing with and solving social and health problems.

(9) Participate in all genuine efforts designed to improve social work standards and practices.

(10) Participate in international social welfare programs.[32]

[32] *Foundations of the AFL-CIO Community Services Program.* New York: Community Services Committee (pamphlet, n.d., no page numbers).

These objectives cannot be accomplished by the national CSC or CSA directly; they can be put into practice only by local unions. Thus, the CSC sponsors the establishment of service committees throughout the union hierarchy. The national and international affiliated unions are asked to establish community services departments, as are city and State central labor bodies, and union locals; all these bodies are asked to "extend full cooperation" to the national committee and department.

Union Participation in Community Services

ACTUAL UNION PARTICIPATION in community services takes a number of forms. Some, such as the union counseling program, are CSC-sponsored throughout the United States. Others, such as volunteer assistance on community projects, take place only in some localities, and may or may not be CSC-sponsored.

In the union counseling program, union counselors serve as a link between other union members and the social agencies and services of the community. They are usually volunteers, working at counseling apart from their regular jobs. Some 40,000 men and women have taken eight-week union courses in counseling, including courses in such subjects as health services, child and family services, public assistance, social security, workmen's compensation, unemployment compensation, and recreational facilities, as well as other community-provided services. Although the immediate recipients of the work of these "referral agents" are usually union members and their families, the agencies themselves and the community as a whole also benefit. Available services and facilities are publicized, and some of the burden of screening requests for assistance is done before the union member reaches the agencies.

More directly concerned with community welfare are the men and women from organized labor on the boards, committees, and staffs of community health and welfare organizations. In the late 1950's it was estimated that 75,000 union members were serving non-governmental community health and welfare organizations, and in the larger cities there were some 125 representatives of organized labor on the staffs of community welfare organizations on a full-time basis, providing a continuing liaison between the organizations and the unions.[33]

In health services, union volunteers and staffs took part in the campaign to establish mass inoculation clinics for the administration of Salk anti-polio serum. Organized labor has often cooperated with the American Red Cross; union members have assisted in establishing the blood bank programs and have contributed large amounts of blood. In times of disaster the unions work in conjunction with the Red

[33] Leo Perlis, "Citizenship in Action," *American Federationist*, November, 1957.

2 5 7

Cross, the Salvation Army, the Federal Civil Defense Administration, and other organizations that can be mobilized to assist disaster victims. Union members have given labor, goods, funds, and equipment in disaster areas. In 1957 the AFL-CIO presented the Red Cross with four mobile canteens to serve in disaster areas. In 1956 a special AFL-CIO Community Service office was opened at Camp Kilmer, New Jersey, to assist Hungarian refugees in finding employment and integrating themselves into American life. Many thousands of them were directly offered assistance by the CSA staff at Camp Kilmer and by Community Service representatives across the nation.[34]

Thousands of members of local unions, building trades unions in particular, have given hundreds of thousands of man-hours to community projects, constructing or rebuilding houses, hospitals, facilities for young people, and many others. In Scranton, Pennsylvania, for example, a CSA representative with the Lackawanna United Fund learned that the Girl Scouts needed a new recreation hall at their day camp and arranged for the Scranton Building Trades Council to supply the needed volunteer labor. In Louisiana, following a 1957 hurricane that damaged or demolished many houses, hundreds of Louisiana Building Trades unionists volunteered to help rebuild homes, working with the Red Cross. Local AFL-CIO affiliates in Camden, New Jersey, became concerned with they learned that the municipal hospital had no dental facilities available. They raised funds to buy equipment and to cover operating expenses for a two-year period, and building tradesmen contributed some $5,000 in labor to put the clinic into operating condition.[35] In 1958, when a school in Clinton, Tennessee, was destroyed by bombs, the presidents of three national labor bodies, the Building Trades Council, the Plasterers' Union, and the Plumbing Union, all promised volunteer labor to help rebuild the school.[36]

Organized Labor and Fund Raising

IN 1956–57 the United Community Campaigns of America, representing 2,100 federated campaigns, reported that members of AFL-CIO unions contributed more than 38 per cent of all funds raised. This amounted to about $120 million, an average of about $7 for each member of American unions. In the 1956 Detroit United Fund campaign, the United Automobile Workers employed by Ford contributed $1,-186,000 from their wages. In such campaigns, most active campaigning

[34] Ibid.
[35] Community Service (AFL-CIO edition), II (Fall, 1957), p. 7.
[36] "Unions Offer Their Help to Blasted Schools," St. Louis Post-Dispatch, Nov. 15, 1958.

and soliciting of union members is done by union volunteers.[37] Union members in a number of communities have worked for and contributed to other fund drives as well. In Dallas, Texas, 400 Communications Workers of America members worked without pay for sixteen hours to handle calls for a Texas telethon in which $250,000 was raised in pledges for cerebral palsy victims.[38]

Organized labor's attitudes toward fund drives have been changing. In the past union members have been subjected to many separate appeals, varying, of course, from one community to another. Although the problems of multiple appeal have been partially reduced by the development of federated campaigns, union leaders have demanded still more unification. Leo Perlis, director of the AFL-CIO CSA, has become the union spokesman for this point of view. His arguments have been directed particularly at the national non-governmental health agencies, which, he has claimed, waste $10 million a year in conducting independent fund drives. He has also argued that the budgeting process of funds and agencies is outdated and that there is a lack of flexibility in programs, which have developed without any real planning for the entire community. The result, he has asserted, is that programs and budgets are designed to meet the needs of agencies, rather than people.[39]

Perlis contends that the solution to these problems is "flexible federation." This would involve a single, united appeal, accompanied by a much greater concern with planning and service than has heretofore been the case. In line with this solution Perlis has proposed a national health fund, a proposal subsequently sponsored officially by the AFL-CIO. It would coordinate the programs of the individual national health agencies, replace the separate publicity campaigns with a single national drive, and allocate funds on the basis of nation-wide needs.[40]

There is another problem concerning fund drives that is of equally great concern to organized labor. This is the fact that the payroll deduction plans currently in use to gather community chest and united fund contributions have become an almost automatic system of taxation. Amounts to be contributed and the organizations to benefit from them are generally suggested or determined by union officials, in keeping with what they believe to be the union members' best interests. All that remains for the union member to do is to say "Yes" or "No" when asked if he is willing to have a certain amount deducted from his

---

[37] *Christian Science Monitor*, Sept. 21, 1957.
[38] Wilbur H. Baldinger, "Big Labor's Biggest Business," *The Kiwanis Magazine*, XIII (Jan., 1957), pp. 33–35.
[39] *New York Times*, April 27, 1958.
[40] Leo Perlis, *Health and Welfare Financing*. Dayton, Ohio: Address at Campaign Leaders' Conference, June 4, 1957.

paycheck. Thus, many workers have come to feel that their "voluntary" contributions are actually seldom voluntary and that they have little part in community welfare.

Some people have argued that a single national fund-raising campaign for all the non-governmental health agencies would increase this tendency. Perlis takes a contrary position. He feels that there should be positive and extensive union participation in planning and education, on all levels in connection with a national health fund. He has said, "I hope we will never lose sight of, or underestimate the importance of citizen participation all the way down the line. We must strive always to build our organizations on the broadest possible base of citizen representation and participation on all levels of policy-making, program development, and in giving. For these agencies are voluntary organizations . . . and the most important part about them is the word 'voluntary.' " [41]

CONCLUDING REMARKS

UNION WELFARE ACTIVITIES have had various effects. The demands of unions and their leaders for increased welfare benefits for members and their families have occasionally been made without consideration of their effects on society as a whole, and some people have argued that union demands have contributed to an inflationary spiral. On the other hand, such demands have lead to a great increase in the wages and benefits shared by much of America's labor force, while union members themselves have made significant contributions to community activity, both financially and in donations of time and energy. Finally, union leaders have established affiliated agencies to contribute to community and regional welfare and to make union members conscious of the role they can play in community welfare.

[41] Ibid.

Chapter Eleven

FOUNDATIONS
AND COMMUNITY TRUSTS

F OUNDATIONS ARE NON-GOVERNMENTAL, NON-PROFIT CORPORATIONS with privately endowed capital, whose customary aims are the promotion or maintenance of educational, research, charitable, or religious activities. They are usually expressions of their donors' wishes to distribute private wealth for public uses, particularly uses for which financial support would otherwise not be available. As such they undertake a multitude of welfare tasks. This chapter discusses the general characteristics of foundations, their types and financial resources, sketches the activities of several specific foundations, and suggests the extent of foundation activity in areas of interest such as education and scientific research. Community trusts and community foundations, organizations closely resembling foundations, are discussed in the final section of this chapter.

GENERAL CHARACTERISTICS

FOUNDATIONS EXIST in many forms; they range in financial size from the Ford Foundation, whose assets exceed $3.3 billion,[1] to many small foundations with assets of only a few thousands of dollars; they go by titles of great variety—the Commonwealth *Fund*, the Duke *Endowment*, the Olin *Foundation*, the Hyams *Trust*, the Research *Corporation*. These variations make it difficult to distinguish foundations from

[1] This is the approximate market value of the stocks that comprise the assets of the Ford Foundation; their 1959 ledger value was about $820 million.

related organizations or to state the number of foundations in existence. Dr. Ernest Hollis of the U.S. Office of Education, speaking before a Congressional investigating committee in 1952, said:

> The number depends on the definition you use for a foundation. . . . My definition initially was any body that is legally chartered or that is created through a charitable trust statute, the purpose of which is to channel private wealth into general welfare channels. That is the broadest possible definition. . . . By this definition the endowment of every college in this country is a foundation. The endowment of every hospital, scientific society, or any other charitable body that has a principal fund that is itself used or the interest from which is used is by that definition a foundation.
>
> It was on the basis of such a definition that I said earlier that between thirty and thirty-five thousand foundations is, in my judgment, a conservative estimate, and that the capital assets of these groups will run between six and one-half and seven billion dollars. . . . If one used a much narrower definition there would be fewer foundations. If only chartered foundations were considered perhaps the number would be nearer five thousand. If only the type of body that makes grants of money to somebody else to do work with, the number also drops very rapidly because a great many foundations are their own operating agencies.[2]

There are three types of related organizations that are excluded from the ranks of the foundations in this chapter. Funds and trusts created for the benefit of single institutions, and trust funds located within an institution and controlled by the trustees of the institution, referred to by Dr. Hollis, are excluded. Examples of such funds that include the word "foundation" in their titles are the Indiana University Foundation and the University of Wichita Foundation for Industrial Research. Also excluded are organizations that solicit for funds, such as the American Foundation for the Blind, Inc., some trade associations that have adopted the name "foundation," and the grant-making programs of many of the large corporations.

The principles and practices of foundations have permitted both narrow and extensive welfare undertakings. The philanthropists who initiated and continue to initiate foundations characteristically have believed that there is some function, institution, or group of persons that needs special assistance, because of its inherent goodness, because of its needs, because of its importance to a part or all of society, or any combination of these. The donors of smaller foundations usually though not always have had relatively limited purposes in mind, for

[2] *Hearings Before the Select (Cox) Committee to Investigate Tax-Exempt Foundations and Comparable Organizations.* U.S. House of Representatives, 82nd Congress, 2nd Session. Washington, D.C.: USGPO, 1953, pp. 14–15.

example, the support of community playgrounds, of certain churches, or of specific welfare agencies and projects.

Donors of the larger foundations have generally held broader pur- poses in mind. The following passage, in Kate Macy Ladd's letter of gift to the Josiah Macy, Jr., Foundation, is of considerable significance in understanding most present-day large foundations:

> Experience seems to show that in an enlightened democracy, private organized philanthropy serves the purposes of human welfare best, not by replacing functions which rightfully should be supported by our communities but by investigating, testing and demonstrating the value of newer organized ideas for sus- tained undertakings from which may gradually emerge social func- tions which in turn should be taken over and maintained by the public. I hope, therefore, that the Foundation will take more interest in the architecture of ideas than in the architecture of buildings and laboratories.
>
> I have faith in the power of human intelligence to relieve much of our social distress by reconciling growing knowledge with tested beliefs and I cherish the hope that the Foundation's best endowment may be its spirit in which it will help in the task of building finer personalities—creation's highest promise.[3]

This general philosophy pervades the majority of large foundations. They conceive of themselves as pioneering in new fields of thought and endeavor. By especially aiding education, research, and similar ac- tivities, they hope indirectly to benefit all of American society and sometimes all the people of the world. Another example of this tenor of thought appears in Simon Guggenheim's letter of gift to the Gug- genheim Memorial Foundation:

> It is Mrs. Guggenheim's and my desire, in memory of our son, through the agency of this Foundation, to add to the educational, literary, artistic and scientific power of this country, and also to provide for the cause of better international understanding. Our thought was that the income of the fund devoted to these pur- poses should be used to provide opportunities for both men and women to carry on advanced study in any field of knowledge, or in any of the fine arts, including music; and that systematic ar- rangements should be made to assure these opportunities under the freest possible conditions, and to make available for the public benefit the results of such studies. Believing as we do that such opportunities may be found in every country of the world, we purposely make no specification of locality, domestic or foreign, for the pursuit of these aims.[4]

[3] Cited in F. Emerson Andrews, *Legal Instruments of Foundations*. New York: Russell Sage Foundation, 1958, p. 273.
[4] *Ibid.*, p. 270.

The concept and practice of pioneering philanthropy have elevated many a foundation into public prominence. A high degree of publicity is often considered a requisite of success, as in directing public attention to a new or neglected purpose, or in the dissemination of ideas. For the quality of their pioneering ventures foundations are dependent on knowledgeable men, and thus seek prominent men from other fields to guide them. The fifteen trustees of the Ford Foundation in 1958 included a college president and a chancellor, a U.S. District Court Judge, three prominent publishers, three chairmen of boards, and the president and a vice-president of the Ford Motor Company.

Not all large foundations have wholeheartedly subscribed to the concept of pioneering new ventures in philanthropy, however. The William Volker Fund, of California, has attempted to maintain the spirit and practice of conventional charity in its activities. Its purposes, briefly, are "to foster and encourage the self-advancement of individuals and individual welfare everywhere through moral, spiritual, mental, and physical improvement." [5] Its grants support research and institutions concerned with the aged, children, health, religion, and social welfare in general; grants are not given a great deal of publicity, however. The Fund does not ordinarily make grants to agencies and institutions receiving portions of their income from government sources, and avoids encouraging any government movement into the areas of its philanthropic interest. The directors have done so in keeping with the belief of the donor that self-advancement and individual welfare are best encouraged through individualized philanthropy.

TYPES OF FOUNDATIONS

ACCORDING TO VARIOUS ESTIMATES within the limits of the definition given at the outset of this chapter, there are between 5,000 and 15,000 foundations. The Foundation Library Center in New York City began in 1956 to establish as complete as possible a record of foundations, and in its first few years of operation accumulated data on about 12,000 foundations and similar organizations. In its 1960 *Foundation Directory*,[6] it listed 5,202 philanthropic foundations, as narrowly defined, excluding 7,000 foundations having neither reported assets of $50,000 nor grants of at least $10,000 per year.

One thing is certain: foundations have had continued growth in size and number over the past several decades and their popularity as

[5] Wilmer Shields Rich. *American Foundations and Their Fields* (Seventh Edition). New York: American Foundations Information Service, 1955, p. 42.
[6] Ann D. Walton and F. Emerson Andrews, eds. *The Foundation Directory* (Edition 1). New York: Russell Sage Foundation, 1960.

a means for making philanthropic contributions is still increasing. One indication of this is the number of foundations listed in various directories published since 1915. In such directories, twenty-seven foundations were listed in 1915; 123 in 1934; 505 in 1946; 899 in 1948; and 4,200 in 1955.[7]

For the purposes of description, foundations can be grouped into six main classes. These classes are somewhat arbitrary, and a given foundation not infrequently changes in status from one to another. Five of these are discussed below: general-purpose foundations, special-purpose foundations, family and personal foundations, corporation foundations, and government foundations. The sixth type, community trusts, is discussed in the final section of this chapter.

General-Purpose Foundations

GENERAL-PURPOSE FOUNDATIONS are those designed to finance any sort of activity deemed meritorious by their directors. Among them are almost all the largest foundations, such as the Ford Foundation, the Rockefeller Foundation, and the Carnegie Corporation. These are the giants among foundations, operating under broad charters and having large endowments and national programs. They are the foundations that are preeminent in the public mind and in the news media. Operating with professional staffs, they finance extensive projects in scientific research, and promote a multitude of educational, charitable, and religious activities. Frequently they cast themselves in the role of innovators, hence the use of the term "venture capital of philanthropy" to describe their expenditures.

Although there are probably no more than 180 general-purpose foundations, they are estimated to control more than 65 per cent of the assets of all foundations. Most of them cannot operate on the scale of the "big three"—Ford, Rockefeller, and Carnegie—but there are many opportunities for smaller foundations to undertake important programs with their relatively limited funds.

Special-Purpose Foundations

SPECIAL-PURPOSE FOUNDATIONS are those intended to support one special kind of field of activity. While most of the general-purpose foundations were established during the lifetimes of their donors, many of the special-purpose foundations have been created by will or trust instrument. Most of them have only limited funds at their disposal. Some of them have had unusually narrow purposes, for instance, "the development of ceramic arts, especially china painting" and the study of

[7] F. Emerson Andrews. *Philanthropic Foundations*. New York: Russell Sage Foundation, 1956, p. 14.

the diseases of horses. Some of these foundations have had purposes that were soon left behind by social change. In 1851 Bryan Mullenphy established the so-called "covered-wagon" fund in St. Louis "to furnish relief to all poor emigrants and travelers coming to St. Louis on their way, bona fide, to settle in the West." [8] Court proceedings subsequently diverted the fund to the more general purpose of travelers' aid, and it later became an initiating factor in the National Travelers Aid Association.

In general, special-purpose foundations have made many useful and significant contributions to welfare. Educational institutions and religious organizations have been the most frequent choices of donors specifying definite purposes, and not all of the trusts are small. Two of the largest are the Edward Drummond Libbey Trust and the Juilliard Musical Foundation, each with assets of about $16 million. The Libbey Trust supports the Toledo, Ohio, Museum of Art; the Juilliard Foundation devotes its income primarily to the Juilliard School of Music. In 1960 there were about 600 special purpose foundations of any size, controlling about 13 per cent of total foundation endowment.

Some people have criticized special-purpose foundations for their narrow restrictions on the use of funds, and trustees of some of them have initiated court actions that they might be given broader discretion in making grants. The donors of general-purpose foundations were usually aware of this problem. For example, Simon Guggenheim's previously cited letter of gift stated:

> The purposes of the Foundation were designedly made very broad in the charter. . . . This course was followed because no one can foresee the future, and limitations which seem wise today might become impracticable or injurious in later years. No man of wisdom would seek perpetually to bind you and your successors [the trustees] to fixed plans and methods involving fixed studies, causes, places or institutions. The history of funds for special purposes has shown the folly of attempting to petrify the ideas of the present.[9]

Family and Personal Foundations

THE INCREASING TAXES on high incomes, combined with the tax provisions for charitable deductions, have led to a notable increase in the number of family foundations. Their greatest advantage is that the donor is not forced to make his charitable contributions immediately, that is, within the year, but may take time for planning and investigating his charitable activity and may accumulate funds for some more

[8] *Ibid.*, p. 25.
[9] *Legal Instruments of Foundations*, pp. 269–70.

266

extensive project. The 1960 *Foundation Directory* listed 3,000 "family and miscellaneous" foundations, holding 11 per cent of foundation assets. The majority of the 7,000 foundations too small to meet the requirements of the *Directory* were of the same type.

These foundations are the vaguely explored hinterland of foundation activity. Often they are simply a channel for the donor's current giving, in which case they expend their capital immediately; frequently they do not outlive their founder. There have been cases of abuse of this type of foundation; at one time it was charged that some of them were established to attain special tax privileges for their donor. This stigma was largely removed following the Revenue Act of 1950, which required public reporting and specifically prohibited certain practices.

Occasionally a family foundation has grown in size and increased its area of interest to become a general-purpose foundation; the three largest foundations did so. Henry Ford II, speaking before a Congressional committee, discussed the growth of the Ford Foundation:

> We believe that the history of the Ford Foundation actually falls into three phases. The first phase covers roughly the twelve years from 1936 to 1948.
>
> During this time our operations were limited in character. The foundation during those years was never in a position to spend in any one year much more than about $1,000,000.
>
> Approximately fifty per cent of the grants during those years were made to educational and charitable institutions which had been established some years before by my grandfather and my father.
>
> This seems, in my estimation at least, a natural thing to have done because certainly the foundation was formed, in part, to provide a convenient means for carrying on the many obligations of the Ford family to education, charity, and scientific progress. . . .
>
> Phase 2 of the foundation's history was forecast as early as 1946 when it became clear that the administration of my father's estate was nearing an end. It was known, of course, that much of his estate would become an asset of the foundation.
>
> With the prospect of enormously increased resources thus available to the foundation, our trustees realized that a careful planning for expanded operations was needed. . . .
>
> The third phase, of course, is the future. . . .[10]

Corporation Foundations

THE CORPORATION FOUNDATION, sometimes known as the company foundation, trust, or fund, in the 1950's became a popular device for

[10] *Hearings Before the Select (Cox) Committee*, pp. 219–20.

channeling corporate giving. Corporation foundations are established as legal entities separate from their parent organizations and are generally provided with broad charters of incorporation. However, their boards of trustees are typically selected from among the officers and directors of the donor corporation. In many respects they resemble the family foundations; most of them have no substantial principal fund but provide a means for current charitable donations. In some few cases they have accumulated substantial capital for more long-range charitable purposes.

The programs of these foundations generally aim at "the portion of that welfare that benefits the corporation, its employees, its stockholders, or its business relationships." In fact, they may be required to do so by law. "Legal restrictions on corporation giving have relaxed in recent years, but it may still be necessary under some corporate laws to show a constructive relation between the gift and the interests of the corporation." [11] However, an equally important factor has been corporate officers' increasing involvement in community problems and interest in social welfare. In many cases they have decided that the attractiveness or prosperity of the community in which their firm is situated will contribute to the profitability of their firm. Thus, for example, they may offer college scholarships to outstanding high school graduates who are children of their employees, partly in the hope of recruiting unusually competent engineers and technicians for their staff.[12]

More than a quarter of the foundations listed in the 1960 *Foundation Directory* were company-sponsored, 1,333 of them. They made about 16 per cent of foundation grants, though they held only about 6 per cent of total reported assets—one reason they are called "in-and-out" foundations. Fully 60 per cent of these corporate foundations were established between 1949 and 1954, most of the rest between 1940 and 1949. Only 80 were set up after 1954, though more are still coming into existence. The largest company foundations in 1960 were the Ford Motor Company Fund, the General Electric Foundation, the Sears-Roebuck Foundation, the Standard Oil Foundation, and the U.S. Steel Foundation, each with assets over $20 million.[13]

5 Government Foundations

GOVERNMENT FOUNDATIONS FALL beyond the definition of foundations, since their financing and ultimate control are in government hands. Nevertheless, some mention should be made of the National Science

[11] *Philanthropic Foundations*, p. 30.
[12] See Richard Eels, *Corporation Giving in a Free Society*, New York: Harper & Brothers, 1956.
[13] Walton and Andrews, *op. cit.*, pp. xxi–xxiv.

Foundation (NSF), the only government foundation presently in operation. Its purposes and practices closely resemble those of many of the large private foundations.

The NSF was established in 1950 by act of Congress. Much of the debate over the NSF Act centered not on the question of government activity in the foundation area but on the question of whether to include the social sciences in the activities of the NSF. As passed, the act authorized the Foundation "to initiate and support basic scientific research in the mathematical, physical, medical, biological, engineering, and other sciences." [14] During its first nine years of operation the NSF largely restricted itself to the physical and biological sciences. However, in 1959 an NSF Office of Social Science was established with funds at its disposal for social science grants. In fiscal 1959–60, $2 million were allocated to social science projects, though excluding political science *per se* so as to avoid public controversy.

The Foundation has no principal fund, but appropriations of $125 million for fiscal 1960 gave it operating funds greater than those of any private foundation. (In 1958 the income of the Ford Foundation available for grants was less than $90 million.) All evidence suggests that the NSF will continue to play an important role in directing increased government expenditures for scientific research, under the direction and advice of the many prominent scientists on its committees. It has also been frequently proposed before Congress that nationally financed foundations be established to operate in the fields of education and the arts, though there seems to be small likelihood that they will be created in the near future.

THE FINANCIAL RESOURCES OF FOUNDATIONS

THE EXTENT OF foundation activity in a field of its interest is determined by the resources available, which are a function both of the *duration type* of the foundation and of its total capital.

Duration Types

ONE OF THE first decisions made by a donor in establishing a foundation concerns the means by which its capital and income are to be used. Depending on this decision, the foundation may be classified as one of four duration types. The first type is the accumulating fund, such as that created by Benjamin Franklin, which not only reserves its capital but also retains all or part of the income. Franklin, fascinated

[14] *National Science Foundation Act of 1950*, Sec. 3.

by the possibilities of compound interest, established funds of £1,000 each in Boston and Philadelphia, to be lent to "young married artificers" at 5 per cent interest. He calculated that if earnings were retained over a 200-year period a sum equivalent to $20 million would accumulate. The funds did not have such success, however, for Franklin had fallen into the trap of being too specific about the means of investment; as the apprentice system passed into oblivion the capital eventually was directed to other, less profitable, investments.

There are several existing funds that accumulate, or have accumulated, some of their income on a temporary basis. The charter of the Duke Endowment provided that 20 per cent of income be retained until the principal reached $40 million. (This point was reached some years ago; in the late 1950's the assets of the Duke Endowment approached $450 million.) The Trexler Foundation stipulates that a fourth of the net income from investments be accumulated to safeguard the investment. However, the Revenue Act of 1950 limited the practice of accumulating funds. Specifically, organizations of the foundation type are denied tax-exempt status if their accumulations are "unreasonable in amount of duration in order to carry out the charitable, educational, or other purpose or function constituting the basis for exemption." [15] Subsequent rulings have interpreted the phrase "unreasonable in amount or duration" in such a way as to give the foundations some leeway in building up principal, using capital gains on investments, and so forth.

A second form of organization is the perpetuity, which, barring accident, is endowed with an immortal but non-accumulating corpus (principal fund). Over the long run the expenditures of foundations established in perpetuity are equal to income on the principal, unless special provision has been made to expend a limited amount of the capital. An unforeseen fate of some perpetuities has been a court proceeding modifying the initial restrictions on capital expenditure. In the opinions of many foundations and their trustees, "trustees or those in control of philanthropic endowments should have, at least, limited rights enabling them to expend capital funds." [16]

The third type is the optional perpetuity: the capital may be gradually expended or the use of the capital may be at the discretion of the trustees. The Rockefeller foundations are optional perpetuities, in accordance with the reported opinion of John D. Rockefeller, Sr.: "Perpetuity is a pretty long time." [17] The Rockefeller Foundation has made

[15] *Internal Revenue Code*, Sec. 3814.
[16] "Answers to Questionnaire" (Questionnaire submitted by the Cox Committee to Investigate Foundations). Cleveland Foundation, p. 34.
[17] *Philanthropic Foundations*, p. 101.

some considerable expenditures from capital, but has more than re-couped them in subsequent market transactions.

The fourth duration type is the liquidating fund: the foundation trustees are directed to spend all the capital. The Julius Rosenwald Fund, established in 1917 as a family foundation, was the first of this type. Julius Rosenwald believed strongly that the generation that was the source of wealth should be the recipient of it, and he specified that the foundation be liquidated within twenty-five years of his death. The Fund had run its course by 1948, lasting a few years beyond the span that he specified. The use of the liquidating fund has been in-creasing. The Children's Fund of Michigan, which initially had an endowment of $10 million, spent $18.5 million over a period of twenty-five years and liquidated itself in 1954. The Max C. Fleischmann Foun-dation of Nevada had a corpus of $67 million in 1959, which was to be expended in its entirety over the two decades following the death of the donor's wife.

Foundation Finances

THE FOUNDATION LIBRARY CENTER study of the late 1950's gathered financial data on some 12,000 foundations. Their total assets were about $11.6 billion, most of them held by a relatively small number of large foundations as noted above. In fact, the ten largest foundations, each worth more than $100 million, held 51 per cent of all foundation assets. The 7,000 smallest foundations, whose average assets were less than $14,000, were together worth less than one per cent of all foundations. There were 747 foundations reporting assets between $1 million and $100 million apiece—total assets about $4.8 billion.

How much foundations spend each year is a question to which there is no exact answer. Reported figures for 5,143 foundations, covering varying years between 1956 and 1960, total $686 million. Of this, $626 million was paid out in grants. The remainder was for operations under-taken by the foundations themselves and for administrative expenses. (By comparison, the aggregate expenditures of 3,800 known founda-tions polled in 1953 were $371.4 million, of which $308.6 million was paid out in grants.) [18]

The American Association of Fund-Raising Counsel has estimated that through the later 1940's and early 1950's foundation grants were about $320 million a year, and approached $400 million in 1953. Grants in 1955 were about $950 million, but this included special grants by the

---

[18] Walton and Andrews, *op. cit.*, pp. xiii–xvii; Rich, *op. cit.*, p. xxiv. In the Walton and Andrews study, most asset figures are given at the estimated market rather than the "book" or ledger value of the foundation's holdings.

TABLE 1

TWENTY LARGE FOUNDATIONS, 1958–1959 [1]

Foundation	Date Founded	Assets [2]	Total Expenditures	Grants
		(*In Thousands of Dollars*)		
Ford Foundation	1936	$3,316,000	$112,146	$109,354
Rockefeller Foundation	1913	648,000	25,106	22,600 [3]
Leonard C. Hanna Fund	1941	11,000	22,739	22,626
Old Dominion Foundation	1941	43,000	17,777	17,631
Carnegie Corporation	1911	261,000	8,716	7,935
W. K. Kellogg Foundation	1930	215,000	8,147	7,747
Duke Endowment	1924	414,000	7,914	7,276
Alfred P. Sloan Foundation	1934	176,000	6,208	5,779
Ford Motor Company Fund	1949	17,000	4,546	4,385
A. W. Mellon Educational and Charitable Trust	1930	44,000	4,201	3,963
Lilly Endowment	1937	157,000	4,128	4,058
Rockefeller Brothers Fund	1940	53,000(L)	4,053	3,841
John A. Hartford Foundation	1929	413,000	3,999	3,946
Commonwealth Fund	1918	120,000	3,973	3,448
Kresge Foundation	1924	95,000	3,624	3,498
U.S. Steel Foundation	1953	22,000	3,299	3,297
Danforth Foundation	1929	110,000	2,914	2,818
James Foundation of New York	1941	78,000	2,619	2,478
Avalon Foundation	1940	74,000	2,474	2,343
Carnegie Institution of Washington	1902	81,000	2,389 [4]	
Totals		$6,348,000	$250,972	$239,023

Source: Ann D. Walton and F. Emerson Andrews, eds. *The Foundation Directory.* New York: Russell Sage Foundation, 1960, various pages.

[1] Listed in order of their total expenditures during the most recent year for which information is available, in all cases either 1958 or 1959. The difference between total expenditures and grants for a given foundation is comprised of administrative expenses and the cost of operating programs, if any.

[2] Asset figures are the approximate market value of securities and other holdings, except in the case of the Rockefeller Brothers Fund, which lists its assets in terms of their ledger value—significantly less than market value.

[3] Includes some operating programs.

[4] The Carnegie Institution is an operating foundation and makes no significant grants.

Ford Foundation of $500 million to private colleges and universities, a once-in-a-lifetime expenditure. (The special Ford grants were announced in 1955 and are thus included in figures for that year; they were actually paid out over a period of several years.) Foundation giving in 1956 has been estimated at $600 million; in 1958, at $505 million; in 1959, at $700 million.[19]

Table 1 lists the assets, total expenditures, and grants of twenty of

[19] *New York Times*, June 13, 1957; *Giving USA*, New York: American Association of Fund-Raising Counsel, 1957, pp. 32–33; 1959, p. 7; 1960, p. 8.

the largest foundations. Some of these foundations are not large in terms of total assets, but are included because of the magnitude of their expenditures. There are some large foundations that have assets of $40 million or more apiece whose annual expenditures did not exceed $2.3 million apiece in recent years—though they may in the near future. Among them are the Charles Hayden Foundation, the Max C. Fleischmann Foundation of Nevada, the Mayo Association, the Guggenheim Memorial Foundation, and the Olin Foundation.

GRANT-MAKING AND OPERATING FOUNDATIONS

THERE ARE TWO functional types of foundations, the operating foundation and the grant-making foundation. Most foundations, large and small, are concerned almost exclusively with grant programs. Several of the large foundations and a number of smaller ones conduct research and provide services, rather than making grants. The activities of several foundations of each type are discussed in this section.

Ford: A Large Grant-Making Foundation

THIS STATEMENT of purpose is taken from *The Ford Foundation Annual Report 1957*:

The Ford Foundation's general purpose is to advance human welfare. More specifically, it serves the public welfare by trying to identify problems of importance to the nation and the world and by supplying funds on a limited scale for efforts directed at their solution. Its activities are mostly in the United States and mostly related to education.

The Foundation is faced with many hard choices in selecting the uses to which its resources may best be put. But it does not devise answers or impose solutions. Its grants, in effect, do no more than underwrite the time and talent of individuals and institutions capable of organizing and pioneering the search for answers to the problems that confront society. It attempts to confine itself to actions and amounts designed to demonstrate the dimensions of these problems and, hopefully to stimulate a public response. . . .

What the foundation can do—what it is uniquely able to do in our society—can be summed up in four characteristics that are both advantages and responsibilities.

First, it can be discriminating. . . . Second, it can pioneer. . . . Third, it can show by example. . . . Fourth, it can be flexible.[20]

[20] *The Ford Foundation Annual Report 1957*. New York: The Ford Foundation, pp. 7–8.

In pursuit of its ideals the Foundation expended nearly $85 million in the fiscal year ending September 30, 1958.[21] It functions primarily as a grant-making foundation; 93 per cent of its total 1958 expenditure, $79,034,000 out of $84,911,000, was given in grants. An examination of these expenditures, which probably comprised one-sixth of all 1958 foundation expenditures, lends insight into the interest of grant-making foundations.[22]

Assistance to education has been a dominant interest of the Foundation. As noted above, Ford gave $500 million in endowment and accomplishment grants to private colleges and universities in the mid-1950's. In 1958 Ford grants for education in the United States were $11.1 million. The Educational Facilities Laboratories was established and was to be supported for five years on an appropriation of $4.5 million. For various experimental programs in the use of educational television, $3.1 million was granted. As a partial result of a 1957 grant of $24.5 million to the Woodrow Wilson National Fellowship Foundation, 1,000 graduate fellowships a year were to be awarded through 1963. In 1959 Ford grants for "Education in the United States" were $29.8 million, more than half of it for teacher training.

In 1958 three national institutions, the Lincoln Center for the Performing Arts, the Brookings Institution, and Resources for the Future, received a total of $21.6 million, the largest group of 1958 grants. Public affairs information and study programs received $2.8 million; twenty-four universities and organizations received $2.2 million for the study of urban and regional problems. Many relatively small grants, totaling $6.6 million, were made to universities in the United States and abroad to study economic development and administration: to achieve "better understanding of the determinants of economic growth and stability" and "improved education for those who make far-reaching public and private economic decisions." [23] Other grant programs made primarily in the United States were for the humanities and the arts, youth development, the study of the problems of the aging, and for science and engineering.

The international sphere is an important concern of the Ford Foundation. International training, research, and legal studies took a $5.6 million share of 1958 grants. The Harvard University Center for International Affairs received $1 million of this, the Cornell Southeast

[21] Ford spent nearly $160 million in the preceding year, but this included an extraordinary grant of $68,250,000 to forty-five private medical schools, most of which was drawn from principal rather than income.
[22] Ford had several small foundation-operated projects, notably in overseas development, which took 1 per cent of its 1958 expenditures. The remaining 6 per cent ($5,034,000) paid program, administrative, and overseas field offices expenses.
[23] *The Ford Foundation Report 1958.* New York: The Ford Foundation, 1958, p. 59.

Asia Studies programs $579,000. There were 187 fellowships granted under the Foreign Area and International Relations Training Fellowship Programs, budgeted at $878,000 for 1958–59. Programs in International Affairs involved $6.6 million in grants, most of them to organizations in foreign countries. Among their major purposes were "strengthening education and research in Europe," "increasing international understanding," and "reducing tensions through East-West exchange."

The largest group of Ford's international programs was initiated in 1950, to aid countries in south and southeast Asia, the Near East, and Africa to raise the living standards of their people. Aid has been given in many forms, including economic and technical assistance; a multitude of training programs for teachers, farmers, craftsmen, children, and others; and many university-centered research and study programs. The total outlay for these programs in 1958 was $16.1 million, India, Pakistan, Iran, Burma, and Indonesia receiving the largest shares. Grants for similar overseas development programs in 1959 were $13.2 million.

The James Clise Fund: A Small Grant-Making Foundation

THE SMALL FOUNDATIONS, those having assets of less than $100,000, are extremely varied in purpose and activity. Their size prevents them from undertaking projects of any wide scope, and they usually content themselves with small grants to churches, educational institutions, hospitals, and the favorite charities of the donor.

The James Clise Fund, of Seattle, Washington, is representative of these small grant-making foundations. Its interests are "to determine and disseminate the fundamental facts most essential to the continuance of our civilization." It makes grants for "adult education, philosophy, and research in economics, political science, social psychology, and sociology relating to human action." Its assets in 1957 were $43,300, and its grants totaled $16,000. As is the case with many other small foundations, it was established primarily as an instrument for its donor's current giving. Its grants far exceeded any possible income from the principal, and the donor himself was one of the Fund's three trustees.[24]

Operating Foundations

OPERATING FOUNDATIONS, such as the Russell Sage Foundation and the Carnegie Institution of Washington, use their funds chiefly for concentrated operations by their own staffs. The Carnegie Institution is the largest of the operating foundations. Its activities are the "Con-

[24] Walton and Andrews, *op. cit.*, p. 653.

duct of research programs principally in the fields of the physical and biological sciences, and the interpretation and dissemination of the results of such investigations." [25] The Institution is currently operating in astronomy, geophysics, terrestrial magnetism, plant biology, embryology, and genetics.

An operating *service* foundation was the Great Books Foundation, whose principal undertaking was the promotion of the Great Books Discussion Seminars program. The Foundation stated that "the surest way to preserve liberty is through the means of reading and discussion," and toward this end it sponsored community group discussion programs throughout the country and also developed reading groups for industry and business.[26]

The Phelps-Stokes Fund is primarily an operating foundation, of the middle range in financial size. Its assets in 1959 were $1,952,000, and expenditures totaled $78,550. The Fund was created to:

> support . . . research and educational activities for the purpose of improving race relations of Negroes, both in Africa and the United States, and North American Indians; also for the support of studies and efforts to improve housing for low-income families in New York City. The Fund maintains consulting services in education and the applied social sciences, sponsors conferences to promote intergroup understanding, undertakes intercultural activities involving Africans in the United States, and disseminates the findings of scientific research about race, human development, and adaptation to social change.[27]

AREAS OF FOUNDATION INTEREST

THE INTERESTS of the larger foundations are concentrated particularly in education, health, and scientific research, though they have many other interests as well, including the arts, recreation, and international relations. Those of the smaller foundations are notably education, the welfare of underprivileged groups, and religion. However, the true extent of foundation contributions to any particular phase of human welfare has proved difficult to determine.

In 1944, 335 foundations were asked, in the Harrison and Andrews study, *American Foundations for Social Welfare*, to indicate which of ten categories of activity had taken more than 15 per cent of their yearly expenditures. For 1954 similar data about 620 foundations were obtained from the Rich study (though the Rich study did not specify

[25] Rich, *op. cit.*, p. 76.
[26] *American Foundations News Service*, I (Jan. 25, 1950), p. 5.
[27] Walton and Andrews, *op. cit.*, p. 426.

any minimum percentage of yearly expenditure for including an activity). Over the ten-year period the largest proportional increase was in the percentage of foundations interested in the physical sciences. Equally significant was the increased interest expressed in health, education, and social welfare, though the latter is a somewhat indeterminate category.[28]

TABLE 2

FOUNDATION GRANTS IN VARIOUS FIELDS, 1957
(In Millions of Dollars)

	129 Large Foundations [1]	651 Medium-Sized Foundations [2]	4,422 Small Foundations [3]	Total Grants	Per Cent
Field of Interest					
Education [4]	$163.5	$42.1	$51.5	$257.1	41%
Health	49.5	22.2	26.6	98.3	16
Social Welfare	30.7	23.8	36.1	90.6	15
Scientific Research	46.7	15.4	9.1	71.2	11
Humanities	14.6	14.4	5.0	34.0	5
Religion	11.9	5.1	11.1	28.1	5
Government	5.6	3.8	4.2	13.6	2
International Affairs	26.2	3.9	2.6	32.7	5
Totals	$348.7	$130.7	$146.2	$625.6	100%

Source: Ann D. Walton and F. Emerson Andrews, eds. *The Foundation Directory.* New York: Russell Sage Foundation, 1960, p. lii.

[1] Based on data from 110 of the 129 foundations having assets over $10 million apiece; the total assets of the 129 were $8,812 million.
[2] Based on a sample of 100 of the foundations having assets between $10 and $100 million; the total assets of the 651 were about $1,855 million.
[3] Based on a sample of 100 of the foundations with assets between $50,000 and $1 million; the total assets of the 4,422 known small foundations were about $850 million.
[4] The extraordinary Ford Foundation grants to college and university endowments, announced in 1957, are excluded from these figures and from the table, since they would raise the totals unusually high in relation to other years.

The most comprehensive, and also the most recent, study of the distribution of foundation grants was made by the Foundation Library Center in the late 1950's. Grants of all but 19 of the 129 largest foundations were tabulated by field, along with sample-based estimates for the 651 medium-sized foundations (those with assets between $1 and $10 million) and for the 4,422 known small foundations (those with assets between $50,000 and $1 million). The target year was 1957. The results are summarized in Table 2; education received the largest portion of all grants, an estimated 41 per cent, followed by health, 16 per cent, and social welfare, 15 per cent. The categories overlap to a considerable

[28] *Philanthropic Foundations*, p. 278.

degree, of course, a fact which led the researchers to admittedly arbitrary decisions in categorizing some grants.

Foundation grants within the various fields of interest have a kaleidoscopic diversity of purpose as well as a wide range of financial magnitude. Some of this is suggested in the following sections, which list representative grants in various fields of interest, most fields being similar to or the same as those given in Table 2.

Education

AID IN THE FIELD of education may take any of a number of forms. It may be an endowment grant, a scholarship program, a contribution to a building fund, or a research program. The *American Foundation News*, a periodical issued by the American Foundations Information Service, in the period from December, 1958, through March, 1959, listed reports of educational grants under the following headings: [29]

General educational purposes	$18,479,000
General support (scholarships, endowment, etc.)	5,751,000
Buildings and facilities	13,125,000
Advancement of teaching	3,868,000
Curriculum and special projects	1,927,000
Educational television	545,000
Secondary education	2,004,000
Adult and continuing education	1,070,000
	$46,769,000

The three largest foundations make extensive grants to education. Some of the Ford Foundation grants to education were cited above. Almost 61 per cent of the Foundation's 1957 expenditures were classified in the Ford annual report under "Education in the United States" and at least half the remaining grants, including a multitude of research programs in public affairs, business, the behavioral sciences, and mental health, were channeled through the nation's colleges and universities. The Carnegie Corporation of New York has been concerned almost exclusively with various aspects of education. In 1957 it granted $7.3 million for various colleges and academic organizations in the United States and the British Commonwealth, numerous travel and study

[29] The "general educational purposes" entry includes grants by the A. W. Mellon Educational and Charitable Trust of $12 million to the University of Pittsburgh and $5 million to the College of Fine Arts of Carnegie Institute of Technology. (The *American Foundation News* ceased publication in the fall of 1960, its function being largely replaced by a new periodical publication of the Foundation Library Center. Also active in collecting and circulating news of foundations and philanthropic activity in general is the John Price Jones Company of New York.)

grants, and the distribution of books to many libraries throughout the British Commonwealth.

The smaller foundations ordinarily cannot equal such contributions, but nevertheless spend significantly for education. The Donner Foundation of Philadelphia in 1958 made a grant of $80,000 to the Foreign Policy Research Institute of the University of Pennsylvania; a grant of $75,000 to the Eisenhower Exchange Fellowships, Inc., of Philadelphia; and $10,000 to the American Economic Foundation of New York, the last "to help extend, through the American film series, the teaching of basic economic principles in secondary schools." [30] The Esso Educational Foundation, established by the Standard Oil Company of New Jersey, in December, 1957, began a three-year $1.5 million program for the development of scientific education. Of the grant for the initial year, $300,000 supported programs for the training of high school teachers of physics, chemistry, the biological sciences, and mathematics.

Some other examples of aid to secondary education are the appropriation of $350,000 by the Carnegie Foundation for the Advancement of Teaching in 1957 for the Educational Testing Service to administer the James B. Conant study of American high schools and the expenditure of $986,000 by the Fund for the Advancement of Education to sponsor the use of television in the public schools.

The education activities of the smaller foundations more typically comprise scholarship aid and student loans, however. The National Scholarship Service and Fund for Negro Students in 1957 helped place 549 Negro high school seniors in colleges and universities, providing nearly $300,000 in scholarship funds; the First Security Foundation of Utah in 1959 granted some $10,000 for scholarships and library aid to universities in Idaho and Utah. Typical foundation loan funds are the Ben Selling Scholarship Loan Fund, limited to students attending colleges in Oregon or rabbinical colleges throughout the country; and the Angier B. Duke Memorial, which provides fellowships, prizes, and scholarships, as well as loans, to students at Duke University.

Within recent years corporation foundations have handled increased educational giving by corporations, much of which has been in the form of scholarship plans. The Phelps-Dodge Foundation is typical of the foundations that have taken advantage of this form of educational giving. In 1957 it awarded ten four-year college scholarships, "giving preference to sons of employees of Phelps-Dodge Corporation and its subsidiaries." [31] In 1955 the Ford Foundation established the National Merit Scholarship Corporation, a national scholarship program based on competitive examinations, which, it was hoped, would gain the

[30] *New York Times*, Feb. 2, 1958.
[31] *American Foundation News*, V (June 15, 1957).

support of corporations, corporation foundations, and private donors.

Graduate study fellowships have long been supported by foundations. A yearly fellowship of $2,500 in the 1950's was adequate to support an unmarried graduate student at most major universities in the United States, and additional grants were quite frequently extended to cover the cost of the student's research. The Procter and Gamble Fund announced, in 1957, that it was granting thirty-one regular fellowships in the fields of chemistry, chemical engineering, and mechanical engineering, with an allocation of $110,000. In the 1957–58 academic year, awards from the Samuel S. Fels Fund totaling $99,400 benefited thirty-four graduate students at eight universities who were completing doctoral dissertations in the humanities and the social sciences. There are fellowships for students working toward their doctorates in almost every field, with the partial exception of medicine. Although medical school is the most expensive of graduate programs, as well as the most demanding, until recently there has been a relatively small amount of fellowship aid available.

Foundations also support postdoctoral study and research, making grants for research in the physical and social sciences, providing extensive funds for overseas study and travel, and supporting various institutes, such as the Center for Advanced Study in the Behavioral Sciences at Stanford University. In 1957 the Center received a Ford Foundation grant of $5 million to extend its work for a second five-year period; it provides a year of study and exchange of experience for about fifty behavioral scientists annually, with the aim of increasing their competence as researchers and teachers.

Foundations have been concerned primarily with education in private colleges and universities, considerably less with public educational institutions, only slightly with secondary education—though this is increasing—and almost not at all with primary education. Foundation directors, and educators as well, do not believe that foundations can or should meet the largest part of the financial requirements of higher education. In 1956–57 the Ford Foundation granted $210 million to the endowment of 615 private colleges and universities for the purpose of raising teachers' salaries, yet it did no more than increase them about 4 or 5 per cent. (This $210 million was part of the exceptional $500 million grant announced in 1955.) Foundations can play an even smaller financial role with respect to lower levels of education.

Rather, foundations have come to consider themselves a major source of innovation in the American educational system. They are more and more responsible for the types of research being undertaken and for the fields of knowledge being investigated in colleges and universities. They are also beginning to believe that there are equally great opportunities, and perhaps a greater need, for experimentation and change in the lower levels of the educational system. If present trends continue, the future will see not only still further foundation interest in higher education and adult education but increasing activity downward in the educational system.

Scientific Research

IN A RUSSELL SAGE survey of seventy-seven large foundations, forty-three reported that they supported research in the physical, biological, and/or social sciences during 1953.[32] The total assets of the seventy-seven were $3,014 million, which provided an income of $166 million, $164 million of which was actually expended for all purposes. Of the

TABLE 3

SCIENTIFIC RESEARCH EXPENDITURES OF LARGE FOUNDATIONS,
1946, 1953, AND 1957 [1]
(*In Thousands of Dollars*)

Field	1957 Amount	*Per Cent*	1953 Amount	*Per Cent*	1946 Amount	*Per Cent*
Social Sciences	$ 9,356	*28%*	$11,009	*42.5%*	$ 2,751	*24.5%*
Medical Sciences	5,874	*18*	7,698	*29.7*	4,038	*36.0*
Biological Sciences	4,588	*14*	3,730	*14.4*	1,695	*15.1*
Physical Sciences	10,401	*31*	2,422	*9.4*	2,464	*21.9*
Agricultural Sciences	3,021	*9*	1,047	*4.0*	284	*2.5*
Totals	$33,241	*100%*	$25,906	*100%*	$11,232	*100%*

Source: *Scientific Research Expenditures by the Larger Private Foundations;* Walton and Andrews, p. xli.

[1] Data from 30 foundations in 1946, 43 in 1953, and 60 in 1957.

latter, $26 million (16 per cent) was for scientific research and development. It was estimated, on the basis of a sample study, that the smaller foundations granted an additional $7 million for research, primarily medical research. Total expenditures on scientific research in the United States in 1953 were about $5 billion, of which the foundations thus contributed about two-thirds of one per cent. The qualitative considerations should not be overlooked, however. About $2 billion of total research funds were spent by the national government, largely for military research, and much of the remainder was applied research within industry. The foundations' two-thirds of one per cent for the

[32] *Scientific Research Expenditures by the Larger Private Foundations,* 1953. Survey by the Russell Sage Foundation for the National Science Foundation. Washington, D.C.: NSF, 1956.

most part was for crucial programs in fundamental research, social sciences, and medical research. Another survey, of scientific research expenditures by sixty large foundations in 1957, showed a total of $33.2 million.

Table 3 indicates relative expenditures for scientific research in five areas over an eleven-year period. Percentage expenditures for biological research declined somewhat over the period; between 1946 and 1953, expenditures in the physical sciences declined somewhat, but increased sharply thereafter. Table 4 gives the distribution of research funds among various recipients in 1953.

TABLE 4

RECIPIENTS OF SCIENTIFIC RESEARCH EXPENDITURES, 1953

Recipient	Per Cent of Total Funds
Colleges and Universities	47%
Health Agencies and Hospitals	10
Other Agencies	23
Individuals [1]	6
Research Programs of Operating Foundations	14

Source: Same as Table 3.

[1] Some foundations make few if any grants directly to individuals, but insist that they be supervised by an institution, such as a college or university.

The following examples suggest the types of research projects supported by foundations. They are a partial listing of those reported in the American Foundations News from September, 1957, to November, 1959:

For research reactors, from the National Science Foundation: $300,000 to Washington State College, $150,000 to the University of Virginia.

From the Ford Foundation: $2.5 million to the National Bureau of Economic Research, $750,000 to Rutgers University for a New Jersey urban research and extension center.

For the carbon-14 dating of archaeological materials, $2,250 to the Smithsonian Institution from the Creole Foundation.

For the study of the social, educational, and attitudinal characteristics of federal executives, $130,000 to the University of Chicago from the Carnegie Corporation.

To further the work of the biophysics research unit at Kings College, University of London, England, $121,000 from the Rockefeller Foundation.

For research on the relation between physical and mental illness

282

at the University of Rochester Medical Center, $355,000 from the Ford Foundation.

From the Hill Family Foundation, $46,740 to Community Research Associates for research on the prevention of dependency in Minnesota counties.

From the Rockefeller Foundation, $285,000 to the Harvard Graduate School of Public Administration for a four-year study of the financial and administrative problems of research in the United States in the application and determination of public policy.

To the Foreign Policy Research Institute of the University of Pennsylvania, $35,000 from the Donner Foundation.

To the University of Miami, for research on plankton and other marine life as a possible food source, $90,000 from the Rockefeller Foundation.

For long-range fundamental research in chemistry, a total of $3.6 million in grants for fifty-one research projects at various institutions from the Robert A. Welch Foundation.

For a world-wide foundation-operated program in the investigation and control of virus diseases, $1,040,750 by the Rockefeller Foundation.

Health

THE FIELD of health and medicine is of interest to almost as many foundations as is education. Grants are made not only for medical research but also to hospitals for construction and equipment, for hospitalization expenses of individuals, for health education, and for training programs for hospital and medical personnel. Some recent grants in the field of health are listed below:

In 1956 the Southern Regional Education Board received $10,000 from the Kellogg Foundation to conduct a survey of dental education resources in the South, in cooperation with the United States Public Health Service and the American Dental Association. Also related to medical education, in 1956–57 the Commonwealth Fund granted nearly $800,000 to twelve universities and other organizations toward increasing knowledge about the "learning process of medical students." These included $300,000 to the Georgetown University School of Medicine to support revisions of the teaching program and $73,000 for designing a new medical center at the University of Kentucky. The Kellogg Foundation in 1957 granted $100,000 to St. Louis University and the Catholic Hospital Association for training and educating a wide variety of hospital personnel, including technicians, dietitians, administrators, and others.

Rehabilitation services also are sponsored by foundations. Late in 1957 the Crotched Mountain Foundation, which provides rehabilitation services for crippled children and handicapped adults, received $525,000 from the Charles Hayden Foundation and $100,000 from the Lilly Endowment. The Avalon Foundation granted the Society for the Rehabilitation of the Facially Disfigured $1 million toward the establishment of an Institute of Plastic Surgery.

Many grants have been made to hospital construction programs. The New York Foundation donated $200,000 and the Lillia Babbitt Hyde Foundation $100,000 to the building program of the New York University Bellevue Medical Center early in 1958; the Fannie E. Ripple Foundation granted $250,000 toward the new building of the New Jersey Orthopaedic Hospital; the Old Dominion Foundation granted $3,000 toward the total cost of $12,000 for the first medical center on the island of Tangier in Chesapeake Bay, "the balance having been more than raised by the Methodist Church and the islanders themselves." [33]

In the field of public health the Rockefeller Foundation granted $150,000 to the American Public Health Association, for the reorganization of its services to cope with new needs.

Other grants have been for mental health. The Grant Foundation and the Hogg Foundation for Mental Hygiene are both particularly interested in this subject. In one recent year the former made grants to organizations such as the Massachusetts General Hospital, the Mental Health Service, and the Mental Health Materials Center, Inc.; the latter made a large number of grants to universities, community projects, and agencies in the State of Texas.

Social Welfare

THERE IS definite foundation interest in "social welfare," expressed in grants specifically designed to benefit groups of underprivileged individuals. Very few large foundations and only some of the smaller ones make grants for direct financial aid and services to individuals, however. Most foundation funds for social welfare are channeled through the medium of established welfare organizations. For example, the Martha Mertz Foundation in 1958 granted $5,200 to the New York Inwood House for unmarried mothers; the Mullen Benevolent Corporation gave $13,561 to the Little Sisters of the Poor. Some family foundations make grants to community chests and other local fund drives. In one recent year the Altman Foundation of New York granted $50,000 to the Federation of Jewish Philanthropies, $25,000 to the

[33] *American Foundation News*, V (June 15, 1957).

Catholic Charities of the Archdiocese of New York, and $10,000 to the Federation of Protestant Welfare Agencies. Homes for the aged and community centers not infrequently receive grants from small foundations. A number of foundations contribute to community funds.

Institutions and organizations concerned with children also sometimes receive foundation grants. The Charles Hayden Foundation gave $150,000 to the Boys Club of the Bronx and $50,000 to a Massachusetts camping reservation, among its total of about $1 million in 1958 for various boys' organizations. The Kresge Foundation in the same year donated $25,000 to the Cleveland YMCA, and the Johnson Foundation contributed $12,000 to the Girl Scouts Camp Fund in Racine, Wisconsin. Grants specifically for underprivileged children include the Doris Duke Foundation gift of $12,000 to a Girl Scouts of America program concerned with "hard to reach" children in urban California; and $125,000 to the New York State Charities Aid Association for aiding in the adoption of children of all races, ages, and religions. The latter two grants differ from most grants for child-related groups; gifts to boys' clubs and YMCA's have typically been for equipment and the construction of facilities.

Larger foundations most often enter the social welfare field in less direct ways than those described above. They finance research on community and social problems, make grants for the training of social welfare workers, and sponsor programs for the physically handicapped, the aged, and others. In this they are sometimes joined by smaller foundations. In 1959 the Lilly Endowment gave $150,000 for graduate training programs in community welfare research; the Rockefeller Brothers Fund contributed $41,000 to the Council on Social Work Education and $25,000 to the American Public Welfare Association. The Ford Foundation has become interested in problems of older persons and in 1958 granted some $900,000 to universities and social welfare groups for research on various aspects of the aged. The Elizabeth McCormick Memorial Fund in one recent year allocated $100,000 for a multitude of research problems relating to child welfare. Such grants are in the foundation tradition of solving problems through applying financial help at crucial points to assist the efforts of others.

Recreation and the Arts

A FEW FOUNDATIONS have been interested in providing or developing public facilities such as auditoriums and parks; more have been interested in the fine arts—music, the visual arts, and the theater. In 1957 the Ford Foundation and the Rockefeller Foundation each granted $2.5 million to the planned Lincoln Center for the Performing Arts in New York City, which will bring together the Metropolitan Opera Association, the New York Philharmonic Symphony Society, and the Juilliard School of Music, among others. These grants were the largest ever made in this area of interest.

Foundations have made contributions to such outdoor facilities as zoos, local parks, gardens and nurseries, and to beach areas. Recreational facilities at Reynolds Memorial Park, in North Carolina, were constructed with the aid of a $175,000 grant from the Z. Smith Reynolds Foundation. A Negro park in South Carolina was made possible by a grant of $22,000 from the Spartanburg County Foundation. In 1956–57 the Rockefeller Brothers Fund gave a total of $1,250,000 to the Jackson Hole Preserve, a conservation foundation. One million dollars of the grants were to be used in the development of the Island of St. John, in the American Virgin Islands, for national park purposes.

The fine arts have attracted the interest of a number of foundations. A program in the humanities and the arts was initiated by the Ford Foundation in 1957. A grant of $150,000 under the program financed "a five-year experiment to determine the proper curriculum for the independent art school, undertaken by the Minneapolis School of Art"; another, of $250,000, was for "a three-year experiment by the American Music Center and six American symphony orchestras in multiple regional performances of new symphonic works." [34] Direct grants totaling $445,000 were made to painters, sculptors, writers, directors, and composers in 1959. The Louis Comfort Tiffany Foundation awarded $22,000 to nineteen applicants in its Competition for Scholarships in Painting, Sculpture, Graphic Arts, and Ceramics in 1957; the William Randolph Hearst Foundation gave the Metropolitan Museum of Art a seventeenth-century choir screen from the Cathedral of Valladolid; and the Walter W. Naumburg Foundation, commissioned by the Koussevitzky Foundation, arranged for the recording of a contemporary composition, Leon Kirchner's *Piano Concerto*.

Religion

MOST FOUNDATIONS that make grants in support of churches and religious activity are small family foundations, which do so usually at the behest of their donors. A few large foundations also contribute to religious bodies; by the terms of its establishment the Duke Foundation directs 12 per cent of its distributable income to churches in the Carolinas, for example, one-sixth of this amount for ministerial pensions and the remainder for the construction and operation of churches. Among other grants, the Rockefeller Brothers Fund has recently spon-

[34] *The Ford Foundation Annual Report 1957*, p. 19.

sored a study of the role religion plays in mental health; and the Sealantic Fund in 1957 granted $110,000 to the American Theological Library Association, to be used in developing a periodical index of theological literature and a microtext system. The family foundations often make small grants to local church groups, but ordinarily local churches have found adequate resources among parishioners for their building and welfare programs. Hence, the outstanding foundation contributions have been almost entirely to broader and more challenging programs of religious study and education.

International Relations and International Welfare

As THE UNITED STATES involvement in the rest of the world has become a matter of increasing concern, foundations have made their influence felt through a number of international programs. The promotion of peace in the early decades of the century prompted the establishment of the Carnegie Endowment for International Peace in 1910, as well as several others, including the World Peace Foundation and the Woodrow Wilson Foundation. The most important current programs of American foundations in the international field are assistance programs, and are discussed in Chapter 15. Here it can be noted that with a few exceptions the foundations concerned with international matters are the largest ones—Ford, Rockefeller, and Carnegie—and a few others such as the Donner Foundation, the Lilly Endowment, the Dodge Foundation, and the Twentieth Century Fund, all of which except the Dodge Foundation have assets over $10 million. A few smaller foundations have been established specifically for international purposes. For example, in 1944 the Li Foundation was incorporated in New York with a capital of $250,000; its special interest is the exchange of American and Chinese students, "with a view to spreading knowledge in each country as to the other, its culture and history, and thereby fostering and promoting mutual good will between the United States of America and the Republic of China." [35]

Race Relations

NUMEROUS FOUNDATIONS have been active in the area of race relations, particularly with respect to the status of Negroes and Jews. The Julius Rosenwald Fund, before its liquidation in 1948, devoted much of its funds to Negro health, education, and welfare; during its lifetime it granted $3 million specifically to the study of Negro race relations. The Phelps-Stokes Fund, cited above, and the Southern Education Founda-

[35] Rich, *op. cit.*, p. 413.

tion have long supported programs for Negroes, especially in education.[36]

The Fund for the Republic, established in 1952 with a $15 million grant from the Ford Foundation, since its beginning has been concerned with civil liberties and has established a number of programs in race relations. It has given $240,000 to the Southern Regional Council for its interracial improvement program; $100,000 for a commission to promote understanding of the American Indian; and $305,000 to the Commission on Race and Housing, for a nation-wide survey of the housing needs of minority groups, particularly of Negroes and Puerto Ricans in metropolitan areas.

Government and Public Administration

TO QUOTE F. EMERSON ANDREWS, who has written the most comprehensive studies of philanthropy, "Government and public administration is an area in which foundations might render notable service as advisory and standard-setting agencies, free from the bias of self-interest. But comparatively few foundations are active in this field." [37]

One of these few is the Fund for the Republic, which has been particularly concerned with the impact of government on individuals and groups. Its major efforts have been within its own offices, where numerous individual collaborators have written many pamphlets on labor unions, the corporation, civil liberties, and other subjects, for distribution to the interested public. In 1959 it established the Center for the Study of Democratic Institutions to continue such studies. The Ford Foundation in 1958 made a grant of $40,000 to the National Civil Service League for a program of public education on career public service. A few foundations are concerned with problems of local government, as are the Ford and Rockefeller Foundations. The Thomas Skelton Harrison Foundation is primarily concerned with promoting good government in Philadelphia.

Generally, however, foundations in this area exert their influence by making grants for research on problems of government. Several such grants were cited above, in the section on research grants. Among others, the Ford Foundation in 1958 granted $47,500 to the Association of the Bar of the City of New York Fund for studies of legal problems in the appointment of qualified private citizens to high-level non-career government offices. In the same year the Samuel S. Fels Fund gave $172,000 to continue the work of the Fels Institute of Local and State Government at the University of Pennsylvania. In 1959 the Ford Foundation gave $400,000 to the Social Science Research Council

[36] *Philanthropic Foundations*, pp. 296–97.
[37] *Ibid.*, p. 297.

for research, training, and conferences on the American government processes; $20,000 each to Kenyon, Union, and Colgate Colleges for public affairs research; and $20,000 to the Eagleton Foundation and Citizenship Clearing House to place twenty-four political science instructors at the 1960 political party conventions.

Economics

AN INCREASING NUMBER of foundations have been initiating programs on economic questions. The Twentieth Century Fund has long been interested in important economic problems in the United States and has produced a number of significant publications, including *America's Needs and Resources*, edited by J. Frederic Dewhurst, as well as frequent reports on current national economic conditions. The interest of the Ford Foundation in economics has been expressed in grants for research and education in business and economics. Some specific grants have been the 1955–57 grants of the Maurice and Laura Falk Foundation to the Brookings Institution for the study of the impact of union policies on management in industry; a Ford Foundation grant of $120,000 for an intercollegiate clearinghouse for economic case studies; and a 1960 Rockefeller grant of $300,000 to the National Bureau of Economic Research. Over a ten-year period the Merrill Foundation for Advancement of Financial Knowledge has granted a total of $1.3 million for thirty-four research projects and programs dealing with commodity markets, economic fluctuations, industrial organization, marketing, securities and securities markets, inflation, taxation, social security, and international economics.

Miscellaneous Activities

THERE REMAIN some foundation activities that cannot be included in the above categories. These include small grants and interests shared by only a few individuals. There are several foundations, such as Resources for the Future and the Charles Lathrop Pack Forestry Foundation, that are interested in conservation. The Pacifica Foundation of Berkeley, California, exists to operate three non-profit, listener-sponsored FM radio stations, two in California and one in New York. There are foundations working on problems of human communication. And among the small foundations are some luxuriant and exotic growths; the Amazonia Foundation of New York is devoted to the promotion of "inter-American cultural and economic relations and scientific cooperation through research in archaeology, paleontology, geology, mineralogy, and related fields, and general good-will activities." [38] There are two

[38] Rich, *op. cit.*, p. 323.

California foundations making grants in support of Confucianism; and in Illinois there is a research foundation whose purpose is "to advance the art of refrigerating commodities."

6 COMMUNITY TRUSTS AND FOUNDATIONS

THE COMMUNITY trusts and foundations are a distinct sub-species of foundations. Their funds are devoted to the welfare interests of a particular community or, more rarely, of a county or State. From their beginning with the Cleveland Foundation in 1914, community trusts slowly increased in number to over 100 by 1950. There were 101 community trusts in the United States in the late 1950's, excluding those with no significant funds. The active capital of these totaled $340 million.[39] The 1960 edition of the publication *Giving USA* reported that in 1958 ninety-seven community trusts in the United States and Canada held assets of $204 million and made grants of $10.3 million.

The initial sources of funds of community trusts are capital gifts or bequests, administered by local banks and trust companies. The income from these funds, and sometimes the capital itself, is distributed under the auspices of citizen committees, whose members are usually chosen for their prominence in community affairs and knowledge of community welfare conditions. Any given community trust may consist of gifts from a number of individuals; some of these gifts may be combined in "composite" funds, others may be separate, named funds designated for particular purposes. Community trusts may have close relations with community chests; in one city—Rochester, New York—a community trust combining some sixty separate funds is a department of the community chest.[40]

The largest of the community trusts is that of Philadelphia, a composite fund with assets of over $70 million, administered by the Philadelphia Board of Directors of City Trusts. The trusts of at least four other cities—Cleveland, New York, Chicago, and Boston—have assets exceeding $20 million. There are also a number of trusts that are quite small in financial size; the active capital of the Trenton (New Jersey) Community Foundation was $62,475 in 1954, for example, and it was far from the smallest. Some community trusts and foundations have little more than a paper existence, the result of enthusiastic schemes that never attracted capital.

Community trusts and foundations are felt to have the same poten-

[39] Walton and Andrews, *op. cit.*, p. xxi.
[40] F. Emerson Andrews. *Philanthropic Giving*. New York: Russell Sage Foundation, 1950, p. 10.

tial for sponsoring new and experimental ventures in welfare on the local level that the large foundations have for national welfare. Their interests are usually more inclusive than those of community chests, and they are willing to support new programs of research, prevention, and treatment. This is a representative listing of activities that might be undertaken by a community trust in a large city: provide for the first year of operation of a center on alcoholism; support a program to furnish teen-age gangs with adult leaders; assist a program for referring the chronically ill to sources of treatment; finance an experimental program to aid migrants to the city to find adequate, inexpensive housing; help recruit and provide financial aid for students in local schools of social work; finance a new program providing vocational counseling for older workers; supply new equipment and modernized programs of care in homes for the aged, children, and unwed mothers. For the most part these are programs that community chests would finance only reluctantly, for the demands of established agencies frequently preclude assistance to new or untried programs.

In summarizing a discussion of community trusts, one writer states:

> . . . the financial support of voluntary social welfare efforts is presently characterized by the tremendous contributions of national foundations and trusts to major undertakings in education, research, and experimentation on a national level. In addition, the national health appeals provide funds for research, education, experimentation, and some treatment, again, mostly on a national level. Local community funds and chests provide substantial support for the operation of established programs in their localities. In addition, other contributions by individuals, corporations, and local trusts help to finance the capital needs of local voluntary organizations; these same sources may provide from time to time for the support of a new venture locally. *In the structure for financing national and local voluntary efforts there is missing the cornerstone—the adequate financing of new and experimental ventures in the local community. The community trust* [can] *. . . . supply this cornerstone.*[41]

The fields of interest of community trusts are suggested in Table 5, which gives percentage breakdowns of community trust grants in two cities, Chicago and San Francisco, by purpose of grants. The San Francisco Foundation in 1957 had assets approaching $1 million and provided $311,000 to local purposes. (Since no investments could provide returns even approaching 31 per cent, some of the Foundation

[41] George K. Herbert, "The Promotion of the Community Trust," in Alfred de Grazia, ed., *Grass Roots Private Welfare*. New York: New York University Press, 1957, p. 266. Author's emphasis.

funds presumably were liquidating.) The Chicago Community Trust in 1956 reported assets of $15 million, and grants totaling $685,000. In the categories of grants that are approximately equivalent, the comparative percentages are quite close, and it is probably safe to assume that most community foundations and trusts follow the same general pattern in their expenditures.

TABLE 5

COMMUNITY TRUST GRANTS IN TWO CITIES

Purpose	Percentage of Total Grants	
	Chicago Community Trust (Total Grants, 1956, $685,000)	San Francisco Foundation (Total Grants, 1957, $311,000)
Health	19.0%	18.0%
Education	16.3	19.0
Community Planning and Specialized Services	15.4	
Family Service	13.3	
Children and Youth	13.0	20.0
Neighborhood Service	12.4	
Age and Handicapped	7.0	5.0
Civic and Cultural Affairs	3.6	3.5
Welfare Planning and Federated Appeals		24.0
Miscellaneous Purposes [1]		5.0
	100%	94.5% [2]

Source: *American Foundation News*, VI (Jan. 15, 1958).

[1] "Miscellaneous expenditures" by the San Francisco Foundation may include grants for some of the other purposes listed. In general, the purposes are not entirely equivalent; for example, the San Francisco Foundation may have listed grants under "Children and Youth" similar to grants that the Chicago Community Trust listed under "Family Service."
[2] The uses of the remaining expenditures by the San Francisco Foundation are not known.

CONCLUDING REMARKS

FOUNDATIONS ARE of several types and have been established in great numbers. Depending upon definitions, there may be five to ten thousand of them, or more. Foundation assets in 1960 were estimated at $12 billion. Foundations spent an estimated $700 million in 1959, about 90 per cent of it in grants and the balance for administration and internally conducted programs of research, publication, education, or welfare.

General-purpose foundations are organized to support any kind of legal activity deemed to be meritorious by their trustees, and about half of all foundation assets are concentrated in such foundations. Special-purpose foundations are chartered to provide aid for a particular problem area, such as the control of a given disease or to support a certain college, religious group, or other institution. The distinguishing characteristic of family and personal foundations is that their control is vested in the donor and his agents or in a family. Often their purpose is to organize and plan the contributions of individuals to education and charity. The boundaries among these three types of foundations are not distinct; many of the large, general-purpose foundations began their existence as family foundations, for example.

Corporation foundations are increasingly popular as a channel for corporate giving. Usually they are wholly controlled by the donor corporations (of course, no one can *own* a foundation, which is a non-profit corporation exempted by law from federal taxes); they lack substantial principal; and they are ordinarily dedicated to a limited range of goals, within the areas of their donor corporations' business interests.

Community trusts are devoted to the concerns of a given locality, and they make grants for purposes similar to those supported by community federated campaigns. They accept funds from a number of different persons, organizations, and other foundations. They number about 150 and hold over $200 million in trust.

The national government's National Science Foundation is distinct from non-governmental foundations in that it was established by law, holds no principal, and obtains annual appropriations for spending on programs described in law. The programs of the NSF, however, resemble those of the larger general-purpose foundations in many ways, and its methods of operation also are similar. Recent annual appropriations to the NSF of about $130 million make it easily the largest operating foundation in the United States. The Ford Foundation, largest of the non-governmental foundations, spent nearly $110 million in 1959 and in doing so far overshadowed the expenditures of the next largest private foundation.

Not all foundations are founded to exist in perpetuity. Some may spend out of principal as well as out of income and some are directed by their charters to spend all of their principal and income within a stated period of time. Most foundations are set up to receive applications for aid, to judge them, and to support some of them by grants. Practice varies on the number and kind of restrictions placed upon money once it has been granted. A common practice is to make grants with no strings attached other than a final report on their use. Some foundations, such as the Twentieth Century Fund, are of an operating type. They accomplish their aims largely by projects organized and executed within the foundation offices.

The laws of the national government and of the States permit foundation funds to be used for a wide variety of purposes, from pure research in astrophysics to the improvement of a church choir. Generally speaking, the larger foundations spend most of their money for the support of education, health studies, and scientific research; lesser amounts are devoted to recreation, the arts, and international relations. For example, in 1959 the Ford Foundation spent $22 million for natural sciences and engineering; $17 million for teacher training experiments; $16.5 million for educational TV projects; $10 million for overseas economic development; $4.2 million for public affairs; $2.6 million for the humanities and the arts; and $1.5 million for urban and regional programs. The smaller foundations appear to spend more of their funds for the direct welfare of needy persons and for the support of religion.

Each foundation record tends to differ at least in part from those of others. The larger foundations set an intellectual pace for most of the others, though there are some maverick foundations that reflect an unusual interest of their founders. Even these, if they are large in financial size, eventually tend to reflect the norm of the larger group in their programs. The same foundation will vary its program from year to year, of course, as it acquires new officers or as the ideas of the old undergo change. Although a primary defense of foundations has been that they pioneer in social welfare programs and help devise new theories and practices, their performance at best is slightly behind the true pioneers of a field of intellectual endeavor or welfare practice. As organizations of large assets, with the intent of prolonging their existence indefinitely, and having staffs that must contain successful businessmen, lawyers, and accountants, their role is almost inevitably that of a quartermaster corps for the vanguards of innovation.

Chapter Twelve

LOCAL GOVERNMENTS

THERE ARE MANY AND VARIOUS LOCAL GOVERNMENTS in the United States, performing numerous welfare functions. They are created and vested with their powers by the State governments, and in general are designed to perform some task for, and as subordinates of, the State governments. The views of William Penn, as noted by a contemporary, serve as an introduction to the welfare roles of local governments in the United States. "William Penn will not give any man his portion separately, but all must dwell together in townships or towns, and this not without weighty reasons. Among these the chief is that in that way the children can be kept at school and much more conveniently brought up well. Neighbors also can better offer each other loving and helpful hands." [1] In most colonial governments the primary purpose for establishing local governments, which was usually done by incorporating towns, was to promote and regulate trade. Penn, on the other hand, saw local government not so much a means to economic prosperity as a means to a satisfying common life. His brief outline of "weighty reasons," though, does not begin to suggest the innumerable welfare functions of the more than one hundred thousand local governmental units in the United States today.

This chapter discusses the types of local governments in the United States; their finances; and their functions, including services for the

[1] From F. D. Pastorius' *Description of Pennsylvania* (1700), cited in Ernest S. Griffith, *History of American City Government: The Colonial Period*. New York: Oxford University Press, 1938, pp. 58–59.

welfare of the general public, services for the welfare of persons in need, and provisions for the welfare of their employees. This chapter includes some data on school districts, which are a form of local government; Chapter 8, "The Educational System," describes the nature and functions of school districts at greater length.

TYPES OF LOCAL GOVERNMENTS

IN 1957 there were 102,243 separately organized local government units in the United States, including Alaska and Hawaii. Nearly half of these were independent school districts, which, having been treated in Chapter 8, are given only passing mention here. Besides these there were over 17,000 municipalities, about the same number of townships, 14,500 special districts, and 3,000 counties, whose wide variety of welfare functions constituted the bulk of the average citizen's contacts with government.

The County

THERE ARE over 3,000 county governments in the United States. Only in Rhode Island and Alaska, the smallest and the largest of the States, are there no counties as such; Rhode Island is divided into three counties, but there are no solely county officers, and Alaska's only major internal subdivisions have been four judicial districts. Counties vary greatly in size, population, and importance. The smallest, Arlington, Virginia, is only twenty-four miles square; San Bernardino, California, has over 20,000 square miles, larger than any one of the nine smallest States. In population they range from 227 (Loving County, Texas, 1950 census) to over four and a half million (Cook County, Illinois, 1950 census).

The relative importance of counties in the scheme of government varies not only with their size and population, but also with the region of the United States in which they are found. In New England, counties are relatively unimportant, towns and townships being the chief political units subordinate to the State. In the southern States, however, the counties are quite powerful and exercise a large number of functions. This is largely the result of the essentially rural nature of the South and of the fact that the settlers of the South were for the most part less cohesive groups than the New Englanders, who settled in towns. In the face of the growth of urban concentrations in the South, the counties have retained much of their dominance, particularly through the controls exercised by the "courthouse gangs" over the State legislatures. The importance of the county in other parts of the United States is determined partly by the origins of the settlers and partly by geographic conditions. In the midwestern States, settled primarily by New Englanders, the county is relatively less important than in the interior southern States. In the trans-Mississippi States, however, counties for the most part have greater importance because towns are relatively few.

There is space here for only a brief glimpse at the complexities of county government. Most counties are governed by central county boards of one type or another, with varying titles and sizes. A relatively few counties have a single officer instead of a board. The central county board, whatever its composition, or the single officer ordinarily levies taxes, appropriates funds, issues bonds, and exercises whatever particular powers are delegated to it by the State; its power may be said to be primarily executive or administrative. Most States have authorized collateral boards to fulfill specific State policies at the county level. These include boards of public welfare, hospitals, schools, highways, recreation, airports, and a variety of others. The county may be compelled to establish such boards or it may be granted discretionary powers. The relations between such boards and the central county board may not be at all clear, however; collateral board members may be popularly elected, appointed by the central board, appointed by the State agency whose function they are to carry out on the county level, or reach office by some other means.

There are also county "row offices," sharing governmental responsibility with the central county board. Two such officers are elected in almost every county in the United States, the sheriff and the county attorney. Among other county officers, who may be either elected or appointed, are the county coroner, the county clerk, the court clerk, and a number of others varying from State to State and county to county.

One of the most serious problems of many counties is the growth of cities within or across their boundaries. As the cities incorporate new areas the counties may find themselves merely a shell, subject to attrition of area and function yet left with a residuum of area and population to serve. They may be overshadowed by the cities or burdened with suburbs and new demands for services. One well-publicized solution has been that of San Francisco County, which has merged entirely with the city government. Other counties have become "metropolitan counties," assuming the features of municipalities.

The Municipality

"A MUNICIPALITY is a public corporation that has been vested with general governing powers over a relatively small, densely populated area. As a public corporation it may sue and be sued, negotiate contracts, own land and other properties, and incur debts." [2] Two-thirds of the people in the United States live in the four loosely defined types of municipalities: cities, villages, towns, and boroughs. Although there are over 17,000 municipalities throughout the country, half the people in the United States reside in 189 areas (1959) defined by the Bureau of the Census as "metropolitan areas," each such area having a central city with over 50,000 inhabitants. The cities, as the counties, are agents of the State, created by the State, and granted powers, usually very explicity, by the State.

There are three principal forms of municipal government in the United States: the mayor-council, the council-manager, and the commission. The mayor-council form of government, the mayor acting as an executive and the council as a legislature, is most common, existing in more than half the cities whose population exceeds 5,000; all but one of the largest cities, those having more than 500,000 inhabitants, are under the mayor-council form. Cincinnati, Ohio, is the only exception, having had a highly efficient and popular council-manager form of government since 1924, when reformers of what is now known as the Charter party took over from Boss Rud Hynica.

The council-manager form of municipal government, with the manager as a non-political executive chosen by the council, which serves as a legislature, by 1955 had been instituted in 30 per cent of the cities having more than 5,000 people. As noted, it is not found among the largest cities, however. The commission form of government is somewhat rarer, and is gradually disappearing. It has no executive head, the commission performing both legislative and executive functions; hence, it often suffers from a lack of firm leadership. Finally, there are a small number of cities (of those having over 5,000 inhabitants) with a town meeting form of government; in 1955 there were ninety-two such cities, all but one of them having fewer than 50,000 people. [3]

At the opposite end of the scale from the large city are the many villages, boroughs, and other incorporated places, each having a few hundred or a few thousand inhabitants. The number of inhabitants necessary for incorporation varies from State to State. In some, New York and Washington for example, a village of 200 persons may be incorporated. In New York, these people must live in an area of one square mile or less. In Illinois, an area of two square miles containing 300 residents may become a village if it wishes, and, after it has 1,000 inhabitants, a city. Village government organization is usually quite simple. Typically there is a board of five to seven members exercising

[2] Alfred de Grazia. *The American Way of Government.* New York: Wiley and Sons, 1957, p. 853.
[3] *Ibid.*, pp. 856–62.

authority over limited activities and services that usually include tax collections, fire department, streets, and sometimes schools and a court; occasionally there is an overseer of the poor. In four States, Connecticut, Minnesota, New Jersey, and Pennsylvania, the term "borough" is used for the village. There are some boroughs and villages of considerable size that have not asked for status as cities but have retained their older form of government. The borough of Princeton, New Jersey, with a population that approached 15,000 in the late 1950's, is one example; perhaps the largest has been Oak Park, Illinois, which, with a population of over 60,000, still retained the village form of government in 1950.[4]

The Township

THE TOWNSHIP is a form of government that may have some of the characteristics of a municipality, of a county, or of both. In general, the township is a government for a given area, rather than a government for a particular concentration of population. Much of New England is a network of "towns," usually unincorporated, that are actually townships. Outside the New England States, the township form of organization is found in sixteen States, primarily the mid-Atlantic States and those fringing the Great Lakes. In New England the township may fulfill many municipal functions, such as police and fire protection, water supply, and waste disposal; townships in other States are primarily rural. In the north central States they are for the most part arbitrary units six miles square and may fulfill, in this more limited area, the functions of the county government. They can be both districts for conducting local affairs and subordinate units for fulfilling county and State functions.

Except in New England, New York, and Michigan, cities, boroughs, and villages are separated from townships on their incorporation; in the latter two States, villages alone remain part of the townships, and in New England practice varies. Of more than 17,000 townships, almost two-thirds had less than 1,000 inhabitants in 1952 and only 3 per cent had more than 10,000. The larger of these included some local units in metropolitan areas in Pennsylvania, the largest being Upper Darby township, outside Philadelphia, with a population of 85,000.

Townships are governed by a variety of means. In New England, town meetings are held, which may be attended by all voters or by a number of delegates; the meeting acts as a legislature, enacting monetary measures, passing ordinances, and electing administrative officers, such as selectmen. Outside New England, townships may be governed by

[4] Marguerite J. Fisher and Donald G. Bishop. *Municipal and Other Local Governments.* New York: Prentice-Hall, 1950, pp. 640–42.

township meetings, by an elected committee or board of supervisors, or a single supervisor or town chairman assisted by a township board. In the more populous townships there are often a number of other elective or appointive officers, including assessors, election inspectors, a clerk and a treasurer, a welfare officer, a health officer, a constable, and sometimes others. Townships with small populations may have no formal government whatsoever.

The Special District

THE SPECIAL DISTRICT is a political unit created or authorized to perform a specific function, or a group of functions. It is a quasi-corporation, usually with power to levy taxes, incur debts, and own property, to carry out its functions. There are three main types of special districts: agricultural, quasi-municipal, and metropolitan. (In addition, school districts are sometimes considered special districts.) Special districts are unevenly distributed. Seven States—California, Illinois, Kansas, Missouri, New York, Washington, and Texas—contained more than half these districts in 1957. Special districts are becoming increasingly popular, having increased in number from 8,300 to 12,300 between 1942 and 1952, and to 14,400 by 1957.

During the 1950's about one-quarter of the districts served agricultural purposes: soil and water conservation, drainage, irrigation, and natural resource protection and development. The quasi-municipal districts are usually small; they provide services such as fire protection, lighting, water and sanitation, cemetery maintenance, mosquito abatement, and others in unincorporated areas. Metropolitan districts have many of the same functions as the quasi-municipal districts, but are established on a larger scale, usually embracing the jurisdictions of numerous other local governments. They often have been established in the belief that certain functions should be independent of local politics or that debt limitations on municipal governments can be evaded by the establishment of an independent governing body. The more important such districts are sanitation, municipal utility, park, bridge and highway, water, housing, port and harbor, and airport districts. One of the largest metropolitan special districts is the Port of New York Authority, established by compact between New York and New Jersey in 1921. Within a twenty-mile radius around the port of New York, the 4,000 employees of the Authority have constructed and operated motor truck terminals, bridges, airports, railroad belt lines, and a number of other projects relating to port development. California has a number of large metropolitan special districts, including the Metropolitan Water District of Southern California, serving at least four million persons in some thirteen cities and their surrounding areas; and the Los Angeles County Air Pollution Control District, covering 4,000 square miles of territory.

Districts may be established in a number of ways, ranging from petition by residents to the State legislature to resolution by the government agencies involved. They are governed by an equally great variety of means. A director or a board may be elected, or appointed; the central county board may directly govern the district; a representative board, with members chosen by several other governmental bodies, may govern. The Port of New York Authority is governed by twelve men, the governors of New Jersey and New York each appointing six of them.[5]

Relations among Governmental Units

SOME OF THE most serious problems of local government today, particularly those of metropolitan governments, arise from their relations with other local governments. The problem is fundamentally one of fragmentation, which may make it very difficult to carry out welfare functions. Cities whose middle- and upper-income families move to suburbs find demands for services and expenses mounting while tax revenues decrease. Local governments compete with other tax-collecting agencies and with other authorities providing similar or identical services in the same area. In the New York metropolitan area there are at least 1,000 separate governments; in Cook County, the metropolitan Chicago area, there are more than 400 independent tax-collecting agencies and over 300 different agencies having police powers. In rural and semi-rural areas similar conditions exist on a somewhat lesser scale; in many such areas the relatively small number of local authorities and overlapping functions have made it possible to achieve coordination of units, by both formal and informal means.

Many solutions to the fragmentation of local authority have been suggested. The movement to consolidate school districts, under way for some years, is one example. The organization of special districts to deal with a single problem in many adjacent units is another. Out of necessity many local officials have set up channels of cooperation, such as joint committees, referral of problems, and sharing of services with adjoining units; such relations are particularly common between county and municipal governments. The most sweeping solutions have been

[5] John C. Bollens, "When Services Get Too Big," *National Municipal Review*, (November, 1949), pp. 498–503, reprinted in Robert L. Morlan, ed., *Capitol, Courthouse and City Hall: Readings in American State and Local Government*, Cambridge, Mass.: Houghton Mifflin, 1954, pp. 223–27; Harold Alderfer, *American Local Government and Administration*, New York: Macmillan, 1956, pp. 320–21.

proposed in urban areas, where the problems are most serious. Concentration of the entire metropolitan area under a single government is most often suggested, though the authority to do so and the willingness of those to be affected have not yet been forthcoming in any city in this country. San Francisco has achieved a partial step in this direction, the city and county governments having merged. There have been efforts to establish a unified government for Dade County, Florida, in which Miami and a number of lesser cities are located.

The process of municipal incorporation of surrounding areas is not a complete solution to metropolitan integration, but it can be reasonably effective. For example, Spokane, Washington, a city of some 170,000, in the 1940's had the largest area of any city in its population class and in the late 1950's was in the process of incorporating large areas, many of them undeveloped, beyond the city limits. In this city the housing and business developments that in other urban areas take place in suburbs outside the reach of municipal taxing authority are taking place on land already incorporated, and can be provided with unified services. A somewhat similar process occurred in the Los Angeles area in the second and third decades of this century, when the municipal government incorporated many sparsely populated areas and small communities because of their desire to receive the benefits of the new municipal water system. The Los Angeles area was not incorporated in a systematic fashion, however, dozens of independent areas being bypassed in the process; partly as a result there is a very large number of local government units in the Los Angeles area today.

LOCAL GOVERNMENT FINANCES

LOCAL GOVERNMENTS IN 1958 spent $34 billion, one-quarter of all government expenditures in the United States. The tables and commentary in this section deal with the *sources* of local government funds (including school district funds); their uses are discussed in the subsequent section on local government welfare functions.

Local governments face a number of restrictions in raising funds. Municipal governments, which received 40 per cent of local government revenue in 1957 ($11.9 billion out of $29.1 billion), find their revenue collections narrowly circumscribed by State constitutions and legislative enactments, and by their own charters. The same is true, to a somewhat lesser extent, of counties and townships; special districts (and school districts) are relatively free in their revenue-raising powers, though generally they must hold special elections if they wish to increase taxes or issue new bonds.

TABLE 1

SOURCES OF LOCAL GOVERNMENT REVENUES, 1957
(*Amounts in Millions of Dollars*)

SOURCE	COUNTIES Amount and Per Cent	CITIES Amount and Per Cent	TOWN-SHIPS Amount and Per Cent	SCHOOL DISTRICTS Amount and Per Cent	SPECIAL DISTRICTS Amount and Per Cent	TOTAL Amount and Per Cent
Intergovernmental Revenue [1]	$2,100 36.3%	$ 1,720 14.6%	$ 320 23.8%	$3,839 41.8%	$ 116 8.3%	$ 7,620 [1] 26.2%
Total Revenue from Own Sources	$3,678 63.7%	$10,147 85.4%	$1,022 76.2%	$5,340 58.2%	$1,280 91.7%	$21,467 73.8%
Property Taxes	$2,635 45.6%	$ 4,251 35.8%	$ 829 61.8%	$4,642 50.6%	$ 261 18.7%	$12,618 43.4%
Other Taxes [2]	$ 176 3.0%	$ 1,609 13.6%	$ 45 3.4%	$ 64 0.7%		$ 1,894 6.5%
Charges, Misc.	$ 744 12.9%	$ 1,586 13.4%	$ 93 7.0%	$ 595 6.5%	$ 490 35.1%	$ 3,507 12.5%
Liquor Stores	$ 56 1.0%	$ 69 0.6%				$ 125 0.4%
Water Systems		$ 1,080 9.2%				$ 1,246 4.3%
Electric Systems	$ 14 0.2%	$ 755 6.4%	$ 50 3.7%		$ 517 37.0%	$ 965 3.3%
Gas Systems		$ 99 0.8%				$ 138 0.5%
Transit Systems		$ 377 3.2%				$ 542 1.9%
Trust Fund Revenues [3]	$ 54 0.9%	$ 323 2.7%	$ 5 0.4%	$ 40 0.4%	$ 12 0.9%	$ 433 1.5%
Total Revenue	$5,778 20.2%	$11,867 41.5%	$1,342 4.7%	$9,179 32.1%	$1,396 4.9%	$29,087 [1]

Note: All figures are subject to sampling variation. Detail does not necessarily add because of rounding.
Source: *Statistical Abstract of the United States 1959.* U.S. Bureau of the Census. Washington, D.C.: USGPO, 1959, p. 402.

[1] To avoid duplication, these figures exclude all transactions between types of local government units; the sums are thus less than the sum of the components listed at the left. "Total revenue" percentages are calculated from the adjusted total, and thus add to more than 100 per cent.
[2] These were primarily city sales and gross receipts taxes ($1,025 million) and license and permit fees ($656 million); others were individual and corporation income taxes, and gift and death taxes.
[3] Largely payments to employee retirement funds and unemployment compensation funds.

The major source of revenue for most local authorities is the property tax, which may be levied on real property (lands and buildings) or against personal property. The property tax, usually a percentage of the assessed valuation of the property, is about 60 per cent of locally-raised revenues, $12.6 out of $21.5 billion. The proportion varied among types of government; the property tax produced about three-quarters of locally raised county funds, about 40 per cent of locally raised municipal funds, and one-fifth of special district funds. It produced nearly 90 per cent of locally raised school district funds.

The sources of revenue of local governments, by type, are given in Table 1. Cities (*i.e.*, municipalities of all sizes) raised the largest portion of revenue among local governments, nearly $12 billion. Independent school districts raised over $9 billion, counties nearly $6 billion. Townships and special districts together raised about $2.7 billion.

TABLE 2

INTERGOVERNMENTAL EXPENDITURES INVOLVING LOCAL GOVERNMENTS,
BY FUNCTION, 1957
(*Amounts in Thousands of Dollars*)

Function	National to Local	States to Local	Local to Local	Local to States
Highways	$ 2,000	$1,071,000	$ 37,000	$ 26,000
Public Welfare	5,000	1,025,000	10,000	25,000
Health and Hospitals	2,000	253,000	42,000	54,000
Natural Resources		11,000	[1]	2,000
Other	173,000	856,000	68,000	181,000
Education	167,000	4,094,000	308,000	16,000
Totals	$350,000	$7,310,000	$464,000	$304,000

Source: *Statistical Abstract 1959*, p. 404.

[1] Less than $500,000.

Local governments received more than a quarter of their income from non-local sources, in the form of grants, subsidies, and subventions from State and national governments. The national government (see Table 2) made relatively minor grants, a third of a billion dollars, compared with State grants of $7.3 billion. County and city governments received nearly half of these funds. Half the national grants and more than half the State grants were for public education; most national grants in education were for construction and maintenance of schools in areas affected by national government operations, State grants were for many purposes. State governments granted more than $1 billion to local governments for public assistance programs, thus meeting two-thirds of the costs of these programs, for which local governments spent about $1.7 billion during the year. Local governments also received over a billion dollars for roads and highways from the States, much of it being subventions, *i.e.*, local shares of State gas taxes and vehicle license fees.

Transfers of funds among local governments included grants to subordinate districts (*e.g.*, counties to townships) and payments for services such as water and fire protection. The relatively minor flow of funds from local to State governments was for the most part in payment for a variety of State services and facilities provided to local units.

The quasi-business operations of local governments, such as government-owned housing, public utilities, toll roads and bridges, fee-charging government hospitals and social service agencies, government-owned liquor stores, and similar operations, had an income of some $6 billion in 1957. Discounting the cost of streets and highways, such revenue-producing operations just about paid for themselves, taken as a group. There were considerable differences within the group, however. Most government hospitals do not approach financial self-sufficiency, nor are they intended to. Liquor stores and the government-owned utilities, on the other hand, are usually operated fairly close to the break-even point. The few liquor stores owned and operated by local governments turned profits of about $21 million into public treasuries in 1957. Utilities— water supply, electric power, transit systems, and gas systems—all operated in the red, however. Their total income was $2.9 billion, their expenses $3.4 billion; in effect, such operations were subsidized $500 million from general tax funds. Some apparent "losses" of these utilities may not be operating losses, though, but capital investments, which are to be repaid from future revenues.

Local governments may also obtain money by issuing bonds, usually in order to raise capital for schools, utilities, highways, and housing developments. Local governments issued $5.3 billion in bonds in 1957, to provide funds for most of their $7.5 billion capital outlay in that year. Total outstanding debt at the end of the year was $38.5 billion; they retired about $2.1 billion of debt in the course of the year. A third of the outstanding debt was for schools and nearly a quarter was for utilities. Another 9 per cent was for sanitation systems, 9 per cent for highways, and 8 per cent for housing and redevelopment. Between 1922 and 1946, local government debts increased from $9 billion to $13.5 billion; between 1946 and 1957 they almost tripled. Among the reasons for the large increase after 1946 were the resumption of postponed capital investment following World War II, when building materials again became available, and the increased demands for school facilities and highway systems. One trend in debt financing is the increasing use of revenue bonds, whose redemption is guaranteed by the income of the facility whose construction will be financed by the bonds; in one recent year nearly half the bond issues were revenue bonds.[6]

LOCAL GOVERNMENT WELFARE FUNCTIONS

EVERY LOCAL GOVERNMENT performs at least one service or function, and usually a large number of them, for the persons under its jurisdiction. Table 3 serves as a guide to the multifarious local government activities: it lists them in detail, following the *Chatters-Hoover Inventory of Governmental Activities in the United States* listing; states the type or types of local government performing them; and gives 1957 local government expenditures for each general type of activity, where available. In this table, township functions are included under the "County" heading, school district functions under the "Special District" heading. Table 4 complements Table 3 by summarizing local government expenditures in 1957, ordering them by major function and by type of local government. The following sections discuss the nature of the various local government welfare functions under these headings: Protective Services, including fire and police protection; Public Health and Welfare, including regulation of businesses, social services, and public hospitals and similar institutions; Recreation; and Public Facilities and Enterprises, including street and highway construction and maintenance, waste disposal, public housing, and public service enterprises.

TABLE 3

THE ACTIVITIES AND EXPENDITURES OF LOCAL GOVERNMENTS, 1957

ACTIVITY [1]	Unit			EXPENDITURES [1]	
	County	Munic- ipality	Spec. Dist.[2]	Amount (In Millions of Dollars)	Per Cent
I. Overhead Activities				$ 1,181	3.8%
A. Passage of Laws	X	X	X		
B. Administration of Law	X	X			
C. Registration of Voters	X	X			
D. Conduct of Elections	X	X			
E. Community Planning and Zoning	X	X			

[6] *Statistical Abstract* 1959, pp. 402–406; de Grazia, *op. cit.*, p. 886.

ACTIVITY [1]	UNIT			EXPENDITURES [1]	
	County	Munic- ipality	Spec. Dist.[2]	Amount *(In Mil- lions of Dollars)*	*Per Cent*
II. Protection					
A. Police Protection and Enforcement				$ 1,299	4.2%
1. Records and Statistics	X	X			
2. Detention of Prisoners	X	X			
3. Police Communications	X	X	X		
4. Crime Control	X	X	X		
5. Vice and Morals Control	X	X			
6. Traffic Control	X	X			
7. International Border Control	X	X			
8. Fish and Game Protection	X				
B. Fire Protection and Fighting				$ 794	2.6%
1. Alarm and Communication Systems	X	X	X		
2. Fire Prevention	X	X	X		
3. Hydrant and Water Service	X	X	X		
4. Fire Fighting Force	X	X	X		
5. Rescue and Emergency Service	X	X			
6. Preventing, Fighting Forest Fires	X				
C. Civil Defense	X	X		(n.a.)	
D. Protective Inspections				(n.a.)	
1. Building and Utilities Inspection		X			
2. Weight and Measure Inspection	X	X			
3. Smoke Inspection		X	X		
E. Regulation of Business and Industry				(n.a.)	
1. Transportation		X			
2. Transmission and Sale of Electricity and Gas		X			
3. Communications		X			
4. Private Employment Bureau		X			
F. Crop Insurance	X			(n.a.)	
G. Other Protection Activities				(n.a.)	
1. Establishment and Administration of Weights and Measures	X	X			
2. Occupational Licensing		X			
3. Coroner and Morgue Services	X	X			
III. Highway Construction and Maintenance				$ 2,877	9.3%
A. Research, Planning, Promotion	X	X	X		
B. Roads, Highways, Streets	X	X	X		
C. Bridges	X	X	X		
D. Other Highway Facilities	X	X			
E. Snow Removal	X	X			
F. Street and Highway Lighting	X	X			

TABLE 3 (*continued*)

ACTIVITY [1]	UNIT			EXPENDITURES [1]	
	County	Munic-ipality	Spec. Dist.[2]	Amount (*In Millions of Dollars*)	*Per Cent*
IV. Natural Resources Development and Conservation				$ 215	0.7%
A. Agriculture					
1. Information Services	X				
2. Plant and Animal Husbandry (Inspection, Disease Control)	X				
3. Advisory Services	X				
4. Farm Youth Activities	X				
B. Water Conservation and Use					
1. Control of Water Rights			X		
2. Drainage	X		X		
3. Irrigation Projects			X		
4. Dams, Reservoirs, Reforestation			X		
5. Levees, Protective Structures	X	X	X		
6. Lake and Stream Improvements	X				
7. River, Harbor, and Waterway Improvement [3]		X	X		
C. Forest Conservation and Use					
1. Reforestation	X	X			
2. Timber Salvage and Control	X	X			
D. Fish and Wildlife Conservation					
1. Predatory Animal Control	X				
2. Game and Fishing Law Enforcement	X				
V. Sanitation and Waste Removal				$ 1,405	4.5%
A. Research		X	X		
B. Sewers and Disposal Facilities	X	X	X		
C. Waste Collection and Disposal		X			
D. Street Sanitation		X			
E. Other					
1. Noxious Weed Control	X	X	X		
2. Comfort Stations	X	X			
VI. Health				$ 350[4]	1.1%
A. Research	X	X			
B. Collection of Vital Statistics	X	X			
C. Laboratories	X	X			
D. Regulation and Inspection					
1. Milk and Dairy Products		X			
2. Meat Products		X			
3. Other Foods		X			
4. Drugs		X			
5. Inspecting Eating and Lodging Places	X	X			
6. Sanitary Inspections		X			
E. Control of Epidemic Diseases	X	X			
F. Control of Communicable Diseases	X	X			

Activity [1]	Unit			Expenditures [1]	
	County	Munic-ipality	Spec. Dist.[2]	Amount (In Millions of Dollars)	Per Cent
G. Prevention of Other Diseases					
1. Malignant		X			
2. Malaria	X				
3. Mosquito Control	X	X	X		
H. Maternal and Child Health Service					
1. Pre-Natal Clinics [3]		X			
2. Licensing of Maternity Homes and Hospitals		X			
3. Pre-School Clinics [3]		X			
4. Inspection of Nurseries and Boarding Homes		X			
5. Medical and Dental Services	X	X	X		
6. Nursing Services	X	X	X		
7. Nutrition Programs			X		
I. Crippled Children Services					
1. Clinic Services [3]	X	X			
2. Hospital Care [3]	X	X			
3. Nursing and Therapy	X	X			
J. Nursing Services and Training	X	X			
K. Dental Clinics	X	X			
L. Health Centers and General Clinics [3]	X	X			
VII. Hospitals				$ 1,135 [4]	3.7%
A. General Hospitals	X	X	X		
B. Special Hospitals	X	X	X		
VIII. Public Assistance and Social Services				$ 1,666	5.4%
A. Services to Children					
1. Institutions for Children	X	X			
2. Aid to Dependent Children	X	X			
3. Foster Home Placement	X	X			
4. Adoption Investigation	X	X			
B. Services to Veterans	X	X			
C. Services to Other Special Groups					
1. Old Age Assistance	X	X			
2. Aid to the Blind	X	X			
D. General Services					
1. Legal Aid		X			
2. General Institutions for Adults	X	X			
3. General Assistance	X	X			
4. Medical Care [3]	X	X			
5. Vocational Rehabilitation	X	X	X		
E. Licensing Private Institutions		X			
F. Disaster Relief	X	X			
IX. Corrections				(n.a.)	
A. Probation and Parole	X	X			
B. Jails	X	X			
C. Prison Camps, Farms, and Industries	X	X			

TABLE 3 (*continued*)

ACTIVITY [1]	UNIT			EXPENDITURES [1]	
	County	Munic-ipality	Spec. Dist.[2]	Amount (*In Millions of Dollars*)	*Per Cent*
D. Juvenile Training Schools	X	X			
E. Detention Homes	X	X			
X. Housing and Urban Redevelopment				$ 458	1.5%
A. Low Rent Housing	X	X	X		
B. Slum Clearance Projects	X	X	X		
C. War Housing	X	X	X		
XI. Educational Activities [2]				$11,952	38.6%
A. Research on Educational Problems	X	X	X		
B. Compiling Statistics on Education	X	X	X		
C. Certification of Teachers	X				
D. In-Service Training for Teachers	X				
E. Pupil Personnel Services					
1. Census	X	X	X		
2. Attendance and Truancy	X	X	X		
3. Guidance Services	X	X	X		
4. Nurse Services	X	X	X		
5. Lunches	X	X	X		
F. Kindergartens and Preschools	X	X	X		
G. Elementary Schools	X	X	X		
H. Secondary Schools	X	X	X		
I. Education of Special Groups					
1. Handicapped	X	X	X		
2. Adult Education	X	X	X		
3. Specially Gifted Children	X	X	X		
4. Mentally Deficient Children	X	X	X		
J. Transportation of School Children	X	X	X		
K. Higher Education				$ 90	0.3%
1. Junior Colleges	X	X	X		
2. Teachers' Colleges	X	X			
3. Colleges and Universities		X			
XII. Library Facilities [3]				(n.a.)	
A. General Libraries	X	X	X		
B. Extension and Traveling Libraries	X				
C. Rural Libraries	X				
D. Historical Commissions		X			
XIII. Public Recreation and Cultural Facilities				$ 585	1.9%
A. Cultural and Scientific Recreation [5]		X			
B. Organized Recreation					
1. Outdoor Activities		X			
2. Indoor Activities		X			
C. Parks, Forests, Monuments	X	X	X		
D. Special Recreational Facilities [6]		X			

Activity [1]	Unit			Expenditures [1]	
	County	Munic-ipality	Spec. Dist.[2]	Amount (In Millions of Dollars)	*Per Cent*
XIV. Public Service Enterprises					
A. Transit Systems				$ 657	2.1%
1. Street Railways and Subways		X			
2. Bus Lines		X			
3. Railroads [3]		X			
B. Electric Power Systems		X	X	$ 1,100	3.5%
C. Water Systems		X	X	$ 1,601	5.2%
D. Gas Supply Systems		X		$ 143	0.5%
E. Liquor Stores	X	X		$ 104	0.3%
F. Non-Highway Transportation				$ 1,481	1.5%
1. Airports	X	X	X		
2. Ports and Harbors		X	X		
3. Ferries [3]	X	X			
4. Bus and Train Terminals		X	X		
G. Markets and Warehouses		X	X	(n.a.)	
H. Grain Elevators		X		(n.a.)	
I. Slaughterhouses		X		(n.a.)	
J. Cemeteries and Crematories		X		(n.a.)	
K. Broadcasting Stations		X		(n.a.)	
L. Telephone Systems		X		(n.a.)	
M. Rural Electrification			X	(n.a.)	
N. Toll Roads and Toll Bridges	X	X	X	(n.a.)	
Other Local Government Expenditures					
Payments to State Governments				$ 304	1.0%
Interest on General Debt				$ 743	2.4%
Insurance-Trust Expenditure				$ 440	1.4%
Other and Unallocable [7]				$ 1,432	4.6%
Total Local Government Expenditures [8]				$31,014,000,000	100%

Note: Detail does not necessarily add because of rounding.
Sources: Expenditure data are from *Statistical Abstract* 1959, p. 402, with some estimates on the basis of 1956 data from *Statistical Abstract* 1958, p. 408. The listing of activities and governmental units performing them are from the *Chatters-Hoover Inventory of Governmental Activities in the United States*, The Hoover Commission on Intergovernmental Affairs, Washington, D.C.: USGPO, 1955. The listing is slightly abridged.

[1] All activities that are sub-categories of given headings are included in the expenditure figure for that heading. Expenditure details are not available (n.a.) for other headings and activities. (See footnote 7.)
[2] The special district heading includes school districts.
[3] Expenditures for these activities may include some funds listed under other headings.
[4] These expenditure figures are estimates.
[5] Includes art galleries, museums, zoos, orchestras, musical performances, and so forth.
[6] Includes auditoriums, stadiums, campsites, trailer camps, yacht harbors, and others.
[7] Includes expenditures for activities on which expenditure data is listed in previous parts of the table as not available (n.a.); detailed breakdowns are not available.
[8] This is a per capita expenditure of $182, based on continental United States population estimates of 170,293,000 in 1957.

TABLE 4

Local Government Expenditures for Major Functions, by Type of Government, 1957

Government	Protective Services	Public Health and Welfare	Education and Recreation	Public Facilities and Enterprises	Other [1]	Totals [1]
	Amount and Per Cent	Amount and Per Cent	Amount and Per Cent	Amount and Per Cent	Amount and Per Cent	Amount and Per Cent
	(Amounts in Millions of Dollars)					
County	$ 214	$1,856	$ 736	$1,361 [2]	$1,333	$ 5,500
	3.9%	33.7%	13.4%	24.7%	24.2%	17.9%
Municipalities	$1,736	$1,147	$1,816	$5,789	$1,997	$12,485
	13.9%	9.2%	14.5%	46.3%	16.0%	40.7%
Townships	$ 130	$ 83	$ 391	$ 454	$ 205	$ 1,263
	10.3%	6.6%	31.0%	36.0%	16.2%	4.1%
School Districts [3]			$9,638		$ 267	$ 9,905
			97.4%		2.6%	32.3%
Special Districts	$ 13	$ 64 [4]	$ 45 [5]	$1,224	$ 212	$ 1,558
	0.9%	4.1%	2.9%	78.5%	13.6%	5.1%
Total						$30,710
						100%

Note: Detail does not necessarily add because of rounding.
Source: *Statistical Abstract 1959*, p. 402.

[1] Excludes payments to State governments.
[2] Most of this, $1,145 million, was for roads and highways.
[3] School district accounting procedure for summary purposes is to list all expenditures as "education," except debt interest and payments into retirement funds.
[4] Primarily for the construction and operation of hospitals.
[5] For parks and recreation only.

Protective Services

THE PROTECTIVE SERVICES comprise the police and fire departments, which shelter persons and property from physical harm and destruction. They are so fundamentally a part of the concept of local government that demand for them has been and sometimes still is an initiating force in the organization of new governmental units. For example, some special districts have been organized for the purpose of providing areas—usually rural areas—with a fire department. The sheriff, police officer, or constable is almost inevitably one of the officials of every organized county, municipal, or township government.

The sheriff, his deputies, and the constable are primarily rural law-enforcement officers; more and more of them, though still by no means a majority, have had some previous police training. Municipal police forces as a rule are quite elaborate and their officers well-trained. Their functions include patrol, the investigation of crime, traffic regulation, and crime prevention. In 1959 the nearly 500 cities in the United States having over 25,000 inhabitants had a total of about 155,000 police personnel. The larger the municipality the more elaborate is the police organization and the more specialized police functions become. The police chief is almost always a career official, and is appointed by his superior, the police commissioner, or, in some smaller cities, the police board or commission. Career policemen are ordinarily recruited and appointed through a career civil service system.

Related to police services are the correctional institutions, found on all levels of government. Jails are found in virtually every municipality and in most counties; they usually house those convicted of minor offenses and those awaiting trial or transfer to State or federal prisons. Prison camps and farms, and juvenile training schools, or reformatories, also are operated by some counties and municipalities.

Fire losses in the United States have been high; in the 1950's there were between 800,000 and 900,000 fires per year in American communities of 2,500 or more, and in 1958 fire losses exceeded $1 billion. Such statistics clearly indicate the reasons for concern with fire departments; they maintain alarm systems and men and equipment to deal with fires, and also engage in extensive and less well-known preventive activities. In municipalities they usually enforce municipal fire codes, granting licenses and permits, and inspecting structures and equipment for hazardous conditions. They also investigate the causes of fires and cases of arson, and supplement prevention programs with popular education in the causes of fires and means of preventing them.

Organization for fire protection, particularly in rural areas, may take several forms. Many cities provide fire protection for adjacent rural areas, either without cost or on some sort of fee basis. Some rural areas combine with small municipalities to form special districts providing blanket fire protective services, while some counties provide fire-fighting services for municipalities within the county.

Public Health and Welfare

PUBLIC HEALTH and welfare services are of several types. They include local government programs designed to benefit persons in need, of course; such programs are often local extensions of State and federal programs. They also include more general activities such as regulating and inspecting businesses whose operations may affect the health and well-being of the general public.

BUSINESS INSPECTION AND REGULATION: Most regulation and inspection is performed by municipal governments, rather than by counties or special districts. This involves inspections of buildings, plumbing, boilers, elevators, and weights; regulation of transportation, communications, and private utilities; the regulation and inspection of dairies, creameries, slaughterhouses and packing houses, canneries, drug laboratories, bakeries, nurseries, boarding homes for children, and homes for the aged; and the zoning of land. Local governments also license members of certain occupations and many hundreds of types of businesses. Still other types of inspection are mentioned in the following section.

PUBLIC HEALTH: Many municipalities, and some counties, engage in what might be termed overhead health activities: research, the collection of health statistics, and the maintenance of laboratories. For the protection of health, most municipalities also regulate and inspect those businesses engaged in the preparation and packaging of foods and drugs, and inspect restaurants and other public eating places.

The American Public Health Association has stated that a local health department should fulfill six fundamental functions: (1) the collection of vital statistics; (2) the control of communicable diseases; (3) supervision of sanitary conditions in food processing and public eating places, and in places of employment; (4) health laboratory services; (5) supervision of hygiene in maternity, infancy, and childhood; (6) health education of the general public.[7] The extent to which any of these functions, or a seventh function, public nursing, are carried out depends on the size and effectiveness of a given local government. As noted, local government is a patchwork of overlapping boundaries, which complicates the fulfillment of any functions, particularly those held to be universally desirable. The municipality usually controls public health work in the United States; rural health work has often been far below municipal standards. It has been strongly recommended by the American Public Health Association that a local health unit contain 50,000 persons, and the Association has consequently suggested the establishment of multi-county units and, in some areas, joint city-county health units. Actually, the majority of counties now have health units but there is considerable question as to the effectiveness of such units in counties with small populations, simply because they cannot afford adequate staffing. In the mid-1950's about 64 per cent of the population were served by public health departments covering a single city or county, 9 per cent were served by multi-county or city-county departments, 6 per cent by district offices of State health departments, and

[7] Alderfer, op. cit., pp. 573–74.

314

the remaining 21 per cent lived in areas where no full-time public health services were maintained.[8]

The maintenance of sanitary conditions by local health departments involves not only the supervision of the production and distribution of foods, milk products in particular, but also the safeguarding of public and non-public water supplies; medical examinations and educational programs for food handlers; checks on the disposal of human and industrial waste; and, in a number of large cities, control of air pollution. In the city of Pittsburgh, for example, a successful campaign for smoke prevention was sponsored by city health officials in conjunction with local businesses.

The control of disease has been fundamental to health programs; public health departments require that physicians report cases of diseases such as typhoid fever, measles, diphtheria, scarlet fever, and a number of others, and frequently undertake investigations to detect the source of infection and its spread. The public health officers do not treat victims of communicable diseases. "It is the duty of the public health officer to diagnose the case and provide whatever medical consultation is necessary, to make home nursing instruction available, and to maintain such records and analyses of the occurrence of these diseases as will protect the health of the general public." [9]

Disease control, the protection of the health of infants and children, and public health education all depend to a considerable extent on the public nurse. The public health nurse, of whom there were some 27,000 in 1955, is the person who most frequently comes in contact with families. Her concerns include the discovery of disease; securing treatment for it; and perhaps most important, teaching health practices to the families with which she comes in contact. She may also work with school health programs.

In 1955 there was, on the average, about one nurse for each 6,000 persons throughout the nation, with considerable differences between regions and between rural and urban areas. There are two general plans. There may be a number of nurses in an area, each specializing in a single field such as maternity care, tuberculosis control, or school hygiene; in such plans, efficient and specialized care is assured. The other plan is to assign a single nurse to a specific area or number of families, fulfilling all types of nursing in this jurisdiction. This is a more personalized system, since families thus come in contact with only one nurse.

The families whom the public nurse helps are for the most part

[8] Leonard A. Scheele, "Public Health," in Russell H. Kurtz, ed., *Social Work Year Book 1957*, New York: National Association of Social Workers. 1957, p. 453.
[9] Fisher and Bishop, *op. cit.*, p. 414.

those that do not know when to seek medical care or do not have the financial resources to do so. It would be clearly impossible for a single nurse to provide even minimal attention to the health of all 6,000 persons in her jurisdiction, and it is not necessary for her to do so. Most families are able to care for their health needs through their own resources, leaving the public nurse to concentrate on those not able to do so. If she works in the school system she may come in contact with all local economic groups, through conducting health education programs; in terms of actual service and in referring children to other health agencies for treatment, though, she is dealing primarily with children from lower-income families.

PUBLIC HOSPITALS AND CLINICS: General and special hospitals, general clinics, dental clinics, pre-natal and pre-school clinics are among the facilities provided by local governments; their expenditures overshadow those of all other local government health programs. In cities in 1957 expenditures on city hospitals were $449 million, of which more than 90 per cent was for current operation; other public health services involved expenditures of only $225 million.[10] In 1958 all local governments in the United States made capital outlays of $205 million for new hospitals and their equipment.

The purpose of local government hospitals and clinics is to supplement rather than supplant non-governmental hospitals and clinics. In 1958 the 1,267 local government hospitals of all types had 197,000 beds, compared with about 500,000 beds in all non-government hospitals. Local governments furnish hospital care and medical services primarily to members of lower-income groups who otherwise could not afford treatment; some municipalities and counties, rather than erect their own hospitals, contract with non-public hospitals to provide such care. Some local governments also provide special hospitals, for the mentally ill, tuberculosis patients, and others. According to one study, the general governmental hospital offers four types of community health service:

(1) It is a general health agency, both for those who can pay and for those who cannot;

(2) it is an institution for the training of nurses and internes, some of whom will go into public health work later;

(3) it is an enterprise in social service, with its clinics for diagnosis, treatment, and rehabilitation; and

(4) it is an institution for research and medical education.[11]

[10] Compendium of City Government Finances in 1957. U.S. Bureau of the Census. Washington, D.C.: USGPO, 1958, p. 9.
[11] Fisher and Bishop, op. cit., p. 419.

Hospitals and clinics may be operated by a municipal health department, a welfare department, or a separate board of control; the same is true of county hospitals. Not infrequently special districts are established to administer public health services and hospitals; there were 371 such districts in 1952.

New York City provides extensive hospital and clinic services, for example. In 1954 the city had seventy-five child health stations, which treated 142,000 children. Medical examinations or treatment were given to over 250,000 children, at twenty-four district health centers and 1,100 public and parochial school clinics. It administered chest X-rays to 314,000 persons and examined 4,400 persons for cancer. The city operated thirty-three hospitals of various types, which had 20,000 beds and a daily average of over 18,000 patients.[12]

PUBLIC SOCIAL SERVICES: The public social services of local governments are traditionally known as "public welfare" and are organized in a welfare department. Local social services, including the administration of some State and national programs, are conducted by counties, municipalities, towns, and townships. Functions are likely to include:

Administration of public assistance
Administration of children's services
Administration of medical care assistance
Administration of institutions for children, the aged, and the ill
Licensing of facilities for the care of children, the aged, and the chronically ill
Referrals to health agencies
Probation services to the courts
Services to persons discharged from mental hospitals and correctional institutions
Services to the handicapped
Participation in cooperative programs with non-governmental agencies (*e.g.*, the disaster program of the Red Cross)
Research on the welfare conditions of the community and evaluation of current programs.[13]

This is only a partial listing, and the content and administration of programs varies greatly among local governments and from State to State.

Many of these programs have been initiated because of concern with family problems and thus directly affect families and their members. The hundreds of millions of dollars spent for public assistance,

[12] Alderfer, *op. cit.*, pp. 578–79.
[13] Wayne Vasey. *Government and Social Welfare*. New York: Henry Holt, 1958, p. 446. Copyright 1958 by Holt, Rinehart and Winston, Inc.

children's care, social casework services, and assistance for the aged have considerable impact on family economics, intra-family relations, and relations between the family and its social environment. In 1958 local governments spent $1.87 billion for these purposes. Payments to families whose wage earners are unemployed help to maintain these families in the face of forces that might otherwise disintegrate them. Most direct financial payments to distressed families are mixed blessings as far as the family is concerned, however: they may detract from the wage earner's role as head of the family; they may decrease family self-reliance; and they may decrease the family's prestige in the eyes of its neighbors. On the other hand these conditions may have already been in existence before the family began to receive aid. Those who practice public welfare are well aware of these problems; hence the growing emphasis on services such as casework, health education, and rehabilitation. For example, in 1959 government welfare agencies (State and local) provided casework services to over 370,000 children in the United States and its territories, about 40 per cent of whom were in homes of parents or relatives, and another 40 per cent of whom were in foster homes. (The others were in institutions.)

Preventive and rehabilitative approaches to distressed families and their members are relatively new, and government agencies have been somewhat slower in implementing them than have non-governmental agencies. Local government agencies have faced something of an impasse on this point. On the one hand simple financial aid is seldom a solution in itself; on the other public authorities have traditionally been reluctant to become involved in private lives.

In general, the administration and financing of social service programs are extremely complex, and it is difficult to say whether a given program is a State program or a local government program. In New Jersey, for example:

Aid to dependent children (called home assistance) is administered by the state through local offices of the state board of child welfare; old age assistance and assistance to the permanently and totally disabled is administered by county welfare boards under the supervision of the Bureau of Assistance of the State Division of Welfare; aid to the blind is administered through county welfare boards under the supervision of the Bureau of Assistance of the Division of Welfare. Child welfare services are the responsibility of the State Board of Child Welfare, which, in addition to aid to dependent children, carries state responsibility for foster home placement and supervision, care and custody, guardianship, special consultation services, and such other matters respecting the care of children as interstate placement of children.

All these . . . are a combination of state-administered and state-supervised but locally-administered services, and are further divided among different types of local units of government.[14]

The funds involved in such programs in New Jersey and other States may include national, State, and local moneys. They may be granted to individuals and families, or used for casework and other services, in keeping with nationally established requirements to which both State and local governments may have added. There are many combinations of sources of funds and auspices. The organization of the county or municipal welfare department may be quite complex, and a single family receiving public assistance, for example, may be in contact with a dozen social workers and other public employees of half a dozen local bureaus and agencies.

This complexity is disturbing to many of the administrators and caseworkers of public welfare programs, for it has often resulted in confusion as to what the actual mission of government social services is, and, of course, it may also be inefficient. Government social work is based on the premise that public assistance should never be a "way of life" for anyone. However, the actual process of providing financial assistance may be so complicated that rehabilitation services are disregarded. Joseph E. Baldwin, director of the Milwaukee County Department of Public Welfare, has commented extensively on this condition:

Any time-motion expert could have a field day in any public welfare department that he might happen to pick throughout the country. First, he would discover the lack of any consistent objective permeating the organization. Then he would discover what he would label "excessive accountability." He would find more than half of the total personnel of the department busily engaged in writing down what had been done. . . .

There appear to be many rationalizations for this excessive accountability. Among them is the acceptance of the idea that this sort of activity is necessary when three levels of government have a part to play. The local administrator must account to the state, the state administrator to the federal government, the federal administrator to Congress, and Congress, presumably, to the people—the same people who were, by the way, in the locality to begin with. This process can get quite complicated. . . . In addition to the routine processes of accounting for actions taken, there are field examinations, studies or audits at the next lower level, which in turn will require detailed re-explanation of whatever actions were taken. . . .

Determining the amount of assistance to be given to an indi-

[14] *Ibid.*, pp. 447–48.

vidual can lead to such a plethora of minutiae that it becomes absurd. For example, a state may get all wrapped up in scientific budgeting to the extent that it recommends a table for utility allowances based on the number of electrical outlets—each one adding a penny or two to the monthly grant. The state can then carefully check each grant to determine whether the caseworker's eye had wandered into the wrong column and added or withheld a few cents. An exception is taken; the caseworker must explain her astigmatism to the supervisor, the supervisor to the director, the director to the state. The state may then determine that the matter was inexcusable and withhold an appropriate amount of funds from the next county allotment; the bookkeepers are then set to work making the necessary adjustments.[15]

Conditions such as this are not typical of all local social services, of course, and efforts are made to reduce them as far as possible. The fact that they exist at all, however, is of some concern to those responsible for local welfare assistance programs.

Local governments are also involved to an important extent with non-governmental welfare organizations and associations. This is particularly true of municipal government welfare offices and agencies. They often participate in community welfare council planning as members of the council, and may offer advisory and other services. They may also grant funds to non-government agencies and in general work in close cooperation with them. Although in some cases this association is expected by one or both groups to result eventually in local government performance of the functions of the non-governmental agency, most typically the purpose is to provide the most comprehensive and integrated service for the community. For example, government welfare offices may be prevented by law or insufficient funds from dealing with certain types of welfare cases, but they are not prevented from encouraging non-governmental agencies to deal with them or from referring such cases to non-governmental agencies.

Recreation

SINCE THE END of the nineteenth century, as leisure time has increased and urban concentrations have expanded, municipal governments in particular have taken an increased interest in public recreation. Vacant lands within the cities have been purchased, or donated to city governments by local philanthropists, and converted into several types of recreation areas. These include neighborhood play lots and playgrounds

[15] Joseph E. Baldwin, "Applying Management Principles to Public Welfare Administration." *Social Service Review*, XXXI (March, 1957), p. 64. Copyright 1957 by the University of Chicago.

for younger children; larger play fields for young people and adults; and large landscaped parks. Reservations, which are large areas usually outside the city limits, also have been acquired, to provide for public picnicking, hiking, and camping. Community centers to provide indoor recreation for all age groups have been established by a number of cities, and other cities sponsor community recreation programs that use schools and other public buildings.

Although public recreation is ordinarily considered a service for the general public, it may sometimes be intended to help special groups of persons who are in need. For example, community centers in lower-income areas of many large cities often have social workers on their staffs and place particular emphasis on programs for prospective or actual juvenile delinquents and for the aged, as well as for other persons. Such community centers may be under the auspices of a separate recreation department or of a public welfare department.

Most municipalities and the other local governments that provide and maintain recreational facilities also have staffs of recreation personnel. Informal, self-initiated activity is encouraged, and this is supplemented by planned games, training in various sports and skills, and special events that may run a gamut from tournaments to Easter-egg hunts. Some, though by no means all, of these recreation programs are financed by fees, which are charged at many public golf courses, swimming facilities, and camping grounds. County recreation facilities, of which there are some, include local parks; regional parks or reservations that may cover large areas; and public ocean beaches, maintained by a number of counties along the seacoasts. There are also special districts established for recreational purposes, one such being the Chicago Park District; generally they are established to maintain and operate all public recreation facilities in a given area, such as a city or county.

Public recreation also takes somewhat more intellectual and cultural forms. Cities may wholly or partially maintain public art galleries, museums, botanical gardens, arboreta, planetaria, aquaria, zoos, community bands, and even symphony orchestras and theater groups. Some of these have been donated to cities by private individuals; others have been established out of civic pride or to attract tourists. In 1955, local governments owned 110 museums, all but twelve of which were owned by municipalities; slightly more than half their financial support came from government sources, the rest from endowments, gifts, and fees.

Among other special recreational facilities provided by municipal governments are auditoriums, stadiums, auto and trailer camps, campsites, and yacht harbors. Here again the motives are both recreational interest and civic boosting. Stadiums and auditoriums attract touring plays, orchestras and ballet companies, athletic contests, fairs, and conventions, any of which may be a boon to city business interests, as well as providing cultural or at least entertainment value. The baseball parks of major league and triple-A league cities are sometimes subsidized, if not actually built, by the city government. Camps of various kinds attract tourists, and yacht harbors in coastal cities and cities on inland waterways may provide for both business and pleasure in a number of ways.

Intermediate between recreation and education are the public libraries, about 7,500 of which are maintained by local governments of all types. Public libraries, as public museums and galleries, have attracted financial support from non-public sources, and many public libraries owe their existence to initial grants made by philanthropists. Municipalities, counties, townships, and special districts have all established libraries; rural areas are often served by traveling libraries, or bookmobiles.

Public Facilities and Enterprises

PUBLIC FACILITIES and enterprises include highway construction and maintenance, waste removal, public housing, and the numerous public service enterprises of local governments. Although they are a somewhat diverse group, they all involve large-scale construction activities (which are almost always let to private firms on contract), heavy capital investment, and continuing operating costs of some magnitude. Public hospitals, which might be included here, are treated elsewhere because of their close functional connection with public health.

ROADS AND HIGHWAYS: Nearly 80 per cent of the 3.45 million miles of streets and highways in the United States in 1957 were under the control of counties, municipalities, townships, and special districts. In 1960 expenditures for the construction and maintenance of these streets and highways by local governments totaled nearly $3.5 billion, more than 10 per cent of their total expenditures. Thirty-nine per cent was for new construction, and slightly less for maintenance. About a third of these funds are aid from State governments, which takes two forms: sharing of highway-user revenues, which are primarily vehicle and gasoline taxes; and direct grants, which may come from the same taxes, from the issue of bonds and notes, and from the national government.

Rural roads make up most of the road mileage under local control, some 2.3 million miles of them (1958); responsibility for them falls on the counties and townships. About half of them have been unpaved; this practice has reduced capital outlay but requires continuing maintenance on the part of the county highway department, which in many counties thus becomes the largest single operating unit.

Although municipalities had less than 400,000 miles of roads and streets in 1958, city streets are relatively much more expensive to construct and maintain. It is a mistake to conceive of city streets as simply a means for moving traffic from one point to another. They conceal a maze of tubing, piping, wiring, and tunnels that are as important to the life of the city as the streets themselves; their sub-surface is almost the only place where this network can be conveniently located, and consequently the street must serve as a means of access to a subterranean world. This has led some disgruntled citizens to define streets as "things to be dug up." Most of all, however, the streets are for people. People must live and work on them, walk and shop along them, primary functions that are often lost sight of by planners viewing rising vehicle registration figures. Some new, and some old, plans for metropolitan development have taken the pedestrian purposes and the aesthetics of city streets into serious consideration; in 1959 certain streets in downtown Toledo and Kalamazoo were transformed into malls that were closed to vehicular traffic. For some cities, for example Fort Worth, plans been made that call for closing all the central business area to vehicular traffic and converting streets into malls and plazas. Other cities have made of some of their streets beautiful parkways and walkways, but some have not attracted as much pedestrian traffic as had been intended and expected.[16]

In fact the streets and roads of both counties and cities are so important that their planning, construction, maintenance, and improvement form the largest public works program of local governments. Tens of thousands of miles of local roads are built or rebuilt each year; bridges, tunnels, overpasses and underpasses, and walkways annually become more elaborate; and there is continuous pressure on local governments to spend more time and energy on their planning and operation.[17]

WASTE REMOVAL: The removal of rubbish, garbage, and sewage is a necessary function of local government, most typically of municipal government. Rubbish and garbage include a miscellany of wastes ranging from abandoned automobiles to vegetable matter. Though a few communities and many rural areas still follow the medieval practice of allowing individuals to dispose of this material as they will, almost

[16] For example, see Jane Jacob, "Downtown is for People," in *The Exploding Metropolis*. Garden City, New York: Doubleday, 1958, pp. 157–84.
[17] Alderfer, *op. cit.*, pp. 548–50; *Statistical Abstract* 1959, pp. 402, 547–52.

all municipalities and a number of counties have refuse collection and disposal services. Collections in about two-thirds of the cities are made by city employees, in most others by contract between the city government and a local businessman. In still other municipalities (about a hundred in the mid-1950's), it is a service provided by private business on contract with individual householders. The results are disposed of in a number of ways; methods such as dumping on open land and barging into the sea are still used, though undesirable in terms of health and aesthetics; incineration and burial by the sanitary-fill method also are used. In a few places new methods such as fermentation or mechanical processes are used to convert organic and even inorganic materials into fertilizers. Such processing, despite its expense, is becoming more and more common.

Most urban areas are also served by extensive sewerage systems to handle wastes that average between 100 and 200 gallons per person per day. Such systems are maintained by either municipalities or special districts; in outlying and rural areas sewage from homes is usually disposed of in privately constructed cesspools or septic tanks, though a few counties maintain sewage systems. The volume of urban waste, as much as half of it industrial, presents a serious disposal problem. Dumping it in waterways, which is still often done, has unpleasant effects on water supplies, water life, and the surrounding atmosphere. Because of widespread pollution, three types of treatment processes have come into use: tank treatment, which removes the approximately one per cent of solid material suspended in sewage; the oxidation of organic sewage materials by various organisms; and sterilization or disinfection by chemicals. The organization and equipment of such systems may be very complex; the Chicago Sanitary District has been named one of the greatest engineering achievements in the world. Charges for sewerage systems and treatment are passed on to urban residents in the form of special assessments or taxes, and periodic charges; industrial plants are usually charged extra fees. The total cost of sewerage and treatment, including capital outlays, was about $6 per urban resident in 1956; other sanitation services, including refuse collection and disposal, cost $5 per capita.[18]

PUBLIC SERVICE ENTERPRISES: Counties, municipalities, townships, and special districts own and operate many thousands of utilities and businesses, including public transportation systems; water supply and distribution systems; electricity and gas systems; airports; terminals; harbor facilities; ferries; toll roads and bridges; markets and warehouses;

[18] Alderfer, op. cit., pp. 556–61; Fisher and Bishop, op. cit., pp. 545–53; Compendium of City Government Finances in 1956, pp. 1, 9.

324

liquor stores; cemeteries; and communication systems. Often, sewers, public auditoriums, recreation facilities, and streets also are considered public enterprises; they are described separately above.

Capital funds for public service enterprises are usually raised by special bond issues; operating costs are met with tax monies and with fees. Sometimes these enterprises are self-supporting through their charges and may retire the initial investment and show a profit. More often, because of either their nature or their administration, their income does not meet even operating costs. It has been suggested that those who are considering government ownership of some public service should consider four matters: whether (1) the services are indispensable to the comfort or welfare of the community as a whole; (2) monopoly is necessary for efficient operation; (3) the services are subject to a high degree of regulation; (4) facilities to provide the service or utility require large capital investments.[19]

The existence of only one of these conditions is seldom regarded as enough to justify public ownership alone, though in the case of government liquor stores, for example, the desire for regulation (and revenue) has been the primary and sometimes the sole motive. Actually, the existence of any given public service enterprise can be explained not merely in terms of conditions or principles but also in terms of local pressures and interests. Importers and exporters in a port city may feel unwilling or unable to provide adequate harbor facilities, and therefore bring pressure to bear on the municipal or other government to provide them; they may be joined by innumerable other civic and business groups, ranging from construction firms that stand to gain from government contracts to clubs and citizens' associations motivated by civic pride. Transportation, gas, electricity, and water services are often governmentally constructed or are purchased from private ownership simply because of consumer dissatisfaction with the price and quality of existing services. Thus, what is a government-owned utility in one city will be a privately owned business in another, with little consistency.

The number and types of certain municipally owned enterprises in cities of various sizes are given in Table 5. Water supply and distribution systems and sewage treatment plants are most frequently government-owned, more than half the cities reporting municipal ownership. Airports, auditoriums, and incinerators also are owned and operated by a number of cities, and larger cities frequently have port facilities. In addition to the facilities listed in Table 5 there are many public service enterprises under the jurisdiction of special districts and counties. The largest special districts in the United States have been established to operate public service enterprises. (Some public enterprises

---

[19] Fisher and Bishop, *op. cit.*, pp. 556–57.

TABLE 5

OWNERSHIP AND OPERATION OF PUBLIC SERVICE ENTERPRISES
IN CITIES OF OVER 5,000 POPULATION, MID-1950's [1]
(*Numbers of Cities Having Particular Utilities and Enterprises*)

UTILITY OR ENTERPRISE	ALL CITIES OVER 5,000 [2]		POPULATION CLASS			
	Number	Per Cent	5,000–25,000	25,000–100,000	100,000–500,000	500,000+
Water Supply and Distribution	1,678	67.4%	1,304	283	75	16
Sewage Treatment	1,261	50.7	1,001	196	52	12
Airport	525	21.1	326	125	61	12
Incinerator	430	17.3	243	125	48	14
Auditorium	413	16.6	283	80	42	8
Electricity Generation and Distribution	280	11.2	227	42	9	2
Electricity Distribution Only	224	9.0	201	19	4	
Water Distribution Only	159	6.4	125	31	3	
Gas Distribution Only	85	3.4	75	8	2	
Port Facilities	66	2.7	15	20	20	10
Gas Manufacturing and Distribution	41	1.6	25	8	6	2
Bus or Trolley Bus	33	1.3	16	12	2	3
Slaughterhouse	26	1.1				
Street Railways	6	0.2	3	1	1	1
Cities Having No Such Public Service Enterprises	319	12.8	282	34	2	1
Total Number of Facilities	5,227					

Source: *1956 Municipal Yearbook.*

[1] Types of public enterprises not included in this table are liquor stores, ferries, markets and warehouses, grain elevators, cemeteries, communication systems, toll roads and toll bridges.

[2] Based on reports from all but seventy cities having over 5,000 inhabitants in 1955. All but three of the non-reporting cities were in the 5,000–25,000 population class.

operated by special districts are believed to be included in Table 5, in cases where the special district is responsible to or was established by the municipal government.)

GOVERNMENT-OWNED HOUSING AND URBAN RENEWAL: Government-owned housing and urban renewal projects are sponsored and financed in part by municipal governments. Both types of projects are directly subsidized by the national government as a rule, and sometimes subsidized by State governments as well.

Government-sponsored housing was initiated in the 1930's when civic groups came to see government projects as a solution to what they considered the lack of adequate housing in urban areas, high crime rates in urban slums, and urban employment. Some force was given to the movement by the appropriation of $800 million by Congress in the Housing Act of 1937, which also established the United States Housing Authority. Local housing authorities could obtain loans from the Authority at low interest rates and direct subsidies of comparatively small amounts. In 1949 a further Housing Act was passed, authorizing loans and capital grants of $1.5 billion, the subsidies making up the difference between what the tenants of public housing paid and the actual cost of operation.

Authorities working with public housing and urban developments often found, however, that their plans did not correspond with the interests of persons affected by "urban blight." A change of emphasis was apparent in the passage by the national government of the Housing Act of 1954 and the subsequent Housing Act of 1959; these acts reflected interest in slum clearance and urban redevelopment, more in keeping with what are now believed to be the actual problems of urban housing.

Such public housing as was constructed in the 1930's and 1940's for the most part represented the "tower and mall" school of architectural aesthetics. The New York City public housing developments, high-rise apartment buildings on relatively open areas of greensward and asphalt, are representative of these early projects. Sponsors of such projects often found, however, that many of the people who were expected to benefit from them apparently preferred the inadequate facilities, crowding, and filth of the slums to the new vertical masses of concrete with their grassy malls surrounded by chains. Most government housing has eventually been filled, of course; low rents have been overriding considerations. Contrary to expectations, however, crime and filth accompanied some tenants, and many public housing developments that have been in use for a few years have come to resemble what some municipal authorities have called vertical slums. What has happened is that public housing of this type not only has not halted but often has contributed to social and family disorganization. Families may be subjected to a wealth of petty restrictions. Tenants' attempts to develop organizations in some cases have been bluntly discouraged. In New York public housing, should any member of the family become involved with the police (usually young people are involved), the family may be automatically evicted. The maximum income permitted public housing tenants has been so low that when a family exceeds the limit it usually must move back to the remaining slums.[20]

Still other criticisms have been made against high-rise public housing. It is claimed to be inordinately expensive to construct and maintain. It has been said that a public housing project is a "cold, impersonal, cheerless place to live in." [21] William H. Whyte, Jr., has summed up some of the criticisms made by local housing authorities:

> Most public-housing experts now agree that the "self-contained" neighborhood that turns its back on the surrounding streets, far from improving the neighborhood around it, depresses the whole area; second, the institutional design, with its lack of stores and small amenities, is a design that does not encourage normal neighborhood life; third, the high-rise buildings are not suited to family needs. Families don't like to live high up; as study after study has demonstrated, what they want is a yard or a porch or a terrace *of their own.*[22]

Certainly, municipal authorities have not given up the attempt to improve local housing. The large and growing blighted, decayed areas in cities are ever more galling impetuses to governmental and non-governmental action. Government-stimulated voluntary action has achieved notable sucesses in some cities, and notable failures in others—the latter due both to disinterest on the part of residents and to refusal of landlords and tenants to cooperate. An earlier chapter describes the success of an entirely non-governmental effort in Chicago's Back of the Yards (Chapter 3). "Spontaneous rehabilitation," as it is called, is generally not believed to provide the entire answer however. Many advocates of government-owned housing now propose "row houses" and low-level or "low-rise" apartments, with few or no unusual regulations on their inhabitants. Some few projects of these types have been built and have proved quite successful. Another approach that is believed to hold considerable promise is "invisible public housing," which has been put into practice in Philadelphia and other cities. Government funds are used to rehabilitate old dwellings, and build new ones, in existing neighborhoods. In connection with government-owned housing and urban redevelopment mention must also be made of ACTION, the American Council to Improve Our Neighborhoods, which is a non-governmental organization working with both governmental and non-governmental groups to remedy urban blight.

[20] Some of these aspects of public housing are documented in Harrison Salisbury's study of juvenile delinquents in New York City, *The Shook-up Generation*, N.Y.: Harper & Brothers, 1958.
[21] Daniel Seligman, "The Enduring Slums," in *The Exploding Metropolis*, p. 125.
[22] "Are Cities Un-American?" in *The Exploding Metropolis*, p. 45.

THE EMPLOYEES OF LOCAL GOVERNMENTS AND THEIR WELFARE

THE EMPLOYEES of local governments, as the employees of business and the State and national governments, are provided certain benefits as a condition of their employment. The most important, other than wages and salaries, is retirement coverage.

In 1958 local governments employed 4.4 million full- and part-time employees; all civilian government employees in the United States totaled 8.1 million. The personal services of their 4.4 million employees cost local governments $17.1 billion, about half their total expenditures. Employment and payroll data, by type of local government, are given in Table 6. On the average, full-time county employees received the

TABLE 6

LOCAL GOVERNMENT EMPLOYMENT AND PAYROLLS, 1958

TYPE OF GOVERNMENT	EMPLOYEES		TOTAL PAYROLL (*In Millions of Dollars*)	AVERAGE ANNUAL SALARY PER FULL-TIME EMPLOYEE [1]
	Number [1]	*Per Cent*		
Counties	679,000	15%	$2,330	$3,720
Municipalities	1,594,000	36	6,110	4,460
School Districts	1,750,000	39	7,360	4,690
Townships and Special Districts	549,000	12	1,250	4,320
Totals	4,423,000 [1,2]		$17,050	

Source: *Statistical Abstract* 1959, pp. 420, 422. Average annual salary figures computed.

[1] Includes 3,694,000 full-time employees and 729,000 part-time employees. There were 294,000 part-time employees in townships and special districts; 234,000 in school districts; 260,000 in municipalities; and 71,000 in counties. The average annual salary figures are based on full-time equivalent employment.
[2] Figures and percentages do not add because numbers for particular types of local governments are based on a sample survey and are subject to sampling variation; the total is known to be accurate.

lowest annual salaries: $3,720. School district employees received the highest: $4,690. The numbers of local government employees by function are given in Table 7; half of all such employees worked for the school systems of various types of local government, about 10 per cent of them with public health, hospitals, and welfare assistance programs.

Local government retirement systems covered about one million local government employees in 1957. Most other local employees were covered by State-administered retirement systems. There are two types of local government retirement programs: those covering all employees of a particular local government unit and those covering only one particular group of employees of a local government, such as firemen. The second type is most common among local governments, and the employees most frequently covered are police and firemen. In 1957 the receipts of locally administered systems came from employees (30 per cent), the governments involved (55 per cent), and investments; their assets at the end of the year were almost $5 billion.

TABLE 7

LOCAL GOVERNMENT EMPLOYMENT BY FUNCTION, 1958

FUNCTION	FULL-TIME EQUIVALENT EMPLOYMENT		AVERAGE ANNUAL SALARY PER FULL-TIME EMPLOYEE [1]
	Number	Per Cent	
Education	1,933,000	50.1%	$4,800
Health and Hospitals	306,000	7.9	3,360
Welfare Programs	67,000	1.7	3,770
Highways	260,000	6.7	3,920
Police Protection	257,000	6.7	4,640
Fire Protection	138,000	3.6	4,940
Sanitation	125,000	3.2	3,920
Water Supply	95,000	2.5	3,120
Other Utilities	131,000	3.4	5,220
Natural Resources	24,000	0.6	4,150
General Control	244,000	6.3	4,240
All Other	281,000	7.3	4,160
Totals	3,859,000	100%	

Source: Same as Table 6.

[1] These figures are estimates, based on October, 1958, earnings of State and local employees, by function.

In 1957 locally administered systems, most of them municipal government systems, paid $368 million in benefits to about 240,000 persons. Most of the beneficiaries were retired employees or their surviving families; they received monthly checks that averaged about $120. Regular payments were also made to some disabled former employees and their families and lump-sum survivor benefits were paid in some instances. Data on employees covered by State-administered retirement programs are given in the next chapter.

CONCLUDING REMARKS

IT MAY BE unfortunate that so much of an introduction to the welfare functions of local governments must consist of lists of activities and the skeletal structure of governmental forms. Yet few citizens appreciate how manifold are the activities of local governments. There is also value in treating governments in the same manner as other institutions dealt with in this survey, by stating their numbers, the sources and uses of their funds, their powers and limitations, and the benefits they provide their employees. As with other large welfare institutions, matters of internal welfare—pay and perquisites—are a significant part of institutional activity. The intergovernmental relations of localities are particularly complicated; units of local government overlap one another, particularly in urban areas, with resulting confusion, inefficiency, lack of accountability, and absence of purpose and coordinated drive even on generally accepted goals.

Students of the American welfare system are inclined to ignore the past welfare achievements of local government. In fact, police systems, fire protection, streets and roads, sanitation, waste removal, utility ownership, and numerous provisions for public health inspection and business regulation are all traditional welfare functions now taken for granted and given relatively little attention where "social work" or "social welfare" is taught, planned, or discussed. There are, of course, good and sufficient reasons for limiting programs of study, provided that the existence and importance of other activities are kept in mind.

Actually, three levels of the "welfare state" are to be found in American local government. In the older tradition of the nineteenth century, the welfare state consists of those protective and regulatory activities just referred to, some of which were regarded as radical innovations when they were first adopted. In keeping with the early twentieth-century conception of the welfare society, local governments have developed numerous programs of the sort concerned with public health, hospitals and clinics, social services, and more extensive education and transportation services. The new era of welfare, finally, finds the localities increasingly concerned with new forms of coordinating nongovernmental and governmental welfare action, with urban planning and renewal, with mass transportation, with recreation, with the problems of the suburbs, and with race relations.

Chapter Thirteen

STATE GOVERNMENTS

T HE FIFTY STATE GOVERNMENTS [1] HAVE an important role in devising, administering, and financing welfare programs of all sorts. The importance of this role stems from the fact that among the powers reserved to the States by the Tenth Amendment to the United States Constitution are the so-called *police powers*—the powers to legislate regarding the public health, welfare, morals, and safety. The national government does not have these broad powers because the Constitution does not vest them in Congress; counties, municipalities, townships, and special districts have such powers only in so far as they have been conferred on them by State legislatures.

Yet the role of the State governments in devising and financing welfare programs has been diminishing relative to the roles of the national and the municipal governments. Certain interests in State governments oppose innovation, and most State governments are approaching exhaustion of their financial resources under their present constitutional and statutory limitations. Hence, welfare programs are increasingly devised by the national government, particularly since the establishment of the Department of Health, Education, and Welfare (HEW). Furthermore, welfare programs are increasingly financed by the national

[1] Unless otherwise specified, data given in this chapter exclude information on Alaska and Hawaii; most statistics available at the time of writing were compiled before statehood was granted to the two former territories, and governmentally compiled statistics on territories and other outlying areas of the Unied States have often been separate from, and not entirely comparable with, data on the continental United States.

government through its grants-in-aid to the State governments; the national Treasury can gather enormous sums by the personal income tax, and by grants it can promote what is believed to be a desirable equalization of welfare funds among high- and low-income States, and promote more equal standards of welfare services. Finally, many municipal governments have been disregarded by rural-dominated State legislatures and have brought their welfare requests directly to Congress. The result of these conditions is that, although the State governments are far from slipping into oblivion, they are more and more becoming administrative units for welfare programs devised and at least partly financed by other governments.

The historical context in which the relative importance of State governments has waxed and waned is well-known. Their predecessors, the British colonial governments, wielded great authority and, for the most part, were responsible only to the distant crown. The States were at the height of their power under the Articles of Confederation, and from the Constitutional Convention down to the Civil War collectively they still far overshadowed the national government. After the Civil War, however, the national government increasingly exercised powers once held reserved to the States, through a series of legislative enactments and Supreme Court decisions. Some landmarks in the assertion of national authority over the States in the past half century have been the passage of the national income tax in 1913, the extraordinary powers assumed by the national government during World War I, the enactment of national prohibition in 1920, the development of national economic and social controls during the depression of the 1930's, the further powers assumed by the national government during World War II, and most recently, the Supreme Court decisions expanding the role of the national government with regard to civil rights.

More quietly, local governments have come to wield power almost independently of the States to which they are legally subordinate. Urban residents have demanded special forms of government and special power to deal with particular, localized problems. To municipalities in particular, State legislatures have granted the power to treat with problems such as zoning, licensing, municipal facilities, and many others —though often reluctantly. To many cities, including most of the largest ones, State legislatures have granted extensive home-rule powers. Many local governments, though only creatures of the State in legal doctrine, thus perform broader welfare functions than the States themselves.

In general, except in higher education, highway law enforcement, protection, and corrections, the States have come to function largely as administrative districts for national government programs or as coordinating bodies for local governments. The States administer public assistance programs in keeping with national requirements and with funds provided in large part by the national government, for example. One State coordinating function is collecting taxes for local governments; in 1958 the States turned over about 30 per cent of their total revenue ($7.9 billion out of $26.2 billion) to local governments, some in the form of subsidies, some as local shares of tax proceeds.

Two fundamental conditions have contributed to making the States middlemen in governmental welfare programs: the essentially arbitrary, non-functional nature of State boundaries and the growing specialization and urbanization of American society. The first of these facts was noted in the nineteenth century, by James Bryce: "The States are not natural growths. Their boundaries are for the most part not natural boundaries due to a series of events, but purely artificial boundaries, determined by an authority which carved the national territory into strips of convenient size." He notes that aside from the original thirteen States only California has true natural boundaries, and none are naturally developed political organisms.[2] (Currently, Hawaii is an exception on both counts.) In itself this condition was not a serious hindrance on the States in a predominantly rural, agricultural society in which government was charged with a minimum of functions. But many problems now deemed to require government solutions are national rather than regional in scope. National economic depression, national concern with health, national mobilization of resources for defense, all have contributed to the rise of national government powers. If problems affect the entire nation, it has been argued in many cases, then the national government should act. There are few problems and interests confined to a single State; even rural interests such as wheat-farming, logging, and mining are generally of a regional nature, encompassing several States.

The growth of cities has also created problems for which inter-State governmental solutions have been demanded. First, many urban concentrations include parts of several States. The New York metropolitan area includes portions of three States; Greater Philadelphia includes large sections of western New Jersey; Chicago is the center of an urban concentration that spills into Wisconsin on the north and Indiana on the east; two Kansas Cities confront each other across the Kansas-Missouri border. There are many urban areas contained within single States, of course. But, secondly, there are many problems common to almost all cities. Almost all cities are plagued by slum conditions, high crime rates, and transportation problems. "Problem families" and the unemployed are heavily concentrated in cities. Where such problems are involved, at least, it is often felt that the United States

[2] James Bryce. *The American Commonwealth*, Vol. 1 (2nd ed., rev.). London and New York: Macmillan, 1891, pp. 402–403.

is a "community of cities," and that when solutions are apparently beyond the capabilities of individual cities, the responsibility lies with the national government rather than with the States.

Despite these many qualifications and limitations of the welfare role of the States, the States continue to perform numerous functions. Often enough they have not initiated these functions, but they nevertheless give to their performance their own particular forms—and often finances. Succeeding sections deal briefly with the structure and demography of the States; their finances; and, at greater length, with their specific functions. A final section discusses the employees of State governments and the social insurance programs provided for them.

THE DEMOGRAPHY AND GOVERNMENTAL STRUCTURE OF THE STATES

Demography and Welfare

THE SIZE AND POPULATION characteristics of a State in large part determine the content of its welfare programs. There are great disparities in size and population among the States. Alaska, with 586,000 square miles, is nearly five hundred times larger than Rhode Island, which has 1,200 square miles. At the same time, the population of Alaska (191,000 in 1959) is only about one eighty-sixth as great as that of New York (16,495,000 in 1959). Stated in another way, in 1959 the nine most populous States (New York, California, Pennsylvania, Illinois, Texas, Ohio, Michigan, New Jersey, and Massachusetts, in that order) contained more inhabitants than the other forty-one States. Ten western States (including Alaska) contain half the land area of the United States. Small States with large populations are predominantly concerned with providing welfare services to individuals on a large scale— education, health services, public assistance, and so forth. Large States with relatively small populations are generally concerned more with indirect welfare services, such as the protection of natural resources, yet to meet national social welfare standards they must maintain fairly elaborate programs that are thus relatively expensive per capita. States such as California and Texas, large in both population and area, maintain elaborate programs for both social welfare and indirect welfare.

The proportions of urban and rural population in a State also affect the character of its welfare services. According to the 1950 census, about 72 per cent of the population lived in urban areas.[3] In 1960 the percent-

[3] The Bureau of the Census in 1950 adopted a definition of "urban" that includes all incorporated or unincorporated places of 2,500 inhabitants or more, plus the densely settled urban fringe surrounding cities of 50,000 or more.

age was about the same: some 130 million out of 180 million Americans lived in or near America's cities. The 1950 census data has been broken down by States:

five States were 80 per cent or more urban;
thirteen States were between 60 and 79 per cent urban;
twenty-one States were between 40 and 59 per cent urban;
nine States were between 20 and 29 per cent urban.
and no States were less than 20 per cent urban.

The more populous States are not necessarily small nor entirely urbanized; in addition to California and Texas, Illinois and New York have significant rural populations, while Pennsylvania, which had the third highest urban population of any State in 1950, also had the largest rural population of *any* State. The eighteen States that were more than 60 per cent urbanized contained 43 per cent of the rural inhabitants of the United States, twenty-three million out of fifty-four million persons.

Rural people usually make different welfare demands on State governments than do urban people. The State may be expected to provide public health services for thinly populated rural areas, to provide special assistance for rural schools, to improve country roads and highways, to ensure flood control and to build irrigation systems, and sometimes to help migrant farm workers and clean up "rural slums." For urban people, particularly in medium- and large-sized cities, State governments may also be expected to provide direct State services such as employment bureaus, child placement agencies, and transportation systems, but more typically urban demands are for grants-in-aid and technical assistance, for example, for municipal health and welfare services.

The Structure of State Governments

THE STATE GOVERNMENTS resemble the national government. Each has a chief executive officer, the governor, who may have the power to appoint a number of officials, to draft and introduce legislation, and to draw up the budget; he is also responsible for the host of State administrative departments, commissions, and boards. Each State except Nebraska has a bicameral legislature, which meets annually or biennially. Each State has a court system, ranging from limited jurisdiction trial courts to appellate courts, that includes all courts in the State not part of the federal court system ("municipal courts" and "county courts" are part of the State court systems, not elements in local government). It is beyond the scope of this survey to consider the State legislative and judicial systems, but a brief sketch of State administrative bodies is relevant.

A State may have a great number of administrative bodies, approaching two hundred in some States. They may be headed by a single official; a commission or board that may perform quasi-legislative or quasi-judicial functions as well as administrative tasks; or a single administrator who shares authority with a commission or board. The last-named type of arrangement is particularly common with bodies that deal with health, education, and social welfare. Almost all States have bodies dealing with finance and administration, education, health, social welfare, public safety, highways, and labor or agriculture. Examples of these and other State administrative bodies are: Department of Administration (North Carolina); Building and Planning Commission (Arizona); Department of Economic Development (Kentucky); Department of Public Assistance (Washington); Department of Health and Welfare (Maine); Water Resources Board (Oklahoma); State Board of Mental Health (Connecticut); Veterans Affairs Commission (Idaho). Bodies with the same or similar titles may be found in many other States, of course.

All States have departments dealing with social welfare but vary greatly with respect to the nature of the agency to which a given function is assigned, the extent to which special-purpose agencies and commissions also carry out social welfare functions, the organization of the agency, and the relations of State agencies to local welfare agencies. Public assistance and child welfare programs are most consistently the responsibility of State public welfare departments, though in thirty-three States (1956) crippled children's services are assigned to State health departments. Vocational rehabilitation may be the responsibility of the department of education, the board of vocational education, an independent commission or department, or even the department of labor. Mental health services may be the province of the department of health or of welfare, or of a separate body. Unemployment insurance and employment service are usually administered by a single body, which may be a separate commission or department or a subordinate division of a department of labor. Health services, corrections, and most other State functions are administered in an equally great variety of ways, but there is a general tendency toward integration of related programs under the auspices of multi-functional departments.

Almost every State welfare department has an associated board of public welfare. In nearly half of them the boards have administrative powers; in others they have policy-making or advisory functions. A few State welfare departments also have boards for one or more of their subordinate divisions.

The most comprehensive State welfare organizations are in New Jersey and Wisconsin, in which public assistance, child welfare, mental health, and corrections are all the responsibility of a single department. The New Jersey Department of Institutions and Agencies is headed by a commissioner and the Board of Control; it has five major divisions, outlined below, which have responsibility for both institutional and non-institutional programs. The five divisions and their subordinate bodies and officers are: [4]

Division of Business Management
Bureau of Accounts
Bureau of Transportation
Bureau of Maintenance Collections
Bureau of Institutional Maintenance
Fire Marshal
Supervising Steward
Farm Supervisor

Division of Correction and Parole
Bureau of Correction
Bureau of State Use
Bureau of Parole

Division of Administration
Bureau of Social Research
Bureau of Community Institutions
Bureau of Personnel
Long Range Planning
Transfer Function
Bureau of Public Relations

Division of Mental Health and Hospitals
Bureau of Mental Deficiency
Bureau of Community Mental Health Services
Psychiatric Research
Psychiatric Education
Consultant in Psychology
Consultant in Psychiatric Social Work
Consultant in Psychiatric Nursing

Division of Welfare
Bureau of Assistance
State Commission for the Blind
State Board of Child Welfare

STATE FINANCING

To MAINTAIN THEMSELVES, to finance their welfare programs and other operations, and to provide grants for the operations of local governments, in 1958 the State governments raised $21.4 billion through taxes and business-type activities; received $4.5 billion in aid from the national

[4] Wayne Vasey. *Government and Social Welfare.* New York: Henry Holt, 1958, pp. 378–99.

government; and borrowed \$2.3 billion. A detailed listing for 1957 is given in Table 1.

TABLE 1

STATE REVENUE AND BORROWING, 1957
(*In Millions of Dollars*)

Source [1]	Amount	Per Cent	Per Capita [2]
Taxation (Total)	\$14,531 [3]	55.5%	\$ 87.31
General Sales Taxes (33)	3,373	12.9	20.28
Motor Fuel Taxes	2,828	10.8	16.99
Other Sales and Gross Receipts Taxes	2,235	8.5	13.43
Motor Vehicle and Operators' Licenses	1,368	5.2	8.22
Other Licenses (Incl. Corporation Licenses	820	3.1	4.93
Individual Income Taxes (31)	1,563	6.0	9.39
Corporation Net Income Taxes (33)	984	3.8	5.91
Property Taxes (45 States in 1958)	479	1.8	2.88
Other Taxes (Death, Gift, etc.)	881	3.4	5.29
Charges for Education, Highways, Hospitals, etc.	1,223 (est.)	4.6	7.35
Earnings on Property and Investments and Other Charges	700 (est.)	2.7	4.21
Liquor Stores Revenue (16)	1,065	4.1	6.40
Insurance Trust Revenue	3,209	12.3	19.28
Intergovernmental Revenue	3,928	15.0	23.60
Borrowing (43 States in 1956)	1,502	5.7	9.02
Totals	\$26,158	100%	\$157.17

Note: Totals do not necessarily add because of rounding.
Sources: *Compendium of State Government Finances in 1957*, U.S. Bureau of the Census, Washington, D.C.: USGPO, 1958, various pages; *Statistical Abstract 1959*, pp. 408–15.

[1] Data are for forty-eight States. Sources were used in all forty-eight States, except as noted.
[2] Based on an estimated population of 166,430,000 on July 1, 1956, excluding military personnel overseas and residents of territories, dependent areas, and the District of Columbia.
[3] State taxation in 1958 totaled \$14,905 million; increases in various types of taxes were roughly proportional, except that corporation net income taxes decreased in absolute magnitude, individual income taxes increased relatively little, and property taxes increased significantly.

Taxation and Licenses

TAXES AND LICENSES provide the largest part of State revenues; in 1959 they provided 68 per cent of the revenues raised by the States themselves (*i.e.*, excluding borrowing and grants from other levels of government). These types of taxes and licenses were used in 1959: [5]

[5] *The Book of the States 1960–61*. Chicago: Council of State Governments, 1960, pp. 216–21. (Data excludes Hawaii.)

Taxes:
   General sales or gross receipts taxes (33 States)
   Motor fuel taxes (49 States)
   Alcoholic beverages taxes (49 States)
   Tobacco products taxes (44 States)
   Insurance taxes (49 States)
   Public utilities taxes (38 States)
   Amusement taxes (28 States)
   Pari-mutuel taxes (23 States)

Licenses:
   Motor vehicles (49 States)
   Motor vehicle operators (49 States)
   Corporations (49 States)
   Public utilities (32 States)
   Alcoholic beverages (49 States)
   Amusements (36 States)
   Hunting and fishing (49 States)
   Chain stores (14 States)

However, the States must compete both with federal income and excise taxes and with the license, sales, and property taxes of local governments. The States once relied heavily on the property tax (more than half of State tax revenue in 1915), but have largely given over that source of revenue to local governments. Individual income taxes and taxes on corporations present the onerous problem of duplicate taxation. States proposing "progressive" personal income taxes must take into account that their high-income citizens might have combined State and national tax bills greater than their total income. The national government allows State income taxes to be deducated from the income subject to national tax, but not all States follow a similar procedure. States taxing corporations do so on different bases, which results in similar problems. One State may tax a corporation on the basis of its income, another its gross sales, and still another its property. Reciprocal tax agreements among the States have been proposed to reduce the inequities that arise from the double taxation on the incomes of persons who work in one State while living in another and on the income of corporations that operate in different States, but most States have been reluctant to enter such agreements.

General sales and gross receipts taxes have been the most productive sources of income for the States that have used them; in the thirty-three States levying such taxes in 1956 they provided from 4 per cent (in Pennsylvania) to 42 per cent (in Washington State) of State general revenue. Such taxes also present a problem, however. Depending on the goods taxed such taxes may be "regressive," *i.e.*, persons with low incomes may be taxed a greater part of their income than persons with higher incomes. This happens especially when food and clothing are taxed. It has been demonstrated, however, that if food is exempted from the tax base, the sales or consumption taxes a person pays are roughly the same percentage of his income, however high or low it may be; *i.e.*, the tax is said to be "proportional." [6]

Grants-in-Aid

GRANTS-IN-AID from the national government added some $3.5 billion to State treasuries in 1957 and well over $4 billion in 1958; they approached $7 billion in 1960. In 1957 nearly half the national grants were for public assistance ($1,552 million); in 1960 such grants were over $2 billion. Federal-aid highway program grants in 1957 were $942 million and became increasingly important in following years; national highway trust fund grants to the States in 1960 were $3.0 billion. Other important grants received by the States in 1960 were $315 million for employment security administration; some $230 million for public health and hospital construction; and over $300 million for aid to agriculture and the protection of agricultural resources.

The States, in turn, make even larger grants to local governments: $7.3 billion in 1957 (see Table 2). In some cases, public assistance for example, the States may merely be middlemen, allocating national grants to local government programs within their boundaries. This is by no means entirely true even of public assistance funds, however. More than half of State grants ($4.1 billion in 1957) have been for local education, and have derived almost entirely from the States' own revenue collections. The States also make sizable grants for highways and roads ($1.1 billion in 1957) and health and hospitals ($253 million in 1957), largely from their own funds. (There is also some reverse flow of funds from local to State governments, $304 million in 1957, largely in payment for special State services; this is included in the Intergovernmental Revenue figure in Table 1.)

Grants-in-aid have various purposes. Through them, for example, the national government can encourage "minimum standards" of social welfare and other services among the States. Highway aid has been designed to bring into being an integrated, inter-State transportation system. Also, in the most general sense, there are believed to be compelling fiscal reasons for grants-in-aid. It is stated that

[6] Kenyon Poole. *Public Finance and Economic Welfare*. New York: Rinehart, 1956, p. 256. This work comprehensively treats the problems of taxation on all levels of government, in terms generally understandable to the layman.

there is no basis for assuming that the states, and more especially
the localities, have at their disposal precisely the taxes necessary
to finance the spending functions that they are best able to perform. In general terms, it can be said that the administrative
ability of the localities to spend greatly surpasses their capacity
to raise revenues. On the other hand, the federal government can
tax much more effectively than it can spend. The states stand
somewhere in between those two extremes.[7]

This is partly a matter of convention and efficiency: convention, in that
there are constitutional and statutory limitations on State and local
taxation; efficiency, in that a national tax system avoids many of the
problems inherent in fifty disparate State tax systems, which have not
yet found solutions to the taxation of inter-State corporations, for example.

Beyond this, by the grant-in-aid the national government can divert
especially large amounts of funds to States with a low level of income
or spending, just as the States can use grants to help equalize welfare
spending among their various local governments. The New Jersey Taxpayers Association has estimated that fifteen States paid more for national aid than they received in subsidies in 1957 (that is, citizens
and corporations of these States paid a relatively larger proportion of
taxes than they received in grants from the national government).
New Jersey headed the list, paying $2.73 for each dollar of national
subsidy; among the others were almost all the highly urban and industrial States, including Connecticut, New York, Illinois, Pennsylvania,
Ohio, Massachusetts, Michigan, and California. New Mexico and
Mississippi taxpayers, however, paid only $.26 for each national aid
dollar.[8] These differences reflect national government concern with low-
income States and their welfare programs; other aspects of this type of
equalization through grants-in-aid are discussed in the following chapter.

On the other hand, many State officials and State and local tax
administrators have argued that each level of government should support its activities from its own revenues, at least to a greater extent than
is presently the case. It is felt that national grants should be reduced
so that States and cities have a tax base large enough to levy sufficient
taxes of their own; the larger the national grants the more funds are taken
from State and locality, and consequently State and local tax bases
are narrowed. "The government responsible for the taxes ought to control the expenditures which it makes possible." [9] Such arguments usually
implicitly involve the assumption that redistribution of funds among

[7] Ibid., p. 355.
[8] "Jersey Pays High for Federal 'Aid,'" Princeton Herald, Nov. 7, 1958.
[9] Poole, op. cit., p. 356.

the States, and among local governments, is undesirable, at least to the extent that it presently takes place.

Expenditures

IN 1957 the States expended $24.9 billion, including grants to local governments (see Table 2), just less than one-fifth of all governmental ex-

TABLE 2

STATE EXPENDITURES, 1957
(*In Millions of Dollars*)

Purpose [1]	Amount	*Per Cent*	Per Capita [2]
Education			
Direct Expenditure	$ 2,459	26.3%	$ 39.37
Grants to Local Governments	4,094		
Highways and Other Transportation			
State Highways, Terminals, etc.	4,945	24.2	36.21
Grants to Local Governments	1,080		
Social Services and Assistance			
Direct State Programs	1,745	*11.1*	16.64
Grants to Local Governments	1,025		
Health and Hospitals			
Direct Expenditure	1,652	7.6	11.45
Grants to Local Governments	253		
Natural Resources [3]	798	3.2	4.79
Public Safety and Corrections [4]	593	2.4	3.56
Employment Security Administration	234	0.9	1.40
Housing and Redevelopment [5] (6 States)	19	0.1	.11
General Legislative and Executive Control	538	2.2	3.23
Judiciary	75	0.3	.45
Other General Expenditure			
Direct Expenditure	730	6.3	9.47
Grants to Local Governments	845		
Insurance Trust Expenditure	2,313	9.3	13.90
Liquor Stores (16 States)	836	3.4	5.02
Debt Redemption	670	2.7	4.02
Total Personal Services [6]	$ 4,490	*18.0%*	$ 26.97
Totals	$24,904	*100%*	$149.64

Note: Totals do not necessarily add because of rounding.
Sources: Same as Table 1, this chapter.

[1] In all forty-eight States, except as noted.
[2] See footnote 3, Table 1, this chapter.
[3] Includes $11 million intergovernmental grants (to local governments).
[4] Includes an estimated $12 million in grants to local governments.
[5] Largely grants to local governments.
[6] Wage and salary payments, included in other figures. Such payments rose markedly after 1957. In April, 1957, the average monthly payroll of State governments was $388 million (equivalent to $4,656 million per year); in October, 1959, it was $506 million (equivalent to $6,072 million per year).

penditures in the United States. On the whole, the States have more than kept pace with the general increase in government spending. In 1913, the States spent some $450 million, about 17 per cent of all governmental expenditures; for 1957, when grants-in-aid from the national government are excluded, the percentage was almost exactly the same. Government spending as a percentage of national income increased more than fourfold between 1913 and 1957, from 8 per cent to 34.7 per cent. The State share quintupled, from 1⅓ per cent to 6.8 per cent of national income. National expenditures have risen very rapidly in relation to local expenditures, however. In 1913 the national share of government spending was about 25 per cent, compared with 58 per cent by local governments; by the late 1950's these percentages were almost exactly reversed. Over the same period State government finances became increasingly interwoven with national and local finances, as noted in the preceding section on grants-in-aid.

Education and highways involved the largest State expenditures in the 1950's—each about a quarter of all State spending in 1957. Both involved extensive fiscal relations with other levels of government. Social services and assistance, public health programs, hospital construction and maintenance, employment security administration, and housing and redevelopment together accounted for about one-fifth of State spending, again with varying degrees of involvement with other levels of government.

Total State expenditures were $150 per person, though this is a somewhat misleading figure, since some of this spending was by the States' self-supporting or partly self-supporting quasi-business operations. For example, in the sixteen States that maintained them, State liquor stores resulted in a net gain in State revenue, and State insurance programs (government employee retirement plans, unemployment compensation programs, workmen's compensation schemes) are generally self-supporting, independent operations. State highway systems have been largely supported by user taxes and provide a study in the flow of funds: in 1956 the States received highway-related funds from six sources, $2.7 billion from gasoline and other fuel taxes, $1.3 billion from vehicle and operators' licenses, $162 million in tolls, $105 million from local governments, and $739 million in subsidies from the national government (in turn derived, in effect, from national gasoline taxes)—a total of $5 billion. New highway construction, current operation of regular and toll highways, State police, and grants to local governments for highway purposes ($1 billion) *cost* the States $5.5 billion, in effect making the State highway systems largely self-supporting.

Other major State functions are not pay-as-you-go operations, of course. Education, the social services and public assistance programs,

344

public health and hospitals, and the management of natural resources are financed only in small part by related business operations and special taxation. The bulk of their support is derived from general tax funds or from grants-in-aid, which in turn come from the general tax collections of the national government.

FUNCTIONS OF THE STATE GOVERNMENTS

SOME OF THE responsibilities with which the States are charged parallel similar responsibilities of both local and national governments; among these are welfare functions such as labor and business regulation, health, public assistance, and, to a very limited extent, housing. The States share responsibility for education, corrections and protection, and the construction and maintenance of highways primarily with local governments. State protection and development of natural resources parallels national programs; there are only a few counterparts at the level of local government. The first two of the following sections deal with education and transportation, the most important items in State budgets. The third discusses health and welfare services for individuals: public health and hospitals; social services and public assistance; public housing; and unemployment and related insurance programs. The fourth section describes State regulation of the family, business and labor, and the use of alcoholic beverages; such regulation is designed primarily to safeguard the welfare of the individual. The final sections briefly describe State activities in natural resources and in protection and corrections.

Education

THE STATE IS legally responsible for public education within its boundaries, but there is great variance in the exercise of that responsibility among the States. All the States contribute some part of the revenue of local school districts, on the average about 40 per cent (1958–59); the range is from less than 5 per cent (Nebraska) to 80 per cent (Delaware). Highly complex formulas determine the distribution of State funds to school districts, formulas whose complexity often derives from the fact that they generally favor poorer districts over wealthier districts and rural areas over urban areas.

As a rule, States also provide research and consultative services to local districts and often exercise considerable control over local schools by the "minimum standards" device. By stating minimum tax rates for school districts to qualify for State grants, minimum salaries for ac-

345

credited teachers, minimum room space per pupil, minimum sanitation standards, and minimum textbook and supply requirements, among others, State legislatures and boards and departments of education may effectively determine the form and content of local education. Local school district groups sometimes protest such controls, claiming that the minimum standards established by the State are contrary to local desires and local abilities to finance. State control of public education is nevertheless increasing. States have been instrumental in consolidating local school districts, and in one State, North Carolina, all public school teachers are employees of the State. The purposes of improving the quality of education and related services provided to school children, and, in some States, of changing patterns of expenditure, are believed by most State legislators and administrators to override any possible bad consequences of increasing control.

Higher education—State universities and teachers' colleges in particular—is supported by State governments, to enable State residents to receive higher education at "less than cost" and to provide vocational and professional training, particularly in medicine, law, engineering, agriculture, and education. State law sometimes requires that the State university or universities and colleges accept any high school graduate of the State who has successfully completed certain courses. Related to education are State library agencies that provide public library extension services of one type or another. Grants-in-aid to the public libraries of local governments also are occasionally made.

Highways and Aviation

THE STATES WERE largely responsible for regulating the some seventy million motor vehicles that swarmed over the nation's highways in 1960, and were responsible for providing many of those highways. State-controlled roads and highways make up only about one-fifth of the total 3.5 million miles of roads in the United States, but this fifth includes most of the highly expensive intrastate and interstate highways. In 1960 the State governments expended two-thirds of all government highway funds ($7.2 billion of $10.9 billion), including expenditures for highway police and safety. During the 1950's the State highway departments constructed between 50,000 and 60,000 miles of new roads annually, almost all of it surfaced; about 40 per cent of the mileage was part of the federal-aid highway systems and was supported in part by national funds.

Highways must be patrolled as well as constructed, and highway safety has been receiving unprecedented attention from State governments. Between 1950 and 1956 highway traffic deaths increased from

34,800 to 39,600, and injuries were well over one million per year; the costs of traffic accidents in 1956 were estimated at $5 billion. The Governors' Conference is one of the groups concerned with the problem, and it has drawn up an elaborate program for immediate and long-range action. Among the consequences of this concern have been legislation in several northeastern States revoking licenses of drivers traveling more than ten miles above the speed limit on non-urban highways, and more stringent automobile insurance requirements. The State of New Jersey does not make such insurance compulsory, but requires payment of a fixed fee by uninsured car owners into the State's Unsatisfied Judgment Fund. In event of an accident involving the uninsured car owner, the injured parties can sue the State and be recompensed from the Fund; the State then garnishees the future earnings of the car owner concerned. The many State safety plans have had some effect. Traffic deaths declined from a high of 39,600 in 1956 to 35,300 in 1959; the death rate per 100 million vehicle miles has undergone a long-range decline, from 7.6 in 1950 to 6.3 in 1956, and to 5.4 in 1959.[10]

Despite all State efforts, however, it is still argued that, in view of rising vehicle registration figures, present and even proposed highway systems are inadequate. The States are called upon to float larger bond issues, acquire more land, raise gas taxes and registration fees, solicit more funds from the national government, institute safety crackdowns, increase highway police forces, and further regulate and enforce automobile insurance coverage. Toll highways have increased in mileage, and more elaborate highway user imposts have been levied on trucking concerns.

An important part of State highway activities is the acquisition of land. In order to construct freeways and new highways, as well as to construct new schools and to provide public beaches and parks, State governments must frequently acquire property from private individuals. In the case of highway construction, in particular, persons holding land in the path of a proposed highway generally are allowed no choice by the State. The State usually initiates condemnation proceedings, which involves the evaluation of the land and any buildings by State assessors and the forced sale of the property to the State at the State-assessed price. The property owner has recourse to the courts if he feels he has been unjustly treated, but in the majority of such cases the State is upheld. The extent of State land purchases is indicated by the experience of the State of California. In the decade 1945–1954 that State acquired about 400,000 acres of land (625 square miles), half for highway rights-of-way. In 1958, the State Division of Highways spent some

[10] *The Book of the States 1958–59*, Chicago: The Council of State Governments, 1958, pp. 297–300; *Statistical Abstract 1960*, pp. 65, 559.

$100 million for rights-of-way in its highway construction program, about 4 per cent of the total State budget. Many other State agencies were legislatively permitted to act independently in land condemnation proceedings, and a California State Senate interim committee remarked, in a 1958 report, that "there are so many agencies which have the power to acquire land that to set them forth would serve no useful purpose." [11]

Since 1945 some State governments have expressed legislative and administrative interest in aviation. From 1947 through 1960 the States provided an average of $35 million a year for the development of airports and related projects, to match funds granted under the federal-aid airport program. A few States have some interest in air traffic control, agricultural aviation, and other aviation matters; in 1960 forty-two States had aeronautics commissions or departments. The national government, however, has long held the initiative with regard to sponsoring and regulating civil aviation, and, because of the distances involved, appears best equipped to do so in the future. In terms of expenditure the Federal Aviation Agency spent $567 million in 1960; all told, the States are believed not to have spent much over $50 million for aviation and related programs in that year.

Health and Welfare Services for Individuals

PUBLIC HEALTH AND HOSPITALS: Public health undertakings include both remedial medicine and preventive medicine. Responsibilities for them may be scattered among various State government agencies or concentrated in a single agency. State health departments in most States are likely to have a considerable staff and substantial amounts of technical equipment. State health agencies may provide local governmental and non-governmental health agencies with technical assistance, such as conducting studies, supplying information, providing laboratory services and health specialists, and maintaining records; they may supervise municipal water supply and sewage disposal systems; and they may distribute financial aid to local governmental health agencies. Some State health agencies furnish direct services where no local services are available; in the mid-1950's it was estimated that about 6 per cent of the population of the United States was served by district offices of State health departments. State health agencies also conduct information programs for the general public and for professional groups; inspect and license agencies, establishments, and enterprises whose activities might affect health conditions; and sometimes supervise State hospital

[11] "State Does Much Land Purchasing," Los Angeles Times, June 17, 1958.

construction programs.[12] In 1959 the States employed 27,000 persons, including both professional and non-professional personnel, in their public health programs.

State hospitals involve greater investments of funds and personnel than other State health programs; in 1958 State hospital expenditures were $1,593 million, compared with other health program expenditures of $254 million; in 1959 State hospitals employed 292,000 persons. Most of the 552 State hospitals (1958) are for mentally ill or deficient persons; others are for victims of tuberculosis or for persons with other special health problems. Some States also maintain clinics, pre-natal clinics for example; some States have arrangements with local government or non-government hospitals and clinics to provide special types of medical services.

The States have almost entirely pre-empted one field of remedial medicine: that of mental illness. Of some 780,000 mentally ill or defective patients in mental hospitals at the end of 1958, more than four-fifths were in State-operated hospitals. This is not surprising considering the long history of State responsibility for the mentally ill, which dates back to the eighteenth century. The philosophy of care has undergone many changes, of course. In the later 1950's extensive new efforts were being made to return partially recovered mentally ill persons to their homes for rehabilitation. This alternative to keeping them in hospitals that have frequently been overcrowded and lacking in personnel for intensive treatment has been made possible in part by recently developed supportive drugs; by the establishment of "halfway houses" by State and local governments and by non-governmental groups; and by psychotherapy provided outside the hospital setting. By 1960 at least twenty States had set up special facilities or treatment for the senile aged, who in the past have comprised a good part of the mental hospital population. As a result of these developments, by mid-1956 thirty-four States had either reduced or stabilized the resident populations of their mental hospitals; nationally, an absolute decline in the number of such patients began in 1956 and continued through 1959.

To complement remedial treatment of mental disease the States have also been placing more and more emphasis on prevention, through a variety of mental health services. Various State agencies and commissions conduct public information and education programs on mental health topics, and they also sponsor community mental health programs. In 1960 State aid on a matching basis was being provided to community mental health programs of local governments in New York,

[12] Leonard A. Scheele, "Public Health," in Russell H. Kurtz, ed., *Social Work Year Book 1957*. New York: National Association of Social Workers, 1957, p. 353.

California, Minnesota, and New Jersey, and there were similar programs in at least six other States. In connection with these programs the States have also established mental health clinics, using both national grants and their own funds, and in turn have made grants to local governments to set up such clinics. These are staffed by psychiatrists, social workers, and psychologists, and offer treatment to those who need therapy but who do not require hospitalization.[13]

SOCIAL SERVICES AND PUBLIC ASSISTANCE: Most government "social welfare" services are characterized by extensive fiscal and administrative relationships among two or more levels of government, and thus there are few such programs that can be called strictly *State* programs. However, there are five important programs in which the States play a major role: child welfare services, crippled children services, maternal and child health services, vocational rehabilitation services, and general assistance. The first four are financed in part by national grants-in-aid, for which States may qualify by meeting minimum standards of service and administration; the States may in turn make grants to local government agencies to provide services directly or they may maintain operating State agencies. The general assistance programs are financed and administered by State and/or local governments, without national aid. (In addition, there are four public assistance programs financed half by the national government and half by the States: old-age assistance, aid to dependent children, aid to the blind, and aid to the disabled. In these programs the States may be considered to function primarily as administrative districts of the national government; the programs are described in Chapter 14.)

Child welfare services include casework, placement, and financial aid for children who are neglected, dependent, or in danger of becoming delinquent. The primary purpose of such services is to strengthen the child's family or foster family; such children are placed in institutions only if all other means fail. In 1959 there were 361,000 children receiving child welfare casework services under this program in the United States (including Alaska and Hawaii); 41 per cent were in the homes of parents or relatives, 43 per cent in foster family homes, and the others, about 63,000, in institutions. The U.S. Children's Bureau makes grants-in-aid to the States for their programs ($11.5 million in 1959). The actual services may be performed by district offices of the State government or by county or municipal agencies under State supervision. Even if the State child welfare program does not involve direct services, it includes some or all of the following: adoption services; specialized services, when not provided by local agencies, for children with physical or

[13] *The Book of the States 1960–61*, pp. 350–56, 379–80; Vasey, *op. cit.*, pp. 223–24.

mental handicaps; licensing and regulating non-governmental agencies, foster homes, day-care facilities, etc.; developing and enforcing standards of care; training personnel and maintaining personnel standards; conducting research and preparing reports on child welfare programs; and maintaining liaison with other State agencies serving children. Most State child welfare agencies also take part in the administration of the aid to dependent children program of the national government.

The crippled children's services programs of the States also are financed in part by the national government ($14.7 million in 1959) and operate primarily in rural areas and areas of "special need." In 1958, 325,000 children with defects of locomotion, hearing, sight, speech, muscle coordination, or heart damage were helped under the State programs. Most were given clinical diagnoses in State-operated clinics, some of which had large staffs of specialists, others of which were staffed by only a physician and a nurse. A number of States also provide for treatment. In 1958, 57,000 children were given corrective or restorative services in hospitals and convalescent homes. Hearing aids, braces, artificial limbs, and other prosthetic equipment are provided under many State programs.

State maternal and child health services may include education of mothers in pre- and post-natal care; well-child clinics; health services for school children; dental hygiene and care; inspection and licensing of maternity homes; and information and assistance on maternity care problems for hospitals. Some States also provide medical facilities and treatment, and training for nurses, nutritionists, and physicians. In 1958 grants-in-aid to the States (including Alaska and Hawaii) for the programs were $15.1 million. School health examinations and immunizations are also part of the maternal and child-health programs in many States. The numbers of mothers or children provided various types of services in 1958 are given in Table 3.

In 1959, 80,000 persons were rehabilitated under State or State-supervised vocational rehabilitation programs (including Alaska and Hawaii); at mid-year another 168,000 persons were in the process of rehabilitation. Grants-in-aid, administered by the U.S. Office of Vocational Rehabilitation, totaled $46.5 million. The 1961 budget proposed for the national government asked $72 million for vocational rehabilitation, largely for grants-in-aid. An estimated 88,000 persons were rehabilitated in 1960. Services have included diagnosis and evaluation, guidance, physical restoration services, provision of training and training materials, maintenance payments, job placement, help in the establishment of small businesses by persons with severe handicaps, transportation, and establishment of workshops. Most of the persons receiving rehabilitation services have been victims of mental or physical

TABLE 3

GOVERNMENT MATERNAL AND CHILD-HEALTH SERVICES, 1958 [1]

Service	States and Areas Providing Services [2]	Persons Receiving Services [3]
Maternity Medical Clinic Service	34	266,000
Maternity Nursing Service	52	562,000
Hospital In-Patient Care	12	41,000
Dental Treatment	12	7,000
Well-Child Conference Service	52	2,065,000
General Pediatric Clinic Service	17	145,000
Special Children's Clinic Service	15	96,000
Children's Nursing Service	52	3,063,000
Topical Fluoride Applications	31	228,000
Dental Treatment	37	509,000
Hospital Care for Premature Infants	14	6,000
Other In-Patient Hospital Care for Children	13	21,000
School Health Examinations by Physicians	41	2,591,000
Other School Examinations		
Tests of Vision	44	5,048,000
Tests of Hearing	43	3,471,000
Dental Checkups	41	2,869,000
Other Tests and Checkups	23	972,000
Immunization		
Smallpox	53	2,737,000
Diphtheria	53	3,181,000
Pertussis	53	2,279,000
Tetanus	53	3,084,000
Poliomyelitis	52	5,152,000
Typhoid	25	770,000
Other	12	44,000

Source: *Statistical Abstract 1960*, p. 292.

[1] Provided by State government agencies or local agencies or institutions under State supervision or contract.
[2] Includes data for the District of Columbia, Alaska, Hawaii, Puerto Rico, and the Virgin Islands.
[3] Includes extensive multiple counting; hence, no total is computed.

disease; about 10 per cent have been victims of accidents. In the mid-1950's State rehabilitation agencies employed some 1,200 rehabilitation counselors in the programs.[14]

The major type of individual social service that is financed and administered solely by State and local governments is general assistance, which comprises aid chiefly for the needy who are ineligible for any of the specific assistance or social insurance programs. It is also sometimes used to supplement the income of recipients of these programs. General assistance is usually directly administered by local government

[14] Vasey, *op. cit.*, pp. 192–217; *Statistical Abstract 1960*, pp. 292–96.

agencies in keeping with State requirements; in some States it is integrated with other programs of assistance and in others it is not. The States pay varying proportions of the cost. In ten States, in the late 1950's, the State welfare department or board paid all costs, and in fifteen, at least half; in another fifteen States, however, local governments met all expenses. The number of persons on general assistance is relatively small but fluctuates widely with economic conditions, and also with the season of the year. Between December, 1950, and December, 1955, general assistance cases declined from 413,000 to 314,000; late in 1957 they began to increase and by the end of 1958 had reached 434,000, the increase being due largely to the recession. By the beginning of 1960 general assistance cases had slacked off to about 400,000. The average monthly payment in 1959 was $69, the total payments $345 million. The proportion of cases varies greatly from State to State, as does the average payment. In 1959 the average monthly payment ranged from $12, in Alabama, to $104, in Michigan.

Some States also have other programs of social service, developed largely on their own initiative to meet special problems or new demands. For the aging, for example, there are relatively new programs concerned with their employment, income maintenance, housing, physical and mental health, and education and recreation, as well as for training and research in geriatrics and chronic illness. There is increased State interest in child and youth welfare, emphasizing new developments in protective services, homemaker services, reform school facilities and practices, day care, and delinquency programs.[15] Such programs are found in only a few States, however, and often consist largely of requirements to be met by local agencies. The responsible State bodies may provide information, attempt to stimulate interest on the part of local governmental and non-governmental agencies, and suggest courses of action; they seldom have had funds for sizable grants or for direct operations.

Some States have expressed interest in veterans' welfare, particularly in the periods immediately after World War II and the Korean War. Some States paid veterans' bonuses, some have given special hospital benefits, certain tax and licenses exemptions, homestead preferences, employment privileges and preferences, and free tuition for children of wounded or disabled veterans. New York State has had a special Veteran Assistance program to provide home relief to veterans and their families with special welfare problems. A number of States have established veterans' service offices. In 1958, however, total State government expenditures under these programs were only about $120 million.[16]

---

[15] *The Book of the States 1960–61*, pp. 376–84.
[16] Vasey, *op. cit.*, pp. 242–43.

THE STATES AND HOUSING: Most public housing and urban renewal projects have been national-local, bypassing the State governments. The States must pass enabling laws permitting municipalities to participate in national aid programs, however. By the beginning of 1958, forty-six States (including Alaska and Hawaii) permitted cities to participate in the national low-rent housing program; by 1960 forty-six permitted participation in urban redevelopment programs. Fifteen States also helped finance housing projects: California, Connecticut, Hawaii, Illinois, Massachusetts, Mississippi, New Hampshire, New Jersey, New York, North Dakota, Ohio, Oregon, Pennsylvania, Washington, and Wisconsin. It is noteworthy that most of these States are highly urbanized; in other States, rural-dominated State legislatures have been unwilling to aid such projects, thus further encouraging municipal governments to turn to the national government for funds.

Four States have had relatively extensive housing programs. Connecticut makes grants to local housing authorities for urban renewal and industrial and commercial redevelopment; the State also finances housing for the elderly, having provided 9,600 low-rental units by 1960, and backs home-mortgage loans. In Massachusetts, the State at one time sponsored a $200 million veterans' rental housing program, through which some 15,000 units were made available; more recently, the State has guaranteed local housing authority bonds to finance housing for older people. The State of Pennsylvania has had a $23 million grant fund for the construction of moderate-rental housing and for financing slum clearance, and in 1959 added a mortgage financing program. The most important State action has been taken by New York, which has had a billion-dollar program to supplement national low-rental public housing. At one point, in 1955, more housing had been erected in New York State with State funds than with national aid. In 1960 the State had 45,000 units of rental housing in occupancy and subsidy contracts for another 13,000 units.

Finally, by early 1960, thirty-three States had urban planning programs, financed in part by matching national grants under the Federal Housing Act of 1954. The programs, then in the rudimentary stages, were to initiate regional or metropolitan planning or to help municipal governments begin such planning.[17]

SOCIAL INSURANCE: The State governments have primary responsibility for three types of social insurance (aside from programs for their own employees, summarized in the final section of this chapter): unemployment insurance, adopted in all fifty States; workmen's compensation, which is required in all States but is State-administered only in

[17] *The Book of the States 1960–61*, pp. 417–21.

some of them; and State temporary disability insurance, provided in four States (1960). The State social insurance programs are distinct from the public assistance and other direct welfare service programs in that they are largely self-financing, through employer and employee contributions; they are distinct from non-govermental insurance plans in that coverage is usually required for almost all classes of employees, and that if the State trust funds prove insufficient, deficits may be made up from general tax funds. For the recipient, one important quality of social insurance may be that it appears to be a normal condition of his employment, to which he has contributed at least indirectly; because of it he does not have to go "on relief," which for many people is undesirable or degrading.

Unemployment insurance was designed to compensate those out of work, through no fault of their own, with weekly sums thought adequate for subsistence but much below the recipient's regular income. By 1958 some forty million employees were covered under State programs; agricultural, domestic, and government employees have been excluded from most State plans. While most government employees have their own compensation programs, the exclusion of the other two groups has often been criticized in recent years. The number of persons receiving payments varies seasonally and with general economic conditions. In 1955 a weekly average of 1,254,000 unemployed persons were receiving compensation. Because of the recession, in 1958 the weekly average rose to 2,537,000 and during the course of the year 7,940,000 persons received first payments. In 1959 the weekly average of insured unemployed persons dropped to 1,682,000. (These and following figures include data for Alaska and Hawaii.) The unemployed person usually receives payments for twenty-six weeks, and State laws generally specify that half of his income loss should be covered. The States also set maximum rates, however, ranging from $25 to $45 per week (in 1957), which are so low that the average worker in most States can receive only 35 to 45 per cent of his weekly wages. This also has been subject to criticism.

The unemployment insurance program is a State-national one, prompted by the national Social Security Act of 1935, which established a framework in which the States could develop their own programs. Each State collects taxes, usually at the rate of 2.7 per cent, on the wages of employees subject to State law, usually up to a wage limit of $3,000 per year. In all but three States only the employer is taxed. The money so collected is held in the U.S. Treasury, in a special fund for each state. The national government collects a 0.3 per cent tax on such payrolls, which is used to finance State administration of the program, carried out in conjunction with the Public Employment Service (cf. Chapter 14). Total benefits paid in 1959 were $2.3 billion, while contributions collected were $1.96 billion. State trust funds had increased to a high of $8.9 billion in 1953 and declined only slightly, to $8.6 billion, by 1957. The heavy inroads of recession unemployment reduced the funds available for benefits to $6.9 billion by early 1959, however, lower than they had been at any time since 1944.

Because unemployment benefits stop after twenty-six weeks in most States, during middle and late 1958 some States established temporary unemployment compensation programs for persons who had exhausted their regular benefits. In five States (Colorado, Connecticut, Illinois, Ohio, and Wisconsin) these were financed without national assistance; in twenty-nine others the national government participated, and in some of these benefits were limited to veterans and federal employees. A total of 2.1 million persons received first payments under these temporary programs and benefits totaled $600 million by the end of 1959. Most of these programs came to an end in June, 1959.

The second type of State social insurance is workmen's compensation, designed to provide benefit payments to injured workers, to provide them with medical care, and to rehabilitate them. The State programs are not supervised or aided by the national government and are quite varied. Some States provide coverage for almost all workers, including those in agriculture; others cover only those in especially hazardous occupations. It is estimated, however, that between 60 and 80 per cent of the employed population of the United States is covered. In about twenty States the State government itself maintains a workmen's compensation fund, but in less than half of them is the employer required to use the State fund. If he wishes, the employer may obtain coverage from a private insurance company. Where there is no State fund, the employer falling within the statutory provision can obtain private insurance; in nearly half the States he may not even be required to do this but can choose to remain without coverage for his employees. In some States, employees themselves decide whether they wish coverage under the provisions of the State law. In fact, however, most employers and employees have taken out coverage. In 1958 compensation payments totaled $1.1 billion, about one-third of which was for medical treatment and care. State funds made only a quarter of the total payments; insurance companies or employers themselves paid the rest.

In California, New Jersey, New York, and Rhode Island the State governments provide for temporary disability insurance for workers who are injured or become ill while off the job. The plans all require employee contributions. Except in Rhode Island, however, an employer has the option of insuring under either the State or a private plan, provided that under the private plan the benefits are equal to those established by State law. Payments under the four temporary disability insurance programs were some $300 million in 1958, including payments from both State funds and insurance companies.[18]

State Regulations for Welfare

THE STATES make extensive use of their police powers in efforts to safeguard the welfare of the individual by regulating the family, business and labor, and the use of alcoholic beverages. These regulations include some of the oldest and fundamental expressions of government's concern for the well-being of its citizens. Because of their essentially limiting nature, however, in contrast to the positive and visible nature of educational, transportation, and social assistance programs, the importance of such regulations is sometimes forgotten.

REGULATION OF THE FAMILY: The regulation of domestic relations is traditionally a State concern, restricted only by certain provisions of the United States Constitution and the Bill of Rights. The States regulate marriage, generally by requiring that the couple obtain a marriage license from civil authorities; a few States still recognize common-law marriages as valid. With five exceptions (1959) the States have required physical examinations of both partners prior to marriage. They also establish the age of consent to marriage and usually fix a minimum waiting period preceding the issuance of the license.

State legal efforts are also made to preserve the family or at least to ensure continued financial support of children. By 1958 all States and dependent areas had passed a reciprocal enforcement act or a support of dependents act, which allow one State to force a father within its jurisdiction to maintain the family he has deserted in another State. Most States have assumed the legal authority, often delegated to local officials, to remove children from their homes in the event of incompetence on the part of the parents, and to place them in a foster home or in a State institution. The States also regulate adoption procedures, in addition to actually making the placements in some cases.

As the States regulate the establishment and issue of marriage they regulate its dissolution. Every State permits divorce on one or more grounds; New York recognizes only adultery as ground for divorce. In other States, the most common grounds for divorce are adultery, cruelty, desertion, alcoholism, impotency, neglect to provide, insanity, and felony conviction or imprisonment. State courts also generally decide whether the wife shall receive alimony, and how much, and determine support payments for any children. Finally, in some States persons who have been divorced are restricted so far as a subsequent marriage is con-

---

[18] Vasey, *op. cit.*, pp. 92–127. Data from *Statistical Abstract 1960*, pp. 263–88.

cerned; oddly enough, in almost every case the restrictions upon the defendent are no more severe than they are upon the plaintiff.

BUSINESS REGULATIONS: State governments have broad powers over corporations, having the power to create corporations and to set the conditions of their existence. States also regulate "foreign" corporations—corporations chartered in other States but operating in the State in question.

Exceptional attention is devoted to the operations of banks, insurance companies, and small loan companies. Several thousand State banks are chartered, regulated, and inspected by State administrative offices; State officials are generally empowered to close a bank whose operations are unsatisfactory. State concern with insurance operations is based upon the same general welfare reasons as its concern with banks: the fact that insurance companies are responsible for vast sums entrusted to them by the public. The States are especially concerned with the ways insurance firms distribute their funds. They also supervise the interest rates collected by small loan companies and by pawnbrokers.

State governments parallel local governments in regulating privately owned public utilities, being concerned chiefly with guaranteeing adequate service and with fixing or at least controlling rates. In practice, proposals for changes in service are commonly initiated by the utility, which then submits the proposals to the appropriate government agency for approval. The reaction of the agency depends to a considerable extent upon the pressure that the utility can bring upon the agency. In almost all the States, utility regulation is administered by a public-utility commission, whose members are usually chosen either by the governor or by election. Rate regulation is extremely complex, turning on what constitutes a "fair return" to the owners on the value of the utility (usually 6 per cent), and in turn on what constitutes the utility's value.

Finally, almost every State has ventured into the field of fair-trade legislation, permitting manufacturers to set minimum retail prices in a given State for any of their products that carry trade-marks or brand names. As such, fair-trade laws constitute exceptions—sanctioned by the Miller-Tydings Act of 1937 and the McGuire Act of 1952—to national antitrust legislation. Originally promoted by independent retailers' associations and various manufacturers' associations, particularly drug houses, appliance manufacturers, and distillers, fair-trade laws have had a checkered career. Chain stores, department stores, and discount houses have strongly opposed them, as have consumers' groups. The high courts of a half dozen States have declared the laws unconstitutional (though in 1955 the United States Supreme Court upheld the constitutionality of the fair-trade law of Louisiana) and several large manufacturers have ceased price-fixing on some or all of their products.

LABOR REGULATIONS: There is a host of State laws regulating wages, hours, and working conditions of employees, applying primarily to workers in intrastate businesses. Early in 1960, for example, the New York State legislature passed into law a required minimum wage rate of $1 an hour, applying to all persons employed in the State. (Workers in interstate business fall under the provisions and amendments of the national Fair Labor Standards Act of 1938.) In general, however, such State laws are less exacting than national requirements, largely because of the great influence agricultural and manufacturing concerns have over State governments. State inspectors enforce safety in various occupations, as well as health conditions. State laws deal with minimum wages for all workers, minimum wages for child labor, maximum hours for women and children, and many other related questions. A few business groups have succeeded in winning exemption from some of these statutes. For example, newspaper publishers have won exemption so far as newsboys are concerned, in part by terming newsboys not "employees" but "independent contractors." Women and children who are migrant farm workers also are often not subject to laws regulating working conditions.

States have passed a group of laws concerning industrial relations and some have established mediation and conciliation services. Some States have also attempted to impose restraints on labor oranizations. In about a third of the States "right-to-work" laws have been passed, which prohibit the union shop. Most of these States are predominantly rural, so that labor unions have had comparatively little political influence at the State capital. In four States there are laws forbidding labor unions to contribute to political campaigns. A few State laws restricting labor unions have been overthrown by the courts, including at least one statute outlawing peaceful picketing, on the ground that such a law was an unconstitutional denial of the freedoms of speech and assembly.

By early 1960 fair employment practices commissions had been established in sixteen States, as well as in some local governments, to help prevent discrimination in employment on the ground of religion, race, or nationality. These commissions investigate complaints and, on finding violations, issue orders that are enforceable in the courts, in the case of the State commissions. In two other States there were antidiscrimination laws that relied upon voluntary compliance. The Rhode Island legislature in 1957 passed legislation prohibiting discrimination against the employment of older workers, and by 1960 similar provisions were in effect in six other States as well.

All State governments license members of certain trades and professions, though which trades and professions are licensed varies from State to State. These persons must be licensed in all States: accountants, architects, attorneys, chiropodists, dentists, dental hygienists, embalmers, engineers, nurses, optometrists, osteopaths, pharmacists, physicians, teachers in elementary and secondary schools, and veterinarians. Such licensing is designed to benefit one or more of at least three groups. One group is the practitioners themselves. Through their associations they often prompt State legislatures to institute licensing. Licensing commissioners are typically chosen from association members or persons sympathetic to its goals, and associations constantly survey the activities of their commissions. One aim of such activities is to prevent the number of practitioners from becoming too great, another is to give present practitioners what is in effect a legal monopoly. They may also feel that their status in the eyes of the public is enhanced by State recognition. The latter reason has been strong in social workers' advocacy of State licensing and regulation of their profession, though their efforts have met with no great success.

Clients of the trade or profession also may benefit from State licensing, of course, by having the assurance that they are dealing with someone who has a statutory minimum of education and practice. On the other hand, the public may suffer when leaders of an association fail to accept new techniques. Third, where admittance to the trade or profession demands a period of formal education or supervised training, licensing benefits the individuals performing the teaching or supervising the training, and also the institutions in which these activities take place.

The industrial accident compensation laws and disability insurance programs cited previously also may be considered a form of labor regulation or protection. In the majority of States the States themselves do not actually administer the programs, but suggest or require that employers provide their workers with coverage.

ALCOHOLIC BEVERAGE CONTROL: The control of alcoholic beverages presumably protects the health and moral integrity of a State's citizens; since the repeal of national prohibition control has been relegated largely to the State and local governments. State law usually establishes the type of beverage to be sold, the days and hours of sale, the minimum age at which a person may be served, and sometimes other stipulations. A number of States have a monopoly on the sale of beverages by the bottle and may in addition require liquor licenses of those who would buy. Most States also provide local option, a device whereby residents of a locality may determine by an election whether or not alcoholic beverages shall be sold in their locality, which shall be sold, and the hours of sale. It is estimated that some twenty-five million people live under State and local option laws that ban the sale of liquor.

Natural Resources

A RELATIVELY SMALL but important State function has been the protection and development of natural resources, including fish and wildlife, water resources and river basins, forests, and mineral deposits. State natural resources programs also include soil conservation, agricultural extension and research, and State parks. The national government has encouraged the development of many of these programs, and foots part of the bill through grant-in-aid programs. The western States have developed the most extensive natural resources programs; average State spending for natural resources in 1957 was 3.2 per cent of all expenditures, while the eleven mountain and Pacific Coast States averaged nearly 7 per cent. Maine, Vermont, New Hampshire, Kentucky, and Florida also have had relatively important programs.

Interstate commissions have been widely used to deal with natural resources problems, primarily through coordinating and fact-finding. Three commissions, numbering among their members all coastal States, have been organized to promote the better utilization of fisheries and to prevent waste: the Atlantic States Marine Fisheries Commission, the Pacific Marine Fisheries Commission, and the Gulf States Marine Fisheries Commission. The Interstate Oil Compact Commission, with thirty-one member States (including Alaska), is interested in conserving oil and gas by preventing physical waste.

Many States attempt to control pollution of water supplies, provide for flood control and public water supplies, and regulate water rights. A number of interstate water compacts have been drawn up, such as the Tennessee River Basin Water Pollution Control Compact and the Great Lakes Basin Compact. One of the oldest is the Colorado River Compact of 1923, regulating the apportionment of water among the seven States party to the Compact. Soil conservation, though of long-standing national interest, has become the object of State programs only fairly recently. State expenditures for conservation operations, river-basin protection, and flood control in 1958 were some $20 million.

Cooperative extension work and agricultural research, initiated by the national government but conducted by States and counties, is partly supported by State governments. They paid about one-third of the $135 million bill for county extension agents in 1959. Agricultural research, conducted at State colleges and universities and at experimental stations, has received about half its financial support from State governments.

Several States became concerned with forests and parks in the 1880's, and by 1960 all but three States had forestry administrative organizations, while all had State parks and recreation areas. State forestry departments are charged with fire control, forest pest control, reforestation, forest administration, and timber management for large areas of both State-owned and privately owned land. It was estimated that in 1957 about 435 million acres of non-federal forest and non-timbered river-basin lands required organized government fire control; almost all of this protection was provided by State forestry departments and cooperating agencies.

Protection and Corrections

ALTHOUGH THE STATES perform myriad services that are "protective" in nature, this section is concerned specifically with State police services and correctional institutions and practices. State protective services are provided chiefly by the State police, whose primary interest is highway patrol and highway safety. In about one-quarter of the States enforcement of highway laws is their only function, though they may sometimes cooperate with local law-enforcement officers in other functions. They exercise general powers of law enforcement only in a handful of States, including New York, New Jersey, Pennsylvania, and West Virginia. Law enforcement in most States is left primarily to local government, but nevertheless the States are legally vested with very considerable protective powers. One exercise of these powers was made by the State of Mississippi in 1947, when Governor Fielding Wright called a special session of the Mississippi legislature to deal with violence that had accompanied a six-month-old bus-drivers' strike. One bill passed by the legislature, at the governor's insistence, gave him the power to establish the "Mississippi Bureau of Investigation," consisting of investigators appointed by and known only to him, who would have the power to investigate and make arrests in crimes of violence or intimidation. Other bills made it a jail offense for two or more persons to conspire to interfere with a transit line's operations and a crime punishable by death for a person to place a bomb in a bus, truck, or filling station.[19]

State correctional institutions and practices involve a more specific set of welfare problems than do police services. At the beginning of 1959 there were 184,000 adult prisoners in State prisons, reformatories,

[19] A. J. Liebling, "The M.B.I.," *The New Yorker*, Jan. 3, 1948, pp. 46–50.

prison camps and farms, and on work gangs, and an estimated 35,000 young people in public training schools for juvenile delinquents. During 1958, 75,000 adult prisoners were received from the courts.

The philosophy underlying most State correctional practices is changing from one based on punishment to one based on rehabilitation. The ancient principle of punishment for those who violate the law is still common, however, as is the related axiom that offenders must be segregated for the protection of society. The application of these principles, unaccompanied by any concept of rehabilitation, has produced many "case-hardened" criminals who have continued their criminal careers quite literally with a vengeance. Helping the criminal to adjust to normal life is often extremely difficult, though. Success is most likely with juvenile delinquents, and many States make relatively major efforts at rehabilitation in reformatories and training schools for young people. It is more difficult effectively to rehabilitate adult offenders, and correctional practices in penitentiaries have only recently achieved a solid foothold.

> Many of the institutions now have reception centers, to which the offender comes for study, diagnosis of his problem, and for a determination of the kinds of treatment he needs. The concept of classification, or individualization of the prisoner, through study of his background, the environmental factors that have influenced his life, and his personality or behavior patterns, has been developing for years, although it is not yet fully developed. The correctional institutions are increasingly being staffed by professional personnel, with psychologists, psychiatrists, social workers, sociologists, and others who contribute to the understanding and treatment of the offender. Education or vocational training are among the features of correctional institutions.[20]

No rehabilitation can be said to be complete while a person is in prison or a reformatory or training school, however. In addition to services in the institutions, three practices are used to implement rehabilitation: probation, indeterminate sentencing, and parole. Probation may be allowed by the court if the court and the probation officer feel that an offender can adjust to his problem best while living in the community; certain conditions are specified for the person, and he is helped and supervised by the probation officer. Probation can be used for juvenile offenders in all States and for adult offenders in most States. In some cases, particularly for young offenders, an indeterminate sentence may be ordered by the court; the prisoner may be released whenever it is thought that he stands a good chance of living a normal, non-

---

[20] Vasey, *op. cit.*, p. 234.

criminal life outside the correctional institution. In the case of both determinate and indeterminate sentencing, the prisoner may be released on parole under the supervision of a parole officer. The parolee must regulate his life according to conditions set down by State parole laws, and it is the task of the parole officer to help him re-establish himself during the period of his parole.

THE EMPLOYEES OF STATE GOVERNMENTS AND THEIR WELFARE

LATE IN 1959 the State governments employed 1,518,000 persons full- or part-time, slightly less than one-fifth of all government employees in the United States. Their payroll, at the rate paid in October, 1959, was some $6.1 billion a year—about one-fifth of all State expenditures. State employment by function in 1958 and average earnings of State and local employees are given in Table 4. About one State employee in four worked for State hospitals or for State health or social service agencies. Of all State and local government employees, the lowest average salaries were received by public school maintenance and custodial personnel, hospital employees, and those working with the social service and assistance programs.

The State governments have retirement and disability programs for their employees and administer similar programs for many of the local governments within their jurisdictions. In 1957 there were 147 such State-administered systems, covering 3,036,000 employees; almost all State employees and nearly two million local employees were included in the plans. The programs were of many types: twelve covered all State employees and fifteen covered all State and local employees in a given State; eight others covered all but local school employees; there were also 102 limited coverage systems for special groups, such as teachers, school employees, firemen, police, and others.

More than 250,000 former government employees were receiving benefits under the State systems in 1957; their average monthly check was about $100. Most of them had retired because of age; about 25,000 were no longer working because of disability. In addition, the families of some 25,000 deceased government employees were drawing benefits from the States systems. Total benefit payments for all groups were $360 million, and assets at the end of fiscal 1957 were over $8 billion. Receipts of the retirement programs in 1957 came from employees (40 per cent), State and local governments (45 per cent), and investments.

TABLE 4

STATE GOVERNMENT EMPLOYMENT BY FUNCTION, 1958

FUNCTION	FULL-TIME EQUIVALENT EMPLOYMENT [1]		AVERAGE ANNUAL SALARY PER FULL-TIME EMPLOYEE [2]
	Number	Per Cent	
Education			
Public School Instructional Personnel	40,000	3.1%	$5,360
Other Public School Personnel	14,000	1.1	3,160
State College and University Personnel	259,000	19.8	5,230
Other	24,000	1.8	4,340
Highways	234,000	17.9	3,920
Hospitals	277,000	21.1	3,180
Health Services	25,000	1.9	4,270
Social Services	44,000	3.4	3,770
Natural Resources	93,000	7.1	4,150
Police Protection	30,000	2.3	4,640
General Control	78,000	6.0	4,240
Other	195,000	14.9	4,160
Totals	1,312,000 [1]	100 %	

Note: Totals do not necessarily add because of rounding.
Source: *Statistical Abstract* 1959, p. 422.

[1] Total employment, both full- and part-time, was 1,469,000; most part-time employment was at State colleges and universities.
[2] Estimated on the basis of October, 1958, payrolls; for most functions, figures are for State *and* local government employee salaries. Breakdowns are not available, but State salaries are believed to be somewhat higher than local salaries, on the average.

CONCLUDING REMARKS

THE FIFTY American States have broad legal powers, but owing to the truly national character of American economy and society the exercise of these powers meets with external restraints. In hypothetical comparison, consider the difficulties of legislating in Sweden if that nation were subject to a federal European government with power to tax and confer benefits on the Swedes, to conduct administrative operations within Sweden, and to maintain a court system with jurisdiction over many of Sweden's internal affairs. The Swedes might take their business elsewhere, move because of high taxes, and confound every legislative debate with arguments that what was proposed was already being done by the European government, or should be, or had failed in Italy or elsewhere. Federalism, in brief, is a most difficult form of government and its relative success in the United States is unique.

Many examples of national-State coordination are given above. Though the States have undertaken few new means of providing welfare and have devised few new forms of welfare organization, in comparison with local and national governments, they have more tasks than ever. They help finance and administer dozens of grants-in-aid programs of the national government, adapting them to regional conditions, and require and supervise dozens of such programs within their own localities. Their education, public highway, and health functions are of great scope. They provide social services of many kinds, especially maternal and child-care programs and dependency programs to aid the poor and aged. They are concerned with mental illness to a greater extent than any other level of government. They also regulate business affairs, labor conditions, alcoholic beverages, the giant insurance business, and many other sectors of human activity. In fact, the State was a "welfare State" long before the term was applied to the national government.

Yet the State governments face serious and perhaps insurmountable problems. Financing State activities in recent years has presented serious difficulties. The States are called upon to meet the "bonuses" offered in the matching grant programs of the national government and to maintain nationally required minimum standards, and their local governments continually call upon them for financial assistance; at the same time the State tax base is being reduced by local and national taxation. A still more serious problem in many States is urban-rural conflict, essentially over who gets what services from the State government: the decreasing rural population, which usually dominates the legislature, or the increasing urban population? The problem is confounded in many States by the existence of metropolitan areas that sprawl across the boundaries of one or more adjacent States. In general, few innovations in welfare are likely to come from the States; their already-extensive connections with national government agencies will increase while their local units of government, cities in particular, will become more self-contained and independent of the State governments.

Chapter Fourteen

THE NATIONAL GOVERNMENT

THE NATIONAL GOVERNMENT, of any single organization in the United States, plays the largest role in the planned distribution of welfare. The majority of the tasks it undertakes are in the name of the general welfare of the American people. This does not mean that all of them bear equally on all citizens or institutions. Rather, the performance of a given government function usually directly affects a small number of persons or organizations and through them presumably has diffuse effects on the general welfare. However, a substantial minority of government functions are specifically designed for the welfare of those who are socially defined as underprivileged. Such programs may simultaneously, if indirectly, contribute to the welfare of persons not viewed as underprivileged. The public assistance programs, for instance, provide funds for individuals and families in economic distress; by doing so they may have incidental effects such as relieving pressures on other levels of government and on voluntary welfare agencies and increasing real estate values in urban slums.

This chapter first summarizes national government finances, pointing out the welfare effects of the tax structure as well as describing the governmental flow of funds. The functions of the national government are described under three headings: regulation, indirect operation, and direct action. The final section deals with internal welfare—the welfare of government employees and veterans.

NATIONAL GOVERNMENT FINANCING

Revenues

THE NATIONAL GOVERNMENT has a variety of receipts from a variety of sources. Usual practice is to list "budget receipts," *i.e.*, income, corporation, and related taxes that are for general uses. Such receipts were predicted in January, 1960, to total $78.6 billion in fiscal 1960. In addition, however, the national government manages a number of trust funds and conducts many business-type operations. The money received by these funds and operations also is part of government receipts. Total national government receipts from the public in fiscal 1960 were predicted at $94.8 billion, including the receipts of trust funds and certain other operations. The 1960 budget receipts of the national government are given in Table 1; the receipts and expenditures of major trust funds are given in Table 2.

TABLE 1

RECEIPTS OF THE NATIONAL GOVERNMENT, 1960

Type of Revenue	Amount (*Millions*)	*Per Cent*	Per Employed Person [1]
Budget Revenues	$78,600	82.9%	$1,173
Individual Income Taxes	40,306	42.5	602
Corporation Income Taxes	22,200	23.4	331
Excise Taxes	9,100	19.6	136
Estate and Gift Taxes	1,470	1.6	22
Customs	1,176	1.2	18
Employment Taxes [2]	333	0.4	5
Miscellaneous Receipts	4,015	4.2	60
Other Receipts from the Public	$16,200	17.1	$ 242
Totals	$94,800	100%	$1,415

Source: "President's Budget Message," *New York Times*, Jan. 19, 1960.

[1] Computed on the basis of an estimated sixty-seven million employed persons receiving wages or salaries in April, 1960, including civilian and military government employees.
[2] Share for national government administrative and related expenses only.

The Old-age, Survivors, and Disability Insurance program is the largest of the trust fund operations; its receipts in 1959 were $9.5 billion, including investment income. Other major trust funds are the unemployment and highway trust funds, each of which has had annual revenues on the order of $2 billion, the former from taxes on employer payrolls and the latter from the highway fuel tax, which was four cents on the gallon in 1960. The Post Office Department is the largest of the many business operations of the national government; its business revenues in 1959 were some $3.1 billion.

TABLE 2

NATIONAL GOVERNMENT TRUST FUNDS, 1958, 1959
(*In Millions of Dollars*)

Trust Fund or Account	Receipts [1] 1958	Expenditures [2] 1958	1959
Old-Age and Survivors	$8,118	$8,521	$10,026
Federal Disability Insurance	991	261	507
Unemployment Compensation State (Deposits in U.S. Treasury to State Accounts)	1,471	3,148	2,954
Federal Employee (UCFE)	(n.a.)	62 [2]	51 [2]
Korea Veterans (UCV)	(n.a.)	82 [2]	17 [2]
Railroad Workers	(n.a.)	169 [2]	193 [2]
Ex-Servicemen (UCX)	(n.a.)	7 [2]	80 [2]
Railroad Retirement and Disability	575	730	776
Federal Employees' Retirement and Disability	(n.a.)	699	836
Veterans' Life Insurance	(n.a.)	664	662
Highway Construction	1,683 [3]	1,602	2,553
Other Trust Accounts and Deposits Funds [4]	(n.a.)	616	1,030
Total Expenditures		$16,561	$19,675

Note: Data do not necessarily agree with other 1958 and 1959 data given in this chapter because most above data are for fiscal years, data elsewhere are sometimes for calendar years.

Source: *Statistical Abstract of the United States* 1959. U.S. Bureau of the Census. Washington, D.C.: USGPO, 1959, pp. 276–77, 280, 284, 366, 370.

[1] Total not computed because data are not available or not comparable.
[2] Benefits paid, administrative costs, refunds, insurance losses, and all other expenses, are included in each item except for four types of unemployment compensation, amounts for which are benefits paid only.
[3] Excise taxes collected on gasoline and diesel fuel.
[4] Includes benefits and administrative expenses not given above plus certain other trust activities such as secondary market operations of the Federal National Mortgage Association.

Income taxes are the major source of national revenue. In 1958 and again in 1960 individual and corporation income taxes provided nearly 80 per cent of budget revenues and, in 1960, over 65 per cent of total receipts. Taxes on the manufacture and sale of goods, including those designated for the highway trust fund, have amounted to about 13 per cent of total receipts from the public in recent years. Social insurance taxes collected or held by the national government have been about the same percentage of total receipts. Nearly all taxes can be considered to be paid directly or indirectly by the individual. The average employed person paid individual income taxes of about $550 in 1958, or 11 per cent of his $5,000 income.[1] He paid indirectly for most of his social insurance, in so far as it was part of his employer's total wage and salary bill; he paid direct taxes for a portion of it. If the employed person is considered as a consumer, he also paid much of the cost of corporation income taxes and excise taxes, which were passed on to him in the form of higher prices. For the entire population rather than just the employed, the national government cost about $460 per person in taxes; by comparison, the personal goods and services purchased by the average person cost about $1,700.

Federal income taxation does not fall evenly on all persons, of course, which constitutes a decided and deliberate benefit for persons in lower-income brackets and for those with children. The federal personal income tax receipts for 1959 *could* have been obtained by an across-the-board tax of 10.9 per cent on all personal income.[2] The present tax structure thus may be said to benefit everyone who paid less than that percentage of his gross income in federal taxes. In this sense, a single person with no dependents benefited if he earned $1,700 or less; if he earned more, he paid more than 11 per cent in taxes, assuming standard deductions. For a married couple with a child, the cutting point was a total income of about $5,000; if they earned less, they paid less than 10.9 per cent in federal income taxes. If a family pays any income tax at all, it receives some tax benefit for each child. For a family whose effective tax rate is 15 per cent, each child is "worth" $90—15 per cent of the permitted $600 income deduction. It might be mentioned that the "average" family, in terms of income, benefits from the present tax structure. In 1958 such a family had an income of $6,220 but, because of deductions, its actual tax was only about 9.8 per cent ($610).

Expenditures

THE ESTIMATED expenditures of the national government for fiscal 1960 are summarized in Table 3. Budget expenditures totaled about $78.4 billion, compared with $64.6 billion in 1955, $71.9 billion in 1958, and

[1] There were about 64 million employed persons in the United States in 1958, including government employees and servicemen but excluding unpaid family workers. Personal income, including wages, salaries, dividends, rental, and interest but excluding fringe benefits, relief payments, and social security benefits, was $320 billion, the figure used in computing average income.
[2] See footnote 1 for definition of "personal income."

$80.7 billion in 1959. Trust funds paid out about $17.7 billion in 1960. Data on public enterprise expenditures are not included because they are not comparable in nature to other national expenditures. Many of these enterprises meet their expenses from their business operations. A few, such as the Post Office, must be subsidized from the general budget; in 1959 the Post Office met about four-fifths of its expenses from reg-

TABLE 3

BUDGET EXPENDITURES OF THE NATIONAL GOVERNMENT, 1960

Purpose	Amount (*Millions*)	*Per Cent*	*Per Capita* [1]
Budget Expenditures	$78,383	82.2%	$432
National Security	45,650	47.9	251
International Affairs and Finance (other than Military Assistance)	2,066	2.2	11
Agriculture and Agricultural Resources	5,113	*5.4*	28
Transportation and Commerce	2,411	*2.5*	13
Natural Resources	1,785	*1.9*	10
Veterans' Services and Benefits	5,157	*5.4*	28
Labor and Social Services	4,441	*4.7*	24
Public Assistance	2,056	*2.2*	11
Public Health	850	*0.9*	5
Promotion of Education, Science, and Research	770	*0.8*	4
Employment Services	323	*0.3*	2
Child and School Lunch Programs	244	*0.3*	1
Other	198	*0.2*	1
Housing and Community Development	591	*0.6*	3
General Government	1,711	*1.8*	9
Interest (Primarily on Public Debt)	9,385	*9.8*	52
Contingency	75	*0.1*	(40¢)
Other Payments to the Public	16,900	*17.7*	93
Totals	$95,300	*100%*	$525

Note: Totals do not necessarily add because of rounding.
Source: Same as Table 1, this chapter.

[1] Based on 181,500,000 estimate of total population, civilian and military, residing in the fifty States, the Commonwealth of Puerto Rico, the Trust Territories, and United States possessions in January, 1960.

ular income. One group of business operations, the public enterprise funds, was established by various appropriations; these funds act as lending or finance agencies, and receive additional funds only when Congress decides to increase their assets. The largest such funds are the Commodity Credit Corporation and the Export-Import Bank.

The activities and programs supported by national expenditures are discussed in subsequent sections; Table 3 serves primarily to show the broad pattern of government spending. In 1960 nearly 60 per cent of the budget was spent for national security; this was consistently the case from the early 1950's on. Of the remainder of the budget it is noteworthy that nearly one-third, about $10.2 billion, was for purposes related to social welfare: public assistance, public health, housing, veterans' services, and education. An additional $1.7 billion (down from $3.4 billion the preceding year) was for technical assistance abroad, also a form of welfare for those who need special attention. Payments and administrative expenses of the social insurance programs were an estimated $13.5 billion. All told, some $25 billion of the 1960 payments of the national government were for social welfare purposes, primarily for Americans but also for peoples in foreign countries. National social welfare spending for the average American was about $130. Comparable figures for previous years (when national spending and the gross national product were less, of course) were $23 in 1935, $24 in 1940, $62 in 1950, and $78 in 1955, with social insurance and veterans' programs accounting for most of the increase. As a percentage of gross national product, such spending has remained remarkably constant: 4.3 per cent in 1935, 3.4 per cent in 1940, 3.6 per cent in 1950, 3.5 per cent in 1955, and about 4.5 per cent in 1960 (including certain social insurance payments not taken into account in previous years).

REGULATION

THE ACTIVITIES of the national government can be divided into three types for ease of presentation: regulation; indirect operations, including consultative and information services; and direct operations. This tripartite classification rests in part on the extent of government involvement in any particular segment of human welfare and in part on the quality of that involvement. Because of the immense scope of national government activities the following discussion is far from complete in its treatment; instead it suggests their extent by giving examples in connection with over-all statistics on expenditures and beneficiaries.

Federal agencies that function in a directly and primarily regulatory capacity include the Federal Communications Commission, the Interstate Commerce Commission, the Bureau of Customs, the Food and Drug Administration, the Patent Office, the Atomic Energy Commission, and some others. Regulation is not entirely distinct from direct and indirect operating programs, however. For example, some of the grants-in-aid programs of the Department of Health, Education, and Welfare are intended to regulate State health, public assistance, and other programs as well as to provide financial assistance. Also, relatively minor functions of a regulatory character are part of some operating programs; the censorship-type activities of the Post Office Department are an example.

Economic Regulation

MOST NATIONAL regulatory activity is directed at maintaining and improving the general welfare by guiding American economic activity into smooth channels. Some regulatory activities also have the effect of promoting business; customs duties are of direct benefit to particular businesses when they keep competing imports off the American market except at relatively high prices. Other types of regulation benefit neither a given business nor its competitors, but the consumer. The Securities and Exchange Commission and the Food and Drug Administration are predominantly consumer-oriented, for example.

One major category of economic regulation is antitrust legislation, notably the Sherman and Clayton Acts, administered by the Antitrust Division of the Justice Department and the Federal Trade Commission, respectively. Public utilities also are subject to special bodies of national regulatory law, administered by separate agencies. Such regulation of business is, theoretically, designed to benefit the general welfare. The consuming public is to be protected from artificially high prices or rates, the small businessman is to be given recourse when he is unjustly squeezed by competitors. In enforcement, however, the antitrust principle is not always upheld.

The antitrust principle is sometimes suspended by Congressional enactment. For instance, the Reed-Bulwinkle Act of 1948 permits railroads to collaborate in fixing their rates. The Webb-Pomerene Export Trade Act allows exporters to form associations that are exempt from antitrust laws, provided that they adhere to certain regulations enforced by the Federal Trade Commission. Congress exempted insurance companies from antitrust laws in the face of a Supreme Court decision that they play a role in interstate commerce. In fact, the chief factor in the enforcement of antitrust legislation seems to have been the conclusion reached by interest groups, and by the government officials over whom these groups have the strongest influence, as to whether or not a competitive situation is advantageous to themselves.

Particularly since the depression of the 1930's, the national government has actively intervened in the financial operations of American businesses, especially of corporations. The Securities and Exchange Commission (SEC) is a quasi-judicial body, exempt from direct partisan control, designed to regulate stock markets and virtually the entire procedure of selling stocks and bonds. The SEC also administers the Public Utility Holding Company Act of 1935. Commodity exchange operations are subject to regulation by two bodies, the Commodity Exchange Commission, an independent agency, and the Commodity Exchange Authority in the Department of Agriculture.

Although only a small number of persons and businesses are directly affected by antitrust and financial operations control, the welfare of large numbers of consumers is the object of rate-fixing and quality regulation by national government agencies. The Interstate Commerce Commission, an independent agency with some 2,300 employees, fixes rates of most forms of transportation engaged in interstate commerce: railroads, ships, buses, trucks, pipelines, etc. In effect the Commission also establishes rates for commerce within a State, wherever that commerce competes with interstate commerce.

The quality of transportation, communication, and goods is regulated under the expanding concept of the constitutional grant of power over interstate commerce to the national government. The licensing powers of the Federal Communications Commission and the Civil Aeronautics Board give them vast authority over radio and television broadcasting and air transport and have largely shaped the development of these two industries. The granting or denying of licenses is nontheless accompanied by considerable political maneuvering, and acquiescence to pressures has been found even among commissioners themselves. The Food and Drug Administration, the Agricultural Marketing Service, and the Federal Trade Commission among them have responsibilities over products ranging from animal pelts and home music-study courses through seeds and cosmetics to aureomycin and peas. A generally unanticipated consequence of some early national regulation of industries and organizations was that unregulated or partially regulated groups chose to regulate themselves, fearing further national intervention. In the case of the film industry, suffering in the early 1920's from severe criticism of the morality to be found in its films, this fear led to self-regulation by the National Board of Review that was probably more severe than any governmental program toward the same end would have been. More recently, groups as diverse as labor unions and the broadcasting industry have vowed to police themselves to avoid national regulation.

In addition to national controls on business and agriculture, some of which have been outlined above, there is a body of national legislation affecting labor. This legislation is both regulatory and promotional. National regulatory legislation directed at workers' organizations consists of the Wagner Act (1935), the Taft-Hartley Act (1947), and the Landrum-Griffin Act (1959). Under the first, the National Labor Relations Board (NLRB) was created to supervise elections by which work-

374

ers might establish unions to negotiate with employers over wages, hours, and working conditions; and to assure that employers did not interfere in such elections. The Taft-Hartley Act, which represented a shift of emphasis in national (*i.e.*, Congressional) concern with union-management relations, attempted to place some restrictions on union power and operations. It outlawed the "closed shop" (though this portion of the act is not strictly enforced), and provided for punishing "unfair labor practices" of unions, among other things. The Landrum-Griffin Act was intended to protect workers and the general public from certain actions of union leaders, particularly in regard to the use of union funds, "sympathy strikes," and so forth; the act was generally acknowledged to be the most restrictive yet passed affecting labor unions.

Under the Republican administration begun in 1953 there began a deliberate shift in emphasis of control over industrial relations from the national government to the State governments. This was done by the simple administrative expedient of raising the minimum size of a plant over whose industrial relations the NLRB would take authority. There are also other national agencies that perform a fundamentally regulatory function in mediating labor disputes. Most prominent of these has been the Federal Mediation and Conciliation Service; it has no powers of enforcement, but merely supplies mediators. This it can do at its own initiation, however. Two other agencies, the National Mediation Board and the National Railroad Adjustment Board, were established to assure industrial peace on the railroads, but neither has powers of enforcement.

The second class of labor-related legislation consists of national regulation of business for the benefit of labor, *e.g.*, the Fair Labor Standards Act. This act and its amendments have provided that any person whose work is involved in interstate commerce must be paid no less than $1 an hour; the act has applied to only a part of the labor force, excluding agricultural workers for example, but there have been continuing efforts to increase its applicability and to raise the minimum to $1.25 an hour. The Bureau of Labor Standards (Department of Labor) administers another section of the act, which provides that goods produced by certain types of industries cannot be transported in interstate commerce if children under sixteen or eighteen (depending on the hazards of the industry) were involved in their manufacture.

Non-Economic Regulation

THERE ARE some national regulatory activities that are initiated for other purposes than regulating the national economy. Some of the activities of the Atomic Energy Commission concerning the peaceful development and use of atomic energy are of this nature. More notable are functions such as the control of immigration, deportation of undesirable aliens, the issuance of passports and visas, the control of narcotics, and certain censorship-type activities of the Post Office Department and the Bureau of Customs.

Censorship activities are only a small part of the activities of the latter two agencies, but such activities are believed to reflect a changing attitude on the part of some administrators toward regulatory functions. Walter Gellhorn, professor of law at Columbia University, has written:

> The subordination of the individual and the exaltation of the state have always impressed Americans as obnoxious. . . . Today, however, too many administrators seek, and too often are given, powers that unduly obscure traditional protections against expedient invasions of individual rights. . . . In the aggregate they reflect a shifting emphasis in governmental activity, a shift away from regulation for the public and toward policing of the public.[3]

The Post Office is, theoretically, not actually engaged in censorship. It is merely deciding on the type of business government chooses to transact. In so deciding, however, it exercises broad powers over what its administrators deem to be foreign propaganda and obscene and seditious writings. Most objections have been to the secrecy of the process. There have been no published regulations concerning the standards of judgment or procedures to be followed in dealing with undesirable materials. Any postal matter other than first-class mail (which cannot be inspected by any person in the Department) may be inspected for "obscenity" or other qualities by any postal employee. Should such a decision be made about any item found in the mails, it may be intercepted and forwarded to the departmental solicitor. It is examined by his staff and, if they uphold the judgment, then and only then is the person who mailed it informed, and notified that he has fifteen days in which to show cause why the material should not be destroyed. There is no provision for formal hearing, though a civil action can be brought against the Post Office in the courts to have the material judged on its merits.

The Bureau of Customs, in contrast, does not make such extreme rulings and its decisions are subject to re-examination by both judge and jury, if desired. Its powers are as broad as those of the Post Office, however. It is permitted to withhold foreign propaganda, obscene materials, and other offensive materials that enter the country other than through the mails. The Bureau also examines some types of mail arriving from

[3] *Individual Freedom and Governmental Restraints.* Baton Rouge: Louisiana State University Press, 1956, pp. 46–47.

overseas, and if it finds material it considers questionable it turns it over to the Post Office for final disposition. Journals and other materials from Communist countries are frequently confiscated at Customs, as have been issues of the *London Economist*. During the early 1950's almost any material printed in Russian, including books by Shakespeare, Chekhov, Dickens, and Tolstoy, as well as more obvious propaganda materials, was likely to be confiscated. In one month in the mid-1950's it was reported that Customs seized 56,500 pieces of "foreign propaganda."[4]

The number of persons aggrieved or harmed by these last two types of regulation is probably a fraction of one per cent of the population. This raises a question that has both theoretical and practical importance, however. When a welfare institution tries to assure the general welfare, or the welfare of particular groups, it may hurt some people and even other organizations. Whenever more support is asked for a particular national welfare program, there is usually that much less support available for some other welfare programs. Every welfare activity thus involves the questions: Who benefits and how much? Who and what suffers, and how much? Finally, does the benefit offset the harm? These questions can be and are asked of both governmental and non-governmental welfare programs, and by many persons, but it may be that they are not asked often enough nor answered well enough.

INDIRECT OPERATIONS

INDIRECT OPERATIONS are those national programs designed to supplement or assist the operations of other social institutions. The practice of agriculture, for example, has remained almost entirely in private hands, but the government has been called upon to institute a number of programs intended to smooth its operation. Assistance is similarly provided business (subsidized airlines, shipping firms, railways), health and welfare (old-age assistance, aid to the disabled, public health services), education (advice, loans, grants for special purposes), and science (National Science Foundation activities, government research contracts). The characteristic devices of supplementary and indirect operation are the grant-in-aid, with concomitant "minimum standards"; expert assistance and advice; and the contract. These are not all, however. The national government has been quite inventive in devising new forms of aid, such as giving tax rebates to particular businesses, passing permissive regulations, refunding certain types of revenue to State and other governments (taxes from dependent areas such as Puerto Rico

[4] *Ibid.*, pp. 83–85, 185–88.

and the Virgin Islands are returned to their governments, for example), administering trust funds such as unemployment insurance for the States, and so forth.

Many indirect national operations are aimed particularly at benefiting specific groups that have been publicly defined as underprivileged or as otherwise needing special assistance. These include such programs as aid to dependent children, aid to the blind, promotion of education, aid to housing and community redevelopment, and assistance to agriculture and transportation, as well as overseas economic and technical assistance programs, discussed in Chapter 15. Other indirect programs are designed primarily to benefit the general welfare; these include public health and medical research programs and the promotion of science and research.

A certain degree of redistribution of the national income takes place in indirect programs, specifically in those involving grants-in-aid. This is not the sort of redistribution that takes place when a person earning $20,000 is taxed at a much higher rate than the person earning $3,000, but a redistribution among the States; grants-in-aid are distributed to State and local governments without reference to the proportions of tax revenues received from their residents and businesses. It is often assumed that national grants-in-aid programs benefit the low-income southern States at the expense of the industrialized States of the Northeast. This is true of some programs administered by the Department of Health, Education, and Welfare, but is only partly true for all grant programs taken together, as the data in Table 4 suggest. The national

TABLE 4

FEDERAL GRANTS-IN-AID TO STATE AND LOCAL GOVERNMENTS, 1957

States (by Decreasing Federal Contribution per Capita)	Federal Contribution Per Capita	Total Income Per Capita [1]	Grants as Percentage of Total State and Local Revenues
Wyoming	$84.88	$2,040	24.8%
New Mexico	66.68	1,690	22.6
Nevada	62.36	2,420 *	17.4
Montana	48.84	1,900	17.7
Oklahoma	40.75	1,620	17.5
Colorado	40.02	2,000	14.8
South Dakota	39.73	1,530	16.4
Oregon	38.53	1,910	13.9
Louisiana	38.28	1,570	14.7
Idaho	36.27	1,630	16.0
California	33.51	2,520 *	10.7
Utah	33.25	1,690	14.5
Alabama	32.16	1,320	19.9

States (by Decreasing Federal Contribution per Capita)	Federal Contribution Per Capita	Total Income Per Capita [1]	Grants as Percentage of Total State and Local Revenues
North Dakota	$31.96	*$1,440*	12.3%
Arizona	31.25	1,750	12.8
Missouri	30.24	1,940	16.7
Washington	29.73	2,130	11.2
Vermont	29.72	*1,670*	13.0
Arkansas	28.38	*1,150*	18.6
Kansas	27.63	1,790	11.7
Mississippi	27.28	960	17.0
North Carolina	26.25	*1,320*	16.1
Georgia	25.75	*1,430*	14.3
Texas	25.47	1,790	12.8
Minnesota	23.88	1,850	9.8
Rhode Island	23.52	1,990	12.1
Tennessee	23.50	*1,380*	14.2
Nebraska	23.50	1,820	12.0
Maine	23.49	1,660	11.7
United States (*Average*)	$22.57	$2,030	10.1%
Iowa	22.27	1,810	9.7
Kentucky	21.87	*1,370*	14.5
Florida	21.25	1,840	9.7
South Carolina	19.76	*1,180*	13.2
West Virginia	19.13	*1,550*	12.7
Delaware	18.78	2,740 *	9.1
Michigan	18.55	2,140	7.9
New Hampshire	18.24	1,860	9.3
Massachusetts	18.21	2,340 *	7.2
Maryland	17.90	2,160	8.6
Virginia	17.29	1,660	9.6
Wisconsin	16.24	1,920	7.1
Ohio	15.99	2,260	8.0
New York	15.74	2,580 *	5.6
Illinois	13.89	2,450 *	6.9
Connecticut	13.38	2,820 *	5.4
Pennsylvania	12.70	2,110	6.4
Indiana	12.54	2,010	6.8
New Jersey	9.97	2,500 *	4.7

Source: *Statistical Abstract* 1959, pp. 311, 371.

[1] Average personal income of the residents of each State. Italicized figures are for the twelve States with the lowest per capita income; asterisked figures are for the eight States with the highest per capita income.

government made grants-in-aid totaling $3.95 billion in 1957, about $22.57 per person in the United States. The States that received the largest contributions per capita were not the low-income southern States, however, but the mountain States. The people of Wyoming received $85 per person from the national government, the people of New Mexico and Nevada $67 and $62, respectively. The States with the lowest per capita income were Mississippi ($960), Arkansas ($1,150), South Carolina ($1,180), and Alabama and North Carolina ($1,320 in both). All but South Carolina received more than the average national grant per person, yet none received more than $32.

There are several reasons for this disparity in the distribution of federal grants to States. One is that the mountain States are sparsely populated, with the result that the operating and overhead costs of a federally sponsored program are higher than in more densely populated areas. Another is that there are natural resources and highway programs in these States whose expenditures are determined by the extent of territory, not by population. Finally, each of the mountain States has a disproportionately large delegation in Congress; they provide sixteen of the senators, almost one-sixth, but contain only one-twenty-fifth of the population, and consequently have benefited from pork-barrel legislation. Some senators from the mountain States have been particularly noteworthy for the amount of federal funds they have helped secure for their States.

In general, however, the low-income States benefit more from grants-in-aid than do high-income States. Nine of the twelve States with the lowest per capita income received more than the average grant per capita and six of the eight States with high incomes received less, some of them much less, than the average federal grant per person.

There are many formulas for the allotment of grant-in-aid funds among the States. For example, the surgeon general is authorized to determine Public Health Service allotments for health services on the basis of population, the extent of a given State's health problems, and its financial need, that is, the State's ability to raise its own funds. This is a very simple allotment scheme, leaving considerable freedom in administrative hands. A few formulas are determined by State contributions on a matching or ratio basis. Most, however, are determined by more complex systems. The Fish and Wildlife Restoration and Management grants-in-aid programs, though they involve only about $13 million in federal aid annually, have an allotment system involving the area of the State, number of fishing licenses issued, percentages in relation to other State percentages, and matching requirements. Some allotments, as in three grant programs administered by the Office of Vocational Rehabilitation, are specified in the appropriation acts.

The remainder of this section discusses some specific indirect programs, including those dealing with health, social services, education, agriculture, and some others.

Health

THE PERFORMANCE of any major national function is so complex a matter that it almost defies description. National health functions, those concerned with public health and medical care activities, are a case in point.

The President's budget message for fiscal 1961 contained a list of about fifty-five major national government functions, and their past and proposed expenditures. Of these, only three appeared to have any direct relation to public health: "Veterans hospitals and medical care"; "Promotion of public health"; and "Promotion of science, research, libraries, and museums." [4] A glance at an organizational chart of federal executive offices suggests a somewhat more complicated picture. The Department of Health, Education, and Welfare (HEW) contains not only the Public Health Service but also such health-related agencies as the Food and Drug Administration, certain offices in the Social Security Administration, the Office of Vocational Rehabilitation (some of whose activities are concerned with health and medical care), and others. The Department of the Navy has a Bureau of Medicine and Surgery. The Bureau of Mines, in the Department of Interior, has a Division of Health. The Tennessee Valley Authority (TVA) has a Division of Health and Safety.[5]

But this is still only a suggestion of national government health activities. A Public Health Service publication notes that, in the early 1950's, all of the departments except the Post Office were engaged in significant health-related activities, as well as sixteen independent agencies, including the Civil Aeronautics Board (air safety programs), the Atomic Energy Commission (research, grants-in-aid, distribution of safety information), and the Railroad Retirement Board (administration of sickness benefits).[6] Within each department and agency there may be from one to dozens of bureaus, offices, divisions, and sections involved in various types of health programs. A partial list of specific health-related activities carried out by these various agencies includes:

(A) Health Services for the General Public
    (1) Control of communicable diseases
    (2) Control of chronic diseases
    (3) Maternal and child health

[4] Reproduced in "President's Budget Message," *New York Times*, Jan. 19, 1960.
[5] *Organization of Federal Executive Departments and Agencies*. Washington, D.C.: USGPO, 1959 (chart).
[6] *Guide to Health Organization in the United States: 1951*. Public Health Service. Washington, D.C.: USGPO, 1953, pp. 5–13.

        (4) School health
        (5) Nutrition
        (6) Dental health
        (7) Mental health
        (8) Occupational health
        (9) Accident prevention
      (10) Environmental sanitation (ranging from water pollution control to food and drug control)
      (11) Epidemic and disaster aid
  (B) Medical and Hospital Care for Specific Beneficiaries
        (1) General illness
        (2) Tuberculosis
        (3) Mental disorders
        (4) Crippled children
        (5) Rehabilitation
        (6) Preventive medicine
        (7) Dental services
  (C) Statistical Reports Related to Health
  (D) Training of Health Personnel
  (E) Construction of Facilities Related to Health
        (1) Hospitals
        (2) Health centers
        (3) Waste treatment works
        (4) Housing
        (5) Research and training facilities
        (6) Water works
        (7) Rural electrification
  (F) Participation in International Health Activities.

There are nine general means of operation that may be used in carrying out these functions; most of them are used by one agency or another in performing any given function listed above. They are:

  (1) Direct provision of medical services
  (2) Grants-in-aid
  (3) Studies and demonstrations
  (4) Regulation
  (5) Conduct of research activities
  (6) Advisory service and the development of standards
  (7) Information and popular education
  (8) Credit and loans for health services
  (9) Loans of personnel.

The Department of Interior, for example, is involved in health-related activities to a relatively minor extent, yet it undertakes a wide variety of such functions; it has three bureaus, an office, and two services involved in health work. The Bureau of Indian Affairs has helped to provide health service and medical care for some 300,000 reservation Indians, including health education, sanitation, disease prevention, and nutrition studies, as well as direct medical care. The Bureau of Mines provides inspection services to mining industries, undertakes studies of health and safety conditions, publishes related information, and trains mineworkers in safety methods. The Bureau of Reclamation includes among its activities the abatement of sedimentation, salination, and pollution of streams and other watercourses. The Office of Territories is involved in all operating medical programs in United States territories and possessions, and in some cases provides public health programs and medical and hospital care. The Fish and Wildlife Service promotes "programs for the destruction of rodents" and for the elimination of stream pollution. It conducts and makes grants for research on the production of vitamins and the processing of fishery products. It promulgates standards of sanitation, quality, and purity in regard to fisheries. It also provides medical and dental services to the inhabitants of the Pribilof Islands and has maintained medical facilities on the islands of St. Paul and St. George, these latter services being provided in connection with the Alaskan fisheries activities. Finally, the National Park Service is concerned with the sanitation of recreational areas and camp facilities throughout the national park system.[7]

Although many health activities are scattered throughout the federal administrative agencies, a number are concentrated in the Public Health Service of HEW. The Public Health Service has four major divisions:

(1) The Office of the Surgeon General is concerned primarily with staff services, such as studying health needs and services, providing advisory services to State and other health agencies, planning, and coordination.

(2) The Bureau of Medical Services operates a number of medical facilities, including sixteen hospitals, twenty-six outpatient clinics, and ninety-eight out-patient offices for merchant seamen, military personnel, and their dependents; it operates fifty-five hospitals for Indians and Eskimos, eighteen Indian health centers, and eighteen Indian school health centers, and some two hundred other field health installations. It enforces quarantine regulations and conducts medical examinations of immigrants. It also provides technical and consultative services to States for the survey, planning, and construction of hospitals and other health facilities and administers a small grants-in-aid program for research on the development and coordination of hospital services and facilities.

(3) Also within the Public Health Service are the seven National

[7] *Ibid.*, pp. 32–33, and *United States Government Organization Manual 1958–59*, General Services Administration. Washington, D.C.: USGPO, 1958, pp. 220–40.

Institutes of Health, which conduct and sponsor research on cancer, heart disease, allergy and infectious diseases, arthritis and metabolic diseases, neurological diseases and blindness, dental care, and mental health. The manufacture and sale of toxins, serums, and vaccines are regulated by the associated Division of Biologics Standards.

(4) The major operating bureau of the Public Health Service is the Bureau of State Services, which directs programs of technical assistance to State and local public health offices, helps train personnel, conducts field surveys and demonstrations, and administers certain grants-in-aid programs. In 1953 State agencies participating in grant programs administered by the Public Health Service expended $280 million, about $35 million of which was in specific grants for venereal disease, cancer, and tuberculosis control, industrial waste studies, hospital survey and planning, and other health purposes.[8]

National expenditures for public health have increased sharply in recent years. In his 1961 budget message, delivered to Congress in January, 1960, President Eisenhower stated that

> the Federal Government has expanded its public health programs and is actively seeking solutions to the Nation's health problems. Expenditures in the fiscal year 1961 are estimated to total $904 million, which is $53 million more than in 1960 and nearly three times the level five years earlier. The largest part of the increase is for medical research and training of research workers through programs of the National Institutes of Health, for which the estimated expenditures of $390 million in 1961 will be four times as great as five years ago. Expenditures for hospital construction grants are estimated at $161 million in 1961, a threefold increase over the same period.[9]

In addition to the health institute and hospital construction expenditures, the 1961 budget called for $29 million for the construction of health research facilities and $45 million for construction of waste treatment facilities. A number of other programs, including a number outside the Public Health Service, involved proposed expenditures of $279 million. In his budget message the President stressed especially programs for the control of water and air pollution and for radiological health control activities.

The most recent health-related federal program, designed to help provide medical care for the needy aged, was passed by the 86th Congress Second Session in September, 1960. The program has two features:

[8] *United States Government Organization Manual 1958–59*, pp. 330–34; Wayne Vasey, *Government and Social Welfare*, New York: Henry Holt, 1958, pp. 361–63; *A Study Committee Report on Federal Aid to Public Health*, Commission on Intergovernmental Relations, Washington, D.C.: USGPO, 1955, pp. 40–46.
[9] "President's Budget Message," *New York Times*, Jan. 19, 1960.

the improvement of medical care presently provided under the federal-State old-age assistance program (described in the following section), and provision for a new medical-care program to aid the aged who are not on the assistance rolls but who cannot pay medical bills. The program operates through a complex grant-in-aid system, which will cost the federal government between $140 and $150 million annually and increase to about $340 million per year by 1965. Essentially, federal grants must be matched by the States, most of which have already provided some medical assistance for the aged. In about half the States, notably the southern and mountain States, State and local funds for these purposes will have to remain the same or be increased, if the States are to receive full benefit of the available federal grants. In the other States, the excess federal funds will take the place of current State and local expenditures, thus releasing the State and local funds for further improving medical care for old-age assistance recipients, or helping provide for others unable to meet medical bills. However, it was only *expected* that the States would use these "released" funds for medical-care purposes; no requirement that they do so was written into the law. This relative lack of federal requirements was one of the criticized features of the program; another was its lack of comprehensiveness.[10]

Finally, two grants-in-aid programs of the Children's Bureau are designed for specific health purposes. These programs, for maternal and child health services and for crippled children's services, are described in the previous chapter; they have involved annual grants to the States of about $30 million. In these as in other health-related grant programs, the extent of aid varies from State to State. Under the maternal and child health services program in 1953, for example, the national government contributed less than 10 per cent of the operating costs of the related agencies in four States—California, Michigan, New York, and Pennsylvania; but it contributed more than 50 per cent of the agency costs in fifteen other States, and more than 60 per cent for those in North Carolina, West Virginia, and the Virgin Islands.[11]

Certain other types of national health activities are discussed below. Trust funds administered by the national government, which involve some payments for medical services, are included under "Direct Operations." Health services for veterans are summarized in the final section. Vocational rehabilitation services, provided by State and local governments and financed in part by national grants (amounting to $46.5 million to all States and territories in 1959), are discussed in the preceding chapter.

[10] "142 Million Set for Needy Aged." *New York Times,* Sept. 15, 1960.
[11] *A Study Committee Report on Federal Aid to Public Health,* pp. 40–46.

Social Services and Assistance

THE NATIONAL GOVERNMENT provides social services and assistance in many forms. It is generally interested in reducing or eliminating the social ills, as they are called, of poverty, poor health, family disintegration, unemployment, and poor living quarters. At least eleven national grants-in-aid programs are directed at manifestations of these problems: medical care for needy aged, public assistance, employment security, school lunches, public health services, construction of health facilities, crippled children's services, child welfare services, vocational rehabilitation, low-rent public housing, and slum clearance and urban renewal. The social insurance funds are another approach to many of the same problems. Similarly, national controls and protections affecting business and labor organizations are in large part directed toward the general goal of social welfare. Proposed national programs such as socialized medicine and national health insurance for the aging would have the object of eliminating social ills, and thus would be part of the national government's social welfare system. Many of these programs are discussed elsewhere in this survey; this section describes five major national programs designed for social welfare purposes in the more restricted sense of the term. These are the four public assistance programs and the employment security program.

PUBLIC ASSISTANCE: The public assistance programs provide financial aid to the aged (old-age assistance, OAA), the blind, dependent children, and the permanently and totally disabled. These programs are operated on a grant-in-aid basis. In most of them the national government pays $24 of the first $30 paid monthly by the State, plus from 50 to 65 per cent of the remainder of the State payment, up to a combined total of $65 per month. In 1959 national grants were $1,957 million, and total payments to beneficiaries, including State contributions, were about $3.34 billion. It was estimated that by 1961 national grants would be about $2.1 billion. Some data on the nationally financed public assistance programs are given in Table 5.

In 1959 more than five million persons received benefits under the four programs; nearly half of them were people over sixty-five. Most of the aged who received OAA were not eligible for Old-Age and Survivors Insurance (OASI); the others, about one-fifth of all OAA recipients, were receiving OASI payments considered insufficient for their needs. Aid also was given to about 2.3 million dependent children of some 780,000 families; these children were about 3.5 per cent of all children under eighteen in the United States.

These four public assistance programs were established by the Social

386

TABLE 5

PUBLIC ASSISTANCE PROGRAMS, 1959 [1]

Program	Federal Grants (*In Thousands of Dollars*)	Number of Recipients	Average Monthly Payment
Old-Age Assistance	$1,132,194	2,394,100	$65.86
Aid to Dependent Children	626,546	2,272,100 [2]	37.70 [2]
Aid to Permanently and Totally Disabled	150,739	350,300	64.64
Aid to Blind	47,619	109,100	71.29
Totals	$1,957,098	5,125,000 est.)	
Total Assistance Payments	$3,340,000 (est.) [3]		

Source: *Statistical Abstract* 1960, pp. 289–91.

[1] Includes data on Alaska, Hawaii, Puerto Rico, and the Virgin Islands. Also see footnote 3, below.
[2] Number of children and average payment per child; the children were members of 778,832 families, whose average monthly payment was $110.
[3] Excludes general assistance payments, which are made under programs that are entirely State and local in administration and financing; general assistance programs are discussed in the previous chapter.

Security Act of 1935 and have been in continuous operation since 1936, though numerous legislative changes have been made in them. The Social Security Act makes nine requirements of the operating programs of each State that wishes to participate in any one of the public assistance programs. These are:

(1) Effectiveness of the plan in all political subdivisions.
(2) Financial participation by the State.
(3) Administration or supervision of administration of the plan by a single State agency.
(4) Provision for a fair hearing to any individual whose claim is denied or not promptly acted upon.
(5) Efficient administrative methods, including the establishment of a classified civil service system for State personnel.
(6) Reports as required by the national government.
(7) Taking into consideration any other income and resources available to the recipient in determining the amount of assistance payments.
(8) Restrictions on the use or disclosure of information on recipients.
(9) Opportunity to apply to all who wish to do so, and provision of assistance with reasonable promptness to all eligible persons.

There are also certain requirements applying to specific programs. For example, in old-age assistance, aid to the blind, and aid to the disabled if payments are made to individuals in governmental or non-governmental institutions there must be State authorities responsible for establishing and maintaining standards for the institutions involved.[12]

These requirements are fairly typical of the administrative strictures of other federal grants-in-aid programs. The sanction that may be applied, should a State agency fail to comply, is the simple one of withholding funds. This sanction is seldom, if ever, imposed once the State has decided to participate in the program, for few State administrators are willing to forgo national funds. State agencies receiving national grants usually work under the watchful eyes of supervisors from regional offices of the national agency; supervisors from the Bureau of Public Assistance (HEW) make full inspections of State public assistance programs once a year, for example, as well as occasional spot checks. National offices at the regional and national level also provide administrative assistance in various forms to State agencies that encounter unusual problems.

Public assistance in general has been one of the most rapidly expanding sectors of government social welfare activity. In terms of spending, for example, federal government expenditures increased 685 per cent between 1939 and 1959, while State and local costs increased 117 per cent (according to a 1960 Tax Foundation study, *Public Assistance: A Survey of Selected Aspects of State Programs*). In 1960, four per cent of the population, nearly seven million persons, were receiving some kind of assistance payment every month, more people than at any time since 1939. (The seven million total includes recipients of State Old-Age Assistance and also the parent or parents of children benefiting from the Aid to Dependent Children program.) The greatest increase has been in the Aid to Dependent Children program; some three million persons, parents included, received about $1 billion in such aid in 1959, as much as was paid out in *all* public assistance programs in 1939. More than one-fifth of the dependent children receiving aid were illegitimate.

EMPLOYMENT SECURITY: The national government shares with the State governments the responsibility for unemployment insurance and public employment offices. The Bureau of Employment Security, in the Department of Labor, is the agency that carries out these responsibilities on the national level. Unemployment insurance is ad-

[12] "Public Assistance," in A *Description of Twenty-five Federal Grant-in-Aid Programs*, Commission on Intergovernmental Relations, Washington, D.C.: USGPO, 1955, pp. 113–14.

ministered directly by the States from taxes collected by them and held on deposit in the U.S. Treasury; this is discussed in the preceding chapter. The Bureau of Employment Security reviews State unemployment legislation and administration, extends various forms of technical assistance and information to related State agencies, and conducts research.

A major function of the Bureau is the coordination and guidance of public employment offices, which is done through the Bureau's U.S. Employment Service. There are about 1,800 full-time and 2,000 part-time local public employment offices in the United States; the Service has assisted in their establishment, prescribes minimum standards of efficiency for them, and provides them with various types of information. More specifically, the Service

> guides and assists the States in their placement functions; in their occupational analysis, counseling, and testing functions; in maximizing employment opportunities for veterans, older workers, youth, handicapped workers, and members of minority groups; in the promotion of community efforts toward the greatest possible use of the labor force; in the compilation, analysis, and dissemination of labor market information; and in the promotion of the use by employers of the public employment service and the providing of employers with materials and techniques for effective use of manpower.[13]

The Service has special units to provide employment services for veterans, operates a farm placement service, and directly maintains employment service facilities in the District of Columbia.

The operating and other costs of the Bureau are met by a 0.3 per cent payroll tax, collected in conjunction with the State unemployment insurance tax on payrolls. A large part of these funds are granted to the States for the administration of unemployment security. Such grants totaled $324 million in 1958, $323 million in 1960.

Other Indirect Operations

THE FOREGOING SECTIONS deal with only some of the federal programs that operate by indirect means. There are many others, involving such fields as education, housing, agriculture, commerce, and even art.

EDUCATION: Most assistance by the national government for education has been provided by indirect means, in grants and loans. In fiscal 1960 the national government spent about $550 million in the promotion of education. A number of educational programs are centered in the Office of Education (HEW), including aid for elementary and

[13] *United States Government Organization Manual 1958–59*, p. 314.

secondary schools in federally affected areas ($234 million in 1960); the defense education program ($134 million in 1960), which makes loans to college students, conducts educational research, and makes grants for fellowships, special teaching equipment, and some types of vocational training; and assistance for general vocational education (about $40 million in 1960). The Office has extensive programs for educational research, collecting and distributing educational information, and providing advisory services.

National Science Foundation grants directly related to education were more than $50 million in 1960, while Indian, Eskimo, and territorial school systems and the educational programs of a few agencies outside the Department of Health, Education and Welfare cost about $60 million. The national government also operates the military academies, Howard University, and schools in the District of Columbia. Veterans' education and training, discussed in a subsequent section, cost $445 million.

There are still other present or proposed forms of national aid to education. One of them is the school lunch program, another is the special milk program (cf. Chapter 8); they cost the national government $234 million in 1960. In one year in the mid-1950's the value of surplus property allocated to various educational institutions was $140 million. One important new plan was outlined in President Eisenhower's 1961 budget message:

> Congressional approval of the administration's proposals for aid to higher educational institutions is . . . essential. The enrollment growth facing colleges and universities from 1960 to 1975 brings a need for additional academic, housing, and related educational facilities. To help colleges finance the construction required, the administration's proposal would authorize Federal guarantees of $1 billion in bonds with interest subject to Federal taxation, and would provide Federal grants, payable over 20 years, equal to 25% of the principal of $2 billion of bonds. This program would provide aid on a much broader basis, and result in the construction of much larger total amounts of college facilities per dollar of Federal expenditures, than the present more limited college housing loan program.[14]

AIDS TO HOUSING: There are three types of federal aid to housing: urban renewal programs, public housing assistance, and loan and mortgage operations. Urban renewal and community development have become of particular interest in recent years; in the decade of the 1950's, when grants for such projects were first authorized, more than a

[14] "President's Budget Message," New York Times, Jan. 19, 1960.

thousand were initiated, but by the beginning of 1960, 647 were still in the planning stage, 355 were in progress, and only 26 had been completed. Sixty-five were scheduled for completion in 1960 and 1961. In 1960 the Urban Renewal Administration spent about $200 million on such projects. Low-rent public housing has been of long-standing concern for the national government. It was estimated that by mid-1961 about half a million federally aided housing units would be occupied, with another 125,000 under contract. The Housing Act of 1959 authorized 37,000 additional units, among them housing for the aged. Expenditures for public housing programs in 1960 were $130 million (also cf. Chapter 12).

A number of national mortgage and loan operations are related to housing. The Housing and Home Finance Agency has been given authority to borrow $100 million from the U.S. Treasury for loans to small communities for public facilities. The Federal Housing Administration underwriters a good share of the mortgages on residential housing and the Federal National Mortgage Association in 1960 borrowed $56 million from the Treasury to purchase mortgages under its special assistance program. There are also loans available for farm housing, college housing loans represented an outlay of $186 million by the national government in 1960, and veterans' housing loans in 1960 amounted to $230 million.

Aɪᴅ ᴛᴏ Aɢʀɪᴄᴜʟᴛᴜʀᴇ: The means of federal assistance to farmers are as varied as the motives for such assistance: purchases of surpluses, the soil-bank program, payments to farmers who leave land fallow, loans, and the less-publicized and relatively inexpensive agricultural conservation, research, and information services. Initially, agriculture was deemed to deserve assistance for various reasons. During the depression, many farmers were in distress—their land was being blown away or washed down rivers; they could not support their families, much less purchase seeds for new plantings. To alleviate their distress the national government developed programs to conserve and develop agricultural land and water resources, and made loans available. Such programs not only alleviated immediate distress, they helped prevent the nation from losing its cropland and much of its food supply along with the skilled persons capable of farming. Agricultural price stabilization, begun in 1933, had a similar combination of purposes. By surplus crop purchases the government could assure individual farmers that they would not be forced into penury by being unable to market their crops at a profit. The stored surpluses were expected to be of general benefit, by leveling out price fluctuations for the consumer between bumper and lean crop years. Furthermore, they provided the government with a backlog of readily available resources for wartime use and for overseas distribution.

But in the 1950's things happened to the farm programs never anticipated by its initiators. Owing largely to repeated bumper crops, corporation farming, and new techniques, far program costs rose from $1 billion in 1952 to $6.5 billion in 1959, then decreased somewhat to $5.1 billion in 1960. The costs of most programs increased relatively little. Conservation and research cost $500 million in 1952, somewhat over $1 billion in 1960; these funds support a great many activities in redirecting land use, preventing erosion, watershed protection, technical assistance to farmers, agricultural research, and rural development. Farm ownership and rural electrification program costs increased from $500 million to $575 million over the same period. The greatest increase came in the price and income stabilization programs, which cost about $5.1 billion in 1959 and $3.5 billion in 1960. (Their anticipated 1961 costs were $4 billion.)

By spring of 1959 the rigid price-support program, administered by the Commodity Credit Corporation, had piled up a $9 billion inventory of wheat, corn, cotton, and other farm surplus products, and there was little prospect short of a span of lean years or dumping on the international market for getting rid of it. By July, 1960, wheat stocks alone were nearly 1.4 billion bushels, enough for more than two years of domestic consumption without additional production. Benefits under the program have by no means been going solely to the small farmers, many of whom are still relatively impoverished. The largest amounts of assistance, at least in terms of direct payments, go to the largest producers, by the nature of the program. For example, ten large farm operators in 1958 received a total of $4 million in price-support and soil-bank funds; 1,200 of Delaware's 6,000 farmers received soil-bank payments totaling $900,000.

There are very strong political demands at least for maintaining if not increasing price supports. A powerful economic motive for these political demands is described in theoretical terms by an economist:

An example of unintended effects of subsidies . . . is to be found in the agricultural price-support program. When a subsidy is not available to all, but is restricted to current owners of land, it becomes a marketable asset. . . . A farmer who already has an allotment discovers that so long as the price-support policy remains in effect the net value of his crops after subsidy is enhanced.

Naturally this increment is capitalized along with his other net receipts in arriving at a valuation of his property. Suppose, however, that in the course of ten years all the farms change hands. The new owners "buy free" of the subsidy. So long as it is believed that the payments will be continued, the original owner can realize a large capital gain. All foreseeable future government price-support payments are capitalized in the sale price. The public is then taxed year after year to reimburse the new owners. But the latter gain nothing from the subsidy, and in fact constitute a powerful pressure group for its continuation, since they would incur a loss if it were given up.[15]

One possible solution to the price-support problem, though previously considered politically unacceptable, would follow the plan proposed in 1949 by Secretary of Agriculture Brannan. Rather than purchase the surpluses the national government would have farmers sell their crops on the market for whatever they would bring, and then reimburse the farmers with periodical checks making up the difference between market prices and support prices. The government thus would be spared storage costs, which have reached about $1.5 million a day, and the lowered market prices would mean cheaper food for the consumer. The system has been opposed for a variety of reasons, among them the contention of farmers that there is some sort of immorality involved in accepting government payments without giving goods to the government in exchange.

AID TO COMMERCE AND BUSINESS: The national government has assumed extensive responsibilities for airways, highways, and water transportation. The airways modernization program of the Federal Aviation Agency, the interstate highway system financed from the Highway Trust Fund, and extensive subsidies for the United States merchant fleet are examples. The 1960 costs of promotion of aviation were $627 million, costs of water transportation promotion were $537 million; the latter included several hundred millions in direct and indirect subsidy. The Highway Trust Fund, built up by the highway fuel tax of four cents a gallon (the 1959–60 rate) and by other excise tax revenues, paid out more than $2.5 billion in grants for State highway construction in 1960; other nationally financed highways, in national forests and on public lands, cost $45 million.

The Small Business Administration provided loans and other forms of financial assistance to small businesses, at a net cost of $102 million in 1960. Regulation of commerce and finance, designed with the general welfare in mind, also benefits the business system as a whole; it cost $58 million in 1960. Still other forms of assistance to business, including various research and information services, special subsidies, and so forth, cost $48 million.

[15] Kenyon Poole. *Public Finance and Economic Welfare.* New York: 1956, Holt, Rinehart and Winston, Inc., pp. 140–41. Copyright 1956 by Kenyon E. Poole.

A noteworthy commentary on the executive and legislative frames of mind is the fact that President Eisenhower's 1961 budget message included space exploration and flight technology projects under the heading of "Commerce and Housing." The National Aeronautics and Space Administration is responsible for these non-military space projects; it is expected to "concentrate on developing the large space vehicle systems essential to the exploration of space." Expenditures for the non-military space program, under way only since 1958, have increased rapidly, from $145 million in 1959 to $325 million in 1960, with estimated costs for 1961 of $600 million.[16]

ART: National assistance for the arts has not only been frequently and seriously proposed, in some cases it has been given. The Work Projects Administration (WPA) of the 1930's had certain projects for writers and artists, for example, and the government in effect partly subsidizes the arts through tax exemptions to foundations and other non-profit organizations that subsidize artists. Some still feel, however, that in a sense Americans are "artistically underprivileged," and particularly that they have inadequate opportunities to experience the performing arts. The practice of government aid to the arts in Western European nations and especially in the Soviet Union are often cited.[17] Such arguments must contend with the fact that most Americans seem to prefer television and films as means of satisfying their desires for entertainment, whatever their artistic qualities, even when "live" performances are available.

It is not often suggested that artists themselves be given direct assistance, but some people have proposed that the tax structure be modified on their behalf. A novelist, playwright, or painter often works for several years to produce a salable work, and thus may have occasional years of high income interspersed among many years of low income; in his high-income years he is nevertheless taxed heavily. A proposed modification would allow him to prorate income from artistic products over a span of years; an administrative and legislative drawback would be determining what is and what is not an artistic product. (Similar tax advantages have been suggested for inventors and professional athletes, for the latter because they have high earning capacity for only a short span of years.) An artists' subsidy *via* tax benefits would cost relatively little, would improve their financial status and hence might implement their work, and would satisfy one concept of social justice.

[16] "President's Budget Message," *New York Times*, Jan. 19, 1960.
[17] For example, cf. Howard Taubman, "Who Should Pay the Bill for the Arts?" *New York Times Magazine*, Dec. 7, 1958, pp. 61 ff.

DIRECT OPERATIONS

THE NATIONAL GOVERNMENT is involved in three types of direct operations. A few functions, notably national security, are almost exclusively pre-empted and performed by the national government. A more varied group of activities, such as the Old-Age and Survivors Insurance system (OASI), the protection and development of natural resources, and the provision of recreational facilities, are undertaken by the national government and also, in comparable forms, by subordinate units of government, or commercial interests, or both. International economic and technical development, an activity of this second type, is discussed in the following chapter. Finally, the national government conducts some 19,000 public enterprises, similar or identical to commercial-type operations but initiated for general welfare purposes or for the purposes of the national government *per se*. Some major activities of this sort are the Post Office, the Tennessee Valley Authority, the Government Printing Office, and the General Services Administration.

National Security and Foreign Affairs

NATIONAL SECURITY is the sole prerogative of the national government, the only possible alternative being its conduct by an independent international authority. In the 1950's it became the largest and most ramified of federal operations. In 1960 it required 58 per cent of federal budget expenditures, $46.65 billion of $78.38 billion; 2.5 million armed services personnel; and more than 45 per cent of the 2.35 million federal civilian employees. The armed forces themselves have the evident purpose of defending the United States from military attack. However, they also carry out certain peacetime welfare tasks. In disaster areas military personnel are often called into action to alleviate disaster conditions. Bodies of regular and reserve personnel occasionally participate in community welfare projects both in the United States and abroad (cf. Chapter 15). Navy "Seabees" (Construction Battalions) have sometimes helped in the construction of religious and civic facilities, for example. Such activities are usually initiated by the officers of the units concerned, frequently for promoting public relations.

The conduct of foreign affairs also is the prerogative of the national government; the administration of foreign affairs by the Department of State has cost about $200 million annually. Related foreign information activities are undertaken by the U.S. Information Agency, which expended $110 million in 1960; it maintains the Voice of America radio stations, numerous overseas libraries, and distributes films, leaflets, books, and other material to enhance the "image of America." International development and exchange programs, which are primarily for the benefit of other countries, are described in Chapter 15.

Social Insurance

THE NATIONAL GOVERNMENT directly operates two social insurance programs, in addition to those for veterans and its own civilian employees: old-age, survivors, and disability insurance; and railroad retirement, disability, and unemployment insurance. It also participates in the State-national unemployment insurance program, in conjunction with which it operates the Bureau of Employment Security, described above.

OLD-AGE, SURVIVORS, AND DISABILITY INSURANCE: Old-age and survivors insurance (OASI) was initiated by the Social Security Act of 1935, to provide continuing income for individuals and their families as partial replacement of earnings lost through retirement, disability, or death. OASI originally applied only to limited groups of workers, but has since been extended to cover virtually all groups except physicians, employees of some non-profit organizations, civilian employees of the national government, some State and local government employees, and railroad workers. Most of those not covered, aside from physicians, have separate pension systems. By 1960 an estimated 85 per cent of the labor force was covered by OASI.

Funds for OASI are collected by the Treasury Department, under the Federal Insurance Contributions Act (FICA, the initials found on most statements of earnings and deductions), from employers, employees, and some self-employed persons. There has been a series of increases in the tax rates for OASI. Beginning in 1959 rates for this compulsory insurance were 2.5 per cent of an employee's salary and wage, up to $4,800; this was matched by employer contributions. The rates were scheduled to increase to 4.5 per cent each by 1969. Self-employed persons have been required to pay one and one-half times the employee rate—3.75 per cent in 1959. Funds so collected, which amounted to $8.5 billion in 1958 and well over $9 billion in the following year, are transferred to two separate funds: the Federal Old-Age and Survivors Insurance and the Disability Insurance Trust Funds, the latter having been established on a separate basis in 1956. All benefits and administrative costs are paid from these funds, which are administered by the Bureau of Old-Age and Survivors Insurance (HEW). At the beginning of 1960 the OASI fund had assets of $20.1 billion and the disability fund $1.8 billion. (The funds have some income from investments in addition to tax income; investment income in 1959 totaled $566 million.)

The worker covered by OASI is protected against a number of unexpected events, as well as being assured of a monthly pension once he reaches the age of sixty-five (or sixty-two in the case of women). If he dies his widow may receive payments when she reaches sixty-two; if she has any dependent children payments begin immediately. The worker also would receive payments if he suffered from disability, though only after he reached the age of fifty. Some recent data on OASI benefits are given in Table 6. In 1959 nearly fourteen million persons were receiving OASI benefits, about seventy-eight out of every thousand persons in the United States. Many were using such payments to help support dependents as well as themselves. Total payments were about $10.3 billion. By 1960 ten million of the sixteen million people aged

TABLE 6

OLD-AGE, SURVIVORS, AND DISABILITY INSURANCE BENEFITS, 1959
(*In Millions of Dollars*)

Type of Benefit	Receiving Payments in December, 1959	Average Monthly Benefit	Total Payments, 1959 (*In Millions of Dollars*)
Old-Age	7,526,000	$72.78	$6,548
Wife's or Husband's	2,208,000	38.16	1,011
Child's	1,832,000	44.07	969
Widow's or Widower's	1,394,000	56.72	921
Mother's	376,000	57.37	263
Parent's	35,000	58.86	25
Disability	334,000	89.00	390
Lump Sum Death Payments			171
Totals	13,704,000 [1]		$10,298

Source: *Statistical Abstract* 1960, pp. 271–75.

[1] Includes some duplication; does not add because of rounding.

sixty-five and over were receiving one form or another of OASI benefits, and it was estimated that in 1961 a total of 14.6 million people of all ages would be receiving benefits with a total value of $11.7 billion.[18]

One interesting feature of the OASI program is that current residence in the United States, or even United States citizenship, is not required for payment of benefits. Thus, a number of immigrants have worked in the United States, making OASI payments, and on reaching the retirement age have returned to their homelands where they are often able to live in relative luxury on old-age payments.

The OASI program is believed to be partly responsible for the growth in industry pension plans. It has stimulated unions to negotiate pension

[18] "President's Budget Message," *New York Times*, Jan. 19, 1960.

plans with business that, in conjunction with OASI payments, will guarantee employees a specified minimum retirement annuity. In 1938 employers paid about $1.7 billion for employee security, all but about a third of which was governmentally-required OASI and unemployment insurance payments. By 1953, however, out of $9.5 billion for employee security $5 billion were employer payments to non-governmental pension and welfare funds, whereas governmentally required payments were about $3.7 billion.

OASI has become a matter of political controversy, not with regard to the fundamental desirability of social insurance but with regard to the directions in which OASI should expand. In Congress in 1958, for example, over 400 bills were presented to extend the system in one direction or another—increased benefits, coverage of new groups, new types of benefits. One criticized feature of the system has been that no beneficiary can earn more than $1,200 annually if he or she wishes to receive the full OASI annuity before reaching the age of seventy-two. If a person who is eligible for OASI is still working at the age of sixty-seven and earning $2,200 a year, for example, $1,000 will be deducted from the OASI payments he would ordinarily be entitled to. The average OASI old-age beneficiary in 1958 received only about $800 in benefits; even if he earned the permitted maximum of $1,200 by working part-time his total income would have been only $2,000, unless he was seventy-two or older, in which case he could have earned as much additional income as he wished without reduction in OASI benefits. Amendments passed by the Congress in 1960 reduced the "penalty" for persons earning over $1,200 per year, but only to a small extent; for example, retired workers earning more than $1,200 are now penalized $1 in benefits for each $2 of earnings up to the first $300.

One feared result of expansion of the OASI program has been that it might cease to be an "insurance" system and would have to be supported in part from general tax funds. By 1955 the OASI unfunded accrued liability was some $300 billion, against a trust fund of about $23 billion. In 1959 disbursements exceeded OASI taxes and other income by about $1.3 billion, and further deficits were expected through the early 1960's. In 1958 Secretary Folsolm of the Department of Health, Education, and Welfare said that the trust funds might drop as low as $19 billion by 1962. After that point, however, increasing contributions are expected to build the funds up beyond any previous level, barring any major expansions in the program.

RAILROAD WORKERS' INSURANCE: The Railroad Retirement Act of 1937 and supplementary legislation provided for national administration of retirement, disability, and unemployment insurance for railroad workers, financed by employer and employee contributions and admin-

The National Government

istered by the Railroad Retirement Board. The present tax rate is 6.25 per cent of the employee's salary, up to $4,200 annually, matched by employer contributions, plus a 1.5 per cent employer contribution for unemployment insurance. The tax rates are much higher than those of the OASI program but coverage is broader and payments generally higher. The system has been termed "the most comprehensive and most adequate social insurance program in the United States." [19]

TABLE 7

RAILROAD WORKERS' SOCIAL INSURANCE BENEFITS, 1959

Type of Benefit	Beneficiaries	Average Monthly Benefits	Total Payments, 1959 (In Thousands of Dollars)
Retirement	501,000 [1]	$99.00 [2]	$ 599,100
Survivor	245,000 [1]	55.00 [2]	163,800
Unemployment	300,000	67.12	193,100
Sickness and Maternity	139,000	76.26	54,800
Lump-Sum Death Benefits	23,000		18,100
Totals	1,200,000 [3]		$1,028,900

Source: *Statistical Abstract 1960*, p. 279.

[1] In current-pay status at end of year.
[2] Estimates.
[3] Includes some double counting; does not add because of rounding.

Some data on railroad workers' benefits in 1959 are given in Table 7. Comparison with Table 6 indicates that railroad retirement benefits are higher by almost half than OASI old-age benefits, for example. In addition, the railroad workers' social insurance plan includes unemployment, sickness, and maternity benefits, which are not provided under OASI (though most persons covered by OASI are also covered by State unemployment insurance plans). All told about 1.2 million persons received benefits of one type or another from railroad insurance in 1959; this is believed to include a small amount of double counting. By comparison the total number of working employees under the system in 1958 was 1.1 million.

Indians and Territorial Populations

THE NATIONAL GOVERNMENT is especially and directly concerned with the welfare of some 300,000 reservation Indians and Eskimos and 60,000 inhabitants of the formerly Japanese Trust Territories of the Pacific

[19] Wilbur J. Cohen, "Social Insurance," in Russell H. Kurtz, ed., *Social Work Year Book 1957*. New York: National Association of Social Workers, 1957, p. 546.

Islands, more so than with any other groups in the population. In their protected status these peoples are provided with extensive medical, social, and educational services, some of which were outlined in a preceding section. They are also provided with economic assistance and technical aid when necessary and, in general, protection against harmful incursions by outsiders. Some 87,500 square miles of Indian land is managed by or for the tribes with the help of the Bureau of Indian Affairs and other federal agencies. To a lesser extent, similar benefits are available to inhabitants of other United States possessions and holdings, e.g., Guam, the Virgin Islands, American Samoa, the Canal Zone, and so forth. Responsibility for Indians and some territorial peoples, who with some exceptions have been unwilling or unable to fit into the main stream of American life, is held to be a permanent function of the national government.

There is one special advantage conferred by the national government on the people of the Commonwealth of Puerto Rico, as well as on the people of some possessions. They either are not subject to the federal income tax or such tax receipts along with corporation and excise taxes are turned directly over the government of the area in question. They still receive other national grants, however, particularly for health, education, and social services and assistance. National grants for health, education, and social welfare to Puerto Rico were $28 million in 1958, for example. However, all national grants to Puerto Rico in 1958 averaged only $15 per capita, considerably less than per capita grants-in-aid of $28 in the continental United States.

Natural Resources and Recreation

THE DEVELOPMENT and preservation of natural resources in the United States are entrusted to the Forest Service and the Soil Conservation Service in the U.S. Department of Agriculture; the Bureau of Land Management, the Bureau of Reclamation, the Fish and Wildlife Service, the National Park Service, and the several area power administrations of the U.S. Department of Interior; and the Tennessee Valley Authority (TVA). In addition, a number of reclamation projects involving the construction of multi-purpose dams have been placed under the authority of the Army Corps of Engineers. The protection of natural resources involves federal ownership of over 400 million acres of land in the continental United States, about one-fifth of its total area, plus other lands in outlying areas. (In Alaska, prior to statehood, some 360 million acres of public domain land were under federal control.)

Almost all present holdings are in the mountain and western States; more than two-thirds of the land area of Idaho, Nevada, and Utah is federally owned, for example. The government has full powers over these public lands and frequently leases them to private interests for exploitation, under strict regulation. Nearly half of the holdings are forest and wildlife lands, and about 170 million acres are for grazing purposes.

Some of the natural resources agencies have considerable impact on local populations. The TVA, for example, has effected some changes in the social and economic conditions of the area. Although in its operations it once had to relocate many families, it has in general helped improve living conditions, health, and employment throughout the valley of the Tennessee. The TVA, the Bonneville Power Administration (in Washington and Oregon), and two smaller power administrations conduct many activities of a commercial nature, notably the production and sale of electric power. Reclamation projects of the Department of Interior and the Corps of Engineers also involve the sale of power and provide irrigation for extensive areas. By the late 1950's the Bureau of Reclamation had completed irrigation projects for over eight million acres and was actually providing irrigation for nearly seven million of them, raising economic conditions in many areas considerably by doing so. The greatest irrigation service land areas were in Idaho, California, Washington, Colorado, and Oregon.

In 1960 national expenditures for natural resources totaled $1.7 billion. This included $860 million to the Corps of Engineers for land and water resource development and $430 million to other agencies, notably the Bureau of Reclamation, for similar purposes. The protection of forest resources cost $223 million, mineral resources $66 million, fish and wildlife resources $70 million.

Both the National Park Service and the Forest Service provide extensive recreational facilities in their 180 national parks and 153 national forests. These undertakings differ in purpose from the many urban recreational programs that have been designed to benefit such particular groups as slum-dwellers and juvenile delinquents. The national programs aim to preserve natural beauty and historical sites for everyone's enjoyment, and the millions of Americans who visit them each year are largely a cross section of the population. In 1958 an estimated 65.5 million Americans visited the national parks, monuments, sites, and recreation areas. The Forest Service estimated that 68.5 million visits were made to the national forests for recreation in the same year. In 1960 the National Park Service spent $87 million in the development of recreational resources.

Business Enterprises

THE BUSINESS OPERATIONS of the national government need only a brief note here. In the mid-1950's there were more than 19,000 governmentally operated facilities providing services or products for government or general public use, employing more than 250,000 government employees. Most such operations were in the Department of Defense, including air transport, naval shipyards, the Panama Steamship Line, commissary stores and post exchanges, and innumerable food, clothing, and other service facilities. Business enterprises in civilian government agencies included the Virgin Islands Corporation and many mining enterprises in the Department of Interior, and the Federal Prison Industries, the Cuba Nickel Company, personal service enterprises, and a number of lending, guaranteeing, and insurance programs operated on a commercial basis in other departments and agencies. Some 450 governmentally-owned, contractor-operated enterprises, mostly connected with the Department of Defense, had capital assets of nearly $9 billion, compared with assets totaling $3 billion for all directly operated government enterprises.[20]

The largest single government business-type operation is the Post Office. It is not operated strictly on business lines, though, for it has run consistently in the red since the turn of the century and must be subsidized from general tax funds. In 1958 it had revenues of $2.55 billion but required national subsidy of $674 million. Despite subsequent rate increases the 1960 postal deficit was some $560 million, and Congress has been reluctant to pass further rate increases. It has been pointed out[21] that the postal deficits of $6.8 billion financed by the national government between 1947 and 1959 were equivalent to almost half the increase in the national debt during the period.

THE WELFARE OF NATIONAL GOVERNMENT EMPLOYEES

SOME OF THE most extensive social welfare programs of the national government are for internal welfare, i.e., for the welfare of veterans, present military personnel, civilian government employees, and their dependents. Services and benefits for veterans are financed from general

---

[20] Business Enterprises: A Report to the Congress. Commission on Organization of the Executive Branch of the Government. Washington, D.C.: USGPO, 1955.
[21] By President Eisenhower in his 1961 budget message to Congress. In recent years, it might be mentioned, the greatest deficits have come from second- and third-class mail services, and hence those businesses and organizations having second- and third-class mail privileges benefit most from the subsidy.

tax revenues and hence are similar in nature to public assistance programs; the veterans' right to them is not based so much on need (except in cases of disability), however, as on the risks they undertook, usually without choice, in serving the government. Benefits for active-duty military personnel are essentially fringe benefits. Civil service benefits are provided under social insurance plans established for the benefit of federal employees.

Veterans and Military Personnel

IN 1960 there were twenty-three million veterans in civilian life, many of whom, along with fifty-eight million dependents and survivors of veterans, were or will be eligible for benefits in one form or another. Some data on veterans' programs are given in Table 8. Almost all such programs are administered by the Veterans Administration (VA), an independent national agency; two special unemployment compensation programs for Korean and other veterans are the responsibility of the Bureau of Employment Service.

An estimated seven million veterans or their dependents received direct benefits or services in 1958. The total financial outlay was some $6 billion, $5 billion of which was provided from tax funds and about $1 billion of which was paid out of insurance and loan funds. Budgetary expenditures of veterans' programs in 1960 were $5.2 billion, one-fifteenth of the entire federal budget and more than was spent for all other health, education, and social welfare programs financed from federal tax funds.

Veterans' benefits are of three general types: First are service-connected benefits, including disability benefits for veterans and their survivors, medical care and treatment, vocational rehabilitation, educational assistance for children of veterans who have died because of service-connected injuries, and certain other benefits. These have been the most important veterans' programs, both in terms of total cost and in terms of number of persons benefiting. In 1958, 2.9 million persons received compensation benefits, most of them living veterans, at a cost of some $2.6 billion. Hospital and domiciliary care was provided to well over 100,000 veterans, primarily in the VA's nation-wide system of modern and well-equipped hospitals. The majority of these veterans were permanently hospitalized, about half of them with neuro-psychiatric disorders. Another 13,400 veterans were undergoing vocational rehabilitation, a relatively small number compared with previous years; in 1950, 111,000 were undergoing rehabilitation, in 1955, 25,500.

The second type of veterans' benefits consists of those that help readjustment to civilian life. Readjustment benefits include partial pay-

ment for education and training, provided for more than ten million
veterans between 1945 and 1958; loan guarantees and direct loans
(terminated on July 25, 1960, for World War II veterans); special unemployment benefits, which helped 9.7 million World War II veterans
and are available for Korean veterans through 1961; homestead and farm
loan preferences; civil service job preferences, applying to 1.15 million
veterans who were civilian employees of the national government in
1958; and a few others. Most readjustment programs have been tem-

TABLE 8

VETERANS' SERVICES AND BENEFITS, 1958

Service or Benefit [1]	Bene-ficiaries [1]	Average Annual Payment or Cost [1]	Total Costs (In Thousands of Dollars [1])
Pensions and Retire-ment Pay	786,700		
Total Disability Com-pensation	114,100	$ 811	$2,300,000
Partial Disability Com-pensation	1,949,600		
Survivors' Compensation	884,400	870	760,000
Hospital Care	110,800 [2]	6,320 [3]	700,000 [3]
Domiciliary Care	16,500 [2]	1,480	24,500
Outpatient Medical Care	2,083,700	62 [3]	130,000 [3]
Vocational Rehabilitation	13,400	1,950	26,100
Education and Training	558,400	1,240	693,200
Korean Veterans Unem-ployment (UCV) [4]	196,000	420	82,035
Ex-Servicemen's Program (UCX) [4]	200,000	400	79,600
Loans Guaranteed and Insured	148,200	540	80,000
Direct Loans	(n.a.)	(n.a.)	229,000
Death Benefits	(n.a.)	(n.a.)	318,900
Other Insurance and Indemnities	(n.a.)	(n.a.)	442,000
Administrative and Other Expenses Not Included Above			90,000 [3]
Totals	7,000,000 [5]		$6,110,000 [6]

Source: *Statistical Abstract 1959*, pp. 255–60, 277.

[1] Original data are not broken down in this manner in all cases and are not entirely comparable. Most average annual figures are calculated from known number of beneficiaries and known or estimated total costs. Some cost figures include administrative expenses, others do not.
[2] Receiving care at end of the year.
[3] Estimates; "Hospital Care" includes $33 million for construction.
[4] Programs administered by Bureau of Employment Security; UCX program data from 1959.
[5] Authors' estimate; adjusted for data not available, multiple counting (persons receiving more than one type of benefit).
[6] Total Veterans Administration expenses plus unemployment benefits.

porary, and most of them in effect in 1960 applied only to Korean
veterans.

Finally, veterans receive certain benefits not connected with their
military service but "based on a general feeling of obligation to the
veteran of wartime service rather than on any specific need or problem
attributable to military service." [22] Among these are medical and hospital care for non-service-connected ailments, provided the veteran cannot pay for them himself; special life insurance programs, notably the
National Service Life Insurance program for veterans of World War II
and later; burial benefits; and a few others. Veterans' pensions also are
included in this group. There has been some increase in non-service-
connected benefits. The Veterans' Pension Act of 1959 provided increased pensions for widows of World War I veterans, and provided
higher benefits for all persons who could demonstrate need under a
"sliding scale income test." Also, by the late 1950's, more than 60 per
cent of the patients in VA hospitals were being treated for non-service-
connected disabilities.

Most veterans' benefits will eventually lapse, barring another war.
Peacetime ex-servicemen receive some benefits, notably pensions for
long-term service and service-connected disability or death compensation, but these involve relatively little expenditure when compared with
the benefits provided wartime veterans. Most readjustment benefits for
World War II veterans have already lapsed, and most for Korean
veterans will have lapsed by the late 1960's. On the other hand, new
or expanded wartime veterans' bills are being passed by Congress or
being requested by veterans' organizations. Increased pension payments
are being provided and in June, 1959, a new bill to allocate $100 million
to the VA for direct loans to veterans was passed. Hence, as compensation, pension, hospital, and medical benefits and services have been
increased, total budget expenditures for veterans have increased and
will probably continue to do so for some time; from a level of $4.3
billion per year immediately after the Korean War they rose to $4.8
billion in 1957, $5.2 billion in 1959, and were expected to reach $5.5
billion in 1961.

Servicemen on active duty and their dependents also receive certain
benefits, which can be quickly summarized. Consumer goods and services are available at or below cost at commissary stores and post exchanges. Special living quarters may be provided to married servicemen
and their families, particularly those stationed abroad. Special allotments are provided for children and other dependents, and free or
below-cost medical services also are available to them. There are also
armed services associations and auxiliaries that provide financial and

[22] Vasey, *op. cit.*, p. 241.

material assistance to distressed families of military personnel and to former military personnel. Finally, retired regular military personnel receive retirement pay (aside from pensions administered by the VA); such retirement pay amounted to $715 million in 1960.

Civil Service Personnel

IN JANUARY, 1960, the national government employed 2,345,000 civilians, 85 per cent of whom were subject to requirements of the Civil Service Act. Their payroll, at the rate paid at that time, was about $13.4 billion a year—17 per cent of total budget expenditures. Their average salary was about $5,700 a year. A relatively small number of national employees were concerned with social welfare services; most of those that were worked for the Veterans Administration (173,000 employees) and for the Department of Health, Education and Welfare (60,000 employees). Some ten thousand employees of the Department of Interior were providing Indian services. All told, an estimated 280,000 national employees in all departments and agencies were involved in providing for health and social welfare.

Government employees also receive a number of welfare benefits, notably retirement and disability pay, and life insurance. The U.S. Civil Service Commission administers these benefits under the Civil Service Retirement Act of 1956 and the Federal Employees Group Life Insurance Act of 1954. Retirement with annuity is provided when the employee reaches a specified age; it is financed by a deduction of between 6 and 10 per cent from salaries (6 per cent is the minimum; up to 10 per cent is optional). Retirement with annuity also is provided in case of total disability. In 1958, 312,000 former national employees and 106,000 survivors were receiving annuities, 84,500 of them for disability. Total payments were $647 million, about $1,550 per person per year. In addition, lump-sum payments of $126 million were made, largely to employees leaving the government before retirement age but also to the beneficiaries of 13,200 deceased employees. Finally, the Bureau of Employment Security operates a special program of unemployment compensation for national employees (UCFE). In 1958, 119,000 persons received benefits totaling $62 million, an average of $30 for each week compensated.

CONCLUDING REMARKS

THE NATIONAL GOVERNMENT will soon be collecting $100 billion annually in taxes and charges to finance its vast array of activities, almost all of which might be termed welfare functions. Actually, about half its receipts are for the maintenance of the defense establishment, while the remainder are used for hundreds of different functions that fall into several major categories. One major group of activities consists of multiform business and labor regulations. The welfare of the consumer is protected through agencies such as the Federal Trade Commission and the Department of Justice's Antitrust Division. Fair labor standards legislation sets minimum wage levels and maximum working hours for many workers. Radio, television, rail and highway transport, the airlines—indeed, a large sector of the American business system—come under federal regulation of one form or another.

Indirect operations of the national government include large expenditures to stabilize agricultural production, less sizable aid to public housing and to State and local welfare programs, to give them support and some measure of uniformity and control. Grants for the support of education and for public assistance are in this group, as are subsidies for transportation through payments to maintain the quality of U.S. shipping and to airlines to reduce the costs of mail.

Direct operations of the national government constitute a third category. OASI is a straightforward national program of insurance for the aged and disabled, with salient differences from business-owned or cooperatively owned insurance operations. The protection and development of natural resources, including important enterprises such as TVA and involving extensive recreational services as well, form another group of direct national operations. The administration and portection of Indians and territorial populations is another. Finally, there are the thousands of service and productive enterprises of the national government that outwardly are very much like private commerical operations.

The national government also has extensive internal welfare programs, covering civil servants, military personnel, veterans, and their families. This is one of the most characteristic features of the socialized welfare state—the extensive provision of direct services and security for its members. Some eleven million persons annually benefit from the internal welfare programs of the national government: over seven million veterans, some two million servicemen, and more than two million former civilian employees and their survivors.

In general, however, there is decreasing emphasis on the provision of *direct* benefits to individuals in need, at least on the part of the national government. Social insurance plans are already supplanting some of the direct assistance programs; social insurance has the advantages of being largely self-supporting, comprehensive in coverage, and fulfilling needs without the onus of being "on relief" for the recipient. Other needs and demands in social welfare, health, and education are being met through indirect operations, especially by controlled grants to State, local, and non-governmental bodies.

The total effect of the myriad operations of the national government is a considerable redistribution of benefits among Americans and among American institutions. Various industries, such as agriculture and shipping, are supported at the cost of other industries. Lower income groups and special segments of the higher income groups are favored over the middle and remaining higher income groups. The poorer and more rural States receive a high level of grants-in-aid assistance at the cost of the wealthier States.

It should be borne in mind that the redistribution occurs by two means: through the tax schedules, especially the personal income tax; and by the mode of conferring benefits, that is, through the laws themselves. Moreover, the net effect is only in modest part to help the poor at the expense of the well-to-do. While redistribution does have this "vertical" effect, it also possesses a "sidewise effect"; that is, benefits are redistributed according to some theory of the general welfare that may prevail at the time the laws are enacted, perhaps continuously thereafter as well, or they are redistributed according to no theory at all but as the unplanned consequences of efforts to help individuals who have a clear and present need. For example, the decision that farmers should receive agricultural price supports to limit their losses in the sale of their products undoubtedly helps many low-income farmers, but it also helps high-income farmers, gentlemen farmers, the agricultural implement industry, and rural towns in agricultural areas. It also constitutes a drain on all other taxpaying individuals and industries in the country. This example could be accompanied by many parallels drawn from an examination of the tax laws and the appropriation laws that take from some and give to others. A review of the full range of supports given by the national government to social welfare confirms that there are very many ways in which social welfare may be affected, controlled, and administered. The welfare channels from giver to receiver are many, and the national government is continuously asked to respond to signals of need.

Chapter Fifteen

AMERICAN WELFARE ABROAD

INDIVIDUALLY AND THROUGH THEIR INSTITUTIONS the people of the United States give assistance in many forms to other peoples throughout the world. Preceding chapters in this book deal with the welfare functions of specific types of institutions in American society; this chapter, in effect, considers the United States itself as an institution, extending welfare benefits to millions of other people.

Then extension of welfare by one country to the people or government of another country, today called foreign aid, is not a new practice, nor is it by any means native to the United States.

Tribes, cities, nations or empires that have been relatively advanced economically have for centuries sent aid, in one form or another, to regions that were less developed. So the citizens of Athens did to Sicily and the shores of Southern Italy, France and Spain; so the Phoenicians, to Carthage; so the Chinese, to Korea and Japan; so the English, French, Spaniards, Portuguese and Dutch, to America, Asia, Africa, and Australasia; so the citizens of the United States to Canada, Latin America and the Middle East; and so, indeed, the Russians to Siberia, and now to China.

They sent foreign aid for reasons that seemed to them good and sufficient, usually for material gain or power or excitement, sometimes as charity. . . .

"Imperialism" also is a form of foreign aid which, though in some cases shamefully abused, has much solid accomplishment on its balance sheet. The United States, Canada and Australia are, after all, off-shoots of imperialism. So are the railroads, roads, water systems, telegraphs, mills and mines, technical knowledge, hospitals and universities of, say, India. There are few material improvements in Iran that are not "aid" from the Anglo-Iranian Oil Company; or in Costa Rica and Guatemala, that did not come from the United Fruit Company.[1]

American foreign aid has been given for many years and in many forms. In 1812 the Congress of the United States appropriated $50,000 to assist earthquake victims in Venezuela. Religious organizations have long supported foreign missions, often including in their programs education, health services, and agricultural aid and instruction. During and immediately after World War I many communities organized "war chests" to provide funds for programs of aid to the starving people of many European nations. In 1919 Congress appropriated $100 million for European food relief, $600,000 for the Near East, and about $1 billion for relief loans, more than 90 per cent of which were never repaid. In 1922 Congress gave $20 million for famine victims in Russia and in 1923 $6 million for the relief of victims of the Japanese earthquake.

Many foundations have made foreign grants, and some American donors have set up foreign foundations. In 1901 Andrew Carnegie endowed his Scottish Universities Trust with $10 million; in 1903 the Palace of Peace at The Hague with $1.5 million; and in 1913 the Carnegie United Kingdom Trust with $10 million. In 1930 Edward S. Harkness of New York established the Pilgrim Trust with an endowment of $10 million to provide for charitable activities in Great Britain and Northern Ireland.[2] Many recent grants of American foundations for foreign purposes are outlined below.

Since 1945 American foreign aid has increased tremendously. By the late 1950's outright foreign aid was at least $5 billion a year, somewhat over one per cent of the gross national product. About 90 per cent of this aid was from the national government ($5.74 billion in 1959, reduced to $3.51 billion in 1960 and about the same amount in 1961), and more than half the government aid was for military assistance. Even discounting military assistance, though, Americans were giving as much as $2.5 billion annually for foreign welfare—individually, through non-governmental organizations, and through the national government. Some comparisons suggest the relative magnitude of this figure: in the late 1950's all community chests and national fund-raising campaigns for the non-governmental health organizations were raising about $650 million per year; the total expenditures of the U.S. Department of Health, Education and Welfare ranged from $2 billion (1955) to $3

[1] "Foreign Aid and Statism," *National Review*, June 6, 1956.
[2] F. Emerson Andrews. *Philanthropic Giving*. New York: Russell Sage Foundation, 1950, pp. 75–76.

billion (1959); the total income of all churches in the United States was about $3.5 billion.

American foreign aid takes many channels. For convenience it is divided here into three categories: assistance provided by individuals and non-governmental American organizations; assistance provided by the national government; and assistance provided by international organizations. International organizations are discussed to the extent that they are financed by Americans and the United States government. In reality these divisions are not entirely clear; overlapping, particularly between governmental and non-governmental aid, is given some attention.

NON-GOVERNMENTAL WELFARE ABROAD

NON-GOVERNMENTAL FOREIGN RELIEF and services may come from individuals, businesses, and national organizations such as church groups and foundations. The volume of non-governmental giving in 1956 was $535 million, somewhat over half from individuals (largely to Western Europe) and more than four-fifths of it in the form of cash. Some foreign remittances, such as aid given by foundations, are not included in this total. In 1959 non-governmental organizations gave over $200 million, again excluding foundations and certain other groups. The amount of individual giving in 1959 is not known, but probably was somewhat less than in 1956.

Individual Contributions

INDIVIDUALS MAY CONTRIBUTE money, goods, or direct services to people in other countries. They make many of these contributions directly, particularly to friends and relatives overseas and to people in countries of the donors' national origins. Hence, much in the way of individual contributions has gone to Western European countries. In addition, individuals give money and goods to various organizations, particularly religious groups, for institutional overseas welfare programs. These institutional programs are in large part for the benefit of Asians and Africans rather than European peoples, as Table 1 indicates. Some individual contributions of money and goods are made directly to foreign missions and to hospitals and clinics operating overseas, though most contributions for such purposes are channeled through other organizations.

Direct services are provided by a number of individuals, usually though not always within the framework of some organization. The

Protestant and Roman Catholic churches have many foreign missions staffed wholly or in part by Americans; in the late 1950's, for example, there were about 5,000 Catholic brothers and sisters from the United States working in foreign missions (cf. Chapter 6). There are also some secular and church-related programs in which young people spend their summers in foreign countries working on projects of a welfare nature.

TABLE 1

NON-GOVERNMENTAL REMITTANCES OF CASH AND GOODS
TO FOREIGN COUNTRIES, 1956, 1959 [1]
(*In Millions of Dollars*)

AREA	INSTITUTIONS, 1956 [2]		INDIVIDUALS, 1956		
	Cash	Value of Goods	Cash	Value of Goods	TOTAL
Western Europe	$ 23	$17	$176	$28	$252
Western European Dependencies	9	2	9	1	20
Eastern Europe	(*)	(*)	7	6	13
Western Hemisphere	17	2	38		57
Other Countries	134	21	26	5	193
Totals	$183	$42	$256	$40	$535

Institutional Remittances, 1959: [1]
   Cash: $42   Goods: $162   Total: $204

Note: Totals do not necessarily add because of rounding; remittances less than $500,000 indicated by (*).
Sources: Jessie L. C. Adams, "Postwar Private Gifts to Foreign Countries Total $6 Billion," *Foreign Commerce Weekly*, LVII (June 17, 1957), pp. 14–15, 32; International Cooperation Administration.

[1] Estimates for fifty-five organizations for first six months of 1959, multiplied by two. Individual 1959 remittances not available.
[2] Ninety per cent of institutional remittances were provided through religious bodies.

There have been many military-initiated welfare activities that were probably as important as the welfare work of foreign missions, at least in the 1950's. Both voluntarily and under military direction, American military personnel stationed in foreign countries have assisted local populations. They have adopted and cared for children. They have provided many varieties of physical and material help to orphanages, hospitals, and other institutions, and have provided direct assistance to families. They have taught Japanese, Koreans, and many others the concepts and practices of community cooperation and provided them technical and material assistance in building community and agricultural facilities. Not all of these efforts have been successful: unwillingness to accept help and the cultural unacceptability of some practices have led to failures. On the whole, however, formal and informal military practices of assisting foreign populations have removed some of the stigma of the presence of military forces and have added considerably to the quantity of American government and non-government international assistance.

Business

AMERICAN BUSINESSES CONTRIBUTE to international welfare in several respects. Some businesses contribute money and goods to organizations such as CARE. Others, particularly those with overseas business interests, may have special educational and assistance programs primarily for the benefit of people in foreign countries. *Aufbau,* a German-language newspaper printed in New York City, uses much of its profits for international welfare purposes; in 1958 it gave $47,700 to refugees in need of assistance.[3] The most important international welfare contributions, however, are made by the American companies that operate overseas. In the "Banana Republics," in Venezuela, in Kuwait, and in other countries American businesses have provided health and hospital services, education, housing, water systems, and similar benefits to many thousands of persons. In Liberia, for example, the Firestone Company has spent more on health and medical services for its 25,000 Liberian employees than the government budgets for public health for all the 1.5 million rural inhabitants of the country. The desire for profitable operation has been the major motive for such services, of course; local employees do better and more skilled work if they are healthy, educated, and well-housed. Profit has not been the *sole* motive, however. Health services for all families in an area and special schools for local children, for example, are motivated by a sincere desire to decrease human misery and raise living standards. American business operations in many underdeveloped countries have also had more general welfare consequences for the people and countries concerned. Highways, railways, and airstrips have been built; mineral and agricultural resources have been developed; and considerable revenue in the form of taxes on exported goods has gone to the governments of these countries. This is the bright side of the coin: American business enterprises in underdeveloped areas usually raise the general economic level and improve the living conditions of at least some of the inhabitants, changes that would be nearly impossible by other means. The other side of the coin is that some of a country's natural resources are lost to it, governments may be subjected to what their citizens consider undue influence, and considerable hostility may be directed at the American business in particular and the United States in general.

[3] "The Refugee's Best Friend," *Time,* LXXIV (Nov. 23, 1959), p. 58.

National Organizations

MANY OF the contributions of individual Americans for overseas welfare are channeled through the relief programs of national non-governmental organizations. According to a study by a sub-committee of the Committee on Foreign Affairs of the United States House of Representatives:

> Private relief ventures abroad have adapted their resources to the meeting of particular needs in local areas. In this they have demonstrated an elasticity that is not found in the over-all programs carried on under public authority. They have shown a capacity for immediate response to emergency situations, demonstrating a speed of action not obtainable in the carefully planned and meticulously controlled programs based upon legislative grants.
>
> Private relief programs, furthermore, are a means of bringing Americans into personal contact with the needs of other countries. They present an opportunity for the individual to do something on his own initiative, and to know the precise purposes for which his particular dollars are spent in relieving needs around the world. The obverse of this is that the recipient abroad knows that the assistance he receives is based upon the personal response of some individual American to his needs. The result is a harvest of good will to the American people.[4]

There are three types of American organizations and agencies active in foreign relief and services: the permanent multi-purpose group, the permanent one-purpose group, and the *ad hoc* group.

THE PERMANENT MULTI-PURPOSE ORGANIZATION: A group participating in international welfare but counting foreign welfare as only one aspect of its accomplishments is of this class. By this definition foundations, religious bodies, universities doing international welfare work, and the Red Cross are multi-purpose organizations.

Altogether, twenty-nine major foundations in the United States made grants for international affairs in one year in the late 1950's. These grants totaled $18.7 million, though a third of the total was for international studies, not specifically for assistance, and another $4.5 million was for exchange of persons. For technical assistance $5.3 million was granted; for economic aid, $1.5 million; and for relief purposes, $385,000.

For example, the Ford Foundation in 1957 spent $15 million in international welfare grants, about a third of such grants being administered by the foreign governments to whose people the aid was directed. These grants are listed by purpose in Table 2. In subsequent

[4] Cited in Andrews, *op. cit.*, pp. 76–77.

years, including both 1959 and 1960, Ford continued to grant about $15 million annually for its overseas programs, following a similar pattern. Some specific grants have been to support the Village and Small Industries Institute of the government of Nepal, to develop a teacher-training program in Jordan, to finance research on Congolese development problems at Louvanium University (Leopoldville), and to plan an international rice research institute in the Philippines. Many founda-

TABLE 2

OVERSEAS FORD FOUNDATION GRANTS, 1957

Purpose	Foreign or International Committees, Councils, etc.	Universities, Institutes, etc.[1]	Governments	Totals
International Exchange of Ideas, Higher Education, Research	$462,610	$8,125,570	$ 297,684	$8,885,864
Adult Training, Teacher Training, Primary and Secondary Education	328,521	325,542	1,944,000	2,598,063
Village, Rural, and Community Development	10,673 [2]	37,400	1,898,286	1,925,013
Government Training			250,917	250,917
Agricultural Development [3]		11,800	102,180	113,980
Grants to Refugees	135,000			135,000
Economic and Industrial Development		234,219	795,790	1,030,009
Totals	$915,458	$8,734,531	$5,288,857	$14,938,846
Percentages	6.1%	58.5%	35.4%	100%

Source: *The Ford Foundation Annual Report* (Oct. 1, 1956–Sept. 30, 1957). New York: The Ford Foundation, 1957.

[1] Includes grants to public universities.
[2] Refund. Subtracted from total.
[3] Other than through education.

tion grants have been for international study, research, and education. The Carnegie Corporation has supported a Cornell University study of technological change in non-industrialized countries; the Rockefeller Foundation has granted $189,500 to the Deccan Postgraduate and Research Institute in southern India for its program in Indian languages. In the period 1953–1959 the Ford Foundation granted $2.4 million to its Foreign Area and International Relations Training Fellowship Program, and has granted $500,000 to the Congress for Cultural Freedom in Paris "for its program of educational activities to strengthen communication and solidarity among intellectual leaders in Europe, Asia, Africa, and the Americas." [5] (These last Ford grants, made under the Foundation's International Training and Research program, are over and above the grants for overseas development listed in Table 2, and have totaled more than $10 million annually in recent years.)

Numerous religious bodies include foreign service in their scope of activities: the American Friends Service Committee (the service branch of the Quaker Churches); the National Catholic Welfare Conference; Lutheran World Relief; United Jewish Appeal; the Mennonite Central Committee; and many others. In the late 1950's religious giving for overseas purposes was approaching $200 million a year (cf. Chapter 6). Forty-seven Protestant church bodies, for example, reported that they gave $73.3 million for foreign missions in 1959.

Church groups cooperate with governmental or quasi-governmental bodies in foreign activities to a considerable degree. For example, the Church of the Brethren states that its members have

> shared in the American Point Four program for underdeveloped countries, and in United Nations agencies like the World Health Organization and the International Children's Emergency Fund. Their participation in projects like these has given Brethren an opportunity to share the spiritual motivation which they believe is essential to the ultimate success also of governmental operations.[6]

The American Friends Service Committee has conducted extensive foreign activities; the type and scope of its work are indicated in the detailed listing of Table 3. The Friends

> have found co-operation with others most fruitful in relief, relocation, and rehabilitation projects. . . . This co-operation has taken the form of relief, of aid to refugees, and of community rehabilitation. . . . Work in these areas has often led also to active co-operation with government agencies in this country, with CRALOG in Europe, with LARA in Japan, and with government agencies in Korea, in India, and in Arabia.[7]

[5] American Foundation News, VI (Oct. 15, 1957); The Ford Foundation Annual Report 1959, pp. 63–87 ff.
[6] E. Theodore Bachmann, ed. The Churches and Social Welfare: The Activating Concern. New York: National Council of Churches, 1955, p. 17.
[7] Ibid., pp. 49–50. CRALOG is the Council of Relief Agencies Licensed for Operation in Germany; LARA is Licensed Agencies for Relief in Asia.

TABLE 3

American Friends Service Committee: International Projects and Expenditures, 1957

General Section Expenditures:
  Relief & Community Development Programs Overseas: Expediting personnel to the field. $ 6,300
  Work & Study Programs: Processing and reviewing applications for volunteer service projects. 8,100

Foreign Service Section Expenditures:
  Relief and Community Development Programs Overseas:
    Middle East—Providing assistance to help meet needs of the Canal Zone refugees and the Jewish community in Egypt. 36,800
    Austria—Operating refugee services, including a farm loan fund and a loan fund for refugee professional and business men; distributing food and clothing; operation of *Quakerhaus* activities. 131,300
    Hungarian Refugees—Operating refugee service projects and distributing food and clothing in cooperation with Friends Service Council of England. 721,100
    Germany—Helping sponsor four neighborhood centers; distributing goods and surplus foods; supervising the School Affiliation Service Program; refugee rehabilitation and integration. 821,700
    Japan—Providing supplies and surplus commodities and assisting in their distribution through the National Council of Social Welfare and Japanese Red Cross; supervising distribution with American personnel; supporting three neighborhood centers with Western staff working with Japanese colleagues and volunteers; organizing International Work Camps and International Seminars. 331,900
    Korea—Shipping clothing, food, school supplies, for distribution by Save the Children Fund and Friends Service Unit; medical training for internes, technicians, and nurses, hospital rehabilitation, housing, and community service projects for refugees, widows, and others by the Friends Service Unit in Kunsan. 298,300
    Central Africa—Cooperation with monthly meetings in Southern Rhodesia promoting race relations. 11,600
    Procuring and Processing Costs—Preparing 8.9 million lbs. of contributed materials and food for shipment. 139,400
  Social and Technical Assistance:
    India—Community development and extension program of agricultural improvement, public health, education, cottage industries, and simple mechanics in forty-four villages in Orissa; staffing this operation with Western and Indian technicians who provided on-the-job training and supervision for some fifty Indian village workers, health workers, and others; limited supervision and supplies for teaching purposes; cooperating with Friends Service Council of London in a community development program of the Friends Rural Center at Rasulia by contributing limited funds and personnel for work in agriculture, dairying, education, health, rural credit, and cooperative activities. 100,600
    Israel—Maintaining a community center in Acre; operating an international voluntary work camp program; informal discussion groups; investigating opportunities for community development in rural Arab villages. 35,400

TABLE 3 *(continued)*

Work and Study Programs:	
Sending sixty American volunteers to some fifty International Work Camps in eighteen countries; finding camp assignments for forty other Americans already in Europe; organizing camps in France, Germany, Italy, and Austria; cooperating with local groups and Committee area teams in sponsoring camps in Africa, Israel, and Japan; providing travel funds and other aid to American and foreign participants.	$ 53,200
Programs Toward World and Domestic Understanding:	
International Centers—Cooperating with local Friends and Friends Service Council of London in operating centers in Paris, Geneva, Amsterdam, Copenhagen, Vienna, Delhi, Dacca, and Washington, D.C.; grants to educational institutions in France; working with UN agencies and persons of various racial, political, and religious backgrounds in the interest of international peace and goodwill; sponsoring a program of Leadership Inter-visitation, utilizing services of qualified observers in two-way interpretations of the United States and various countries visited.	152,000
Conferences for Diplomats—Two conferences in Switzerland for Foreign Office officials and preparing for a conference in Ceylon.	65,100
Conference for Parliamentarians—Conference in Switzerland for parliamentarians of some fifteen countries.	13,700
School Affiliation Services—Promoting the exchange of classroom projects, individual correspondence, and persons between schools in foreign countries and schools in the United States; providing personal contacts through conferences, visits of exchange students, and development of mutual understanding, respect, and friendship among teachers and young people in the various countries.	76,200
Grants to Persons and Organizations	4,900
Transmittals to Designated Organizations	16,600
General Services: General Administration	34,800
Total (subject to rounding errors)	$3,059,100

Source: Materials supplied by American Friends Service Committee, Inc., Philadelphia.

Many American universities, both public and private, have student exchange programs with foreign universities; they also may provide technical experts to foreign countries under government contract. For example, Harvard has an exchange-of-students program with the Free University of Berlin and Stanford has exchange arrangements with Keio University in Japan. There are also some exchange programs of schools of social work. The American branch of the World University Service provides used clothing and books for students in underdeveloped countries and serves as a medium for the exchange of information and ideas with other universities throughout the world.

The American National Red Cross conducts an active overseas aid program. Since the beginning of World War II it has sent an estimated $250 million worth of food, clothing, medical and sanitary supplies, prisoner-of-war packages, milk for children, and ambulance and auto-motive equipment to people throughout the world under its civilian relief operations programs. Emergency relief has been provided in some sixty countries. The Red Cross has also provided distribution facilities for substantial quantities of government-purchased supplies.

THE PERMANENT ONE-PURPOSE ORGANIZATION: There are certain entirely American non-governmental agencies that operate only in the international welfare field. Among them are the Cooperative for Ameri-can Remittances to Everywhere (CARE), the Foreign Missions Con-ference of North America, World Neighbors, Inc., and "Seeds for Democracy."

CARE was developed during World War II to solve the difficulties faced by individuals who were attempting to assemble and ship packages abroad. In November, 1945, twenty-two American agencies combined to form a non-profit cooperative; by the beginning of 1958 CARE had shipped overseas some twenty million packages valued at over $265 million.[8] In 1958 CARE spent $39 million, the second-greatest annual amount spent in its twelve years of existence. Officials of the organiza-tion have stated that the work of CARE is not finished. It has expanded from its emergency shipping programs to include shipments labeled "self-help" packages: school kits, agricultural and vocational tools and machines, health equipment, livestock, fertilizer, medicines, and drugs. Ultimately, it is the aim of the organization to "fade out" and let people take care of themselves with their new knowledge. In Costa Rica, for example, after CARE completed two years of a school-feeding program, "the Government of Costa Rica took over." [9]

A large portion of Protestant overseas aid is channeled through the Foreign Missions Conference of North America, which represents some fifty religious denominations. In 1956 the Conference spent $45 mil-lion on overseas work.[10] A publication of the Conference states that its members "are convinced that the secret of permanent peace and security is One World in Christ—a world united through a common faith in God through Christ and so thoroughly 'in Christ' that His commandment to love one another is fulfilled in all human relation-ships." [11]

A new single-purpose organization, founded with the support of the

[8] *New York Times,* Dec. 15, 1957.
[9] *New York Times,* Aug. 31, 1958.
[10] *Report of the Eighth Annual Meeting of the Division Assembly, Division of Foreign Missions, and the Sixty-Fourth Annual Meeting of the Foreign Missions Conference of North America.* New York: National Council of the Churches of Christ in the U.S.A., 1958, p. 73.
[11] Cited in Andrews, *op. cit.,* p. 89.

419

International Rescue Committee in 1958, is Medical International Cooperation (MEDICO). MEDICO sends teams of physicians and medically trained assistants to African and Asian countires that request them, to help build clinics and small hospitals and to train local staffs. It receives its support from the International Rescue Committee, which raises funds specifically for this purpose, from pharmaceutical firms, which donate drugs and equipment, and from its own fund-raising campaigns in the U.S. Host governments are expected to provide duty-free entry for medical equipment and pay interior transportation and postage costs.

World Neighbors, Inc., a privately financed group, has spent some $120,000 annually encouraging self-help in the villages of the Philippines, India, and Ethiopia, helped 700,000 persons in 1,500 villages between 1952 and 1957. The group was formed in 1952 by a committee including the Rev. Dr. Norman Vincent Peale, Representative Walter Judd of Minnesota, and several prominent clergymen, and in 1957 was supported by about 10,000 private subscribers.[12]

Another relatively small-scale program encouraging self-help is Seeds for Democracy, sponsored by a larger permanent one-purpose organization, the Asia Foundation. Seeds for Democracy was begun in 1950 as a result of an Asian survey by American agricultural specialists. Boy and Girl Scouts, Four-H Clubs, garden clubs, church groups, and numerous civic groups in the United States now send a million packets of seeds annually to the Philippines, Burma, Pakistan, and Ceylon.[13]

THE "Ad Hoc" ORGANIZATION: It is sometimes difficult to distinguish between "temporary" and "permanent" one-purpose international welfare organizations; interests and needs are continually changing and older organizations are frequently replaced by new. Groups such as CRALOG (Council of Relief Agencies Licensed for Operation in Germany), LARA (Licensed Agencies for Relief in Asia), and ARK (American Relief for Korea) definitely have been more temporary than permanent in nature. They may be termed quasi-governmental: supported by non-governmental funds, they have acted to coordinate non-governmental welfare with the regulations set down by American authorities, usually military, in the foreign areas concerned. Their avowed purpose has been "efficiency in the framework of voluntarism," and they have expected to disband themselves on the return of a semblance of normalcy to the countries in which they have been operating.[14]

[12] New York Times, July 9, 1957.
[13] St. Louis Post-Dispatch, July 27, 1958.
[14] Materials in this section have been drawn in part from Irving J. Fasteau, "International Social Welfare," in Russell H. Kurtz, ed., Social Work Year Book 1957. New York: National Association of Social Workers, 1957, pp. 311–24.

GOVERNMENTAL EXPENDITURES ABROAD

THE GOVERNMENT of the United States is very extensively concerned with international assistance; in 1958 it extended net grants and credits of $4.8 billion to foreign countries. Most such aid takes the form of direct grants of supplies, services, and funds to foreign governments. The net total of such grants in 1958 was $4.2 billion. Credits, *i.e.*,

TABLE 4

UNITED STATES GOVERNMENT FOREIGN AID, 1941–1960
(In Billions of Dollars)

Programs	Gross Expenditure	Net Grants and Credits
1941–1945:		
Wartime Lend-Lease	$46.8	$39.0
Civilian Supplies Occupied Areas Refugee Relief, etc.	2.3	1.9
Total Wartime Outlays	49.1	40.9
1945–1950:		
Famine Relief UNRRA Interim Aid Marshall Plan Greek-Turkish Aid	28.6	26.3
1950–1960:		
Military Assistance	25.6	
Non-Military Aid (Including technical assistance, defense support, relief funds, etc.)	27.2	40.9
Total Postwar Outlays (through Fiscal 1960)	$81.4	$67.2

Sources: William T. Stone, "Extension of Foreign Aid," *Editorial Research Reports*, II (Dec. 12, 1956), p. 876; *Statistical Abstract of the United States 1959*, U.S. Bureau of the Census, Washington, D.C.: USGPO, p. 878; "President's Budget Message," *New York Times*, Jan. 19, 1960.

loans, are extended to both foreign governments and non-governmental organizations; new credits extended in 1958 were $1.2 billion, but were partly balanced by repayments, so that *net* credits were about $580 million. The general types and extent of United States foreign aid from 1941 to 1960 is given in Table 4. The differences between the "gross expenditure" and "net grants and credits" figures represent repaid loans. A more detailed listing of foreign aid for 1958, by program, is given in Table 5.

TABLE 5

UNITED STATES GOVERNMENT FOREIGN AID PROGRAMS, 1958 [1]
(*In Millions of Dollars*)

Program		
GRANT PROGRAMS		$4,213 [2]
Mutual Security (and Related Programs)	$4,013 [2]	
Military Aid:		
Military Supplies and Services	2,512	
Multilateral Construction	81	
Military Equipment Loans (Actually, Transfers on an Indeterminate Basis)	20	
Economic and Technical Aid:		
Technical Cooperation and Special Assistance	1,295	
Foreign Currencies under Agricultural Trade Development and Assistance Act	99	
Famine and Other Urgent Relief	77	
Civilian Supplies	2	
Agricultural Surpluses (Through Private Welfare Organizations)	159	
Inter-American Programs	10	
International Children's Assistance	6	
Libyan Special Purpose Funds	4	
CREDIT PROGRAMS		$ 577 [3]
Export-Import Bank	751	
Mutual Security (Including Development Loan Fund)	227	
Agricultural Trade Development and Assistance	236	
Gross New Grants and Credits	$5,498	
Net Grants and Credits		$4,791 [2,3]

Note: Totals do not necessarily add because of rounding.
Source: *Statistical Abstract 1959*, p. 878.

[1] Does not include most U.S. government contributions to international organizations.
[2] These figures are adjusted downward by $71 million in reverse grants and returns.
[3] These figures are adjusted downward by $636 million in principal collections (primarily repayments on loans).

Mutual Security

MOST FOREIGN ASSISTANCE in the 1950's was provided under the mutual security programs, not all of which have been concerned even indirectly with defense. Types of mutual security assistance have included: (1) military supplies and services; (2) multilateral construction program contributions; (3) defense support (designed to sustain and increase military efforts, although commodities may be utilized by civilians); (4) technical cooperation, including what was once known as the Point 4 Program (advice, teaching, training, and the exchange of information to further the economic development and living standards of less-developed areas); (5) special assistance (a variety of grants, services, and material for the "maintenance or promotion of political or economic stability" in foreign countries); and (6) development assistance (loans to encourage economic development). Except for the last, these programs have involved outright grants of goods, services, or funds.

Direct military aid amounted to about 55 per cent of net grants and credits in 1958 (cf. Table 5) and 1959. Two-thirds of this was for military supplies, services, and construction, and was administered by the Department of Defense. The remainder, the Defense Support program, was administered by the International Cooperation Administration (ICA), a semi-autonomous agency within the Department of State. These programs have relatively few direct effects on foreign peoples except in the preventive sense: they may deter aggression by neighboring countries.

The most important non-military foreign aid programs, in terms of long-range consequences, are the technical assistance and special assistance programs, which are administered by the ICA. Their most general purpose is to raise the living standards of the peoples of less-developed countries, which they attempt to do by a variety of means. American technicians, either government personnel or employees of American universities and management firms having contracts with the United States government, work to improve health conditions, educational practices, and to develop new agricultural practices. They assist in the training of indigenous personnel; there have also been grants for the training of persons from participating countries in the United States or elsewhere. A number of training centers for social welfare workers have been established in these countries, for example. American technicians, equipment, and funds are used to sponsor rural and village community development projects; to help construct highways, dams, and irrigation systems; and to assist in the development of industrial operations.

In connection with its non-military assistance programs the ICA purchases large quantities of commodities, both in the United States and abroad, for the benefit of foreign countries. A list of such expenditures, totaling over $1 billion, is given in Table 6, for 1958. Raw materials, machinery, and vehicles are the most important items, having been used in various development projects. Some of the agricultural commodities were United States surpluses sold for foreign currencies under a special program.

The purposes of the mutual security loan funds are much the same as those of the direct assistance programs. These and other loan funds for foreign economic development are discussed in a subsequent section.

Since the early 1950's the non-military aid provided under the mutual security program has been primarily for the benefit of the less-developed countries, particularly in the Near and Far East. Prior to that time most

TABLE 6

INTERNATIONAL COOPERATION ADMINISTRATION PURCHASES OF
COMMODITIES FOR FOREIGN ASSISTANCE AND DEVELOPMENT, 1958
(*In Thousands of Dollars*)

Type of Commodity	Expenditure	*Per Cent*
Foodstuffs	$ 151,667	15.0%
Feed and Fertilizer	73,104	7.2
Fuel	96,346	9.5
Cotton, Wool, Other Fibers, Hides, Fabricated Textiles	178,249	17.6
Iron, Steel, Chemicals, Lumber, Paper, and Related Products and Raw Materials	237,534	23.5
Machinery and Vehicles	215,736	21.3
Miscellaneous	60,114	5.9
Totals	$1,012,753 [1]	100%

Source: *Statistical Abstract* 1959, p. 882.

[1] Total does not add because of rounding.

aid had gone to Europe. Table 7 lists the non-military aid given by the International Cooperation Administration between 1954 and 1958, inclusive, by country and area. This aid totaled $8.1 billion; during the same period other agencies administered non-military mutual secrity aid totaling $518 million.

Other Foreign Aid Grants and Assistance

IN ADDITION to the mutual security programs, the United States government extends certain other types of assistance to foreign countries and their inhabitants. In 1958, for example, agricultural surpluses valued at $159 million were sent overseas through private welfare organizations and $2.2 million was budgeted to help pay ocean freight charges of non-governmental relief agency shipments. A relatively new program is Atoms for Peace, for which $10 million was budgeted in 1958 and 1959.

A number of government offices and agencies other than the ICA have international responsibilities. The Department of Health, Educa-

TABLE 7

COUNTRIES RECEIVING NON-MILITARY AID FROM THE INTERNATIONAL
COOPERATION ADMINISTRATION, 1954–1958 [1]

Country, Area, or Program	Amount	Per Cent
Korea	$1,311,000,000	16.2%
Viet-Nam	962,000,000	11.8
Indochina (1954–55 Obligations; Undistributed)	726,000,000	8.9
China (Taiwan)	456,000,000	5.6
Laos	165,000,000	2.0
Thailand	147,000,000	1.8
Cambodia	145,000,000	1.8
Philippines	123,000,000	1.5
Other Far East (3 Countries; Regional Programs)	92,000,000	1.1
Turkey	407,000,000	5.0
Iran	282,000,000	3.5
Israel	170,000,000	2.1
Greece	124,000,000	1.5
Other Near East (5 Countries; Regional Programs)	220,000,000	2.7
India	379,000,000	4.7
Pakistan	347,000,000	4.3
Other South Asia (3 Countries)	72,000,000	0.9
Africa (7 Countries; [2] Regional Programs)	177,000,000	2.2
Bolivia	90,000,000	1.1
Other Latin America (19 Countries; Regional Programs)	199,000,000	2.4
Spain	355,000,000	4.4
United Kingdom	235,000,000	2.9
Yugoslavia	160,000,000	2.2
West Berlin	95,000,000	1.2
Other Europe (4 Countries; Regional Programs)	255,000,000	3.1
Asian Economic Development Fund	86,000,000	1.1
Inter-Regional Programs [3]	344,000,000	4.2
Totals	$8,108,000,000 [4]	100%

Source: *Statistical Abstract* 1959, pp. 880–81.

[1] Fiscal years, inclusive. All figures are net, *i.e.*, grants minus returns and adjustments. Included are $102 million in 1958 loans from the Development Loan Fund. Excluded are all grants for military purposes and allocations to or from other United States government agencies.

[2] Other than the United Arab Republic and the Sudan (included in Near East figures).

[3] Includes administrative expenses, ocean freight, and special programs, *e.g.*, malaria eradication, refugee care, atoms for peace.

[4] Does not add because of rounding and some double counting.

tion, and Welfare has a coordinator of international activities; the Office of Education recruits American educators to go abroad under the ICA technical assistance programs and the Smith-Mundt and Fulbright programs, arranges for teacher exchanges, and arranges for programs of study and observation for persons from other countries; the Children's Bureau also cooperates in the technical assistance programs and "carries responsibility for developing programs of study and observation for specialists from other countries desiring to study maternal and child health and child welfare services . . . in the United States." [15] Some foreign assistance activity is conducted by the Office of International Labor Affairs of the Department of Labor. All foreign assistance programs, of course, are carried out in cooperation with various offices in the Department of State, which serve as advisory and coordinating bodies.

Loans for Foreign Assistance

LOANS FOR economic development and other purposes comprise a significant part of United States government assistance abroad. Between 1945 and 1951 such loans, or credits, averaged about $1.6 billion a year; in the early and middle 1950's they fell to as low as $400 million a year, but by the late 1950's, were once again increasing. New credits in 1958 totaled $1.2 billion, in 1959, $1.0 billion.

The two major instruments for foreign loans are the Export-Import Bank of Washington, an independent government agency, and the Development Loan Fund of the ICA. The Export-Import Bank is not primarily concerned with economic development as such but rather finances and facilitates trade between the United States and foreign countries, and their agencies and nationals. Its loans, which can total as much as $6 billion at any one time, are expected to supplement rather than compete with non-governmental capital; in 1959 the bank authorized loans of $890 million and collected $286 million. (Authorizations dropped to $406 million in 1960.)

The Development Loan Fund (DLF), which began operations in 1958, makes loans to foreign businessmen or foreign governments for specific projects requiring investment capital. Its general purpose is "to encourage the economic development of the less developed countries of the free world," which it does by "financing investments that can spark the mobilization of unused resources." [16] In 1958 the DLF extended credits to the governments or businesses of India ($75 million), Pakistan ($5.5 million), Honduras ($5 million), and Ceylon ($1.6

[15] *United States Government Organization Manual* 1958–59. General Services Administration. Washington, D.C.: USGPO, 1958, p. 344.
[16] *Ibid.*, p. 93.

426

million). Total funds appropriated to the DLF in fiscal 1958 and 1959 were $880 million. In 1959 the DLF approved loans of $568 million, primarily for the benefit of countries in the Near East and Asia; in 1960 about $700 million.

Foreign credits are also extended under the mutual security programs other than the DLF ($103 million in 1959), in some cases relating to military assistance. Under the Agricultural Trade Development and Assistance Act, United States agricultural commodities are sold for foreign currencies and the funds thereby obtained are used by the United States to finance military or other grants and credits for foreign countries. To the extent that the countries involved do not have to use their holdings of dollars to purchase the commodities, they receive short-term assistance, which was valued at $236 million in 1958.

The Value and Uses of Government Aid

One type of question concerning United States foreign assistance is the extent to which the government should encourage non-governmental investment abroad as a complement of or substitute for non-military government grants and credits. There has been considerable discussion over (1) the use of non-government firms on a fee basis for carrying out mutually agreed contracts; (2) government insurance of transfer of profits and repatriation of capital; (3) government-negotiated guarantees against confiscation without compensation; (4) tax treaties to eliminate double taxation of profits (it has been estimated that it would cost the United States $200 million a year to drop all United States taxes on foreign profits of American businesses [17]); (5) exchange convertibility guarantees; (6) coordination of United States tariff policy with United States development policy; (7) elimination of cargo preferences to the Merchant Marine; [18] and (8) requirements that funds for foreign governments and businesses be spent for American goods, a requirement that, late in 1959, was made for DLF loans. Such measures would encourage further investment and participation by American businesses in overseas development. Against such increased participation is the fact that businesses operating overseas are primarily interested in profitable activities, only secondarily in improving living conditions; also cited is the widespread hostility of other peoples to American business operations in their countries.

Certain criticisms have been made against loan programs in so far as they help government rather than private business, and against the

[17] *Time*, LXXII (July 21, 1958).
[18] *The Objectives of United States Economic Assistance Programs.* Center for International Studies, Massachusetts Institute of Technology. Washington, D.C.: USGPO, 1957, pp. 43–46.

technical assistance programs: government-financed development programs may waste scarce resources as a perhaps inevitable by-product of government direction of the growth of entire economies; non-governmental initiative may be discouraged; local efforts for improvement may be decreased; and United States government aid may encourage socialism by employing governmental channels for aid. In answer to such criticisms it has been argued that countries receiving government aid for the most part lack the personnel, the experience, the capital, the business and financial institutions to embark extensively on free private enterprise; that democratic socialism is further removed from communism than it is from modern American capitalism; and that foreign peoples frequently do not share the American distinction between public and private enterprise, and sometimes hold the latter in disrepute.[19]

Criticisms such as the above have been primarily internal ones, *i.e.*, from within the United States. Foreign criticism of United States overseas assistance has taken different forms. Aid itself is seldom criticized; its nature and distribution often are. Some countries, for example, have asked for less military assistance and more technical assistance. Many countries have asked for more economic development assistance; as Table 7 indicates, the proportion of non-military aid for Africa and Latin America has been relatively small (5.7 per cent), though both areas have considerable potential for economic growth. Also serious are criticisms that non-military aid is not always suited to the needs of a country, though of course aid is not given in forms greatly different from those requested by foreign governments or businesses. It has been suggested that less emphasis be placed on heavy industrial development and the construction of major projects such as dams and highways, and more on small pilot projects, demonstration teams, and training of indigenous personnel. Such projects and instruction should be in keeping with the cultural and social background of the country in question, both to ensure their acceptance and to avoid disruption of established ways of life. One writer has summed up the requirements that foreign aid should meet to answer some of these and other criticisms: "the primary criteria for determining an optimum allocation of foreign technical assistance would be . . . economic efficiency; absorbability in the recipient economies; and conformity with the overall interests of the donors." [20]

[19] *The Cost of Peace Is Your Business.* Public Affairs Institute. Washington, D.C.: Public Affairs Institute, 1957, p. 18.
[20] Jahangir Amuzegar, "Foreign Technical Assistance: Sense and Nonsense," *Social Research*, XXVI (Autumn, 1959), p. 270.

INTERNATIONAL ORGANIZATIONS

AMERICAN CITIZENS and the United States government participate in a number of international organizations. Such participation may involve individual or governmental financial contributions; information and technical assistance; or the use of goods, equipment, and facilities. Generally speaking there are two groups of international bodies: those comprised of non-governmental organizations and individual citizens of various countries and those comprised of representatives of various governments.

International Non-Governmental Organizations

THERE ARE four types of international non-governmental bodies concerned wholly or in part with social welfare. One type comprises organizations that provide a forum for international discussion of information on social welfare subjects. An example is the International Conference of Social Work, which has constituent national committees in some twenty-five countries and holds biannual meetings; its purpose is to promote improved social work methods throughout the world. The theme of its 1956 conference in Munich was: "Man and the Machine—Industrialization and Its Impact on Social Welfare." Another small group of organizations promotes governmental and intergovernmental action; among these bodies is the International Alliance of Women Voters for Suffrage and Equal Citizenship.

A third, more important, group of organizations comprises federations of national organizations to provide coordination and exchange of information; they correspond on the international level to the nationwide staff organizations in the United States, discussed in Chapter 5. The League of Red Cross Societies is an example; it provides liaison and coordination in program development, disaster assistance, and technical aid for eighty-two national Red Cross, Red Crescent, Red Lion, and Sun Societies. (The International Committee of the Red Cross is not a federation of agencies but rather a Swiss committee designed to safeguard the principles of the Red Cross and to give official recognition to national Red Cross societies.) [21] Another body of this general type is the Commission of the Churches on International Affairs, established in 1948 as "the agent to represent the World Council of Churches and the International Missionary Council in international affairs." It serves

[21] For the Common Weal: A Ten-Year Report on the International Activities of the American Red Cross. Washington, D.C.: American National Red Cross, 1955, p. 13.

429

liaison purposes and acts as a representative of its parent groups before the United Nations and related intergovernmental bodies. In the latter capacity it provides "leaders of the world-wide Christian fellowship" with information on matters of international concern to churches and serves as a means for "effective Christian witness when international decisions are made." [22]

The International Conference of Catholic Charities promotes the collaboration and coordination of the national charitable and assistance organizations of forty-three countries. It maintains a Center of Study and Information at its offices in Rome to deal with such subjects as youth welfare, housing and population, and emergency relief. The International Federation of Settlements and Neighborhood Centers sponsors cooperation among such agencies in some twenty countries. The International Association of Schools of Social Work sponsors high standards of social work education through information services, forums, and study courses; in 1960 its members were 257 schools of social work in thirty-two countries and eleven associations of such schools.[23]

Finally, there are international non-governmental bodies that provide relief and services; one of these is the International Rescue Committee, whose primary purpose is to aid refugees from the "Iron Curtain" countries. It has provided food, clothes, medical care, and cash allotments; has operated migration and resettlement projects and retraining programs; and has sponsored and maintained children's homes.[24] There are a number of international Jewish agencies, supported largely but not entirely by American contributions, that give direct assistance. The Organization for Rehabilitation through Training (ORT), in cooperation with the fund-raising and -dispersing Joint Distribution Committee and other international Jewish agencies, in 1957 spent $4.8 million on training programs for occupational and social rehabilitation.[25] (Also cf. Chapter 6, section on "Jewish Communal and Social Services.")

There are a few international bodies that provide both relief, and coordination and information. The International Union for Child Welfare, comprising sixty-nine organizations in thirty-eight countries (1960), provides both disaster relief and assistance in program development and methods of work. Its clearinghouse functions are relatively new; leaders of the organization expect it to evolve into a specialized body for guidance in improvement of services, and they plan to initiate conferences and small working groups for the betterment of techniques and

[22] *The Commission of the Churches on International Affairs, 1956–57.* New York: The Commission of the Churches on International Affairs, 1957, pp. 5, 25.
[23] Russell H. Kurtz, ed. *Social Work Year Book 1960.* New York: National Association of Social Workers, 1960, pp. 626–29.
[24] *Ibid.,* p. 628.
[25] *ORT Yearbook 1958.* New York: American ORT Federation, 1958.

services.[26] International Social Service is an organization with branches or correspondent agencies in 102 countries (1960) that gives "intercountry social casework service to families and individuals whose problems require such service." It also makes studies, provides information to various groups, and encourages legislation and social welfare programs that "will lessen the destructive effects of migration and facilitate satisfactory adjustment." [27]

International Governmental Organizations

THE UNITED NATIONS, with its specialized agencies and programs, is the principal international organization that involves the United States. There are a number of others, however, some of which have important social welfare and health functions, notably the Intergovernmental Commission for European Migration. American support for such organizations comes largely from the United States government, which in 1959 contributed $123.9 million to a variety of international bodies. Contributions for 1958 are given in Table 8. There have also been private American contributions to international governmental bodies, particularly to the United Nations. The most-publicized gift to the UN from an American was the donation of the site of the present UN building by John D. Rockefeller, Jr., the value of which was set at $8.5 million. Among businesses, the Ford Motor Company has sponsored televised coverage of General Assembly sessions; Eastman-Kodak has sponsored a 3,500-member Rochester, New York, Committee for the UN; Charles Pfizer and Company has donated penicillin and other antibiotics to the UN Children's Fund and the World Health Organization.[28] Beginning in 1960, a growing number of Americans have contributed a self-imposed one per cent tax on their incomes to the UN.

The UN is active in several broad areas of welfare. Relief and servives for refugees have been of considerable importance. The Children's Fund (UNICEF) has helped initiate projects in maternal and child welfare services and training, child health and nutrition programs, and emergency assistance programs; in 1960 it was assisting 350 child health and welfare programs in some 100 countries. The World Health Organization is a specialized body that offers advisory services and directly conducts programs to reduce specific diseases such as tuberculosis, malaria, venereal diseases, and others, as well as to improve general health conditions. The UN Educational, Scientific and Cultural

---

[26] "Reorganization of the Activities of the International Union for Child Welfare," *International Social Service Review* #3 (October, 1957), p. 58.
[27] Kurtz, *op. cit.*, p. 628.
[28] *New York Times*, April 19, 1958.

Organization (UNESCO) and the UN Food and Agriculture Organization (FAO) are essentially staff bodies, conducting research and educational programs and furnishing technical assistance on request to member nations.

TABLE 8

UNITED STATES GOVERNMENT CONTRIBUTIONS TO INTERNATIONAL
ORGANIZATIONS, 1958 [1]
(In Thousands of Dollars)

Organization or Program	Amount	Per Cent
All United Nations Programs and Agencies	*$105,921*	*85.3%*
United Nations	16,361	13.2
Food and Agriculture Organization	2,035	1.6
International Civil Aviation Organization	1,912	1.5
International Labor Organization	1,750	1.4
International Telecommunication Union	146	0.1
Relief and Works Agency for Palestine Refugees in the Near East	22,996	18.5
Expanded Program of Technical Assistance	14,088	11.3
Children's Fund	11,000	8.9
World Health Organization [2]	9,168	7.4
UN Educational, Scientific, and Cultural Organization	3,383	2.7
Refugee Fund	2,233	1.8
Relief for Hungarian Refugees	1,225	1.0
High Commissioner for Refugees (special projects)	100	0.1
United Nations Emergency Force	19,441	15.6
Others (2 organizations)	83	0.1
Intergovernmental Commission for European Migration	*8,562*	*6.9*
Inter-American Organizations	*8,211*	*6.5*
Pan-American Health Organization [3]	3,518	2.8
Pan-American Union	2,830	2.3
Organization of American States Technical Cooperation Program	1,212	1.0
Tropical Tuna Commission	353	0.3
Institute of Agricultural Sciences	214	0.2
Others (6 organizations)	85	0.1
Other Regional Organizations	*1,397*	*1.1*
North Atlantic Treaty Organization	1,032	0.8
Caribbean Commission	138	0.1
Others (3 organizations)	228	0.2
Other International Organizations (19) [4]	*218*	*0.1*
Totals	$124,310	100%

Note: Totals do not add because of rounding.
Source: *Statistical Abstract* 1959, p. 953.

[1] Includes both assessments ($54.6 million) and contributions ($69.7 million). Capital subscriptions to organizations such as the International Monetary Fund are excluded.
[2] Includes $5 million for a malaria eradication program.
[3] Includes $2 million for a malaria eradication program.
[4] For example, $64,570 for International Atomic Energy Agency fellowship programs, $14,847 to the Bureau of Weights and Measures, $9,997 to the Hydrographic Bureau, and so forth.

The UN Technical Assistance Administration is primarily concerned with economic development and long-range improvement in social services and the quality of public administration. Among other special UN agencies whose primary purpose is economic development are the International Bank for Reconstruction and Development and its associated International Finance Corporation (IFC). The funds of both organizations are subscribed by member countries; for example, the United States has contributed $635 million to the International Bank, one-third its paid-in capital. The Bank makes loans, primarily to governments, for various productive purposes, particularly to finance power and transportation projects; between 1947 and mid-1958 it made 193 loans, with a value equivalent to $3.6 billion, to forty-six countries and overseas territories. The IFC is an investment institution, established in 1956 to deal directly with private businessmen and investors rather than with or through governments; its investments have been predominantly in manufacturing, processing, and mining, and by 1960 totaled $26 million. In 1958 the UN Special Fund was established to assist less developed countries in the planning and training for development projects, the United States contributing 40 per cent of its budget. Most recently, in 1960, the International Development Association was established as an affiliate of the World Bank to provide capital assistance to less-developed countries, the United States to meet one-third of its $1 billion subscription.

In a study of the United Nations published by the Brookings Institution the general nature and concern of UN welfare activities was stated as follows:

> The common denominator of most of the programs and activities in the field of welfare and social defense is the emphasis on assistance to the individual. This emphasis makes for an almost infinite variety of possible programs and approaches, dependent on the special needs of the individual and the social and cultural pattern in which he lives. The temptation to engage in activities beyond the scope and powers of an intergovernmental organization such as the United Nations is, therefore, great. . . .
>
> Considering these pressures, the United Nations has, on the whole, been surprisingly successful in developing basic programs and adapting them to national and local needs. Major requirements, such as the need for trained welfare personnel, have been ascertained and programs to meet them have been initiated. Long-range programs are increasingly taking the place of earlier short-term activities. The emphasis now is on assistance to governments in the development of integrated programs of their own. Brakes are being applied to the preparation of studies that are not essential to the formulation of policy recommendations on the part of the United Nations or are of only limited value to national gov-

ernments as they confront their major tasks in improving the lot of their people.[29]

The contribution of the United States government to the activities of the UN can most readily be measured in financial terms. In 1959 the total income of the UN (excluding its specialized agencies) was some $72 million; of this, $61.5 million was assessed from members. The United States share was $20 million, about 32.5 per cent. The United States contributed roughly the same percentage of the $8.3 million assessed budget of the Food and Agriculture Organization; of the $12.6 million assessed budget of UNESCO; and of the $15 million budget of the World Health Organization. The U.S.S.R. was assessed about 13 per cent of the budgets of these bodies (except the FAO, to which it did not contribute); the United Kingdom about 8 per cent. The great majority of member nations of the UN were assessed less than 0.5 per cent apiece of the various budgets.

A number of non-UN international organizations also are supported in part by the government of the United States. Among these is the Intergovernmental Committee for European Migration, established in 1951 to help move migrants (including refugees) from Europe to countries of resettlement. Between 1952 and 1957 the Committee helped process and provide transportation for 770,000 migrants. It has also helped to develop further opportunities for resettlement by providing specialists in fields such as land settlement to various countries.[30] The United States participates in as many as fifty other international bodies that are not agencies of the UN. They include groups such as the Consultative Committee on Economic Development in South and Southeast Asia, and Permanent Court of Arbitration, and the International Sugar Council; most of them have no direct bearing on special problems of health and welfare, though in a wider sense they may have a great deal to do with the general welfare of man, as does the United Nations.

Finally, the United States participates in certain inter-American organizations, notably the Organization of American States (OAS, better known under the name of its general secretariat, the Pan American Union). The OAS is, formally, a regional agency of the UN, though in fact it is a cooperating but independent organizational entity. The welfare interests of the OAS include the economic, social, juridical, and cultural relations among its twenty-one member republics; its most important direct activity is its technical assistance program. Another inter-American organization is the Pan American Sanitary Organiza-

[29] Robert E. Asher, et al. The United Nations and Promotion of the General Welfare. Washington, D.C.: The Brookings Institution, 1958, pp. 548–49.
[30] United States Government Organization Manual 1958–59, p. 552.

tion, which by argeement with the World Health Organization serves as the regional office of that body. The Pan American Sanitary Bureau, the operating arm of the Sanitary Organization, conducts health studies and conferences; provides consultative services to member governments; and extends technical assistance to public health programs.

CONCLUDING REMARKS

WITHOUT EXCEPTION, the welfare institutions discussed in this survey participate in welfare abroad to some extent. Prior to World War II there were some examples of American governmental aid extended to other peoples but the pattern of participation in foreign welfare efforts was essentially religious. Even today, the proportion of American non-governmental to governmental aid for foreign assistance is greater than it is for social welfare and education at home. Annual individual contributions for welfare abroad amount to a quarter of a billion dollars a year, while foundations, churches, and other institutions contribute at least that amount. Church effort is of especial significance because it is usually carried out by men and women who are paid very little in proportion to their skill and devoted energies. The efforts of the Friends Service Committee, for example, cost American donors only $3 million in one recent year, but any objective measure of their immediate impact would probably be several times the impact of a similar amount of governmental aid to industrial development, for instance. The difficulties encountered by governmental aid in general suggest a revaluation of the efforts of "missionaries" abroad. A similar reassessment might be made of the often-extensive contributions of American business enterprises, both as payers of taxes and as providers of income, skills, and social service to foreign employees overseas.[31]

The national government expended a total of $3.7 billion in grants and credits abroad in 1959. Of this, 56 per cent was for direct military assistance, however, and in recent years the U.S. Congress has showed an increasing disposition to cut foreign assistance expenditures, particularly for non-military purposes. It is also the case that much of the non-military assistance given as direct grants has gone to a relatively small number of countries around the perimeter of the Soviet bloc—countries that also receive much U.S. military assistance. The major long-term impact of U.S. foreign aid has come from programs of credit

[31] For example, see *United States Business and Labor in Latin America*, University of Chicago Research Center in Economic Development and Cultural Change, prepared for the U.S. Senate Committee on Foreign Relations. Washington, D.C.: USGPO, 1960.

to assist countries in the development of public works and industry, of grants for technical assistance in all phases of agriculture, commerce, and industry, and of loans for the construction of economic facilities. In addition, one consequence of the huge surpluses accumulated by the government's farm price-support program has been the program for giving and selling at low prices American agricultural commodities to countries whose food supplies and foreign exchange holdings are low.

Meanwhile, the contribution of the United States to international organizations extending aid to the less-developed nations has been proportionate to the great wealth of this nation. There is a growing network of social welfare organizations throughout the world corresponding to similar groups in the United States, usually formed from U.S. groups and their foreign counterparts. Some of these are nongovernmental, some governmental, and some represent both interests. The United Nations itself has a growing program of aid to its less-developed member nations. It appears that a larger proportion of U.S. foreign aid expenditures in the future will be channeled through international agencies such as the UN, the International Bank, the International Monetary Fund, and new organizations such as the International Development Association that was being organized in 1960. The government of the United States has thus far been reluctant to assure the granting of one indirect but effective form of foreign aid. It has declined participation in several international boards established to set prices for certain types of raw materials and agricultural products, prefering to let the prices for such products find their "natural level." The effect of U.S. participation would be to raise generally the prices paid to primary and secondary producers of raw commodities in the less-developed countries, hence increasing their national incomes; the countereffect would be to raise slightly the consumer prices of goods such as rubber, tin, cocoa, sugar, and others.

Chapter Sixteen

THE FUTURE OF WELFARE
IN AMERICA

IN BRINGING THIS SURVEY TO A CLOSE, it is fitting to make some general remarks on welfare in America—its prospects, problems, and trends. One matter of some concern is the relative success of the welfare institutions described in this survey. Is it true, as is sometimes alleged, that the national government is absorbing more and more of the welfare functions of society and that many of the other institutions will soon cease to perform significant roles? Are churches declining? Are voluntary agencies things of the past?

Some brief opinions may be ventured on these questions. First of all, welfare is continually being redefined. Health insurance was not an element in the welfare concerns of the ancients, and they were not in an unhappy state for want of it. Good race relations were not considered by nineteenth-century Americans as the chief problem confronting them, although they were coming to be very well aware of the social situation of the Caucasian immigrant from Europe. Thus, the continual redefinition of needs provides ever-new competitive opportunities. If a welfare agency or institution has failed to do well on a past problem, if it has given up its functions to more successful, powerful, or efficient institutions, it may still undertake new welfare functions.

Granted this possibility, the question of the relative growth and power of the several institutions of welfare may be considered. Several institutions of the twelve general types described in this survey have advanced notably in scope and influence. The national government is the outstanding example. A second growing system of philanthropy and welfare is the foundation. Fifty years ago, the foundation was a rare and generally unknown instrument. Today foundations and related non-profit corporations are being formed annually by the hundreds. Their assets may be added to at the rate of a billion dollars a year for the next few years. Foundations are not a fad; they have proved to have great facility for directing organized, orderly human effort, either for the most precise or for the most general welfare needs.

The business corporation is characterized by an equally brisk development of welfare enterprise. America is already a corporate economy in every sector of enterprise, including grocery stores and farming. Even the professions are being "corporatized" under new laws. Although small corporations are far greater in number, the large corporations are the dominant factor in all branches of industry. Because of its structure, the larger corporation has developed internal and external welfare motives resembling those that were once thought to be the sole province of philanthropists and mutual-aid societies. Consider the non-market behavior of the large corporation today: it requires an increasing proportion of resources, time, and leadership; it resembles more and more the medieval *corporatio*, or guild, and the mutual-aid society in the benefits it provides members and more and more the modern philanthropic, non-profit organization that gives to scholars, schools, churches, governments, and other agencies of society. Doing business "in a favorable climate" may seem to be a vague and intangible basis for decision, scorned by hardheaded businessman and cynical professor alike, but it nevertheless is the driving over-all policy that explains the enormous expansion in the non-market activity of business.[1]

It is probable that the local governments of the United States will be increasingly called upon to coordinate the welfare activities within their geographical area. What this area must be is itself an important question. The authors believe that the artificial barriers among local communities within a single interdependent and natural larger community must be broken down. Even as new hundreds of thousands of people crowd into them, the suburbs of America are proving to be failures as human and economic settlements. There must be an organic concept of the metropolis if anything approaching a "welfare society" can be achieved for the middle classes of America. The middle classes of America are paying a twofold price in the great game of welfare exchanges in society: they are paying heavily to make minimum standards possible for the poor and they are paying an unconscionable cost to remain middle-class at work and at home in the suburbs. It seems likely

[1] For an interpretation of the changes taking place in modern economic activity, see A. A. Berle, Jr., *The 20th-Century Capitalist Revolution* (1954).

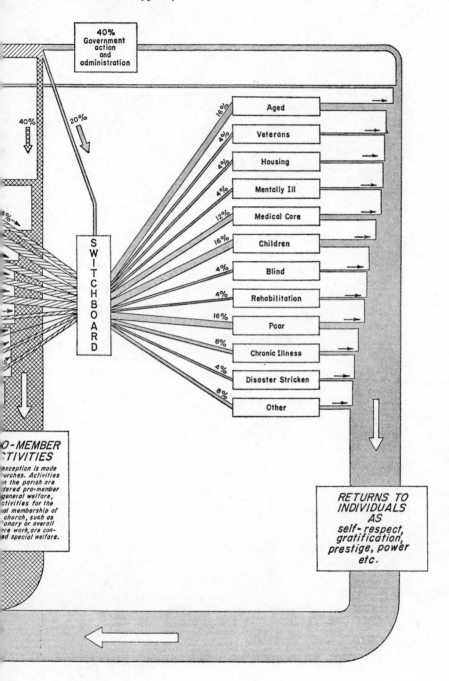

40%
Government
action
and
administration

40%

20%

16% Aged

4% Veterans

4% Housing

4% Mentally Ill

12% Medical Care

16% Children

4% Blind

4% Rehabilitation

16% Poor

8% Chronic Illness

4% Disaster Stricken

8% Other

S
W
I
T
C
H
B
O
A
R
D

O-MEMBER
TIVITIES

exception is made
urches. Activities
n the parish are
dered pro-member
general welfare,
ctivities for the
al membership of
church, such as
onary or overall
re work, are con-
ed special welfare.

RETURNS TO
INDIVIDUALS
AS
self-respect,
gratification,
prestige, power
etc.

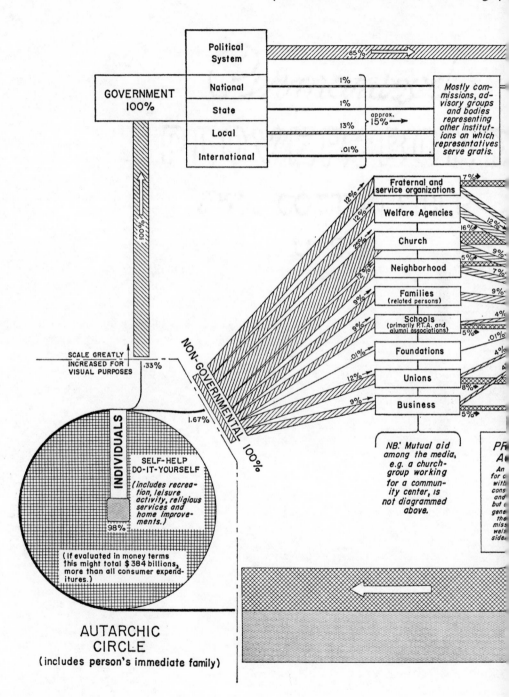

FIGURE

THE ANNUAL FLOW OF VOLUNTARY, NON-MONE
(Time and work estimated for an average ye

Political System — 85%

GOVERNMENT 100%

National — 1%
State — 1%
Local — 13%   approx. >15%→
International — .01%

Mostly commissions, advisory groups and bodies representing other institutions on which representatives serve gratis.

Fraternal and service organizations — 7%→   12%
Welfare Agencies — 16%   12%
Church — 5%   9%
Neighborhood — 7%
Families (related persons) — 9%
Schools (primarily P.T.A. and alumni associations) — 4%   5%   .01%
Foundations — 4%
Unions — 8%
Business — 5%

12%
12%
2%
12%
9%
9%
.01%
12%
9%

100%

SCALE GREATLY INCREASED FOR VISUAL PURPOSES   .33%

NON-GOVERNMENTAL 100%

1.67%

INDIVIDUALS

SELF-HELP DO-IT-YOURSELF
(includes recreation, leisure activity, religious services and home improvements.)

98%

(If evaluated in money terms this might total $384 billions, more than all consumer expenditures.)

AUTARCHIC CIRCLE
(includes person's immediate family)

NB. Mutual aid among the media, e.g. a church-group working for a community center, is not diagrammed above.

PR
A
An
for a
with
cons
and
but a
gene
the
miss
welf
side

that the invention and development of new mechanisms for coordinating the hundreds of separate governments of the metropolis and the hundreds of distinct welfare agencies that operate within the metropolitan chaos will find support among the middle classes.

International organizations are a progressively stronger factor in the national and international welfare picture. The United Nations and a host of special institutions will probably assemble an increasing proportion of the world resources for international aid. The weaker and poorer nations desire aid from international institutions in preference to aid from single nations, such as the United States and the Soviet Union would provide alone; their influence is sufficient to bring about this turn of events. Furthermore, the very reluctance of the U.S.S.R., as evidenced in the speeches of Premier Khrushchev in 1960, to collaborate with other nations or groups in foreign development aid is bound to incite an opposite reaction by the United States and may end in a surrender of the U.S.S.R. to world opinion. The underdeveloped nations and the moderately well-to-do nations have much to gain by seeking aid through the United Nations and similar international collectivities rather than directly from a single nation. The numerous failures and disappointments of the United States in using foreign aid directly as "an extension of foreign policy by other means" will encourage this nation to still further participation in collective international effort. Concretely, this means that the annual American contribution for international welfare will be increasingly channeled through international organizations and the work managed by collaborative efforts of the nations.

In contrast to foundations, business, the national government, international government, and some others, the fraternal orders and service organizations seem to be somewhat outdated as means of dispensing social welfare. It may be premature to predict a decline in the influence of such august and powerful groups as the Masonic orders, the Lions, and the American Legion. Nevertheless, the conventional mode of American society seems to be moving away from special groups that are formal in their rituals, historic in their hold upon their members, or based on the camaraderie of their fellows. There are other successful competitors for the attention of the ordinary man, who has been the favorite of such organizations. No doubt their power will continue, much as the agrarian power has continued in American life long after the United States has become a nation of city-dwellers, but it will probably undergo a gradual but constant decline.

There are also a number of institutions of welfare that appear likely to remain stable, neither advancing greatly nor retrogressing; these include the neighborhood and community welfare organizations, national non-governmental welfare organizations, the churches, the educational system, labor unions, and State governments. Some of these institutions, for example the national welfare bodies, the educational system, and the labor unions, have developed rapidly in the past few decades but now seem to have reached a point at which they will not undergo major changes, at least not in their present form. The others have been holding their positions in relation to other institutions for some time and will probably continue to do so.

First, neighborhood and non-governmental community welfare organizations often prosper and are continually being developed. There have been many intelligent innovations in small-scale neighborhood and community welfare organizations in the past few decades. Less and less frequently, however, do such undertakings have lengthy independent existences. More typically, both old and new small-scale organizations are being increasingly integrated and coordinated with other institutions, including local governments. Coordination, one of the most striking structural developments in local welfare in recent years, is discussed further below.

The coordinating and fund-raising welfare organizations of national scope, including the heart, cancer, and other associations, are not likely to decline, because they are the centers of skilled personnel in their fields, have powerful apparatuses, are concerned with important problems, and provide outlets for civic energies of a voluntary sort not encompassed by church groups, governments, or other movements of a political kind in this apolitical age. But they will probably not advance beyond their present stature, because they already cover the widespread felt needs of this time. Perhaps they do so excessively; there appears to be an organization of this type for every conceivable need. Furthermore, they will be increasingly under fire from interests wishing to coordinate metropolitan areas in a reliable way. They have aroused much opposition because some of them have engaged in bitterly competitive activities. Also, governments continue to take their functions away. Finally, many foundations are being set up to manage the philanthropy of individuals and corporations; the "free giving" of the public may become so constricted and channelized that the appeals of many national and local organizations may be moderated and become applications to trusts, corporations, and formal and "scientific" foundations.

The prospect of the churches of America, as Americans have traditionally known them, seems to be fairly constant. A great deal is known about church welfare in America. A marvelous history and fair present performance are evident. Yet the will to suffer for charity (which is the peculiar claim of the church) is largely absent. The Roman Catholic and Mormon churches appear almost alone in their claim to divine missions *as institutions* to organize and conduct welfare in the context of religion. Most religious groups regard the church as a vehicle, intrinsically neither better nor worse than others, for performing acts of charity. This attitude, with the movements of individual churches to the suburbs and the rather complete *de facto* separation of churches from the large province of mental health, have limited the progress of religious groups in social welfare.

The educational institutions and school systems of the country have probably reached their peak so far as their control of other institutions and individuals for welfare purposes is concerned. They also have reached their financial peak as an independent group of fund-gathering agencies. Private institutions will probably undergo a financial decline relative to State-supported institutions, and indeed, from the standpoint of the future, the private institutions must depend more and more upon foundations and corporations for their continuing annual support. The power of educators as a class in American life, however, will tend to increase, partly by virtue of the coalition of universities with foundations and businesses (every action has its reaction: the controlled controls the controller). Therefore, the problems of education will continue to receive prominence in the policies of government but it will no longer be the independent intellectual authority of the educators that will produce such impact but rather their influence as intellectuals plus their membership in a more tightly knit community and national leadership network.

The unions of the country are just rising to the challenge of the welfare society. They started, of course, as mutual-aid societies, and continue a great many such functions, but in recent years they have depended for more and more of their welfare contributions to their members upon periodic agreements with employers. Here they are strong, and perhaps should be classified as a growing type of organization, inasmuch as every year sees an increasing number of cooperative and bargained welfare plans. But this is generally a tendency away from traditional unionism and in the long run seems to result in corporatism, that is, a blending of union leaders' power with the power of management, or in innocuous trusteeship, a form of welfare operation in which the union itself gains little in power and wealth but rather acts as an annual bargaining agent for a group of employees. Such a statement may seem questionable in view of the newspaper headlines of the past few years, proclaiming the immense power secured by unions through the new welfare schemes. More responsible studies, however, have indicated that typically the union loses much of its control over trusteed funds, especially when compared with what its control would have been had it continued in the old tradition of the union as a mutual-aid society. Essentially, the distinction between the labor unions and businesses as sources of employee benefits is becoming blurred.

The State governments appear to be a more certain case of welfare stagnation than the unions; the latter are at least active agents for bringing about tremendous changes on the American welfare scene. The States, however, continue to be handmaidens of the national government. To the extent that they no longer are characterized by the strong control of rural interests over urban interests, they may be expected to produce more legislation of a permissive sort for urban centers. But it is difficult to see in what way the States may be more useful than they have been in the past thirty years in assuming *new* functions of a welfare kind or in acting as agents of other groups for welfare. The States continue to be, for objective students, a fascinating display of an old and decayed type of politics trying to feed upon technical and administrative issues. A new philosophy, really a new "operational code," is needed in American State politics.

The original question asked of the welfare process in this survey was, Who gives what to whom by what means? In answer, the welfare procedures of each major welfare institution have been elaborated. From time to time it has been necessary to take up activities jointly performed by two or more institutions. Thus, foundation grants for overseas aid are sometimes involved with United States government action overseas. National, State, and local governmental activities are often intertwined. But the full extent of this interrelation of the institutions of welfare is nowhere commented upon in detail.

The mutual operating dependence of welfare institutions might be called the *coordination* of welfare media. The collaboration of educators and family members in a PTA is a simple example of media coordination. More complex coordination takes place when several agencies of the national government, local government, the Red Cross, and volunteer neighborhood groups rally to fight a flood disaster. Institutional coordination is of two structural types:

First, it is accomplished by largely independent agencies of the same institutional type. For example, the U.S. Corps of Engineers and the U.S. Forest Service, both federal agencies, may cooperate in establishing better recreational use of a watershed area.

Secondly, different types of institutions may collaborate; for example, a church and an association of doctors that establish a hospital.

Too much should not be made of this distinction. There are so many striking differences among groups within the same general institutional setting that they are often as different from one another as they are from a wholly different type of institution. For instance, a small-town government may have more in common in its operations with a neighborhood voluntary group than with a large city.

There are many thousands of instances of institutional and agency collaboration in American welfare activities. In fact, a new type of personnel has arisen on the American scene, a composite of the social worker, the promoter, and the businessman, whose function has been to join together community forces performing similar or related operations. An example may be seen in the mental health field. In Kansas City mental health was a problem with which all governments were concerned but none urgently; there was a need to combine promotion, research, treatment, and education on mental health in an integrated operation; numerous private and voluntary associations and unorganized but interested individuals were active; the need for flexibility of operations in a complex field was apparent. Such conditions foster the emergence of a new kind of leadership that can cut its way through the entanglements of law, finance, conflicting and overlapping jurisdictions, and divergent and often hostile community elements. The result may be, as it was in Kansas City, the formation of a special agency, a non-profit corporation. It is empowered to deal with governments of all kinds, foundations, agencies, hospitals, and individuals—in short, with every conceivable kind of institution—in pursuing its multiple aims in the mental health field. Agencies of this type are increasing in number throughout the American welfare system. The organizational problems encountered call forth the greatest skills of leadership and management. They constantly raise the questions: What kind of governmental system is emerging? What kind of welfare system is evolving? It may be too early to comment on the proliferation of coordinated institutional activities in the welfare field, but it is surmised that this may be how America will continue its twentieth-century movement toward a functionally organized and organically coordinated society; as such it would stand in contrast, ultimately in sharp contrast, to the individualistic, geographically organized society of the nineteenth century in which institutions were separatistic.[2]

All exchanges of goods and services in American society can be considered part of a great welfare cycle. The major institutions of society, the subjects of this survey, take energy and funds from individuals, or are given them, transform them, and pass them back to the same

[2] For a more detailed treatment of this trend, with illustrations and evidence, see Alfred de Grazia, *Public and Republic* (New York: Alfred Knopf, 1950), especially the last three chapters, and the *Elements of Political Science*, by the same author (New York: Alfred Knopf, 1952), pages 497–508. Unfortunately, an account of this trend so far as it concerns private welfare and private-public social welfare agencies is not available.

people or along to others. Actually, the cycle is composed of two sections, a larger and a smaller one. The larger includes the exchanges that take place through the market system and the general activities of government, such as national defense; human, material, and financial inputs are used by government and business to provide Americans with food, clothing, shelter, protection, and other welfare services. About nine-tenths of American production and consumption is part of this, the general welfare process. The smaller cycle is especially organized for social welfare purposes. Derived from the same input base, human, material, and financial resources are used by the institutions described in this survey (including elements of the business and governmental systems) to provide special services and goods for certain groups of people, many of whom would not otherwise get them.

Some major features of the American welfare cycle are described in previous chapters; certain other characteristics may be summarized here.

There is no such thing as a "one-institution" welfare problem. Every welfare problem is taken up by at least two institutions, most are the concern of several. Examples are legion. For instance, the national, State, and local governments as well as many individuals and non-governmental agencies extend help to the mothers of dependent children.

A problem that one institution takes as its own at one time is assumed by another agency at another time. The shift of education from family to school is only one of a hundred such shifts that have taken place in the past two centuries.

The same welfare function may be performed in fundamentally different ways: by charitable contributions, by bargaining, by authoritative rule, or by self-help. For example, one unemployed person may receive support from his parents, children, or neighbors; another from an insurance policy he contracted for while employed; a third by virtue of legislation appropriating tax receipts to pay unemployed persons an income for an extended period of time; and a fourth by turning his hand to subsistence farming. A single welfare setting can provide examples of all the different welfare transactions. For instance, an unpaid volunteer in a privately capitalized hospital, subsidized by government funds, helps to attend a patient who receives medical insurance benefits and pays from savings whatever costs cannot be met by insurance benefits. In this case, the "cooperative attitude of the patient" in his own cure constitutes the major element of self-help.

Every institution has many means of managing welfare that it does not use to the fullest. Churches could do a great deal more than they do, for example, as could labor unions. Almost any type of welfare matter might be assigned to the national government, or to a local

444

government for that matter. In this sense, every welfare institution that Americans have evolved has great unused capacity.

An important question is whether one institution is better suited than another to perform a given task. The present study, which is primarily descriptive, suggests only some of the more obvious cases of institutional superiority. There is little question that the family is the best mechanism for dealing with the welfare of the young, yet there are exceptional cases: a family may suffer moral disintegration; the need for technical training fosters special schools; premature death of parents demands social attention to the hardships facing the surviving children. In fact, the distinction between the welfare scope of the family and of other institutions of society is blurred and disputed; a number of welfare functions, because of their kind or because they constitute individual cases of hardship, are subject to examination and controversy. Proof of the superiority of a welfare institution such as the national government or a community council to do a certain job is most difficult to obtain. Any definitive judgment of the specific superiorities of each institution, when compared with the others, requires years of research and evaluation, while individual values are the source of still further controversy.

However, the materials of the present survey suggest several nearly universal problems that beset welfare organizations. A few remarks about them may serve to focus attention on the dangers and possibilities in the "government" of welfare institutions.[3] The primary problem is that of the use and abuse of power in welfare institutions. Related to this is the question of bureaucracy. The problem of voluntarism, its practice and limits, leads to the question of the present and potential strength of civic participation in American welfare institutions.

The problem of concentration of power in regard to welfare organization must be considered. The broadest danger from power in society, as history clearly demonstrates, comes from the unchecked, centralized state when equipped with the apparatus of coercion and modern communications. All functions undertaken by the government, particularly a national government, run a risk of being subverted to the ends of power, that is, to persons who are more interested in irrelevant goals, often seeking a domineering position, than they are in the provision of services to those intended to have them. Since this is not an analysis of the complex problem of the organization and philosophy of power, but rather an inventory of welfare operations in America, it can only

---

[3] A recent and thoughtful treatise on this subject is F. A. Hayek's *The Constitution of Liberty* (Chicago: University of Chicago Press, 1960). See also the series of books on ethics and economic life published by Harper & Brothers under the sponsorship of the National Council of Churches.

be suggested that the shadow of potential abuse comes particularly from those functions that are assigned to the government without measures to assure a maximum of decentralization, divorce from autocratic procedures, and adaptation to individual needs. Furthermore, there should be constant study of means of relieving the state, at least in its traditional form, of whatever activities may be reliably performed by non-national government agencies. Some measure of inconvenience is a cheap price to pay for removing the shadow of power.

It would be incorrect, however, to suggest that all problems of power concern the national government. Some of the worst problems of power begin in the family; nor are the community council, the neighborhood center, or the Quaker meetinghouse free of concern over them. Perhaps the only general prescription of use to all welfare organizations is that their potential leaders should be educated to suppress or control their temptation to power and then screened to assure rejection of any pure power-types, that is, persons lacking all principle save the expansion of their own or their group's power in any given situation.[3]

Power is the ability to command the behavior of others. Voluntarism is its opposite. It is the ability of each to act as he thinks best. Hence, to put the matter another way, maximum emphasis can be given to voluntary effort, plans, and activities in the total area of welfare. In many cases, pluralism is perhaps the ideal compromise for a clash between total control and total libertarianism. By its workings, the worst kind of power—total power—is avoided and the worst kind of libertarianism —irresponsible anarchy—is contained. To a great extent, pluralism now exists in the multiform autonomous structure of American welfare media.

The best protection of a society against abuses of power is a large measure of determined civic participation. Bureaucratic organization in government and other institutions becomes less blind and rigid in the presence of a vociferous and active citizenry. However, American society needs a larger number of active citizens than it has at the present. In the round, there are about four million people who give several hours or more a week to public affairs.

For a separate study, not yet published, the senior author has prepared a chart of non-monetary welfare. (See Figure 1, facing page 456.) It gives a "book value" of $3.5 billion to the annual non-monetary welfare of Americans, excluding unpaid self-help activities of the "do-it-yourself" type. About one-sixth of this unpaid public activity

[3] Cf. Harold D. Lasswell, "Political Constitution and Character," *Psychoanalysis and the Psychoanalytic Review*, XLVI, No. 4 (1959), pp. 3–18; and "Democratic Character," in *Political Writings*, Glencoe, Ill.: The Free Press, 1951, pp. 465–525.

is estimated to go into government at all levels and five-sixths into the public activities of the non-governmental institutions. Some of such activity benefits principally the members of welfare institutions; the balance aids the several categories of needs.

Considering how badly the active citizenry is organized and how bootless much of their effort is, and recalling the great many areas of national life that require some active, general constituency, it would seem that their number should be doubled and their efficiency and power markedly increased through non-governmental and governmental measures alike. At one time it was thought that suffrage was the way to controlled and limited government. Merely to give more people the vote was considered the way to increase the accountability of government. The same logic was applied to large private groups such as churches, business corporations, labor unions, and welfare agencies. Yet sheer membership of a formal kind only adds some ultimate control to the actions of an agency. A middle level of activism, "politism," is required for any extensive and enduring control of institutional operations. The search for means of creating such a large body of politists is perhaps the key quest of modern democracy. That and the functional reorganization of the system of government, referred to above, are together the avenue to a new kind of welfare society competent to manage its affairs without the attrition of morale and the weight of authoritarianism.

The past successes and future development of the welfare society in America could best be ensured by some budget of goals that would direct people's energies, giving precedence to some activities over others. A schedule of priorities should be added to the controls over power, the increased voluntarism, increased politism, and functional reorganization that are proposed above. However, lacking a systematic statement of a philosophy of welfare at the present time, the task is not simple. The greatest goal—universal charity—is still most remote. It is an ancient injunction, expressed in the early days of religious altruism. It is the doctrine of brotherly love, with good works as its external and material expression, and with the good material life as the external framework in which an attitude guaranteeing the dignity of all men might develop. Charity in this sense appears to be beyond the abilities of the welfare society of yesterday and today to provide directly, yet it was the fundamental desire that led to the development of the welfare society and, however differently it may be expressed in the present time, it remains the ultimate goal of the welfare society.

Progress toward human dignity and well-being is certainly apparent. Within a very few years, every American may expect that as a matter of course he will receive an income sufficient to subsist modestly in his old age out of the proceeds of his life's work plus or minus other payments from other sources. By the standards of the generation into which he was born, he can expect an education as good as that of the next man, up to the point where he may no longer usefully continue. He can expect to rely on medical services whenever sick and to seek guidance whenever in distress, and not be denied these services by shame or poverty. He can expect useful employment almost all of his working life, and when not employed he will be certain of maintenance by money payments from insurance and other sources. If disabled and unemployable, he may expect a permanent income somewhat above the level of subsistence.

This survey shows these trends to be established and the promise almost accomplished. What is it, then, that this "luckiest man ever to have lived" *cannot* expect? One fact of modern life that is largely beyond the scope of this survey is that the average man today has the greatest likelihood of sudden death of any average man in history. The newly devised means of death by warfare are as potent as the newly contrived means of the good material life.

Moreover, a certain uniformity and mediocrity may be introduced into the enjoyment of the routine pleasures of life. Everyone alike will consume certain minimal goods, with some resulting standardization of ways of life and a loss of some of the zest that economic peril, like other perils, brings to some men. Most people will not regret this loss, nor will they regret the loss of that small chance of being vastly successful through luck or skill. Men will take more of their chances in groups rather than as individuals. Men will no longer read of those who "struck it rich" or "made a million" but that "the gross national product rose a quarter of a point more than expected last year."

The common man will probably have no more chance of developing genius and a high order of creativity than he did before the achievement of a decent minimal level of security. Improved mass standards are not necessarily productive of more highly accomplished individuals on the top levels of literature, science, and art.

There are other problems with which the newly secure man of American society is most likely to be concerned. He will become more and more conscious of that great part of the world whose hunger and desperation contrast so sharply with his own security and well-being. All his past efforts to improve those conditions through taxes and foreign aid have been only enough to suggest what could be done. He must now sacrifice some of his "capital," that is, draw upon the resources and production upon which his security is based, thereby losing some of it shortly after gaining it, or he must risk the hostility of much of the world and the assaults of conscience, and even the ultimate decline of his own economic system.

More immediate to him will be domestic problems that will sometimes make his modest economic independence seem to be only a small gain. If he lives in the city, as he is more and more likely to do, he will be increasingly uncomfortable, beset by a most exasperating set of problems. Cramped housing, slow transportation, crowded recreational facilities, and confused administrative and governmental situations will be his lot. Thus far, herculean efforts seem to have brought only a maintenance of inadequate levels of performance in all these respects. It is difficult to say how much physical discomfort, controversy, mental distress, monotony, and downright unhappiness he must endure before the gigantic steps necessary to solve these problems are conceived, brought to public attention, taken, and their effects felt.

The tensions and unhappiness of race conflict will be felt particularly in metropolitan areas, one more addition to the already distressing problems of the American cities. The human relations problems produced by the efforts of one-tenth of the nation to achieve nondiscriminatory treatment are a welfare issue of grave proportions. Certainly, Negroes will eventually participate equally in the fundamental economic security programs and receive the benefits of decent education and medical care. Still, the fact that Negroes and other ethnic minorities share the minimum standards of life and care will not suppress but will increase their agitation over discriminatory treatment in social and economic affairs generally.

It must be remembered that the distresses of ethnic minorities are not felt by them alone. The pain of discrimination is felt vicariously by a great many Caucasians, both in their own lives and when in touch with the world outside their country's boundaries. Beyond this, for every problem of race relations there is a Caucasian who suffers as much as a Negro or a non-white Puerto Rican. This is often misunderstood and leads to an underestimation of the extent of welfare problems produced by racial conflict. Scientifically conducted studies would almost certainly show that literally millions of Caucasian Americans suffer as constantly, either sympathetically or out of hostilities and fears, as the ethnic minorities to whom the problem is usually thought to be confined. As matters stand now, several Negro children in a southern school can strike dismay, despair, and fear into the hearts and minds of thousands of white Southerners. That this situation is objectively absurd does not dissolve it, but even intensifies it. Multiply the illustration a thousandfold, for all the schools, hotels, houses changing tenants, restaurants opening their service to members of minority groups, and newly integrated recreational facilities, and a serious threat to the stability

449

of society and the individual's mind is posed. Obviously, some major and radical plan needs to be evolved and a new kind and order of leadership is required to deal responsibly with race relations in America.

Yet another problem will plague the materially secure man of the late twentieth century. He will be threatened by mental illness. One out of ten Americans is now believed to be suffering the handicaps of definable and disruptive mental imbalance. It is unlikely that a general increase in material prosperity will reduce this proportion. Probably economic well-being stimulates more manifestations of mental illness than economic insecurity produces, though the causal connections of the former may be more varied and obscure. The conditions of life in America continue to impose strains on the individual mind. It is unlikely that the important new developments in drug therapy, and more rapid and effective techniques of clinical therapy, will alone solve the problem.

Faced by these many problems and conditions, the common man and the uncommon man must both be aware that today America is achieving a welfare society only in terms of early twentieth-century expectations. Mid-century American experiences and new and developing circumstances suggest new concepts of the welfare society. The *new* welfare society is still far off, separated from the present by lack of knowledge, thought, and resources as well as by time. Those who work at its creation must then face the probability that once it has been achieved their heirs must turn to still other problems on man's road to peace, prosperity, and harmony.

Appendix

A WELFARE BIBLIOGRAPHY

THE WORKS LISTED BELOW are of several types. Some describe particular types of welfare activities or organizations; others are general studies of specific institutions; a few are collections of articles and essays on social welfare problems. Certain general reference works also are included, among them the most useful of government publications. Concerning publications of the national government, frequent reference is made in this work to the *Statistical Abstract of the United States*. This volume, which appears in annual editions, is a compilation of a very wide variety of statistical materials from governmental and non-governmental sources, and as such is a secondary source of data. Original sources can be identified by reference to the *Statistical Abstract*, and more recent data on much of the American welfare system can be obtained by consulting the 1961 and subsequent editions of the *Statistical Abstract*. The initials "USGPO" that occur in many citations in this survey and in the following bibliography refer to the United States Government Printing Office, which publishes almost all materials prepared by federal agencies.

Alinsky, Saul David. *Reveille for Radicals.* Chicago: University of Chicago Press, 1946.
American Jewish Year Book 1960. New York: The American Jewish Committee, 1960, and other editions.
Anderson, Odin W., and Jacob J. Feldman. *Family Medical Costs and Voluntary Health Insurance: A Nation-wide Survey.* New York: McGraw-Hill, 1956.

Andrews, F. Emerson. *Attitudes Toward Giving.* New York: Russell Sage Foundation, 1953.

Andrews, F. Emerson. *Philanthropic Foundations.* New York: Russell Sage Foundation, 1956.

Andrews, F. Emerson. *Philanthropic Giving.* New York: Russell Sage Foundation, 1950.

Bachman, George, and Associates. *Health Resources in the United States.* Washington, D.C.: The Brookings Institution, 1952.

Bachman, E. Theodore, ed. *Churches and Social Welfare: I. The Activating Concern; II. The Changing Scene; III. The Emerging Perspective.* New York: National Council of Churches, 1955.

Biennial Survey of Education in the United States 1952–54. U.S. Office of Education. Washington, D.C.: USGPO, 1956, and other editions. (Appears in separately bound chapters.)

The Book of the States 1960–1961 (Volume XIII). Chicago: Council of State Governments, 1960, and other editions.

Bornet, Vaughn Davis. *California Social Welfare.* Englewood Cliffs, N.J.: Prentice-Hall, 1956.

Bowen, Howard R. *Social Responsibilities of the Businessman.* New York: Harper & Brothers, 1953.

Bremner, Robert H. *From the Depths: The Discovery of Poverty in the United States.* New York: New York University Press, 1956.

Bruno, Frank J. *Trends in Social Work, 1874–1956.* New York: Columbia University Press, 1957.

Buell, Bradley, and Associates. *Community Planning for Human Services.* New York: Columbia University Press, 1952.

Burns, Eveline M. *Social Security and Public Policy.* New York: McGraw-Hill, 1956.

Cary, Sturges R., ed. *New Challenges to Our Schools.* (The Reference Shelf, XXV, Number 1.) New York: H. W. Wilson, 1953.

Daland, Robert T. *Government and Health: The Alabama Experience.* University, Ala.: University of Alabama Press, 1955.

de Grazia, Alfred. *The American Way of Government.* New York: Wiley and Sons, 1957.

de Grazia, Alfred, ed., *Grass Roots Private Welfare.* New York: New York University Press, 1958.

Dewhurst, J. Frederic, and Associates. *America's Needs and Resources: A New Servey.* New York: The Twentieth Century Fund, 1955.

Drake, Joseph T. *The Aged in American Society.* New York: Ronald Press, 1958.

Dunham, Arthur. *Community Welfare Organization: Principles and Practice.* New York: Thomas Y. Crowell, 1958.

Economic Security of Americans. The American Assembly. New York: Graduate School of Business, Columbia University, 1955.

The Exploding Metropolis. New York: Doubleday, 1958.

Feldman, Frances Lomas. *The Family in a Money World.* New York: Family Service Association of America, 1957.

Fitch, John A. *Social Responsibilities of Organized Labor*. New York: Harper & Brothers, 1957.

Freeman, Roger A. *Financing the Public Schools, Volume I: School Needs in the Decade Ahead*. Washington, D.C.: Institute for Social Science Research, 1958.

Freidlander, Walter. *Introduction to Social Welfare*. Englewood Cliffs, N.J.: Prentice-Hall, 1955.

Giving USA 1960. New York: American Association of Fund-Raising Counsel, 1960, and other editions.

Glueck, Sheldon and E. T. *Delinquents in the Making: Paths to Prevention*. New York: Harper & Brothers, 1952.

Glueck, Sheldon and E. T. *Unraveling Juvenile Delinquency*. Cambridge, Mass.: Commonwealth Fund, Harvard University Press, 1950.

Glueck, Sheldon, ed. *The Welfare State and the National Welfare*. Cambridge, Mass.: Addison-Wesley, 1952.

Historical Statistics of the United States 1789–1957. U.S. Bureau of the Census. Washington, D.C.: USGPO, 1960.

Hogan, John D., and Francis A. J. Lanni. *American Social Legislation*. New York: Harper & Brothers, 1956.

International Conference of Social Work Proceedings. Various titles, 1952, 1954, 1956, 1958, and other editions. New York: International Conference of Social Work.

Kasius, Cora, ed. *New Directions in Social Work*. New York: Harper & Brothers, 1954.

Keith-Lucas, Alan. *Decisions about People in Need*. Chapel Hill: The University of North Carolina Press, 1957.

Kiger, Joseph C. *Operating Principles of the Larger Foundations*. New York: Russell Sage Foundation, 1954.

Kutner, Bernard, *et al. Five Hundred Over Sixty—A Community Survey on Aging*. New York: Russell Sage Foundation, 1956.

Kurtz, Russell H., ed. *Social Work Year Book 1960*. New York: National Association of Social Workers, 1960, and other editions.

Landis, Benson Y., ed. *Yearbook of American Churches for 1960*. New York: National Council of the Churches of Christ in the U.S.A., 1959, and other editions.

Lester, Richard A. *As Unions Mature*. Princeton, N.J.: Princeton University Press, 1958.

Link, Henry C. *The Way of Security*. Garden City, N.Y.: Doubleday, 1951.

Maves, Paul B., ed. *The Church and Mental Health*. New York: Charles Scribner's Sons, 1953.

McKee, Elmore. *The People Act*. New York: Harper & Brothers, 1955.

Naftalin, Arthur, *et al.*, eds. *An Introduction to Social Science*. Chicago: J. B. Lippincott, 1953.

The National Catholic Almanac. Paterson, N.J.: St. Anthony's Guild, 1960, and other editions.

Neumeyer, Martin H. *Social Problems and the Changing Society*. New York: D. Van Nostrand, 1953.

Poole, Kenyon E. *Public Finance and Economic Welfare*. New York: Rinehart & Company, 1957.

Russell, James E., ed. *National Policies for Education, Health and Social Services*. Garden City, N. Y.: Doubleday, 1955.

Seeley, John R., Buford H. Junker, and R. Wallace Jones, Jr., *et al. Community Chest, A Case Study in Philanthropy*. Toronto, Ont.: University of Toronto Press, 1957.

Sills, David L. *The Volunteers*. Glencoe, Ill.: The Free Press, 1957.

Smith, Bradford. *A Dangerous Freedom*. Philadelphia: J. B. Lippincott, 1952.

The Social Welfare Forum. Official Proceedings of National Conference on Social Welfare. New York: Columbia University Press, annual editions.

Steiner, Peter O., and Robert Dorfman. *The Economic Status of the Aged*. Berkeley, Calif.: University of California Press, 1957.

Stevenson, George S. *Mental Health Planning for Social Action*. New York: McGraw-Hill, 1956.

Stokes, Dillard. *Social Security—Fact and Fancy*. Chicago: Henry Regnery, 1956.

Taylor, Eleanor K. *Public Accountability of Foundations and Charitable Trusts*. New York: Russell Sage Foundation, 1953.

Turnbull, John G., S. Arthur Williams, and Earl F. Cheit. *Economic and Social Security*. New York: Ronald Press, 1957.

Tyler, Poyntz, ed. *Social Welfare in the United States*. (The Reference Shelf, XXVII, Number 3.) New York: H. W. Wilson, 1955.

Vasey Wayne. *Government and Social Welfare*. New York: Henry Holt, 1958.

Ward, A. Dudley, ed. *Goals of Economic Life*. New York: Harper & Brothers, 1953.

Whyte, William H., Jr. *The Organization Man*. New York: Simon and Shuster, 1956.

Wilensky, Harold, and Charles N. Lebaux. *Industrial Society and Social Welfare*. New York: Russell Sage Foundation, 1958.

Wilton, Ann D., and F. Emerson Andrews, eds. *The Foundation Directory*. New York: Russell Sage Foundation, 1960.

Wirth, Louis. *Community Life and Social Policy*. Chicago: University of Chicago Press, 1956.

Wood, Robert C. *Suburbia: Its People and their Politics*. Boston: Houghton Mifflin, 1959.

INDEX

Adult education, 186
Aged: Catholic care for, 121–22; community services for, 62; Elks home for, 148; employment for, 56, 62, 79; family care for, 27–28; foundation grants for, 285; national medical-care program for, 384–85; number of, 27; public assistance for, 386–88; social insurance payments to, 397–98; State housing for, 354
Agricultural Marketing Service, U.S., 374
Agricultural Trade Development and Assistance Act, 427
Agriculture, federal aid for, 391–93
Agriculture, U.S. Dept. of, 184, 202, 400
Aid Retarded Children, Inc., 63
Aid to Dependent Children (ADC), 26, 388
Alcoholic beverage control, by States, 360–61
Alcoholics Anonymous, 61–62, 168–69
Alcoholics, services for, 169
Alexian Brothers, 122
Alinsky, Saul, 43
Altman Foundation of New York, 284
Amalgamated Clothing Workers' Union, 252
Amalgamated Housing Corporation, 252
Amalgamated Meat Cutters, 252; Local 88 Medical Institute, 249–50
Amazonia Foundation, 289
America-Israel Cultural Foundation, 134

American Alumni Council, 199
American Cancer Society, 63, 70, 87
American Civil Liberties Union, 61
American Council to Improve Our Neighborhoods (ACTION), 86, 328
American Dental Association, 283
American Economic Foundation, 279
American Farm Bureau Federation, 139
American Federation of Labor, 243, 250, 251, 254, 255
American Federation of Labor-Council of Industrial Organizations (AFL-CIO), 239–41, 244, 255, 258, 259
American Federation of State, County and Municipal Employees, 253
American Foundation for the Blind, 262
American Foundations Information Service, 278
American Friends Service Committee, 416, 435
American Heart Association, 63, 70
American Industrial Hygiene Association, 90
American Institute of Public Opinion, 98
American Jewish Committee, 131
American Jewish Congress, 131
American Jewish Historical Society, 133
American Jewish Joint Distribution Committee, 133, 430
American Labor Educational Service, 255
American Legion, 62, 69, 138, 163–67

455

American Legion Child Welfare Foundation, 165–66
American Legion Endowment Fund Corporation, 166
American Medical Association, 139
American Music Center, 286
American National Committee to Aid Homeless Armenians, 61
American Public Health Association, 6, 284, 314
American Public Welfare Association, 87, 285
American Recreation Society, 90
American Red Cross: 5, 59–79 *passim*; foreign aid, 418–19; and labor unions, 257–58; national membership and activities, 85–86; participation in federated campaigns, 70
American Relief in Korea (ARK), 420
American Telephone and Telegraph Co., 206
American Theological Library Association, 287
American University, 144
American Veterans of World War II and Korea (AMVETS), 163, 164
American Women's Voluntary Services, 90–91
Ancient Order of United Workmen, 141
Andrews, F. Emerson, 288
Angier B. Duke Memorial, 279
Anglican Church and colonial welfare, 4; *see also* Protestant Episcopal Church
Anglo-Iranian Oil Co., 410
Anti-Defamation League, *see* B'nai B'rith
Apostleship of the Sea, 62
Arequipa Sanitorium, 62
Army Corps of Engineers, U.S., 400, 401, 442
Art, federal assistance for, 394
Asia Foundation, 420
Association of the Bar of the City of New York Fund, 288
Atlantic States Marine Fisheries Commission, 361
Atomic Energy Commission (AEC), 202, 372, 375, 381
Avalon Foundation, 284
Avery-Fuller Children's Center, 63
Aviation Agency, Federal, 348, 393
Aviation: federal aid for, 393, 394; State aid for, 348

Back of the Yards Council (Chicago), 36–37, 39, 40, 43–44, 46, 328
Baldwin, Joseph E., 319
Baylor University, 144

Bayse, Walter, 142
Benedictine Sisters, 122
Ben Selling Scholarship Loan Fund, 279
Berkeley Big Brother Project, 53
Biologics Standards, U.S. Public Health Service Division of, 384
Blind: community services for, 53; educational services for, 83; federal assistance for, 386–88; Lions services for, 159
Blue Cross and Blue Shield health insurance plans, 231
B'nai B'rith, 131, 139, 150–51; B'nai B'rith National Youth Service, 132
Boards of education: local, 172, State, 173
Bonneville Power Administration, 401
Boys Club of America, 160
Boys Club of the Bronx, 285
Boy Scouts of America, 69, 86, 148, 166
Boys Town, Nebraska, 146
Brandeis University, 132
Brookings Institution, 274, 289, 433
Brookwood Labor College, 254
Bryce, James, 334
Building Trades Council, 258
Burns, Eveline, 14
Businesses: community services, 224–25; employees of, 206–207; federal aid for, 393–94; federal regulation of, 373–74; growth of welfare functions, 438; local government regulation of, 314; number of, 206–208
Businesses and foreign aid, 413, 427–28
Businessmen's service clubs, 151–63; *see also* specific organizations
Business operations, federal government, 402

Camping programs, in public schools, 186
Canisius College, 149
Carnegie, Andrew, 410
Carnegie Corporation, 265, 278, 282, 415
Carnegie Endowment for International Peace, 287
Carnegie Foundation for the Advancement of Teaching, 279
Carnegie Institution of Washington, 275–76
Carnegie United Kingdom Trust, 410
Casework services: by community agencies, 59–64 *passim*, 121; international, 431; local government, 318–20; in public schools, 183; State, 350

Catholic Alumni, International Federation of, 168
Catholic Apostleship of the Sea Conference, National, 124
Catholic Big Brothers, 125
Catholic Camping Association, National, 120
Catholic Charities, International Conference of, 430
Catholic Charities, National Conference of (CC), 91, 119, 121
Catholic Charities of the Archdiocese of New York, 285
Catholic Church: contributions to, 100; dioceses and archdioceses, 119–23; education, 26, 120, 123–24, 188–89; health and welfare organizations, 119–22, 124–26; membership in, 96–97, 118; missionaries, 126; national organizations, 120, 121, 122, 124–26; parishes, 118; see also Children and youth; Catholic services for, Foreign assistance, etc., and specific organizations
Catholic Community Service, National, (NCCS), 86, 124
Catholic Daughters of America, 95, 125, 150
Catholic Deaf Association, International, 125
Catholic Hospital Association, 283
Catholic Kolping Society, 60
Catholic Men, National Council of, 122, 125
Catholic Missions, American Board of, 125
Catholic Nurses, National Council of, 125
Catholic Relief Services, 125–26
Catholic Social Services of San Francisco, 59, 64–65, 121
Catholic University of America, 149
Catholic War Veterans of the U.S.A., 164
Catholic Welfare Conference, National, 125
Catholic Women, National Council of, 122, 125
Catholic Workers for the Blind, American Federation of, 125
Censorship, by federal agencies, 376–77
Census, U.S. Bureau of the, 97, 298
Center for Advanced Study in the Behavioral Sciences, 280
Center for the Study of Democratic Institutions, 288
Central West End Association, 40, 42

Chambers of Commerce, 154, 161–63
Chamber of Commerce of the United States, 162, 213
Charity: as Christian doctrine, 4; as goal of welfare society, 447; as source of welfare funds, 9
Charles Pfizer and Co., 431
Chicago Community Trust, 292
Chicago Park District, 321
Chicago Sanitary District, 324
Child Welfare, International Union for, 430
Children and youth: administration of State services for, 337; American Legion services for, 165–66; Big Brother project for, 53; casework services for, 318–19; Catholic services for, 119–21, 419–20; community services for, 57–61; family care for, 24–27; federal health programs for, 385; federal assistance for, 12, 386–87; foundation grants for, 285; international services for, 430, 431; Jewish services for, 129–30; Kiwanis services for, 157; neighborhood recreation for, 41, 44, 45; Optimist services for, 160–61; Salvation Army services for, 113; special public education services for, 178–86; Protestant services for, 107, 111; State regulation to ensure care for, 357; State welfare services for, 350–51; see also Recreation, Handicapped children, Health services
Children and Youth, National Advisory Council on State and Local Action for, 88
Children's Bureau, U.S., 180, 350, 385
Children's Emergency Fund, International, 416
Children's Fund of Michigan, 271
Christian Family Movement, 121
Church councils, State and local, 111–12, 113–14
Churches: attendance, 37, 98–99; contributions to, 99–101, 127–28, 132, 134–35; and education, 26, 117, 120, 123–24, 130–31, 188–89; foreign aid by, 116, 125–26, 132, 133–34, 416–18, 419, 430; membership in, 6, 96–98, 101–102, 118; and social services, 101–16, 119–33; trends in, 440–41; see also specific denominations and organizations
Church of the Brethren, 416
Church World Service, 116
Cities, population of, 52
Citizenship Clearing House, 289

City of Hope, 82
Civil Aeronautics Board, U.S., 374, 381
Civil Defense Administration, Federal, 258
Civil Service Act, 406
Civil Service Commission, U.S., 406
Civil Service League, National, 288
Civil Service Retirement Act of 1956, 406
Class size, in public schools, 173
Cleveland Foundation, 290
Cleveland Society for the Blind, 53
Clinics, see Hospitals and clinics
Clise, James, Fund, 275
Collective bargaining, benefits achieved through, 243–50; see also Labor unions
Colleges and universities, see Higher education
Colorado River Compact, 361
Commerce, U.S. Dept. of, 201–202, 213, 402, 423
Commercial schools, 190
Commission of the Churches on International Affairs, 429
Committee on Community Services, AFL-CIO, 241, 256
Committee on Political Education (COPE), AFL-CIO, 240–41, 255
Commodity Credit Corporation, U.S., 371, 392
Commodity Exchange Authority, U.S., 374
Commodity Exchange Commission, U.S., 374
Commonwealth Fund, 261, 283
Communications Commission, Federal, 372, 374
Communications Workers of America, 254, 259
Community assistance, by military personnel, 395, 412–13
Comunity centers: Jewish, 129–30; local government, 321
Community chests, 67–69, 70; see also United funds
Community, defined, 48
Community Research Associates, 87, 283
Community Services Activities (CSA), AFL-CIO, 256–58, 259
Community services: by businesses, 224–25; by higher education, 202–203; by labor union members, 256–58; see also Volunteers
Community Services Committee (CSC), AFL-CIO, 256–57

Community Service Society of New York City, 55–56
Community trusts and foundations, 290–92
Community welfare: coordination of, 73–75, 76–77, 442–43; trends in, 440; see also specific organizations and types of services
Community welfare councils, 49, 65–67, 72–76
Congress for Cultural Freedom, 416
Conservation: federal programs, 391–92; local government programs, 308; State programs, 361
Conservative Jewish congregations, 127, 130, 131
Consultative Committee on Economic Development in South and Southeast Asia, 434
Consumption, by families, 23
Cooperative action, 35, 39–40
Cooperative agricultural extension program, 202
Cooperative for American Remittances to Everywhere (CARE), 413, 419
Cooperative Health Federation of America, 88
Cooperative housing, see Housing
Cornell University, 415
Cornell University Southeast Asia Studies Program, 274–75
Corporate foundations, 221, 267–68
Corporate managers: motives for giving, 223–24; restrictions on contributions by, 221
Corporate philanthropy, 11, 198–99, 219–24, 267–68, 413, 431
Correctional institutions, 313, 362–64
Cottey Junior College for Women, 169
Council for Financial Aid to Education, 198
Council for Independent School Aid, 189
Council of Community Associations, Norwalk, Conn., 71
Council of Relief Agencies Licensed for Operation in Germany (CRALOG), 420
Council of State Governments, 202
County governments, 296–97
Court systems, State, 336
Creole Foundation, 282
Crippled children, see Handicapped and crippled children
Crotched Mountain Foundation, 284
Cuba Nickel Company, 402
Customs, U.S. Bureau of, 372, 376
Curriculums, high school, 177–78

Industrial Areas Foundation, 44
Industrial revolution, in the U.S., 5
Information Agency, U.S., 395
Institute of Plastic Surgery, 284
Institute of Welfare Research of the New York City Community Service Society, 72
Insurance, non-governmental: in general, 225–33; for labor union members, 141; *see also* Fraternal insurance, Health insurance, Life insurance, Social insurance
Intergovernmental Commission for European Migration, 431, 434
Interior, U.S. Dept. of, 381, 382, 400, 401, 402
Internal Revenue Act of 1950: and foundations, 267, 270; regulation of charitable contributions, 220–21
International Association of Machinists, 251, 254
International Bank for Reconstruction and Development, 433
International Brotherhood of Electrical Workers, 251, 252, 254
International Concatenated Order of Hoo Hoo, 143
International Cooperation Administration (ICA), 423–26 *passim*
International Development Association, 433
International Finance Corporation (IFC), 433
International Institute, 60, 64
International Labor Affairs, U.S. Office of, 426
International Ladies' Garment Workers Union (ILGWU), 251, 253, 254
International Longshoremen's and Warehousemen's Union, 244
International organization, 429–35, 439; *see also* specific organizations
International relations and welfare, foundation grants for, 287
International Rescue Committee, 420, 430
International Social Service, 431
International Sugar Council, 434
International Typographical Union (ITU), 241
Interstate Commerce Commission, 372, 374
Interstate commissions, 361; *see also* specific organizations
Interstate Oil Compact Commission, 361

"invisible public housing," 328
Italian Welfare Agency, 64

Jackson Hole Preserve, 286
Jewish Center Workers, National Association of, 90
Jewish Committee for Personal Service, 61
Jewish communal and social services: contributions to, 127–28, 132, 134–35; education, 130–31, 189; local organizations, 127–30; national and international organizations, 131–33; *see also* specific organizations; Children and youth, Jewish services for; Foreign aid, etc.
Jewish Communal Service, National Conference of, 91, 132
Jewish Community Center, 60, 61
Jewish Education, American Association for, 132
Jewish Family Service Agency, 61, 64
Jewish Federation and Welfare Funds, Council of, 71, 127
Jewish Labor Committee, 131
Jewish Philanthropies, Federation of, 284
Jewish Philanthropies, New York City Federation of, 71
Jewish Publication Society, 133
Jewish Research, American Academy for, 133
Jewish Theological Seminary, 133
Jewish War Veterans of America, 131, 163
Jewish Welfare Board, National, 86, 132
Jewish Women, National Council of, 134
John Howard Association, 82–83
Johnson Foundation, 285
Jones, Melvin, 153
Judd, Rep. Walter, 420
Julliard Musical Foundation, 266
Junior chambers of commerce, 65, 154
Junior Leagues of America, Inc., 91, 168
Junior Optimist Clubs, 160
Juvenile delinquency, 26, 42, 52, 53, 60–61, 111, 291, 321, 327, 363; *see also* Children and youth

Keio University, 418
Kellogg Foundation, 283
Kenny, Elizabeth, Polio Foundation, 63
Khrushchev, Premier Nikita, 439
Kingsborough Houses Tenant Organization, 41–42

Mental Health services: administration of, 337; community programs, 349–50, 443; in public schools, 182; State programs, 349–50; *see also* Mental illness, Rehabilitation

Mental illness: community rehabilitation of, 79–80; extent of, 29–31, 452; family care for, 31; State responsibility and care for, 349–50; *see also* Mental health services, Rehabilitation

Mentally retarded, public education for, 179–80

Merrill Foundation for the Advancement of Financial Knowledge, 289

Mertz, Martha, Foundation, 284

Methodist Church, 45–46, 99

Metropolitan areas, defined, 298

Metropolitan Museum of Art, 286

Metropolitan Water District of Southern California, 300–301

Migrants, immigrants, and refugees: Catholic services for, 126; integration into community, 45–46; international services for, 430, 434; Jewish services for, 128–29; labor union services for, 258; Protestant services for, 116

Migrant workers, Protestant services for, 115

Military Order of the Purple Heart, 163

Miller-Tydings Act of 1937, 358

Milwaukee County Department of Public Welfare, 319

Mines, U.S. Bureau of, 383

Minimum wage laws: federal, 375; State, 359

Minneapolis School of Art, 286

Minority group welfare problems, 169, 451–52; *see also* Negroes, Race relations

Missionaries, 126, 412

Missionary Council, International, 429

Mississippi Bureau of Investigation, 362

Modern Woodmen of America, 168

Moose, Loyal Order of, 168

Morgan, Arthur, 225

Morrison Center for Rehabilitation, 63

Mullen Benevolent Corporation, 284

Mullenphy, Bryan, 266

Municipal governments, 297–99; *see also* Local governments

Muscular Dystrophy Association, 62, 63

Muscular Dystrophy Foundation, 146

Museums, local government, 321

Mutual security programs, 422–24

National Aeronautics and Space Administration, 394

National Association for the Advancement of Colored People (NAACP), 61, 139

National Association of Housing and Redevelopment Officials, 92

National Association of Manufacturers, 138, 139

National Association of Veterans' Employment Councils (NAVEC), 163–64

National Audubon Society, 168

National Better Business Bureau, 223

National Board of Review, 374

National Budget and Consultation Committee, 89, 93

National Bureau of Economic Research, 282, 289

National CIO War Relief Committee, 256

National Committee for Labor Israel, 134

National Conference of the Churches of Christ (NCCC), 101, 108–10, 112, 114–16

National Congress of Colored Parents and Teachers, 175

National Council of Independent Schools, 188

National Council on Agricultural Life and Labor, 92

National Defense Education Act, 198

National Education Association (NEA), 173

National Foundation for Infantile Paralysis, 13–14, 63, 85

National government: 304–452 *passim*; employees of, 402–403, 406; finances, 368–72; regulation by, 372–77; welfare and related programs, 377–402; *see also* specific programs

National Grange, 138, 139

National health agencies, non-governmental: in general, 83–86; labor union attitudes toward, 259; trends in, 440; *see also* Fund-raising, specific organizations

National Health and Welfare Retirement Association, 90

National Health Council, 92

National Industries for the Blind, 86

National Information Bureau, 93

National Labor Relations Board (NLRB), 374

National Legion of Decency, 125

National Mediation Board, 375

National Merit Scholarship Foundation, 279–80

National Multiple Sclerosis Society, 63

National Planning Association, 87

Social Welfare, National Conference on, 91
Social welfare spending, summaries, 12, 372
Social work: as a profession, 89–93; in public schools, 183; and religion, 105–106; 110–11, 113; *see also* specific organizations
Social Work, Church Conference of, 91
Social Work, International Association of Schools of, 430
Social Work, International Conference of, 429; U.S. Committee of, 92
Social Work, National Conference of, 6
Social Work, State Conferences of, 80
Social Work Education, Council on, 89, 92, 110, 285
Social Workers, National Association of: in general, 83; objectives of, 90; School Social Work Section, 183
Social Work Vocational Bureau, 90, 92
Society for the Rehabilitation of the Facially Disfigured, 284
Society of St. Vincent de Paul, 125
Soil Conservation Service, U.S., 54
Southern Baptist Convention, 99
Southern Education Foundation, 287–88
Southern Regional Council, 288
Southern Regional Education Board, 283
Spartanburg County Foundation, 286
Special district governments, 300–301; *see also* Education
"spontaneous rehabilitation" of housing, 328
Standard Oil Foundation, 268
Stanford University, 280, 418
State, U.S. Dept. of, 395
State colleges and universities, 193, 201; *see also* Higher education
State governments: employees of, 364–65; federal grants to, 378–80; financing, 338–45; functions, 345–64; and higher education, 197; and private education, 188, 190–92; and public education, 173, 175, 180, 183, 184; relations to other levels of government, 332–35; unemployment payments and guaranteed annual wage plans, 247; welfare administration, 336–38; *see also* specific programs
State Services, U.S. Bureau of, 384
Strike benefits for labor union members, 250–51
Strikes, 243
Student loans, 169, 198, 200
Supreme Court, U.S., 6, 186, 190, 333, 373

Supreme Forest Woodmen Circle, 168
Surgeon General, U.S. Office of the, 383
Synagogue Council of America, 127, 134

Taft-Hartley Act of 1947, 374, 375
Taxation: effective rates, 10, 12; federal, 6, 9, 11, 368–70; local government, 302–304; State, 334, 338–41
Tax Foundation, 388
Teachers: in private schools, 188; in public schools, 173; in special education programs, 179–80
Technical assistance: by federal government, 423, 426, 428; by foundations, 414–15; by Protestant churches, 116; by the UN, 433
Temporary disability insurance, State programs of, 356–57
Tennessee River Basin Water Pollution Control Compact, 361
Tennessee Valley Authority (TVA), 381, 400, 401
Tenth Amendment to the U.S. Constitution, 332
Territories, U.S. Office of, 383
Tiffany, Louis Comfort, Foundation, 286
Township governments, 299–300
Trade Commission, Federal, 373, 374
Traffic accidents, 346–47
Travelers' Aid Society for San Francisco, 64
Treasury, U.S., 389, 391
Trenton Community Foundation, 290
Trexler Foundation, 270
Trust territories, U.S., welfare services in, 399–400
Twentieth Century Fund, 289, 293

Unemployment insurance: federal administration of, 369, 388–89; for railroad workers, 369, 398–99; State programs, 355–56; for veterans and federal employees, 369, 403–404, 406
Union and union members, *see* Labor unions
Union of Czech Catholic Women of Texas, 143
United Automobile Workers (UAW), 241, 254, 258
United Cerebral Palsy, 63
United Church Women, 114
United Community Campaigns of America, 258
United Community Funds and Councils of America (UCFC), 68, 87, 92, 93
United Fruit Co., 410

468